PROJECT MANAGEMENT

The Irwin/McGraw-Hill Series

Operations and Decision Sciences

OPERATIONS MANAGEMENT

Bowersox and Closs
Logistical Management: The Integrated Supply Chain Process
First Edition

Chase, Aquilano, and Jacobs
Production and Operations Management
Eighth Edition

Chu, Hottenstein, and Greenlaw
PROSIM for Windows
Third Edition

Cohen and Apte
Manufacturing Automation
First Edition

Davis, Aquilano, and Chase
Fundamentals of Operations Management
Third Edition

Dobler and Burt
Purchasing and Supply Management
Sixth Edition

Flaherty
Global Operations Management
First Edition

Fitzsimmons and Fitzsimmons
Service Management: Operations, Strategy, Information Technology
Second Edition

Gray and Larson
Project Management: The Managerial Process
First Edition

Hill
Manufacturing Strategy: Text & Cases
Third Edition

Hopp and Spearman
Factory Physics
Second Edition

Lambert and Stock
Strategic Logistics Management
Third Edition

Leenders and Fearon
Purchasing and Supply Chain Management
Eleventh Edition

Melnyk and Denzler
Operations Management
First Edition

Moses, Seshadri, and Yakir
HOM Operations Management Software for Windows
First Edition

Nahmias
Production and Operations Analysis
Third Edition

Nicholas
Competitive Manufacturing Management
First Edition

Pinedo and Chao
Operations Scheduling
First Edition

Sanderson and Uzumeri
Managing Product Families
First Edition

Schroeder
Operations Management: Contemporary Concepts and Cases
First Edition

Schonberger and Knod
Operations Management: Customer-Focused Principles
Sixth Edition

Simchi-Levi, Kaminsky, and Simchi-Levi
Designing and Managing the Supply Chain: Concepts, Strategies, and Cases
First Edition

Stevenson
Production/Operations Management
Sixth Edition

Sterman
Business Dynamics: Systems Thinking and Modeling for a Complex World
First Edition

Vollmann, Berry, and Whybark
Manufacturing Planning & Control Systems
Fourth Edition

Zipkin
Foundations of Inventory Management
First Edition

QUANTITATIVE METHODS AND MANAGEMENT SCIENCE

Bodily, Carraway, Frey, Pfeifer
Quantitative Business Analysis: Casebook
First Edition

Bodily, Carraway, Frey, Pfeifer
Quantitative Business Analysis: Text and Cases
First Edition

Bonini, Hausman, and Bierman
Quantitative Analysis for Business Decisions
Ninth Edition

Hesse
Managerial Spreadsheet Modeling and Analysis
First Edition

Hillier, Hillier, Lieberman
Introduction to Management Science: A Modeling and Case Studies Approach with Spreadsheets
First Edition

PROJECT MANAGEMENT
The Managerial Process

Clifford F. Gray
Oregon State University

Erik W. Larson
Oregon State University

Irwin
McGraw-Hill

Boston   Burr Ridge, IL   Dubuque, IA   Madison, WI   New York   San Francisco   St. Louis
Bangkok   Bogotá   Caracas   Lisbon   London   Madrid
Mexico City   Milan   New Delhi   Seoul   Singapore   Sydney   Taipei   Toronto

McGraw-Hill Higher Education

A Division of The **McGraw-Hill** Companies

PROJECT MANAGEMENT
The Managerial Process

This book is printed on acid-free paper.

1 2 3 4 5 6 7 8 9 0 DOW/DOW 9 0 9 8 7 6 5 4 3 2 1 0 9

ISBN 0-07-365812-X

Vice president/Editor-in-Chief: *Michael W. Junior*
Publisher: *Jeffrey J. Shelstad*
Senior sponsoring editor: *Scott Isenberg*
Developmental editor: *Wanda J. Zeman*
Senior marketing manager: *Colleen J. Suljic*
Project manager: *Margaret Rathke Bogovich*
Senior production supervisor: *Lori Koetters*
Designer: *Jennifer McQueen Hollingsworth*
Supplement coordinator: *Betty Hadala*
Compositor: *ElectraGraphics, Inc.*
Typeface: *10.5/12 Times Roman*
Printer: *R. R. Donnelley & Sons Company*
Photos for Chapters 1, 2, 3, 5, 6, 7, 8, 9, 11, 12, and 14 are © Copyright 1999 PhotoDisc, Inc. All rights reserved.
Cover image: © *The Image Bank, Team Work Puzzle, Pierre Goavec*

Library of Congress Cataloging-in-Publication Data

Gray, Clifford F.
    Project management: the managerial process/Clifford F. Gray, Erik W. Larson.
        p. cm. — (The Irwin/McGraw Hill series, operations and decision sciences)
        Includes bibliographical references and index.
        ISBN 0-07-365812-X
        1. Industrial project management. 2. Time management. 3. Risk management. I. Larson, Erik W., 1952–   . II. Title.
III. Series: Irwin/McGraw Hill series in operations and decision sciences.
HD69.P75G72   2000
659.4'04—dc21
                                              99-27905

www.mhhe.com

ABOUT THE AUTHORS

CLIFFORD F. GRAY is professor emeritus of management at the College of Business, Oregon State University. He continues to teach undergraduate and graduate project management courses overseas and in the United States; he has personally taught more than 100 executive development seminars and workshops. His research and consulting interests have been divided equally between operations management and project management; he has published numerous articles in these areas, plus a text on project management. He has also conducted research with colleagues in the International Project Management Association. Cliff has been a member of the Project Management Institute since 1976 and was one of the founders of the Portland, Oregon, chapter. He has been the president of Project Management International, Inc. (a training and consulting firm specializing in project management) since 1977. He received his BA in economics and management from Millikin University, MBA from Indiana University, and doctorate in operations management from the College of Business, University of Oregon.

ERIK LARSON is professor and chairman of the department of management, marketing, and international business at the College of Business, Oregon State University. He teaches executive, graduate, and undergraduate courses on project management, organizational behavior, and leadership. His research and consulting activities focus on project management. He has published numerous articles on matrix management, product development, and project partnering. He has been a member of the Portland, Oregon, chapter of the Project Management Institute since 1984. In 1995 he worked as a Fulbright scholar with faculty at the Krakow Academy of Economics on modernizing Polish business education. He received a BA in psychology from Claremont McKenna College and a PhD in management from State University of New York at Buffalo.

To Mary, Kevin, and Robert
C.F.G.
To Ann, Mary, Rachel, and Tory
E.L.

PREFACE

Our motivation for writing this text was to provide for our students a text built around a holistic, integrative view of project management. A holistic view of project management focuses on how projects contribute to the strategic goals of the organization. The linkages for integration include the process of selection of projects that best support organizational strategy and all the technical and managerial processes to complete those projects. The goals for prospective project managers are to clearly understand the role of a project in their organizations and to master project management tools/techniques and interpersonal skills necessary to orchestrate projects to completion.

The role of projects in organizations is receiving increasing attention. Projects are becoming the major tool for reaching the strategic goals of the organization. Given savage worldwide competition, many organizations have reorganized around a philosophy of innovation, renewal, and organizational learning to survive. This philosophy suggests an organization that is flexible and project driven. Project management has developed to the point where it is a professional discipline having its own body of knowledge and skills. Today it is nearly impossible to imagine anyone at any level in the organization who would not benefit from some degree of expertise in the process of managing projects.

AUDIENCE

This text is written for a wide audience. Students and prospective project managers will find the text useful to understand why organizations have developed a formal project management process to gain a competitive advantage. Readers will find the concepts and techniques discussed in enough detail to be immediately useful in new-project situations. Practicing project managers will find the text a useful guide and reference for typical problems that pop up. Managers will also find the text useful to understand the role of the project in the mission of their organization. Analysts will find the text useful in explaining the data needed and the operations of inherited or purchased software. Members of the Project Management Institute will find the text a useful handbook when preparing for project management certification. People at all levels in the organization assigned to work on projects will find the text useful in providing the rationale behind project management tools and techniques and will gain insights on how to enhance their contributions to project success.

Our emphasis is not only on *how* the management process works, but more importantly *why* it works. The concepts, principles, and techniques are universally applicable. That is, the text does not specialize by project type—for example, construction, product development, large, small. Rather, the text is written for the individual who will be required to manage a variety of projects. In the case of some small projects, a few of the steps of the techniques can be omitted, but the conceptual framework applies to all organizations in which projects are important to survival. The approach can be used in pure project organizations such as construction, research organizations, and consultant engineering firms. Organizations that spend most of their daily effort producing products or services will find the text useful in managing the many small projects that are going on while the daily production continues.

CONTENT

The text addresses the major questions and issues the authors have encountered over their 50 combined years of teaching project management and consulting with practicing project managers in domestic and foreign environments. The following questions represent the issues and problems practicing project managers find consuming most of their effort: What is the strategic role of projects in contemporary organizations? How are projects prioritized? What organizational and managerial styles will improve chances of project success? How do project managers orchestrate the complex network of relationships involving vendors, subcontractors, project team members, senior management, functional managers, and customers that affect project success? What factors contribute to the development of a high-performance project team? What project management system can be set up to gain some measure of control? How do managers prepare for a new international project in a foreign culture? Can senior management change the organizational culture to support projects?

Project managers must deal with all these concerns to be effective. All of these issues and problems represent linkages to an integrative project management view. The chapter content of the text has been placed within an overall framework that integrates these topics in a holistic manner. Cases and snapshots are included from the experiences of practicing managers. The future for project managers appears to be promising. Careers will be determined by success in managing projects.

ACKNOWLEDGMENTS

The text includes contributions from numerous students, colleagues, friends, and managers gleaned from professional conversations. We want them to know we sincerely appreciate their counsel and suggestions. Almost every exercise, case, and example in the text is drawn from a real-world project. Special thanks to managers who graciously shared their current project as ideas for exercises, subjects for cases, and examples for the text. Shlomo Cohen, Pat Taylor, and John Wold, whose work is printed, are gratefully acknowledged. Special gratitude is due Robert Breitbarth of Interact Management, who shared invaluable insights on prioritizing projects. University students and managers deserve special accolades for identifying problems with earlier drafts of the text and exercises.

We would like to thank the reviewers of this book who contributed significantly to the final product. They include S. Narayan Bodapati, Southern Illinois University at Edwardsville; Warren J. Boe, University of Iowa; Burton Dean, San Jose State University; Kwasi Amoako-Gyampah, University of North Carolina–Greensboro; Owen P. Hall, Pepperdine University; Michael R. Godfrey, Winona State University; Bruce C. Hartman, University of Arizona; Richard Irving, York University; Robert T. Jones, DePaul University; Richard L. Luebbe, Miami University of Ohio; William Moylan, Lawrence Technological College of Business; Edward Pascal, University of Ottawa; James H. Patterson, Indiana University; Art Rogers, City University; Christy Strbiak, U.S. Air Force Academy; David A. Vaughan, City University; and Ronald W. Witzel, Keller Graduate School of Management.

In addition, we would like to thank our colleagues in the College of Business at Oregon State University for their support and help in completing this project. In particular, we recognize Carol Brown, Dan Brown, Ashok Chandrashekar, Jack Drexler, Dave Gobeli, Chandra Mishra, and Mary Alice Seville for their helpful comments and suggestions. Special thanks go to Karen Bruder, Ann Leen, and Eva Hofenbredl who helped prepare the manuscript. We also wish to thank the many students who helped us at different stages of this project, most notably Kitty Taghon, Nel Young, Rebecca Keepers, Katherine Knox, and Phong Duong. Mary Gray deserves special credit for editing and working under tight deadlines.

Finally, we want to extend our thanks to all the people at Irwin/McGraw-Hill for their efforts and support. We'd like to thank Scott Isenberg for championing the project during the early development stage and Wanda Zeman and Maggie Rathke Bogovich for managing the final development/production phase of the project.

Clifford F. Gray
Erik W. Larson

NOTE TO STUDENT

You will find the content of this text highly practical, relevant, and current. The concepts discussed are relatively simple and intuitive. As you study each chapter we suggest you try to grasp not only *how* things work, but *why* things work. You are encouraged to use the text as a handbook as you move through the three levels of competency:

I know.

I can do.

I can adapt to new situations.

Project management is both people and technical oriented. Project management involves understanding the cause-effect relationships and interactions among the sociotechnical dimensions of projects. Improved competency in these dimensions will greatly enhance your competitive edge as a project manager.

The field of project management is growing in importance and at an exponential rate. It is nearly impossible to imagine a future management career that does not include management of projects. Résumés of managers will soon be primarily a description of the individual's participation in projects and their respective contributions.

Good luck on your journey through the text and on your future projects.

BRIEF CONTENTS

TABLE OF CONTENTS

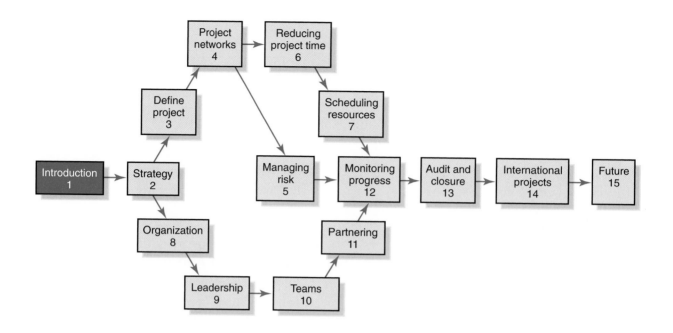

CHAPTER ONE

Modern Project Management

Managing projects is one of the oldest and most respected accomplishments of mankind. We stand in awe of the achievements of the builders of pyramids, the architects of ancient cities, the masons and craftsmen of great cathedrals and mosques; of the might and labour behind the Great Wall of China, and other wonders of the world.
—Peter W. G. Morris, *The Management of Projects*[1]

This is an exciting time to be reading a text on project management. Business leaders and experts have proclaimed that "Project management is the wave of the future." Stewart, in *Fortune* magazine, asserts that the corporate jungle has a new species: the *project manager* who will fill the void created by the extinction of middle management:

> If the old middle managers are dinosaurs, a new class of manager mammal is evolving to fill the niche they once ruled: project managers. Unlike his biological counterpart, the project manager is more agile and adaptable than the beast he's displacing, more likely to live by his wits than throwing his weight around.[2]

Likewise, *The Wall Street Journal* reports that more and more of the work in America is project oriented with a beginning, a middle, and an end.[3] They go on to describe the emergence of project junkies, a growing band of professional gypsies whose careers consist of a series of independent projects. Rodney Turner, editor of the *International Journal of Project Management,* predicts, "into the 21st century, project-based management will sweep aside traditional functional line management."[4]

The project approach has long been the style of doing business in the construction industry, U.S. Department of Defense contracts, and Hollywood as well as at big consulting firms. Now project management is spreading to all avenues of work. Today, project teams carry out everything from port expansions to hospital restructuring to upgrading information systems. The "Big Three" automakers credit their ability to recapture a significant share of the auto market to the use of project management teams, which quickly develop new cars that incorporate the latest automotive technology. The impact of project management is most profound in the area of information technology, where the new folk heroes are young professionals whose Herculean efforts lead to the constant flow of new hardware and software products.

Project management is not limited to the private sector. Project management is also a vehicle for doing good deeds and solving social problems. Endeavors such as providing emergency aid to a region devastated by a hurricane, devising a strategy for reducing crime and drug abuse within a city, or organizing a community effort to renovate a public playground would and do benefit from the application of modern project management skills and techniques.

Perhaps the best indicator of the sudden growth and interest in project management can be seen in the rapid expansion of the Project Management Institute (PMI), a professional organization for project management specialists. Between 1993 and 1997, membership quadrupled to more than 24,000, with membership growing at a rate of 1,200 per month; current membership is now past 40,000. PMI's goal is 100,000 by 2002![5] In 1985 two-thirds of the PMI members were in construction-related industries. Now construction represents only about one third of the membership, with the most rapidly growing areas being telecommunications, software engineering, and product development.

The growth of project management can also be seen in the classroom. Ten years ago major universities offered one or two classes in project management, primarily for engineers. Today, many universities offer multiple sections of project management classes, with the core group of engineers being supplemented by business students majoring in marketing, management information systems (MIS), and finance, as well as students from other disciplines such as oceanography, health sciences, computer sciences, and liberal arts. These students are finding that their exposure to project management is providing them with distinct advantages when it comes time to look for jobs. More and more employers are looking for graduates with project management skills. The logical starting point for developing these skills is understanding the uniqueness of a project and of project managers.

WHAT IS A PROJECT?

What do the following headlines have in common?

Two hundred million plus TITANIC breaks box-office record

Mars Lunar Landing Produces First Pictures

Nintendo 64 and Sony PlayStation games compete for Christmas market

FARM AID concert raises millions for family farmers

Chunnel celebrates five millionth customer

All these events resulted from the management of projects. A project can be defined as follows:

> A project is a complex, nonroutine, one-time effort limited by time, budget, resources, and performance specifications designed to meet customer needs.

Like most organizational effort, the major goal of a project is to satisfy a customer's need. Beyond this fundamental similarity, the characteristics of a project help differentiate it from other endeavors of the organization. The major characteristics of a project are as follows:

1. An established objective.
2. A defined life span with a beginning and an end.
3. Usually, the involvement of several departments and professionals.
4. Typically, doing something that has never been done before.
5. Specific time, cost, and performance requirements.

First, projects have a defined objective—whether it is constructing a 12-story apartment complex by January 1 or releasing version 2.0 of a specific software package as quickly as possible. This singular purpose is often lacking in daily organizational life in which workers perform repetitive operations each day. Second, because there is a specified objective, projects have a defined endpoint, which is contrary to the ongoing duties and responsibilities of traditional jobs. In many cases, individuals move from one project to the next as opposed to staying in one job. After helping to construct a desalination installation along the Gulf of Mexico, an engineer may next be assigned to construct an oil refinery plant in Malaysia. Third, unlike much organizational work that is segmented according to functional specialty, projects typically require the combined efforts of a variety of specialists. Instead of working in separate offices under separate managers, project participants, whether they be engineers, financial analysts, marketing professionals, or quality control specialists, work closely together under the guidance of a project manager to complete a project.

The fourth characteristic of a project is that it is nonroutine and has some unique elements. This is not an either/or issue but a matter of degree. Obviously, accomplishing something that has never been done before, such as putting a man on the moon, requires solving previously unsolved problems and breakthrough technology. On the other hand, even basic construction projects that involve established sets of routines and procedures require some degree of customization that makes them unique. Finally, specific time, cost, and performance requirements bind projects. Projects are evaluated according to what was accomplished, what it cost, and how much time it took. These triple constraints impose a higher degree of accountability than you typically find in most jobs. These three also highlight one of the primary functions of project management, which is balancing the trade-offs between time, cost, and performance while ultimately satisfying the customer.

The Project Life Cycle

Another way of illustrating the unique nature of project work is in terms of the project life cycle. Some project managers find it useful to use the project life cycle as the cornerstone for managing projects. The life cycle recognizes that projects have a limited life span and that there are predictable changes in level of effort and focus over the life of the project. There are a number of different life-cycle models in project management literature. Many are unique to a specific industry or type of project. For example, a new software development project may consist of five phases: definition, design, code, integration/test, and maintenance. A generic cycle is depicted in Figure 1–1.

The project life cycle typically passes sequentially through four stages: definition, planning, execution, and delivery. The starting point begins the moment the project is given the go ahead. Project effort starts slowly, builds to a peak, and then declines to delivery of the project to the customer. In the *definition* stage, specifications of the project are defined; project objectives are established; teams are formed; major responsibilities are assigned. In the *planning* stage, the level of effort increases, and plans are developed to determine what the project will entail, when it will be scheduled, whom it will benefit, what quality level should be maintained, and what the budget will be. During the *execution* stage, a major portion of the project work takes place—both physical and mental. The physical product is produced (a bridge, a report, a software program). Time, cost, and specification measures are used for control. Is the project on schedule, on budget, and meeting specifications? What are the forecasts of each of these measures? What revisions/changes are necessary? The *delivery* stage usually includes the two activities: delivering the project product to the customer and redeploying project resources. Delivery of the project might include

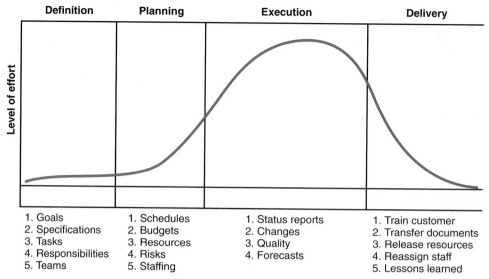

Definition	Planning	Execution	Delivery
1. Goals	1. Schedules	1. Status reports	1. Train customer
2. Specifications	2. Budgets	2. Changes	2. Transfer documents
3. Tasks	3. Resources	3. Quality	3. Release resources
4. Responsibilities	4. Risks	4. Forecasts	4. Reassign staff
5. Teams	5. Staffing		5. Lessons learned

FIGURE 1–1   Project Life Cycle

customer training and transferring documents. Redeployment usually involves releasing project equipment/materials to other projects and finding new assignments for team members.

In practice, the project life cycle is used by some project groups to depict the timing of major tasks over the life of the project. For example, the design team might plan a major commitment of resources in the definition stage, while the quality team would expect their major effort to increase in the latter stages of the project life cycle. Because most organizations have a portfolio of projects going on concurrently, each at a different stage of each project's life cycle, careful planning and management at the organization and project level are imperative.

The Project Manager

Management decides and implements the ways and means to effectively and efficiently utilize human and nonhuman resources to reach predetermined objectives. In a small sense project managers perform the same functions as other managers. That is, they plan, schedule, motivate, and control. Various types of managers exist because they fill special needs. For example, the marketing manager specializes in distributing a product or service; the production manager specializes in conversion of resource inputs to outputs; the financial manager ensures adequate funds are available to keep the organization viable. The project manager is unique because she/he manages temporary, nonrepetitive activities and frequently acts independently of the formal organization.

Project managers are expected to marshal resources to complete a fixed-life project on time, on budget, and within specifications. Project managers are the direct link to the customer and must manage the interface between customer expectations and what is feasible and reasonable. They provide direction, coordination, and integration to the project team, which is often made up of part-time participants loyal to their functional departments. Project managers are responsible for performance (frequently with too little authority). They must ensure that appropriate trade-offs are made between the time, cost, and performance requirements of the project. At the same time, unlike their functional counterparts, project managers generally possess only rudimentary technical knowledge to make such decisions. Instead, they must orchestrate the completion of the project by inducing the right people, at the right time, to address the right issues and make the right decisions. Clearly, project management is a unique and challenging profession. This text is intended to provide the necessary knowledge, perspective, and tools to enable students to accept the challenge.

THE IMPORTANCE OF PROJECT MANAGEMENT

Project management is no longer a special-need management. It is rapidly becoming a standard way of doing business. An increasing percentage of the typical firm's effort is being devoted to projects. The future promises an increase in the importance and the role of projects in contributing to the strategic direction of organizations. An influential project management scholar, David Cleland, has declared that this is the dawning of the "Age of Project Management"; several of the reasons this is likely to be the case are briefly discussed in the following paragraphs (see Figure 1–2).[6]

Compression of the Product Life Cycle   One of the most significant driving forces behind the demand for project management is the shortening of the product life cycle. Instantaneous, worldwide flows of information reduce the competitive advantage of new products, which are more easily imitated. Computer-aided design (CAD) and manufacturing (CAM) have also forced radical changes in the product life cycle. For example, today in high-tech industries the product life cycle is averaging 1.5 to 3 years. Only 30 years ago, life cycles of 10 to 15 years were not uncommon. Given the

FIGURE 1–2   The Age of Project Management

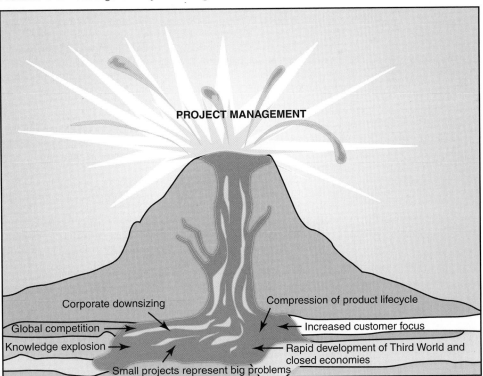

Snapshot from Practice
THE BEST WIRELESS PHONE ON THE MARKET[9]

In the spring of 1996, a tense team of Nokia Corp. researchers gathered outside of Helsinki, Finland. Their charter: to create a new "icon" among cell phones—something jazzy, like Apple Computer's first Macintosh. The marketing division presented a wish list of grueling specs: featherweight, long battery life, and whizzy new features to attract techies. Then came the clincher: It was to be unveiled in Beijing in November 1997, just 20 months away. "We knew that time was our enemy," says project manager Arto Kiema.

What they came up with is Nokia's 6100 series—powerful 4.5-ounce phones about the size and shape of a slim pack of cigarettes. The saga of the 6100 set a new standard for conquering high-tech markets. Developers began with a simple precept: First, to save money and time, they recycled everything from the complex decoding software to ring menus from the earlier 2100 series of phones. For panache, they added new features. But they confined the innovations to things that wouldn't tax the battery, such as simple computer games, an alarm clock, and an infrared modem for downloading e-mail from data networks.

Most important, Nokia listened to key customers. The Finns went straight to big service providers, such as AT&T, which buys thousands of cell phones and resells them in subscription packages. Such providers want their customers to be able to communicate across frequency bands used by different formats, such as analog and digital cellular lines and personal computers (PCs). They also want phones switched on for as many hours as possible to maximize the number of calls received.

Nokia concentrated on ratcheting down power consumption in the handset. For help, it enlisted Texas Instruments, Inc. The Dallas-based chip giant came up with proprietary power-saving circuits that brought Nokia handset power requirements down from six volts to three. Nokia then scrambled to redesign other components to run on less power.

The most arduous task Nokia faced was customizing the phone for every major market. Developers built in rudimentary voice recognition for Asia, where keyboards are problematic, and raised the ring volume so the phone could be heard on crowded Asian streets. A bigger challenge was building in extra receivers so the regional models could accommodate all the different formats: GSM digital in Europe and much of Asia and one analog and two digital modes for the splintered U.S. market. "To work through all of the protocols was painful," says Kiema. "Sometimes they're in conflict."

The phones debuted on schedule in China, and since then, consumers from Sidney to Seville have snapped up an estimated 3+ million units. Daniel Hesse, CEO of AT&T Wireless, proclaimed that the Nokia 6100 was ". . . the best wireless phone on the market, bar none."

much shorter life cycle, it is imperative that firms keep a constant chain of new products in the pipeline and get each product to market before their competitors. A common rule of thumb in the world of high-tech product development is that a six-month project delay can result in a 33 percent loss in product revenue share. *Time to market* for new products with short life cycles has become increasingly important to all product organizations because of the velocity with which technology is changing. Speed is becoming a competitive advantage; more and more organizations are relying on cross-functional project teams and project management methods to get new products and services to the market as quickly as possible.

Global Competition   The transformation from national or regional economies to one global economy during the 1970s has not only led to dramatic technological innovations but has also created tremendous pressures on quality improvement and cost containment. Today's open market demands not only *cheaper* products and services but also *better* products and services. This has led to the emergence of the quality movement across the world with ISO 9000 certification a requirement for doing business. ISO 9000 is a family of international standards for quality management and assurance. These standards cover design, procurement, quality assurance, and delivery processes for everything from banking to manufacturing. Quality management and improvement invariably involve project management. For many, their first exposure to project management techniques has been in quality workshops. Increased pressures to reduce costs have not only led to the migration of U.S. manufacturing operations to Mexico and the Far East, which by itself is a significant project, but also a transformation in how organizations try to achieve results. More and more work is being classified as projects. Individuals are being assigned responsibility to achieve a specific objective within a given budget and by a specified deadline. Project management, with its triple focus on time, cost, and performance, is proving to be an efficient, flexible way to get things done.

Knowledge Explosion   The growth in new knowledge has increased the complexity of projects because projects encompass the latest advances. For example, building a road 30 years ago was a somewhat simple process. Today, each area has increased in complexity, including materials, specifications, codes, aesthetics, equipment, and required specialists. Not only has basic project work become more complex, requiring greater degrees of coordination, but existing products and services are also more technologically complex. In today's digital, electronic age it is becoming hard to find a new product that does not contain at least one microchip. Product complexity has increased the need to integrate divergent technologies. Project management has emerged as an important discipline for achieving this task.

Corporate Downsizing   After years of stressing growth and "big is better," organizations have begun to face the harsh reality that big is also more costly. The last decade has seen a dramatic restructuring of organizational life. Downsizing (or rightsizing if you are still employed) and sticking to core competencies have become necessary for survival for many firms. Middle management is a mere skeleton of the past. In today's flatter and leaner organizations, where change is a constant, project management is replacing middle management as a way of ensuring that things get done. Corporate downsizing has also led to a change in the way organizations approach projects. It is rare today to find any major project performed totally in-house. Companies outsource significant segments of project work, and project managers have to manage not only their own people but also their counterparts in different organizations.

Increased Customer Focus   Increased competition has placed a premium on cus-tomer satisfaction. Customers no longer simply settle for generic products and ser-vices. They want customized products and services that cater to their specific needs. This mandate requires a much closer working relationship between the provider and the receiver. Account executives and sales representatives are assuming more of a proj-ect manager's role as they work with their organization to satisfy the unique needs and requests of clients. This change has also prompted the development of customized products and services. For example, 10 years ago buying a set of golf clubs was a rel-atively simple process: You picked out a set based on price and feel. Today, there are golf clubs for tall players and short players, clubs for players who tend to slice the ball and clubs for those who hook the ball, high-tech clubs with the latest metallurgic dis-covery guaranteed to add distance, and so forth. Project management is critical both to development of customized products and services and to sustaining lucrative rela-tionships with customers.

Rapid Development of Third World and Closed Economies   The collapse of the Soviet Empire and the gradual opening of Asian communist countries have created an explosion in pent-up demand within these societies for all manner of consumer goods and infrastructure development. Western firms are scrambling to introduce their prod-ucts and services to these new markets, and many firms are using project management techniques to establish distribution channels and foreign bases of operations. Like-wise, these historical changes have created a tremendous market for core project work in the areas of heavy construction and telecommunications as these countries strive to revitalize their inefficient industries and decrepit infrastructures. To reduce some of the risk and maximize individual talents, more and more firms are entering into joint ventures with indigenous firms to complete large- and small-scale foreign projects. These foreign ventures have placed a premium on the adaptive capacity of project management personnel to work in foreign cultures with vastly different values, work habits, and orientations.[7]

Small Projects Represent Big Problems   The velocity of change required to remain competitive or simply keep up has created an organizational climate in which hun-dreds of projects are implemented concurrently. This climate has created a multi-project environment and a plethora of new problems. Sharing and prioritizing re-sources across a portfolio of projects is a major challenge for senior management. Those who manage small projects often face a greater variety of problems than do managers of single megaprojects. Frequently, the organizational culture does not sup-port small projects, and control systems are nonexistent. Thousands of product and service companies are faced with multiple projects continuously in process. Many firms have no idea of the problems involved with inefficient management of small projects. Small projects typically carry the same or more risk as do large projects. Small projects are perceived as having little impact on the bottom line because they do not demand large amounts of scarce resources and/or money. Because so many small projects are going on concurrently and because the perception of the inefficiency im-pact is small, measuring inefficiency is usually nonexistent. Unfortunately, many small projects soon add up to large sums of money. Many customers and millions of dollars are lost each year on small projects in product and service organizations.

Many small projects can eat up the people resources of a firm and represent hidden costs not measured in the accounting system. Organizations with many small projects going on concurrently face the most difficult project management problems. A key

Snapshot from Practice

THE EMERGENCE OF e.SCHWAB

Main Street in the 1950s, malls in the 1970s, superstores in the 1990s—since World War II we have seen a fundamental shift in the retailing paradigm with each new generation, and now we are on the verge of another revolution: e-commerce. Experts agree that Internet retail operations will fundamentally change customer's expectations about convenience, speed, comparability, price, and service. Furthermore, project management will be a driving force behind this revolution. A case in point is the development of e.Schwab and the transformation of a discount brokerage firm into an on-line brokerage firm.

Charles R. Schwab founded The Charles Schwab Corporation in 1971 as a traditional brokerage company and in 1974 became a pioneer in the discount brokerage business. Schwab's journey into e-commerce began in late 1995 with a series of messages to chief information officer Dawn Lepore from one of her research teams. The group wanted to show her some experimental software that would allow Schwab's different computer systems to talk to one another. It was the sort of project that software designers love: challenging, technically complicated, and intended to solve an obscure problem that was difficult to explain to anyone but other techies. Lepore scheduled a demonstration and invited one of the company's biggest technology nuts, Charles Schwab himself, to attend.

The application the engineers chose was a very simple Web-based stock trade. Their program allowed a Schwab server to take an order from a Web browser on a PC, route it through all of Schwab's sophisticated backend systems and mainframes, execute it, and send a confirmation back to the PC. At the time, most existing Web trading systems required that orders be printed out and entered by hand into another system, defeating the point of automated trading. As it turns out, Lepore's computer researchers were less interested in on-line brokerage than in winning Lepore's approval to continue research on their obscure middleware project. But Lepore and Schwab instantly recognized the implications of the patched-together demo. Says Schwab, "I fell off my chair."

Within weeks an independent project team was assigned to get Web trading up and running at Schwab. The team consisted of Schwab executives and an Israeli engineer named Gideon Sassoon, whom Lepore had hired away from IBM to head technology development for the team. Working in secrecy at first, the team grew to 30 people and evolved into a separate electronic brokerage unit, called e.Schwab, which bypassed Schwab's normal hierarchy and reported directly to co-CEO David Pottruck.

A handful of deep-discount brokerages, such as E*Trade and Ameritrade, were racing to perfect Web trading at the same time. "We had to figure out how to compete with these small brokerages," says Pottruck. "So we needed a group that felt like they did: nimble, unshackled from the larger bureaucracy." And indeed, the early days were packed with intense, freewheeling meetings in which everyone could fit into one room and shout ideas back and forth.

By the middle of 1996, e.Schwab was ready. Investors had to send in a physical check (or wire transfer) to open an e.Schwab account, but after that they could trade any security available through a regular account—stocks, mutual funds, options—by logging onto e.Schwab's Web site. They would pay a flat $39 (quickly dropped to $29.95) for any stock trade up to 1,000 shares. The only publicity for the launch of e.Schwab was an announcement at the annual shareholders' meeting.

Despite the lack of fanfare, the new service was an immediate success. Says Sasson, "We were totally unprepared. Customers began voting with their keyboards, and in two weeks we reached 25,000 Web accounts—our goal for the entire year." By the end of 1997, all on-line accounts, both at e.Schwab and at regular Schwab, had grown to 1.2 million. By the end of the third quarter of 1998, 58 percent of total trades at Schwab were Web transactions.

Source: Adapted from Erick Schonfeld, "Schwab Puts It All Online," *Fortune* (December 7, 1998), pp. 94–99.

question becomes one of how to create an organizational environment that supports multiproject management. A process is needed to prioritize and develop a portfolio of small projects that supports the mission of the organization.

In summary, there are a variety of environmental forces interacting in today's business world that contribute to the increased demand for good project management across all industries and sectors. Project management appears to be ideally suited for a business environment requiring accountability, flexibility, innovation, speed, and continuous improvement. However, people do not embrace change easily or quickly; the next section traces the gradual adoption of project management methods within organizations over time.

THE EVOLUTION OF PROJECT MANAGEMENT SYSTEMS

Implementing project management in an organization almost always occurs in small, incremental phases. Different models exist that attempt to capture this evolution. Both the Software Engineering Institute and the Project Management Institute have developed "maturity" models that trace the evolution of project management practices in an organization.[8] A three-phase model based on the authors' observations is presented in this section.

Phase One: Ad Hoc Use   This phase typically begins with an individual or department champion initiating the use of one or more of the basic project management tools in a project. A variety of reasons exist for this first venture. For example, often a special project is picked in which timing or control is important, competitors are successfully using the project management tools, or the company senses a lack of control on all its projects. The tools appear to hold potential for improving project success. These early efforts will use project management tools such as networks and the assignment of project activities to organization units. Top management will have little or no involvement in the decision to use these tools. In a few cases, these attempts end in failure. The blame may be placed on the tools, but other circumstances are found to be the cause in most cases. The cause is usually the complete lack of coordination between projects and resources. Sometimes project management tools are abandoned for a period, but they are usually tried again in a few years. Near the end of this phase, conflicts across functional lines often appear as tensions arise over the control and direction of projects.

Phase Two: Formal Application   Getting through the first phase in an organization may take two to five years. In phase two various needs and inadequacies are recognized as barriers to project success. Typical of this phase is the recognition that project management training is needed for every management level in the organization. Attending project management workshops of all types is encouraged. Managers know that many projects are running concurrently and that multiproject resource scheduling is imperative. Deliverables and time to market for projects receive constant attention. Top management takes an interest in better management of projects. The need for quality control becomes an issue. The concept of a customer or client for each project becomes part of the organizational culture. Project managers are given more control over the projects; functional managers are less fearful of giving up power to project managers. Questions relating to the effectiveness of the current organization structure are heard in private conversations. An ad hoc group is studying how to transform the organization into a formal matrix structure. More attention is given to project leadership. Top management is not active in project selection and prioritizing projects. The relationship between strategic planning and projects is difficult to discern. Management needs a retreat to integrate strategic planning and projects.

Phase Three: Project-Driven Organizations   In phase three the outlook is long run. Top management is now playing a significant role in setting strategy, in developing a balanced project portfolio, and in setting project priorities. The prioritized projects relate directly to the strategic plan of the organization. Project management is a part of the organizational culture. Everyone is speaking the same language and is focused and working as a team. The organizational structure has shifted toward a project matrix and project teams with dedicated resources. Resources are balanced across all projects by their priority. Projects are integrated with accounting. Good project leaders are recognized and valued by top management. Evaluation and incentive systems are tied to individual contributions to the project team and the group effort of the project team. Training and policy manuals have been written for each phase of the project life cycle. Training in all dimensions of project management is ongoing; the goal is excellence in managing projects. Termination of projects includes a project audit and evaluation of time, cost, and technical performance as well as management performance. The outcome of this 5- to 10-year, sometimes painful, effort is a disciplined, integrated, organizational approach to managing and implementing projects linked to strategic plans. Organizations can be reasonably certain this integrated approach will improve controls over time and budget; however, it is likely the internal operations of the organization may become more complex.

These three phases occur at different times depending on the type and size of the firm. For example, some large organizations may resemble a mosaic with different departments in various phases at any given time. Every organization that finds projects to be a major part of its effort (as, for example, software, hardware, product, construction, engineering, service, consulting, or research and development [R&D] firms) constantly tries to improve its approach to managing projects. It is probably not practical to expect to leapfrog to phase three immediately. Movement through these phases can be incremental. However, it is probably desirous to move to phase three as quickly as possible to compete more effectively. Migration to excellence can be expedited by developing the skills and capabilities of every manager in the organization through training in project management—not as a set of disjointed concepts but as an integrated whole.

PROJECT MANAGEMENT TODAY—AN INTEGRATIVE APPROACH

Some project managers have used pieces of systems that are useful for managing projects. For example, networks, bar charts, job costing, task forces, partnering, and scheduling all have been used—sometimes very successfully and other times with poor results. As the world becomes more competitive, the importance of managing the process of project management and "getting it right the first time" takes on new meaning. Piecemeal systems fail to tie to the overall strategies of the firm. Piecemeal project priority systems fail to prioritize project selection to resources and those projects that contribute most to the strategic plan. Piecemeal tools and techniques fail to be integrated throughout the project life cycle. Piecemeal approaches fail to balance the application of project planning and control methods with appropriate adjustments in the organization's culture to support project endeavors.

Today emphasis is on development of an integrated project management process that focuses all project effort toward the strategic plan of the organization and reinforces mastery of both the project management tools/techniques and the interpersonal skills necessary to orchestrate successful project completion. For some organizations, integrating projects with strategy will require reengineering the entire business management process. For others, integration will mean carefully establishing linkages among the piecemeal systems already in place and altering the focus to one of a total system. At the individual level, for some professionals to become effective project managers will require augmenting their leadership and team-building skills with modern project planning and control methods. For others it will require complementing their administrative skills with the capacity to inspire and lead a divergent cast of professionals to project completion.

Integration in project management directs attention to two key areas. The first area is integration of projects with the strategic plan of the organization. The second area is integration within the process of managing actual projects. Each of these areas is examined next.

Integration of Projects with the Strategic Plan

In some organizations, selection and management of projects often fail to support the strategic plan of the organization. Strategic plans are written by one group of managers, projects selected by another group, and projects implemented by another. These independent decisions by different groups of managers create a set of conditions leading to conflict, confusion, and—frequently—an unsatisfied customer. Under these conditions, resources of the organization are wasted in non-value-added activities/projects.

An integrated project management system is one in which all of the parts are interrelated. A change in any one of the parts will influence the whole. Every organization has a customer it is seeking to satisfy. The customer sets the raison d'être for the organization. Mission, objectives, and strategies are set to meet the needs of customer(s). Development of a mission, objectives, and organization strategies depend on the external and internal environmental factors. External environmental factors are usually classified as political, social, economic, and technological; they signal opportunities or threats in setting the direction for the organization. Internal environmental factors are frequently classified as strengths and weaknesses such as management, facilities, core competencies, and financial condition. The outcome of the analysis of all these environmental factors is a set of strategies designed to best meet the needs of customers. But this is only the first step (see Figure 1–3).

Implementing strategies is the most difficult step. Strategies are typically implemented through projects. Creative minds always propose more projects than there are resources. The key is selecting from the many proposals those projects that make the largest and most balanced contribution to the objectives and strategies (and thus, customers) of the organization. This means prioritizing projects so that scarce resources are allocated to the right projects. Once a project has been selected for implementation, the focus switches to the project management process that sets the stage for how the project will be implemented or delivered.

Integration within the Process of Managing Actual Projects

There are two dimensions within the project management process. The first dimension is the technical side of the management process, which consists of the formal, disciplined, pure logic parts of the process. The technical side relies on the formal information system available. This dimension includes planning, scheduling, and control-

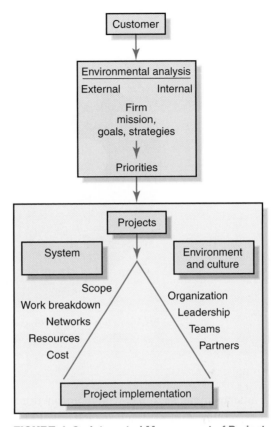

FIGURE 1–3 Integrated Management of Projects

ling projects. Clear project scope statements are written to link the project and customer and to facilitate planning and control. Creation of the deliverables and work breakdown structures facilitate planning and monitoring the progress of the project. The work breakdown structure serves as a database that links all levels in the organization, major deliverables, and all work—right down to the tasks in a work package. Effects of project changes are documented and traceable. Thus, any change in one part of the project is traceable to the source by the integrated linkages of the system. This integrated information approach can provide all project managers and the customer with decision information appropriate to their level and needs. A successful project manager will be well trained in the technical side of managing projects (see Figure 1–4).

The second dimension is the sociocultural side of the project management process. In contrast with the orderly world of project planning, this dimension involves the much messier, often contradictory and paradoxical world of implementation. It centers on creating a temporary social system within a larger organizational environment that combines the talents of a divergent set of professionals working to complete the project. Project managers must shape a project culture that stimulates teamwork and high levels of personal motivation as well as a capacity to quickly identify and resolve problems that threaten project work. This dimension also involves managing the interface between the project and external environment. Project managers have to assuage and shape expectations of customers, sustain the political support of top

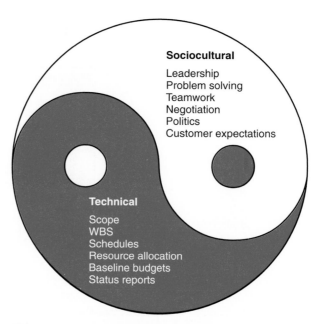

FIGURE 1–4 The Technical and Sociocultural Dimensions of the Project Management Process

management, negotiate with their functional counterparts, monitor subcontractors, and so on. Overall, the manager must build a cooperative social network among a divergent set of allies with different standards, commitments, and perspectives.

Some suggest that the technical dimension represents the "science" of project management while the sociocultural dimension represents the "art" of managing a project. To be successful, managers must be a master of both. Unfortunately, some project managers become preoccupied with the planning and technical dimension of project management. Often their first real exposure to project management is through project management software, and they become infatuated with network charts, Gantt diagrams, and performance variances and attempt to manage a project from a distance. Conversely, there are other managers who manage projects by the "seat of their pants," relying heavily on team dynamics and organizational politics to complete a project. Good project managers balance their attention to both the technical and sociocultural dimensions of project management.

SUMMARY

There are powerful environmental forces contributing to the rapid expansion of project management approaches to business problems and opportunities. A project is defined as a nonroutine, one-time effort limited by time, resources, and performance specifications designed to meet customer needs. One of the distinguishing characteristics of project management is that it has both a beginning and an end and typically consists of four phases: definition, planning, execution, and delivery. Effective project management begins with selecting and prioritizing projects that support the firm's mission and strategy. Successful implementation requires mastering both the technical and the sociocultural dimensions of the process.

RESEARCH HIGHLIGHT
Chaos: Software Projects

The Standish Group International is a market research and advisory firm specializing in mission-critical software and electronic commerce. They have conducted and published extensive research on the success and failure of software development/application projects. Their research, code name "Chaos," shows that a staggering 31 percent of software projects will be canceled before they ever get completed. In addition, 53 percent of projects will cost 189 percent of their original estimates. In terms of success, on the average only 16 percent of software projects are completed on time and within budget. In larger companies, the success rate is much worse—9 percent. The Standish Group estimated that in 1995 American companies and government agencies spent $81 billion for canceled software projects.

The Chaos research is based on "key findings" from research surveys and personal interviews. The respondents were information technology (IT) executive managers. The sample included large, medium, and small companies across major industry segments, for example, banking; securities; manufacturing; retail; wholesale; health care; insurance service; and local, state, and federal organizations. The total sample size was 365 respondents and represented 8,380 projects.

Based on an in-depth comparison of successful versus unsuccessful software projects, the Standish Group created a success potential chart that identifies key factors associated with project success. The success criteria were weighted based on the input from the surveyed IT managers. The most important criterion, "user involvement," was given 19 success points, while the least important, "hard-working, focused staff," was given 3 success points. The following chart lists the criteria in order of importance:

Success Criteria	Points
1. User involvement	19
2. Executive management support	16
3. Clear statement of requirements	15
4. Proper planning	11
5. Realistic expectations	10
6. Smaller project milestones	9
7. Competent staff	8
8. Project team ownership	6
9. Clear vision and objectives	3
10. Hard-working, focused staff	3
Total	100

Source: Used by permission of the Standish Group International, Inc., 586 Olde King's Highway, Dennis, MA 02638.

TEXT OVERVIEW

This text is written to provide the reader with a comprehensive, integrative understanding of the project management process. The text focuses both on the science of project management and the art of managing projects. Following this introductory chapter, Chapter 2 focuses on how organizations go about evaluating and selecting projects. Special attention is devoted to the importance of linking project selection to the mission and strategy of the firm.

The next five chapters focus on developing a plan for the project; after all, project success begins with a good plan. Chapter 3 deals with defining the scope of the project, developing a work breakdown structure (WBS), and formulating cost and time estimates. Chapter 4 focuses on utilizing the information from the WBS to create a project plan in the form of a timed and sequenced network of activities. Risks are a potential threat to project management, and Chapter 5 examines how organizations and managers identify and manage risks associated with project work. Chapter 6 examines strategies for reducing ("crashing") project time either prior to the initiation of the project or in response to problems or new demands placed on the project. Finally, resource allocation is added to the project plan in Chapter 7, with special attention devoted to how resource limitations impact the schedule and budget of the project.

Chapters 8 through 11 focus on project implementation and the sociocultural side of project management, beginning with Chapter 8, which examines how organizations go about managing projects. The traditional discussion of matrix management and other organizational forms is augmented by a detailed discussion of the significance the culture of the organization plays in the implementation of projects. Chapter 9 focuses on the role of the project manager as a leader and stresses the importance of managing project interfaces within the organization. Chapter 10 focuses on the core project team. It combines the latest information on team dynamics with leadership skills/techniques for developing a high-performance project team. Chapter 11 continues the theme of managing project interfaces by extending it to the management of extra-organizational project relationships (that is, contractors, customers, suppliers). This chapter also focuses on the art of negotiating, which is a core competency for project management.

Chapter 12 focuses on the kinds of information managers use to monitor project progress, with special attention devoted to the key concept of earned value. Issues surrounding the termination or completion of the project are dealt with in Chapter 13. Implementation of project management in multicultural, international environments is the subject of Chapter 14. Finally, Chapter 15 looks toward the future of project management, includes a special segment on pursuing a career in project management, and tries to put the management of projects in a holistic perspective.

Throughout this text you will be exposed to the major aspects of the project management system. However, a true understanding of project management comes not from what a scope statement is, or the critical path, or partnering with contractors, but from trying to understand how the different elements of the project management system interact to determine the fate of a project. The key to success, then, becomes managing conflicting demands and the interaction among different elements of a project (scope, plans, schedule, risk, customer, team, other stakeholders, and so on), not the elements themselves. For example, project managers must manage the interactions among scope, cost, schedule, and customer expectations. They must manage the interactions between the project management information system and the people who provide the data and use it. They must manage the interactions between the core project team and the outsiders they depend on. If, by the end of this text, you come to appreciate these key points of balancing your skills in the technical and sociocultural dimensions and managing the interactions among them, you should have a distinct competitive advantage over others aspiring to work in the field of project management.

REVIEW QUESTIONS

1. Define a project. What are four characteristics that help differentiate projects from other functions carried out in the daily operations of the organization?

2. What are some of the key environmental forces that have changed the way projects are managed? What has been the effect of these forces on the management of projects?
3. Why is the implementation of projects important to strategic planning and the project manager?
4. The technical and sociocultural dimensions of project management are two sides to the same coin. Explain.
5. Implementing project management techniques into an organization appears to be evolutionary rather than revolutionary. Why is it improbable that an organization will be able to leapfrog to a holistic project management system in one year?
6. What is meant by an integrative approach to project management? Why is this approach important in today's environment?

EXERCISES

1. Review the front page of your local newspaper, and try to identify all the projects contained in the articles. How many were you able to find?
2. Individually identify what you consider to be the greatest achievements accomplished by mankind in the last five decades. Now share your list with three to five other students in the class, and come up with an expanded list. Review these accomplishments in terms of the definition of a project. What does your review suggest about the importance of project management?
3. Check out the Project Management Institute's home page at *www.pmi.org*.
    a. Review general information about PMI as well as membership information.
    b. See if there is a PMI chapter in your state. It not, where is the closest one?
    c. From the news link, access information on PMI's Project Management Body of Knowledge (PMBOK), or go directly to it at *www.pmi.org/publictn/pmboktoc.htm*. What is PMBOK?
    d. Explore other links that PMI provides. What do these links tell you about the nature and future of project management?

Note: If you have any difficulty accessing any of the Web addresses listed here or elsewhere in the text, you can find up-to-date addresses on the home page of Dr. Erik Larson, coauthor of this text: *www.bus.orst.edu/faculty/larson*.

ENDNOTES

1. Peter W. G. Morris, *The Management of Projects* (London: Thomas Telford Services Ltd., 1994), p. 1.
2. Thomas A. Stewart, "The Corporate Jungle Spawns a New Species: The Project Manager," *Fortune* (September 1996), pp. 14–15.
3. Bernard Wysocki, "Flying Solo: High-Tech Nomads Write New Program for Future of Work," *The Wall Street Journal* (August 19, 1996), p. 1.
4. Jeffrey K. Pinto and Om P. Kharbanda, "Lessons for an Accidental Profession," *Business Horizons,* vol. 38, no. 2 (March–April 1995), p. 36.
5. William S. Ruggles, PMI president, "President's Report," *PM Network,* vol. 11, no. 10 (October 1997), p. 52.
6. David I. Cleland, "The Strategic Pathway of Project Management," *Proceedings of the 28th Annual PMI Symposium* (Newtown Square, PA: PMI, 1997), pp. 519–23.
7. For a convincing statement on the need to enhance project managers' cross-cultural sensitivity see: Dragan Milosevic, "Echoes of the Silent Language of Project Management," *Project Management Journal,* vol. 30, no. 1 (March 1999), pp. 27–39.
8. Anita Fincher and Ginger Levin, "Project Management Maturity Model," *Proceedings of the 28th Annual PMI Symposium (*Newtown Square, PA: PMI, 1997), pp. 1028–35.
9. Stephen Baker, "The Best Wireless Phone on the Market," *Business Week* (August 10, 1998), p. 60.

South American Adventures Unlimited

SA Adventures Unlimited was formed four years ago by Michael and Jill Rodriguez. Michael was a trained geologist, while Jill had a masters degree in Spanish. They were both avid outdoor enthusiasts and fell in love while trekking across the Andes in Chile. Upon graduation they seized upon the idea of starting their own specialized tour business that would focus on organizing and leading "high-end" adventure trips in South America. Their first trip was a three-week excursion across Ecuador and Peru. The trip was a resounding success, and they became convinced that they could make a livelihood doing something they both enjoyed.

After the first year, Adventures Unlimited began to slowly expand the size and scope of the business. The Rodriguezes' strategy was a simple one. They recruited experienced, reliable people who shared their passion for South America and the outdoors. They helped these people organize specific trips and advertised the excursion over the Internet and in travel magazines.

Adventures Unlimited has grown from offering 4 trips a year to having 16 different excursions scheduled, including trips to Central America. They now had an administrative support staff of 3 people and a relatively stable group of 5 trip planners/guides whom they hired on a trip-by-trip contract basis. The company enjoyed a high level of repeat business and often used their customers' suggestions to organize future trips.

Although the Rodriguezes were pleased with the success of their venture, they were beginning to encounter problems that worried them about the future. A couple of the tours went overbudget because of unanticipated costs, which eroded that year's profit. In one case, they had to refund 30 percent of the tour fee because a group was stranded five days in Blanco Puente after missing a train connection. They were also having a hard time maintaining the high level of customer satisfaction to which they were accustomed. Customers were beginning to complain about the quality of the accommodations and the price of the tours. One group, unfortunately, was struck by a bad case of food poisoning. Finally, the Rodriguezes were having a hard time tracking costs across projects and typically did not know how well they did until after their taxes were prepared. This made it difficult to plan future excursions.

The Rodriguezes shared these concerns around the family dinner table. Among the members in attendance was Michael's younger brother, Mario, a student at a nearby university. After dinner, Mario approached Michael and Jill and suggested that they look into what business people called "project management." He had been briefly exposed to project management in his Business Operations class and felt that it might apply to their tour business.

1. To what extent does project management apply to Adventures Unlimited?
2. What kind of training in project management should the Rodriguezes, the administrative staff, and tour guides receive to improve the operation of Adventures Unlimited? Try to identify major topics or skill sets that should be addressed.

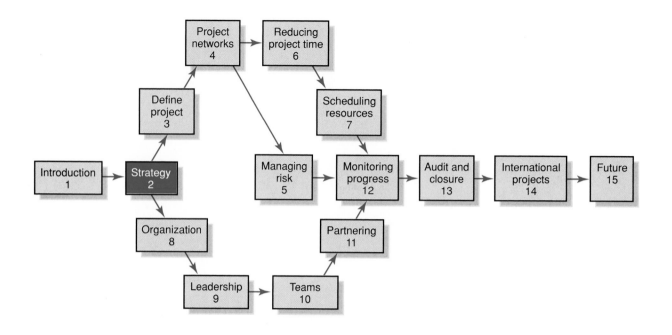

Integration of Organization Strategy with Projects

The Strategic Management Process: An Overview
Absence of a Priority System Linked to Strategy Creates Problems
Moving to an Effective Organizational Priority System
A Generic Selection and Priority System
Assessing the Effectiveness of the Priority System Over the Long Haul—The Balanced Scorecard Model
Case Study: A Detailed Selection Priority Model from Practice
Summary
Appendix 2–1: Sample: Interface Roles and Responsibilities of Key Players
Appendix 2–2: Sample: Interview Questionnaire

CHAPTER TWO

Integration of Organization Strategy with Projects

Strategy is implemented through projects. Every project should have a clear link to organization strategy.

Today's savage global competition has altered organizational culture and business processes. Business has been forced to downsize and decentralize operations. The resulting changes are most obvious in organizations strongly influenced by time to market—for example, Bechtel, Cable Network News (CNN), Electronic Data Systems (EDS), and Hewlett-Packard (HP). In the late 1980s and early 1990s these and other organizations addressed this environmental transformation by shifting their organization culture to be project driven and results oriented. Dinsmore coined the phrase "managing organizations by projects" to describe this evolving shift in organization cultures.[1] It is clear that the intent is to use projects to move organizations toward their strategic targets. Linking all projects to the strategic direction of the organization is crucial to success.

Every project should contribute to the organization's strategic plan, which is designed to meet the future needs of its customers. However, there are few medium or large organizations in which many managers can identify a project's priority and link it with the strategic plan. Ensuring a strong linkage between the strategic plan and projects is a very tedious task that demands a great deal of continuous attention from top and middle management. The larger and more diverse an organization, the more difficult it is to create and maintain this strong link. There is ample evidence that many organizations have not developed a process that clearly links project selection to the strategic plan. The result is poor utilization of the organization's resources—people, money, equipment, and core competencies.

How can an organization ensure this linkage? The answer requires integration of projects within the strategic plan. Integration assumes the existence of a strategic plan and a process for prioritizing projects by their contribution to the plan. A major factor that will ensure the success of integrating the plan with projects lies in the creation of a process that is open and published for all participants to review. This chapter presents an overview of the importance of strategic planning and the process for developing a strategic plan. Typical problems encountered when strategy and projects are not linked are noted. A generic methodology that ensures integration by creating very strong linkages of project selection and priority to the strategic plan is then discussed.

Finally, a priority selection model used in practice is explained. The intended outcomes are clear organization focus, best use of scarce organization resources (people, equipment, capital), and a vehicle for motivation.

Why Project Managers Need to Understand the Strategic Management Process

In today's world of organization *downsizing*, the process of strategic planning has come to include participants from nearly every level of the organization—as opposed to only senior management. There is a distinct trend toward a top-down *and* bottom-up approach to strategic management that encourages commitment from stakeholders at every level. Project managers are finding themselves a part of this process and are becoming more involved in strategic planning and the project selection process. This participation is good for several reasons. First, involvement gives the project manager an overall perspective of the organization focus, which typically leads to professional growth and more reasoned decisions. Second, experienced project managers can provide valuable insights concerning organizational capabilities and resource constraints. Next, each project manager can see his or her project in relation to other projects. Finally, awareness of the selection criteria and process facilitates reassignment of resources and priorities among projects in a less hostile manner. Hence, project managers find it valuable to have a keen understanding of strategic management and project selection process. The latter is discussed next.

THE STRATEGIC MANAGEMENT PROCESS: AN OVERVIEW

Strategic management is the process of assessing "what we are" and deciding and implementing "what we intend to be and how we are going to get there." Strategy describes how an organization intends to compete with the resources available in the existing and perceived future environment.

Two major dimensions of strategic management are responding to changes in the external environment and allocating scarce resources of the firm to improve its competitive position. Constant scanning of the external environment for changes is a major requirement for survival in a dynamic competitive environment. The second dimension is the internal responses to new action programs aimed at enhancing the competitive position of the firm. The nature of the responses depends on the type of business, environment volatility, competition, and the organizational culture.

Strategic management provides the theme and focus of the future direction of the organization. It supports consistency of action at every level of the organization. It encourages integration because effort and resources are committed to common goals and strategies. It is a continuous, iterative process aimed at developing an integrated and coordinated long-term plan of action. Strategic management positions the organization to meet the needs and requirements of its customers for the long term. With the long-term position identified, objectives are set, and strategies are developed to achieve objectives and then translated into actions by implementing projects. Strategy can decide the survival of an organization. Most organizations are successful in *formulating* strategies for what course(s) they should pursue. However, the problem in many organizations is *implementing* strategies—that is, making them happen. Integration of strategy formulation and implementation often does not exist.

The components of strategic management are closely linked, and all are directed toward the future success of the organization. Strategic management requires strong links among mission, goals, objectives, strategy, and implementation. The mission gives the general purpose of the organization. Goals give global targets within the mis-

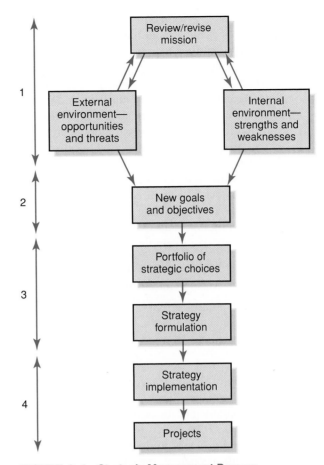

FIGURE 2–1   Strategic Management Process

sion. Objectives give specific targets to goals. Objectives give rise to formulation of strategies to reach objectives. Finally, strategies require actions and tasks to be implemented. In most cases the actions to be taken represent projects. Figure 2–1 shows a schematic of the strategic management process and major activities required.

Strategic Management Process Includes Four Activities

The typical sequence of activities of the strategic management process is outlined here; a description of each activity then follows:

1. Review and define the organizational mission.
2. Set long-range goals and objectives.
3. Analyze and formulate strategies to reach objectives.
4. Implement strategies through projects.

Review and Define the Organizational Mission   The mission identifies "what we want to become" or the raison d' être. Mission statements identify the scope of the organization in terms of its product or service. Everyone in the organization should be keenly aware of the organization's mission. For example, at Arthur Andersen Consulting, partners who fail to recite the mission statement on demand are required to buy lunch. A written mission statement provides focus for decision making when shared by organizational managers and employees. The mission statement communicates and identifies the purpose of the organization to all stakeholders. Mission statements can be used for evaluating organization performance.

Traditional components found in mission statements are major products and services, target customers and markets, and geographical domain. In addition, statements frequently include organizational philosophy, key technologies, public image, and contribution to society. Researchers Pearce and David found that mention of such factors in mission statements related to business success.[2] Mission statements change infrequently. However, when the nature of the business changes or shifts, it may require a revised mission statement. For example, the breakup of American Telephone and Telegraph (AT&T) required a shift in mission from one of telecommunications to information handling. More specific mission statements tend to give better results because of a tighter focus. Mission statements decrease the chance of false directions by stakeholders. For example, compare the phrasing of the following mission statements:

Provide bridge design services.

Provide waste plant design services.

Provide engineering services.

Increase shareholder value.

Provide high-value products to our customer.

Clearly, the first two statements leave less chance for misinterpretation than the others. A rule-of-thumb test for a mission statement is, if the statement can be anybody's mission statement, it will not provide the guidance and focus intended. The mission sets the parameters for developing objectives.

Long-Range Goals and Objectives   Objectives translate the organization mission into specific, concrete, measurable terms. Organizational objectives set targets for all levels of the organization. Objectives pinpoint the direction managers believe the organization should move toward. Objectives answer in detail *where* a firm is headed and *when* it is going to get there. Typically, objectives for the organization cover markets, products, innovation, productivity, quality, finance, profitability, and people. In every case, objectives should be as operational as possible. That is, objectives should include a time frame, be measurable, be an identifiable state, and be realistic. Doran created the memory device shown in Exhibit 2–1 which is useful when writing objectives:[3]

Each level below the organizational objectives should support the higher-level objectives in more detail. For example, if a firm making leather luggage sets an objective of achieving a 40 percent increase in sales through a research and development strat-

EXHIBIT 2–1		
CHARACTERISTICS OF OBJECTIVES		
S	**Specific**	Be specific in targeting an objective
M	**Measurable**	Establish a measurable indicator(s) of progress
A	**Assignable**	Make the objective assignable to one person for completion
R	**Realistic**	State what can realistically be done with available resources
T	**Time related**	State when the objective can be achieved, that is, duration

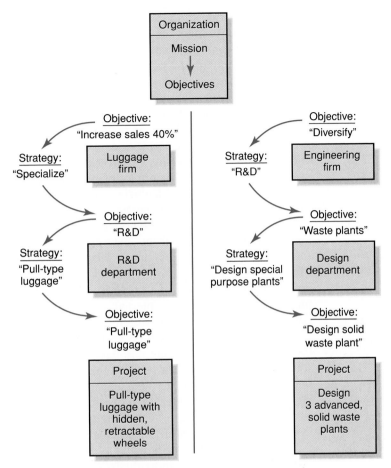

FIGURE 2–2 Strategy, Objectives, and Project Linkages

egy, this charge is passed to the marketing, production, and R&D departments. The R&D department accepts the firm's strategy as their objective, and their strategy becomes the design and development of a new "pull-type luggage with hidden retractable wheels." At this point the objective becomes a project to be implemented—to develop the retractable wheel luggage for market within six months within a budget of $200,000. See Figure 2–2 for a schematic of the linkages. A similar schematic is also shown for an engineering firm in Figure 2–2. The engineering firm sets an objective to diversify by entering the waste-treatment-plant market. This objective becomes the strategy for their design department. In turn, this strategy becomes an objective for the engineering department, which decides on a strategy of specializing in the design and construction management of solid-waste plants. Implementation becomes a project of designing three technologically advanced solid-waste plants to meet the needs of local governmental groups, within eight months at a budget of $500,000.

Analyze and Formulate Strategies to Reach Objectives   Formulating strategy answers the question of *what* needs to be done to reach objectives. Strategy formulation includes determining and evaluating alternatives that support the organization's objectives and selecting the best alternative. The first step is a realistic evaluation of the past and current position of the enterprise. This step typically includes an analysis of "who are the customers" and "what are their needs as they (the *customers*) see them."

The next step is an assessment of the internal and external environments. What are the internal strengths and weaknesses of the enterprise? Examples of internal strengths or weaknesses could be core competencies, such as technology, product quality, management talent, low debt, and dealer networks. Managers can alter the strengths and weaknesses. Opportunities and threats usually represent external forces for change such as technology, industry structure, and competition. Competitive benchmarking tools are sometimes used here to assess current and future directions. Opportunities and threats are the flip sides of each other. That is, a threat can be perceived as an opportunity, or vice versa. Examples of perceived external threats could be a slowing of the economy, a maturing life cycle, exchange rates, or government regulation. Typical opportunities are increasing demand, emerging markets, and demographics. Managers or individual firms have limited opportunities to influence such external environmental factors; however, in recent years notable exceptions have been new technologies (laser scanning, computers) and alliances (the Kodak and Fuji joint development of film standards for the industry).[4] The keys are to attempt to forecast fundamental industry changes and stay in a proactive mode rather than a reactive one. This assessment of the external and internal environments is known as the SWOT analysis (strengths, weaknesses, opportunities, and threats).

From this analysis, critical issues and a portfolio of strategic alternatives are identified. These alternatives are compared with the current portfolio and available resources; strategies are then selected that should support the basic mission and objectives of the organization. Critical analysis of the strategies includes asking questions: Does the strategy take advantage of our core competencies? Does the strategy exploit our competitive advantage? Does the strategy maximize meeting customers' needs? Does the strategy fit within our acceptable risk range?

Strategy formulation ends with cascading objectives or tasks assigned to lower divisions, departments, or individuals. Strategy formulation is a relatively straightforward process when compared with planning how strategies will be implemented. A rule of thumb for management effort in formulating strategy might range around 20 percent, while determining *how* strategy will be implemented might consume 80 percent of management's effort.

Implement Strategies through Projects   Implementation answers the question of *how* strategies will be realized, given available resources. The conceptual framework for strategy implementation lacks the structure and discipline found in strategy formulation. Implementation requires action and completing tasks; the latter frequently means mission-critical projects. Therefore, implementation must include attention to several key areas.

First, completing tasks requires allocation of resources. Resources typically represent funds, people, management talents, technological skills, and equipment. Frequently, implementation of projects is treated as an "addendum" rather than an integral part of the strategic management process. However, multiple objectives place conflicting demands on organizational resources. Second, implementation requires a formal and informal organization that complements and supports strategy and projects. Authority, responsibility, and performance all depend on organization structure and culture. Third, planning and control systems must be in place to be certain project activities necessary to ensure strategies are effectively performed. Fourth, motivating project contributors will be a major factor for achieving project success. Finally, an area receiving more attention in recent years is prioritizing projects. Although the strategy implementation process is not as clear as strategy formulation, all managers realize that, without implementation, success is impossible.

RESEARCH HIGHLIGHT
Muddling

Although there are cases of good luck or simply "muddling through," there is credible evidence that effective strategic planning practices have a positive impact on organizational performance. Organizations that are good at strategy formulation and implementation tend to perform better than those that are not. Research supports this conclusion. Rhyne studied 210 *Fortune* 500 firms to find if those conforming to "good" strategic management practices performed better than those not conforming.* He found a positive relationship between good strategic management practice and financial performance in the long run. Four other studies found similar results for firms using strategic management practices and financial performance.†

There is growing awareness of this phenomenon among managers. Armstrong found the number of firms using strategic planning has increased dramatically.‡ The format or process used to formulate and implement strategy may differ, but careful attention to the process itself can ignite support for the organization's objectives. Simply working through the strategic management process can be of major benefit. The process forces evaluation of the external and internal environments—opportunities and threats, strengths and weaknesses—in deciding the future positioning of the organization.

---

*Lawerence C. Rhyne, "The Relationship of Strategic Planning to Financial Performance," *Strategic Management Journal,* vol. 7 (September–October 1986), pp. 423–36.

†Richard B. Robinson, Jr., "The Importance of 'Outsiders' in Small Firm Strategic Planning," *Academy of Management Journal,* vol. 25, no. 1 (March 1982), pp. 80–93, Jonathan B. Welch, "Strategic Planning Could Improve Your Price Share," *Long Range Planning* (April 1984), pp. 144–47, J. S. Bracker and J. N. Pearson, "Planning and Financial Performance of Small Manufacturing Firms," *Strategic Management Journal* (November–December 1986), pp. 503–22, and Donald W. Beard and Gregory G. Dess, "Corporate Business Strategy, Business Level Strategy, and Firm Performance," *Academy of Management Journal,* vol. 24, no. 4 (December 1981), pp. 663–88.

‡J. S. Armstrong, "The Value of Formal Planning for Strategic Decisions," *Strategic Planning Journal* (1982), pp. 197–212, and Gary Hamel and C. K. Prahalad, *Competing for the Future* (Boston, MA: Harvard Business School Press, 1995).

ABSENCE OF A PRIORITY SYSTEM LINKED TO STRATEGY CREATES PROBLEMS

Connection of Projects to Strategic Plan—The Implementation Gap

In organizations with short product life cycles, it is interesting to note that frequently participation in strategic planning and implementation includes participants from all levels within the organization. However, in perhaps 80 percent of the remaining product and service organizations, top management pretty much formulates strategy and leaves strategy implementation to functional managers. The fact that these objectives and strategies are made *independently* at different levels by functional groups within the organization hierarchy causes manifold problems. There may be some logical explanations for this apparent void. Missions, objectives, and organizational strategies set by top managers tend to lack specificity, give only general direction, and set major constraints; frequently resource availability and allocations are not part of the

SNAPSHOT FROM PRACTICE
THE SAS TURNAROUND

During the early 1980s Jan Carlzon was appointed chief operating officer for Scandinavian Airlines (SAS). At this time, the entire airline industry was in the midst of a slump, and SAS was about to record a second straight year of losses. Carlzon halted the practice of instituting across-the-board cuts and instead focused on developing a strategic mission that would make SAS profitable during a time of zero market growth. The strategy was to make SAS known as the best airline in the world for the frequent business traveler. SAS realized that business travelers were the most stable part of the market and tended to purchase full-fare tickets as opposed to discounted tickets. Furthermore, business travelers tended to have unique needs that would allow SAS to develop services to attract their full-fare business.

Under Carlzon's leadership, SAS scrutinized every project and expense as to whether it contributed to improving the service to the frequent business traveler. If the answer was no, no matter what it was or how dear it was to those within SAS, it was cut. Projects such as developing vacation packages to the Mediterranean were eliminated, and overall SAS was able to cut $40 million in nonessential expenses. At the same time, Carlzon persuaded the SAS board to invest $45 million and increase operating expenses $12 million a year for 147 different projects designed to attract and serve the frequent business traveler. They launched a comprehensive punctuality campaign, improved the traffic hub in Copenhagen, and offered customer service courses for more than 12,000 staff members.

SAS dropped first-class seating and created "Euro-Class" at full-fare coach prices. They installed movable partitions in their aircraft to separate the Euro-Class section from the others. They were among the first airlines to create comfortable lounges at the terminals with telephone and telex services for Euro-Class passengers. They gave Euro-Class travelers separate, express check-in counters, more comfortable seats, and better food.

The results were startling. Within three years SAS increased the number of full-fare business passengers by 23 percent at a time when the overall market was stagnant. *Fortune* magazine conducted a survey that named SAS the best airline for business travelers in the world. The SAS story illustrates how a clear mission allows an organization to concentrate its limited resources on those projects that increase the profitability and success of the firm.

Source: Jan Carlzon, *Moments of Truth* (New York: Harper & Row, 1987).

equation at this level. Top management assumes that if the strategic plan is given, the plan will be implemented. However, can middle managers of different functional areas interpret and understand what to do? For example, the strategic plan seldom tells which project has first priority. Regardless, within these broad constraints more detailed strategies and objectives are developed by the next level of managers. This process filters down the organization until specific projects are identified.

At this point some of the painful problems created by this approach begin to raise their ugly heads—projects are not getting done on time or within budget; resources are not adequate; some projects do not contribute to the major objectives and strategies of the organization as a whole. Because clear linkages do not exist, the organizational environment becomes dysfunctional, confused, and ripe for ineffective implementation of organization strategy and, thus, of projects. Well documented by researchers, these phenomena are categorized as the "implementation gap."

The implementation gap refers to the lack of understanding and consensus of organization strategy among top and middle-level managers.[5] If this condition exists, how is it possible to effectively implement strategy? The problem is serious. One study found that only about 25 percent of *Fortune* 500 executives believe there is a strong linkage, consistency, and/or agreement between the strategies they formulate and implementation.[6] Another large study found that middle managers considered organizational strategy to be under the purview of others or not in their realm of influence.[7] It is the responsibility of senior management to set policies that show a distinct link between organizational strategy and objectives and projects that implement those strategies. The research of Fusco suggests the implementation gap and prioritizing projects are still overlooked by many organizations. He surveyed 280 project managers and found that 24 percent of their organizations did not even publish or circulate their objectives; in addition, 40 percent of the respondents reported that priorities among competing projects were not clear, while only 17 percent reported clear priorities.[8] The link between strategy and projects cannot be overlooked if the firm intends to compete in today's turbulent, competitive world.

Project Selection and Organizational Politics

Politics exist in every organization and can have a significant influence on all kinds of decisions. The existence of power politics can determine if a project receives funding and high priority. Organizational politics has been defined as actions by individuals or groups of individuals to acquire, develop, and use power and other resources in order to obtain preferred outcomes when there is uncertainty or disagreement over choices.[9] Furthermore, political behavior is much more likely to occur when decision-making procedures and performance measures are highly uncertain and when the competition among individuals for scarce resources is high.[10] If so, project selection is ripe for politics, given the uncertainty surrounding the feasibility of projects and the competition between projects for funding. Such selection will be based not so much on facts and sound reasoning, but rather on the persuasiveness and power of the people presenting the facts.

Studies on innovation highlight the role that project sponsors play in the selection and successful execution of projects.[11] Project sponsors are typically high-ranking managers who endorse and lend political support for the completion of a specific project. They are instrumental in winning approval of the project and in protecting the project during the critical development stage. Savvy project managers recognize the importance of having "friends in higher courts" who can advocate for their case and protect their interests.

Within companies, the term "sacred cow" is often used to denote a project that a powerful, high-ranking official is advocating. For example, a marketing consultant confided that he was once hired by the marketing director of a large firm to conduct an independent, external market analysis for a new product the firm was interested in developing. His extensive research indicated that there was insufficient demand to warrant the financing of this new product. The marketing director chose to bury the report and made the consultant promise never to share this information with anyone. The director explained that this new product was the "pet idea" of the new CEO, who saw it as his legacy to the firm. He went on to describe the CEO's irrational obsession with the project and how he constantly referred to it as his "new baby." Like a parent fiercely protecting his child, the marketing director believed that he would lose his job if such critical information ever became known.

The significance of corporate politics can be seen in the ill-fated ALTO computer project at Xerox during the mid-1970s. The project was a tremendous technological success; it developed the first workable mouse, the first laser printer, the first user-friendly software, and the first local area network. All of these developments were five years ahead of their nearest competitor. Over the next five years this opportunity to dominate the nascent personal computer market was squandered because of internal in-fighting at Xerox and the absence of a strong project sponsor.[12]

Politics can play a role not only in project selection but also in the aspirations behind projects. Individuals can enhance their power within an organization by managing extraordinary and critical projects.[13] Power and status naturally accrue to successful innovators and risk takers rather than to steady producers. Similarly, managers can become heroes within their organization by leading projects that contribute significantly to the organization's mission or solve a pressing crisis. Many ambitious managers pursue high-profile projects as a means for moving quickly up the corporate ladder. For example, Lee Iococca's career was built on successfully leading the design and development of the highly successful Ford Mustang.

Many would argue that politics and project management should not mix. A more proactive response is that projects and politics invariably mix and that effective project managers recognize that any significant project has political ramifications. Likewise, top management needs to develop a system for identifying and selecting projects that reduces the impact of internal politics and fosters the selection of the best projects for achieving the mission and strategy of the firm.

Multiple Projects and Resource Contentions

In Chapter 1, it was noted that most organizations have many projects in process at any given point in time. The number of small and large projects in a portfolio almost always exceeds the available resources (typically by a factor of three to four times the available resources). This capacity overload inevitably leads to confusion and inefficient use of scarce organizational resources. The presence of an implementation gap and of power politics add to the problem of which projects are allocated resources first. Employee morale and confidence suffer because it is difficult to make sense of an ambiguous system. A multiproject organization environment faces major problems without a priority system that is clearly linked to the strategic plan.

MOVING TO AN EFFECTIVE ORGANIZATIONAL PRIORITY SYSTEM

How can the implementation gap be narrowed so that understanding and consensus of organizational strategies run through all levels of management? How can power politics be minimized? Can a process be developed in which projects are consistently prioritized to support organizational strategies? Can the prioritized projects be used to allocate scarce organizational resources—for example, people, equipment? Can the process encourage bottom-up initiation of projects that support clear organizational targets?

What is needed is a set of integrative criteria and a process for evaluating and selecting projects that support higher-level strategies and objectives. A single-project priority system that ranks projects by their contribution to the strategic plan would make life easier. Easily said, but difficult to accomplish in practice.

There are always more project proposals than available resources permit. Therefore, some centralized process is needed to allocate the scarce resources of the organization to those projects that contribute more value than other alternative projects. Survival of the organization depends on a process that accomplishes this successfully. Selection of any project among alternative projects implies a decision model related to specific criteria.

The key is having criteria that support the strategic direction of the organization and that are recognized and used by every member of the organization. The authors are convinced a major key to success of projects is careful development of project selection priority criteria. At a minimum, carefully selected criteria will facilitate the following:

1. Keeping organization stakeholders focused on the strategic bull's-eye of the organization.
2. Consensus as to which projects are highest priority.
3. Use of organization resources more effectively and resource planning.
4. Portfolio selection of projects that balance risk, given available capital.
5. Openness in the project selection process.
6. A mechanism for controlled change through criteria selection.

The absence of such project selection criteria leads to confusion, power politics, and poor or misuse of an organization's resources.

Building Commitment for a Central Project Priority System

The suggestion that a rigorous project priority system be used to select which projects will be budgeted and staffed is frequently met with skepticism and resistance.[14] Typical responses include the following:

1. We already have a priority system. All of our projects are very important.
2. Come on. We all know which projects have first priority.
3. Our business world changes each day. We don't need a system that locks us out of opportunities. Priorities change.
4. Let's not rock the boat. We're getting along. The cream projects always rise to the top.

Resistance responses such as these almost always suggest a deep need for a project priority system. Developing a project priority system will not materialize without top management support and a demonstrated need for all stakeholders. Two approaches used by consultants for establishing a need to change are an *interview questionnaire* (see Appendix 2–2 for a simplified questionnaire example) and a *survey of current projects*. (Note: The same information can be collected and summarized internally.) Individuals or small groups at *all* levels in the organization are asked to address the general problem of why projects do not achieve their desired impact through the questionnaire. The outcomes can be consolidated into one table and/or a fishbone diagram, which is then communicated to major stakeholders. Typical results of one survey of interviews for projects not achieving the desired impact are summarized in Table 2–1.

Sometimes the same information can be more clearly summarized in a fishbone diagram to demonstrate the need for a priority system, as shown in Figure 2–3. The fishbone diagram is also an excellent tool for analyzing and isolating symptoms and causes of problems.

An interesting observation is the commonality of answers, regardless of industry or organization size; all groups tend to identify similar problems and even major classifications of problems. The result of the survey is the reinforcement of project problems and an identification of some of the causes—especially the absence of a priority system. The use of the survey questionnaire should have major stakeholders agreeing there is a problem and reaching a consensus that change is needed.

Another factor that can support buy-in of stakeholders to a project priority system is an additional survey of projects in process and proposed projects accepted. Consultants or an internal task force collect a list of all of the projects in process and planned for an organization. The outcome is usually enlightening and startling! The projects easily fall into three categories. Here are the figures for one such inquiry:

1. Repetitive operations that are not projects—e.g., quarterly financial statements	180
2. Projects less than $50,000 or projects less than 500 labor hours	109
3. "Real" projects	72
Total	361

These results are typical in product and service organizations.[15] First, many projects are repetitive and represent the basic daily operations of the organization. These recurring activities should be handled and scheduled by the departments responsible and not be treated as projects. Second, projects that require few man-hours or represent a relatively small dollar value do not individually sabotage implementation of high-impact projects. However, such projects in total can have a profound effect on important projects by gobbling up critical resources. Analysis of these small projects regularly points out that they contribute little or nothing to the strategic plan or to meeting the needs of the customer; many could then be eliminated. Finally, the remaining

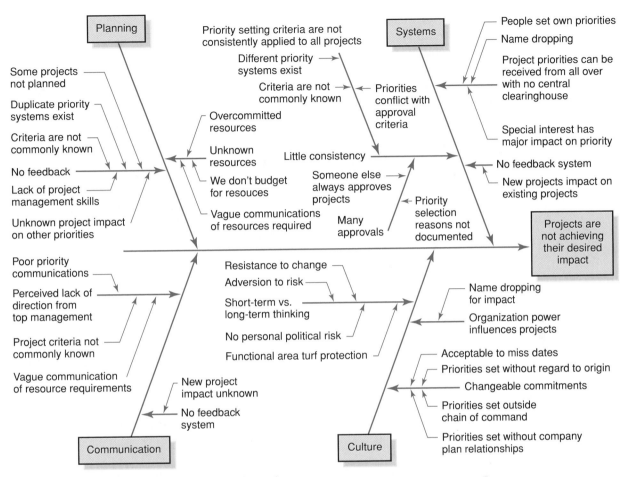

FIGURE 2–3 Cause-and-Effect Worksheet Example

"real" projects are those that clearly contribute significantly to the organization's mission, goals, and strategies. The linkage can be identified. In reality most real projects were selected from a list of proposals *without* criteria for selection.

TABLE 2-1

SUMMARY OF SURVEY RESULTS

1. No consistent project approval system exists.
2. Many individuals can approve projects.
3. There is little evidence that project priority is communicated downward.
4. Priorities are set outside the chain of command—several priority systems exist.
5. Functional areas protect turf.
6. Human resources for projects are not budgeted.
7. Priorities are set without regard to strategic plan.
8. No consistency in applying criteria to projects exists.
9. It is not acceptable to refuse project assignments because of lack of resources.
10. No feedback system exists for impact of new projects on current projects.
11. Pet projects of powerful individuals receive higher priority.
12. No central clearing system of projects exists.
13. Production is always first.

The results and implications of this particular inquiry are serious! Planned and proposed real projects typically overcommit resources by a factor of four over a five-year planning horizon. Some projects need to be eliminated. The total set of real projects lacks focus. This situation suggests the strategic plan had not been communicated effectively to middle management. The hierarchical arrangement of objectives and strategies had not taken place, and the middle managers were not active contributors to the process. No formal system existed for prioritizing projects to optimize their contribution to the strategic plan. The results of using the processes just described are usually earthshaking enough to gain buy-in that some kind of priority system is needed to select and monitor projects. A generic priority system is described in the next section.

A GENERIC SELECTION AND PRIORITY SYSTEM

Selection Criteria

The variety of models available to practitioners is unlimited. Picking a selection model depends on the nature of the organization. For example, factors such as industry, organization size, risk aversion level, technology, competition, markets, and management style may strongly influence the form of the model used to select projects.

In the past, financial criteria were used almost to the exclusion of other criteria. However, in the last two decades we have witnessed a dramatic shift to include multiple criteria in project selection. Succinctly, profitability alone is simply not an adequate measure of contribution; however, it is still an important criterion. A detailed discussion is beyond the scope of this text; however, two financial models are briefly mentioned here to give the reader a sense of the nature and potential problems of financial models.

1. The *payback model* measures the time it will take to recover the project investment. Shorter paybacks are more desirable. Payback is the simplest and most widely used model. Payback emphasizes cash flows, a key factor in business. Some managers use the payback model to eliminate unusually risky projects (those with lengthy payback periods). The major limitations of payback are that it ignores the time value of money, assumes constant cash flows for the investment period (and not beyond), and does not consider profitability.
2. The *net present value (NPV) model* uses management's minimum desired rate of return discount rate (for example, 20 percent) to compute the present value of all cash inflows and outflows. If the result is positive, and the project meets the minimum desired rate of return, it is eligible for further consideration. Higher positive NPV's are desirable. Exhibit 2–2 presents simple examples of the payback and NPV models.

From Exhibit 2–2 the payback method suggests project B because it has a payback of 3.3 years. However, the NPV model rejects both projects, which have negative present values of –$346,130 and –$61,620, because it considers the time value of money. The NPV model is more realistic because it considers the time value of money, cash flows, and profitability. This example demonstrates the major shortcoming of the payback model and why model selection is important.

Models such as payback and NPV represent one criterion useful in screening alternative projects. However, financial criteria alone obviously cannot serve as a project screening process that establishes a clear link between strategy and project selection.[16]

EXHIBIT 2-2

FINANCIAL PROJECT SELECTION CRITERIA

Given data for two potential projects:

	Project A	Project B
Cost of project	$720,000	$600,000
Estimated annual cash inflow	$125,000	$180,000
Estimated useful life of project	5 years	5 years
Required rate of return	20%	20%

Payback Period

		Project A	Project B
Payback Period $= \dfrac{\text{Investment}}{\text{Annual net savings}}$		= 5.8 years	3.3 years
Rate of return[a]		17.4%	30.0%

NPV (Net Present Value)

	Project A	Project B
Present value of annual net cash inflows		
Project A $125,000 × 2.991[b]	$383,870	
Project B $180,000 × 2.991		$538,380
Investment	(− 720,000)	(− 600,000)
NPV	(−$346,130)	(−$ 61,620)

Outcomes

Payback
   Project A—5.8 years; reject, longer than life of project (5 years)
   Project B—3.3 years; accept, less than 5 years and exceeds 20% desired rate of return

Net present value
   Reject both projects because they have negative net present values

---

[a] The reciprocal of payback yields the average rate of return (e.g., 125/720 × 100 = 17.4%).
[b] Present value of an annuity of $1 for 5 years at 20 percent. These values can be found in annuity tables of standard accounting and finance texts.

Other factors such as researching a new technology, public image, ethical position, protection of the environment, core competencies, and strategic fit might be important criteria for selecting and prioritizing projects. The trend toward using multiple screening criteria models is quickly gaining acceptance—especially in project-driven organizations. One impetus supporting this trend was the advent of Y2K projects (the millennium date bug).

Selection Process

Under rare circumstances, there are projects which "must" be selected. "Must" projects are those which must be implemented or the firm will fail or will suffer dire consequences. For example, a manufacturing plant must install an electrostatic filter on top of a smoke stack in six months or close down. Other examples could be a large software firm must open its software architecture to allow other competing software to be compatible and to interact with Y2K projects. Any project placed in the "must" category ignores other selection criteria. A rule of thumb for placing a proposed project in this category is that 99 percent of the organization stakeholders should agree that the project must be implemented; there is no perceived choice but to implement the

SNAPSHOT FROM PRACTICE
Y2K PROJECTS

Anecdotal remarks of Y2K pundits and informal surveys suggested that about 80 percent of Y2K project managers believed they had too little time to complete proper testing of their projects by December 31, 1999. Advocates of multiple screening criteria for selection of projects were quick to point out that many Y2K projects were started too late. Their explanation was that Y2K projects did not add to the bottom line. Therefore, those organizations depending on the return on investment (ROI) criterion for project selection never allowed Y2K projects to rise to the top of the priority list. Finally, when national attention focused on the seriousness of the problem and the year 2000 neared, organizations bypassed the ROI criterion and used criteria such as urgency, improved customer service, and minimization of loss to justify Y2K projects.

Most of the Y2K latecomers found their projects costing much more because of the necessity to crash activity times and the unavailability of qualified human resources. In fact, some IT managers found it necessary to visit retirement homes to recruit old-timers who had COBOL programming skills that could be used to reprogram older business programs. Because the cost of Y2K projects ran into billions of dollars, earlier recognition of the seriousness of the problem and earlier implementation of Y2K projects would have resulted in significant savings and avoided the very real business risks of not meeting the year 2000 deadlines.

project. All other projects are selected using criteria linked to organization strategy. A project selection process which uses multiple screening criteria is discussed next.

Project Proposals   Suggestions for projects come from many internal and external sources. It is a rare organization that does not have more project proposals than are feasible. This is especially true in project-driven organizations. Culling through so many proposals to identify those that add the most value requires a structured process. Figure 2–4 shows a flow chart of a screening process, beginning with the creation of an idea for a project. Data and information are collected to assess the value of the proposed project to the organization and for future backup. If the sponsor decides to pursue the project on the basis of the collected data, it is forwarded to the project priority team (or sometimes a project office). Given the selection criteria and current portfolio of projects, the priority team rejects or accepts the project. If accepted, the priority team sets implementation of the project in motion.

Priority Team Role   The role of the priority team includes more than accepting or rejecting project proposals on the basis of selected criteria. The priority team is responsible for publishing the priority of every project and ensuring that the process is open and free of power politics. For example, most organizations using a priority team or project office use an electronic bulletin board to disperse the current portfolio of projects, the current status of each project, and current issues. This open communication discourages power plays. In addition, the priority team is responsible for balancing the portfolio of projects for the organization. Hence, a proposed project that satisfies most criteria may not be selected because the organization portfolio already includes too many projects with the same characteristics—for example, project risk level, use of key resources, high cost, non–revenue producing, long durations. Such projects may be put on hold. Over time the priority team evaluates the progress of the

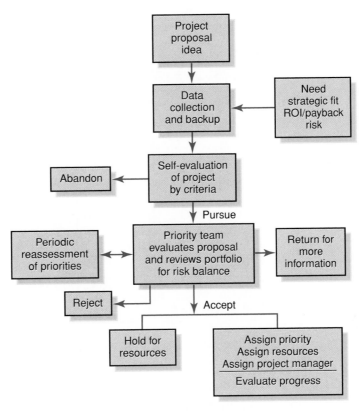

FIGURE 2–4 Project Screening Process

projects in the portfolio. The priority team is also responsible for reassessing organizational goals and priorities and changing priorities if conditions dictate. How well this whole process is managed can have a profound impact on the success of an organization.

Selection Criteria   Selection criteria need to mirror the critical success factors of an organization. For example, 3M set a target that 25 percent of the company's sales would come from products fewer than four years old versus the old target of 20 percent. Their priority system for project selection strongly reflects this new target. On the other hand, failure to pick the right factors will render the screening process "useless" in short order. Figure 2–5 represents a hypothetical project scoring matrix. The screening criteria selected are shown across the top of the matrix (stay within core competencies . . . ROI of 18 percent plus). Management weights each criterion (a value of 0 to a high of, say, 3) by its relative importance to the organization's objectives and strategic plan. Project proposals are then submitted to a project priority team or project office.

Each project proposal is then evaluated by its relative contribution/value added to the selected criteria. Values of 0 to a high of 10 are assigned to each criterion for each project. This value represents the project's fit to the specific criterion. For example, project 1 appears to fit well with the strategy of the organization since it is given a value of 8. Conversely, project 1 does nothing to support reducing defects

Criteria Weight	Stay within core competencies	Strategic fit	Urgency	25% of sales from new products	Reduce defects to less than 1%	Improve customer loyalty	ROI of 18% plus	Weighted total
	2.0	3.0	2.0	2.5	1.0	1.0	3.0	
Project 1	1	8	2	6	0	6	5	66
Project 2	3	3	2	0	0	5	1	27
Project 3	9	5	2	0	2	2	5	56
Project 4	3	0	10	0	0	6	0	32
Project 5	1	10	5	10	0	8	9	102
Project 6	6	5	0	2	0	2	7	55
⋮								
Project n	5	5	7	0	10	10	8	83

FIGURE 2–5 Project Screening Matrix

(its value is 0). Finally, this model applies the management weights to each criterion by importance using a value of 1 to 3. For example, ROI and strategic fit have a weight of 3, while urgency and core competencies have weights of 2. Applying the weight to each criterion, the priority team derives the weighted total points for each project. For example, project 5 has the highest value of 102 $[(2 \times 1) + (3 \times 10) + (2 \times 5) + (2.5 \times 10) + (1 \times 0) + (1 \times 8) + (3 \times 9) = 102]$ and project 2 a low value of 27. If the resources available create a cutoff threshold of 50 points, the priority team would eliminate projects 2 and 4. (Note: Project 4 appears to have some urgency, but it is not classified as a "must" project. Therefore, it is screened with all other proposals.) Project 5 would receive first priority, project n second, and so on. In rare cases where resources are severely limited and project proposals are similar in weighted rank, it is prudent to pick the project placing less demand on resources. Weighted multiple criteria models similar to this one are rapidly becoming the dominant choice for prioritizing projects.[17]

In summary, centralized project priority systems support a holistic approach to linking organizational projects to organizational strategy. The system is proactive rather than reactive. The project portfolio represents a process for controlling the use of scarce resources and balancing risk. Regardless of the criteria used for selection, each project should be evaluated by the same criteria. The project priority system ties resource requirements directly to resource availability. Enforcing the project priority system is critical. Keeping the whole system open and aboveboard is important to maintaining the integrity of the system. For example, communicating which projects are approved, project ranks, current status of in-process projects, and any changes in priority criteria will keep people from bypassing the system. Project-driven organizations are integrating organizational goals and strategy with projects using a portfolio of projects selected by a proactive project priority system.

ASSESSING THE EFFECTIVENESS OF THE PRIORITY SYSTEM OVER THE LONG HAUL—THE BALANCED SCORECARD MODEL

Project priority models select which actions (projects) best support organizational strategy. The balanced scorecard model compliments the project priority selection process. It is more "macro" in perspective than project priority selection models.[18] This model measures the *results* of major activities taken to support the overall vision, mission, and goals of the organization. The scorecard model limits measures of performance to goals in four main areas: customer, internal, innovation and learning, and financial measures. For example, a performance measure for a customer might be industry ranking for sales, quality, or on-time projects. Internal measures that influence employees' actions could be time to market or reduction of design time to final product. Innovation and learning measures frequently deal with process and product innovation and improvement. For example, the percent of sales or profit from new products is often used as a performance goal and measure. Project improvement savings from partnering agreements are another example of an innovation and learning measure. Finally, financial measures such as ROI, cash flow, and projects on budget reflect improvement and actions that contribute value to the bottom line.

These four perspectives and performance measures keep vision and strategy at the forefront of employees' actions. The basic assumption underlying the balanced scorecard model is that people will take the necessary actions to improve the performance of the organization on the given measures and goals. The balanced scorecard model and project priority selection models should never be in conflict with each other. If a conflict exists, both models should be reviewed and conflicts eliminated. When both models are used in project-driven organizations, focus on vision, strategy, and implementation are reinforced. Both models encourage employees to determine the actions needed to improve performance.

CASE STUDY: A DETAILED SELECTION PRIORITY MODEL FROM PRACTICE*

This case study from practice describes a multiple-criteria selection process to prioritize projects so organizational objectives are optimized. The model forces all levels of management to contribute by identifying what is strategically important in a *relative* sense. Working through the model quickly points out areas where there is consensus and areas where agreement does not exist. Continuous dialogue and probing of what is and what should be moves all levels of management toward a list of strategic priorities that can be used to select projects to directly support organizational goals, strategies, and objectives. The model suggested may appear to some as too detailed and dependent on numbers; however, it is effective when used. The observation concerning the use of numbers misses the major point. Basically the model quickly points out differences among organizational groups and individuals. The numbers used to develop the model are not as important as the exercise of developing the model. The exercise requires clarification at every point and consensus at all levels of the organization. The final model is published for everyone in the organization to use in proposing projects. The model ranks (prioritizes) projects by their contribution to the strategic plan and is tied to resource availability (people and capital). Periodically working through the model serves to integrate strategy formulation and its implementation.

---

*We are grateful to Robert Breitbarth of Interact Management for his outline and diagrams of the system.

FIGURE 2–6 Project Priority System

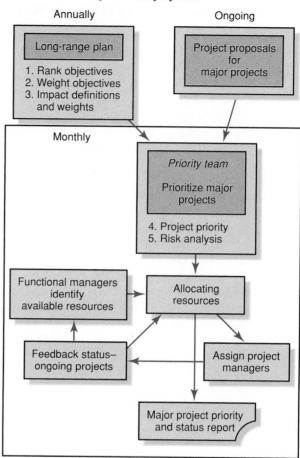

Developing the Project Selection Model

Figure 2–6 presents an overview of the project priority system. The diagram shows the interface among the five stakeholder groups—top management, project originator, priority team, functional managers, and project manager. (The interface roles of key stakeholders are found in Appendix 2–1 of this chapter.) The small numbers (1–5) represent the steps necessary to develop a project priority system. These steps are discussed in detail herein. Basically, senior management evaluates and weights organizational objectives (and, implicitly, strategies) so the priority team can prioritize new project proposals (given organizational resources). It is important to note that the system supports a bottom-up approach for project proposals (see top right box of Figure 2–6). In addition, the project priority team assigns project managers, reports project status, and monitors projects in process. The priority system encourages projects that support organizational goals.

1. **Rank objectives.** Given the organization objectives, the first aim is to achieve consensus on the importance of an individual objective. A direct process is used to gain consensus on the ranking of each objective. Senior management, such as the CEO and vice presidents, is asked to rank each objective by three independent criteria—seriousness, urgency, and future seriousness. A scale of 1 to 10 is used for each cri-

FIGURE 2–7 Rank Objectives

Analyze objectives independently in three dimensions

1. Seriousness—What is the current impact of the results of the objective on the organization?

0 ├───────────────────┤ 10
   Small impact   Large impact

2. Urgency–time factor. What will be the relative consequences of not taking action over the next 12 months?

0 ├───────────────────┤ 10
   Can defer   Must take action

3. Future seriousness—What is the chance of the objective's seriousness changing over time?

0 ├───────────────────┤ 10
   Decrease or   Dramatically
   remain same   increase

Objectives	Seriousness	Urgency	Future seriousness	Total score
Improve external customer service	5	4	6	15
10% decrease in production costs	7	6	4	17
All activities meet current legal, safety, and environmental standards				MUST
Create $5 million in new sales	8	4	6	18
Provide immediate response to field problems	10	10	10	30
Develop/document policies, systems, procedures	7	10	6	23

terion. Figure 2–7 presents a modified format and outcome for an organization. Note that these evaluations treat each objective as *independent* of the others, not relative to each other. The outcome is a ranking of each objective.

2. **Weight objectives.** In this second step, objectives are viewed *relative* to each other. Weighting objectives is necessary so projects can be evaluated by a relative numeric process. This step is simply a further refinement of ranking the objectives (see Figure 2–8). The senior management group is asked to organize objectives in order of importance using a relative point scale of 1 to 100. This step uses "must" and "want" objectives as suggested by Kepner and Tregoe.[19] The first want objective is ranked 99; the second, 88; and the third, 83. This process breaks ties and gives a better indication of the relative differences of importance among objectives. This refined weighted ranking by senior management provides a powerful

statement; it indicates what management believes is the relative worth of its strategic plan objectives. In addition, working through the process forces senior management to focus on what is important to position the organization to compete in the future. Senior management passes the weighted objectives to the priority team, which develops a scheme for evaluating the impact or contribution of projects to the organization's objectives.

3. **Impact definitions and weights.** This step represents an even further refinement of the earlier steps. The priority team is made up of managers below the level of vice presidents, often functional managers. In step 3 the priority team or project office must decide how an individual project will affect specific objectives. The assumption is that projects that affect more objectives in a significant way should be placed higher on a priority list than those that have less of an effect. The relative impact of each potential project on an individual objective can be determined by setting up single-project impact definitions for each objective.

Basically, each project will be assessed to determine its effect on each objective by classifying the project in one of three categories:

0	No impact
1	Unknown impact
2	Have an impact

These impact categories must be specifically redefined for each objective by the priority team. Some examples of single impact definitions for ranking a specific project are shown in Figure 2–8. Note that the impact weight (0,1,2) is used to compute a weighted score for any project's contribution toward the objective. This list is available to individuals or groups proposing projects so they may prescore how their project will affect organization objectives and the strategic plan.

4. **Project priority.** This step is completed by both project proposal individuals and the priority team. For example, project 26 in Figure 2–8 has been rated with a 1 on the first objective, a 0 on the second objective, and a 2 on the third objective. The weighted scores for these objectives are 99, 0, and 166, respectively (1×99, 0×88, and 2×83, respectively). The final outcome is the total weighted scores for all objectives. This total score is used to screen new projects for possible inclusion on the priority list. Embedded in the project score is a very strong link and consensus between senior and middle management because each group has contributed to the weighting scheme. Figure 2–9 shows the first page of the project proposal sheet.

5. **Risk analysis.** Prioritizing projects by the priority team is more than a process of selecting projects with the highest total weighted scores. These projects could all be high risk projects and/or not meet minimum financial thresholds. Therefore, the priority team is responsible for ensuring that the portfolio of projects is balanced with some high-, medium-, and low-risk projects. Figure 2–10 shows the second page of the project proposal sheet and the "risk analysis" section. The process used is simplistic, but it avoids the possibility of ignoring project risk. Care should be taken not to allow the risk factor to be used as a way around the system by power centers, hidden agendas, or squeaky wheels.

In addition to risk, the priority team must consider the availability of organization resources to implement projects. No project is placed on the priority list without documented availability of the resource by functional managers. Anyone can check the system to ensure the resource is being used on the highest-priority project. One project audit scheme gives a rough estimate of project resource usage. Each week project participants allocate hours spent on *prioritized* projects. These hours do not have to add up to 40 hours; they represent only hours spent on prioritized projects. This information is used to assess cost and schedule variance and to catch projects getting out of control. Unfortunately, the scheme requires getting over the paranoid "timecard phobia" professionals have.

Prioritizing projects becomes a straightforward task for the priority team. In practice, once the process is in place, the priority team may meet as little as once a month for one or two hours to handle new project proposals, revise priorities, and report status of all projects via an e-mail attachment. The system has self-checking aspects. First, those submitting proposals are able to assess for themselves the chances of a project being accepted and its possible priority. Second, because the whole process is open, those who might choose to go around the system become obvious. If these

FIGURE 2–8 Priority Analysis

Project number

Must objectives	Must meet if impacts	...26	27	28	29
All activities meet current legal, safety, and environmental standards	Yes-Meets objective No-Does not meet obj N/A-No impact	n/a			
All new products will have a complete market analysis	Yes-Meets objective No-Does not meet obj N/A-No impact	yes			
Want objectives	Relative Importance 1-100	**Single project impact definitions**	Weighted score	Weighted score	Weighted score	Weighted score
Provides immediate response to field problems ㉚	99	0 ≤ Does not address ①= Opportunity to fix 2 ≥ Urgent problem	99			
Create $5 million in new sales by 199x ⑮	88	⓪≤ $100,000 1 = $500,000 2 ≥ $500,000	0			
Improve external customer service ⑱	83	0 ≤ Minor impact 1 = Significant impact ②≥ Major impact	166			
◯						
Total weighted score						
Priority						

Date _____   Number _____

Project Title _____

Responsible Manager _____ Project Manager _____

☐ _____	☐ General support	☐ Quality	☐ Legal	☐ New product
☐ _____	☐ _____	☐ Cost reduction	☐ Replacement	☐ Capacity
☐ _____	☐ _____	☐ _____	☐ _____	☐ _____

YES ☐ NO ☐   The project will take more than 500 labor hours?
YES ☐ NO ☐   The project is a one-time effort? (will not occur on a regular basis)
YES ☐ NO ☐   The project proposal was reviewed by the product manager?

Problem definition
Describe the problem/opportunity.

Goal definition
Describe the project goal.

Objective definition
Performance: Quantify the savings/benefits you expect from the project.

Cost: Labor hours, materials, methods, equipment?

Schedule: Overall duration in months.

FIGURE 2–9 Major Project Proposal

self-checking methods are not a deterrent, senior management must step in and maintain the integrity of the system.

Prioritizing can be an uncomfortable exercise for managers. Prioritizing means discipline, accountability, responsibility, constraints, reduced flexibility, and loss of power. Top management commitment means more than giving a blessing to the priority system; it means management will have to rank and weigh, in concrete terms, the objectives and strategies they believe to be most critical to the organization. This public declaration of commitment can be risky if the ranked objectives later prove to be poor choices, but setting the course for the organization is top management's job. The good news is, if management is truly trying to direct the organization to a strong future position, a good project priority system supports their efforts and develops a culture in which everyone feels a part of contributing to the goals of the organization.

What are the three major risks for this project?		
1.		
2.		
3.		

		Risk 1 above	
What is the probability of the above risks occurring?	0 to 1.0 none high	Risk 2 above	
		Risk 3 above	
What is the impact on project success if these risks do occur?	0 to 10 none high	Risk 1 above	
		Risk 2 above	
		Risk 3 above	

Resources available? _____ Yes _____ No

Current project status

Start date _____ Estimated finish date _____

Status: ☐ Active ☐ On hold

Update:

Priority team action: ☐ Accepted ☐ Returned

☐ Discovery—project not defined   ☐ Duplicate to: _____

☐ Operational—proposal not a project   Project # [   ]

☐ Need more information—to prioritize project   ☐ Completed project

FIGURE 2–10 Risk Analysis

SUMMARY

The priority system focuses attention on the mission and major goals of the organization. The system forces management to develop a mission and goals that are highly operative, not motherhood and apple pie statements such as "maximize shareholder's wealth." A single-project priority system that links strategy formulation and implementation fills a void found in many product and service organizations. The important point is to develop a relative ranking system that ties the long-range plan to projects. The major value of the system described in the case study is not in the numbers but rather in identifying areas of disagreement and gaining consensus on direction. The resultant priority system provides focus at all levels in the organization and furnishes the basis for effective allocation of scarce human and nonhuman resources. The system results in bottom-up proposals from front-line managers who have the expertise, who are closest to the customer, and who have a clear vision of where the organization is headed. The process encourages the entrepreneurial spirit and allows individual project initiators to flourish.

The system described in detail is only one example of many priority systems found in practice. Linking strategy formulation and projects using a priority system helps to ensure that everyone will stay focused on the organization's objectives. Many organizations have gained considerable insight from the use of their priority system. The benefits of projects to the long-term strategic direction of the organization are more easily evaluated *before* and *after* they occur with a priority system.

Only one priority system can exist. It is important to ensure all projects are evaluated by the same consistent criteria. It is critical to communicate priority criteria to all organizational stakeholders. Every project selected should be ranked and the results published. Senior management must take an active role in setting priorities and supporting the priority system. Going around the priority system will destroy its effectiveness. The project priority team needs to consist of seasoned managers who are capable of asking tough questions and distinguishing facts from fiction. Resources (people, equipment, and capital) for major projects must be clearly allocated and not conflict with daily operations or become an overload task. The priority system must respond quickly to changes. An appeal process should be included in the system; all appeals and responses should be open and documented.

When strategy and projects are closely linked and projects are readily recognized as the primary vehicle to implement strategy, the next challenge is to establish a consistent, formal, disciplined process for managing the implementation of projects. In theory this may appear to be a contradiction since all projects are different and teams need autonomy to act freely. However, the absence of strategy linkage and a consistent process for managing projects is known to create serious problems. It is possible to meet both conditions and not strangle organization innovation and the motivation of self-directed teams.

REVIEW QUESTIONS

1. Describe the major components of the strategic management process.
2. Explain the role projects play in the strategic management process.
3. How are projects linked to the strategic plan?
4. Why does the priority system described in this chapter require that it be open and published? Does the process encourage bottom-up initiation of projects? Does it discourage some projects? Why?
5. Describe an operative system that will prioritize projects by their contribution to the strategic plan. How does this system assist in allocating organization resources and avoiding overcommitment of resources? How does your system differ from the case study model?
6. Why should an organization not rely only on ROI to select projects?

ENDNOTES

1. Paul C. Dinsmore, "Up and Down the Organization: Tom Peters Is Behind Times," *PM Network,* vol. 10, no. 9 (September 1996), p. 11.
2. John A. Pearce II and Fred David, "Corporate Mission Statements: The Bottom Line," *Academy of Management Executive,* vol. 1, no. 2 (1987), pp. 109–13.

3. George T. Doran, "There's a Smart Way to Write Management Goals and Objectives," *Management Review* (November 1981), pp. 35–36.
4. J. Schmeidawind, "Kodak Joins Fuji, Others for Project," *USA Today* (March 1992), p. B1.
5. Donald W. Beard and Gregory G. Dess, "Corporate Business Strategy, Business Level Strategy, and Firm Performance," *Academy of Management Journal,* vol. 24, no. 4 (December 1981), pp. 663–88.
6. This is an excellent article describing the implementation gap and how it is measured. Steven W. Floyd and Bill Wooldridge, "Managing Strategic Consensus: The Foundation of Effective Implementation," *Academy of Management Executives,* vol. 6, no. 4 (1992), pp. 27–39.
7. Booz-Allen & Hamilton Inc., "Making Strategy Work: The Challenge for the 1990s" (1990).
8. Joseph C. Fusco, "Better Policies Provide the Key to Implementing Project Management," *Project Management Journal,* vol. 28, no. 3 (1997), pp. 38–41.
9. Jeffrey Pfeffer, *Power in Organizations* (Boston: Pitman, 1981), p. 7.
10. D. R. Beemon and T. W. Sharkey, "The Use and Abuse of Corporate Politics," *Business Horizons* (March–April 1987), pp. 26–30.
11. See Edward B. Roberts, "Entrepreneurship and Technology," *Research Management,* vol. 11, no. 4 (July 1968), pp. 249–66; Edward B. Roberts and Alan R. Fusefield, "Critical Functions: Needed Roles in the Innovation Process," *Career Issues in Human Resource Management,* R. Katz, ed. (Englewood Cliffs, NJ: Prentice Hall, 1982), pp. 182–207; David H. Gobeli and William Rudeluis, "Managing Innovation: Lessons Learned from the Cardiac-Pacing Industry," *Sloan Management Review* (Summer 1985), pp. 29–43.
12. O. P. Kharbanda and Jeffrey K. Pinto, *What Made Gertie Gallop: Learning from Project Failures* (New York: Van Nostrand Reinhold, 1996), pp. 106–11, 263–83.
13. Rosebeth M. Kanter, *Men and Women of the Corporation* (New York: Basic Books, 1977), pp. 176–81.
14. Sandra E. Chillous, "Project Prioritization—Why Not Do It," *PM Network* (March 1994), pp. 41–42.
15. Steven C. Wheelwright and Kim B. Clark, "Creating Project Plans to Focus Product Development," *Harvard Business Review* (March–April 1992), pp. 70–82.
16. Roy E. Johnson, "Scrap Capital Project Evaluations," *Chief Financial Officer* (May 1998), p. 14. See also July 1998 issue, pp. 6–7, for responses.
17. For other variations in screening and priority systems, see Wheelwright and Clark, reference cited, and Charles H. Kepner and Benjamin B. Tregoe, *The New Rational Manager* (Princeton, NJ: Princeton Research Press, 1981), pp. 87–88.
18. Robert S. Kaplan and David P. Norton, "The Balanced Scorecard—Measures That Drive Performance," *Harvard Business Review* (January–February 1992), pp. 73–79. (Note: An interactive CD simulation is available from Harvard Customer Service, product #8397. This interactive simulation provides hands-on experience for learning more about the method.)
19. Kepner and Tregoe, reference cited.

BIBLIOGRAPHY

1. William R. King, "The Role of Projects in Implementation of Business Strategy," in D. Cleland and W. R. King, *Project Management Handbook* (New York: Van Nostrand, 1988), pp. 129–34.
2. Joan Knutson and Alan M. Gump, "Project Prioritization Process: Developing Criteria for Assessing and Evaluating Project Requests," *PMI 27th Annual Seminar/Symposium Proceedings* (Newtown Square, PA: PMI, October 1996), pp. 301–6.
3. Bruce Miller, "Linking Corporate Strategy to the Selection of IT Projects," *Proceedings of 28th Annual Project Management Institute 1997 Seminars and Symposium* (Newtown Square, PA: PMI, 1997), pp. 803–7.

4. J. Reddy Nukalapti, "Resource Allocation Information System for the Next Century," *Proceedings of 28th Annual Project Management Institute 1997 Seminars and Symposium* (Newtown Square, PA: PMI, 1997), pp. 873–78.

Jarvis Communication Corporation

Background

Jarvis Communication is a startup firm that develops, manufactures, and markets a miniature telephone. Last year's sales revenue was $6.5 million, resulting in its first profitable year in its first three years of business. The phone is unique because it is only two inches long, weighs two ounces, and a miniature receiver is worn in the ear. The phone speaker and microphone carry out all the normal functions of a phone (except dialing) without the use of a mouthpiece. The phone uses bone conduction technologies that detect small, minute vibrations in the skull when a person talks. The phone sells for $99. Jarvis's markets have grown quickly and have become worldwide; analysts believe the market will grow 50 percent per year for the next five years.

Most of the development of the miniature phone was done by the founder, Ms. Carly Jarvis, an electrical engineer. She is also the primary source for more than 20 new products already designed with accompanying engineering drawings. Jarvis believes innovation in modes of telecommunications is the key to future success of the company. She believes quality is number one; profits and returns to stockholders will follow.

Only last month the company purchased a small circuit board company that specializes in bonding small silicon chips on printed circuit boards. Jarvis Communication stock sells over the counter. Management is thinking it will be necessary to become listed on the New York Stock Exchange if large expansion becomes desirable.

Management

The company employs 120 people and is organized in a matrix form to facilitate the project environment. Every employee behaves as if quality is an obsession. Jarvis believes the management style should be collegial, the workplace environment should be one employees enjoy, and the company should provide products that make life easier and more productive. Marketing is responsible for direct and original equipment manufacturer (OEM) sales. Engineering is responsible for design and improvement of all products. Manufacturing controls production and product quality.

Future

External The market for telecommunication products is expected to grow by 20 percent for the next seven years. Although Jarvis Communication has no competitors today, many new entrées in the market are expected in the near future. Time to market will become more important with each passing day. Keeping a flow of new products will be necessary to survive. Strategic alliances with computer and communications firms appear inevitable as the industry and product lines develop. The biggest threat comes from the Orient.

Internal   The most exciting new product prototype is the cordless miniature telephone. This phone will allow people to walk around and use their hands while wearing the phone. The phone fits in the ear and requires the user to carry a small pack about the size of a chewing gum pack and weighing approximately one ounce. Marketing expects to sell the phone for $150. The next step is setting up for manufacturing large quantities as quickly as possible. Manufacturing is asking, "Do you want the new phone good, fast, or cheap? Pick any two."

Another product is a miniature phone that uses voice-activated technology for computers—to dial customers and to record and transmit data. This prototype has been demonstrated with the Apple line of computers. Because the phone uses bone conduction technology (not air), background noise is virtually filtered out, so sound is significantly improved over traditional phones. Marketing believes this phone can sell for about $200.

Other products designed, but not developed as prototypes, are listed here:

1. Voice imprint documentation.
2. Miniature programmable phones to hold more than 100 telephone numbers.
3. Special sets for major surgery operations to send and receive instant information, for example, to and from Mayo Clinic or Texas Cancer Clinic. This product is dubbed the "socially conscious" product.
4. Voice-activated cellular phone communications for the military and police, the elimination of the traditional microphone, voice activation, and ability to "wear the phone" all have attracted many classes of target customers.
5. Reduction of printed circuit board size by 75 percent by the new acquisition has unlimited potential.

Jarvis Communication management feels now is the time to prepare for full-scale manufacturing and a marketing thrust into the communications and computer industries. The company currently has $2 million in cash reserves to start this effort. Additional funds for future expansion are available through stock issues.

Jarvis has asked your management team to develop a mission statement, three major goals, and objectives for Jarvis Communication. She also wishes each functional area to develop four key objectives that support your corporate objectives. Be prepared to justify the document you submit to her.

CASE

Hector Gaming Company

Hector Gaming Company (HGC) is an educational gaming company specializing in young children's educational games. HGC has just completed their fourth year of operation. This year was a banner year for HGC. The company received a large influx of capital for growth by issuing stock privately through an investment banking firm. It appears the return on investment for this past year will be just over 25 percent with zero debt! The growth rate for the last two years has been approximately 80 percent each year. Parents and grandparents of young children have been buying HGC's products almost as fast as they are developed. Every member of the 56-person firm is enthusiastic and looking forward to helping the firm grow to be the largest and best educational gaming company in the world. The founder of the firm, Sally Peters, has been written up in *Young Entrepreneurs* as "the young entrepreneur to watch." She has been able to develop an organization culture in which all stakeholders are committed to innovation, continuous improvement, and organization learning.

Last year, 10 top managers of HGC worked with McKinley Consulting to develop the organization's strategic plan. This year the same 10 managers had a retreat in Aruba to formulate next year's strategic plan using the same process suggested by McKinley Consulting. Most executives seem to have a consensus of where the firm should go in the intermediate and long term. But there is little consensus on how this should be accomplished. Peters, now president of HGC, feels she may be losing control. The frequency of conflicts seems to be increasing. Some individuals are always requested for any new project created. When resource conflicts occur among projects, each project manager believes his or her project is most important. More projects are not meeting deadlines and are coming in over budget. Yesterday's management meeting revealed some top HGC talent have been working on an international business game for college students. This project does not fit the organization vision or market niche. At times it seems everyone is marching to his own drummer. Somehow more focus is needed to ensure everyone agrees on *how* strategy should be implemented, given the resources available to the organization.

Yesterday's meeting alarmed Peters. These emerging problems are coming at a bad time. Next week HGC is ramping up the size of the organization, number of new products per year, and marketing efforts. Fifteen new people will join HGC next month. Peters is concerned that policies be in place that will ensure the new people are used most productively. An additional potential problem looms on the horizon. Other gaming companies have noticed the success HGC is having in their niche market; one company tried to hire a key product development employee away from HGC. Peters wants HGC to be ready to meet any potential competition head on and to discourage any new entries into their market. Peters knows HGC is project driven; however, she is not as confident that she has a good handle on how such an organization should be managed—especially with such a fast growth rate and potential competition closer to becoming a reality. The magnitude of emerging problems demands quick attention and resolution.

Peters has hired you as a consultant. She has suggested the following format for your consulting contract. You are free to use another format if it will improve the effectiveness of the consulting engagement.

> What is our major problem?
> Identify some symptoms of the problem.
> What is the major cause of the problem?

Provide a detailed action plan that attacks the problem. Be specific and provide examples that relate to HGC.

Film Prioritization

The purpose of this case is to give you experience in using a project priority system that ranks proposed projects by their contribution to the organization's objectives and strategic plan.

Company Profile

The company is the film division for a large entertainment conglomerate. The main office is located in Anaheim, California. In addition to the feature film division, the conglomerate includes theme parks, home videos, a television channel, interactive games, and theatrical productions. The company has been enjoying steady growth over the past 10 years. Last year total revenues increased by 12 percent to $21.2 billion. The company is engaged in negotiations to expand its theme park empire to mainland China and Poland. The film division generated $274 million in revenues, which was an increase of 7 percent over the past year. Profit margin was down 3 percent to 16 percent because of the poor response to three of the five major film releases for the year.

Company Mission

The mission for the firm:

> Our overriding objective is to create shareholder value by continuing to be the world's premier entertainment company from a creative, strategic, and financial standpoint.

The film division supports this mission by producing four to six high-quality, family entertainment films for mass distribution each year. In recent years, the CEO of the company has advocated that the firm take a leadership position in championing environmental concerns.

Company "Must" Objectives   Every project must meet the must objectives as determined by executive management. It is important that selected film projects not violate such objectives of high strategic priority. There are three must objectives:

1. All projects meet current legal, safety, and environmental standards.
2. All film projects should receive a PG or lower advisory rating.
3. All projects should not have an adverse effect on current or planned operations within the larger company.

Company "Want Objectives"   Want objectives are assigned weights for their relative importance. Top management is responsible for formulating, ranking, and weighting objectives to ensure that projects support the company's strategy and mission. The following is a list of the company's want objectives:

1. Be nominated for and win an academy award for Best Picture of the Year.
2. Create at least one new animated character each year that can star in a cartoon or TV series.
3. Generate additional merchandise revenue (action figures, dolls, interactive games, music CDs).
4. Raise public consciousness about environmental issues and concerns.
5. Generate profit in excess of 18 percent.
6. Advance the state of the art in film animation, and preserve the firm's reputation.
7. Provide the basis for the development of a new ride at company-owned theme park.

Assignment

You are a member of the priority team in charge of evaluating and selecting film proposals. Use the provided evaluation form to formally evaluate and rank each proposal. Be prepared to report your rankings and justify your decisions.

Assume that all of the projects have passed the estimated hurdle rate of 14 percent ROI. In addition to the brief film synopsis, the proposals include the following financial projections of theater and video sales: 80 percent chance of ROI, 50 percent chance of ROI, and 20 percent chance of ROI.

For example, for proposal #1 (Dalai Lama) there is an 80 percent chance that it will earn at least 8 percent return on investment (ROI), a fifty-fifty chance the ROI will be 18 percent, and a 20 percent chance that the ROI will be 24 percent.

Film Proposals

Project Proposal 1: My Life with Dalai Lama   An animated, biographical account of the Dalai Lama's childhood in Tibet based on the popular children's book, *Tales from Nepal.* The Lama's life is told through the eyes of "Guoda," a field snake, and other local animals who befriend the Dalai and help him understand the principles of Buddhism.

Probability	80%	50%	20%
ROI	8%	18%	24%

Project Proposal 2: Heidi   A remake of the classic, children's story with music written by award-winning composers Syskle and Obert. The big-budget film will feature top-name stars and breathtaking scenery of the Swiss Alps.

Probability	80%	50%	20%
ROI	2%	20%	30%

Project Proposal 3: The Year of the Echo   A low-budget documentary that celebrates the career of one of the most influential bands in rock-and-roll history. The film will be directed by new-wave director Elliot Cznerzy and will combine concert footage and behind-the-scenes interviews spanning the 25-year history of the rock band, the Echos. In addition to great music, the film will focus on the death of one of the founding members from a heroin overdose and reveal the underworld of sex, lies, and drugs in the music industry.

Probability	80%	50%	20%
ROI	12%	14%	18%

Project Proposal 4: Escape from Rio Japuni   An animated feature set in the Amazon rainforest. The story centers around Pablo, a young jaguar who attempts to convince warring jungle animals that they must unite and escape the devastation of local clear cutting.

Probability	80%	50%	20%
ROI	15%	20%	24%

Project 5: Olga!   The story of Olga Korbut, the famous Russian gymnast who won three gold medals at the 1971 Summer Olympic Games. The low-budget film will document her life as a small child in Russia and how she was chosen by Soviet authori-

ties to join their elite, state-run, athletic program. The film will highlight how Korbut maintained her independent spirit and love for gymnastics despite a harsh, regimented training program.

Probability	80%	50%	20%
ROI	8%	15%	20%

Project 6: Keiko—One Whale of a Story   The story of Keiko, the famous killer whale, will be told by an imaginary offspring Seiko, who in the distant future is telling her children about their famous grandfather. The big-budget film will integrate actual footage of the whale within a realistic animated environment using state-of-the-art computer imagery. The story will reveal how Keiko responded to his treatment by humans.

Probability	80%	50%	20%
ROI	6%	18%	25%

Project 7: Grand Island   The true story of a group of junior-high biology students who discover that a fertilizer plant is dumping toxic wastes into a nearby river. The moderate-budget film depicts how students organize a grassroots campaign to fight local bureaucracy and ultimately force the fertilizer plant to restore damage to the local ecosystem.

Probability	80%	50%	20%
ROI	9%	15%	20%

PROJECT PRIORITY EVALUATION FORM

Must objectives	Must meet if impacts	1	2	3	4	5	6	7
Meets all safety and environmental standards	Y = yes N = no N/A = not applicable							
PG or P rating	Y = yes N = no N/A = not applicable							
No adverse effect on other operations	Y = yes N = no N/A = not applicable							

Want objectives	Relative Importance 1–100	Single project impact definitions	Weighted Score	Weighted Score	Weighted Score	Weighted Score	Weighted Score	Weighted Score	Weighted Score
Be nominated for Best Picture of the Year	60	0 ≤ No potential 1 ≥ Low potential 2 > High potential							
Generate additional merchandise	10	0 ≤ No potential 1 ≥ Low potential 2 > High potential							
Create a new, major animated character	20	0 ≤ No potential 1 ≥ Low potential 2 > High potential							
Raise environmental concerns	55	0 ≤ No potential 1 ≥ Low potential 2 > High potential							
Generate profit greater than 18%	70	0 ≤ 18% 1 ≥ 18% 2 > 22%							
Advance state of film animation	40	0 ≤ No impact 1 ≥ Some impact 2 > Great impact							
Provide basis for new theme ride	10	0 ≤ No potential 1 ≥ Low potential 2 > High potential							
		Total weighted score							
		Priority							

Sample: Interface Roles and Responsibilities of Key Players

CEO
Role: Final arbitrator
Responsibilities
    Maintain integrity of system
    Resolve deadlocks
    Veto of priority team decisions

Project Originator
Role: Identify project idea
Responsibilities:
    Develop project proposal
    Define proof of need
    Present proposal to functional manager

Vice President
Role: Establish priority criteria
Responsibilities:
    Delegate responsibility to priority team to set priorities, allocate resources, and approve plans for all major projects
    Select priority team
    Sponsor priority system
    Communicate strategic plan

Functional Managers
Role: Manage available resources
Responsibilities:
    Identify project resource conflicts
    Plan and communicate allocated resources for projects
    Refuse major project work based on available resources
    Forward project proposals from functional areas to priority team

Project Priority Team
Role: Manage the project priority system
Responsibilities—priority related:
    Recommend resources for major projects
    Represent functional areas on team
    Track available resources
    Gain top-management approval of priority lists
Responsibilities—project related:
    Approve/reject/hold major projects
    Approve major project plans
    Publish a priority and project status report
    Approve project managers
    Approve cost, schedule, and performance changes
    Act as sponsors for major project managers
    Plan and communicate allocated resources for projects
    Refuse major project work based on resources available

Sample: Interview Questionnaire

Priority Questions

1. Define your responsibilities and authority.
2. How do you distinguish between projects and operational activities?
3. Where do your projects come from?
4. Who sets your priorities?
5. What do you base your priority on?

Project Questions

1. Who plans projects?
2. Who approves projects?
3. Who evaluates the availability and assignment of resources to projects?

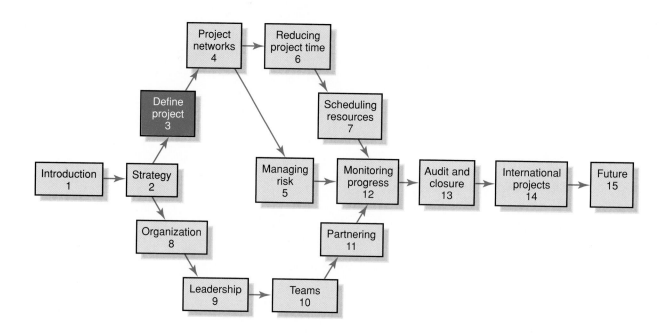

CHAPTER THREE

Defining the Project

Select a dream
Use your dream to set a goal
Create a plan
Consider resources
Enhance skills and abilities
Spend time wisely
Start! Get organized and go

. . . it is one of those acro-whatevers,
said Pooh.[1]

One of the best ways to meet the needs of the customer and major project stake-holders is to use an integrated project planning and control system that requires selective information. Project managers who manage a single, small project can plan and schedule the project tasks without a formal planning and information system. However, when the project manager must manage several small projects or a large, complex project, a threshold is quickly reached in which the project manager can no longer cope with the detail.

This chapter describes a disciplined, structured method for selectively collecting information to use through all phases of the project life cycle, to meet the needs of all stakeholders (e.g., customer, project manager), and to measure performance against the strategic plan of the organization. The method suggested is a selective outline of the project called the *work breakdown structure.* The early stages of developing the outline serve to ensure that all tasks are identified and that participants of the project have an understanding of what is to be done. Once the outline and its detail are defined, an integrated information system can be developed to schedule work and allocate budgets. This baseline information is later used for control.

The five generic steps described herein provide a structured approach for collecting the project information necessary for planning, scheduling, and controlling the project. These steps and the development of project networks found in the next chapters all take place concurrently, and several iterations are typically required to develop dates and budgets that can be used for control of the project. The old saying, "We can control only what we have planned" is true; therefore, defining the project is the first step.

STEP 1: DEFINING THE PROJECT SCOPE

Defining the project scope sets the stage for developing a project plan. Project scope is a definition of the end result or mission of your project—a product or service for your client/customer. The primary purpose is to define as clearly as possible the deliverable(s) for the end user and to focus project plans. As fundamental and essential

61

as scope definition appears, it is frequently overlooked by project leaders of well-managed, large corporations.

Research clearly shows that a poorly defined scope or mission is the most frequently mentioned barrier to project success. A study by Smith and Tucker of a large petroleum refinery plant project found that poor scope definition for major segments of the project had the greatest negative impact on cost and schedule.[2] Pinto and Slevin found that a clear mission statement is a predictor of more than 50 percent of project success in the concept, planning, and execution stages of the project.[3] Ashley et al. found that outstanding, successful projects exhibit clear scope and work definitions.[4] A survey by Posner found lack of clear goals as a major problem mentioned by more than 60 percent of project manager respondents.[5] In a large study of more than 1,400 project managers in the United States and Canada, Gobeli and Larson found that approximately 50 percent of the planning problems relate to unclear definition of scope and goals.[6] These studies suggest a strong correlation between project success and clear scope definition. The scope document directs focus on the project purpose throughout the life of the project for the customer and project participants.

The scope should be developed under the direction of the project manager and customer. The project manager is responsible for seeing that there is agreement with the owner on project objectives, deliverables at each stage of the project, technical requirements, and so forth. For example, a deliverable in the early stage might be specifications; for the second stage, three prototypes for production; for the third, a sufficient quantity to introduce to market; and finally, marketing promotion and training.

Your project scope definition is a document that will be published and used by the project owner and project participants for planning and measuring project success. *Scope* describes what you expect to deliver to your customer when the project is complete. Your project scope should define the results to be achieved in specific, tangible, and measurable terms.

Employing a Project Scope Checklist

Clearly, project scope is the keystone interlocking all elements of a project plan. To ensure that scope definition is complete, you may wish to use the following checklist:

Project Scope Checklist

1. Project objectives
2. Deliverables
3. Milestones
4. Technical requirements
5. Limits and exclusions
6. Reviews with customer

---

1. **Project objectives.** The first step of project scope definition is to define the major objectives to meet your customer's need(s). For example, as a result of extensive market research a computer software company decides to develop a program that automatically translates verbal sentences in English to Russian. The project should be completed within three years at a cost not to exceed $1.5 million. Another example is to design and produce a completely portable, hazardous waste, thermal treatment system in 13 months at a cost not to exceed $13 million.

2. **Deliverables.** The next step is to define deliverables—the expected outputs over the life of the project. For example, deliverables in the early design phase of a proj-

ect might be a list of specifications. In the second phase deliverables could be software coding and a technical manual. The next phase could be to test prototypes. The final phase could be final tests and approved software. Deliverables typically include time, quantity, and/or cost estimates.

3. **Milestones.** A milestone is a significant event in a project that occurs at a point in time. The milestone schedule shows only major segments of work; it represents first, rough-cut estimates of time, cost, and resources for the project. The milestone schedule is built using the deliverables as a platform to identify major segments of work and an end date—for example, testing complete and finished by July 1 of the same year. Milestones should be natural, important control points in the project. Milestones should be easy for all project participants to recognize. The milestone schedule should identify which major organizational divisions will assume responsibility for the major segments of work and provide the necessary resources and technical expertise. The organizational units may be internal or external—for example—companies may rely on consultants to test Y2K compliance.

4. **Technical requirements.** More frequently than not, a product or service will have technical requirements to ensure proper performance. For example, a technical requirement for a personal computer might be the ability to accept 120-volt alternating current or 240-volt direct current without any adapters or user switches. Another well-known example is the ability of 911 emergency systems to identify the caller's phone number and location of the phone.

5. **Limits and exclusions.** The limits of scope should be defined. Failure to do so can lead to false expectations and to expending resources and time on the wrong problem. Examples of limits are data that will be collected by the client, not the contractor; a house that will be built, but no landscaping or security devices added; software that will be installed, but no training given.

6. **Reviews with customer.** Completion of the scope checklist ends with a review with your customer—internal or external. The main concern here is the understanding and agreement of expectations. Is the customer getting what he or she desires in deliverables? Does the project definition identify key accomplishments, budgets, timing, and performance requirements? Are questions of limits and exclusions covered? Clear communication in all these issues is imperative to avoid claims or misunderstanding.

In summary, close liaison with your customer is necessary to develop a project definition that meets all the requirements of the customer. Clear scope definition ensures you will know when a change in scope occurs. A clear project scope definition is the primary prerequisite for development of your work breakdown structure. Scope definition provides an administrative plan that is used to develop your operational plan. Scope definition should be as brief as possible but complete; one or two pages are typical for small projects.

STEP 2: ESTABLISHING PROJECT PRIORITIES

Quality and the ultimate success of a project are traditionally defined as meeting and/or exceeding the expectations of the customer and/or upper management in terms of cost (budget), time (schedule), and performance (scope) of the project (see Figure 3–1). The interrelationship among these criteria varies. For example, sometimes it is necessary to compromise the performance and scope of the project to get the project done quickly or less expensively. Often the longer a project takes, the more expensive it becomes. However, a positive correlation between cost and schedule may not always be true. Sometimes project costs can be reduced by using cheaper, less efficient labor

Snapshot from Practice
SCOPE STATEMENT

PROJECT OBJECTIVE

To construct a high-quality, custom home within five months at cost not to exceed $150,000.

DELIVERABLES

- A 2,200-square-foot, 2½-bath, 3-bedroom, finished home.
- A finished garage, insulated and sheetrocked.
- Kitchen appliances to include range, oven, microwave, and dishwasher.
- High-efficiency gas furnace with programmable thermostat.

MILESTONES

1. Permits approved—March 5
2. Foundation poured—March 14
3. Dry in. Framing, sheathing, plumbing, electrical, and mechanical inspections passed—May 25
4. Final inspection—June 7

TECHNICAL REQUIREMENTS

1. Home must meet local building codes.
2. All windows and doors must pass NFRC class 40 energy ratings.
3. Exterior wall insulation must meet an "R" factor of 21.
4. Ceiling insulation must meet an "R" factor of 38.
5. Floor insulation must meet an "R" factor of 25.
6. Garage will accommodate two large-size cars and one 20-foot Winnebago.
7. Structure must pass seismic stability codes.

LIMITS AND EXCLUSIONS

1. The home will be built to the specifications and design of the original blueprints provided by the customer.
2. Owner responsible for landscaping.
3. Refrigerator is not included among kitchen appliances.
4. Air conditioning is not included but prewiring is included.
5. Contractor reserves the right to contract out services.
6. Contractor responsible for subcontracted work.
7. Site work limited to Monday through Friday, 8:00 A.M. to 6:00 P.M.

CUSTOMER REVIEW

John and Joan Smith

FIGURE 3–1 Project Management Trade-Offs

or equipment that extends the duration of the project. Likewise, as will be seen in Chapter 6, project managers are often forced to expedite or "crash" certain key activities by adding additional labor, thereby raising the original cost of the project.

One of the primary jobs of a project manager is to manage the trade-offs among time, cost, and performance. To do so, project managers must define and understand the nature of the priorities of the project. They need to have a candid discussion with the project customer and upper management to establish the relative importance of each criterion. One technique that is useful for this purpose is completing a priority matrix for the project that identifies which criterion is constrained, which should be enhanced, and which can be accepted:

Constrain. The original parameter is fixed. The project must meet the completion date, specifications and scope of the project, or budget.

Enhance. Given the scope of the project, which criterion should be optimized? In the case of time and cost, this usually means taking advantage of opportunities to either reduce costs or shorten the schedule. Conversely, with regards to performance, enhancing means adding value to the project.

Accept. For which criterion is it tolerable not to meet the original parameters? When trade-offs have to be made, is it permissible for the schedule to slip, to reduce the scope and performance of the project, or to go over budget?

Figure 3–2 displays the priority matrix for the development of a new high-speed modem. Because *time* to market is important to sales, the project manager is instructed to take advantage of every opportunity to reduce completion time. In doing so, going over *budget* is acceptable though not desirable. At the same time, the original *performance* specifications for the modem as well as reliability standards cannot be compromised.

Some would argue that all three criteria are always constrained and that good project managers should seek to optimize each criterion. If everything goes well on a project and no major problems or setbacks are encountered, their argument may be valid. However, this situation is rare, and project managers are often forced to make tough decisions that benefit one criterion while compromising the other two. The purpose of this exercise is to define and agree on what the priorities and constraints of the project are so that when "push comes to shove," the right decisions can be made.

There are likely to be natural limits to the extent managers can constrain, optimize, or accept any one criterion. It may be acceptable for the project to slip one month behind schedule but no further or to exceed the planned budget by as much as $20,000.

FIGURE 3–2 Project Priority Matrix

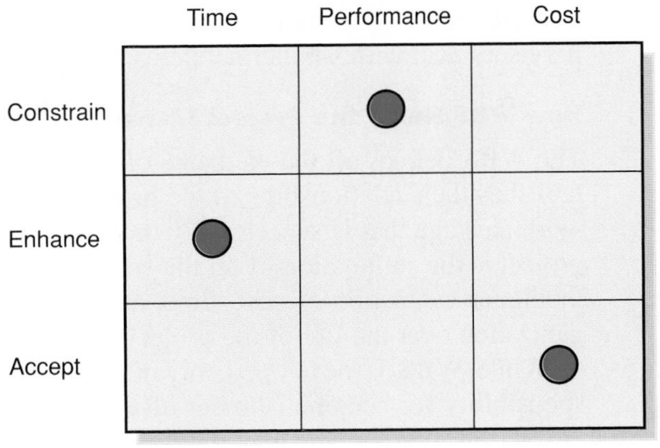

Likewise, it may be desirable to finish a project a month early, but after that cost conservation should be the primary goal. Some project managers document these limits as part of creating the priority matrix.

In summary, developing a decision priority matrix for a project is a useful exercise. (Note: This matrix is also useful midway in the project for approaching any problem or decision that must be made.) It provides a forum for clearly establishing priorities with customers and top management so as to create shared expectations and avoid misunderstandings. The priority information is essential to the planning process, where adjustments can be made in the scope, schedule, and budget allocation. Finally, the matrix provides a basis for monitoring and evaluating progress so that appropriate corrective action can be taken. Still, one caveat must be mentioned: During the course of a project, priorities may change. The customer may suddenly need the project completed one month sooner, or new directives from top management may emphasize cost saving initiatives. The project manager needs to be vigilant in order to anticipate and confirm changes in priorities and make appropriate adjustments.

STEP 3: CREATING THE WORK BREAKDOWN STRUCTURE

Major Groupings Found in a WBS

Once the scope and deliverables have been identified, the work of the project can be successively subdivided into smaller and smaller work elements. The outcome of this hierarchical process is called the work breakdown structure (WBS). The WBS is a map of the project. Use of WBS helps to assure project managers that all products and work elements are identified, to integrate the project with the current organization, and to establish a basis for control. Basically, the WBS is an outline of the project with different levels of detail. Figure 3–3 shows the major groupings commonly used in the field to develop a hierarchical WBS. The WBS begins with the project as the final deliverable. Major project work deliverables/systems are identified first; then the subdeliverables necessary to accomplish the larger deliverables are defined. The process is repeated until the subdeliverable detail is small enough to be manageable and where one person can be responsible. This subdeliverable is further divided into work packages. Because the lowest subdeliverable usually includes several work packages, the work packages are grouped by type of work—for example, hardware, programming, testing. These groupings within a subdeliverable are called cost accounts. This grouping facilitates a system for monitoring project progress by work and responsibility. The hierarchical structure later provides management with a database for planning, executing, monitoring, and controlling the work of the project. In addition, the hierarchical structure provides management with information appropriate to each level. For example, top management deals primarily with major deliverables, while first-line supervisors deal with smaller subdeliverables and work packages.

How WBS Helps the Project Manager

The WBS defines all the elements of the project in a hierarchical framework and establishes their relationships to the project end item(s). Think of the project as a large work package that is successively broken down into smaller work packages; the total project is the summation of all the smaller work packages. This hierarchical structure facilitates evaluation of cost, time, and technical performance at all levels in the organization over the life of the project.

While WBS is developed, organizational units and individuals are assigned responsibility for accomplishment of work packages. This integrates the work and the

Snapshot from Practice
YEAR 2000 OLYMPIC GAMES—SYDNEY, AUSTRALIA[7]

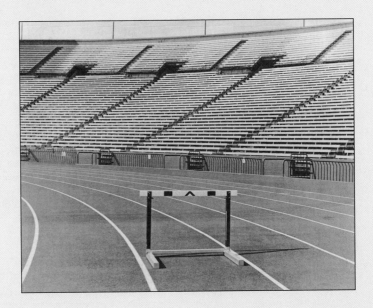

In the realm of event project management, the Olympic Games rank as one of the premier achievements.

OBJECTIVE

To stage the Year 2000 Olympic Games at specified locations in Sydney beginning September 15 at a cost of $1.4 billion.

CLIENT

No clearly defined client. Activities are underwritten by the government of New South Wales (NSW). Many stakeholders and customers, e.g., citizens of New South Wales, the NSW government, the Australian people, the International Olympic Organization, the international community as a whole, the athletes, and Australian and international business communities.

SCOPE

Organizing all Games and ceremonies. Putting in place all technology and resources required to stage the Games. Handling public relations and fundraising.

CRITERIA FOR SUCCESS

Trouble-free performance of Games. Level of public enthusiasm and enjoyment. Economic activity generated within NSW and Australia. Continued interest in future Olympic Games.

PROJECT TEAM

SOCOG was appointed as the project managers by legislation. Other organizations directly contributing to the success of the Games, such as the International Olympic Committee, Australian Olympic Committee, Sydney City Council, and Olympic Coordination Authority (NSW government) have been made party to the Host City Contract. Olympic Coordination Authority is responsible for all the infrastructure projects, most of which are either already under way or are being reprogrammed to accommodate the Games. Completion of these projects on time is vital to the success of the Olympic Games.

WORK BREAKDOWN STRUCTURE

The WBS for the project includes the following major areas: events; venues and facilities, including accommodation; transport; media facilities and coordination; telecommunications;

Snapshot from Practice

YEAR 2000 OLYMPIC GAMES—SYDNEY, AUSTRALIA (concluded)

security arrangements; medical care; human resources, including volunteers; cultural olympiad; pre-Games training; information technology projects; opening and closing ceremonies; public relations; financing; test games and trial events; and sponsorship management and control of ambush marketing. Each of these items could be treated as a project in its own right. Precision coordination will be necessary to ensure that these, and therefore the entire Games project, are delivered on time.

PRIORITIES

Time, obviously, is the most critical dimension of the Sydney 2000 Olympic Games project. Any shortcomings in the time dimension will have to be offset by sacrificing either cost or quality. However, performance on all three dimensions is vital to success of the Games. Worldwide opinion will be shaped by the perceived quality of the facilities, the efficacy of event management, and the treatment of foreign athletes and spectators. The Games budget in nominal terms is $1.4 billion, and any major cost overruns will alienate the public and overshadow the spectacle. Still, if a compromise has to be made, the cost aspect will be the first dimension sacrificed.

FIGURE 3–3 Hierarchical Breakdown of the WBS

Level	Hierarchical breakdown	Description
1	Project	Complete project
2	Deliverable	Major deliverables
3	Subdeliverable	Supporting deliverables
4	Lowest subdeliverable	Lowest management responsibility level
5	Cost account*	Grouping of work packages for monitoring progress and responsibility
	Work package	Identifiable work activities

*This breakdown groups work packages by type of work within a deliverable and allows assignment of responsibility to an organizational unit. This extra step facilities a system for monitoring project progress (discussed in Chapter 12).

organization. In practice, this process is sometimes called OBS, the organization breakdown structure, which will be further discussed later in the chapter.

The WBS also makes it possible to plan, schedule, and budget. It gives a framework for tracking cost and work performance. Use of the structure provides the opportunity to "roll up" (sum) the budget and actual costs of the smaller work packages into larger work elements so that performance can be measured by organizational units and work accomplishment.

The WBS defines communication channels and assists in understanding and coordinating many parts of the project. The structure shows the work and organizational units responsible and suggests where written communication should be directed. Problems can be quickly addressed and coordinated because the structure integrates work and responsibility.

WBS Development

Figure 3–4 shows a simplified WBS for development of a new personal computer project. At the top of the chart (level 1) is the project end item—a deliverable product or service. Note how the levels of the structure can represent information for different levels of management. For example, level 1 information represents the total project objective and is useful to top management; levels 2, 3, and 4 are suitable for middle management; and level 5 is for first-line managers.

Level 2 shows a partial list of deliverables necessary to develop the personal computer. One deliverable is the disk storage unit (shaded), which is made up of three

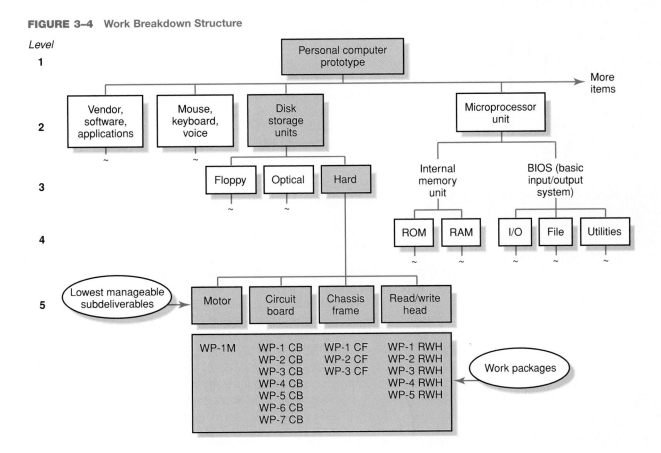

FIGURE 3–4 Work Breakdown Structure

subdeliverables—floppy, optical, and hard disks. Finally, the hard disk requires four subdeliverables—motor, circuit board, chassis frame, and read/write head. These subdeliverables represent the lowest manageable elements of the project. Each subdeliverable requires work packages that will be completed by an assigned organizational unit. Each deliverable will be successively divided in this manner. It is not necessary to divide all elements of the WBS to the same level.

The lowest level of the WBS is called a *work package.* Work packages are short duration tasks that have a definite start and stop point, consume resources, and represent cost. Each work package is a control point. A work package manager is responsible for seeing that the package is completed on time, within budget, and according to technical specifications. Practice suggests a work package should not exceed 10 workdays or one reporting period. If a work package has a duration exceeding 10 days, check or monitoring points should be established within the duration, say, every three to five days, so progress and problems can be identified before too much time has passed. Each work package of the WBS should be as independent of other packages of the project as possible. No work package is described in more than one subdeliverable of the WBS.

There is an important difference between the last work breakdown subdeliverable and a work package. Typically, a work breakdown subdeliverable includes the outcomes of more than one work package from perhaps two or three departments. Therefore, the subdeliverable does not have a duration of its own and does not consume resources or cost money directly. (In a sense, of course, a duration for a particular work breakdown element can be derived from identifying which work package must start first [earliest] and which package will be the latest to finish; the difference becomes the duration for the subdeliverable.) The resources and costs for the subdeliverable are simply the summation of the resources and costs for all the work packages in the work subdeliverable. This is the basis for the term *project rollup—* starting with the work package, costs and resources can be "rolled up" into the higher elements. The higher elements are used to identify deliverables at different phases in the project and to develop status reports during the execution stage of the project life cycle. Thus, the work package is the basic unit used for planning, scheduling, and controlling the project.

To review, each work package in the WBS

1. Defines work (what).
2. Identifies time to complete a work package (how long).
3. Identifies a time-phased budget to complete a work package (cost).
4. Identifies resources needed to complete a work package (how much).
5. Identifies a single person responsible for units of work (who).
6. Identifies monitoring points for measuring progress.

Project managers developing their first WBS frequently forget that the structure should be end-item, output oriented. First attempts often result in a WBS that follows the organization structure—design, marketing, production, finance. If a WBS follows the organization structure, the focus will be on the organization function and processes rather than the project output or deliverables. In addition, a WBS with a process focus will become an accounting tool that records costs by function rather than a tool for "output" management. Every effort should be made to develop a WBS that is output oriented in order to concentrate on concrete deliverables. Organizational unit responsibility can be tied to the WBS by grouping the work packages of a deliverable into a cost account while still maintaining the focus on completing the deliverable. This process is discussed next.

STEP 4: INTEGRATING THE WBS WITH THE ORGANIZATION

An integral part of the WBS is to define the organizational units responsible for performing the work. In practice, the outcome of this process is the organization breakdown structure (OBS). The OBS depicts how the firm has organized to discharge work responsibility. The purposes of the OBS are to provide a framework to summarize organization unit work performance, identify organization units responsible for work packages, and tie the organizational unit to cost control accounts. Recall, cost accounts group similar work packages (usually under the purview of a department). The OBS defines the organization subdeliverables in a hierarchical pattern in successively smaller and smaller units. Frequently, the traditional organization structure can be used. Even if the project is completely performed by a team, it is necessary to break down the team structure for assigning responsibility for budgets, time, and technical performance.

As in the WBS, the OBS assigns the lowest organizational unit the responsibility for work packages within a cost account. Herein lies one major strength of using WBS and OBS; they can be *integrated* as shown in Figure 3–5. The intersection of work packages and the organizational unit creates a project control point (cost account) that integrates work and responsibility. The intersection of the WBS and OBS represents the set of work packages necessary to complete the subdeliverable located immediately above and the organizational unit on the left responsible for accomplishing the packages at the intersection. Later we will use the intersection as a cost account for management control of projects. For example, the circuit board element requires completion of work packages whose primary responsibility will include the design, production, test, and software departments. Control can be checked from two directions—outcomes and responsibility. In the execution phase of the project, progress can be tracked vertically on deliverables (client's interest) and tracked horizontally by organization responsibility (management's interest). Although it is possible for the authors to graphically show an integrated WBS/OBS (e.g., Figure 3–5) for demonstration purposes, software programs do not draw diagrams as we have shown. The graphic output requirements for large projects make such graphic descriptions impractical by sheer size alone. Typical software packages allow project managers to sort by WBS and/or OBS, which simply presents the information in another form. See Tables 3–1 A and 3–1 B.

TABLE 3-1A

SORTED BY WBS

		Direct Labor Budget	
1.1.3	Hard drive	1,660	
1.1.3.1	Motor	10	
	Purchasing		10
1.1.3.2	Circuit board	1000	
	Design		300
	Production		400
	Testing		120
	Software		180
1.1.3.3	Chassis frame	50	
	Production		50
1.1.3.4	Read/write head	600	
	Design		300
	Production		200
	Testing		100

FIGURE 3–5 Integration of WBS and OBS

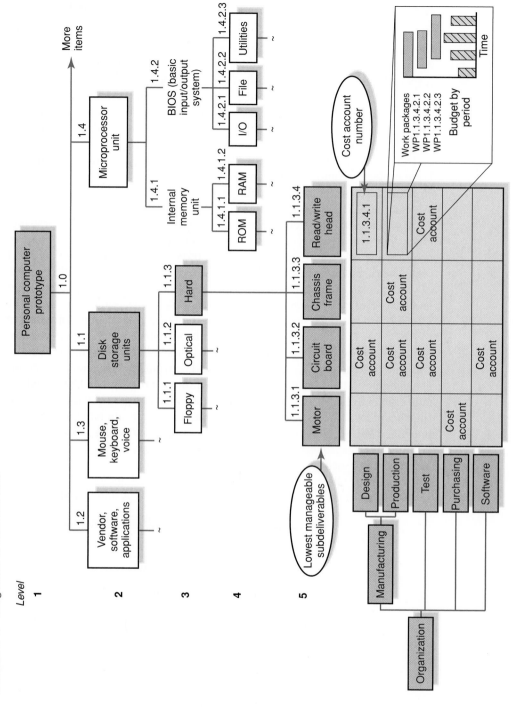

TABLE 3–1B

SORTED BY OBS

		Direct Labor Budget	
Design		600	
1.1.3.2	Circuit board		300
1.1.3.4	Read/write head		300
Production		650	
1.1.3.2	Circuit board		400
1.1.3.3	Chassis frame		50
1.1.3.4	Read/write head		200
Testing		220	
1.1.3.2	Circuit board		120
1.1.3.4	Read/write head		100
Purchasing		10	
1.1.3.1	Motor		10
Software		180	
1.1.3.2	Circuit board		180
Total		1,660	

STEP 5: CODING THE WBS FOR THE INFORMATION SYSTEM

Gaining the maximum usefulness of a breakdown structure depends on a coding system. The codes are used to define levels and elements in the WBS, organization elements, work packages, and budget and cost information. The codes allow reports to be consolidated at any level in the structure. The most commonly used scheme in practice is numeric indention. An example for the new computer project and the "Disk storage units" in Figure 3–5 is presented here:

1.0 Computer project
    1.1 Disk storage units
        1.1.1 Floppy
        1.1.2 Optical
        1.1.3 Hard
            1.1.3.1 Motor
                1.1.3.1.1 Sourcing work package
                •
                •
                •
            1.1.3.4 Read/write head
                1.1.3.4.1 Cost account
                1.1.3.4.2 Cost account
                      1.1.3.4.2.1 WP
                      1.1.3.4.2.2 WP
                      1.1.3.4.2.3 WP
                1.1.3.4.3 Cost account
                  •
                  •
                  •
                  etc.

Note the project identification is 1.0. Each successive indention represents a lower element or work package. Ultimately the numeric scheme reaches down to the work package level, and all tasks and elements in the structure have an identification code. The "cost account" is the focal point because all budgets, work assignments, time, cost, and technical performance come together at this point.

This coding system can be extended to cover large projects. Additional schemes can be added for special reports. For example, adding a "–3" after the code could indicate a site location, an elevation, or a special account such as labor. Some letters can be used as special identifiers such as "M" for materials or "E" for engineers. You are not limited to only 10 subdivisions (0–9); you can extend each subdivision to large numbers—for example, .1–.99 or .1–.9999. If the project is small, you can use whole numbers. The following example is from a large, complex project:

$$3R–237A–P2–33.6$$

where 3R identifies the facility, 237A represents elevation and the area, P2 represents pipe two inches wide, and 33.6 represents the work package number. In practice most organizations are creative in combining letters and numbers to minimize the length of WBS codes.

PROJECT ROLLUP

Recall that the intersection of the WBS and OBS represents a control point, called a cost account by project managers. The work packages and cost accounts serve as a

FIGURE 3–6   Work Package Estimates

WP Description *Final version*   Page *1* of *1*

WP ID *1.1.3.2*   Project *PC proto*

Deliverable *Circuit board*   Date *9/29/XX*

Original Unit *Software*   Estimator *RMG*

WP Duration *3* work weeks   Total Budget $ *465*

Time-Phased Budget ($)

Work periods

Direct costs	Rate	1	2	3	4	5	Total
Code	$ XX/hr	50	30	20			$100
Document	$ XX/hr		10	15			25
Publish	$ XX/hr			5			5
Total labor		50	40	40			$130
Materials			20				20
Equipment	$ XX/hr	50	15	50			115
Other _____							
Total direct		100	75	90			$265

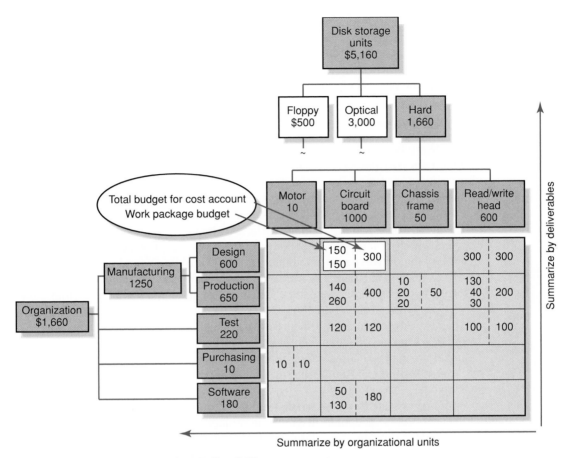

FIGURE 3-7 Direct Labor Budget Rollup (000)

database from which all other planning, scheduling, and controlling processes are co-ordinated. Cost accounts represent work packages. Each work package has time, budget, resource, responsibility, and control points that can be used to track project progress. Figure 3–6 shows an example of an oversimplified version of a work package with a time-phased budget (without dates). This work package represents one work package in the circuit board deliverable assigned to the software department. Using only the direct labor cost factor, you can get an overview of how it is possible to roll up the project costs for the circuit board and across organizational units.

Figure 3–7 shows hypothetical labor costs and work packages for the hard disk storage element of the personal computer prototype project. The intersection of circuit board and production shows two work packages in the cost account with budgets of $140 and $260, which total $400. Rollup to the circuit board element (summation of all cost accounts below the element) is $1,000. The hard disk element, which includes all first-level elements, has a budget of $1,660. The rollup for the organizational units operates in a similar fashion. For example, the design department has responsibility for the work packages found in the circuit board and read/write head cost accounts. These accounts each have a labor budget of $300, or a total of $600. The manufacturing section has a total budget of $1,250. Of course, the total for the organization delivering the hard disk element is the same as the total budget of all elements rolled up to the hard disk element. This ability to consolidate and integrate using the rollup process demonstrates the potential value of the WBS for managing the project. Remember, the units do not have to be money; the units can be resources, labor hours, materials, time, or any units that contribute to the completion of deliverables. However, at the cost account level, the units have to be the same throughout the structure.

TOP-DOWN VERSUS BOTTOM-UP ESTIMATING

Readers who have tried to imagine applying the breakdown structure to a project of their own may perceive a conflict between the top-down estimating of the WBS and practice. Good sense suggests project estimates should come from the people most knowledgeable about the estimate needed. Early users of project management techniques emphasized milestone schedules with accompanying estimates of costs and time based on top-down estimates. These estimates were frequently made by top managers who had very little knowledge of the processes. For example, a mayor of a major city making a speech noted that a new law building would be constructed at a cost of $13 million and be ready for occupancy in 2.5 years. Although the mayor probably asked for an estimate from someone, the estimate could have come from a luncheon meeting with a local contractor who wrote an estimate (guesstimate) on a napkin. This is an extreme example, but in a relative sense this scenario is frequently played out in the development of scope definition and WBS. The customer and project manager define deliverables, estimate total project duration, estimate total cost, and identify major responsibilities. But the question is, do these estimates represent low-cost, efficient methods?

It is important to recognize that these first, macroestimates are only a rough cut and occur in the "conceptual" stage of the project. The top-down estimates are helpful in initial development of a complete plan. However, such estimates are sometimes significantly off the mark because little detailed information was gathered. At this level, individual work items are not identified. Or, in a few cases, the top-down estimates are not realistic because top management "wants the project." Nevertheless, the initial top-down estimates are helpful in giving a quick overview and establishing project parameters.

The next step is to push the estimating process down to the work package level for bottom-up estimates, which establish low-cost, efficient methods. This process can take place after the project has been defined in detail. The bottom-up approach at the work package level can serve as a check on cost elements in the WBS by rolling up the work packages and associated cost accounts. Resource requirements can be checked similarly. The time, resource, and cost estimates from the work packages can later be consolidated into time-phased networks, resource schedules, and budgets.

The ideal approach is for the project manager to allow enough time for both the top-down and bottom-up estimates to be worked out so a complete plan based on reliable estimates can be offered the customer. In this way false expectations are minimized for all participants, and negotiation is reduced. The bottom-up approach also provides the client with an opportunity to compare the low-cost, efficient method approach with any imposed restrictions. For example, if the project completion duration is imposed at 2 years and your bottom-up analysis tells you the project will take 2.5 years, the client can now consider the trade-off of the low-cost method versus compressing the project to 2 years. Similar trade-offs can be compared for different levels of resources or increases in technical performance. The assumption is that any movement away from the low-cost, efficient method will increase costs—for example, overtime. The preferred approach in defining the project is to make rough top-down estimates, develop the WBS/OBS, make bottom-up estimates, develop schedules and budgets, and reconcile differences between top-down and bottom-up estimates. Hopefully, these steps will be done *before* final negotiation with either an internal or external customer. With both top-down and bottom-up approaches, managers must be sensitive to factors that can influence project estimates.

ESTIMATING COSTS AND DEVELOPING BUDGETS

Accurate costs and budgets are the lifeline for control; they serve as the standard for comparison of actual and plan throughout the life of the project. Project rollup and project status reports depend on reliable cost estimates and budgets as the major input for measuring variances and taking corrective action.

Cost Estimates

The accuracy of the cost estimate improves as you move from the conceptual phase of the project to the point where individual items (work packages) are defined. Assuming work packages are defined, detailed cost estimates can be made. Here are typical kinds of costs found in a project:

1. Direct costs
    A. Labor
    B. Materials
    C. Equipment
    D. Other
2. Project overhead costs
3. General and administrative (G&A) overhead costs

The total project cost estimate is broken out in this fashion to sharpen the control process and improve decision making.

Direct Costs   These costs are clearly chargeable to a work package. Direct costs can be influenced by the project manager, project team, and individuals implementing the work package. These costs represent real cash outflows and must be paid as the project progresses; therefore, direct costs are usually separated from overhead costs. Lower-level project rollups frequently include only direct costs.

Project Overhead Costs   Project overhead represents project costs that cannot be tied to a specific deliverable but serve the entire project. Examples of project overhead are consultants, the project manager, training, and travel.

General and Administrative (G&A) Overhead Costs   These represent organizational costs that are not directly linked to a specific project and are also called fixed costs. Although overhead is not an immediate out-of-pocket expense, it *is* real and must be covered in the long run if the firm is to remain viable. These costs are carried for the duration of the project. Allocation of G&A costs varies from organization to organization. G&A costs are usually allocated as a percentage of total direct cost. For example, if the total direct cost is $400,000, a blanket G&A rate of 50 percent would be added for a total project cost of $600,000.

In larger organizations the application of such a blanket rate may cause the total project cost to be excessive because the project is being charged with G&A (fixed) costs which are not relevant to the project. For example, if the project does not include inventory or maintenance facilities used by another division, the project should not have these costs included in its total cost. To avoid this problem, larger firms frequently break their G&A (fixed) costs down into categories known as Direct Overhead Costs that more closely pinpoint which resources of the organization infrastructure are being used in the project. Direct overhead costs can be tied to project deliverables or work packages. Selective direct overhead charges provide a more accurate total project cost based on deliverables or work packages rather than using a blanket G&A overhead rate for the whole project.

Given the totals of direct and overhead costs for an individual deliverable, it is possible to cumulate the total costs for the entire project. A percentage can be added for profit if you are a contractor. It is important to remember that only direct costs should be used for measuring project schedule and cost performance, since direct costs are the only costs the project manager or project team can influence.

Cost Estimating Methods

Ratio methods are often used in the concept phase of a project to get an initial cost estimate for the project. Top-down estimates frequently use this method. Three common examples are the cost estimate for a house by square feet, the cost of a new plant estimated by capacity size, and a software product estimate by lines of code. However, these ratio methods are not very accurate for control or for developing budgets because these methods neither recognize differences among projects nor identify specific deliverables.

If the project is similar to past projects, the costs from past projects can be used as a starting point for the new project. Differences in the new project can be noted and old costs adjusted to reflect these differences. For example, a ship repair dry-dock firm has a set of standard repair projects (e.g., boilerplate projects) that are used as a starting point for estimating the cost and duration of any new project. Differences from the appropriate standardized project are noted for times, costs, and resources, and changes are made. This approach enables the firm to develop a potential schedule, estimate costs, and develop a budget in a very short time span. Unfortunately, the approach applies to only a small number of projects.

A typical statement in the field is the desire to "have 95 percent probability of meeting time and cost estimates." Past experience is a good starting point for developing time and cost estimates. But past experience estimates must almost always be refined by other considerations to reach the 95 percent probability level. Project, people, and external factors all need to be considered to improve quality of estimates for project times and costs.

Factors related to the uniqueness of the project will have a strong influence on the accuracy of estimates. For example, time to implement new technology has a habit of expanding in an increasing, nonlinear fashion. Sometimes poorly written scope specifications for new technology result in errors in estimating times and costs. Environmental conditions for a project also can produce errors. Long-duration projects increase the uncertainty in estimates. A predetermined imposed time-to-market duration can profoundly influence time and cost estimates for the project.

The people factor can also introduce errors in estimating times and cost. A close match of people skills to the task will influence productivity and learning time. People dedicated full time or part time to the project influence estimates—full timers tend to be more productive. Physical closeness of team members and organizational infrastructure will influence communication and thus project estimates (i.e., they may in-

Work package cost estimate

Cost

Direct costs	Low	Average	High
Design engineers	$ 80	$100	$150
Proto engineers	130	150	280
Materials	25	25	25
Equipment rental	25	25	30
Total direct costs	$260	$300	$485

FIGURE 3–8 **Read/Write Head Design**

fluence how long it takes to make decisions). Sometimes factors such as staff turnover can influence estimates.

Finally, factors external to the project can refine time and cost estimates. For example, equipment downtime can alter time estimates. National holidays, vacations, and legal limits can influence project estimates. Estimates of the time and cost together allow the manager to develop a budget.

The most reliable method for estimating cost is to ask the people responsible for the work. They know from experience or know where to find the information to estimate work package costs. When work packages have significant uncertainty associated with the cost to complete the work package, it is a prudent policy to require three cost estimates—best, average, and high. Figure 3–8 presents a hypothetical example using three time estimates for a work package. This cost estimating approach gives the project manager and owner an opportunity to assess the risks associated with project costs. The approach helps to reduce cost surprises as the project progresses. It also provides a basis for determining the contingency fund. (See Chapter 5 for a detailed discussion.)

Time-Phased Budgets

Cost estimates are not a budget. A cost estimate becomes a budget when it is time phased. For example, the budget for a project may be $500,000. The money is dispensed as the project is implemented. A procedure is needed to determine *when* the money must be available. Each work package estimate requires a time-phased budget. In Figure 3–6, the work package has a duration of three weeks; at this point there is *no way of knowing when* the work package time-phased expenses will be incurred. This work package duration and others are used to develop the project network, which schedules when work packages will start and finish. The time-phased budgets for work packages are then assigned to scheduled time periods to determine the financial requirements for each period over the life of the project.

Perceptions of costs and budgets vary depending on their users. The project manager must be very aware of these differences when setting up the project budget and when communicating these differences to others. Figure 3–9 depicts these different perceptions.[8] The left line represents funds committed before actual use in the project. For example, the placing of an order for a large custom pump for an oil line may take place six months before it is needed, but the order has been placed and there is a legal obligation to pay when it is ready for shipment and use in the project. In this case, the link between money committed does not mirror the cash flow of the project schedule. This information is useful to the financial officer of the organization in forecasting

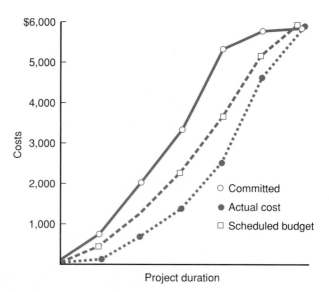

FIGURE 3–9 Three Views of Cost

future cash outflows. The middle line, scheduled budget, represents the planned direct costs as they are expected to occur. The actual cost line represents actual direct costs as they occur as the project is implemented. The respective timings of these three costs are useful to forecast future cash needs, measure project schedule, and track actual cost variances.

LEVEL OF DETAIL

Level of detail is different for different levels of management. At any level the detail should be no more than is necessary and sufficient. Top management interests usually center on the total project and major milestone events that mark major accomplishments—for example, "build oil platform in the North Sea" or "complete prototype." Middle management might center on one segment of the project or one milestone. First-line managers' interests may be limited to one task or work package. One of the beauties of WBS is the ability to aggregate network information so that each level of management can have the kind of information necessary to make decisions.

Practicing project managers advocate keeping the level of detail to a minimum. But there are limits to this suggestion. One of the most frequent mistakes new project managers make is to forget that the task time estimate will be used to control schedule and cost performance. A frequent rule of thumb used by practicing project managers says that a task duration should not exceed 5 workdays or at the most 10 workdays, if workdays are the time units used for the project. Such a rule will probably result in a more detailed network, but the additional detail pays off in controlling schedule and cost as the project progresses. Suppose the task is "build prototype computer-controlled conveyor belt," the time estimate is 40 workdays, and the budget $300,000. It may be better to divide the task into seven or eight smaller tasks for control purposes. If one of the smaller tasks gets behind because of problems or a poor time estimate, it will be possible to take corrective action quickly and avoid delaying successive tasks and the project. If the single task of 40 workdays is used, it is possible that no corrective action would be taken until day 40, since many people have a tendency to wait and see if progress improves or to avoid admitting they are behind; the result may mean the project will fall far more than five days behind schedule. The 5- to 10-day rule of thumb applies to cost and performance goals. A similar check is needed on cost and performance goals at short time intervals to avoid losing control.

If following the rule of thumb just suggested results in too many network tasks, an alternative is available, but it has conditions. The activity time can be extended beyond the 5- to 10-day rule **if** control monitoring checkpoints for segments of the task can be established so that clear measures of progress can be identified by a specific percent complete. This information is invaluable to the control process of measuring schedule and cost performance—for example, payments for contract work are paid on "percent complete." Defining a task with start and end points and intermediate points enhances the chances of early detection of problems, corrective action, and on-time project completion.

Getting the level of detail in the WBS to match management needs for effective implementation is crucial, but the delicate balance is difficult to find. The level of detail in the WBS varies with the complexity of the project; the need for control; the project size, cost, and duration; and other factors. If the structure reflects excessive detail, there is a tendency to break the work effort into department assignments. This tendency can become a barrier to success because the emphasis will be on departmental outcomes rather than on deliverable outcomes. Excessive detail also means more unproductive paperwork. Note that if the level of the WBS is increased by one, the number of cost accounts may increase geometrically. On the other hand, if the level of detail is not adequate, an organizational unit may find the structure falls short of meeting its needs. Fortunately, the WBS has built-in flexibility. Participating organizational units may expand their portion of the structure to meet their special needs. For example, the engineering department may wish to further break their work on a deliverable into smaller packages by electrical, civil, and mechanical.

ESTIMATING GUIDELINES FOR TIMES, COSTS, AND RESOURCES

Managers recognize that time, cost, and resource estimates must be accurate if project planning, scheduling, and controlling are to be effective. Therefore, every effort should be made to see that initial estimates are as accurate as possible because the choice of no estimates leaves a great deal to luck and is not palatable to serious project managers. Even though a project has never been done before, a manager can follow six guidelines to develop useful work package estimates:

1. **Responsibility.** *At the work package level, estimates should be made by the person(s) most familiar with the task.* Except for extremely technical tasks, those responsible for getting the job done on schedule and within budget are usually first-line supervisors or technicians who are experienced and familiar with the type of work involved. These people will not usually have a preconceived, imposed duration for a deliverable in mind. They will give an estimate based on their experience and best judgment. A secondary benefit of using those responsible is the hope they will "buy in" to seeing that the estimate materializes when they implement the work package. If those involved are not consulted, it will be difficult to hold them responsible for failure to achieve the estimated time. Reliable time estimates deserve the careful attention of those responsible.

   Because projects represent one-time efforts, depending on other sources for task time, resource, and cost estimates has some inherent dangers. Historical estimates, although low cost and easy to obtain, assume the past represents the future and may miss uncertainties that go with a new task.

2. **Normal conditions.** When task time, cost, and resource estimates are determined, they are based on certain assumptions. *Estimates should be based on normal conditions, efficient methods, and a normal level of resources.* Normal conditions are sometimes difficult to discern, but it is necessary to have a consensus in the organization as to what "normal conditions" mean in each project. If the normal workday is eight hours, the time estimate should be based on an eight-hour day. Similarly, if the normal workday is two shifts, the time estimate should be based on a two-shift workday. Any time estimate should reflect efficient methods for the resources normally available. The time estimate should represent the normal level of resources—people or equipment. For example, if three programmers are available for coding or two roadgraders available for road construction, time and cost estimates should be based on the normal level of resources, unless it is anticipated the project will change what is currently viewed as "normal." In addition, possible conflicts in demand for resources on parallel or concurrent activities should not be considered at this stage. The need for adding resources will be examined when resource scheduling is discussed in Chapter 7.

3. **Time units.** Time units to use should be selected early in the development phase of the project network. *All task time estimates need consistent time units.* Estimates of time must consider if normal time is calendar days, workdays, workweeks, mandays, single shift, hours, minutes, and so forth. In practice, the use of "workday" is the dominant choice for expressing task duration. However, in projects such as a heart transplant operation, minutes probably would be more appropriate as a time unit. One such project that used minutes as the time unit was the movement of patients from an old hospital to an elegant new one across town. Because there were several life-endangering moves, minutes were used to ensure patient safety so that proper emergency life-support systems would be available if needed. The point is, network analysis requires a standard unit of time. When computer programs allow more than one option, some notation should be made of the variance from the standard unit of time. If the standard unit of time is a five-day workweek and the estimated activity duration is in calendar days, it must be converted to the normal workweek. For example, if the shipment of a large pump to an Alaskan oilfield takes 14 calendar days from a Seattle port, the activity duration would be 10 workdays.

4. **Independence.** Estimators should treat the task as independent of other tasks that might be integrated by the WBS. Use of first-line managers usually results in considering tasks independently; this is good. Top managers are prone to aggregate many tasks into one time estimate and then deductively make the individual task time estimates add to the total. If tasks are in a chain and performed by the same group or department, it is best not to ask for all the time estimates in the sequence at once to avoid the tendency for a planner or a supervisor to look at the whole path and try to adjust individual task times in the sequence to meet an arbitrary imposed schedule or some rough "guesstimate" of the total time for the whole path or segment of the project. This tendency does not reflect the uncertainties of individual activities and generally results in optimistic task time estimates. In summary, *each task time estimate should be considered independently of other activities.*

5. **Contingencies.** *Work package estimates should not include allowances for contingencies.* The estimate should assume normal or average conditions even though every work package will not materialize as planned. For this reason, top manage-

ment has an extra fund for contingencies that can be used to cover unforeseen events.

6. **Estimate errors.** Finally, *the project management culture should allow estimate mistakes and errors to occur.* Punishment produces quick results—the next request for an estimate probably will include a large cushion for extra time, resources, and cost! A strong element of trust in the project management culture will result in more realistic estimates.

SUMMARY

The project scope definition and breakdown structure are the keys to nearly every aspect of managing the project. The scope definition provides focus and emphasis on the end item(s) of the project. The structure helps ensure all tasks of the project are identified and provides two views of the project—one on deliverables and one on organization responsibility. The WBS avoids having the project driven by organization function or by a finance system. The structure forces attention to realistic requirements of personnel, hardware, and budgets. Use of the structure provides a powerful framework for project control that identifies deviations from plan, identifies responsibility, and spots areas for improved performance. No well-developed project plan or control system is possible without a disciplined, structured approach. The WBS, OBS, and cost account codes provide this discipline. The WBS will serve as the database for developing the project network which establishes the timing of work, people, equipment, and costs.

REVIEW QUESTIONS

1. What kinds of information are included in a cost account?
2. What kinds of information are included in a work package?
3. What is a time-phased budget in a work package?
4. What is the meaning of the term "project rollup," and what is its significance to the project manager?

EXERCISES

1. Develop a WBS matrix for a local stage play. Be sure to identify the deliverables and organizational units (people) responsible. How would you code your system? Give an example of the work packages in one of your cost accounts.
2. Use an example of a project you are familiar with or are interested in. Identify the deliverables and organizational units (people) responsible. How would you code your system? Give an example of the work packages in one of your cost accounts.

ENDNOTES

1. Roger E. Allen and Stephen D. Allen, *Winnie-the-Pooh on Success* (New York: Penguin, 1997), p. 10.
2. M. A. Smith and R. L. Tucker, "Early Project Problem—Assessment of Impact and Cause," *1984 Proceedings* (Newtown Square, PA: Project Management Institute, 1984), p. 226.
3. Jeffrey K. Pinto and Dennis P. Slevin, "Critical Success Factors across the Project Life Cycle," *Project Management Journal,* vol. 19, no. 3 (June 1988), p. 72.
4. David B. Ashley et al., "Determinants of Construction Project Success," *Project Management Journal,* vol. 18, no. 2 (June 1987), p. 72.

5. Barry Z. Posner, " What It Takes to Be a Good Project Manager," *Project Management Journal,* vol. 18, no. 1 (March 1987), p. 52.

6. David Gobeli and Erik Larson, "Barriers Affecting Project Success," in R. Brunies and P. Menard, eds., *Measuring Success* (Newtown Square, PA: Project Management Institute, 1986), pp. 22–29.

7. David Eager, "Aussie Project Management: The Sidney 2000 Olympic Games," *PM Network,* vol. 12, no. 9 (September 1998), pp. 63–66.

8. For a more detailed discussion, see David Hamburger, "Three Perceptions of Project Cost—Cost Is More Than a Four-Letter Word," *Project Management Journal,* vol. 17, no. 3 (June 1986), pp. 51–58.

CASE

Manchester United Soccer Club

Nicolette Larson was loading the dishwasher with her husband, Kevin, and telling him about the first meeting of the Manchester United Tournament Organizing Committee. Larson, a self-confessed "soccer mom," had been elected tournament director and was responsible for organizing the club's first summer tournament.

Manchester United Soccer Club (MUSC) located in Manchester, New Hampshire, was formed in 1992 as a way of bringing recreational players to a higher level of competition and prepare them for the State Olympic Development Program and/or high school teams. The club currently has 24 boys and girls (ranging in age from under 9 to 16) on teams affiliated with the Hampshire Soccer Association and the Granite State Girl's Soccer League. The club's board of directors decided in the fall to sponsor a summer invitational soccer tournament to generate revenue. Given the boom in youth soccer, hosting summer tournaments has become a popular method for raising funds. MUSC teams regularly compete in three to four tournaments each summer at different locales in New England. These tournaments have been reported to generate between $50,000 and $70,000 for the host club.

MUSC needs additional revenue to refurbish and expand the number of soccer fields at the Rock Rimmon soccer complex. Funds would also be used to augment the club's scholarship program, which provides financial aid to players who cannot afford the $450 annual club dues.

Nicolette gave her husband a blow-by-blow account of what transpired during the first tournament committee meeting that night. She started the meeting by having everyone introduce themselves and by proclaiming how excited she was that the club was going to sponsor its own tournament. She then suggested that the committee brainstorm what needed to be done to pull off the event; she would record their ideas on a flipchart.

What emerged was a free-for-all of ideas and suggestions. One member immediately stressed the importance of having qualified referees and spent several minutes describing in detail how his son's team was robbed in a poorly officiated championship game. This was followed by other stories of injustice on the soccer field. Another member suggested that they needed to quickly contact the local colleges to see if they could use their fields. The committee spent more than 30 minutes talking about how they should screen teams and how much they should charge as an entry fee. An argument broke out over whether they should reward the winning teams in each age bracket with medals or trophies. Many members felt that medals were too cheap, while others thought the trophies would be too expensive. Someone suggested that they seek local corporate sponsors to help fund the tournament. The proposed sale of tournament T-shirts and sweatshirts was followed by a general critique of the different shirts parents had acquired at different tournaments. One member advocated that they recruit an artist he knew to develop a unique silk-screen design for the tournament. The meeting adjourned 30 minutes late with only half of the members remaining until the end. Nicolette drove home with seven sheets of ideas and a headache.

As Kevin poured a glass of water for the two aspirin Nicolette was about to take, he tried to comfort her by saying that organizing this tournament would be a big project not unlike the projects he works on at his engineering and design firm. He offered to sit down with her the next night and help her plan the project. He suggested that the first thing they needed to do was to develop a WBS for the project.

1. Develop a draft of the work breakdown structure for the tournament that contains at least three levels of detail. What are the major deliverables associated with hosting an event such as a soccer tournament?
2. How would developing a WBS alleviate some of the problems that occurred during the first meeting and help Nicolette organize and plan the project?
3. Where can Nicolette find additional information to help her develop a WBS for the tournament?
4. How could Nicolette and her task force use the WBS to generate cost estimates for the tournament? Why would this be useful information?

Computer Project Exercise, Part 1

Exercise Design

The computer exercises found in Chapters 3, 4, 7, and 12 are designed to help learners *apply* the principles found in these chapters. A major overall goal of the exercises is to develop an *integrated* information system needed for decision making and for tracking a project's progress. Understanding the key linkages and connections of all the segments of the exercises should be a key objective of the student, rather than learning a particular project software. This understanding is extremely useful on projects that use software and those that do not. The exercises and questions are set up to develop the ability to make connections.

The exercises are designed to allow students to use most commercial software packages that are network-based and include routines for resource constraints and earned value. Each exercise uses the information developed in earlier exercises; therefore, make sure all files are *saved* so output from previous exercises can be used as a starting point or input in future exercises.

Exercise Structure and Assumptions

In developing the exercises, trade-offs had to be made to enrich the learning experience. One of the major problems students initially encounter is data and detail overload. This reduces their ability to identify project and data problems and to compare alternatives. Although the project found in the exercises is real, it has been reduced and detail has been eliminated many times to concentrate on applying project management principles and understanding linkages. In addition, other simplifying assumptions have been made so that students and instructors can trace problems and discuss outcomes. These assumptions detract from reality, but they keep the focus on the objectives of the exercises and reduce student frustration with software intricacies. Moving from these exercises to real projects is primarily one of increasing detail. The simplifying assumptions are given below (make sure they are included in "default," "preferences," and/or "options" sections of the software used):

- Each activity will represent a work package.
- Resources will be considered in terms of teams—not individuals. There are seven teams available (initially): one team for documentation, assembly/test, and purchasing, plus two design teams and two development teams.
- A 7-day workweek is used for the whole year; no holidays.
- An 8-hour workday, or 56-hour workweek, is used. Overtime is not allowed.
- The project should start January 1 of the next year.
- There are no overhead costs included in this project. Use only the costs of resources stated in costs per unit of usage time.

Warning: Experience has taught students to frequently make separate backup files for each exercise. The software is never as friendly as users expect!

COMPUTER-CONTROLLED CONVEYOR BELT PROJECT

Project Description

The new computer-controlled conveyor belt is an exciting project that moves and positions items on the conveyor belt within <1 millimeter. The proposed project will produce a new system for future installations, and for replacement of those in the field, at a low cost. The computer-controlled conveyor belt has the potential to be a critical unit in 30 percent of the systems installed in factories. The new system is also easier to update with future technologies. Tables A3–1, A3–2, and A3–3 have been developed for you to use in completing the project exercises.

Assignment

Develop the WBS outline using the software available to you. (Note: You do not need the OBS at this time.) You may input duration, resources, costs, and preceding activities at this time if your software asks for this information.

Question

Does this information (WBS) allow you to define any milestones of the project? Why and what are they? Or why not?

Remember: Save your file for future exercises!

TABLE A3-1

COMPUTER-CONTROLLED CONVEYOR BELT PROJECT

Activity	Description	Resource	Duration (days)	Preceding activity
1	Architectural decisions	Design	25	—
2	Hardware specifications	Development, design	50	1
3	Kernel specifications	Design	20	1
4	Utilities specifications	Development, design	15	1
5	Hardware design	Design, development	70	2
6	Disk drivers	Assembly, development	100	3
7	Memory management	Development	90	3
8	Operating system documentation	Development, documentation	25	3
9	Routine utilities	Development	60	4
10	Complex utilities	Development	80	4
11	Utilities documentation	Documentation, design	20	4
12	Hardware documentation	Documentation, design	30	5
13	Integration first phase	Assembly, development	50	6,7,8,9,10,11,12
14	Prototypes	Assembly, development	80	13
15	Serial I/O drivers	Development	130	13
16	System hard/software test	Assembly	25	14,15
17	Order printed circuit boards	Purchasing	5	16
18	Network interface	Development	90	16
19	Shell	Development	60	16
20	Project documentation	Documentation, development	50	16
21	Assemble preproduction	Assembly, development	30	17F-S, lag 50 days
22	Integrated acceptance test	Assembly, development	60	18,19,20,21

TABLE A3-2

COMPUTER-CONTROLLED CONVEYOR BELT PROJECT

Hardware	Hardware specifications
	Hardware design
	Hardware documentation
	Prototypes
	Order circuit boards
	Assemble preproduction models
Operating system	Kernel specifications
	Drivers
	Disk drivers
	Serial I/O drivers
	Memory management
	Operating system documentation
	Network interface
Utilities	Utilities specifications
	Routine utilities
	Complex utilities
	Utilities documentation
	Shell
System integration	Architectural decisions
	Integration first phase
	System hard/software test
	Project documentation
	Integration acceptance testing

TABLE A3-3

ORGANIZATION RESOURCES

Name	Group	Cost ($/hr)
Research and Development		
Design	R&D (2 teams)	$100
Development	R&D (2 teams)	70
Documentation	R&D	60
Assembly/test	R&D	70
Purchasing		40

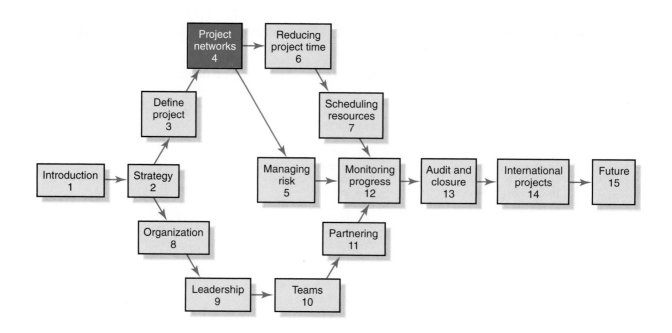

CHAPTER FOUR

Developing a Network Plan

Time is the scarcest resource, and unless it is managed nothing else can be managed.
—Peter Drucker

DEVELOPING THE PROJECT NETWORK

The project network is the tool used for planning, scheduling, and monitoring project progress. The network is developed from the information collected for the WBS and is a graphic flowchart of the project job plan. The network depicts the project activities that must be completed, the logical sequences, the interdependencies of the activities to be completed, and in most cases the times for the activities to start and finish along with the longest path(s) through the network—the *critical path*. The network is the framework for the project information system that will be used by the project managers to make decisions concerning project time, cost, and performance.

Developing the project networks takes time for someone or some group to develop; therefore, they cost money! Are networks really worth the struggle? The answer is definitely yes, except in cases where the project is considered trivial or very short in duration. The network is easily understood by others because the network presents a graphic display of the flow and sequence of work through the project. Once the network is developed, it is very easy to modify or change when unexpected events occur as the project progresses. For example, if materials for an activity are delayed, the impact can be quickly assessed and the whole project revised in only a few minutes with the computer. These revisions can be communicated to all project participants quickly.

The project network provides other invaluable information and insights. It provides the basis for scheduling labor and equipment. It enhances communication that melds all managers and groups together in meeting the time, cost, and performance objectives of the project. It provides an estimate of project duration rather than picking a project completion date from a hat or someone's preferred date. The network gives the times when activities can start and finish and when they can be delayed. It provides the basis for budgeting the cash flow of the project. It identifies which activities are "critical" and, therefore, should not be delayed if the project is to be completed as planned. It highlights which activities to consider if the project needs to be compressed to meet a deadline.

There are other reasons project networks are worth their weight in gold. Basically, project networks minimize surprises by getting the plan out early and allowing corrective feedback. A commonly heard statement from practitioners is that the project network represents three quarters of the planning process. Perhaps this is an exaggeration, but it signals the perceived importance of the network to project managers in the field.

FROM WORK PACKAGE TO NETWORK

Networks are built using nodes (boxes) and arrows. In Figure 4–1 the node (box) depicts an activity, and the arrow shows dependency and project flow. The activity represents one or more tasks that consume time.

The network process is similar to the WBS process. That is, the work packages are used to develop a detailed network for the first-line managers (see Level 3—Plans in Figure 4–1). The detailed network of two projects can be shown in a more aggregate network for the department manager (level 2) and, in turn, is summarized to a level needed for the project manager, top management, and the client. This top level is usu-

FIGURE 4–1 Rollup of Network Plans

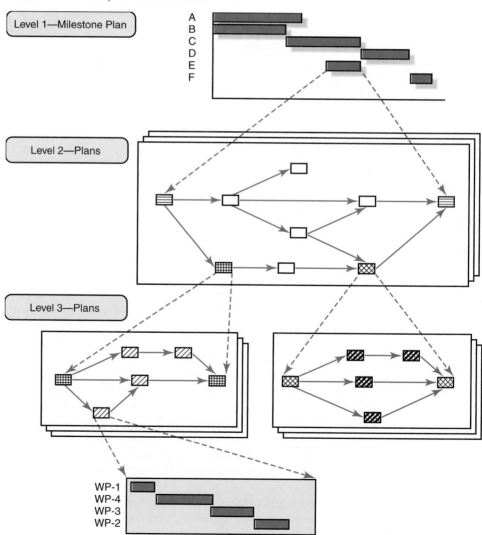

ally depicted as a bar chart and is called a *milestone plan.* Validity of the information at each summary level relies on the accuracy of the work packages and activities.

Integrating the work packages and the network represents a point where the management process often fails in practice. The primary explanations for this failure are that (1) different groups (people) are used to define work packages and activities and (2) the WBS is poorly constructed and not deliverable/output oriented. Integration of the WBS and project network is crucial to effective project management. The project manager must be careful to guarantee continuity by having some of the same people who defined the WBS and work packages develop the network activities.

Networks provide the project schedule by identifying dependencies, sequencing, and timing of activities, which the WBS is not designed to do. The primary inputs for

FIGURE 4–2 WBS/Work Packages to Network

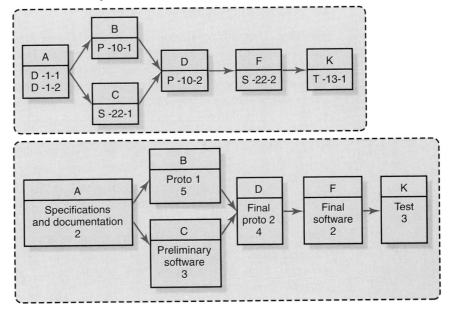

developing a project network plan are work packages. Remember, a work package is defined independently of other work packages, has definite start and finish points, requires specific resources, includes technical specifications, and has cost estimates for the package. However, dependency, sequencing, and timing of each of these factors are not included in the work package. A network activity can include one or more work packages.

Figure 4–2 shows a segment of the WBS example from Chapter 3 and how the information is used to develop a project network. The lowest level deliverable in Figure 4–2 is "circuit board." The cost accounts (design, production, test, software) denote project work, organization unit responsible, and time-phased budgets for the work packages. Each cost account represents one or more work packages. For example, the design cost account has two work packages (D-1-1 and D-1-2)—specifications and documentation. The software and production accounts also have two work packages. Developing a network requires sequencing tasks from all work packages that have measurable work.

Figure 4–2 traces how work packages are used to develop a project network. You can trace the use of work packages by the coding scheme. For example, activity A uses work packages D-1-1 and D-1-2 (specifications and documentation), while activity C uses work package S-22-1. This methodology of selecting work packages to describe activities is used to develop the project network, which sequences and times project activities. Care must be taken to include all work packages. *The manager derives activity time estimates from the task times in the work package.* For example, activity B (proto 1) requires five weeks to complete; activity K (test) requires three weeks to complete. After computing the activity early and late times, the manager can schedule resources and time-phase budgets (with dates).

CONSTRUCTING A PROJECT NETWORK

Terminology

Every field has its jargon that allows colleagues to communicate comfortably with each other about the techniques they use. Project managers are no exception. Here are some terms used in building project networks.

Activity.   For project managers, an *activity* is an element of the project that requires time. It may or may not require resources. Typically an activity consumes time—either while people work or while people wait. Examples of the latter are time waiting for contracts to be signed, materials to arrive, drug approval by the government, budget clearance, etc. Activities usually represent one or more tasks from a work package. Descriptions of activities should use a verb/noun format: for example, develop product specifications.

Merge activity.   This is an activity that has more than one activity immediately preceding it (more than one dependency arrow flowing to it).

Parallel activities.   These are activities that can take place at the same time, if the manager wishes. However, the manager may choose to have parallel activities *not* occur simultaneously.

Path.   A sequence of connected, dependent activities.

Critical path.   When this term is used, it means the longest path(s) through the network; if an activity on the path is delayed, the project is delayed the same amount of time.

Event.   This term is used to represent a point in time when an activity is started or completed. It does not consume time.

Burst activity.   This activity has more than one activity immediately following it (more than one dependency arrow flowing from it).

Two Approaches

The two approaches used to develop project networks are known as *activity-on-node (AON)* and *activity-on-arrow (AOA). Both methods use two building blocks—the arrow and the node.* Their names derive from the fact that the former uses a node to depict an activity, while the second uses an arrow to depict an activity. From the first use of these two approaches in the late 1950s, practitioners have offered many enhancements; however, the basic models have withstood the test of time and still prevail with only minor variations in form.[1]

In practice, the activity-on-node (AON) method has come to dominate most projects. Hence, this text will deal primarily with AON. However, for those who find their organization using the activity-on-arrow (AOA) approach, the chapter includes an appendix demonstrating AOA methods (Appendix 4–2). There are good reasons for students of project management to be proficient in both methods. Different departments and organizations have their "favorite" approaches and are frequently loyal to software that is already purchased and being used. New employees or outsiders are seldom in a position to govern choice of method. If subcontractors are used, it is unreasonable to ask them to change their whole project management system to conform to the approach you are using. The point is, a project manager should feel comfortable moving among projects that use either AON or AOA.

Basic Rules to Follow in Developing Project Networks

The following eight rules apply in general when developing a project network:

1. Networks flow typically from left to right.
2. An activity cannot begin until all preceding connected activities have been completed.
3. Arrows on networks indicate precedence and flow. Arrows can cross over each other.
4. Each activity should have a unique identification number.
5. An activity identification number must be larger than that of any activities that precede it.
6. Looping is not allowed (in other words, recycling through a set of activities cannot take place).
7. Conditional statements are not allowed (that is, this type of statement should not appear: If successful, do something; if not, do nothing).
8. Experience suggests that when there are multiple starts, a common start node can be used to indicate a clear project beginning on the network. Similarly, a single project end node can be used to indicate a clear ending.

ACTIVITY-ON-NODE (AON) FUNDAMENTALS

The wide availability of personal computers and graphics programs has served as an impetus for use of the Activity-on-Node (AON) method (sometimes called the *precedence diagram method*). Figure 4–3 shows a few typical uses of building blocks for the AON network construction. An **activity** is represented by a *node* (box). The node

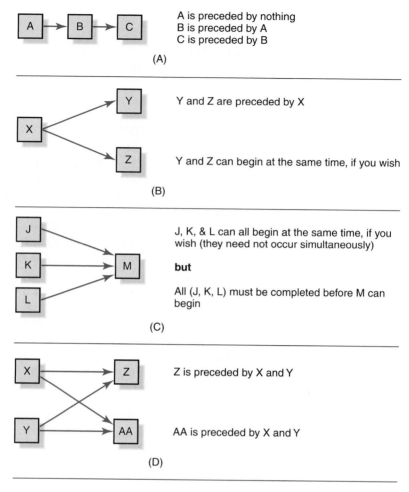

FIGURE 4–3 Activity-on-Node Network Fundamentals

can take many forms, but in recent years the node represented as a rectangle (box) has dominated. The dependencies among activities are depicted by *arrows* between the rectangles (boxes) on the AON network. The arrows indicate how the activities are related and the sequence in which things must be accomplished. The length and slope of the arrow are arbitrary and set for convenience of drawing the network. The letters in the boxes serve here to identify the activities while you learn the fundamentals of network construction and analysis. In practice, activities have identification numbers and descriptions.

There are three basic relationships that must be established for activities included in a project network. The relationships can be found by answering the following three questions for each activity:

1. Which activities must be completed immediately *before* this activity? These activities are called *predecessor* activities.
2. Which activities must immediately *follow* this activity? These activities are called *successor* activities.
3. Which activities can occur *while* this activity is taking place? This is known as a *concurrent* or *parallel* relationship.

Sometimes a manager can use only questions 1 and 3 to establish relationships. This information allows the network analyst to construct a graphic flowchart of the sequence and logical interdependencies of project activities.

Figure 4–3A is analogous to a list of things to do where you complete the task at the top of the list first and then move to the second task, etc. This figure tells the project manager that activity A must be completed before activity B can begin, and activity B must be completed before activity C can begin.

Figure 4–3B tells us that activities Y and Z cannot begin until activity X is completed. This figure also indicates that activities Y and Z can occur concurrently or simultaneously if the project manager wishes; however, it is not a necessary condition. For example, pouring concrete driveway (activity Y) can take place while landscape planting (activity Z) is being accomplished, but land clearing (activity X) must be completed before activities Y and Z can start. Activities Y and Z are considered *parallel* activities. Parallel paths allow concurrent effort, which may shorten time to do a series of activities. Activity X is sometimes referred to as a *burst* activity because more that one arrow bursts from the node. The number of arrows indicates how many activities immediately follow activity X.

Figure 4–3C shows us activities J, K, and L can occur simultaneously if desired, and activity M cannot begin until activities J, K, and L are all completed. Activities J, K, and L are parallel activities. Activity M is called a *merge* activity because more than one activity must be completed before M can begin. Activity M could also be called a milestone.

In Figure 4–3D, activities X and Y are parallel activities that can take place at the same time; activities Z and AA are also parallel activities. But activities Z and AA cannot begin until activities X and Y are both completed.

Given these fundamentals of AON, we can practice developing a simple network. Remember, the arrows can cross over each other (e.g., Figure 4–3D), be bent, or be any length or slope. Neatness is not a criterion for a valid, useful network—only accurate inclusion of all project activities, their dependencies, and time estimates. Information for a simplified project network is given in Table 4–1. This project represents a new business center that is to be developed and the work and services the county engineering design department must provide as it coordinates with other groups—such as the business center owners and contractors.

Figure 4–4 shows the first steps in constructing the AON project network from the

TABLE 4-1

NETWORK INFORMATION

KOLL BUSINESS CENTER
County Engineers Design Department

Activity	Description	Preceding activity
A	Application approval	None
B	Construction plans	A
C	Traffic study	A
D	Service availability check	A
E	Staff report	B, C
F	Commission approval	B, C, D
G	Wait for construction	F
H	Occupancy	E, G

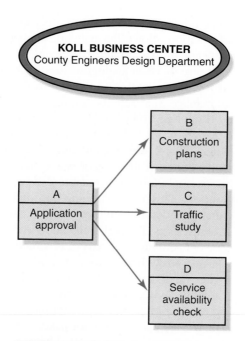

FIGURE 4–4 Koll Business Center—
Partial Network

information in Table 4–1. We see that activity A (application approval) has nothing preceding it; therefore, it is the first node to be drawn. Next, we note that activities B, C, and D (construction plans, traffic study, and service availability check) are all preceded by activity A. We draw three arrows and connect them to activities B, C, and D. This segment shows the project manager that activity A must be completed before ac-

FIGURE 4–5 Koll Business Center—Complete Network

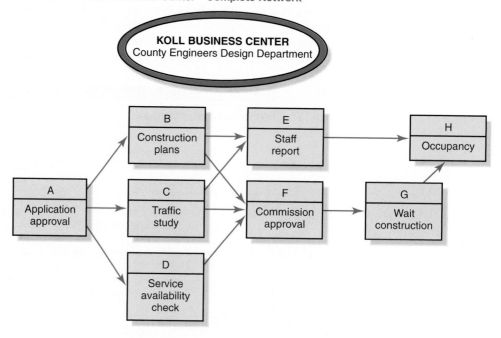

tivities B, C, and D can begin. After A is completed, B, C, and D can go on concurrently, if desired. Figure 4–5 shows the completed network with all of the activities and precedences depicted.

Snapshot from Practice
THE YELLOW STICKY APPROACH
(FOR CONSTRUCTING A PROJECT NETWORK)

In practice small project networks (25 to 100 activities) are frequently developed using yellow Post-it® stickers. The meeting requirements and process for the project team are described herein.

The following are the requirements for such a project:

1. Project team members and a facilitator.
2. One yellow sticker (3 × 4 inches or larger) for each activity with the description of the activity printed on the sticker.
3. Erasable whiteboard with marker pen (a long, 4-foot-wide piece of butcher paper can be used in place of the whiteboard).

All of the yellow stickers are placed in easy view of all team members. The team begins by identifying those activity stickers that have no predecessors. Each of these activity stickers is then attached to the whiteboard. A start node is drawn, and a dependency arrow is connected to each activity.

Given the initial network start activities, each activity is examined for immediate successor activities. These activities are attached to the whiteboard and dependency arrows drawn. This process is continued until all of the yellow stickers are attached to the whiteboard with dependency arrows. (Note: The process can be reversed, beginning with those activities that have no successor activities and connecting them to a project end node. The predecessor activities are selected for each activity and attached to the whiteboard with dependency arrows marked.)

When the process is complete, the dependencies are recorded in the project software, which develops a computer-designed network along with the critical path(s) and early, late, and slack times. This methodology sensitizes team members early to the interdependencies among activities of the project.

START AND FINISH NETWORK COMPUTATIONS

At this point our project network presents us with a graphic map of the project activities with sequences and dependencies. This information is tremendously valuable to those managing the project. However, estimating the duration for each activity will further increase the value of the network. A realistic project plan and schedule require reliable time estimates for project activities. The addition of time to the network allows us to estimate how long the project will take. When activities can or must start, when resources must be available, which activities can be delayed, and when the project is estimated to be complete are all determined from the times assigned. Deriving an activity time estimate necessitates early assessment of resource needs in terms of material, equipment, and people. In essence the project network with activity time estimates links planning, scheduling, and controlling of projects.

NETWORK COMPUTATION PROCESS

Drawing the project network places the activities in the right sequence for computing start and finish times of activities. Activity time estimates are taken from the task times in the work package and added to the network (review Figure 4–2). Performing a few simple computations allows the project manager to complete a process known as the forward and backward pass. Completion of the *forward and backward pass* will answer the following questions:

Forward Pass—Earliest Times

1. How soon can the activity start? (early start—ES)
2. How soon can the activity finish? (early finish—EF)
3. How soon can the project be finished? (expected time—TE)

Backward Pass—Latest Times

1. How late can the activity start? (late start—LS)
2. How late can the activity finish? (late finish—LF)
3. Which activities represent the critical path (CP)? This is the longest path in the network which, when delayed, will delay the project.
4. How long can the activity be delayed? (slack or float—SL)

The terms in parentheses represent the acronyms used in most texts and computer programs and by project managers. The forward and backward pass process is presented next.

Forward Pass—Earliest Times

The forward pass starts with the first project activity(ies) and traces each path (chain of sequential activities) through the network to the last project activity(ies). As you trace along the path, you *add* the activity times. The longest path denotes the project completion time for the plan and is called the critical path (CP). Table 4–2 lists the activity times in workdays for the Koll Business Center example we used for drawing a network.

Figure 4–6 shows the network with the activity time estimate found in the node (see "Dur" for duration in the legend). For example, activity A has an activity duration of 5 workdays, and activity G has a duration of 170 workdays. The forward pass begins with the project start time, which is usually time zero. (Note: Calendar times can

TABLE 4-2

NETWORK INFORMATION

KOLL BUSINESS CENTER
County Engineers Design Department

Activity	Description	Preceding activity	Activity time
A	Application approval	None	5
B	Construction plans	A	15
C	Traffic study	A	10
D	Service availability check	A	5
E	Staff report	B, C	15
F	Commission approval	B, C, D	10
G	Wait for construction	F	170
H	Occupancy	E, G	35

be computed for the project later in the planning phase.) In our Koll Center example, the early start time for the first activity (activity A) is zero. This time is found in the upper left corner of the activity A node in Figure 4–7. The early finish for activity A is 5 (ES + Dur = EF or 0 + 5 = 5). Next, we see that activity A is the predecessor for activities B, C, and D. Therefore, the earliest these activities can begin is the instant in time when activity A is completed; this time is 5 workdays. You can now see in Figure 4–7 that activities B, C, and D can all start the moment activity A is complete and, therefore, have an early start (ES) of 5. Using the formula ES + Dur = EF, the early finish (EF) times for activities B, C, and D are 20, 15, and 10. What is

FIGURE 4–6 Activity-on-Node Network

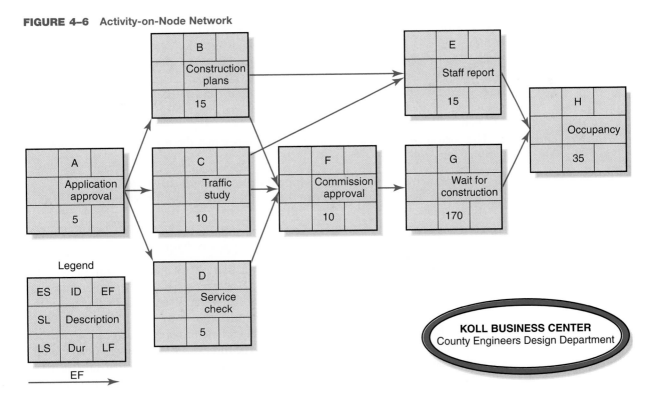

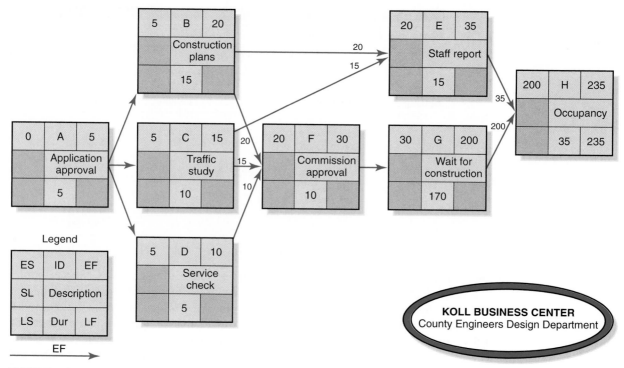

FIGURE 4–7 Activity-on-Node Network Forward Pass

the ES for activity E, then, which is a merge activity? Is it 15 or 20? The answer is 20 because all activities immediately preceding activity E (B and C) must be completed before activity E can begin. Because activity B will take the longest to complete, it controls the ES of activity E. The same process is used for determining the ES for activity F. It is preceded by activities B, C, and D. The controlling early finish (EF) time is activity B, which has the longer early finish (20 versus 15 and 10) of the immediate predecessors (activities B, C, and D) of activity F. Stated differently, the forward pass assumes every activity will start the instant in time when the last of its predecessors is finished.

The forward pass requires that you remember just three things when computing early activity times:

1. You *add* activity times along each path in the network (ES + Dur = EF).
2. You carry the early finish (EF) to the next activity where it becomes its early start (ES), *unless*
3. The next succeeding activity is a *merge* activity. In this case you select the *largest* early finish number (EF) of *all* its immediate predecessor activities.

In our example in Figure 4–7, the EF for activity F (30) is carried to activity G, where it becomes its ES (30). We see activity H is a merge activity and therefore find the largest EF of its immediate predecessors (activities E and G). In this case, the choice is between the EF times of 35 and 200; the choice for the ES of activity H is 200. The EF for activity H (235) becomes the earliest the project can be expected to be completed (TE) under normal conditions. The three questions derived from the forward pass have been answered; that is, early start (ES), early finish (EF), and the project duration (TE) times have been computed. The backward pass is the next process to learn.

Backward Pass—Latest Times

The backward pass starts with the last project activity(ies) on the network. You trace backward on each path *subtracting* activity times to find the late start (LS) and finish times (LF) for each activity. Before the backward pass can be computed, the late finish for the last project activity(ies) must be selected. In early planning stages, this time is usually set equal to the early finish (EF) of the last project activity (or in the case of multiple finish activities, the activity with the largest EF). In some cases an imposed project duration deadline exists, and this date will be used. Let us assume for planning purposes we can accept the EF project duration (TE) equal to 235 workdays. The LF for activity H becomes 235 workdays (EF = LF) (see Figure 4–8).

The backward pass is similar to the forward pass; you need to remember three things:

1. You *subtract* activity times along each path starting with the project end activity (LF – Dur = LS).
2. You carry the LS to the next preceding activity to establish its LF, *unless*
3. The next preceding activity is a *burst* activity; in this case you select the *smallest* LS of all its immediate successor activities to establish its LF.

Let's apply these rules to our Koll Center example. Beginning with activity H (occupancy) and an LF of 235 workdays, the LS for activity H is 200 workdays (LF – Dur = LS or 235 – 35 = 200). The LS for activity H becomes the LF for activities E and G. The LS for activities E and G becomes 185 (200 – 15 = 185) and 30 workdays (200 – 170 = 30), respectively. Next, the LS for activity G becomes the LF for activity F, and its LS becomes 20. At this point we see that activities B and C are *burst* activities that tie to activities E and F. The late finish for activity B is controlled by the LS of activities E and F. The LS for activity E is 185 days and for activity F, 20 days. Follow

FIGURE 4–8 Activity-on-Node Network Backward Pass

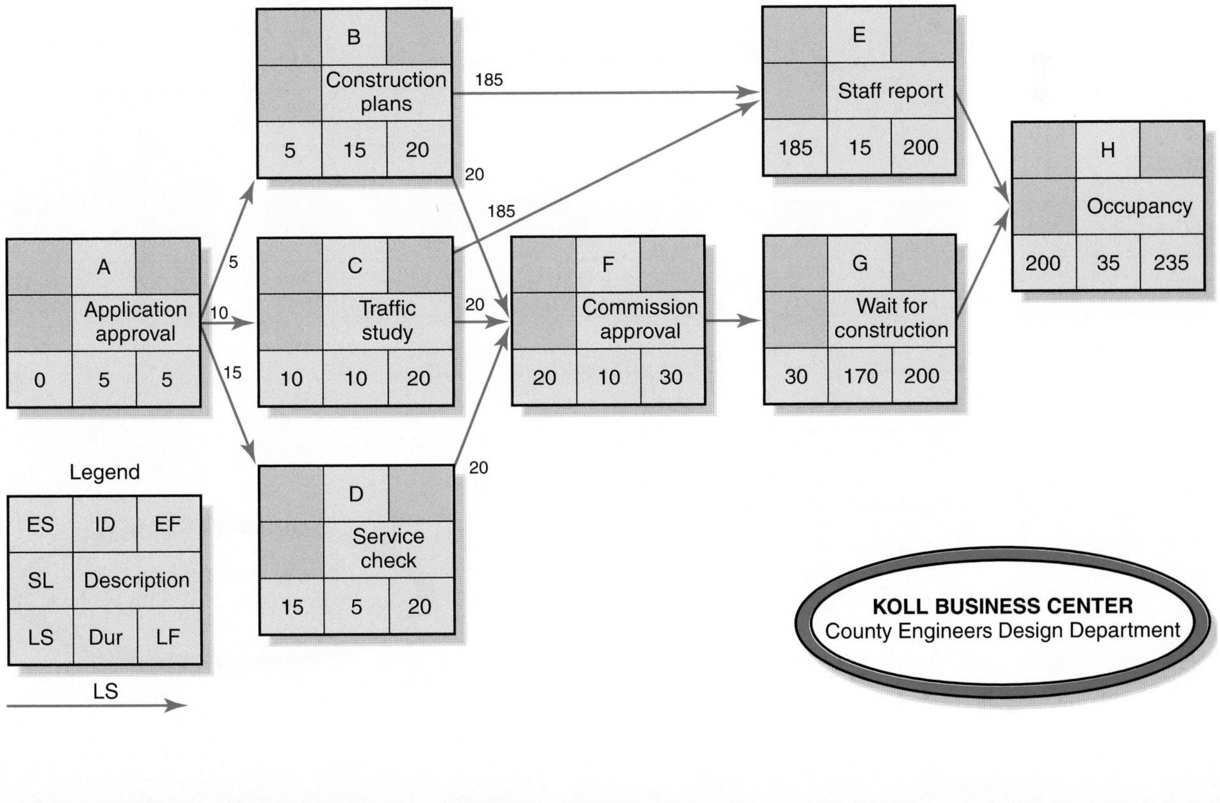

the arrows backward from activities E and F to activity B. Note that LS times for activities E and F have been placed to the right of the node so you can select the *smallest* time—20 days. The latest activity B can finish is 20 days, or activity F will be delayed and hence the project. The LF for activity C is identical to activity B because it is also controlled by the LS of activities E and F. Activity D simply picks up its LF from activity F. By computing the LS (LF – Dur = LS) for activities B, C, and D, we can determine the LF for activity A, which is a *burst* activity. You see that the finish of activity A is controlled by activity B, which has the smallest LS of activities B, C, and D. Because the LS for activity B is time period 5, the LF for activity A is 5, and its LS is time period zero. The backward pass is complete, and the latest activity times are known.

Determining Slack (or Float)

When the forward and backward passes have been computed, it is possible to determine which activities can be delayed by computing "slack" or "float." Total slack or float for an activity is simply the difference between the LS and ES (LS – ES = SL) or between LF and EF (LF – EF = SL). For example, the slack for activity C is 5 days, for activity D is 10 days, and for activity G is zero (see Figure 4–9). *Total slack* tells us the amount of time an activity can be delayed and yet not delay the project. If slack of one activity in a path is used, the ES for all activities that follow in the chain will be delayed and their slack reduced. Use of total slack must be coordinated with all participants in the activities that follow in the chain.

After slack for each activity is computed, the critical path(s) is (are) easily identified. When the LF = EF for the end project activity, the critical path can be identified as those activities that also have LF = EF or a slack of zero (LF – EF = 0) (or LS – ES

FIGURE 4–9 Activity-on-Node Network with Slack

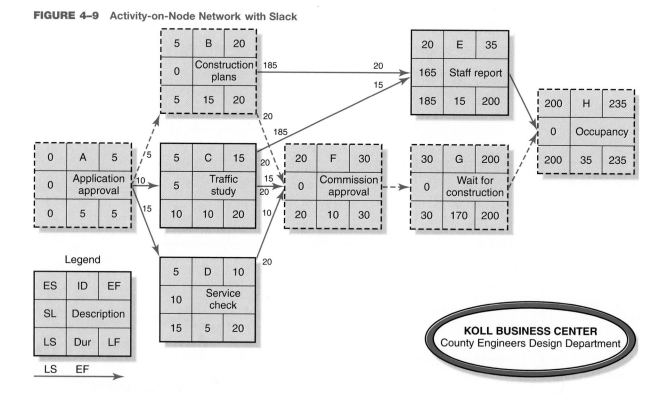

Snapshot from Practice

THE CRITICAL PATH

The critical path method (CPM) has long been considered the "Holy Grail" of project management. Here are comments made by veteran project managers when asked about the significance of the critical path in managing projects:

- I try to make it a point whenever possible to put my best people on critical activities or on those activities that stand the greatest chance of becoming critical.
- I pay extra attention when doing risk assessment to identifying those risks that can impact the critical path, either directly or indirectly, by making a noncritical activity so late that it becomes critical. When I've got money to spend to reduce risks, it usually gets spent on critical tasks.
- I don't have time to monitor all the activities on a big project, but I make it a point to keep in touch with the people who are working on critical activities. When I have the time, they are the ones I visit to find out firsthand how things are going. It's amazing how much more I can find out from talking to the rank and file who are doing the work and by reading the facial expressions of people—much more than I can gain from a number-driven status report.
- When I get calls from other managers asking to "borrow" people or equipment, I'm much more generous when it involves resources from working on noncritical activities. For example, if another project manager needs an electrical engineer who is assigned to a task with five days of slack, I'm willing to share that engineer with another project manager for two to three days.
- The most obvious reason the critical path is important is because these are the activities that impact completion time. If I suddenly get a call from above saying they need my project done two weeks earlier than planned, the critical path is where I schedule the overtime and add extra resources to get the project done more quickly. In the same way, if the project schedule begins to slip, it's the critical activities I focus on to get back on schedule.

= 0). *The critical path is the network path(s) that has (have) the least slack in common.* This awkward arrangement of words is necessary because a problem arises when the project finish activity has an LF that differs from the EF found in the forward pass—for example, an imposed duration date. If this is the case, the slack on the critical path will *not* be zero; it will be the difference between the project EF and the imposed LF of the last project activity. For example, if the EF for the project is 235 days, but the imposed LF or target date is set at 220 days, all activities on the critical path would have a slack of *minus* 15 days. Of course, this would result in a late start of −15 days for the first project activity—a good trick if the project is to start now. Negative slack occurs in practice when the critical path is delayed.

In Figure 4–9 the critical path is marked with dashed arrows and nodes—activities A, B, F, G, and H. Delay of any of these activities will delay the total project by the same number of days. Critical activities typically represent about 10 percent of the activities of the project. Therefore, project managers pay close attention to the critical path activities to be sure they are not delayed.

Free Slack (Float)

An activity with free slack is unique because the activity can be delayed without delaying the ES of activities following it. Free slack is defined as the difference between the EF of an activity and the ES of the activity that follows it. Free slack can never be negative. Only activities that occur at the end of a chain of activities (usually where you have a merge activity) can have free slack. For example, if a single chain (path) of activities has 14 days slack, the last activity will have free slack, and the others will have none. Sometimes the chain is not very long; it can be only one activity. For example, in the Koll Business Center network (Figure 4–9), activity E is a chain of one and has free slack of 165 workdays (200 – 35 = 165). Activities C and D also have free slack of 5 and 10 days, respectively. The beauty of free slack is that changes in start and finish times for the free slack activity require less coordination with other participants in the project and give the project manager more flexibility than total slack. Because the activity is the last in the chain, delaying the activity up to the slack amount will not influence any following activities.

HOW THE INFORMATION OF THE FORWARD AND BACKWARD PASS IS USED

What does a slack of 10 workdays for activity D mean for the project manager? In this specific case it means activity D can be delayed 10 days. In a larger sense the project manager soon learns that slack is important because it allows flexibility in scheduling scarce project resources—personnel and equipment— that are used on more than one parallel activity.

Knowing the four activity times of ES, LS, EF, and LF is invaluable for the planning, scheduling, and controlling phases of the project. The ES and LF tell the project manager the time interval in which the activity should be completed. For example, activity E must be completed within the time interval 20 and 200 workdays; the activity can start as early as day 20 or finish as late as day 200. Conversely, activity F (commission approval), must start on day 20, or the project will be delayed.

When the critical path is known, it is possible to tightly manage the resources of the activities on the critical path so no mistakes are made that will result in delays. In addition, if for some reason the project must be expedited to meet an earlier date, it is possible to select those activities, or combination of activities, that will cost the least to shorten the project. Similarly, if the critical path is delayed and the time must be made up by shortening some activity or activities on the critical path to make up any negative slack, it is possible to identify the activities on the critical path that cost the least to shorten. If there are other paths with very little slack, it may be necessary to shorten activities on those paths also.

LEVEL OF DETAIL FOR ACTIVITIES

Time-phasing work and budgets of the project mandate careful definition of the activities that make up the project network. Typically an activity represents one or more tasks from a work package. How many tasks you include in each activity sets the level of detail. In some cases it is possible to end up with too much information to manage, and this can result in increased overhead costs. Managers of small projects have been able to minimize the level of detail by eliminating some of the preliminary steps to drawing networks. Larger firms also recognize the cost of information overload and are working to cut down the level of detail in networks and in most other dimensions of the project.

Small Projects

Small projects that are closely managed and have participants who clearly feel they are part of a team effort can reduce the level of detail and still track performance. Emphasis is still on deliverables. A simplified WBS (responsibility matrix) is used (see Figure 4–10). A work package becomes an activity assigned to one organizational unit. However, if the activity duration extends beyond five workdays, clear monitoring points of short intervals are imperative to measure time and cost performance within

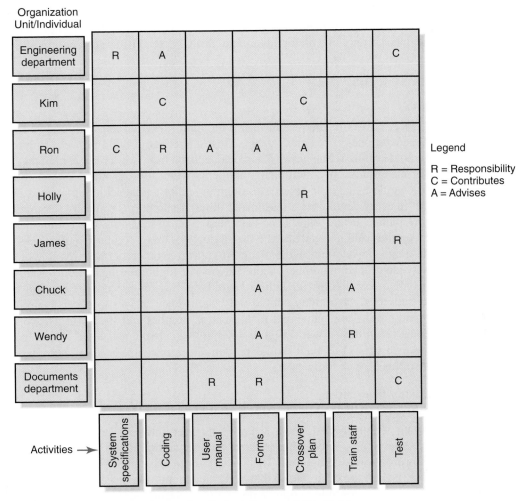

Organization
Unit/Individual

	System specifications	Coding	User manual	Forms	Crossover plan	Train staff	Test
Engineering department	R	A					C
Kim		C			C		
Ron	C	R	A	A	A		
Holly					R		
James							R
Chuck				A		A	
Wendy				A		R	
Documents department			R	R			C

Activities →

Legend

R = Responsibility
C = Contributes
A = Advises

FIGURE 4–10   Software Conversion Project Responsibility Matrix

the activity duration. This approach is possible in small projects where coordination is relatively easy. The responsibility matrix will be discussed in detail in Chapter 7. Note that the network is still used as a valuable tool.

Partnering or Teaming with Contractors

A recent phenomenon in the project management world is *partnering,* an agreement between project owner and contractor to file no claims but rather work out all problems. Partnering is based on the premise of a high degree of trust between a contractor and project owner. For example, assuming a high degree of trust exists, the level of detail for work packages and activities does not have to be as intricate because control and monitoring points do not have to be as tight in this environment. In addition, the level of design specifications can be reduced because problem resolution occurs quickly and fairly. For example, in a large partnering construction project, the owner was able to reduce the number of drawings and specifications (level of detail) due to the contractor by more than 30 percent; the high level of trust between the owner and contractor was supported by the partnering agreement to file no claims.

Partnering is becoming more common in project management as a way of sharing responsibility and risk with contractors. It appears to have potential for a win-win situation and improvement in project performance. Reducing the level of plan and schedule detail is only one major advantage. See Chapter 11 for a discussion of this process.

LOOSE ENDS

Network Logic Errors

Project network techniques have certain logic rules that must be followed. One rule is that conditional statements such as "if test successful build proto, if failure redesign" are not permitted. The network is not a decision tree; it is a project plan that we assume will materialize. If conditional statements were allowed, the forward and backward pass would make little sense. Although in reality a plan seldom materializes as we expect in every detail, it is a reasonable initial assumption. You shall see that once a network plan is developed, it is an easy step to make revisions to accommodate changes.

Another rule that defeats the project network and computation process is *looping*. Looping is an attempt by the planner to return to an earlier activity. Recall that the activity identification numbers should always be higher for the activities following an activity in question; this rule helps to avoid the illogical precedence relationships among the activities. An activity should only occur once; if it is to occur again, the activity should have a new name and identification number and should be placed in the right sequence on the network. Figure 4–11 shows an illogical loop. If this loop were allowed to exist, this path would perpetually repeat itself. Many computer programs catch this type of logic error.

Activity Numbering

Each activity needs a unique identification code—usually a number. In practice very elegant schemes exist. Most schemes number activities in ascending order, that is, each succeeding activity has a larger number so that the flow of the project activities is toward project completion. It is customary to leave gaps between numbers (1, 5, 10, 15 . . .). Gaps are desirable so that you can add missing or new activities later. Because it is nearly impossible to draw a project network perfectly, numbering networks is frequently not done until after the network is complete.

In practice you will find computer programs that accept numeric, alphabetic, or a combination of activity designations. Combination designations are often used to identify cost, work skill, departments, and locations. As a general rule, activity numbering systems should be ascending and as simple as possible. The intent is to make it as easy as you can for project participants to follow work through the network and locate specific activities.

Use of Computers to Develop Networks

All of the tools and techniques discussed in this chapter can be used with computer software currently available. Three examples are shown in Figures 4–12, 4–13, and

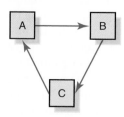

FIGURE 4–11 Illogical Loop

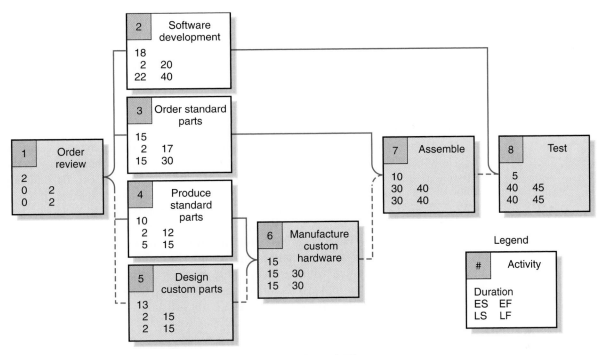

FIGURE 4–12 Air Control Inc. Custom Order Project—Network Diagram

4–14. Figure 4–12 presents a generic AON computer output for the "custom order project." The critical path is identified by the shaded nodes and dashed dependency arrows. The activity identification is found in the top left corner. Immediately below the activity number is the duration, and below the duration are the activity times—ES,EF,LS,LF (reading top row then bottom row).

Figure 4–13 presents an early start Gantt bar chart. Bar charts are popular because they present an easy-to-understand, clear picture on a time-scaled horizon. They are

FIGURE 4–13 Air Control Inc. Custom Order Project—Gantt Chart

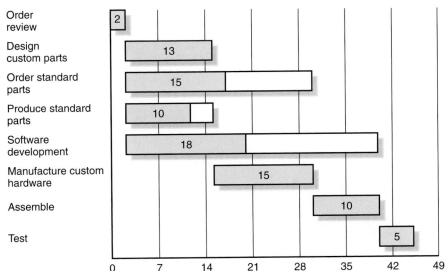

used during planning, resource scheduling, and status reporting. The format is a two-dimensional representation of the project schedule, with activities down the rows and time across the horizontal axis. For example, "software development" has a duration of 18 time units (shaded area of the bar). The bar also indicates the activity can start at time period 2, would end in period 20, but can finish as late as period 40 because it has 20 time units of slack (clear area of the bar). When calendar dates are used on the time axis, Gantt charts provide a clear overview of the project schedule and can be often found posted on the walls of project offices.

The major weakness of the bar chart format is the absence of dependency relationships among project activities. For example, if float is used on an earlier activity in the network chain, it cannot be used on a later activity in the same chain. This dependency is not shown on a bar chart. Therefore, a bar chart should always be used with a network. Although some computer software will develop bar charts with dependency lines, the dependency lines soon become overwhelming and defeat the simplicity of the bar chart. Note that the bar chart is derived from the project network—not vice versa.

Project management software can be a tremendous help in the hands of those who understand and are familiar with the tools and techniques discussed in this text. However, there is nothing more dangerous than someone using the software with little or no knowledge of how the software derives its output. Mistakes in input are very common and require someone skilled in the concepts, tools, and information system to recognize that errors exist so false actions are avoided.

Calendar Dates

Ultimately you will want to assign calendar dates to your project activities. If a computer program is not used, dates are assigned manually. Lay out a calendar of workdays (exclude nonworkdays), and number them. Then relate the calendar workdays to

FIGURE 4–14 Air Control Inc. Custom Order Project—Network with Dates

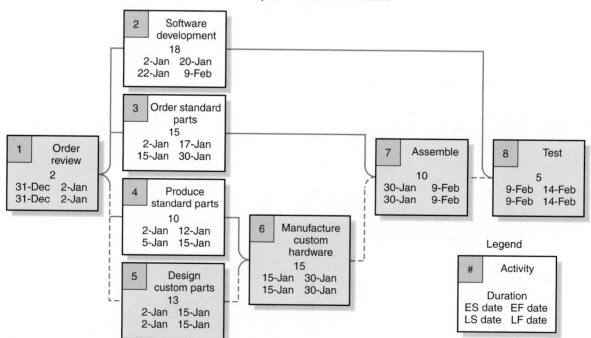

the workdays on your project network. Most computer programs will assign calendar dates automatically after you identify start dates, time units, nonworkdays, and other information. Figure 4–14 shows the network for the custom order project with dates.

Multiple Starts and Multiple Projects

Some computer programs require a common start and finish event in the form of a node—usually a circle or rectangle—for a project network. Even if this is not a requirement, it is a good idea because it avoids "dangler" paths. Dangler paths give the impression that the project does not have a clear beginning or ending. If a project has more than one activity that can begin when the project is to start, each path is a dangler path. The same is true if a project network ends with more than one activity; these unconnected paths are also called danglers. Danglers can be avoided by tying dangler activities to a common project start or finish node.

When several projects are tied together in an organization, using a common start and end node helps to identify the total planning period of all projects. Use of pseudo or dummy wait activities from the common start node allows different start dates for each project.

EXTENDED NETWORK TECHNIQUES TO COME CLOSER TO REALITY

The method for showing relationships among activities in the last section is called the finish-to-start relationship because it assumes all immediate preceding connected activities must be completed before the next activity can begin. In an effort to come closer to the realities of projects, some useful extensions have been added. The use of *laddering* was the first obvious extension practitioners found very useful.

Laddering

The assumption that all immediate preceding activities must be 100 percent complete is too restrictive for some situations found in practice. This restriction occurs most frequently when one activity overlaps the start of another and has a long duration. Under the standard finish-to-start relationship, when an activity has a long duration and will delay the start of an activity immediately following it, the activity can be broken into segments and the network drawn using a *laddering* approach so the following activity can begin sooner and not delay the work. This segmenting of the larger activity gives the appearance of steps on a ladder on the network, thus the name. The classic example used in many texts and articles is laying pipe, because it is easy to visualize. The trench must be dug, pipe laid, and the trench refilled. If the pipeline is one mile long, it is not necessary to dig one mile of trench before the laying of pipe can begin or to lay one mile of pipe before refill can begin. Figure 4–15 shows how these

FIGURE 4–15 Example of Laddering Using Finish-to-Start Relationship

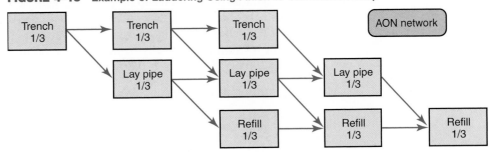

overlapping activities might appear in an AON network using the standard finish-to-start approach.

Use of Lags

The use of *lags* has been developed to offer greater flexibility in network construction. *A lag is the minimum amount of time a dependent activity must be delayed to begin or end.* The use of lags in project networks occurs for two primary reasons:

1. When activities of long duration delay the start or finish of successor activities, the network designer normally breaks the activity into smaller activities to avoid the long delay of the successor activity. Use of lags can avoid such delays and reduce network detail.
2. Lags can be used to constrain the start and finish of an activity.

The most commonly used relationship extensions are start-to-start, finish-to-finish, and combinations of these two. These relationship patterns are discussed in this section.

Finish-to-Start Relationship   The finish-to-start relationship represents the typical, generic network style used in the early part of the chapter. However, there are situations in which the next activity in a sequence must be delayed even when the preceding activity is complete. For example, removing concrete forms cannot begin until the poured cement has cured for two time units. Figure 4–16 shows this lag relationship for AON networks. Finish-to-start lags are frequently used when ordering materials. For example, it may take 1 day to place orders but take 19 days to receive the goods. The use of finish-to-start allows the activity duration to be only 1 day and the lag 19 days. This approach ensures the activity cost is tied to placing the order only rather than charging the activity for 20 days of work. This same finish-to-start lag relationship is useful to depict transportation, legal, and mail lags.

The use of finish-to-start lags should be carefully checked to ensure their validity. Conservative project managers or those responsible for completion of activities have been known to use lags as a means of building in a "slush" factor to reduce the risk of being late. A simple rule to follow is that the use of finish-to-start lags must be justified and approved by someone responsible for a large section of the project. The legitimacy of lags is not usually difficult to discern. The legitimate use of the additional relationship shown can greatly enhance the network by more closely representing the realities of the project.

Start-to-Start Relationship   An alternative to segmenting the activities as we did earlier is to use a start-to-start relationship. Typical start-to-start relationships are shown in Figure 4–17. Figure 4–17A shows the start-to-start relationship with zero lag, while Figure 4–17B shows the same relationship with a lag of five time units. It is important to note that the relationship may be used with or without a lag. If time is assigned, it is usually shown on the dependency arrow of an AON network.

In Figure 4–17B, activity Q cannot begin until five time units after activity P begins. This type of relationship typically depicts a situation in which you can perform a portion of one activity and begin a following activity before completing the first.

FIGURE 4–16   Finish-to-Start Relationship

A
B
Activity M
Activity N
Activity P
Lag 5
Activity Q

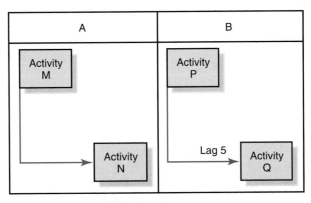

FIGURE 4–17 Start-to-Start Relationship

This relationship can be used on the pipe laying project. Figure 4–18 shows the project using an AON network. The start-to-start relationship reduces network detail and project delays by using lag relationships.

It is possible to find compression opportunities by changing finish-to-start relations to start-to-start relationships. A review of finish-to-start critical activities may point out opportunities that can be revised to be parallel by using start-to-start relationships. For example, in place of a finish-to-start activity "design house, then build foundation," a start-to-start relationship could be used in which the foundation can be started, say, five days (lag) after design has started—assuming the design of the foundation is the first part of the total design activity. This start-to-start relationship with a small lag allows a sequential activity to be worked on in parallel and to compress the duration of the critical path. This same concept is frequently found in construction projects in which concurrent engineering is used to speed completion of a project. Concurrent engineering basically breaks activities into smaller segments so that work can be done in parallel and the project expedited.[2] Start-to-start relationships can depict the concurrent engineering conditions and reduce network detail. Of course, the same result can be accomplished by breaking an activity into small packages that can be implemented in parallel, but this latter approach increases the network and tracking detail significantly.

FIGURE 4–18 Use of Lags to Reduce Detail

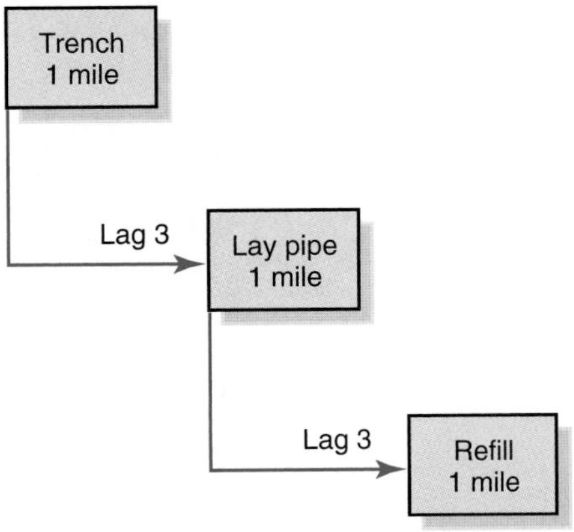

Trench 1 mile
Lag 3
Lay pipe 1 mile
Lag 3
Refill 1 mile

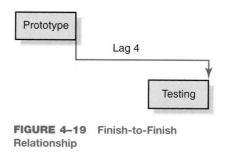

FIGURE 4–19   Finish-to-Finish
Relationship

Finish-to-Finish Relationship   This relationship is found in Figure 4–19. The finish of one activity depends on the finish of another activity. For example, testing cannot be completed any earlier than four days after the prototype is complete.

Start-to-Finish Relationship   This relationship represents situations in which the finish of an activity depends on the start of another activity. For example, system documentation cannot end until three time units after testing has started (see Figure 4–20).

Combinations of Lag Relationships   More than one lag relationship can be attached to an activity. These relationships are usually start-to-start and finish-to-finish combinations tied to two activities. For example, debug cannot begin until two time units after coding has started. Coding must be finished four time units before debug can be finished (see Figure 4–21).

An Example Using Lag Relationships—The Forward and Backward Pass

The forward and backward pass procedures are the same as explained earlier in the chapter for finish-to-start relationships (without lags). The modifying technique lies in the need to check each new relationship to see if it alters the start or finish time of another activity.

An example of the outcome of the forward and backward pass is shown in Figure 4–22. Activities C and D depend on the start of activity B (start-to-start). The start of activity C must lag the start of B by 10 time units, and the start of D must lag activity B by 5 time units. Activity E must lag the finish of activity C by 5 time units (finish-to-finish). Activity G cannot finish until 10 time units after the start of activity F (start-to-finish). Finally, the finish of activity H depends on the finish of activity G by 10 time units.

Note how an activity can have a critical finish or start. Activity H has a critical finish (zero slack) of 50 time units, but the activity has a start that has 5 units of slack. It is only the finish of activity H that is critical. Conversely, activity F has zero slack to start but has 5 time units of slack to finish. The critical path follows activity start and

FIGURE 4–20   Start-to-Finish
Relationship

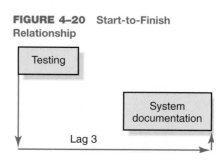

FIGURE 4–21 Combination Relationships

finish constraints that occur due to the use of the additional relationships available and the imposed lags. You can identify the critical path by following the dotted line on the network.

If a lag relationship exists, each activity must be checked to see if the start or finish is constrained. For example, in the forward pass the EF of activity G (40) is controlled by the start of activity F and the lag of 10 time units (30 + 10 lag = 40). The EF (40 + 10 lag = 50) of activity H depends on the finish of activity G and the lag of 10, which is 50 rather than 45 time units using the *ES + Dur = EF* approach. In the backward pass, the LS of activity F is constrained by the LF (40) of activity G and the lag of 10 time units (40 − 10 lag = 30), which imposes an LS of 30 for activity F.

Hammock Activities

Another of the extended techniques uses a *hammock activity*. The major use of a hammock activity is to identify the use of fixed resources or costs over a segment of the project. Typical examples of hammock activities are inspection services, consultants, or construction management services. A hammock activity derives its duration from the time span between other activities. For example, a special color copy machine is needed for a segment of a tradeshow publication project. A hammock activity can be used to indicate the need for this resource and to apply costs over this segment of the

FIGURE 4–22 Network Using Lags

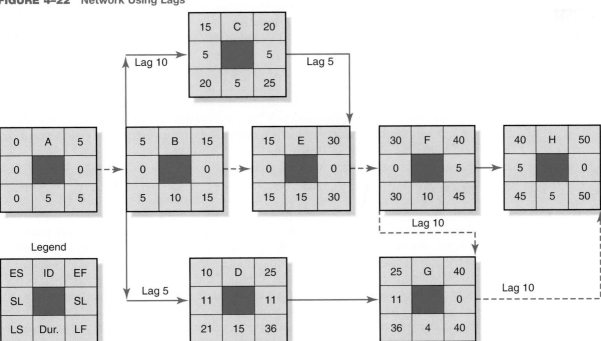

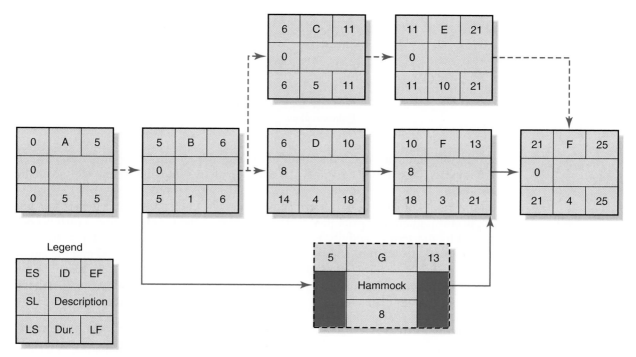

FIGURE 4–23 Hammock Activity Example

project. This hammock is linked from the start of the first activity in the segment that uses the color copy machine to the end of the last activity that uses it. The hammock duration is simply the difference between the EF for the last activity and the ES of the first activity. The duration is computed after the forward pass and hence has no influence on other activity times. Figure 4–23 provides an example of a hammock activity used in a network. The duration for the hammock activity is derived from the early start of activity B and the early finish of activity F; that is, the difference between 13 and 5, or 8 time units. The hammock duration will change if any ES or EF in the chain-sequence changes. Hammock activities are very useful in assigning and controlling indirect project costs.

Another major use of hammock activities is to aggregate sections of a project. This is similar to developing a subnetwork, but the precedence is still preserved. This approach is sometimes used to present a "macro network" for upper management levels. Using a hammock activity to group activities can facilitate getting the right level of detail for specific sections of a project.

SUMMARY

Many project managers feel the project network is their most valuable exercise and planning document. Project networks sequence and time-phase the project work, resources, and budgets. Work package tasks are used to develop activities for networks. Every project manager should feel comfortable working in an AON environment. The AON method uses nodes (boxes) for activities and arrows for dependencies. The forward and backward passes establish early and late times for activities and events. Although most project managers use computers to generate networks and activity times, they find a keen understanding of network development and the ability to compute activity times is invaluable in the field. Computers break down; input errors give false information; some decisions must be made without computer "what if" analysis. Project managers who are well acquainted with network development and AON methods and who are able to compute activity times will encounter fewer problems than project managers less well acquainted. Project networks help to ensure there are no surprises.

Several extensions and modifications have been appended to the original AON method. Lags allow the project planner to more closely replicate the actual conditions found in practice. The use of lags can result in the start or finish of an activity becoming critical. Some computer software simply calls the whole activity critical rather than identifying the start or finish as being critical. Caution should be taken to ensure that lags are not used as a buffer for possible errors in estimating time. Finally, hammock activities are useful in tracking costs of resources used for a particular segment of a project. Hammock activities can also be used to reduce the size of a project network by grouping a group of activities. All of the discussed refinements to the original AON methodology contribute toward better planning and control of projects.

REVIEW QUESTIONS

1. How does the WBS differ from the project network?
2. How are WBS and project networks linked?
3. Why bother creating a WBS? Why not go straight to a project network and forget the WBS?
4. Why is slack important to the project manager?
5. Why are lags used in developing project networks?
6. What is a hammock activity, and when is it used?

EXERCISES

Drawing AON Networks

1. Given the following information, draw a project network.

Activity	Predecessor
A	None
B	None
C	A
D	A
E	B
F	B
G	C, D, E, F

2. Draw a project network from the following information.

Activity	Predecessor
A	None
B	None
C	A, B
D	A, B
E	A, B
F	C, D
G	E
H	F
I	F, G

3. Use the following information to draw a project network.

Activity	Predecessor
A	None
B	None
C	None
D	A, B
E	B, C
F	D, E
G	F
H	F
I	G
J	H, I

4. Given the following information, draw a project network.

Activity	Predecessor
A	None
B	A
C	A
D	A
E	B
F	B
G	C
H	D
I	F, G
J	E, I, H

Creating a Project Network

5. Here is a work breakdown structure for a wedding. Use the yellow sticky approach described in the Snapshot from Practice (see p. 97) to create a network for this project.

Note: Do not include summary tasks in the network (i.e., 1.4, ceremony, is a summary task; 1.2, marriage license, is not a summary task). Do not consider who would be doing the task in building the network. For example, do not arrange "hiring a band" to occur after "florist" because the same person is responsible for doing both tasks. Focus only on technical dependencies between tasks.

Hint: Start with the last activity (wedding reception), and work your way back to the start of the project. Build the logical sequence of tasks by asking the following question: In order to have or do this, what must be accomplished immediately before this? Once completed, check forward in time by asking this question: Is this task(s) the only thing that is needed immediately before the start of the next task?

Work Breakdown Structure

1. Wedding project
    1.1 Decide on date
    1.2 Marriage license
    1.3 Bridal arrangements
        1.3.1 Select attendants
        1.3.2 Order dresses
        1.3.3 Fit dresses
    1.4 Ceremony
        1.4.1 Rent church

1.4.2 Florist
1.4.3 Create/print programs
1.4.4 Hire photographer
1.4.5 Wedding ceremony
1.5 Guests
1.5.1 Develop guest list
1.5.2 Order invitations
1.5.3 Address and mail invitations
1.5.4 Track RSVPs
1.6 Reception
1.6.1 Reserve reception hall
1.6.2 Food and beverage
1.6.2.1 Choose caterer
1.6.2.2 Decide on menu
1.6.2.3 Make final order
1.6.3 Hire band
1.6.4 Decorate reception hall
1.6.5 Wedding reception

AON Network Times

6. From the following information, develop an AON network. Complete the forward and backward pass, compute the activity slack, and identify the critical path.

Activity	Duration	Predecessor
A	5	None
B	10	None
C	15	A
D	10	A
E	5	B
F	20	C
G	20	E
H	5	D, E, F
I	15	G

7. The project information for the custom order project of the Air Control Company is presented here. Draw a project network for this project. Compute the early and late activity times and the slack times. Identify the critical path.

ID	Activity	Predecessor	Time
A	Order review	None	2
B	Order standard parts	A	15
C	Produce standard parts	A	10
D	Design custom parts	A	13
E	Software development	A	18
F	Manufacture custom hardware	C, D	15
G	Assemble	B, F	10
H	Test	E, G	5

8. J. Wold, project manager of Print Software, Inc., wants you to prepare a project network; compute the early, late, and slack activity times; determine the planned project duration; and identify the critical path. His assistant has collected the following information for the Color Printer Drivers Software Project:

ID	Description	Predecessor	Time
A	External specifications	None	8
B	Review design features	A	2
C	Document new features	A	3
D	Write software	A	60
E	Program and test	B	60
F	Edit and publish notes	C	2
G	Review manual	D	2
H	Alpha site	E, F	20
I	Print manual	G	10
J	Beta site	H, I	10
K	Manufacture	J	12
L	Release and ship	K	3

9. A large Eastern city is requesting federal funding for a park-and-ride project. One of the requirements in the request application is a network plan for the design phase of the project. Catherine Walker, the chief engineer, wants you to develop a project network plan to meet this requirement. She has gathered the activity time estimates and their dependencies shown here. Show your project network with the activity early, late, and slack times. Mark the critical path.

ID	Description	Predecessor	Time
A	Survey	None	5
B	Soils report	A	20
C	Traffic design	A	30
D	Lot layout	A	5
E	Approve design	B, C, D	80
F	Illumination	E	15
G	Drainage	E	30
H	Landscape	E	25
I	Signing	E	20
J	Bid proposal	F, G, H, I	10

10. Given the project network that follows, complete a bar chart for the project. Use the time-line to align your bars. Be sure to show slack for noncritical activities.

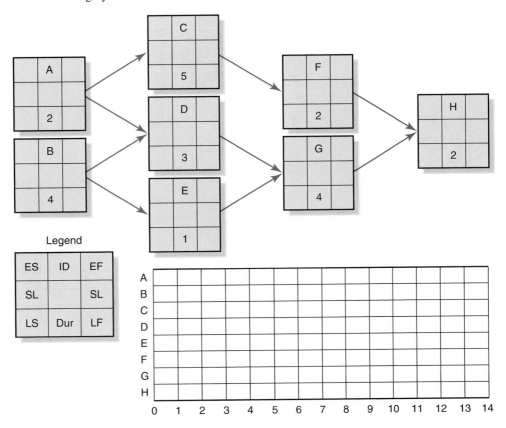

Legend

ES	ID	EF
SL		SL
LS	Dur	LF

11. Given the project network that follows, complete a bar chart for the project. Use the time-line to align your bars. Be sure to show slack for noncritical activities.

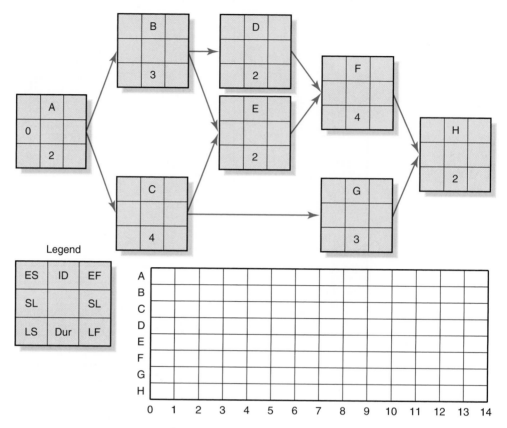

Legend

ES	ID	EF
SL		SL
LS	Dur	LF

Lag Exercises

12. From the following information, draw the project network. Compute the early, late, and slack times for each activity. Identify the critical path. (Hint: Draw the finish-to-start relationships first.)

ID	Duration	Finish-to-start predecessor	Finish-to-start lag	Additional lag relationships	Lag
A	5	None	0	None	0
B	10	A	0	None	0
C	15	A	0	Start-finish C to D	20
D	5	B	5	Start-start D to E	5
				Finish-finish D to E	25
E	20	B	0	Finish-finish E to F	0
F	15	D	0	None	0
G	10	C	10	Finish-finish G to F	10
H	20	F	0	None	

13. Given the following information, draw the project network. Compute the early, late, and slack times for the project network. Which activities on the critical path have only the start or finish of the activity on the critical path?

ID	Duration	Finish-to-start predecessor	Finish-to-start lag	Additional lag relationships	Lag
A	2	None	0	None	0
B	4	A	0	None	0
C	6	A	0	Finish-finish C to F	7
D	8	A	0	None	0
E	18	B	0	Finish-finish E to G	9
		C	10		
F	2	D	0	None	
G	5	F	0	Start-start G to H	10
H	5	None	0	None	0
I	14	E	0	Finish-finish I to J	5
J	15	G, H	0	None	

14. Given the information in the following lag exercises, compute the early, late, and slack times for the project network. Which activities on the critical path have only the start or finish of the activity on the critical path?

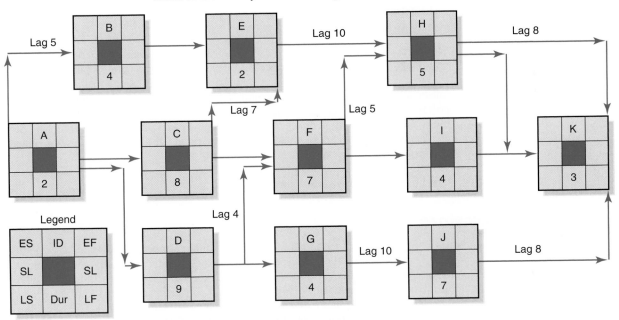

Optical Disk Preinstallation Project

15. The optical disk project team has started gathering the information necessary to develop the project network—predecessor activities and activity times in weeks. The results of their meeting are found in the following table.

Activity	Description	Duration	Predecessor
1	Define scope	6	None
2	Define customer problems	3	1
3	Define data records and relationships	5	1
4	Determine mass storage requirements	5	2, 3
5	Analyze consultant needs analysis	10	2, 3
6	Prepare installation network	3	4, 5
7	Estimate costs and budget	2	4, 5
8	Design section "point" system	1	4, 5
9	Write request proposal	5	4, 5
10	Compile vendor list	3	4, 5

Unfortunately, the project champion and most knowledgeable team member, Pat Taylor, has been promoted and placed in charge of a multinational project in South America. The team has asked Bob Bryant to telephone Pat and record the information needed to complete the network along with his best estimate of activity times. The following is an edited version of the conversation. The project team has requested that you complete the table, work up a network for the project, and determine if the project can be completed in 45 weeks.

After you have completed <u>Prepare installation network</u> and have estimated costs and budgets, you can start the <u>Prepare management control system</u> activity, which should take 5 weeks. You can begin <u>Prepare comparison report,</u> which will take 5 weeks as soon as <u>Write request proposal</u> and <u>Compile vendor list</u> are completed. When <u>Design section "point" system</u> and <u>Prepare comparison report</u> are finished, you can begin four activities concurrently:

<u>Compare system "philosophies"</u>

<u>Compare total installation</u>

<u>Compare cost of support</u>

<u>Compare customer satisfaction level</u>

The durations for these activities are 3, 2, 3, and 10 weeks, respectively. <u>Assign philosophies points</u> (1 week) is preceded by <u>Compare system "philosophies."</u>

You can begin <u>Assign installation cost</u> (1 week) when <u>Compare total installation</u> is finished. Similarly, you can <u>Assign support cost</u> (1 week) when <u>Compare cost of support</u> is complete and <u>Assign customer satisfaction points</u> (1 week) when <u>Compare customer satisfaction level</u> is finished. When all the preceding activities are complete, <u>Select best system</u> can start (1 week). Finally, the last activity is to <u>Order system,</u> which will require only 1 week.

Bob, this should be enough for you and the project team to draw up a project plan. Good luck, and best wishes to the team!

ENDNOTES

1. James E. Kelly, "Critical Path Planning and Scheduling: Mathematical Basis," *Operations Research,* vol. 9, no. 3, 1961 (May–June), pp. 296–321; James E. Kelly and Morgan R. Walker, "Critical Path Planning and Scheduling," Proceedings: Eastern Computer Conference, Boston, 1–3 December 1959, pp. 160–70; J. J. Moder and C. R. Phillips, *Project Management with CPM and PERT,* 1964, 1968, and 1970 editions (New York: Van Nostrand Reinhold); and *DoD and NASA Guide PERT/Cost Systems Design,* Office of the Secretary of Defense (Washington, DC: U.S. Government Printing Office), June 1962.
2. Quentin C. Turtle, *Implementing Concurrent Project Management* (Englewood Cliffs, NJ: Prentice Hall), 1994.

CASE

Nightingale Project—A

You are the assistant project manager to Rassy Brown, who is in charge of the Nightingale project. Nightingale was the code name given to the development of a handheld electronic medical reference guide. Nightingale would be designed for emergency medical technicians and paramedics who need a quick reference guide to use in emergency situations.

Rassy and her project team were developing a project plan aimed at producing 30 working models in time for MedCON, the biggest medical equipment trade show each year. Meeting the MedCON October 25 deadline was critical to success. All the major medical equipment manufacturers demonstrated and took orders for new products at MedCON. Rassy had also heard rumors that competitors were considering developing a similar product, and she knew that being first to market would have a significant sales advantage. Besides, top management made funding contingent upon developing a workable plan for meeting the MedCON deadline.

The project team spent the morning working on the schedule for Nightingale. They started with the WBS and developed the information for a network, adding activities when needed. Then the team added the time estimates they had collected for each activity. Here is the preliminary information for activities with duration time and predecessors:

Activity	Description	Duration	Predecessor
1	Architectural decisions	10	None
2	Internal specifications	20	1
3	External specifications	18	1
4	Feature specifications	15	1
5	Voice recognition	5	2,3
6	Case	4	2,3
7	Screen	2	2,3
8	Speaker output jacks	2	2,3
9	Tape mechanism	2	2,3
10	Database	40	4
11	Microphone/soundcard	5	4
12	Pager	4	4
13	Barcode reader	3	4
14	Alarm clock	4	4
15	Computer I/O	5	4
16	Review design	10	5,6,7,8,9,10,11,12,13,14,15
17	Price components	5	5,6,7,8,9,10,11,12,13,14,15
18	Integration	15	16,17
19	Document design	35	16
20	Procure prototype components	20	18
21	Assemble prototypes	10	20
22	Lab test prototypes	20	21
23	Field test prototypes	20	19,22
24	Adjust design	20	23
25	Order stock parts	2	24
26	Order custom parts	2	24
27	Assemble first production unit	10	25, FS—8 time units 26, FS—13 time units
28	Test unit	10	27
29	Produce 30 units	15	28
30	Train sales representatives	10	29

Use any project network computer program available to you to develop the schedule for activities (See the Case Appendix for further instructions)—noting late and early times, the critical path, and estimated completion for the project.

Prepare a short memo that addresses the following questions:

1. Will the project as planned meet the October 25th deadline?
2. What activities lie on the critical path?
3. How sensitive is this network?

Nightingale Project—B

Rassy and the team were concerned with the results of your analysis. They spent the afternoon brainstorming alternative ways for shortening the project duration. They rejected outsourcing activities because most of the work was developmental in nature and could only be done in-house. They considered altering the scope of the project by eliminating some of the proposed product features. After much debate, they felt they could not compromise any of the core features and be successful in the marketplace. They then turned their attention to accelerating the completion of activities through overtime and adding additional technical manpower. Rassy had built into her proposal a discretionary fund of $200,000. She was willing to invest up to half of this fund to accelerate the project, but wanted to hold on to at least $100,000 to deal with unexpected problems. After a lengthy discussion, her team concluded that the following activities could be reduced at the specified cost:

- Development of voice recognition system could be reduced from 15 days to 10 days at a cost of $15,000.
- Creation of database could be reduced from 40 days to 35 days at a cost of $35,000.
- Document design could be reduced from 35 days to 30 days at a cost of $25,000.
- External specifications could be reduced from 18 days to 12 days at a cost of $20,000.
- Procure prototype components could be reduced from 20 days to 15 days at a cost of $30,000.
- Order stock parts could be reduced from 15 days to 10 days at a cost of $20,000.

Ken Clark, a development engineer, pointed out that the network contained only finish-to-start relationships and that it might be possible to reduce project duration by creating start-to-start lags. For example, he said that his people would not have to wait for all of the field tests to be completed to begin making final adjustments in the design. They could start making adjustments after the first fifteen days of testing. The project team spent the remainder of the day analyzing how they could introduce lags into the network to hopefully shorten the project. They concluded that the following finish-to-start relationships could be converted into lags:

- Document design could begin 5 days after the start of the review design.
- Adjust design could begin 15 days after the start of field tests.
- Ordering stock parts could begin 5 days after the start of adjust design.
- Ordering custom parts could begin 5 days after the start of adjust design.
- Training sales personnel could begin 5 days after the start of unit test and completed 5 days after the production of 30 units.

As the meeting adjourns, Rassy turns to you and tells you to assess the options presented and try to develop a schedule that will meet the October 25th deadline. You are to prepare a report to be presented to the project team that answers the following questions:

1. Is it possible to meet the deadline?
2. If so, how would you recommend changing the original schedule (Part A) and why? Assess the relative impact of crashing activities versus introducing lags to shorten project duration.
3. What would the new schedule look like?
4. What other factors should be considered before finalizing the schedule?

CASE APPENDIX: TECHNICAL DETAILS

Create your project schedule and assess your options based on the following information:

1. The project will begin the first working day in January.
2. The following holidays are observed: January 1, Memorial Day (last Monday in May), July 4th, Labor Day (first Monday in September), Thanksgiving Day (fourth Thursday in November), December 25 and 26.
3. If a holiday falls on a Saturday, then Friday will be given as an extra day off; if it falls on a Sunday, then Monday will be given as a day off.
4. The project team works Monday through Friday.
5. If you choose to reduce the duration of any one of the activities mentioned, then it must be for the specified time and cost (i.e., you cannot choose to reduce database to 37 days at a reduced cost; you can only reduce it to 35 days at a cost of $35,000).
6. You can only spend up to $100,000 to reduce project activities; lags do not contain any additional costs.

APPENDIX 4–1

Computer Project Exercise, Part 2

COMPUTER-CONTROLLED CONVEYOR BELT PROJECT

Using your file from Part 1 (Chapter 3), add all the information to complete this exercise.

1. Develop an AON project network for the Computer Controlled Conveyor Belt Project. Print out your network. If your software allows activity times on the node, include ES, LS, free slack, and duration in your printout. (Hint: The software used for this exercise has a finish date of 6/13/year 2 or 530 work days. Your software may vary one to three days. Do you have any ideas why?)
2. Identify the critical path.
3. Print out ES, LS, EF, LF, and slack times in table form.
4. Print out a bar (Gantt) chart for the project. Months seem to work best as a time unit here.
5. Define (sensible) milestones and give arguments for your choice.
6. How sensitive is this network?
7. What are the advantages of displaying the network versus a Gantt chart?

Remember: Save your file for future exercises!

APPENDIX 4–2

Activity-on-Arrow Method

Description

The activity-on-arrow (AOA) approach also uses the arrow and node as network building blocks. However, in this approach *the arrow represents an individual project activity that requires time.* The length and slope of the arrow have no significance. *The node represents an event; it is usually presented as a small circle.* Events represent points in time but do not consume time. Each activity on the network has a start and

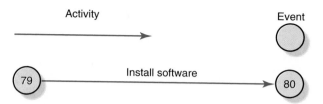

FIGURE A4–1 AOA Network Building Blocks

end event node. For example, if the activity were "install software," the start event could be "start installing software" and the end event could be "finish software installation." Event nodes are numbered with the start node having a smaller number than the end event node (see Figure A4–1). These two numbers are used to identify the activity start node to finish node (79–80). As we shall see shortly, an event node can

FIGURE A4–2 Activity-on-Arrow Network Fundamentals

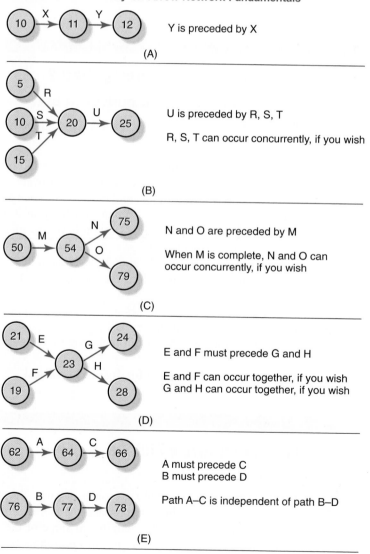

serve as a start or end node for one or more activities, and an end event node can serve as a start node for one or more activities that immediately follow.

Figure A4–2 illustrates several methods for showing AOA activity relationships in a project network. Figure A4–2A simply tells the project manager that activity X must be completed before activity Y can begin. Activity X can also be identified as activity 10–11. Note that event 11 is the finish event for activity X and the start event for activity Y. All AOA networks use this method to link activities and establish dependencies among activities.

Figure A4–2B tells us that activities R, S, and T are parallel, that is, independent, and can occur concurrently if the project manager wishes; however, activities R, S, and T must all be completed before activity U can begin. Observe how event 20 is a common ending event for activities R, S, and T and the start event for activity U. Figure 4–2C shows that activity M must be completed before activities N and O can begin. When activity M is complete, activities N and O are considered independent and can occur simultaneously if you wish. Event 54 is called a burst event because more than one activity arrow leaves (bursts from) it. Figure A4–2D tells us activity E and F can go on together, but both must be completed before activities G and H can begin. Event 23 is both a merge event and a burst event. Theoretically, an event is unlimited in the number of activities (arrows) that can lead into (merge) or out of (burst from) it. Figure A4–2E illustrates parallel paths A–C and B–D. Activity A must precede activity C and B precede D. Paths A–C and B–D are independent of each other. Let us apply these fundamentals to the simple Koll Business Center project.

Design of an AOA Project Network

You are now ready to use the information in Table A4–1 to draw an AOA network of the Koll Business Center. From the information given, the first four activities can be drawn as shown in Figure A4–3. Activity A (1–2) (application approval) must be completed before activities B (2–4), C (2–3), and D (2–6) can begin.

At this point we run into a problem common in AOA networks. Activity E is preceded by activities B and C. The natural inclination is to draw your activity arrows for B and C from event 2 straight to event 4, which is the beginning event for activity E. However, the result would be that activities B and C would both have the same identification numbers (2–4). In cases like this where two or more activities are parallel and have the same start and finish nodes, a dummy activity is inserted to ensure each activity has its unique identification number. A dummy activity is depicted by a dashed

---

TABLE A4–1

NETWORK INFORMATION

KOLL BUSINESS CENTER
County Engineers Design Department

Activity	Description	Preceding activity	Activity time
A	Application approval	None	5
B	Construction plans	A	15
C	Traffic study	A	10
D	Service availability check	A	5
E	Staff report	B, C	15
F	Commission approval	B, C, D	10
G	Wait for construction	F	170
H	Occupancy	E, G	35

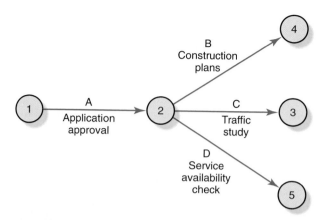

FIGURE A4–3 Partial Koll Business Center AOA Network

arrow and its duration is zero. The dummy activity could be inserted before or after either activity B or C as shown in Figure A4–4 (see parts A through D). In Figure A4–4E we placed it after activity C with its own identification of X or 3–4.

Activity F in Figure A4–4E denotes another network problem in which activity dependencies exist but it is not convenient to connect the activities. In this case, the dummy activity can be used to maintain the logic of the network dependencies. Activity F is preceded by activities B, C, and D. Dummy activity Y (4–5) is necessary because activity B precedes both E and F. The dummy activity maintains the intended logic and sequence. Dummy activity 3–5 can be removed because it is redundant; that is, its removal does not change the intended relationships—the end event 4 precedes activity F. Typically, the first pass in drawing your network will include many dummy activities. After several passes forward and backward through the network, you will find ways to remove some of the dummy activities that are there solely to maintain logic. However, when two or more parallel activities have the same beginning and ending event nodes, dummy activities cannot be avoided. Figure A4–5 has a completed network for the Koll design project.

In this simple project network no activity networks cross over each other, a situation which is very rare. Remember the length and slope of the arrows is arbitrary. The activity durations are included and found below the arrows, near the middle. You should work through the AOA network exercises before moving to the next section. Your familiarity with the activity/event approach will help your initial understanding of the forward and backward pass on an AOA network.

Forward Pass—Earliest Times   The forward pass in AOA uses the same concepts found in the AON procedure. The major difference lies in recognition and use of events to set early and late start and finish times for activities. Figure A4–6 shows the Koll design project with all the activity durations and early start and finish times. Also near each event is a box that will allow us to record event times and slack. In the field this box is sometimes called a "T-box" because the shape within the box forms the letter T. There are many variations of the T-box found in the field, but they all use the basic T format.

The forward pass starts with the first activity(ies) and traces each path through the network. As in AON, you *add* (cumulate) the activity times along the path. When you come to a merge event, you select the largest early finish (EF) of all the activities merging to that event. Let's work through Figure A4–6. Event 1 is the project start event; therefore, the earliest that event can occur is time zero. This early event time for event 1 is placed in the lower left side of the event box. The early event time is also the ES for any activity bursting from an event. Therefore, the zero in the box for event 1 is also the early start for activity A. The early finish for activity A is 5 workdays (ES + Dur = EF or 0 + 5 = 5). The EF for the activity is placed at the head of the arrow. The earliest event 2 can occur is the instant activity A is complete, which is 5 workdays; therefore, this time is placed in the lower left T-box of event 2. Again, note that

FIGURE A4–4 Partial AOA Koll Network

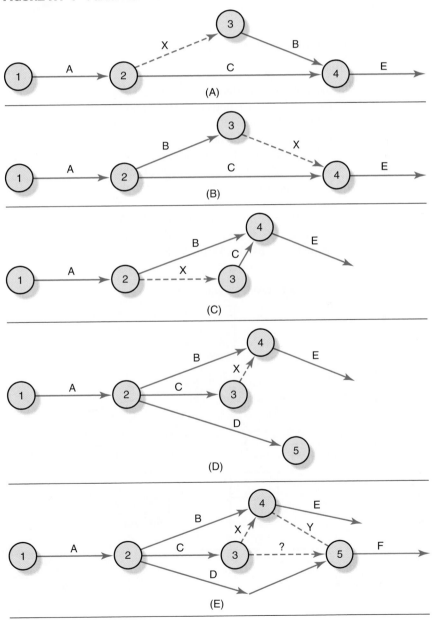

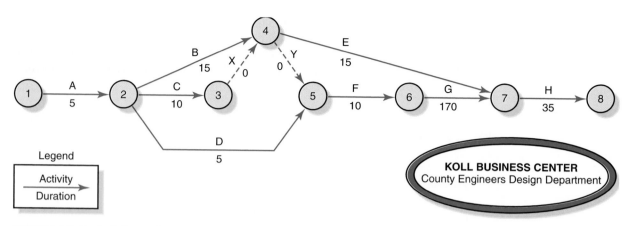

FIGURE A4–5 Activity-on-Arrow Network

the early event time is also the ES for any activity using the event as a start event. Hence, the ES for activities B, C, and D is 5 workdays. The EF for activity B is 20 (ES + Dur = EF), for activity C is 15, and for activity D is 10. (See the head of the arrow for each activity.) The ES for the dummy activity (3–4) is 15, and its EF is 15 (15 + 0 = 15). Although the dummy activity has zero duration, it must be included in the forward and backward pass computations.

At this point you must determine the early event times for events 4 and 5. Both are merge events that require selection among activities merging into these events. Event 4 has B and X, the dummy activity (3–4). The largest EF for these two activities (20 and 15) is 20, which controls the early event time for event 4. Similarly, event 5 is controlled by activities D and Y. Because activity Y has the largest early finish (20 versus

FIGURE A4–6 Activity-on-Arrow Network Forward Pass

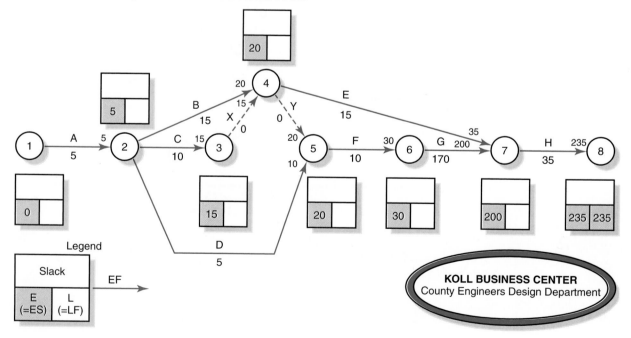

10 workdays for activity D), it establishes the early event time for event 5 and activity F. Times are cumulated until merge event 7. The EFs for activities E and G are 35 and 200 workdays, respectively. Thus, event 7 and activity H have early times of 200 workdays. The early finish for the project is 235 workdays. Assuming we accept this planned duration of 235 days for the project, the LF for event 8 becomes 235 days, and you are ready to compute the backward pass.

Backward Pass—Latest Times The backward pass procedure is similar to that used in the AON procedure. You start with the last project event node(s) and *subtract* activity times along each path (LF – Dur = LS) until you reach a burst event. When this happens, you pick the *smallest* LS of all the activities bursting from the event; this number denotes the latest that event can occur and not delay the project. Let's trace the backward pass for part of the Koll design project.

Figure A4–7 displays the late times for the events and activities. The late start for activity H is 200 days (LF – Dur = LS or 235 – 35 = 200). This time is found at the tail of the arrow. Because event 7 is not a burst event, the late start for activity H becomes the late time for event 7. This procedure continues until you reach event 4, which is a burst event. The LS for activity E is 185 and for activity Y is 20. The smallest time is 20 days and is the late time for event 4. The next burst event is event 2. Here the LS for activities B, C, and D are 5, 10, and 15 days, respectively. Activity B controls the late event time for event 2, which is 5 workdays. The late event time is also the LF for any activity using the event as an end event. For example, the late time for event 7 is 200 workdays; thus, activities E and G can finish no later than day 200, or the project will be delayed.

With the backward pass complete, the slack and critical path can be identified. Figure A4–8 presents the completed network. The event slack is entered above the T in the event box. Activity slack is the difference between LS and ES or LF and EF. For

FIGURE A4–7 Activity-on-Arrow Network Backward Pass

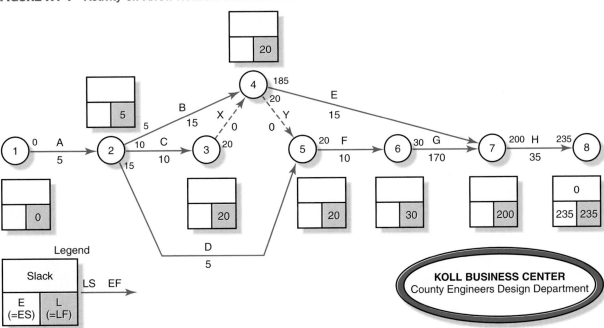

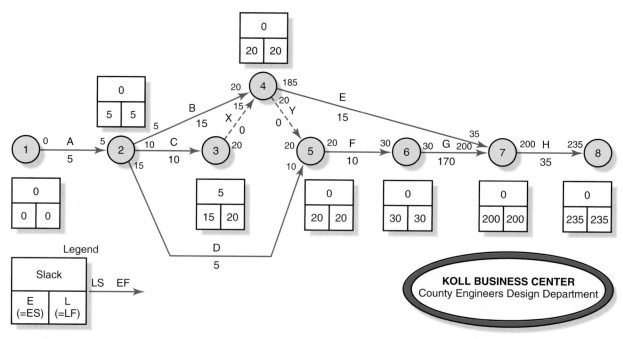

FIGURE A4–8 Activity-on-Arrow Network Backward Pass, Forward Pass, and Slack

example, the slack for activity E is 165 days—LS – ES (185 – 20 = 165) or LF – EF (200 – 35 = 165). What are the slack values for activities B, C, and D? The answers are zero workdays (5 – 5 = 0 or 20 – 20 = 0), 5 workdays (10 – 5 = 5 or 20 – 15 = 5), and 10 workdays (15 – 5 = 10 or 20 – 10 = 10), respectively. The critical path is A, B, Y, F, G, H.

Compare the networks found in Figure A4–8 and in chapter text Figure 4–9 to see the similarities between the AOA and AON methods. As in the AON method, if the

FIGURE A4–9 Air Control Inc. Custom Order Project—AOA Network Diagram

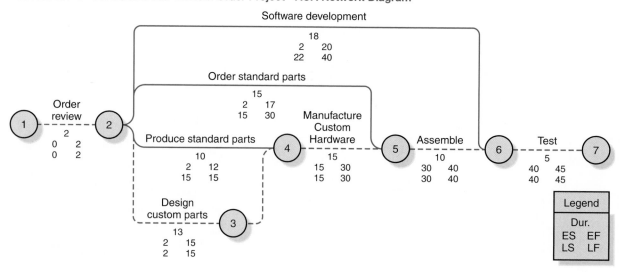

TABLE A4–3

COMPARISON OF AON AND AOA METHODS

AON method

Advantages
1. No dummy activities are used.
2. Events are not used.
3. AON is easy to draw if dependencies are not intense.
4. Activity emphasis is easily understood by first-level managers.
5. The CPM approach uses deterministic times to construct networks.

Disadvantages
1. Path tracing by activity number is difficult. If the network is not available, computer outputs must list the predecessor and successor activities for each activity.
2. Network drawing and understanding are more difficult when dependencies are numerous.

AOA method

Advantages
1. Path tracing is simplified by activity/event numbering scheme.
2. AOA is easier to draw if dependencies are intense.
3. Key events or milestones can easily be flagged.

Disadvantages
1. Use of dummy activities increases data requirements.
2. Emphasis on events can detract from activities. Activity delays cause events and projects to be late.

---

early and late time for the end project event are the same (L = E or LF = EF), the slack on the critical path will be zero. If the times are not the same, the slack on the critical path will equal the difference (L – E or LF – EF).

Computer-Generated Networks   Figure A4–9 presents a generic AOA computer output for the custom order project. AOA networks identify activities by the beginning and ending nodes—for example, the software development activity is identified as activity 2–6. Its duration is 18 time units; ES = 2; EF = 20; LS = 22; and LF = 40 time units. The critical path is 1, 2, 3, 4, 5, 6, 7. Compare the AOA computer output in Figure A4–9 with the AON computer output in chapter Figure 4–12. Bar charts are identical to those developed for AON networks.

Choice of Method—AON or AOA

Your choice of method depends on the importance of various advantages and disadvantages of each method. Table A4–3 will assist you in making your choice.

Summary

In AOA networks, dummy activities meet two needs. First, when two parallel activities have the same start and end nodes, a dummy must be inserted to give each activity a unique identification number (see activity X in Figure A4–8). Next, dummy activities can be used to clarify dependency relationships (see activity Y in Figure A4–8). Dummy activities are very useful when activity dependencies are far apart on the network. In AOA networks the early event time is the ES for any activity emanating from the event. Conversely, the late event time is the LF for any activity merging to the event. The major advantage of the AOA method is the avoidance of having to list all the predecessor and successor activities for each activity in the network so activity sequence and dependency can be traced when a network is not available or shows incomplete information. Computer output is reduced manyfold.

Review Questions

1. How do the building blocks of AON and AOA differ?
2. What are the purposes of dummy or pseudo activities?
3. How do activities differ from events?

Appendix Exercises

1. Use the information found in the text exercises 4–2 and 4–3 to draw AOA networks. Include the activity and event times on the network as shown in Figure A4–8.
2. Use the information found in the text exercise 4–9 to draw an AOA network. Include the activity and event times on the network as shown in Figure A4–8.
3. Given the project network that follows, compute the early, late, and slack times for the project. Be sure to show the early finish and late start times on your network.

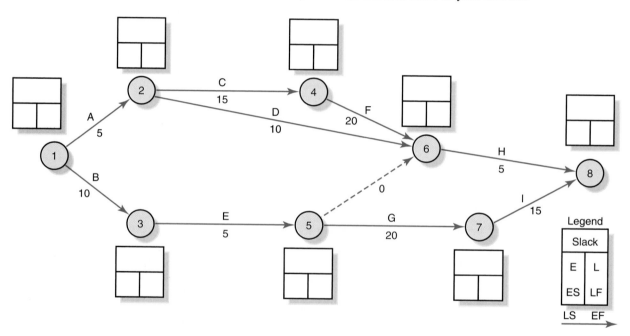

4. Given the project network that follows, compute the early, late, and slack times for the project. Be sure to show the early finish and late start times on your network.

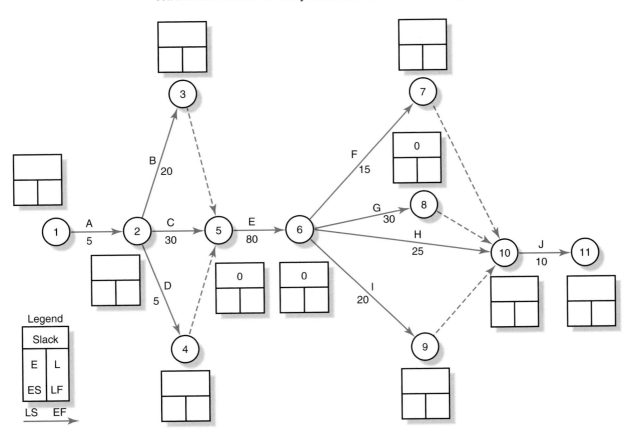

5. Given the project network that follows, complete the bar chart for this project. Use the time-line to align your bars. Be sure to use the legend to show slack for noncritical activities.

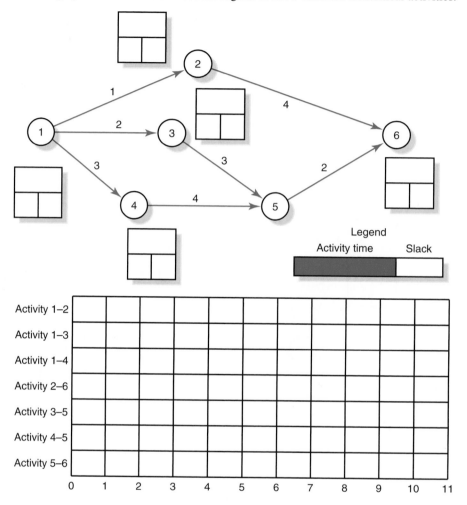

6. Given the project network that follows, draw a bar chart for this project. Use the timeline to align your bars. Be sure to show slack for noncritical activities.

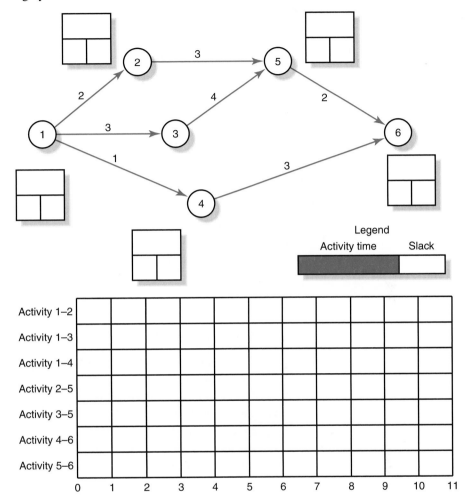

Legend

Activity time   Slack

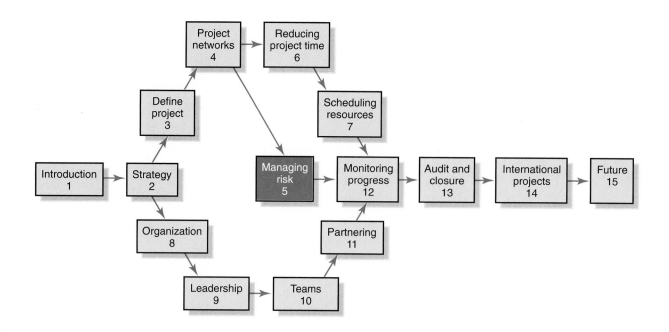

CHAPTER FIVE

Managing Risk

Great deeds are usually wrought at great risk.
—Herodotus, Greek historian

Every project manager understands risks are inherent in projects; all risks cannot be eliminated. No amount of planning can overcome *risk,* or the inability to control chance events. Plans are essentially lists of things to do. More often than not, what is missing from plans is serious consideration of potential project risks. In the context of projects, *risk is the chance that an undesirable event will occur and the consequences of all its possible outcomes.* Project risks are those events that, if they materialize, can delay or kill a project. Some of these possible undesirable events can be identified before the project starts, while a few may be unforeseen and beyond imagination. Project risk events typically have a negative effect on the project objectives of schedule, cost, and specification. (Note: There is the possibility of positive risk events, but project managers' major concerns center on *what can go wrong.*) Risk management identifies as many risk events as possible (what can go wrong), minimizes their impact (what can be done about the event before the project begins), manages responses to those events that do materialize (contingency plans), and provides contingency funds to cover risk events that actually materialize.

Figure 5–1 presents a graphic model[1] of the risk management dilemma. The chances of a risk event occurring (e.g., an error in time estimates, cost estimates, or design technology) are greatest in the concept, planning, and startup phases of the project. The cost impact of a risk event in the project is less if the event occurs earlier rather than later. The early stages of the project represent the period when the opportunity for minimizing the impact or working around a potential risk exists. Conversely, as the project passes the halfway mark, the cost of a risk event occurring increases rapidly. For example, the risk event of a design flaw occurring after a prototype has been made has a greater cost or time impact than if the event occurred in the startup phase of the project. Clearly, identifying project risk events and deciding a response before the project begins is a more prudent approach than not attempting to manage risk.

IDENTIFYING AND ASSESSING PROJECT RISK

Planning for project risk formally addresses identification and analysis and assessment of potential trouble spots before implementing a project. It is a proactive approach

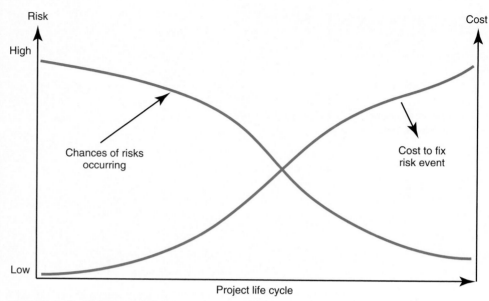

FIGURE 5–1 Risk Event Graph

rather than reactive. It is a preventive process designed to ensure that surprises are reduced and that negative consequences associated with undesirable events are minimized. It also prepares the project manager to take risk when a time, cost, and/or technical advantage is possible. Successful management of project risk gives the project manager better control over the future and can significantly improve chances of reaching project objectives of on time, within budget, and meeting required technical (functional) performance.[2]

The major components of the risk management process are as follows:

- Identifying sources of risk.
- Analyzing and assessing risk.
- Responding to risk.
- Contingency planning.
- Establishing contingency reserves.

These components will be examined in more detail in the remainder of the chapter.

IDENTIFYING SOURCES OF RISK

Basically, risk identification begins by making a list of all areas that might cause project delays or failure and their respective outcomes. Things that have not been done before are potential trouble spots. The entire management team should participate in this exercise. Questionnaires and checklists can be used to ensure all aspects of the project are covered. It is usually better to start with risks associated with the whole project rather than one specific section. That is, keep team members thinking big; don't restrict their thinking to a specific section of the project or network. Questions to ask might be these:

- How adequate are our core competencies to meet the needs of this project?
- Is the degree of novelty of this project high, about average, or lower than most of our projects?

- When you look at the cost, time, and functional performance factors of this project, which one suggests the biggest risk to you? Why?

After the macro risks have been identified, specific areas can be checked. The effective tool to identify specific risks is the work breakdown structure (WBS). Use of the WBS reduces the chance a risk event will be missed. In some projects, practitioners use a technical breakdown structure (TBS) to ensure all technical risks are examined. A TBS uses the WBS as the framework and identifies technical risk events for tasks and deliverables.

The sources of project risks are unlimited. There are sources external to the organization such as inflation, market acceptance, exchange rates, and government regulations. Because such external risks are considered before the decision to go ahead with the project, they will be excluded from the discussion of project risks. However, external risks are extremely important and must be addressed. Other risk sources exist that depend on the specific type of project—e.g., construction, design, software, system, or process. These project-specific risk events will be passed over so that we can limit the discussion to generic risk situations that apply to most projects found in practice.

The following types of information should be developed for each identified risk:

1. The undesirable event.
2. All the outcomes of the event's occurrence.
3. The magnitude or severity of the event's impact.
4. Chances/probability of the event happening.
5. When the event might occur in the project.
6. Interaction with other parts of this or other projects.

For example, assume the chances of a resource shortage of a particular skill are about 80 percent. The outcomes could be a delayed project, tighter scheduling and less flexibility, increased cost, etc. The impact could be a 10 percent increase in cost and a 5 percent delay in project duration. The shortage will show up in the design stage of the project. A delay in this project may delay other projects or require a change in priorities. Having this information available facilitates the assessment of each risk event worthy of attention. Risk identification has major benefits even if there is no follow-through on the remaining steps of the risk management process.

ANALYZING AND ASSESSING RISK

The next step of risk assessment selects potential foreseen risk events that need attention because they exhibit a high probability of occurrence and have a high consequence of loss. Risk analysis attempts to quantify the severity of the impact of an identified risk event, sometimes its probability, and its sensitivity to change. A matrix similar to Figure 5–2 can be developed as a starting point to brainstorm assessment of project risks. This figure is a partial example of a risk assessment matrix used on an IS (Information Systems) project involving the upgrade from Windows Office 97 to Windows Office 2000. The project team identified risks, including the system freezing after installation, end-users resisting and complaining about the changes, and hardware equipment malfunctioning. In addition to assessing the chances, severity, and time the event is likely to occur, the project team also assessed whether they would be able to detect that the event was going to occur in time to take mitigating action. Note that the team rated the detection difficulty "high" for the system freezing because

Risk event	Chance—LMH	Severity—LMH	Detection difficulty—LMH	When
System freezing	Low	High	High	Startup
User backlash	High	Medium	Medium	Post-installation
Hardware malfunctioning	Low	High	High	Installation

FIGURE 5–2　Risk Assessment Matrix

systems crash without warning, while "user backlash" was rated medium because a groundswell of resistance could be detected before such a backlash reached disastrous proportions.

The risk assessment matrix is one of many approaches to risk assessment. Basically, assessments are either subjective or quantitative. "Expert opinion" or "gut feeling" estimates are used the most, but they can carry serious errors depending on the skill of the person(s) making the judgment call. Quantitative methods usually require more detailed analysis of facts and tend to be more reliable. Typical quantitative methods are ratio analysis, probability analysis, and sensitivity analysis. Unfortunately, quantitative methods require serious data collection, are frequently limited in scope, and have low acceptance levels by practicing managers. Hybrid expert systems, which utilize quantitative data and rules of thumb derived from experience, are being used more today. Whether a subjective or quantitative approach is used depends on the source of risk, possible outcomes, effects of a risk event, and management attitude toward risk assessment.

Many analysis techniques are used to identify and assess the impact of a risk event; a few of the most recognized techniques are examined next to give the flavor of approaches used by some project managers. Techniques that require sophisticated and elegant mathematical analysis have been excluded—not because they are invalid but because they require specialized training, data that are often very difficult and expensive to collect, and are used less frequently. In addition, the accuracy of data for a project never done before leaves the numerical answer of questionable value to some practitioners.

Scenario Analysis (A): Nonquantitative

This is the easiest and most used technique. Basically, this technique identifies what might go wrong, the magnitude of the threatening event, and the chance of the event occurring. Given the subjective judgment of these variables, an assessment is made of the alternatives of accepting or reducing, sharing, or transferring risk using a subjective cost-benefit thought process. Although risks are not quantified, they are based on experience, which in most cases is reliable. However, when experience and knowledge among "experts" differ, assessments of risk can be inconsistent.

Ratio/Range Analysis

This technique is also widely used by project managers. The technique uses data from prior projects that are similar to the proposed project. It assumes a ratio between the old and new project to make a point estimate of time, cost, or technology and a low and high range for the estimate. The ratio typically serves as a constant. For example, if past projects have taken 10 minutes per line of computer code, a constant of 1.10 (which represents a 10 percent increase) would be used for the proposed project time estimates because the new project will be more difficult than prior projects. Given the computed estimate for the new project, the percentage ranges for past projects can also be reviewed and the downside risk of the range assessed.

Hybrid Analysis Approaches

Managers are often reluctant to accept quantitative methods because of their restrictive assumptions and scope. To these managers such models fail to utilize the full breadth and knowledge they have gained from experience. Acceptance of heuristic models that utilize the manager's knowledge and rules of thumb is increasing. For example, time to build a printer assembly line in foreign countries may take longer than building one in the United States. Thus, U.S. managers may need to multiply the U.S. project duration by 1.3 or another number based on historical data for the project duration in the country where the line is to be built. Managers are comfortable using rules of thumb combined with subjective judgments and will continue to use them. A few researchers have included these rules of thumb in knowledge-based expert systems to pick up the benefits of the manager's experience/knowledge and historical quantitative databases. The expert system uses a hierarchical inference network for the manager to select general risk factors and ultimately work through to courses of action.[3]

Probability Analysis

There are many statistical techniques available to the project manager that can assist in assessing project risk. Decision trees have been used to assess alternative courses of action using expected values. Statistical variations of net present value (NPV) have been used to assess cash flow risks in projects. Correlations between past projects' cash flow and S-curves (cumulative project cost curve—baseline—over the life of the project) have been used to assess cash flow risks. Finally, PERT (program evaluation review technique) and PERT simulation can be used to review activity and project risk. The use of PERT simulation is increasing because it uses the same data required for PERT, and software to perform the simulation is readily available. (See Appendix 5–1 at the end of this chapter for a more detailed discussion of PERT and PERT simulation.)

Scenario Analysis (B): Semiquantitative

Project managers are often reluctant to use or provide probabilities for risk analysis. Such information would allow risk analysis to be more rigorous, robust, and valuable. The challenge is to get the project team to articulate risk in words. This information can be very practical and, at the same time, provide some of the benefits of probability and utility theory.

One approach used by practicing project managers, semiquantitative scenario analysis, is described in the accompanying Snapshot from Practice. This approach uses time because most risk events are time dependent, impact project delays, and are easily understood by risk team members. (Note that a similar approach can be used for budget.)

The quasiquantitative scenario approach described in the Snapshot from Practice takes basic scenario analysis one step further. By using numbers to verify impacts, it serves as a reality check on identified risks and analysis. A major outcome of the process is a "bracketing" of the project risk and possible durations. By running the

Snapshot from Practice
SEMIQUANTITATIVE RISK APPROACH

The scenario analysis begins with the *baseline schedule,* which typically represents average time and implies there is a 50/50 chance of completing the project schedule early or late. Risk team members are checked to be sure they are 90 (or 95) percent confident that the schedule's duration is about average.

Second, the risk team assesses the baseline schedule assuming "everything goes right." A new *best-case schedule* is developed. The team is asked to confirm they are 90 percent confident that there is at least a 10 percent chance that the best-case schedule can be reached if everything goes right. Note that this schedule actually represents an opportunity for project compression by taking steps to avoid or reduce risks.

Third, the risk team assumes the worst case, which implies that the identified risk events will occur. Murphy's Law will dominate the project. A *worst-case schedule* is developed. The team is asked to confirm they are 90 percent confident that there is a 90 percent chance they can meet the worst-case schedule if the risk events occur.

Finally, as a reality check on the three schedules—best, baseline, and worst—team members are asked to suggest how much of their own money they would be willing to wager on each schedule. This open process usually results in some small revisions of schedules, but it also brings the team close to agreeing that the schedules are reasonable. Figure 5–3 depicts three hypothetical schedules for a project, known as 10, 50, and 90 percent schedules. That is, the team is 90 percent confident there is a 10 percent chance of reaching the best-case schedule of 470 days, a 50 percent chance of meeting the baseline schedule of 500 days, and a 90 percent chance of meeting the worst-case schedule of 590 days. Graphing these three schedules and documenting time estimates, costs, and assumptions is a powerful mechanism that is very useful in explaining to the customer and senior management the uncertainties and effects of risk on a project.

FIGURE 5–3 Risk Schedules

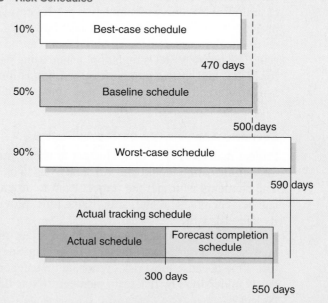

While the project is implemented, the actual schedule can be plotted against the 10, 50, and 90 percent schedules. The bottom section of Figure 5–3 shows an "actual" tracked schedule for the hypothetical project. On day 300 it is estimated that the project will take 250 more days; this is 50 days more than the baseline and 40 days less than the worst-case schedule.

three schedules before the project begins, it is possible to examine what decisions may have to be made; "what if" questions can be addressed. For example, if a risk event occurs, what impact will it have on other projects? This approach is also very useful in explaining to project members the risks inherent in a project.

Sensitivity Analysis

This approach can incorporate techniques from the very simple to highly complex. Fundamentally, project variables are given different values to identify different outcomes and the severity of each. It is similar to scenario analysis, but it typically uses a modeling approach that is very detailed and numerically oriented.

RESPONDING TO RISK

When a risk event is identified and assessed, a decision must be made concerning which response is appropriate for the specific event. Responses to risk can be classified as reducing or retaining, transferring, or sharing.

Reducing or Retaining Risk

Reducing risk is usually the first alternative considered. An example from a bridge-building project illustrates risk reduction. A new bridge project for a coastal port was to use an innovative, continuous cement-pouring process developed by an Australian firm to save large sums of money and time. The major risk was that the continuous pouring process for each major section of the bridge could not be interrupted. Any interruption would require that the whole cement section (hundreds of cubic yards) be torn down and started over. An assessment of possible risks centered on delivery of the cement from the cement factory. Trucks could be delayed, or the factory could break down. Such risks would result in tremendous rework costs and delays. Risk was reduced by having two additional portable cement plants built nearby on different highways within 20 miles of the bridge project in case the main factory supply was interrupted. These two portable plants carried raw materials for a whole bridge section, and extra trucks were on immediate standby each time continuous pouring was required. Similar risk reduction scenarios are apparent in system and software development projects where parallel innovation processes are used in case one fails.

In some cases a conscious decision is made to retain the risk of an event occurring. Some risks are so large it is not feasible to consider transferring or reducing the event (e.g., an earthquake or flood). The project owner thus assumes the risk because the chance of such an event occurring is slim. In other cases risks identified in the budget reserve can simply be absorbed if they materialize. The risk is retained by developing a contingency plan that would be implemented if the risk materializes. In a few cases a risk event can be ignored and a cost overrun accepted should the risk event occur.

Transferring Risk

Passing risk to another party is common; this transfer does not change risk. Passing risk to another party almost always results in paying a premium for this exemption. Fixed-price contracts are the classic example of transferring risk from an owner to a contractor. The contractor understands his or her firm will pay for any risk event that materializes; therefore, a monetary risk factor is added to the contract bid price. Before deciding to transfer risk, the owner should decide which party can best control activities that would lead to the risk occurring. Also, is the contractor capable of absorbing the risk? Clearly identifying and documenting responsibility for absorbing risk is imperative. Another more obvious way to transfer risk is insurance. However, in most cases this is impractical because defining the project risk event and conditions to an insurance broker who is unfamiliar with the project is difficult and usually expensive. Of course, low-probability and high-consequence risk events such as acts of God are more easily defined and insured.

Sharing Risk

Risk sharing allocates proportions of risk to different parties. An example of risk sharing was the Airbus A300B. Research and development risks were allocated among European countries including Britain and France. Alternatively, the entertainment industry formed a consortium to define a common operating format for Digital Video Disc (DVD) to ensure compatibility across products. Other forms of risk sharing are emerging.

Sharing risk has drawn more attention in recent years as a motivation for reducing risk and, in some cases, cutting project cost. Partnering (see Chapter 11) between an owner and contractors has prompted the development of continuous improvement procedures to encourage contractors to suggest innovative ways for project implementation. The new method will probably include additional startup costs and the risk that the new process may not work. Usually the risk costs and benefits of the improved process are shared on a 50/50 basis between the owner and contracting firms.

The more effort given to risk response before the project begins, the better the chances are for minimizing project surprises. Knowing that the response to a risk event will be retained, transferred, or shared greatly reduces stress and uncertainty when the risk event occurs. Again, control is possible with this structured approach.

CONTINGENCY PLANNING

A contingency plan is an alternative plan that will be used if a possible foreseen risk event becomes a reality. The contingency plan represents preventive actions that will reduce or mitigate the negative impact of the risk event. Like all plans, the contingency plan answers the questions of what, where, when, and how much action will take place. The absence of a contingency plan, when a risk event occurs, can cause a manager to delay or postpone the decision to implement a remedy. This postponement can lead to panic, crisis mismanagement, and acceptance of the first remedy suggested. Such after-the-event decision making under pressure can be potentially dangerous and costly. Contingency planning evaluates alternative remedies for possible foreseen events before the risk event occurs and selects the best plan among alternatives. This early contingency planning facilitates a smooth transition to the remedy or workaround plan. The availability of a contingency plan can significantly increase the chances for project success.

Conditions for activating the implementation of the contingency plan should be decided and clearly documented. The plan should include a cost estimate and identify the source of funding. All parties affected should agree to the contingency plan and have authority to make commitments. Because implementation of a contingency plan embodies disruption in the sequence of work, all contingency plans should be communicated to team members so that surprise and resistance are minimized.

Here is an example: A high-tech niche computer company intends to introduce a new "platform" product at a very specific target date. The project's 47 teams all agree delays will not be acceptable. Their contingency plans for two large component suppliers demonstrate how seriously risk management is viewed. One supplier's plant sits

Risk event	Accept, reduce, share, transfer	Contingency plan	Trigger
System freezing	*Reduce*	*Reinstall OS*	*Still frozen after 1 hour*
User backlash	*Reduce*	*Increase staff support*	*Call from top management*
Equipment malfunctioning	*Transfer*	*Order different brand*	*Replacement doesn't work*

FIGURE 5–4   Responses to Risk Matrix

on the San Andreas Fault. The contingency plan has an alternative supplier, who is constantly updated, producing a replica of the component in another plant. Another supplier in Toronto, Canada, presents a delivery risk on their due date because of potential bad weather. This contingency plan calls for a chartered plane (already contracted to be on standby) if overland transportation presents a delay problem. To outsiders these plans must seem a bit extreme, but in high-tech industries where time to market is king, risks of identified events are taken seriously.

Risk response matrices such as the one shown in Figure 5–4 are useful for summarizing how the project team plans to manage risks that have been identified. Again, the Windows Office 2000 project (see Figure 5–2) is used to illustrate this kind of matrix. The first step is to identify whether to reduce, share, transfer, or accept the risk. The team decided to reduce the chances of the system freezing by experimenting with a prototype of the system. Prototype experimentation not only allows them to identify and fix conversion "bugs" before the actual installation, but it also yields information that could be useful in enhancing acceptance by end-users. The project team is then able to identify and document changes between the old and new system that will be incorporated in the training the users receive. The risk of equipment malfunctioning is transferred by choosing a reliable supplier with a strong warranty program.

The next step is to identify contingency plans in case the risk still occurs. For example, if the system freezes after installation, the team will first try to reinstall the software. If user dissatisfaction is high, then the IS department will provide more staff support. If the team is unable to get reliable equipment from the original supplier, then it will order a different brand from a second dealer. Finally, the team needs to discuss and agree what would "trigger" implementation of the contingency plan. In the case of the system freezing, the trigger is not being able to unfreeze the system within one hour or, in the case of user backlash, an angry call from top management.

Unplanned Risk Events—Go/No-Go Situations

Sometimes unforeseen risk events occur midway in a project. Because no contingency plan is available, one must quickly be developed. For example, a new computer chip plant halfway through construction faced an injunction to stop construction because of an environmental lawsuit claiming damage to wetlands. Development of a contingency plan required a go/no-go decision and a whole additional set of new players in the project—biologists, hydrologists, lawyers, etc. The new contingency plan involved heavy damage control and a go-ahead on construction with significant changes in design and cost. As in this example, risk events that arise from sources external to the project tend to cause more disruption than internal risk events. Contingency plans that respond to external events frequently involve new team players. Such players

Snapshot from Practice
RISK MANAGEMENT AT THE TOP OF THE WORLD

Into Thin Air, Jon Krakauer's gripping account of an ill-fated attempt to climb Mount Everest in which six climbers died, provides testimony to the risks of extreme mountain climbing. Thirteen days after the tragedy, David Breashears successfully led a film crew to the summit. Their footage can be seen in the spectacular IMAX film, *Everest.*

Accounts of Mount Everest expeditions provide insights into project risk management. First, most climbers spend more than three weeks acclimating their bodies to high-altitude conditions. Native Sherpas are used extensively to carry supplies and set up each of the four base camps that will be used during the final stages of the climb. To reduce the impact of hypoxia, lightheadness, and disorientation caused by shortage of oxygen, most climbers use oxygen masks and bottles during the final ascent. If lucky enough not to be one of the first expeditions of the season, the path to the summit should be staked out and roped by previous climbers. Climbing guides receive last-minute weather reports by radio to confirm whether the weather conditions warrant the risk. Finally, for added insurance, most climbers join their Sherpas in an elaborate *puja* ritual intended to summon the divine support of the gods before beginning their ascent.

All of these efforts pale next to the sheer physical and mental rigors of making the final climb from base camp IV to the summit. This is what climbers refer to as the "death zone" because beyond 26,000 feet the mind and body begin to quickly deteriorate despite supplemental oxygen. Under fair conditions it takes around 18 hours to make the round trip to the top and back to the base camp. Climbers leave as early as 1:00 A.M. in order to make it back before night falls and total exhaustion sets in.

The greatest danger in climbing Mount Everest is not reaching the summit but making it back to the base camp. One out of every five climbers who make it to the summit dies during their descent. The key is establishing a contingency plan in case the climbers encounter hard going or the weather changes. Guides establish a predetermined turnaround time (i.e., 2:00 P.M.) to ensure a safe return no matter how close the climbers are to the summit. Accepting the time takes tremendous discipline. One who was caught up by time was solo climber Goran Krupp. He turned back 1,000 feet from the top—a twenty-nine-year-old Swede who had bicycled 8,000 miles from Stockholm to Katmandu! Many lives have been lost by failing to adhere to the turn-back time and pushing forward to the summit. As one climber put it, "With enough determination, any bloody idiot can get up the hill. The trick is to get back down alive."[4]

(although necessary) may be unfamiliar with the project organization and have goals in conflict with project goals, presenting still another problem.

Contingency plans are designed to ensure that project goals are reached. Plans typically cover schedule, cost, and technical risks. Some considerations for teams developing contingency plans are discussed next. Some are caveats that represent misdirections managers often take in practice. Clearly, all projects are different; therefore, project managers need to pick and choose those considerations that are relevant to their project (see the accompanying Snapshot from Practice).

Schedule Risks

Use of Slack When some managers see network slack, they cease to worry about completing their activity on time—why worry if there are 10 days of slack! Unfortunately, that slack may be needed by another activity on the path that now must start later and leave little or no slack available because the path slack has already been used up. Managing slack can be an excellent method for reducing schedule risk.[5] Remember, use of slack moves more activities nearer their late start, and thus the risk of project delay is increased.

Managing scheduling risk usually requires trade-off decisions. It is ironic that practicing managers actually increase risk by some of their decisions. Two of those situations are examined below.

Imposed Duration Dates Our experience suggests that about 80 percent of all projects have imposed duration dates. Usually this means someone (with authority) has determined that the project or milestone(s) can or must be completed by a specific date. Examples might be completing a road by January 1 or developing a video game for the Christmas market. The specified project duration is frequently a top-down decision that does not include bottom-up planning and often understates the normal time required to complete the project. If this is the case, meeting the required, specified project duration will result in activities being performed more rapidly than the normal, low-cost method. This hurried approach increases cost and the chance of activities being late and reduces flexibility in the total scheduling system. There are times when completing a project by an imposed duration is necessary (e.g., time to market to beat competition), but in almost all cases of imposed project durations, both risks of being late and greater costs are increased. The question is, "Is this simply poor planning, or is there a real necessity to manage projects by imposed durations?"

Compression of Project Schedules Sometimes before or midway through the project, the need to shorten the project duration arises. Shortening project duration is accomplished by shortening (compressing) one or more activities on the critical path. Shortening an activity/work package duration increases direct cost. In addition, compressing the critical path decreases total slack on other paths, and more paths become critical or near critical. The more critical activities or near-critical activities there are, the higher the risk of delaying project completion. Some contingency plans can avoid costly procedures. For example, schedules can be altered by working activities in parallel or using start-to-start lag relationships. Also, using the best people for high-risk tasks can relieve or lessen the chance of some risk events occurring. Techniques for managing this situation are discussed in Chapter 7.

Cost Risks

Given some of the reported cost overruns, cost risks are significant and carry heavy consequences. Most cost risks are created in schedule and technical estimate errors and omissions. In addition, some management decisions actually increase cost risks. A few selected cost risks found in practice are discussed here.

Time/Cost Dependency Link   There is a dependency link between time and cost and technical problems and cost. For example, if the activity "develop process prototype" requires 50 percent more time than the original estimate, it can be expected that costs will also increase. Thus, time and cost do not occur independently. Neglecting to consider this interactive dependency can result in significant cost risk errors.

Cash Flow Decisions   Some cash flow decisions can heighten schedule risks. For example, financial analysts will make comparisons of an early-start schedule versus a late-start schedule. Theoretically, they conclude that by delaying activities, the future value of the money is greater than its value today (the money can earn interest). Alternatively, the money can be used elsewhere. The increased risk of reducing slack is sometimes ignored or significantly underestimated. Using the schedule to solve cash flow problems should be avoided if possible; it should be done with clear recognition of an increase in schedule risk and the fact that late schedules usually result in higher costs.

Final Cost Forecasts   A frequent scenario occurs when the project is about 20 percent complete. Management asks, "How close to budget will we be when the project is finished?" Because reestimating all costs is too time consuming, three quick methods are used to estimate cost at completion.

The first and most used method is also the most dangerous. This method compares budget versus actual cost at a particular point in time—say, 30 percent complete. If the actual cost is 4 percent over budget to date, the conclusion is the project completion cost will be 4 percent over total budget. Experience shows this is seldom true. If the project is 4 percent over budget early in the project, it can expected the percentage overrun at completion will be greater than 4 percent. The reason is fundamental. If the estimates to date are in error by 4 percent, it is unlikely that the estimates for the remainder of the project will be better. In most cases, the percentage overrun only increases as the project progresses toward completion. Of course, corrective action can be taken, but improvement is difficult and will require serious management attention to change the direction of a cost overrun.

Another more accurate and reliable approach is to forecast final project cost using the earned value concept, which will be developed in Chapter 12. This model applies a cost performance index based on completed work to predict the costs remaining.[6] The cost remaining plus actual costs to date predict the final project cost at completion. Again, this model will be explained in greater detail in Chapter 12, which covers progress and performance measurement and evaluation.

Finally, some analysts use the S-shaped phenomenon of the cumulative project cost curve to forecast final project cost and cash flows. This approach uses complex statistical techniques (e.g., nonlinear regression) that compare budget and actual costs to date to predict cost at completion. Given its complexity, this method has not gained wide acceptance. The S-curve method is sometimes used on a few large projects as one input estimate along with others. In the field, the cost forecasting risks with this model appear to be greater than with the model suggested earlier that depends on the more reliable cost performance index. (See Chapter 12 for a more complete discussion of the cost forecast methods.)

Price Protection Risks   Projects of long duration need some contingency for price changes—which are usually upward. The important point to remember when reviewing price is to avoid the trap of using one lump sum to cover price risks. For example, if inflation has been running about 3 percent, some managers add 3 percent for all resources used in the project. This lump-sum approach does not address exactly where price protection is needed and fails to provide for tracking and control. Price risks should be evaluated item by item. Some purchases and contracts will not change over the life of the project. Those that may change should be identified and estimates made of the magnitude of change. This approach ensures control of the contingency funds as the project is implemented.

Technical Risks

Technical risks are problematic; they can often be the kind that cause the project to be shut down. What if the system or process does not work? Contingency or backup plans are made for those possibilities that are foreseen. For example, Carrier Transicold was involved in developing a new Phoenix refrigeration unit for truck-trailer applications. This new unit was to use rounded panels made of bonded metals, which at the time was new technology for Transicold. Furthermore, one of its competitors had tried unsuccessfully to incorporate similar bonded metals in their products. The project team was eager to make the new technology work, but it wasn't until the very end of the project that they were able to get the new adhesives to bond adequately to complete the project.[7] Throughout the project, the team maintained a welded-panel fabrication approach just in case they were unsuccessful. If this contingency approach had been needed, it would have increased production costs, but the project still would have been completed on time.

In addition to backup strategies, project managers need to develop methods to quickly assess whether technical uncertainties can be resolved. The use of sophisticated CAD programs has greatly helped resolve design problems. At the same time, Smith and Reinertsen, in their book *Developing Products in Half the Time,* argue that there is no substitute for making something and seeing how it works, feels, or looks. They suggest that one should first identify the high-risk technical areas, then build models or design experiments to resolve the risk as quickly as possible. By isolating and testing the key technical questions early on in a project, project feasibility can be quickly determined and necessary adjustments made such as reworking the process or in some cases closing down the project.[8] Usually the owner and project manager make decisions concerning technical risks.

ESTABLISHING CONTINGENCY RESERVES

Contingency funds are established to cover errors in estimates, omissions, and uncertainties that may materialize as the project is implemented. When, where, and how much money will be spent is not known until the risk event occurs. Project "owners" are often reluctant to set up project contingency funds that seem to imply the project plan might be a poor one. Some perceive the contingency fund as an add-on slush fund. Some say they will face the risk when it materializes. Usually such reluctance to establish contingency reserves can be overcome with documented risk identification, assessment, contingency plans, and plans for when and how funds will be disbursed.

The size and amount of contingency reserves depends on "newness" of the project, inaccurate time and cost estimates, technical problems, minor changes in scope, and problems not anticipated. In practice, contingencies run from 1 to 10 percent in projects similar to past projects. However, in unique and high-technology projects it is not uncommon to find contingencies running in the 20 to 60 percent range. Use and rate of consumption of reserves must be closely monitored and controlled. Simply picking a percentage of the baseline, say, 5 percent, and calling it the contingency reserve is not a sound approach. Also, adding up all the identified contingency allotments and throwing them in one pot is not conducive to sound control of the reserve fund. In practice, the contingency reserve fund is typically divided into budget and management reserve funds for control purposes. Budget reserves are those allocated to specific segments or deliverables of the project. Management reserves are those allocated to risks associated with the total project.

Budget Reserves

These reserves are identified for specific work packages or segments of a project found in the baseline budget or work breakdown structure. Budget reserves are for *identified* risks that have a low chance of occurring. Examples of variations covered by budget reserves are small design changes and time and cost estimate errors. For example, a reserve amount might be added to "computer coding" to cover the risk of "testing" showing a coding problem. The reserve amount is determined by costing out the accepted contingency or recovery plan. The budget reserve should be communicated to the project team. This openness suggests trust and encourages good cost performance. However, distributing budget reserves should be the responsibility of both the project manager and the team members responsible for implementing the specific segment of the project. If the risk does not materialize, the funds are returned to the management reserve. Thus, budget reserves decrease as the project progresses.[9]

Management Reserves

These reserve funds are needed to cover major unforeseen and potential risks and, hence, are applied to the total project. For example, a major scope change may appear necessary midway in the project. Because this change was not anticipated or identified, it is covered from the management reserve. Management reserves are established *after* budget reserves are identified and funds established. These reserves are independent of budget reserves and are controlled by the project manager and the "owner" of the project. The "owner" can be internal (top management) or external to the project organization. Most management reserves are set using historical data and judgments concerning the uniqueness of the project.

Placing technical contingencies in the management reserve is a special case. Identifying possible technical (functional) risks is often associated with a new, untried, in-

TABLE 5–1

CONTINGENCY FUND ESTIMATE (THOUSANDS OF DOLLARS)

Activity	Budget baseline	Budget reserve	Project budget
Design	$500	$15	$515
Code	900	80	980
Test	20	2	22
Subtotal	$1,420	$97	$1,517
Management reserve	—	—	50
Total	$1,420	$97	$1,567

novative process or product. Because there is a chance the innovation may not work out, a fallback plan is necessary. This type of risk is beyond the control of the project manager. Hence, technical reserves are held in the management reserve and controlled by the owner or top management. The owner and project manager decide when the contingency plan will be implemented and the reserve funds used. It is assumed there is a high probability these funds will never be used.

Table 5–1 shows the development of a contingency fund estimate for a hypothetical project. Note how budget and management reserves are kept separate; control is easily tracked using this format.

RESPONSIBILITY FOR PROJECT RISKS

Responsibility for risk is frequently passed on to others with the statement, "That is not my worry." This mentality is dangerous. One of the major keys for controlling the cost of risks is documenting responsibility. Each identified risk should be assigned (or shared) by mutual agreement of the owner, project manager, and the contractor or person having line responsibility for the work package or segment of the project. It is best to have the line person responsible approve the use of budget reserve funds and monitor their rate of usage. If management reserve funds are required, the line person should play an active role in estimating additional costs and funds needed to complete the project. If risk management is not formalized, responsibility and responses to risk will be ignored.

Table 5–2 shows common categories of risk assignments for a generic owner/contractor project; there are also project specific risks that are not included in this table. It is not uncommon for an owner and contractor to have conflicting objectives—lowest cost versus quality. Each has a preferable course of action. Sharing may hold the best potential for reducing risk. Planning should isolate the risks controllable by the owner, those by the contractor, and those best shared.

CHANGE CONTROL MANAGEMENT

Every detail of a project plan will not materialize as expected. Coping with and controlling project changes present a formidable challenge for most project managers.

TABLE 5-2

RISK ASSIGNMENTS

Owner/project manager	Contractor
1. Inflation	1. Schedule
2. Acts of God	2. Cost
3. Scope changes	
4. Technical	

Shared
1. Safety
2. Innovation—costs and gains

Changes come from many sources such as the project customer, owner, project manager, team members, and occurrence of risk events. Most changes easily fall into three categories:

1. Scope changes in the form of design or additions represent big changes; for example, customer requests for a new feature or a redesign that will improve the product.
2. Implementation of contingency plans, when risk events occur, represent changes in baseline costs and schedules.
3. Improvement changes suggested by project team members represent another category.

Because change is inevitable, a well-defined change review and control process should be set up early in the project planning cycle.

Basically, change control systems involve reporting, controlling, and recording changes to the project baseline. (Note: Some organizations consider change control systems part of configuration management.) In practice most change control systems are designed to accomplish the following:

1. Identify proposed changes.
2. List expected effects of proposed change(s) on schedule and budget.
3. Review, evaluate, and approve or disapprove changes formally.
4. Negotiate and resolve conflicts of change, conditions, and cost.
5. Communicate changes to parties affected.
6. Assign responsibility for implementing change.
7. Track all changes that are to be implemented.

An example of a simplified change request form is depicted in Figure 5–5.

Change requests should be reviewed and approved or disapproved within a short time limit. If the project is large, a review team may be needed to oversee project changes. Changes more often than not increase cost, cause delays, increase stress among team members, and disrupt the sequence of work; therefore, change proposals are often resisted by team members.

Every approved change must be identified and reflected in the project WBS and baseline. If the change control system is not integrated with the WBS and baseline, project plans and control will soon self-destruct. Thus, one of the keys to a successful change control process is document, document, document! The benefits derived from change control systems are the following:

1. Inconsequential changes are discouraged by the formal process.
2. Costs of changes are maintained in a log.
3. Integrity of the WBS and performance measures is maintained.
4. Allocation and use of budget and management reserve funds are tracked.
5. Responsibility for implementation is clarified.
6. Effect of changes is visible to all parties involved.
7. Implementation of change is monitored.
8. Scope changes will be quickly reflected in baseline and performance measures.

Clearly, change control is important and requires that someone or some group be responsible for approving changes and keeping the process updated. Project control depends heavily on keeping the change control process current. This historical record can be used for satisfying customer inquiries, identifying problems in post-project audits, and estimating future project costs.

Project _Y2K–Machine Dept._		Date _3/29/_
Originator _CEG_		Phone _Ext. 4942_

Impact Areas		Baseline Impact	
Deliverable # _1.3M_	Scope ☐	Contingency ☐
Work package # _1.313M_	Budget ☒	Staff ☒
Cost account # _1.31M_	Schedule ☒	Equipment ☒
Organization unit _IS-M Dept._		

Description of change

Install Y2K compatible chip in six computer controlled milling machines

Justification (include impact if not implemented)

Reprogramming cost is higher than estimated, and risk of old chips failing is higher than estimated.
(Eliminating reprogramming cost is –$10,000. Cost of Y2K chips installed is +$15,000)

Disposition	Priority	Funding Source	
☒ Approve	☐ Emergency	Mgmt. reserve	$ _____
☐ Approve as amended	☒ Urgent	Budget reserve	$ _5,000._
☐ Disapprove	☐ Routine	Other	$ _____
☐ Deferred			

Authorized _S.P_	Scheduled start _4/7/_
Date _4/3/_	Scheduled finish _5/10/_

FIGURE 5-5 Change Request

SUMMARY

Every manager understands that risks are inherent in projects. Risk management reduces the number of surprises and leads to a better understanding of the most likely outcomes of negative events. Although many managers believe that in the final analysis risk assessment and contingency depend on subjective judgment, some standard method for identifying, assessing, and responding to risks should be included in all projects. The very process of identifying project risks forces some discipline at all levels of project management and improves project performance.

Contingency plans increase the chance that the project can be completed on time and within budget. Contingency plans can be simple "work-arounds" or elaborate detailed plans. Responsibility for risks should be clearly identified and documented. It is desirable and prudent to keep a reserve as a hedge against project risks. Budget reserves are linked to the WBS and should be communicated to the project team. Control of management reserves should remain with the owner, project manager, and line person responsible. Use of contingency reserves should be closely monitored, controlled, and reviewed throughout the project life cycle.

Risk management can be handled before the project begins or when the risk occurs. Experience clearly indicates that using a formal, structured process to handle possible foreseen and unforeseen project risk events minimizes surprises, costs, delays, stress, and misunderstandings. When risk events occur or changes are necessary, using an effective change control process to quickly approve and record changes will facilitate measuring performance against schedule and cost.

REVIEW QUESTIONS

1. Project risks can/cannot be eliminated if the project is carefully planned. Explain.
2. The chances of risk events occurring and their respective costs increasing change over the project life cycle. What is the significance of this phenomenon to a project manager?
3. Explain the difference between budget reserves and management reserves.
4. How are the work breakdown structure and change control connected?
5. What are the likely outcomes if a change control process is not used? Why?

EXERCISES

1. Gather a small team of students. Think of a project most students would understand; the kinds of tasks involved should also be familiar. Identify and assess major and minor risks inherent to the project. Decide on a response type. Develop a contingency plan for two to four identified risks. Estimate costs. Assign contingency reserves. How much reserve would your team estimate for the whole project? Justify your choices and estimates.
2. You have been assigned to a project risk team of five members. Because this is the first time your organization has formally set up a risk team for a project, it is hoped that your team will develop a process that can be used on all future projects. Your first team meeting is next Monday morning. Each team member has been asked to prepare for the meeting by developing, in as much detail as possible, an outline that describes how you believe the team should proceed in handling project risks. Each team member will hand out their proposed outline at the beginning of the meeting. Your outline should include but not be limited to the following information:
   a. Team objectives.
   b. Process for handling risk events.
   c. Team activities.
   d. Team outputs.

ENDNOTES

1. Adapted from *Project Management Body of Knowledge* (Newtown Square, PA: Project Management Institute, 1994), p. 6.
2. Charles H. Kepner and Benjamin B. Tregoe, *The New Rational Manager* (Princeton, NJ: Kepner-Tregoe, Inc., 1981); Steve J. Simister, "Usage and Benefits of Project Risk Analysis," *International Journal of Project Management,* vol. 12, no. 1 (February 1994), p. 8.
3. Roozbeh Kangari and LeRoy T. Boyer, "Risk Management by Expert Systems," *Project Management Journal,* vol. 20, no. 1 (1989), pp. 40–47.
4. Jon Krakauer, *Into Thin Air* (New York: Doubleday, 1997), p. 190; Broughton Coburn, *Everest: Mountain without Mercy* (New York: National Geographic Society, 1997).
5. Harvey A. Levine, "Risk Management for Dummies: Managing Schedule, Cost and Technical Risk, and Contingency," *PM Network,* vol. 9, no. 10 (October 1995), pp. 31–33.

6. Quentin W. Flemming and Joel M. Koppelman, "Forecasting the Final Cost and Schedule Results," *PM Network,* vol. 10, no. 1 (January 1996), pp. 13–19.
7. Preston G. Smith and Donald G. Reinertsen, *Developing Products in Half the Time* (New York: Van Nostrand, 1995), pp. 218–19.
8. *Ibid.,* pp. 219–20.
9. David H. Hamburger, "The Project Manager: Risk Taker and Contingency Planner," *Project Management Journal,* vol. 21, no. 4 (1990), pp. 11–16.
10. David T. Hulett, "Project Schedule Risk Assessment," *Project Management Journal,* vol. 26, no. 1 (1995), pp. 21–31; John R. Schuler, "Decision Analysis in Projects: Monte Carlo Simulation," *PM Network,* vol. 8, no. 1 (January 1994), pp. 30–36; Clifford F. Gray and Robert Reiman, "PERT Simulation: A Dynamic Approach to the PERT Technique," *Journal of Systems Management* (March 1969), pp. 18–23.

CASE

Alaska Fly-Fishing Expedition*

You are sitting around the fire at a lodge in Dillingham, Alaska, discussing a fishing expedition you are planning with your colleagues at Great Alaska Adventures (GAA). Earlier in the day you received a fax from the president of BlueNote, Inc. The president wants to reward her top management team by taking them on an all-expense-paid fly-fishing adventure in Alaska. She would like GAA to organize and lead the expedition.

You have just finished a preliminary scope statement for the project (see below). You are now brainstorming potential risks associated with the project.

1. Brainstorm potential risks associated with this project. Try to come up with at least 5 different risks.
2. Use a risk assessment matrix similar to Figure 5–2 to analyze identified risks.
3. Develop a risk response matrix similar to Figure 5–4 to outline how you would deal with each of the risks.

Project Scope Statement

Project Objective
To organize and lead a 5-day fly-fishing expedition down the Tikchik River system in Alaska from June 21 to 25 at a cost not to exceed $18,000.

Deliverables
- Provide air transportation from Dillingham, Alaska, to Camp I and from Camp II back to Dillingham.
- Provide river transportation consisting of two 8-man drift boats with outboard motors.
- Provide 3 meals a day for the 5 days spent on the river.
- Provide 4 hours fly-fishing instruction.
- Provide overnight accommodations at the Dillingham lodge plus three 4-man tents with cots, bedding, and lanterns.
- Provide 4 experienced river guides who are also fly fishermen.
- Provide fishing licenses for all guests.

---

*This case was prepared with the assistance of Stuart Morigeau.

Milestones
1. Contract signed January 22.
2. Guests arrive in Dillingham June 20.
3. Depart by plane to Base Camp I June 21.
4. Depart by plane from Base Camp II to Dillingham June 25.

Technical Requirements
1. Fly in air transportation to and from base camps.
2. Boat transportation within the Tikchik River system.
3. Digital cellular communication devices.
4. Camps and fishing conform to state of Alaska requirements.

Limits and Exclusions
1. Guests are responsible for travel arrangements to and from Dillingham, Alaska.
2. Guests are responsible for their own fly-fishing equipment and clothing.
3. Local air transportation to and from base camps will be outsourced.
4. Tour guides are not responsible for the number of king salmon caught by guests.

Customer Review
The president of BlueNote, Inc.

CASE

Silver Fiddle Construction

You are the president of Silver Fiddle Construction (SFC), which specializes in building high-quality, customized homes in the Grand Junction, Colorado, area. You have just been hired by the Czopeks to build their dream home. You operate as a general contractor and employ only a part-time bookkeeper. You subcontract work to local trade professionals. Housing construction in Grand Junction is booming. You are tentatively scheduled to complete 11 houses this year. You have promised the Czopeks that the final costs will range from $290,000 to $320,000 and that it will take 5 months to complete the house once groundbreaking has begun. The Czopeks are willing to have the project delayed in order to save costs.

You have just finished a preliminary scope statement for the project (see below). You are now brainstorming potential risks associated with the project.

1. Identify potential risks associated with this project. Try to come up with at least 5 different risks.
2. Use a risk assessment matrix similar to Figure 5–2 to analyze identified risks.
3. Develop a risk response matrix similar to Figure 5–4 to outline how you would deal with each of the risks.

Project Scope Statement

Project Objective
To construct a high-quality, custom home within 5 months at a cost not to exceed $320,000.

Deliverables
- A 2,500-square-foot, 2½-bath, 3-bedroom, finished home.
- A finished garage, insulated and sheet rocked.
- Kitchen appliances to include range, oven, microwave, and dishwasher.
- High-efficiency gas furnace with programmable thermostat.

Milestones
1. Permits approved July 5.
2. Foundation poured July 12.
3. "Dry in"—framing, sheathing, plumbing, electrical, and mechanical inspections— passed September 25.
4. Final inspection November 7.

Technical Requirements
1. Home must meet local building codes.
2. All windows and doors must pass NFRC class 40 energy ratings.
3. Exterior wall insulation must meet an "R" factor of 21.
4. Ceiling insulation must meet an "R" factor of 38.
5. Floor insulation must meet an "R" factor of 25.
6. Garage will accommodate two cars and one 28-foot long Winnebago.
7. Structure must pass seismic stability codes.

Limits and Exclusions
1. The home will be built to the specifications and design of the original blueprints provided by the customer.
2. Owner is responsible for landscaping.
3. Refrigerator is not included among kitchen appliances.
4. Air conditioning is not included, but house is prewired for it.
5. SFC reserves the right to contract out services.

Customer Review:
"Bolo" and Izabella Czopek.

CASE

Javacom LAN Project*

Javacom is a small, information systems consulting firm located in Meridian, Louisiana. Javacom has just been hired to design and install a local area network (LAN) for the city of Meridian's social welfare agency. You are the manager for the project, which includes two Javacom professionals and one intern from a local university. You have just finished a preliminary scope statement for the project (see below). You are now brainstorming potential risks associated with the project.

1. Identify potential risks associated with this project. Try to come up with at least 5 different risks.

---

*This case was prepared with the assistance of Budiyoso Kurniawai.

2. Use a risk assessment matrix similar to Figure 5–2 to analyze identified risks.
3. Develop a risk response matrix similar to Figure 5–4 to outline how you would deal with each of the risks.

Project Scope Statement

Project Objective

To design and install a local area network (LAN) within 1 month with a budget not to exceed $82,000 for the Meridian Social Service Agency.

Deliverables
- Twenty workstations.
- Server with dual Pentium processor.
- Two Hewlett-Packard laser jet Si/Si MX printers.
- Windows NT server and workstation operating system.
- Four hours of introduction training for client's personnel.
- Sixteen hours of training for client network administrator.
- Fully operational LAN system.

Milestones
1. Hardware January 22.
2. Setting users priority and authorization January 26.
3. In-house whole network test completed February 1.
4. Client site test completed February 2.
5. Training completed February 16.

Technical Requirements
1. Workstations with 17-inch monitors, Pentium II processor, 128 MB RAM, 4 MB SVGA, 32X CD-ROM, zip drive, Ethernet card, 4.0 GB hard drive.
2. PCI 64 Ethernet LAN interface cards and Ethernet connections (must transmit at least 100 mbps).
3. System must support Windows NT platform and be Y2K compliant.

Limits and Exclusions
1. System maintenance and repair only up to 1 month after final inspection.
2. Warranties transferred to client.
3. Only responsible for installing software designated by the client 2 weeks before the start of the project.
4. Client will be billed for additional training beyond that prescribed in the contract.

Customer Review

Director of the city of Meridian's Social Service Agency.

APPENDIX 5–1

PERT and PERT Simulation

PERT—Program Evaluation Review Technique

In 1958 the Special Office of the Navy and the Booze, Allen, and Hamilton consulting firm developed PERT (Program Evaluation Review Technique) to schedule the

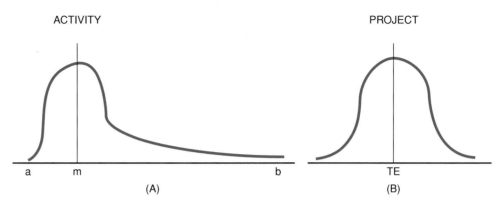

FIGURE A5–1   Activity and Project Frequency Distributions

more than 3,300 contractors of the Polaris submaine project and to cover uncertainty of activity time estimates.

PERT is almost identical to the critical path method (CPM) technique except it assumes each activity duration has a range that follows a statistical distribution. PERT uses three time estimates for each activity. Basically, this means each activity duration can range from an optimistic time to a pessimistic time, and a weighted average can be computed for each activity. Because project activities usually represent work, and because work tends to stay behind once it gets behind, the PERT developers chose an approximation of the *beta distribution* to represent activity durations. This distribution is known to be flexible and can accommodate empirical data that do not follow a normal distribution. The activity durations can be skewed more toward the high or low end of the data range. Figure A5–1A depicts a *beta* distribution for activity durations that is skewed toward the right and is representative of work that tends to stay late once it is behind. The distribution for the project duration is represented by a normal (symmetrical) distribution shown in Figure A5–1B. The project distribution represents the sum of the weighted averages of the activities on the critical path(s).

Knowing the weighted average and variances for each activity allows the project planner to compute the probability of meeting different project durations. Follow the steps described in the hypothetical example given next. (The jargon is difficult for those not familiar with statistics, but the process is relatively simple after working through a couple of examples.)

The weighted average activity time is computed by the following formula:

$$t_e = \frac{a + 4m + b}{6} \tag{5–1}$$

where t_e = weighted average activity time
   a = optimistic activity time (1 chance in 100 of completing the activity earlier under *normal* conditions)
   b = pessimistic activity time (1 chance in 100 of completing the activity later under *normal* conditions)
   m = most likely activity time

When the three time estimates have been specified, this equation is used to compute the weighted average duration for each activity. The average (deterministic) value is placed on the project network as in the CPM method and the early, late, slack, and project completion times are computed as they are in the CPM method.

The variability in the activity time estimates is approximated by the following equations: Equation 5–2 represents the standard deviation for the *activity*. Equation 5–3 represents the standard deviation for the *project*. Note the standard deviation of the activity is squared in this equation; this is also called variance. This sum includes only activities on the critical path(s) or path being reviewed.

$$\sigma_{t_e} = \left(\frac{b-a}{6}\right) \tag{5-2}$$

$$\sigma_{T_E} = \sqrt{\Sigma\sigma_{t_e}^2} \tag{5-3}$$

Finally, the average project duration (T_E) is the sum of all the average activity times along the critical path (sum of t_e), and it follows a normal distribution.

Knowing the average project duration and the variances of activities allows the probability of completing the project (or segment of the project) by a specific time to be computed using standard statistical tables. The equation below (Equation 5–4) is used to compute the "Z" value found in statistical tables (Z = number of standard deviations from the mean), which, in turn, tells the probability of completing the project in the time specified.

$$Z = \frac{T_S - T_E}{\sqrt{\Sigma\sigma_{t_e}^2}} \tag{5-4}$$

where T_E = critical path duration
T_S = scheduled project duration
Z = probability (of meeting scheduled duration) found in statistical Table A5–2

A Hypothetical Example Using the PERT Technique

The activity times and variances are given in Table A5–1. The project network is presented in Figure A5–2.

The expected project duration (T_E) is 64 time units; the critical path is 1, 2, 3, 5, 6. With this information, the probability of completing the project by a specific date can easily be computed using standard statistical methods. For example, what is the probability the project will be completed before a scheduled time (T_S) of 67? The normal curve for the project would appear as shown in Figure A5–3.

TABLE A5-1

ACTIVITY TIMES AND VARIANCES

Activity	a	m	b	t_e	$[(b-a)/6]^2$
1–2	17	29	47	30	25
2–3	6	12	24	13	9
2–4	16	19	28	20	4
3–5	13	16	19	16	1
4–5	2	5	14	6	4
5–6	2	5	8	5	1

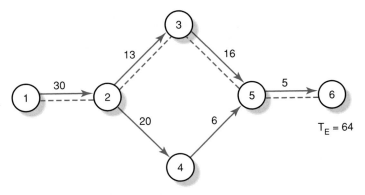

FIGURE A5–2 Hypothetical Network

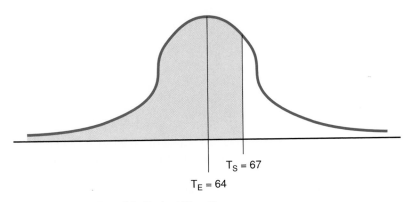

FIGURE A5–3 Possible Project Durations

Using the formula for the Z value, the probability can be computed as follows:

$$Z = \frac{T_S - T_E}{\sqrt{\Sigma \sigma_{t_e}^2}}$$

$$= \frac{67 - 64}{\sqrt{25 + 9 + 1 + 1}}$$

$$= \frac{+3}{\sqrt{36}}$$

$$= +0.50$$

$$P = 0.69$$

Reading from Table A5–2, a Z value of + 0.5 gives a probability of 0.69, which is interpreted to mean there is a 69 percent chance of completing the project on or before 67 time units.

Conversely, the probability of completing the project by time period 60 is computed as follows:

TABLE A5-2			
Z VALUE	**PROBABILITY**	**Z VALUE**	**PROBABILITY**
−2.0	0.02	+2.0	0.98
−1.5	0.07	+1.5	0.93
−1.0	0.16	+1.0	0.84
−0.7	0.24	+0.7	0.76
−0.5	0.31	+0.5	0.69
−0.3	0.38	+0.3	0.62
−0.1	0.36	+0.1	0.54

$$Z = \frac{60 - 64}{\sqrt{25 + 9 + 1 + 1}}$$

$$= \frac{-4}{\sqrt{36}}$$

$$= -0.67$$

$$P \approx 0.26$$

From Table A5–2, a Z value of –0.67 gives an approximate probability of 0.26, which is interpreted to mean there is about a 26 percent chance of completing the project on or before 60 time units. Note that this same type of calculation can be made for any path or segment of a path in the network.

When such probabilities are available to management, trade-off decisions can be made to accept or reduce the risk associated with a particular project duration. For example, if the project manager wishes to improve the chances of completing the project by 64 time units, at least two choices are available. First, management can spend money up front to change conditions that will reduce the duration of one or more activities on the critical path. A more prudent, second alternative would be to allocate money to a contingency fund and wait to see how the project is progressing as it is implemented.

PERT Simulation

This analysis technique requires computer software to simulate the project time, cost, and/or resource availability using the Monte Carlo technique. For example, using the same time estimates developed for PERT, simulation generates the probability of any activity or path becoming critical. The software uses a simple triangular distribution to represent the range and average of each activity duration. Simulating each activity duration distribution for a project gives one set of activity values used to compute the critical path. This process is repeated hundreds of time to determine the *criticality* of any activity or path. Cost can be simulated similarly by using the high and low estimates of costs for each activity and each simulation trial. By using a resource-constrained program with the duration PERT simulation program, potential resource conflicts are identified and assessed. Risk retention or transfer decisions are made using information gained from time, cost, and resource simulations. Computer software is readily available for both PERT and PERT duration simulation. PERT and PERT simulation are useful in projects that are extremely important, include a great deal of inherent uncertainty, and have reasonably accurate time estimates for activities.[10]

Review Questions

1. How does the information in PERT differ from the CPM technique?
2. How is the probability of completing a project by a specific duration computed using PERT? What assumptions underlie this technique?
3. Why is the PERT technique seldom used in practice?

Exercises

1. The following information has been collected by your project team. You have been asked to determine the probabilities of completing the project by time periods 20 and 23. Draw a project network using the method found in Appendix 4–2 of Chapter 4.

Activity	a	m	b	t_e	$[(b - a)/6]^2$
1–2	1	7	13	_____	_____
1–3	4	7	10	_____	_____
1–4	16	19	28	_____	_____
2–5	6	9	24	_____	_____
3–6	2	5	14	_____	_____
6–7	5	8	17	_____	_____

2. The following information has been collected by your project team. Draw a project network using the method found in Appendix 4–2 of Chapter 4. You have been asked to determine the probabilities of completing the project by time periods 50 and 61. In addition, you are asked to assess other risks that may exist in this project. What would be your advice to senior management?

Activity	a	m	b	t_e	$[(b - a)/6]^2$
1–2	3	6	9	_____	_____
2–3	6	9	24	_____	_____
2–4	15	27	45	_____	_____
2–5	2	5	14	_____	_____
3–6	17	29	47	_____	_____
4–6	5	8	17	_____	_____
5–6	4	10	28	_____	_____
6–7	5	8	11	_____	_____

CASE

International Capital, Inc.—Part A

International Capital, Inc. (IC), is a small investment banking firm that specializes in securing funds for small- to medium-sized firms. IC is able to use a standardized project format for each engagement. Only activity times and unusual circumstances change the standard network. Beth Brown has been assigned to this client as project manager partner and has compiled the network information and activity times for the latest client below:

Activity	Description	Immediate predecessor
A	Start story draft using template	—
B	Research client firm	—
C	Create "due diligence" rough draft	A, B
D	Coordinate needs proposal with client	C
E	Estimate future demand and cash flows	C
F	Draft future plans for client company	E
G	Create and approve legal documents	C
H	Integrate all drafts into first-draft proposal	D, F, G
I	Line up potential sources of capital	G, F
J	Check, approve, and print final legal proposal	H
K	Sign contracts and transfer funds	I, J

Time in Workdays

Activity	Optimistic	Most likely	Pessimistic
A	4	7	10
B	2	4	8
C	2	5	8
D	16	19	28
E	6	9	24
F	1	7	13
G	4	10	28
H	2	5	14
I	5	8	17
J	2	5	8
K	17	29	45

Managerial Report

Brown and other broker partners have a policy of passing their plan through a project review committee of colleagues. This committee traditionally checks that all details are covered, times are realistic, and resources are available. Brown wishes you to develop a report that presents a planned schedule and expected project completion time in workdays. Include a project network in your report. The average duration for a sourcing capital project is 70 workdays. IC partners have agreed it is good business to set up projects with a 95 percent chance of attaining the plan. How does this project stack up with the average project? What would the average have to be to ensure a 95 percent chance of completing the project in 70 workdays?

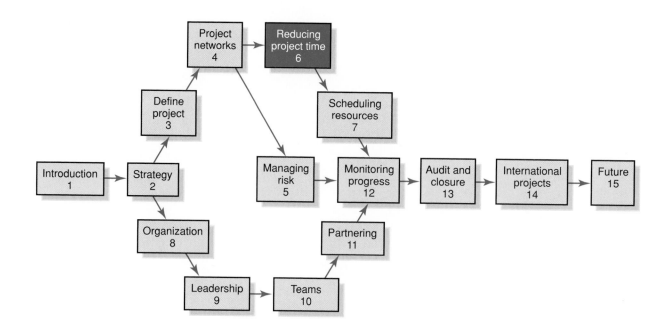

Reducing Project Time

Rationale for Reducing Project Time
Project Time Reduction Procedure
Constructing a Project Cost-Time Graph
Practical Considerations
Summary

CHAPTER SIX

Reducing Project Time

When do you need it?
  Yesterday.

RATIONALE FOR REDUCING PROJECT TIME

There are few circumstances in which a project manager or owner would not wish to reduce the time to complete a project. Reducing the time of a critical activity in a project can be done but almost always results in a higher direct cost; thus, the manager faces a cost-time trade-off problem—is the reduction in time worth the additional cost? Cost-time situations focus on reducing the critical path that determines the project completion date.

There are many good reasons for attempting to reduce the duration of a project. One of the more common reasons is known in the field as an "imposed" project duration date. For example, a politician makes a public statement that a new law building will be available in two years. Or the president of a software company remarks in a speech that new technologically advanced software will be available in one year. Such statements too often become imposed project duration dates—without any consideration of the problems or cost of meeting such a date. The project duration time is set while the project is in its "concept" phase before or without any detailed scheduling of all the activities in the project. This phenomenon is very common in practice! Unfortunately, this practice almost always leads to a higher-cost project than one that is planned using low-cost, efficient methods and detailed planning. In addition, quality is sometimes compromised to meet deadlines. More importantly, these increased costs of imposed duration dates are seldom recognized or noted by project participants. Imposed project durations are a fact of life for project managers.

In recent years emphasis on time-to-market has taken on new importance because of intense global competition and rapid technological advances. The *market* imposes a project duration date. For example, a rule of thumb for moderate- to high-technology firms is that a six-month delay in bringing a product to market can result in a gross profit loss or market share of about 30 percent. In these cases, high-technology firms typically assume that the time savings and avoidance of lost profits are worth any additional costs to reduce time without any formal analysis. It is interesting to observe how more serious analysis occurs in recession periods when cash flows are tight.

Snapshot from Practice
RESPONDING TO THE NORTHRIDGE EARTHQUAKE[1]

On January 17, 1994, a 6.8-magnitude earthquake struck the Los Angeles basin, near suburban Northridge, causing 60 deaths, thousands of injuries, and billions of dollars in property damage. Nowhere was the destructive power of nature more evident than in the collapsed sections of the freeway system that disrupted the daily commute of an estimated 1 million Los Angelians. The Northridge earthquake posed one of the greatest challenges to the California Department of Transportation (CalTrans) in its nearly 100-year history. To expedite the recovery process, Governor Pete Wilson signed an emergency declaration allowing CalTrans to streamline contracting procedures and offer attractive incentives for completing work ahead of schedule. For each day that the schedule was beaten, a sizable bonus was to be awarded. Conversely, for each day over the deadline, the contractor would be penalized the same amount. The amount ($50,000 to $200,000) varied depending on the importance of the work.

The incentive scheme proved to be a powerful motivator for the freeway reconstruction contractors. C. C. Myers, Inc., of Rancho Cordova, California, won the contract for the reconstruction of the Interstate 10 bridges. Myers pulled out all stops to finish the project in a blistering 66 days—a whopping 74 days ahead of schedule—and earning a $14.8 million bonus! Myers took every opportunity to save time and streamline operations. It greatly expanded the workforce. For example, 134 ironworkers were employed instead of the normal 15. Special lighting equipment was set up so that work could be performed around the clock. Likewise, the sites were prepared and special materials were used so that work could continue despite inclement weather that would normally shut down construction. The work was scheduled much like an assembly line so that critical activities were followed by the next critical activity. A generous incentive scheme was devised to reward teamwork and reach milestones early. Carpenters and ironworkers competed as teams against each other to see who could finish first.

Although C. C. Myers received a substantial bonus for finishing early, they spent a lot of money on overtime, bonuses, special equipment, and other premiums to keep the job rolling

Incentive contracts and continuous improvement incentives in partnering arrangements can make reduction of project time rewarding—usually for both the project contractor and owner. For example, a contractor finished a bridge across a lake 18 months early and received more than $6 million for the early completion. The availability of the bridge to the surrounding community 18 months early to reduce traffic gridlock made the incentive cost to the community seem small to users. In another example, in a partnering continuous improvement arrangement, the joint effort of the owner and contractor resulted in early completion of a river lock and a 50/50 split of the savings to the owner and contractor.

Another reason for reducing project time occurs when unforeseen delays—for example, adverse weather, design flaws, and equipment breakdown—cause substantial delays midway in the project. Getting back on schedule usually requires compressing the time on some of the remaining critical activities. The additional costs of getting back on schedule need to be compared with the costs of being late.

Sometimes very high overhead or goodwill costs are recognized before the project begins. In these cases it is prudent to examine the direct costs of shortening the critical path versus the overhead and/or goodwill cost savings. Usually there are opportunities to shorten a few critical activities at less than the daily overhead rate or perceived goodwill cost. Under specific conditions (which are not rare), huge savings are possible with little risk.

Finally there are times when it is important to reassign key equipment and/or people to new projects. Under these circumstances, the cost of compressing the project can be compared with the costs of not releasing key equipment or people.

Nothing on the horizon suggests that the need to shorten project time will change. The challenge for the project manager is to use a quick, logical method to compare the benefits of reducing project time with the cost. When sound, logical methods are absent, it is difficult to isolate those activities that will have the greatest impact on reducing project time at least cost. This chapter describes a procedure for identifying the costs of reducing project time so that comparisons can be made with the benefits of getting the project completed sooner. The method requires gathering direct and indirect costs for specific project durations. Critical activities are searched to find the lowest direct-cost activities that will shorten the project duration. Total cost for specific project durations are computed and then compared with the benefits of reducing project time—*before the project begins or while it is in progress.*

PROJECT TIME REDUCTION PROCEDURE

Explanation of Project Costs

The general nature of project costs is illustrated in Figure 6–1. The total cost for each duration is the sum of the indirect and direct costs. Indirect costs continue for the life of the project. Hence, any reduction in project duration means a reduction in indirect costs. Direct costs on the graph grow at an increasing rate as the project duration is reduced from its original planned duration. With the information from a graph such as this for a project, managers can quickly judge any alternative such as meeting a time-to-market deadline. Further discussion of indirect and direct costs is necessary before demonstrating a procedure for developing the information for a graph similar to the one depicted in Figure 6–1.

Project Indirect Costs   Indirect costs generally represent overhead costs such as supervision, administration, consultants, and interest. Indirect costs cannot be associated with any particular work package or activity, hence the term. Indirect costs vary directly with time. That is, any reduction in time should result in a reduction of indirect costs. For example, if the daily costs of supervision, administration, and consultants are $2,000, any reduction in project duration would represent a savings of $2,000 per day. If indirect costs are a significant percentage of total project costs, reductions in project time can represent very real savings (assuming the indirect resources can be utilized elsewhere).

Project Direct Costs   Direct costs commonly represent labor, materials, equipment, and sometimes subcontractors. Direct costs are assigned directly to a work package and activity, hence the term. The ideal assumption is that direct costs for an activity time represent normal costs, which typically mean low-cost, efficient methods for a normal time. When project durations are imposed, direct costs may no longer represent low-cost, efficient methods. Costs for the imposed duration date will be higher

FIGURE 6–1   Project Cost-Time Graph

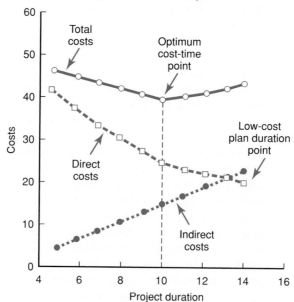

than for a project duration developed from ideal normal times for activities. Because direct costs are assumed to be developed from normal methods and time, any reduction in activity time should add to the costs of the activity. The sum of the costs of all the work packages or activities represents the total direct costs for the project. The major plight faced in creating the information for a graph similar to Figure 6–1 is computing the direct cost of shortening individual critical activities and then finding the total direct cost for each project duration as project time is compressed; the process requires selecting those critical activities that cost the least to shorten.

Shortening the Project Time

Methods for shortening project time (activities on the critical path) are limited. Reducing quality is one alternative that may reduce the time of an activity on the critical path. However, sacrificing quality is rarely an acceptable or used method. Another method for shortening the project time is to subcontract an activity. The subcontractor may have access to superior technology or expertise that will accelerate the completion of the activity. Subcontracting also frees up resources that can be assigned to a critical activity and can result in a shorter project duration. However, it is likely this alternative was considered in the early planning stages, so it may not be a viable means for shortening the schedule at a later date.

The most common method for shortening project time is to assign additional manpower and equipment to the remaining activities. There are limits, however, as to how much speed can be gained by adding manpower. The relationship between manpower and progress is not linear; doubling the size of the workforce will not necessarily reduce completion time by half. The relationship would be correct only when tasks can be partitioned so no communication is needed between workers, as in harvesting a crop by hand. Most projects are not set up that way; additional workers increase the communication requirements to coordinate their efforts. For example, doubling a team by adding two workers requires six times as much pair-wise intercommunication than is required in the original two-person team. Not only is more time needed to coordinate and manage a larger team, but there is the additional delay of training the new people and getting them up to speed on the project. The relationship between manpower and progress is, in fact, curvilinear, and there is a threshold point where additional labor will actually slow down progress. The end result is captured in Brooks's law: "Adding manpower to a late software project makes it later."[2] Frederick Brooks formulated this principle based on his experience as a project manager for IBM's System/360 software project during the early 1960s. Subsequent research concluded that adding more people to a late project always makes it more costly, but late additions may not *always* cause the project to be completed later.[3] Adding extra manpower early in the schedule is a much safer maneuver than adding it later, because the new people always have an immediate negative effect on progress (e.g., training, communication, startup) that may take weeks to overcome.

Sometimes it is possible to rearrange the logic of the project network so that critical activities are done in parallel (concurrently) rather than sequentially. This alternative is a good one if the project situation is right. When this alternative is given serious attention, it is amazing to observe how creative project team members can be in finding ways to restructure sequential activities in parallel. As noted in Chapter 4, one of the most common methods for restructuring activities is to change a finish-to-start relationship to a start-to-start relationship. For example, instead of waiting for the final design to be approved, manufacturing engineers can begin building the production line as soon as key specifications have been established. Changing activities from sequential to parallel usually requires closer coordination among those responsible for the activities affected.

Finally, another common method for meeting critical deadlines is to reduce the scope of the project. For example, the Rose Garden stadium in Portland, Oregon, was supposed to be completely finished in time for the start of the 1995–1996 National Basketball Association (NBA) season. Delays made this impossible, so the construction crew set up temporary bleachers to accommodate the opening night crowd. Likewise, software firms release products that do not meet the original performance specifications, only to add the missing features in subsequent versions. Care should be exercised in reducing the scope of the project to accelerate progress so that essential requirements are not compromised.

If all of these alternatives are ruled out, shortening project time comes down to reducing specific, critical activity times to reduce project time. This alternative means paying a premium cost to cut activity time. A logical method for evaluating this cost-time trade-off condition is presented next.

CONSTRUCTING A PROJECT COST-TIME GRAPH

There are three major steps required to construct a project cost-time graph:

1. Find total direct costs for selected project durations.
2. Find total indirect costs for selected project durations.
3. Sum direct and indirect costs for these selected durations.

The graph is then used to compare additional cost alternatives for benefits. Details of these steps are presented here.

Determining the Activities to Shorten

The most difficult task in constructing a cost-time graph is finding the total direct costs for specific project durations over a relevant range. The central concern is to decide which activities to shorten and how far to carry the shortening process. Basically, managers need to look for critical activities that can be shortened with the *smallest increase in cost per unit of time*. The rationale for selecting critical activities depends on identifying the activity's normal and crash times and corresponding costs. *Normal time* for an activity represents low-cost, realistic, efficient methods for completing the activity under normal conditions. Shortening an activity is called *crashing*. The shortest possible time an activity can realistically be completed in is called its *crash time*. The direct cost for completing an activity in its crash time is called *crash cost*. Both normal and crash times and costs are collected from personnel most familiar with completing the activity. Figure 6–2 depicts a hypothetical cost-time graph for an activity.

The normal time for the activity is 10 time units, and the corresponding cost is $400. The crash time for the activity is 5 time units and $800. The intersection of the normal time and cost represents the original low-cost, early-start schedule. The heavy line connecting the normal and crash points represents the slope, which assumes the cost of reducing the time of the activity is constant *per unit of time*. The assumptions underlying the use of this graph are as follows:

1. The cost-time relationship is linear.
2. Normal time assumes low-cost, efficient methods to complete the activity.

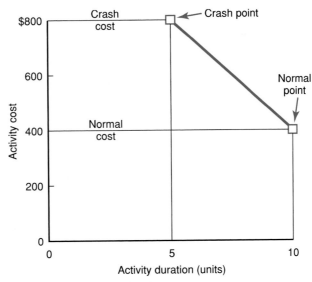

FIGURE 6–2 Activity Graph

3. Crash time represents a limit—the greatest time reduction possible under realistic conditions.
4. Slope represents cost *per unit of time.*
5. All accelerations must occur within the normal and crash times.

Knowing the slope of activities allows managers to compare which critical activities to shorten. The less steep the cost slope of an activity, the less it costs to shorten one time period; a steeper slope means it will cost more to shorten one time unit. The cost per unit of time or slope for any activity is computed by the following equation:

$$\text{Cost slope} = \frac{\text{Rise}}{\text{Run}} = \frac{\text{Crash cost} - \text{Normal cost}}{\text{Normal time} - \text{Crash time}}$$

$$= \frac{\text{CC} - \text{NC}}{\text{NT} - \text{CT}} = \frac{\$800 - \$400}{10 - 5}$$

$$= \frac{\$400}{5} = \$80 \text{ per unit of time}$$

In Figure 6–2 the rise is the *y* axis (cost) and the run is the *x* axis (duration). The slope of the cost line is $80 for each time unit the activity is reduced; the limit reduction of the activity time is five time units. Comparison of the slopes of all critical activities allows us to determine which activity(ies) to shorten to minimize total direct cost. Given the preliminary project schedule (or one in progress) with all activities set to their early-start times, the process of searching critical activities as candidates for reduction can begin. The total direct cost for each specific compressed project duration must be found.

A Simplified Example

Figure 6–3a presents normal and crash times and costs for each activity, the computed slope and time reduction limit, the total direct cost, and the project network with a

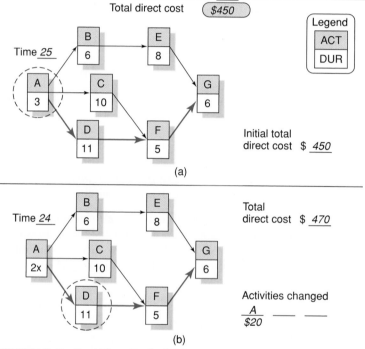

Activity ID	Slope	Maximum crash time	Direct costs			
			Normal		Crash	
			Time	Cost	Time	Cost
A	20	1	3	$50	2	$70
B	40	2	6	80	4	160
C	30	1	10	60	9	90
D	25	4	11	50	7	150
E	30	2	8	100	6	160
F	30	1	5	40	4	70
G	0	0	6	70	6	70

Total direct cost $450

FIGURE 6–3 Cost-Time Trade-Off Example

duration of 25 time units. Note the total direct cost for the 25-period duration is $450. This is an anchor point to begin the procedure of shortening the critical path(s) and finding the total direct costs for each specific duration less than 25 time units. The maximum time reduction of an activity is simply the difference between the normal and crash times for an activity. For example, activity D can be reduced from a normal time of 11 time units to a crash time of 7 time units, or a maximum of 4 time units. The positive slope for activity D is computed as follows:

$$\text{Slope} = \frac{\text{Crash cost} - \text{Normal cost}}{\text{Normal time} - \text{Crash time}} = \frac{\$150 - \$50}{11 - 7}$$

$$= \frac{\$100}{4} = \$25 \text{ per period reduced}$$

The network shows the critical path to be activities A, D, F, G. Because it is impossible to shorten activity G, activity A is circled because it is the least-cost candidate; that is, its slope ($20) is less than the slopes for activities D and F ($25 and $30). Reducing activity A one time unit cuts the project duration to 24 time units but increases the total direct costs to $470 ($450 + $20 = $470). Figure 6–3b reflects these changes. The duration of activity A has been reduced to two time units; the "x" indicates the activity cannot be reduced any further. Activity D is circled because it costs the least ($25) to shorten the project to 23 time units. Compare the cost of activity F. The total direct cost for a project duration of 23 time units is $495 (See Figure 6–4a).

Observe that the project network in Figure 6–4a now has two critical paths—A, C, F, G and A, D, F, G. Reducing the project to 22 time units will require that activity F be reduced; thus, it is circled. This change is reflected in Figure 6–4b. The total direct cost for 22 time units is $525. This reduction has created a third critical path—A, B, E, G; all activities are critical. The least-cost method for reducing the project duration to 21 time units is the combination of the circled activities C, D, E which cost $30, $25, $30, respectively, and increase total direct costs to $610. The results of these

FIGURE 6–4   Cost-Time Trade-Off Example (continued)

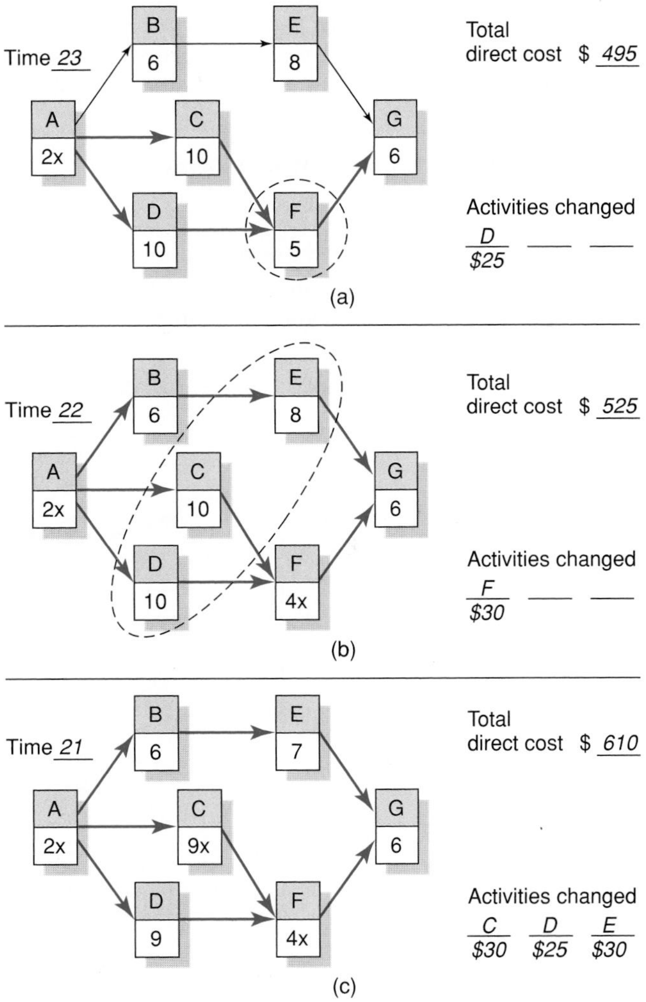

Project duration	Direct costs	+	Indirect costs	=	Total costs
25	450		400		$850
24	470		350		820
23	495		300		795
(22)	525		250		(775)
21	610		200		810

FIGURE 6–5 Summary Costs by Duration

changes are depicted in Figure 6–4c. Although some activities can still be reduced (those without the "x" next to the activity time), no activity or combination of activities will result in a reduction in the project duration.

With the total direct costs for the array of specific project durations found, the next step is to collect the indirect costs for these same durations. These costs are typically a rate per day and are easily obtained from the accounting department. Figure 6–5 presents the total direct costs, total indirect costs, and total project costs. These same costs are plotted in Figure 6–6. This graph shows that the optimum cost-time duration is 22 time units and $775. Assuming the project will actually materialize as planned, any movement away from this time duration will increase project costs. The movement from 25 to 22 time units occurs because, in this range, the absolute slopes of the indirect costs are greater than the direct cost slopes.

PRACTICAL CONSIDERATIONS

Crash Times

Collecting crash times for even a moderate-size project can be difficult. The meaning of crash time is difficult to communicate. What is meant when you define crash time as "the shortest time you can realistically complete an activity"? Crash time is open to

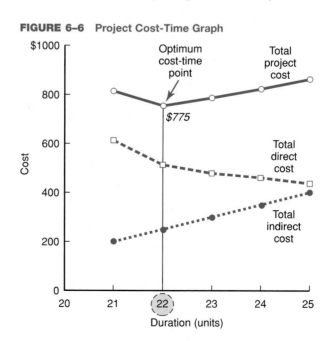

FIGURE 6–6 Project Cost-Time Graph

different interpretations and judgments. Some estimators feel very uncomfortable providing crash times. Regardless of the comfort level, the accuracy of crash times and costs is frequently rough at best, when compared with normal time and cost.

Timing of Crashing Activities

Sometimes a wait-and-see strategy is the wise move. Crashing a critical activity early in the project may result in wasted money if some other critical activity is finished early or some noncritical path becomes the new critical path. In such cases the money spent early is gone, and no benefit comes from early completion by crashing the activity. Conversely, it may be wise to crash an early critical activity when later activities are likely to be delayed and absorb the time gained. Then the manager would only have the option of crashing final activities to get back on schedule. Ultimately, the timing of crashing activities is a judgment call requiring careful consideration of the options available, the risks involved, and the importance of meeting a deadline.

Linearity Assumption

Because the accuracy of compressed activity times and costs is questionable, the concern of some theorists—that the relationship between cost and time is not linear but curvilinear—is seldom a concern for practicing managers. Reasonable, quick comparisons can be made using the linear assumption. The simple approach is adequate for most projects. In a few rare cases of very large, complex, long-duration projects, the use of present value techniques may be useful; such techniques are beyond the scope of this text.

Computer Solutions

Care must be taken against depending too heavily on a computer solution. The computer solution does not consider uncertainty or risk. Some critical activities can be crashed with less chance of something going wrong than others. The computer solution only deals with slopes. In addition, in large, complex project networks collecting the data can be overwhelming and costly. In these situations a group meeting of key managers of the project can identify a small segment of the project in which the greatest opportunities for time reduction on the critical path exist at relatively low cost. The computer can be used to develop a cost-time graph for this section. Using the suggested formal approach ensures indirect (overhead) costs are included in the analysis. Some project managers fail to consider indirect costs in project compression situations.

The Bottom Line

Should the project owner or project manager go for the optimum cost-time? The answer is, "It depends." Risk must be considered. Recall from our example that the optimum project time point represented a reduced project cost and was less than the original normal project time (review Figure 6–6). The project direct-cost line near the normal point is usually relatively flat. Because indirect costs for the project are usually greater in the same range, the optimum cost-time point is less than the normal time point. Logic of the cost-time procedure suggests managers should reduce the project duration to the lowest total cost point and duration.

How far to reduce the project time from the normal time toward the optimum depends on the *sensitivity* of the project network. A network is sensitive if it has several critical or near-critical paths. In this situation project movement toward the optimum

Snapshot from Practice
I'LL BET YOU . . .

The focus of this chapter has been on how project managers crash activities by typically assigning additional manpower and equipment to cut significant time off of scheduled tasks. Project managers often encounter situations in which they need to motivate individuals to accelerate the completion of a specific, critical task. Imagine the following scenario.

Pegi Young just received a priority assignment from corporate headquarters. The preliminary engineering sketches that were due tomorrow need to be e-mailed to the West Coast by 4:00 P.M. today so that the model shop can begin construction of a prototype to present to top management. She approaches Danny Whitten, the draftsman responsible for the task, whose initial response is, "That's impossible!" While she agrees that it would be very difficult she does not believe that it is as impossible as Danny suggests nor that Danny truly believes that. What should she do?

She tells Danny that she knows this is going to be a rush job, but she is confident that he can do it. When Danny balks, she responds, "I tell you what, I'll make a bet with you. If you are able to finish the design by 4:00, I'll make sure you get two of the company's tickets to tomorrow night's Celtics–Knicks basketball game." Danny accepts the challenge, works feverishly to complete the assignment, and is able to take his daughter to her first professional basketball game.

Conversations with project managers reveal that many use bets like this one to motivate extraordinary performance. These bets range from tickets to sporting and entertainment events to gift certificates at high-class restaurants to a well-deserved afternoon off. For bets to work they need to adhere to the principles of expectancy theory of motivation.[4] Boiled down to simple terms, expectancy theory rests on three key questions:

1. Can I do it (Is it possible to meet the challenge)?
2. Will I get it (Can I demonstrate that I met the challenge and can I trust the project manager will deliver his/her end of the bargain)?
3. Is it worth it (Is the payoff of sufficient personal value to warrant the risk and extra effort)?

If in the mind of the participant the answer to any of these three questions is no, then the person is unlikely to accept the challenge. However, when the answers are affirmative, then the individual is likely to accept the bet and be motivated to meet the challenge.

Bets can be effective motivational tools and add an element of excitement and fun to project work. But, the following practical advice should be heeded:

1. The bet has greater significance if it also benefits family members or significant others. Being able to take a son or daughter to a professional basketball game allows that individual to "score points" at home through work. These bets also recognize and reward the support project members receive from their families and reinforces the importance of their work to loved ones.
2. Bets should be used sparingly; otherwise everything can become negotiable. They should be used only under special circumstances that require extraordinary effort.
3. Individual bets should involve clearly recognizable individual effort, otherwise others may become jealous and discord may occur within a group. As long as others see it as requiring truly remarkable, "beyond the call of duty" effort, they will consider it fair and warranted.

time requires spending money to reduce critical activities, resulting in slack reduction and/or more critical paths and activities. Slack reduction in a project with several near critical paths increases the risk of being late. The practical outcome can be a higher total project cost if some near-critical activities are delayed and become critical; the money spent reducing activities on the original critical path would be wasted. Sensitive networks require careful analysis. The bottom line is that compression of projects with several near-critical paths reduces scheduling flexibility and increases the risk of delaying the project. The outcome of such analysis will probably suggest only a partial movement from the normal time toward the optimum time.

There is a positive situation where moving toward the optimum time can result in very real, large savings—this occurs when the network is *insensitive*. A project network is insensitive if it has a dominate critical path, that is, no near-critical paths. In this project circumstance, movement from the normal time point toward the optimum time will *not* create new or near-critical activities. The bottom line here is that the reduction of the slack of noncritical activities increases the risk of their becoming critical only slightly when compared with the effect in a sensitive network. Insensitive networks hold the greatest potential for real, sometimes large, savings in total project costs with a minimum risk of noncritical activities becoming critical.

Insensitive networks are not a rarity in practice; they occur in perhaps 25 percent of all projects. For example, a light rail project team observed from their network a dominant critical path and relatively high indirect costs. It soon became clear that by spending some dollars on a few critical activities, very large savings of indirect costs could be realized. Savings of several million dollars were spent extending the rail line and adding another station. The logic found in this example is just as applicable to small projects as large ones. Insensitive networks with high indirect costs can produce large savings.

Using the Project Cost-Time Graph

This graph, as presented in Figure 6–1, is valuable to compare any proposed alternative or change with the optimum cost and time. More importantly, the creation of such a graph keeps the importance of indirect costs in the forefront of decision making. Indirect costs are frequently forgotten in the field when the pressure for action is intense. Finally, such a graph can be used before the project begins or while the project is in progress. Creating the graph in the pre-project planning phase without an imposed duration is the first choice because normal time is more meaningful. Creating the graph in the project planning phase with an imposed duration is the second choice because normal time is made to fit the imposed date and is probably not low cost. Creating the graph after the project has started is the last choice because some alternatives may be ruled out of the decision process. Managers may choose not to use the formal procedure demonstrated. However, regardless of the method used, the principles and concepts inherent in the formal procedure are highly applicable in practice and should be considered in any cost-time trade-off decision.

SUMMARY

The need for shortening the project duration occurs for many reasons such as imposed duration dates, time-to-market considerations, incentive contracts, key resource needs, high overhead costs, or simply unforeseen delays. These situations are very common in practice and are known as cost-time trade-off decisions. This chapter presented a logical, formal process for assessing the implications of situations that involve shortening the project duration. Reducing the project duration increases the *risk* of being late. How far to reduce the project duration from the normal time toward the optimum depends on the *sensitivity* of the project network. A sensitive network is one that has several critical or near-critical paths. Great care should be taken when shortening sensitive networks to avoid increasing project risks. Conversely, insensitive networks represent opportunities for potentially large project cost savings by eliminating some overhead costs with little downside risk.

REVIEW QUESTIONS

1. Identify five indirect costs you might find on a moderately complex project. Why are these costs classified as indirect?
2. How can a cost-time graph be used by the project manager? Explain.
3. When compressing project durations, you should avoid providing across-the-board funds. Why?
4. Reducing the project duration increases the risk of being late. Explain.
5. It is possible to shorten the critical path and save money. Explain how.
6. Why are indirect costs significant in analysis of potential project alternatives?
7. Sensitive and insensitive networks should be viewed differently when considering compressing a project. Explain in detail the risks involved in crashing each type of project network.

EXERCISES

Note: Use the procedure presented in the chapter example to compute exercises; that is, compress *one* time unit per move using the least-cost method.

1. Assume the network and data that follow. Compute the total direct cost for each project duration. If the indirect costs for each project duration are $400 (18 time units), $350 (17), $300 (16), $250 (15), $200 (14), and $150 (13), compute the total project cost for each duration. Plot the total direct, indirect, and project costs for each of these durations on a cost-time graph. What duration represents the lowest total project cost? What is this cost?

Activity ID	Slope	Maximum crash time	Direct costs			
			Normal		Crash	
			Time	Cost	Time	Cost
A	____	____	2	$ 50	1	$ 70
B	____	____	4	80	2	160
C	____	____	8	70	4	110
D	____	____	6	60	5	80
E	____	____	7	100	6	130
F	____	____	4	40	3	100
G	____	____	5	100	4	150

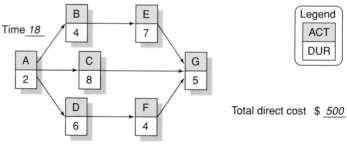

Time 18

Legend

| ACT |
| DUR |

Total direct cost $ 500

2. Given the data and information that follow, compute the slope and maximum reduction time for each activity and the total direct costs for durations 32, 31, 30, 29, 28, and 27 time units. Assume indirect costs of $170, $150, $129, $122, $118, and $110, respectively, for each listed duration. What are the optimum project duration and cost?

Activity ID	Slope	Maximum crash time	Direct costs			
			Normal		Crash	
			Time	Cost	Time	Cost
A	____	____	7	$50	5	$70
B	____	____	16	14	15	20
C	____	____	12	4	10	12
D	____	____	8	21	7	30
E	____	____	6	10	3	19
F	____	____	13	22	12	30
				$121		

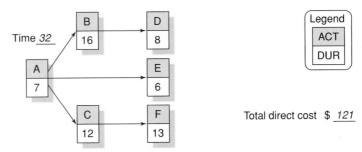

Total direct cost $ _121_

3. Assume the network and data that follow. Compute the total direct cost for each project duration. If the indirect costs for each project duration are $150 (17 time units), $140 (16), $130 (15), $120 (14), $110 (13), and $100 (12), compute the total project cost for each duration. What duration represents the lowest total project cost? What is this cost?

Activity ID	Slope	Maximum crash time	Direct costs			
			Normal		Crash	
			Time	Cost	Time	Cost
A	____	____	4	$10	3	$20
B	____	____	5	30	3	50
C	____	____	7	10	5	30
D	____	____	6	20	4	50
E	____	____	4	30	3	45
F	____	____	5	20	4	50
G	____	____	6	50	4	60

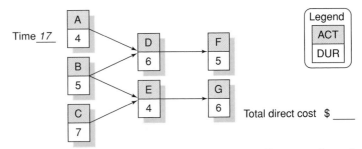

Total direct cost $ ____

4. Assume the network and data that follow. Compute the total direct cost for each project duration. If the indirect costs for each project duration are $300 (20 time units), $250 (19), $200 (18), $150 (17), $100 (16), and $50 (15), compute the total project cost for each duration.

What duration represents the lowest total project cost? What is this cost? Create a cost-time graph for the project owner that shows direct, indirect, and total costs for the project.

Activity ID	Slope	Maximum crash time	Direct costs			
			Normal		Crash	
			Time	Cost	Time	Cost
A	___	___	4	$ 50	4	$ 50
B	___	___	3	80	2	120
C	___	___	5	60	3	180
D	___	___	7	20	4	200
E	___	___	6	40	4	200
F	___	___	5	100	3	160
G	___	___	6	20	5	170

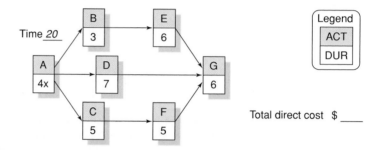

5. Assume the network and data that follow. Compute the total direct cost for each project duration. If the indirect costs for each project duration are $450 (21 time units), $400 (20), $350 (19), 300 (18), $250 (17), and $200 (16), compute the total project cost for each project duration. What duration represents the lowest total project cost? What is this cost?

Activity ID	Slope	Maximum crash time	Direct costs			
			Normal		Crash	
			Time	Cost	Time	Cost
A	___	___	5	$ 90	4	$120
B	___	___	9	100	5	140
C	___	___	8	80	7	120
D	___	___	7	60	6	80
E	___	___	4	70	2	190
F	___	___	6	50	4	190
G	___	___	3	200	2	280

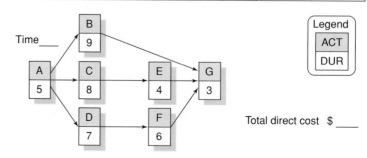

ENDNOTES

1. Jerry B. Baxter, "Responding to the Northridge Earthquake," *PM Network* (November 1994), pp. 13–22.
2. Frederick P. Brooks, Jr., *The Mythical Man-Month: Essays on Software Engineering Anniversary Edition* (Reading, MA: Addison-Wesley Longman, Inc., 1994), pp. 15–26.
3. T. Abdel-Hamid and S. Madnick, *Software Project Dynamics: An Integrated Approach* (Englewood Cliffs, NJ: Prentice Hall, 1991).
4. V. H. Vroom, *Work and Motivation* (New York: John Wiley & Sons, 1964).

CASE

International Capital, Inc.—Part B

Given the project network derived in Part A of the case from Chapter 5, Brown also wants to be prepared to answer any questions concerning compressing the project duration. This question will almost always be entertained by the accounting department, review committee, and the client. To be prepared for the compression question, Brown has prepared the following data in case it is necessary to crash the project. (Use your weighted average times (t_e) computed in Part A of the International Capital case found in Chapter 5.)

Activity	Normal cost	Maximum crash time	Crash cost/day
A	$ 3,000	3	$ 500
B	5,000	2	1,000
C	6,000	0	—
D	20,000	3	3,000
E	10,000	2	1,000
F	7,000	1	1,000
G	20,000	2	3,000
H	8,000	1	2,000
I	5,000	1	2,000
J	7,000	1	1,000
K	12,000	6	1,000

Total normal costs = $103,000

Using the data provided, determine the activity crashing decisions and best time cost project duration. Given the information you have developed, what suggestions would you give Brown to ensure she is well prepared for the project review committee? Assume the overhead costs for this project are $700 per workday. Will this alter your suggestions?

CASE

Whitbread World Sailboat Race

Each year countries enter their sailing vessel in the 9-month Round the World Whitbread Sailboat Race. In recent years, about 14 countries entered sailboats in the race.

Each year's sailboat entries represent the latest technologies and human skills each country can muster.

Bjorn Ericksen has been selected as a project manager because of his past experience as a master helmsman and because of his recent fame as the "best designer of racing sailboats in the world." Bjorn is pleased and proud to have the opportunity to design, build, test, and train the crew for next year's Whitbread entry for his country. Bjorn has picked Karin Knutsen (as chief design engineer) and Trygve Wallvik (as master helmsman) to be team leaders responsible for getting next year's entry ready for the traditional parade of all entries on the Thames River in the United Kingdom, which signals the start of the race.

As Bjorn begins to think of a project plan, he sees two parallel paths running through the project—design and construction and crew training. Last year's boat will be used for training until the new entry can have the crew on board to learn maintenance tasks. Bjorn calls Karin and Trygve together to develop a project plan. All three agree the major goal is to have a winning boat and crew ready to compete in next year's competition at a cost of $3.2 million. A check of Bjorn's calendar indicates he has 45 weeks before next year's vessel must leave port for the United Kingdom to start the race.

The Kickoff Meeting

Bjorn asks Karin to begin by describing the major activities and the sequence required to design, construct, and test the boat. Karin starts by noting that design of the hull, deck, mast, and accessories should only take 6 weeks—given the design prints from past race entries and a few prints from other countries' entries. After the design is complete, the hull can be constructed, the mast ordered, sails ordered, and accessories ordered. The hull will require 12 weeks to complete. The mast can be ordered and will require a lead time of 8 weeks; the 7 sails can be ordered and will take 6 weeks to get; accessories can be ordered and will take 15 weeks to receive. As soon as the hull is finished, the ballast tanks can be installed, requiring 2 weeks. Then the deck can be built, which will require 5 weeks. Concurrently, the hull can be treated with special sealant and friction resistance coating, taking 3 weeks. When the deck is completed and mast and accessories received, the mast and sails can be installed, requiring 2 weeks; the accessories can be installed, which will take 6 weeks. When all of these activities have been completed, the ship can be sea tested, which should take 5 weeks. Karin believes she can have firm cost estimates for the boat in about 2 weeks.

Trygve believes he can start selecting the 12-man or woman crew and securing their housing immediately. He believes it will take 6 weeks to get a committed crew on site and 3 weeks to secure housing for the crew members. Trygve reminds Bjorn that last year's vessel must be ready to use for training the moment the crew is on site until the new vessel is ready for testing. Keeping the old vessel operating will cost $4,000 per week as long as it is used. Once the crew is on site and housed, they can develop and implement a routine sailing and maintenance training program, which will take 15 weeks (using the old vessel). Also, once the crew is selected and on site, crew equipment can be selected, taking only 2 weeks. Then crew equipment can be ordered; it will take 5 weeks to arrive. When the crew equipment and maintenance training program are complete, crew maintenance on the new vessel can begin; this should take 10 weeks. But crew maintenance on the new vessel cannot begin until the deck is complete and the mast, sails, and accessories have arrived. Once crew maintenance on the new vessel begins, the new vessel will cost $6,000 per week until sea training is complete. After the new ship maintenance is complete and while the boat is being tested, initial sailing training can be implemented; training should take 7 weeks. Finally, after the boat is tested and initial training is complete, regular sea training can be implemented—weather permitting; regular sea training requires 8 weeks. Trygve believes he can put the cost estimates together in a week, given last year's expenses.

Bjorn is pleased with the expertise displayed by his team leaders. But he believes they need to have someone develop one of those critical path networks to see if they can safely meet the start deadline for the race. Karin and Trygve agree. Karin suggests the cost estimates should also include crash costs for any activities that can be compressed and the resultant costs for crashing. Karin also suggests the team complete the following priority matrix for project decision making:

FIGURE C6-1 Project Priority Matrix: Whitbread Project

	Time	Performance	Cost
Constrain			
Enhance			
Accept			

Two Weeks Later

Karin and Trygve submit the following cost estimates for each activity and corresponding crash costs to Bjorn (costs are in thousands of dollars):

Activity	Normal time	Normal cost	Crash time	Crash cost
A Design	6	$ 40	4	$ 160
B Build hull	12	1,000	10	1,400
C Install ballast tanks	2	100	2	100
D Order mast	8	100	7	140
E Order sails	6	40	6	40
F Order accessories	15	600	13	800
G Build deck	5	200	5	200
H Coat hull	3	40	3	40
I Install accessories	6	300	5	400
J Install mast and sails	2	40	1	80
K Test	5	60	4	100
L Sea trials	8	200	7	450
M Select crew	6	10	5	20

Activity	Normal time	Normal cost	Crash time	Crash cost
N Secure housing	3	30	3	30
O Select crew equipment	2	10	2	10
P Order crew equipment	5	30	5	30
Q Routine sail and maintenance	15	40	12	130
R Crew maintenance training	10	100	9	340
S Initial sail training	7	50	5	350

Bjorn reviews the materials and wonders if the project will come in within the budget of $3.2 million and in 45 weeks. Advise the Whitbread team of their situation.

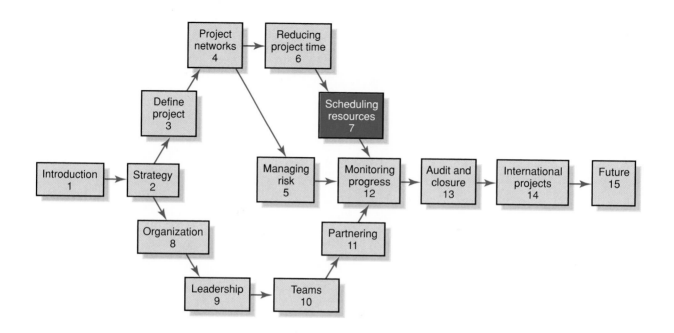

			Scheduling Resources		

Scheduling Resources

The Problem
Types of Project Constraints
Kinds of Resource Constraints
Classification of a Scheduling Problem
Resource Allocation Methods
Splitting/Multitasking
The Critical Chain Approach
Benefits of Scheduling Resources
Assigning Project Work
Multiproject Resource Schedules
Summary
Appendix 7–1: Computer Project Exercise, Part 3

CHAPTER SEVEN

Scheduling Resources

Project network times are not a schedule until resource availability has been assured.

There are always more project proposals than there are available resources. The priority system needs to select projects that best contribute to the organization's objectives, within the constraints of the resources available. If all projects and their respective resources are computer scheduled, the feasibility and impact of adding a new project to those in process can be quickly assessed. With this information the project priority team will add a new project only if resources are available and formally committed to that specific project. This chapter examines methods of scheduling resources so the team can make realistic judgments of resource availability and project durations. The project manager uses the same schedule for implementing the project. If changes occur during project implementation, the computer schedule is easily updated and the effects easily assessed.

THE PROBLEM

One frustrated project director listed the following questions he needed to be able to answer at any point in time:

> If another project is added to our ongoing and planned projects, which, if any, projects will be delayed?
>
> Is an imposed date realistic?
>
> Which resources have priority?
>
> Will existing labor and/or equipment be adequate and available to deal with a new project?
>
> Where is the critical path? Do unforeseen dependencies exist?
>
> If slack is used up, what happens to the risk of being late?
>
> Will outside contractors have to be used?

Clearly, this project director has a good understanding of the problems he is facing. Any project scheduling system should facilitate finding quick, easy answers to these questions.

The planned network and activity project duration times found in previous chapters fail to deal with resource usage and availability. The time estimates for the work packages and network times were made independently with the implicit assumption that resources would be available. This may or may not be the case. If resources are adequate but the demand varies widely over the life of the project, it may be desirable to even out resource demand by delaying noncritical activities (using slack) to lower peak demand and, thus, increase resource utilization. This process is called *resource leveling*. On the other hand, if resources are not adequate to meet peak demands, the late start of some activities must be delayed, and the duration of the project may be increased. This process is called *resource-constrained scheduling*. One research study of more than 50 projects reports that planned project network durations were increased 38 percent when resources were scheduled.[1]

Because the costs of failing to consider resource usage and availability are hidden or not obvious, resource scheduling in practice is often not done or does not get the attention it deserves. The consequences of failing to schedule limited resources are costly activity and project delays that usually manifest themselves midway in the project when quick corrective action is difficult. An additional consequence of failing to schedule resources is the failure to reduce the peaks and valleys of resource usage over the duration of the project. Because project resources are usually overcommitted and because resources seldom line up by availability and need, procedures are needed to deal with these problems. This chapter addresses methods available to project managers for dealing with resource utilization and availability through resource leveling and resource-constrained scheduling.

TYPES OF PROJECT CONSTRAINTS

Project constraints impede or delay the start of activities. The result is a reduction in slack shown on the planned network, a decrease in scheduling flexibility, a possible decrease in the number of parallel activities, and an increase in the likelihood of delaying the project. Three project constraints need to be considered in scheduling.

Technical or Logic Constraints

These constraints usually address the *sequence* in which project activities must occur. The project network depicts technical constraints. A project network for framing a house might show three activities of (1) pour foundation, (2) build frame, and (3) cover roof in a sequence. A network for a new software project could place the activities of (1) design, (2) code, and (3) test in the network as a sequence. In other words, you cannot logically perform activity 2 until 1 is completed, etc. (see Figure 7–1A).

Resource Constraints

The absence or shortage of resources can drastically alter technical constraints. A project network planner may assume adequate resources and show activities occurring in parallel. However, parallel activities hold potential for resource conflicts. For example, assume you are planning a wedding reception that includes four activities—(1) plan, (2) hire band, (3) decorate hall, and (4) purchase refreshments. Each activity takes one day. Activities 2, 3, and 4 could be done in parallel by different people. There is no technical reason or dependency of one on another (see Figure 7–1B). However, if one person must perform all activities, the resource constraint requires the activities be performed in sequence or series. Clearly the consequence is a delay of these activities and a very different set of network relationships (see Figure 7–1C). Note that the resource dependency takes priority over the technological dependency but *does not vio-*

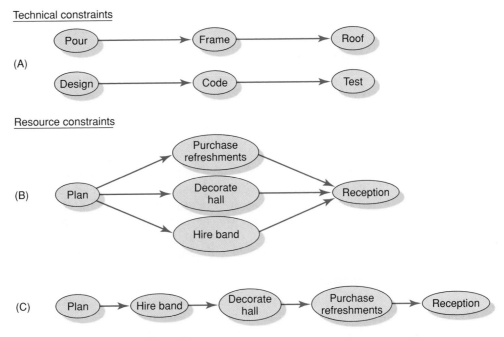

FIGURE 7–1 Constraint Examples

late the technological dependency; that is, hire, decorate, and purchase may now have to take place in sequence rather than concurrently, but they must all be completed before the reception can take place.

Physical Constraints

In rare situations there are physical constraints that cause activities that would normally occur in parallel to be constrained by contractual or environmental conditions. For example, renovation of a ship compartment might allow only one person to perform an activity because of space limitations. The procedures for handling physical constraints are similar to those used for resource constraints.

The interrelationships and interactions among time and resource constraints are complex for even small project networks. Some effort to examine these interactions before the project begins frequently uncovers surprising problems. Project managers who do not consider resource availability in moderately complex projects usually learn of the problem when it is too late to correct. A deficit of resources can significantly alter project dependency relationships, completion dates, and project costs. Project managers must be careful to schedule resources to ensure availability in the right quantities and at the right time. Fortunately there are computer software programs that can identify resource problems during the early project planning phase when corrective changes can be considered. These programs only require activity resource needs and availability information to schedule resources.

KINDS OF RESOURCE CONSTRAINTS

People

This is the most obvious project resource. Human resources are usually classified by the skills they bring to the project—for example, programmer, mechanical engineer, welder, inspector, marketing director, supervisor. In rare cases some skills are interchangeable, but usually with a loss of productivity. The many differing skills of human resources add to the complexity of scheduling projects.

Materials

Material shortages have been blamed for the delay of many projects. When it is known that a lack of availability of materials is important and probable, materials should be included in the project network plan and schedule. For example, delivery and placement of an oil rig tower in a Siberian oil field has a very small time window during one summer month. Any delivery delay means a one-year, costly delay. Another example in which material was the major resource scheduled was the resurfacing and replacement of some structures on the Golden Gate Bridge in San Francisco. Work on the project was limited to the hours between midnight and 5:00 A.M. with a penalty of $1,000 per minute for any work taking place after 5:00 A.M. Scheduling the arrival of replacement structures was an extremely important part of managing the five-hour work-time window of the project. Scheduling materials has also become important in developing products where time-to-market can result in loss of market share.

Equipment

Equipment is usually presented by type, size, and quantity. In some cases equipment can be interchanged to improve schedules, but this is not typical. Equipment is often overlooked as a constraint. The most common oversight is to assume the resource pool is more than adequate for the project. For example, if a project needs one earth-moving tractor six months from now and the organization owns four, it is common to assume the resource will not delay the pending project. However, when the earth-moving tractor is due on site in six months, all four machines in the pool might be occupied on other projects. In multiproject environments it is prudent to use a common resource pool for all projects. This approach forces a check of resource availability across all projects and reserves the equipment for specific project needs in the future. Recognition of equipment constraints before the project begins can avoid high crashing or delay costs.

Working Capital

In a few project situations such as construction, working capital is treated as a resource because it is limited in supply. If working capital is readily available, a project manager may work on many activities concurrently. If working capital is in short supply because progress payments are made monthly, materials and labor usage may have to be restricted to conserve cash. This situation represents a cash flow problem.

CLASSIFICATION OF A SCHEDULING PROBLEM

Most of the scheduling methods available today require the project manager to classify the project as either *time constrained* or *resource constrained*. Project managers need to consult their priority matrix (see Figure 3–2) to determine which case fits their project. One simple test to determine if the project is time or resource constrained is to ask, "If the critical path is delayed, will resources be added to get back on schedule?" If the answer is yes, assume the project is time constrained; if no, assume the project is resource constrained.

> A time-constrained project is one that must be completed by an imposed date. If required, resources can be added to ensure the project is completed by a specific date. Although time is the critical factor, resource usage should be no more than is necessary and sufficient.

A resource-constrained project is one that assumes the level of resource available cannot be exceeded. If the resources are inadequate, it will be acceptable to delay the project, but as little as possible.

In scheduling terms, time constrained means time (project duration) is fixed and resources are flexible, while resource constrained means resources are fixed and time is flexible. Methods for scheduling these projects are presented in the next section.

RESOURCE ALLOCATION METHODS

Assumptions

Ease of demonstrating the allocation methods available requires some limiting assumptions to keep attention on the heart of the problem. The rest of the chapter depends entirely on the assumptions noted here. First, splitting activities will not be allowed. This means once an activity is placed in the schedule, assume it will be worked on continuously until it is finished; hence, an activity cannot be started, stopped for a period of time, and then finished. Second, the level of resource used for an activity cannot be changed. These limiting assumptions do not exist in practice, but simplify learning. It is easy for new project managers to deal with the reality of splitting activities and changing the level of resources when they meet them on the job.

Time-Constrained Projects

Scheduling time-constrained projects focuses on resource *utilization*. When demand for a specific resource type is erratic, it is difficult to manage, and utilization may be very poor. Practitioners have attacked the utilization problem using resource leveling techniques that balance or smooth demand for a resource. Basically, all leveling techniques delay noncritical activities by using slack to reduce peak demand and fill in the valleys for the resources. A hypothetical example will demonstrate the basic procedure.

For the purpose of demonstration, this example uses only one resource class (e.g., carpenters); within the class, all resources are interchangeable. The starting point for leveling resources is the early start (ES) network plan. Figure 7–2 presents the example network, an ES resource loading chart, and a resource profile. The shaded areas in the loading chart represent the scheduling boundaries for each activity. The resource profile follows the typical pattern of growing to a peak and then declining. Note the fluctuations in demand. Because this project is declared time constrained, the goal will be to reduce the peak requirement for the resource and thereby increase the utilization of the resource. A quick examination of the ES resource load chart suggests only two activities have slack that can be used to reduce the peak—activities B and D. Either B or D can be delayed to lower the peak resource of 5 to 4 by using 2 time units of slack. The choice will probably center on the activity that is perceived as having the least risk of being late (probably activity D because it has the most slack). Figure 7–3a shows the results of delaying activity B. Figure 7–3b presents the outcome of delaying activity D. Note the differences in the resource profiles. The important point is the resources needed over the life of the project have been reduced from 5 to 4 (20 percent), and the utilization of the resource has increased from 57 percent [34 total resource units required/(5 × 12)] to 71 percent [34/(4 × 12)]. In addition the profile has been smoothed, which should be easier to manage.

The downside of leveling is a loss of flexibility that occurs from reducing slack. The risk of activities delaying the project also increases because slack reduction can create more critical activities and/or near-critical activities. Pushing leveling too far for a perfectly level resource profile is risky. Every activity then becomes critical.

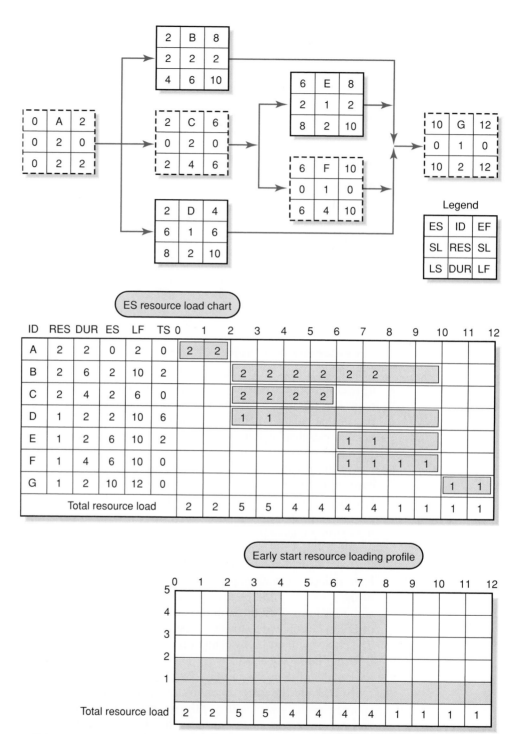

FIGURE 7–2 Time-Constrained Network

This simple, trivial example gives a sense of the time-constrained problem and the leveling approach. However, in practice the magnitude of the problem is very complex for even small projects. Manual solutions are not practical. Fortunately, the software packages available today have very good routines for leveling project resources. Typ-

FIGURE 7-3 Leveled Resource Schedule

Leveled resource schedule A

ID	RES	DUR	ES	LF	TS	0	1	2	3	4	5	6	7	8	9	10	11	12
A	2	2	0	2	0	2	2											
B	2	6	2	10	2			X	X	2	2	2	2	2	2	2		
C	2	4	2	6	0			2	2	2	2							
D	1	2	2	10	6			1	1									
E	1	2	6	10	2								1	1				
F	1	4	6	10	0								1	1	1	1		
G	1	2	10	12	0												1	1
Total resource load						2	2	3	3	4	4	4	4	3	3	3	1	1

(a)

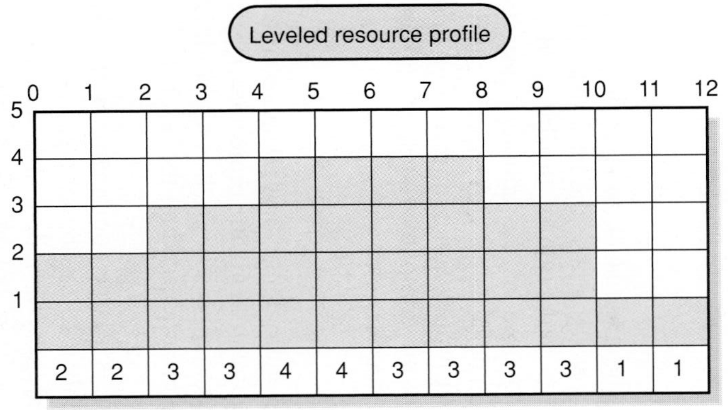

Leveled resource profile

	1	2	3	4	5	6	7	8	9	10	11	12
	2	2	3	3	4	4	3	3	3	3	1	1

Leveled resource schedule B

ID	RES	DUR	ES	LF	TS	0	1	2	3	4	5	6	7	8	9	10	11	12
A	2	2	0	2	0	2	2											
B	2	6	2	10	2			X	X	2	2	2	2	2	2	2		
C	2	4	2	6	0			2	2	2	2	2						
D	1	2	2	10	6			X	X	X	X	X	X	X	1	1		
E	1	2	6	10	2								X	X	1	1		
F	1	4	6	10	0							1	1	1	1	1		
G	1	2	10	12	0												1	1
Total resource load						2	2	4	4	4	4	3	3	3	3	3	1	1

(b)

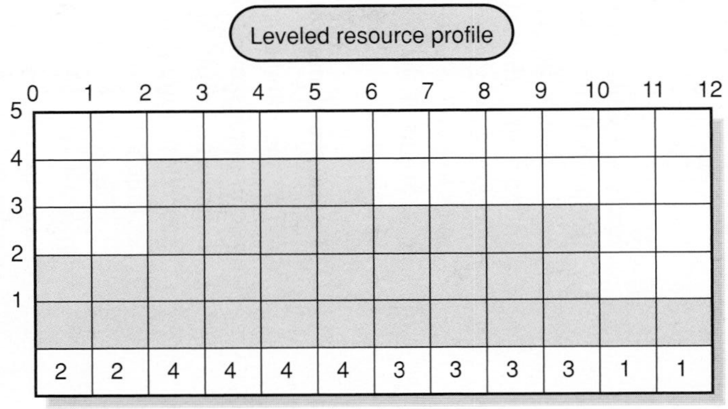

Leveled resource profile

	1	2	3	4	5	6	7	8	9	10	11	12
	2	2	4	4	4	4	3	3	3	3	1	1

ically, they use activities that have the most slack to level project resources. The rationale is those activities with the most slack pose the least risk. Although this is generally true, other risk factors such as reduction of flexibility to use reassigned resources on other activities or the nature of the activity (easy, complex) are not addressed using such a simple rationale. It is easy to experiment with many alternatives to find the one that best fits your project and minimizes risk of delaying the project. Some of the procedures used in the computer routines are found in the original classic studies. (See Endnotes 1, 2, and 3.)

Resource-Constrained Projects

When the number of people and/or equipment is not adequate to meet peak demand requirements and it is impossible to obtain more, the project manager faces a resource-constrained problem. Something has to give. The trick is to prioritize and allocate resources to minimize project delay without exceeding the resource limit or altering the technical network relationships.

The resource scheduling problem is a large combinatorial one. This means even a modest-size project network with only a few resource types might have several thousand feasible solutions. A few researchers have demonstrated *optimum* mathematical solutions to the resource allocation problem but only for small networks and very few resource types.[2] The massive data requirements for larger problems make pure mathematical solutions (e.g., linear programming) impractical. An alternative approach to the problem has been the use of heuristics (rules of thumb) to solve large combinatorial problems. These practical decision or priority rules have been in place for many years. Heuristics do not always yield an optimal schedule, but they are very capable of yielding a "good" schedule for very complex networks with many types of resources. The efficiency of different rules and combinations of rules has been well documented.[3] However, because each project is unique, it is wise to test several sets of heuristics on a network to determine the priority allocation rules that minimize project delay. The computer software available today makes it very easy for the project manager to create a good resource schedule for the project. A simple example of the heuristic approach is illustrated here.

Heuristics allocate resources to activities to minimize project delay; that is, heuristics prioritize which activities are allocated resources and which activities are delayed when resources are not adequate. The following scheduling heuristics have been found to consistently minimize project delay over a large variety of projects.[4] Schedule activities using the following heuristic priority rules in the order presented:

1. Minimum slack.
2. Smallest duration.
3. Lowest activity identification number.

The parallel method is the most widely used approach to apply heuristics. The parallel method is an iterative process that starts at the first time period of the project and schedules period-by-period any activities eligible to start. In any period when two or more activities require the same resource, the priority rules are applied. For example, if in period 5 three activities are eligible to start (i.e., have the same ES) and require the same resource, the first activity placed in the schedule would be the activity with the least slack (rule 1). However, if all activities have the same slack, the next rule would be invoked (rule 2), and the activity with the smallest duration would be placed in the schedule first. In very rare cases, when all eligible activities have the same slack and the same duration, the tie is broken by the lowest activity identification number (rule 3), since each activity has a unique ID number. When a resource limit has been reached, the early start (ES) for succeeding activities not yet in the schedule will be delayed (and all successor activities not having free slack) and their slack reduced. In subsequent periods the procedure is repeated until the project is scheduled. The procedure can be applied to the earlier time-constrained project example (see Figures 7–3A and B), *except now the resource pool is limited to three.* Follow the actions described in Figures 7–4 and 7–5. Refer to Figure 7–4 now.

Period	Action
0–1	Only activity A is eligible. It requires 2 resources. Load activity A into schedule.
1–2	No activities are eligible to be scheduled.
2–3	Activities B, C, and D are eligible to be scheduled. Activity C has the least slack (0)—apply rule 1. Load Activity C into schedule. Activity B is next with slack of 2; however, activity B requires 2 resources and only 1 is available. Delay activity B. Update ES = 3, slack = 1. The next eligible activity is activity D, since it only requires 1 resource. Load activity D into schedule.

————————————————— See Figure 7–5 —————————————————

Period	Action
3–4	Activity B is eligible but exceeds limit of 3 resources in pool. Delay activity B. Update ES = 4, slack = 0.
4–5	Activity B is eligible but exceeds limit of 3 resources in pool. Delay activity B. Update ES = 5, slack = –1. Delay activity G. Update ES = 11, slack = –1.
5–6	Activity B is eligible but exceeds limit of 3 resources in pool. Delay activity B. Update ES = 6, slack = –2. Delay activity G. Update ES = 12, slack = –2.
6–7	Activities B, E, and F are eligible with slack of –2, 2, and 0, respectively. Load activity B into schedule (rule 1). Because activity F has 0 slack, it is the next eligible activity. Load activity F into schedule (rule 1). The resource limit of 3 is reached. Delay activity E. Update ES = 7, slack = 1.
7–8	Limit is reached. No resources available. Delay activity E. Update ES = 8, slack = 0.
8–9	Limit is reached. No resources available. Delay activity E. Update ES = 9, slack = –1.
9–10	Limit is reached. No resources available. Delay activity E. Update ES = 10 slack = –2.
10–11	Activity E is eligible. Load activity E into schedule. (Note: Activity F does not have slack because there are no resources available—3 maximum.)
11–12	No eligible activities.
12–13	Activity G is eligible. Load activity G into schedule.

Observe how it is necessary to update each period to reflect changes in activity early start and slack times so the heuristics can reflect changing priorities. The

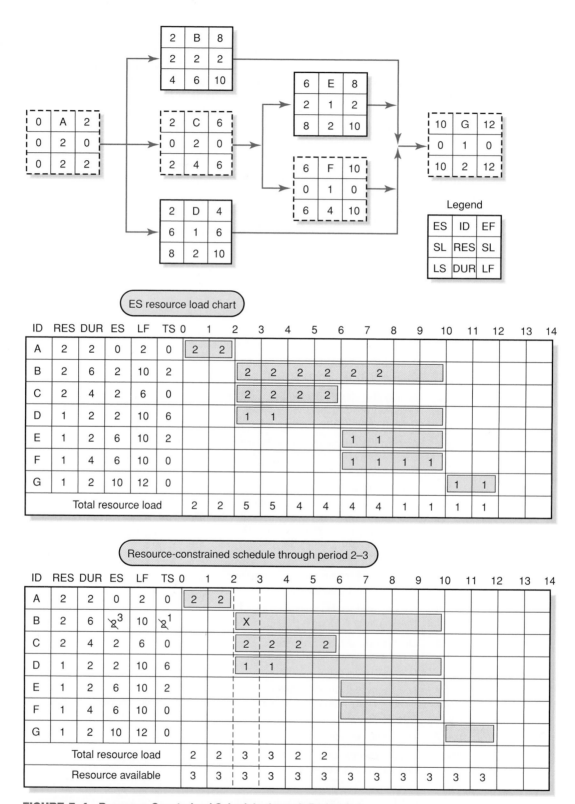

FIGURE 7–4 Resource-Constrained Schedule through Period 2–3

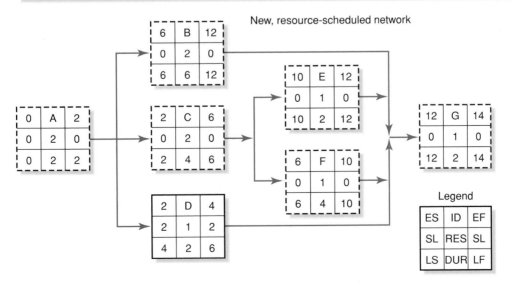

FIGURE 7–5 Resource-Constrained Schedule through Period 5–6

network in Figure 7–5 on the preceding page reflects the new schedule date of 14 time units, rather than the time-constrained project duration of 12 time units. The network has also been revised to reflect new start, finish, and slack times for each activity. Note that activity F is still critical and has a slack of 0 time units because no resources are available (they are being used on activities B and E). Compare the slack for each activity found in Figures 7–4 and 7–5; slack has been reduced significantly. Note that activity D has only 2 units of slack rather than what appears to be 6 slack units. This occurs because only three resources are available, and they are needed to satisfy the resource requirements of activities B and E. Note that even though the project duration has increased from 12 to 14 time units, the number of critical activities (A, B, C, E, F, G) has increased from four to six.

Figure 7–6 illustrates another project network that utilizes three different types of resources (A, B, and C); each type has two resources in its pool. The network shows the original critical path with a dashed line. The resource constrained set of critical activities has heavy, thick lines around the activity box. Below the network is the resource loading chart. The time ("plan") and resource schedules are shown at the bottom of Figure 7–6. The time limited critical path is 3, 5, 8, and 11, and the project duration is 17 time units. The resource limited critical set of activities is 1, 4, 5, 7, 8, and 10 with a project duration of 20 time units. Note activities 3 and 11 are no longer critical and have slack time. Activities 4, 5, 7, and 8 are no longer in parallel, but are now sequential. Slack has decreased. Resources A, B, and C are each critical at some point in the project. Although the examples in Figures 7–5 and 7–6 are hypothetical, the conditions illustrated occur frequently in practice.

The Impacts of Resource-Constrained Scheduling

Like leveling schedules, the limited resource schedule usually reduces slack, reduces flexibility by using slack to ensure delay is minimized, and increases the number of critical and near-critical activities. Scheduling complexity is increased because resource constraints are added to technical constraints; start times may now have two constraints. The traditional critical path concept of sequential activities from the start to the end of the project is no longer meaningful. The resource constraints can break the sequence and leave the network with a set of disjointed critical activities. Conversely, parallel activities can become sequential. Activities with slack on a time-constrained network can change from critical to noncritical, while some identified as critical activities can become noncritical with slack.

SPLITTING/MULTITASKING

Splitting or multitasking is a scheduling technique used to get a better project schedule and/or to increase resource utilization. A planner splits the continuous work included in an activity by interrupting the work and sending the resource to another activity for a period of time and then having the resource resume work on the original activity. Splitting can be a useful tool if the work involved does not include large startup or shutdown costs—for example, moving equipment from one activity location to another. The most common error is to interrupt "people work," where there are high conceptual startup and shutdown costs. For example, having a bridge designer take time off to work on the design problem of another project may cause this individual to lose four days shifting conceptual gears in and out of two activities. The cost may be hidden, but it is real. Figure 7–7 depicts the nature of the splitting problem. The original activity has been split into three separate activities: A, B, and C. The shut-

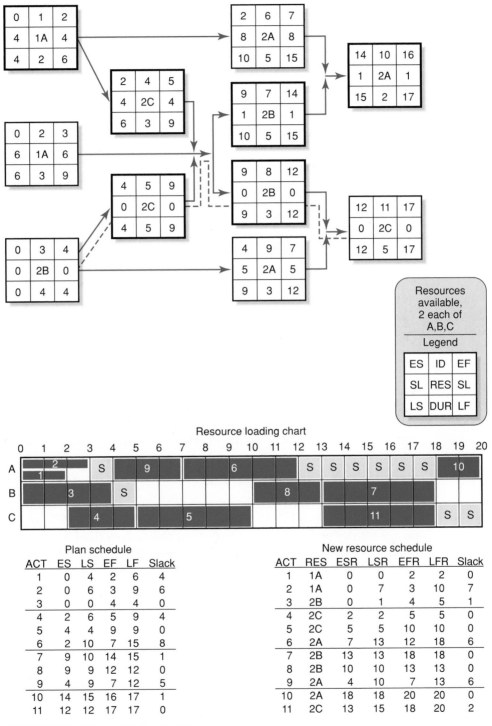

FIGURE 7–6 Original Network Plan

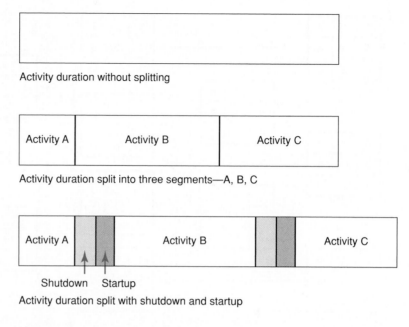

Activity duration without splitting

Activity duration split into three segments—A, B, C

Shutdown   Startup
Activity duration split with shutdown and startup

FIGURE 7–7   Splitting/Multitasking

down and startup times lengthen the time for the original activity. Planners should avoid the use of splitting as much as possible, except in situations where splitting costs are known to be small or when there is no alternative for resolving the resource problem. Computer software offers the splitting option for each activity; use it sparingly.

THE CRITICAL CHAIN APPROACH

In practice project managers carefully manage slack on sensitive resource-constrained projects. For example, some managers use an early start schedule and prohibit slack on any activity or work package to be used unless authorized by the project manager. Progress by percent complete and by remaining time is carefully monitored and reported to catch any activities that beat estimated completion times so that succeeding activities can start ahead of schedule—on critical and noncritical activities. Monitoring and encouraging of early completion of estimated times ensure that the time gained is used to start a succeeding activity earlier and time is not wasted. The intent is to save the slack as a time buffer to complete the project early or to cover delay problems that may creep up on critical activities or paths.

Eliyahu Goldratt advocates an alternative approach to managing slack.[5] Goldratt argues that there is a natural tendency for people to add safety (just-in-case) time to their estimations. It is believed that those who estimate activity times provide an estimate that has about an 80 to 90 percent chance of being completed on or before the estimated time. Hence, the median time (50/50 chance) is overestimated by approximately 30 to 40 percent. For example, a programmer may estimate that there is a 50/50 chance that he can complete an activity in five days. However, to ensure success and to protect against potential problems, he adds two days of safety time and reports that it will take seven days to complete the task. In this case the median (50/50) time is overestimated by approximately 40 percent. If this hidden contingency is pervasive across a project, then most activities in theory should be completed ahead of schedule. Remember, the programmer still has a 50/50 chance of completing the assignment within five days or less.

This situation raises an interesting paradox. Why, if there is a tendency to overestimate activity durations, do so many projects come in behind schedule? Goldratt offers several explanations. First, work fills the time available. Why hustle to complete a task today when it isn't due until tomorrow? Second, there may be disincentives within the organization for reporting early finishes: The quality of the work may come into question, or workers will be expected to always come in under the estimated time. Third, early finishes may not lead to the start of the next activity because people assigned to perform the next activity are not ready to start work early. Time gained is wasted. Finally, excessive multitasking will add time to the completion of individual tasks.

Goldratt's solution to reducing project time overruns is to insist on people using the "true 50/50" activity time estimates (rather than estimates that have an 80 to 90 percent chance of being completed before the the estimated time); the 50/50 estimates result in a project duration about one-half the low risk 80 to 90 percent estimates. He then suggests inserting "time buffers" or safety time only where potential problems can occur. Time buffers are inserted in the network to cover three conditions:

1. Because all activities have inherent *uncertainty* that is difficult to predict, project duration is uncertain. Therefore, a project time buffer is added to the expected project duration—say, 40 percent of the aggregate of the hidden contingencies of activity durations on the critical path.
2. *Merge* time (feeder) buffers are added to the network where noncritical paths merge with the critical path. These buffers serve to protect the critical path from being delayed.
3. A *resource* time buffer (flag) is inserted where a scarce resource is needed for an activity. The nonavailability of a resource can create a resource critical path that may be very different from the original critical path and may cause a delay of the project.

Recall that the resource path can appear to jump randomly over the network because it sequentially follows the activities that employ the resource; however, the technical dependencies must still remain intact. Eliyahu Goldratt has coined the phrase "critical chain" (C-C) to recognize that the project network may be constrained by both resource and technical dependencies. All of these buffers reduce the risk of the project duration being late and increase the chance of early project completion.

Support to date for the C-C method of planning projects is limited, but promising. For example, Harris Semiconductor was able to build a new automated wafer fabrication facility within 13 months using C-C methods when the industry standard for such a facility is 26 to 36 months. The Israeli aircraft industry has used C-C techniques to reduce average maintenance work on aircraft from two months to two weeks.[6] Successful implementation requires that project participants reduce their time estimates to eliminate "just-in-case" time and use "true 50/50" time. This means that management must feel comfortable accepting that roughly half the activities of a project will take longer than estimated. The C-C approach depends heavily on close, frequent monitoring of critical chain progress by percent complete and remaining time so that time is not wasted between succeeding activities. Buffers must be carefully managed and multitasking of people reduced as much as possible.

Snapshot from Practice

UNITED STATES FOREST SERVICE RESOURCE SHORTAGE

A major segment of work in managing U.S. Forest Service (USFS) forests is selling mature timber to logging companies that harvest the timber under contract conditions monitored by the Service. The proceeds are returned to the federal government. The budget allocated to each forest depends on the two-year plan submitted to the U.S. Department of Agriculture.

Olympic Forest headquarters in Olympia, Washington, was developing a two-year plan as a basis for funding. All of the districts in the forest submitted their timber sale projects (numbering more than 50) to headquarters, where they were compiled and aggregated into a project plan for the whole forest. The first computer run was reviewed by a small group of senior managers to determine if the plan was reasonable and "doable." Management was pleased and relieved to note all projects appeared to be doable in the two-year time frame until a question was raised concerning the computer printout. "Why are all the columns in these projects labeled 'RESOURCE' blank?" The response from an engineer was, "We don't use that part of the program."

The discussion that ensued recognized the importance of resources in completing the two-year plan and ended with a request to "try the program with resources included." The new output was startling. The two-year program turned into a three-and-a-half-year plan because of the shortage of specific labor skills such as road engineer and environmental impact specialist. Analysis showed that adding only three skilled people would allow the two-year plan to be completed on time. In addition, further analysis showed hiring only a few more skilled people, beyond the three, would allow an extra year of projects to also be compressed into the two-year plan. This would result in additional revenue of more than $3 million. The Department of Agriculture quickly approved the requested extra dollars for additional staff to generate the extra revenue.

BENEFITS OF SCHEDULING RESOURCES

It is important to remember that, if resources are truly limited and activity time estimates are accurate, the resource-constrained schedule *will* materialize as the project is implemented—*not* the time-constrained schedule! Therefore, failure to schedule limited resources can lead to serious problems for a project manager. The benefit of creating this schedule *before* the project begins leaves time for considering reasonable alternatives. If the scheduled delay is unacceptable or the risk of being delayed too high, the assumption of being resource constrained can be reassessed. Cost-time trade-offs can be considered. In some cases priorities may be changed.

Resource schedules provide the information needed to prepare time-phased work package budgets with dates. Once established, they provide a quick means for a project manager to gauge the impact of unforeseen events such as turnover, equipment breakdowns, or transfer of project personnel. Resource schedules also allow project managers to assess how much flexibility they have over certain resources. This is useful when they receive requests from other managers to borrow or share resources. Honoring such requests creates goodwill and an "IOU" that can be cashed in during a time of need.

ASSIGNING PROJECT WORK

So far the discussion of resources has been directed at analyzing how resource availability affects the project plan and schedule. Once these issues have been resolved and the project manager has a pretty firm idea of the personnel available to complete the project, the project manager needs to finalize the assignment of specific project responsibilities. One very useful tool for doing so is the responsibility matrix (RM). This tool was briefly mentioned in Chapter 3 and deserves more attention.

The RM (sometimes called a linear responsibility chart) summarizes who is responsible for what on a project. In its simplest form an RM would consist of a chart listing all the project activities and the participants responsible for each activity. For example, Figure 7–8 illustrates an RM for a market research study. In this matrix "R" is used to identify the committee member who is responsible for coordinating the efforts of other team members assigned to the task and making sure that the task is

FIGURE 7–8   Responsibility Matrix for a Market Research Project

> R = Responsible
> S = Supports/assists

Project team

Task	Richard	Dan	Dave	Linda	Elizabeth
Identify target customers	R	S		S	
Develop draft questionnaire	R	S	S		
Pilot-test questionnaire		R		S	
Finalize questionnaire	R	S	S	S	
Print questionnaire					R
Prepare mailing labels					R
Mail questionnaires					R
Receive and monitor returned questionnaires				R	S
Input response data			R		
Analyze results		R	S	S	
Prepare draft of report	S	R	S	S	
Prepare final report	R		S		

completed. The "S" is used to identify members of the five-person team who will support and/or assist the individual responsible. Simple RMs like this one are particularly useful for organizing and assigning responsibilities for small projects or subprojects of larger, more complex projects.

More complex RMs not only identify individual responsibilities but also clarify critical interfaces between units and individuals that require coordination. For example, Figure 7–9 is an RM for a larger, more complex project involving developing a new piece of test equipment. Note that within each cell a numeric coding scheme is used to define the nature of involvement on that specific task. Such an RM extends the WBS/OBS found in Chapter 3 and provides a clear and concise method for depicting responsibility, authority, and communication channels.

Responsibility matrices provide a means for all participants in a project to view their responsibilities and agree on their assignments. They also help clarify the extent or type of authority exercised by each participant in performing an activity in which two or more parties have overlapping involvement. By using an RM and by defining authority, responsibility, and communications within its framework, the relationship among different organizational units and the work content of the project is made clear.

Although RMs are effective tools for organizing and communicating individual assignments, the project manager must still decide who should do what on a project. When making individual assignments, project managers should match, as best they can, the demands and requirements of specific work with the qualifications and experience of available participants. In doing so, there is a natural tendency to assign the best people the most difficult tasks. Project managers need to be careful not to overdo this. Over time these people may grow to resent the fact that they are always given the toughest assignments. At the same time, less experienced participants may resent the fact that they are never given the opportunity to expand their skill/knowledge base.

FIGURE 7–9   Responsibility Matrix for the Computer-Controlled Conveyor Belt Project

Legend

1 Responsible
2 Support
3 Consult
4 Notification
5 Approval

Organization

Deliverables	Design	Development	Documentation	Assembly	Testing	Purchasing	Quality assurance	Manufacturing
Architechural design	1	2			2		3	3
Hardware specifications	2	1				2	3	
Kernel specifications	1	3						3
Utilities specifications	2	1			3			
Hardware design	1			3		3		3
Disk drivers	3	1	2					
Memory management	1	3			3			
Operating system documentation	2	2	1					3
Prototypes	5		4	1	3	3	3	4
Integrated acceptance test	5	2	2		1		5	5

Project managers need to balance task performance with the need to develop the talents of people assigned to the project.

Project managers not only need to decide who does what but who works with whom. A number of factors need to be considered in deciding who should work together. First, to minimize unnecessary tension, managers should pick people with compatible work habits and personalities but who complement each other (i.e., one person's weakness is the other person's strength). For example, one person may be brilliant at solving complex problems but sloppy at documenting his or her progress. It would be wise to pair this person with an individual who is good at paying attention to details. Experience is another factor. Veterans should be teamed up with new hires—not only so they can share their experience but also to help socialize the newcomers to the customs and norms of the organization. Finally, future needs should be considered. If managers have some people who have never worked together before but who have to later on in the project, they may be wise to take advantage of opportunities to have these people work together early on so that they can become familiar with each other.

MULTIPROJECT RESOURCE SCHEDULES

For clarity we have discussed key resource allocation issues within the context of a single project. In reality resource allocation generally occurs in a multiproject environment where the demands of one project have to be reconciled with the needs of other projects. Organizations must develop and manage systems for efficiently allocating and scheduling resources across several projects with different priorities, resource requirements, sets of activities, and risks. The system must be dynamic and capable of accommodating new projects as well as reallocating resources once project work is completed. While the same resource issues and principles that apply to a single project also apply to this multiproject environment, application and solutions are more complex, given the interdependency among projects.

The following lists three of the more common problems encountered in managing multiproject resource schedules. Note that these are macro manifestations of single-project problems that are now magnified in a multiproject environment:

1. **Overall schedule slippage.** Because projects often share resources, delays in one project can have a ripple effect and delay other projects. For example, work on one software development project can grind to a halt because the coders scheduled for the next critical task are late in completing their work on another development project.
2. **Inefficient resource utilization.** Because projects have different schedules and requirements, there are peaks and valleys in overall resource demands. For example, a firm may have a staff of 10 electricians to meet peak demands when, under normal conditions, only 5 electricians are required.
3. **Resource bottlenecks.** Delays and schedules are extended as a result of shortages of critical resources that are required by multiple projects. For example, at one Lattice Semiconductor facility, project schedules were delayed because of competition over access to test equipment necessary to debug programs. Likewise, several projects at a U.S. forest area were extended because there was only one silviculturist on the staff.

To deal with these problems, more and more companies create project offices or departments to oversee the scheduling of resources across multiple projects. One approach to multiple project resource scheduling is to use a first come–first served rule.

A project queue system is created in which projects currently underway take precedence over new projects. New project schedules are based on the projected availability of resources. This queuing tends to lead to more reliable completion estimates and is preferred on contracted projects that have stiff penalties for being late. The disadvantages of this deceptively simple approach are that it does not optimally utilize resources nor take into account the priority of the project. See the Snapshot from Practice box, "Multiple Project Resource Scheduling."

Many companies utilize more elaborate processes for scheduling resources to increase the capacity of the organization to initiate projects. Most of these methods approach the problem by treating individual projects as part of one big project and adapting the scheduling heuristics previously introduced to this "megaproject." Project schedulers monitor resource usage and provide updated schedules based on progress and resource availability across all projects. One major improvement in project management software in recent years is the ability to prioritize resource allocation to specific projects. Projects can be prioritized in ascending order (e.g., 1, 2, 3, 4, . . .), and these priorities will override scheduling heuristics so that resources go to the project highest on the priority list. (Note: This improvement fits perfectly with organizations that use project priority models similar to those described in Chapter 2.) Centralized project scheduling also makes it easier to identify resource bottlenecks that stifle progress on projects. Once identified, the impact of the bottlenecks can be documented and used to justify acquiring additional equipment, recruiting critical personnel, or delaying the project.

Finally, many companies are using outsourcing as a means for dealing with their resource allocation problems. In some cases, a company will reduce the number of projects they have to manage internally to only core projects and outsource noncritical projects to contractors and consulting firms. In other cases, specific segments of projects are outsourced to overcome resource deficiencies and scheduling problems. Companies may hire temporary workers to expedite certain activities that are falling behind schedule or contract project work during peak periods when there are insufficient internal resources to meet the demands of all projects. The ability to more efficiently manage the ebbs and flows of project work is one of the major driving forces behind outsourcing today.

SUMMARY

Usage and availability of resources are major problem areas for project managers. Attention to these areas in developing a project schedule can point out resource bottlenecks before the project begins. Project managers should understand the ramifications of failing to schedule resources. The results of resource scheduling are frequently significantly different from the results of the standard CPM method.

With the rapid changes in technology and emphasis on time-to-market, catching resource usage and availability problems before the project starts can save the costs of crashing project activities later. Any resource deviations from plan and schedule that occur when the project is being implemented can be quickly recorded and the effect noted. Without this immediate update capability, the real negative effect of a change may not be known until it happens. Tying resource availability to a multiproject, multiresource system supports a project priority process that selects projects by their contribution to the organization's objectives and strategic plan.

Assignment of individuals to projects may not fit well with those assigned by computer software routines. In these cases overriding the computer solution to accommodate individual differences and skills is almost always the best choice. Responsibility matrices can be effective tools for communicating and clarifying individual responsibilities on a project.

REVIEW QUESTIONS

1. How does resource scheduling tie to project priority?
2. How does resource scheduling reduce flexibility in managing projects?
3. Present six reasons scheduling resources is an important task.
4. How can outsourcing project work alleviate the three most common problems associated with multiproject resource scheduling?
5. Explain the risks associated with leveling resources, compressing or crashing projects, and imposed durations or "catchup" as the project is being implemented.

EXERCISES

1. Given the network plan that follows, compute the early, late, and slack times. What is the project duration? Using any approach you wish, develop a loading chart for resource A and

resource B. Assume only one of each resource exists. Given your resource schedule, compute the early, late, and slack times for your project. Which activities are now critical? What is the project duration now? Could something like this happen in real projects?

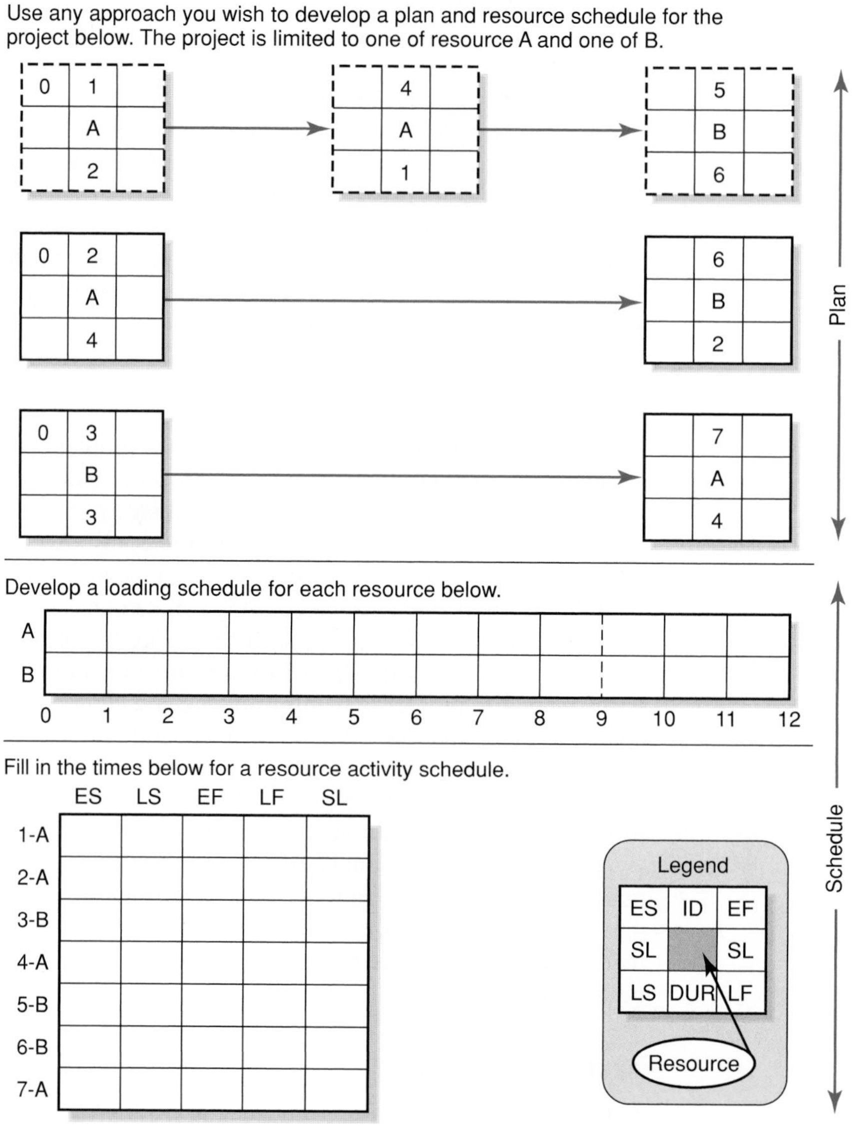

Use any approach you wish to develop a plan and resource schedule for the project below. The project is limited to one of resource A and one of B.
0
1
A
2
4
A
1
5
B
6
0
2
A
4
6
B
2
0
3
B
3
7
A
4
Plan
Develop a loading schedule for each resource below.
A
B
0 1 2 3 4 5 6 7 8 9 10 11 12
Fill in the times below for a resource activity schedule.
ES LS EF LF SL
1-A
2-A
3-B
4-A
5-B
6-B
7-A
Legend
ES ID EF
SL SL
LS DUR LF
Resource
Schedule

2. Given the network plan that follows, compute the early, late, and slack times. What is the project duration? Using any approach you wish, develop a loading chart for resources A and B. Assume only one of resource A is available and two of resource B are available. Given your resource schedule, compute the early, late, and slack times for your project. Which activities are now critical? What is the project duration now?

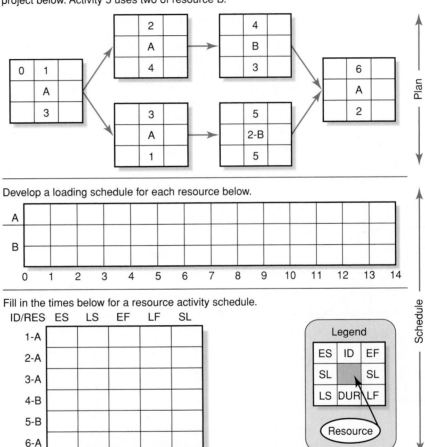

Use any approach you wish to develop a plan and resource schedule for the project below. Activity 5 uses two of resource B.

3. Compute the early, late, and slack times for the activities in the network that follows, assuming a time-constrained network. Which activities are critical? What is the time constrained project duration?

Assume you are a computer using a software that schedules projects by the parallel method and following heuristics. Schedule only one period at a time!

Minimum slack

Smallest duration

Lowest identification number

Keep a log of each activity change and update you make each period—e.g., period 0–1, 1–2, 2–3, etc. The log should include any changes or updates in ES and slack times each period, activities scheduled, and activities delayed. (Hint: Remember to maintain the technical dependencies of the network.)

List the order in which you scheduled the activities of the project. Which activities of your schedule are now critical?

Recompute your slack for each activity given your new schedule. What is the slack for activity 1? 4? 5?

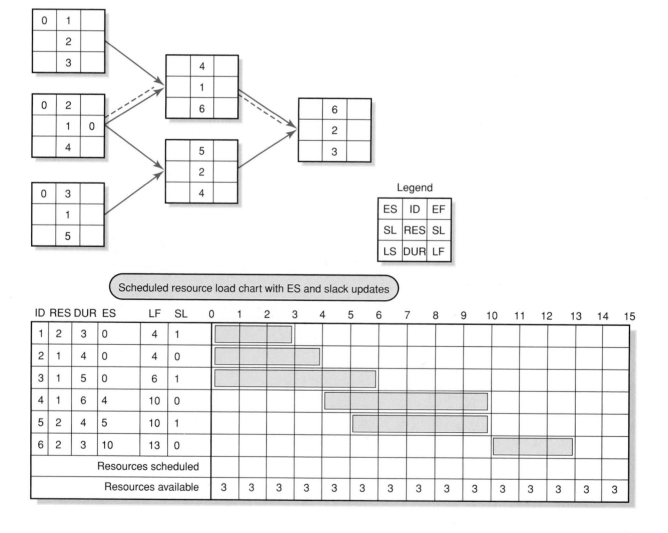

Legend

ES	ID	EF
SL	RES	SL
LS	DUR	LF

Scheduled resource load chart with ES and slack updates

ID	RES	DUR	ES	LF	SL	0	1	2	3	4	5	6	7	8	9	10	11	12	13	14	15
1	2	3	0	4	1																
2	1	4	0	4	0																
3	1	5	0	6	1																
4	1	6	4	10	0																
5	2	4	5	10	1																
6	2	3	10	13	0																
		Resources scheduled																			
		Resources available				3	3	3	3	3	3	3	3	3	3	3	3	3	3	3	3

4. Develop a resource schedule in the loading chart that follows. Use the parallel method and heuristics given. Be sure to update each period as the computer would do. Note: Activities 2, 3, 5, and 6 use two of the resource skills. Three of the resource skills are available.

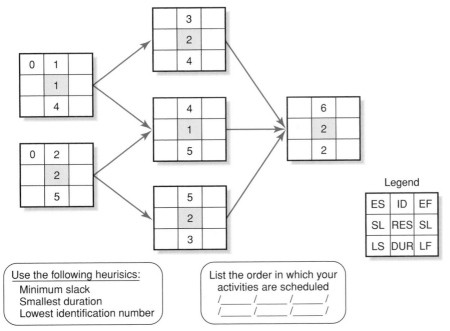

Legend

ES	ID	EF
SL	RES	SL
LS	DUR	LF

Use the following heurisics:
Minimum slack
Smallest duration
Lowest identification number

List the order in which your activities are scheduled
/_____/_____/_____/
/_____/_____/_____/

Develop a resource-constrained schedule in the loading chart below.

ID	RES	DUR	ES	LF	SL	0	1	2	3	4	5	6	7	8	9	10	11	12	13	14	15
1	1	4	0	5	1																
2	2	5	0	5																	
3	2	4	4	10																	
4	1	5	5	10																	
5	2	3																			
6	2	2																			
Resources scheduled																					
Resources available						3	3	3	3	3	3	3	3	3	3	3	3	3	3	3	

What is the schedule slack for 1_____, 3_____, and 4_____?
Which activities are critical now? _____

5. Develop a resource schedule in the loading chart that follows. Use the parallel method and heuristics given. Be sure to update each period as the computer would do. Note: Activities 1, 2, 3, 5, and 6 use two of the resource skills. Three of the resource skills are available.

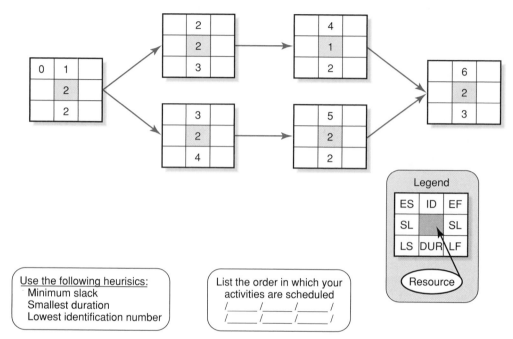

Use the following heurisics:
  Minimum slack
  Smallest duration
  Lowest identification number

List the order in which your activities are scheduled
  /_____/_____/_____/
  /_____/_____/_____/

Develop a resource schedule in the loading chart below.

ID	RES	DUR	ES	LF	SL	0	1	2	3	4	5	6	7	8	9	10	11	12	13	14	15	16
1	2	2	0	2	0	2	2															
2	2	3	2	6	1																	
3	2	4	2	6	0																	
4	1	2																				
5	2	2																				
6	2	3																				
Resources scheduled																						
Resources available					3	3	3	3	3	3	3	3	3	3	3	3	3	3	3	3	3

ENDNOTES

1. A. R. Burgess and J. B. Kellebrew, "Variations in Activity Level on Cyclical Arrow Diagrams," *Journal of Industrial Engineering,* vol. 13 (March–April 1962), pp. 76–83; J. D. Wiest, "A Heuristic Model for Scheduling Large Projects with Limited Resources," *Management Science,* vol. 18 (February 1967), pp. B359–77; and Bruce M. Woodworth and C. J. Willie, "A Heuristic Algorithm for Resource Leveling in Multiproject, Multiresource Scheduling," *Decision Sciences,* vol. 6 (July 1975), pp. 525–40.
2. Kenneth J. Arrow and L. Hurowicz, *Studies in Resource Allocation Processes* (New York: Cambridge University Press, 1977); A. Charnes and W. W. Cooper, "A Network Interpre-

tation and Direct Subdual Algorithm for Critical Path Scheduling," *Journal of Industrial Engineering* (July–August 1962); B. F. Talbot and J. H. Patterson, "Optimal Methods for Scheduling under Resource Constraints," *Project Management Journal* (December 1979); and Bruce M. Woodworth and Sean Shanahan, "Identifying the Critical Sequence in a Resource Constrained Project," *International Journal of Project Management,* vol. 6, no. 2 (1988), pp. 89–96.

3. L. G. Fendly, "Towards the Development of a Complete Multiproject Scheduling System," *Journal of Industrial Engineering,* vol. 19 (October 1968), pp. 505–15; and T. L. Pascoe, "Heuristic Methods for Allocating Resources," unpublished Ph.D. dissertation, University of Cambridge, United Kingdom (1965).

4. L. G. Fendly, reference cited.

5. For a complete and interesting discussion of the theory of constraints see Eliyahu Goldratt, *Critical Chain* (Great Barrington, MA: North River Press, 1997). See also Robert C. Newbold, "Leveraging Project Resources: Tools for the Next Century," *Proceedings of 28th Annual Project Management Institute 1997 Seminars and Symposium* (Newtown, PA: Project Management Institute, 1997), pp. 417–21; Eric Noreen, Debra Smith, and James Mackey, *The Theory of Constraints and Its Implication for Management Accounting* (Barrington, MA: North River Press, 1995), and Lawrence P. Leach, "Critical Chain Project Management," *Proceedings of 29th Annual Project Management Institute, 1998, Seminars and Symposium* (Newtown, PA: Project Management Institute, 1998), pp. 1239–44.

6. Cited in materials developed by the Eliyahu Goldratt Institute (New Haven, CT) for a workshop entitled, "Project Management: The TOC Way" (1998).

CASE

Power Train, Ltd.

We have smashing systems for reporting, tracking, and controlling costs on design projects. Our planning of projects is better than any I have seen at other companies. Our scheduling seemed to serve us well when we were small and we had only a few projects. Now that we have many more projects and schedule using multiproject software, there are too many occasions when the right people are not assigned to the projects deemed important to our success. This situation is costing us big money, headaches, and stress!

Claude Jones
VP, Design and Operations

History

Power Train, Ltd. (PT), was founded in 1960 by Daniel Gage, a skilled mechanical engineer and machinist. Prior to founding PT he worked for 3 years as design engineer for a company that designed and built transmissions for military tanks and trucks. It was a natural transition for Dan to start a company designing and building power trains for farm tractor companies. Today, Dan is no longer active in the management of PT but is still revered as its founder. He and his family still own 25 percent of the company, which went public in 1988. PT has been growing at a 6 percent clip for the last 5 years but expects industry growth to level off as supply exceeds demand.

Today, PT continues its proud tradition of designing and building the best-quality power trains for manufacturers of farm tractors and equipment. The company employs 178 design engineers and has about 1,800 production and support staff. Contract design projects for tractor manufacturers represent a major portion of PT's revenue. At any given time, about 45 to 60 design projects are going on concurrently. A small portion of their design work is for military vehicles. PT only accepts military contracts that involve very advanced, new technology and are cost plus.

A new phenomenon has attracted management of PT to look into a larger market. Last year a large Swedish truck manufacturer approached PT to consider designing power trains for its trucks. As the industry consolidates, the opportunities for PT should increase because these large firms are moving to more outsourcing to cut infrastructure costs and stay very flexible. Only last week a PT design engineer spoke to a German truck manufacturing manager at a conference. The German manager was already exploring outsourcing of drive trains to Porsche and was very pleased to be reminded of PT's expertise in the area. A meeting is set up for next month.

Claude Jones

Claude Jones joined PT in 1989 as a new MBA from the University of Edinburgh. He worked as a mechanical engineer for U.K. Hydraulics for 5 years prior to returning to school for the MBA. "I just wanted to be part of the management team and where the action is." Jones moved quickly through the ranks. Today he is the vice president of design and operations. Sitting at his desk, Jones is pondering the conflicts and confusion that seem to be increasing in scheduling people to projects. He gets a real rush at the thought of designing power trains for large trucks; however, given their current project scheduling problems, a large increase in business would only compound their problems. Somehow these conflicts in scheduling have to be resolved before any serious thought can be given to expanding into design of power transmissions for truck manufacturers.

Jones is thinking of the problems PT had in the last year. The MF project is the first to come to mind. The project was not terribly complex and did not require their best design engineers. Unfortunately, the scheduling software assigned one of the most creative and expensive engineers to the MF project. A similar situation, but reversed, happened on the Deer project. This project involved a big customer and new hydrostatic technology for small tractors. In this project the scheduling software assigned engineers who were not familiar with small tractor transmissions. Somehow, thinks Jones, the right people need to be scheduled to the right projects. Upon reflection, this problem with scheduling has been increasing since PT went to multiproject scheduling. Maybe a project office is needed to keep on top of these problems.

A meeting with the information technology team and software vendors was positive but not very helpful because these people are not really into detailed scheduling problems. The vendors provided all sorts of evidence suggesting the heuristics used— least slack, shortest duration, and identification number—are absolutely efficient in scheduling people and minimizing project delays. One project software vendor, Lauren, kept saying their software would allow PT to customize the scheduling of projects and people to almost any variation selected. Lauren repeated over and over, "If the standard heuristics do not meet your requirements, create your own heuristics that do." Lauren even volunteered to assist in setting up the system. But she is not willing to spend time on the problem until PT can describe to her exactly what criteria will be used (and their sequence) to select and schedule people to projects.

What Next?

Potential expansion into the truck power train business is not feasible until the confusion in project scheduling is solved or reduced significantly. Jones is ready to tackle this problem, but he is not sure where to start.

Computer Project Exercise, Part 3

COMPUTER-CONTROLLED CONVEYOR BELT PROJECT

Remember the old saying, "A project plan is not a schedule until resources are committed." This exercise illustrates this subtle, but very important, difference.

Part A

1. Using your files from Part 2 in Chapter 4, input resources and their costs if you have not already done so. All information is found in Tables 1, 2, and 3 from Part 1 in Chapter 3.
2. Which if any of the resources are overallocated?
3. Try to resolve the over-allocation problems without extending the duration of the project. (Hint: level within slack.) What happens?

Question: What is the impact of leveling within slack on the sensitivity of the network?

4. Assume you cannot add additional resources (resource constrained). How long will the project take after resolving all overallocation problems?

Note: No splitting of activities is allowed.

Question: How does this duration compare with the outcome of Part 2? What are the managerial implications of the problems you observe? What options would generally be available to the manager at this stage?

Part B

When you show the resource-constrained network to top management, they are visibly shaken. After some explanation and negotiation they make the following compromise with you:

- The project must be completed no later than June 13, second year (530 days).
- You may assign two additional development teams.
- If this does not suffice, you may hire other development teams from the outside. Hire as few external teams as possible because they cost $50 more per hour than your inside development people.

Internal Development

1. Add as many development units (teams) as needed to stay within the 530 days. If you need more than the two units, examine all possibilities. Select the cheapest possibilities! Change as few activities as possible. It is recommended you keep work packages which require cooperation of several organizational units inside your company. You decide how best to do this.
2. Once you have obtained a schedule that meets the time and resource constraints:
   a. Print out your final project network.
   b. Identify the critical path and the new finish time.
   c. Print out your new ES, LS, EF, LF, and slack times for all activities in tabular form.
   d. Report the rolled-up costs for the project by deliverable as well as by resource.
   Explain the new output and the changes to your project owner in narrative form.

Question: How did these changes affect the sensitivity of the network? How confident are you that you will complete the project on time? Explain.

Save your file and printouts—you will need them for the next exercise to develop a baseline!

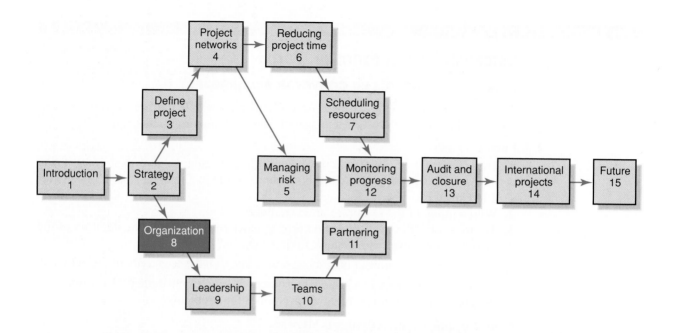

Organization

Project Management Structures
Choosing the Appropriate Project Management Structure
Organizational Culture
Implications of Organizational Culture for Organizing Projects
Summary
Appendix 8–1: How Culture Is Created and Communicated in Organizations

CHAPTER EIGHT

Organization

Matrix management works, but it sure is difficult at times. All matrix managers must keep up their health and take Stress-Tabs.
—a project manager[1]

This chapter examines how enterprises organize to manage projects. More specifically it describes and discusses three different project management structures used by firms to implement projects: functional organization, dedicated project teams, and matrix structure. Although not exhaustive, these structures and their variant forms represent the major approaches for organizing projects. The advantages and disadvantages of each of these structures are discussed as well as some of the critical factors that might lead a firm to choose one form over others.

Whether a firm chooses to complete projects within the traditional functional organization or with independent project teams or even through some form of matrix arrangement is only part of the story. Anyone who has worked for more than one organization realizes that there are often considerable differences in how projects are managed within certain firms with similar structures. Working in a matrix system at AT&T is significantly different from working in a matrix environment at Hewlett-Packard. Many researchers attribute these differences to the organizational culture at AT&T and Hewlett-Packard. A simple explanation of *organizational culture* is that it reflects the "personality" of an organization. Just as each individual has a unique personality, so each organization has a unique culture. Toward the end of this chapter, we examine in more detail what organizational culture is and the impact that the culture of the parent organization has on organizing and managing projects.

Both the project management structure and the culture of the organization constitute major elements of the environment in which projects are implemented. It is important for project managers and participants to know the "lay of the land" so that they can avoid obstacles and take advantage of pathways to complete their projects.

PROJECT MANAGEMENT STRUCTURES

A project management system provides a framework for launching and implementing project activities within a parent organization. A good system appropriately balances the needs of both the parent organization and the project by defining the interface between the project and parent organization in terms of authority, allocation of resources, and eventual integration of project outcomes into mainstream operations.

221

Many business organizations have struggled with creating a system for organizing projects while managing ongoing operations. One of the major reasons for this struggle is that projects contradict fundamental design principles associated with traditional organizations. First, projects are unique, one-time efforts with a discrete beginning and end. Most organizations are designed to efficiently manage ongoing activities. Efficiency is achieved primarily by breaking down complex tasks into simplified, repetitive activities, as symbolized by assembly-line production methods. Projects by their very nature are not routine and are therefore an anomaly in these work environments.

A second reason businesses find it difficult to effectively organize projects is that most projects are multidisciplinary in nature because they require the coordinated efforts of a variety of specialists to be completed. For example, a new-product development project will likely involve the combined efforts of people from design, marketing, manufacturing, and finance. However, most organizations are departmentalized according to functional expertise with specialists from design, marketing, manufacturing, and finance residing in different units. Many researchers have noted that these groupings naturally develop unique customs, norms, values, and working styles that inhibit "integration" across functional boundaries.[2] Not only are there "hidden walls" between departments, but managing projects poses the additional dilemma of who is in charge of the project. In most organizations authority is distributed hierarchically across functional lines. Because projects span across functional areas, identifying and legitimizing project management authority is often problematic.

Organizing Projects within the Functional Organization

One approach to organizing projects is to simply manage them within the existing functional hierarchy of the organization. Once management decides to implement a project, the different segments of the project are delegated to the respective functional units with each unit responsible for completing its segment of the project (see Figure 8–1). Coordination is maintained through normal management channels. For example, a tool manufacturing firm decides to differentiate its product line by offering a series of tools specially designed for left-handed individuals. Top management decides to implement the project, and different segments of the project are distributed to appropriate areas. The industrial design department is responsible for modifying specifications to conform to the needs of left-handed users. The production department is responsible for devising the means for producing new tools according to these new design specifications. The marketing department is responsible for gauging demand and price as well as identifying distribution outlets. The overall project will be managed within the normal hierarchy, with the project being part of the working agenda of top management.

The functional organization is also commonly used when, given the nature of the project, one functional area plays a dominant role in completing the project or has a dominant interest in the success of the project. Under these circumstances, a high-ranking manager in that area is given the responsibility of coordinating the project. For example, the transfer of equipment and personnel to a new office would be managed by a top-ranking manager in the firm's facilities department. Likewise, a project involving the upgrading of the management information system would be managed by the information systems department. In both cases, most of the project work would be done within the specified department and coordination with other departments would occur through normal channels.

There are advantages and disadvantages for using the existing functional organization to administer and complete projects.[3] The major advantages are the following:

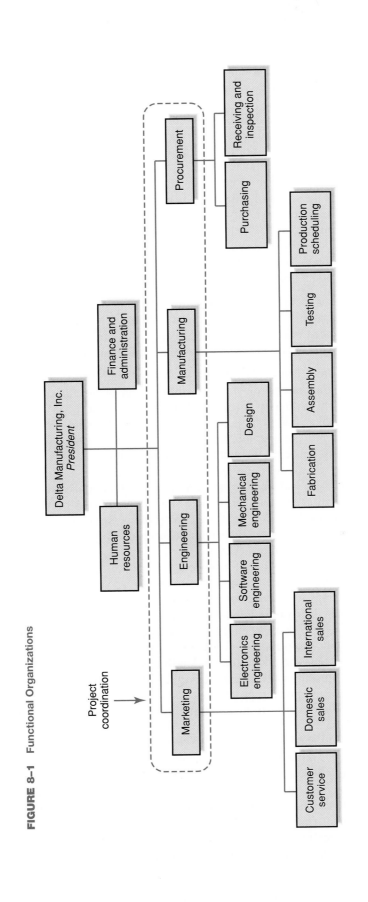

FIGURE 8-1 Functional Organizations

1. Projects are completed within the basic functional structure of the parent organization. There is no radical alteration in the design and operation of the parent organization.
2. There is maximum flexibility in the use of staff. Appropriate specialists in different functional units can temporarily be assigned to work on the project and then return to their normal work. With a broad base of technical personnel available within each functional department, people can be switched among different projects with relative ease.
3. If the scope of the project is narrow and the proper functional unit is assigned primary responsibility, then in-depth expertise can be brought to bear on the most crucial aspects of the project.
4. Normal career paths within a functional division are maintained. While specialists can make significant contributions to projects, their functional field is their professional home and the focus of their professional growth and advancement.

Just as there are advantages for organizing projects within the existing functional organization, there are also disadvantages. These disadvantages are particularly pronounced when the scope of the project is broad and one functional department does not take the dominant technological and managerial lead on the project:

1. Projects often lack focus. Each functional unit has its own core routine work to do; sometimes project responsibilities get pushed aside to meet primary obligations. This difficulty is confounded when the project has different priorities for different units. For example, the marketing department may consider the project urgent while the operations people considered it only of secondary importance. Imagine the tension if the marketing people wait for the operations people to complete their segment of the project before they proceed.
2. There may be poor integration across functional units. Cross-functional communication and coordination are slow and limited at best in most hierarchical organizations. Furthermore, there is a tendency to suboptimize the project with respective functional specialists being concerned only with their segment of the project and not the total project.
3. It generally takes longer to complete projects through this functional arrangement. This is in part attributable to slow response time—project information and decisions have to be circulated through normal management channels. Furthermore, the lack of horizontal, direct communication among functional groups contributes to rework as specialists realize the implications of others' actions after the fact.
4. The motivation of people assigned to the project can be weak. The project may be seen as an additional burden that is not directly linked to their professional development or advancement. Furthermore, because they are working on only a segment of the project, professionals do not identify with the project. Lack of ownership discourages strong commitment to project-related activities.

Organizing Projects as Dedicated Teams

At the other end of the structural spectrum is the creation of independent project teams. These teams operate as separate units from the rest of the parent organization. Usually a full-time project manager is designated to pull together a core group of specialists who work full time on the project. The project manager recruits necessary personnel from both within and outside the parent company. The subsequent team is physically separated from the parent organization and given the primary directive of accomplishing the objectives of the project (see Figure 8–2).

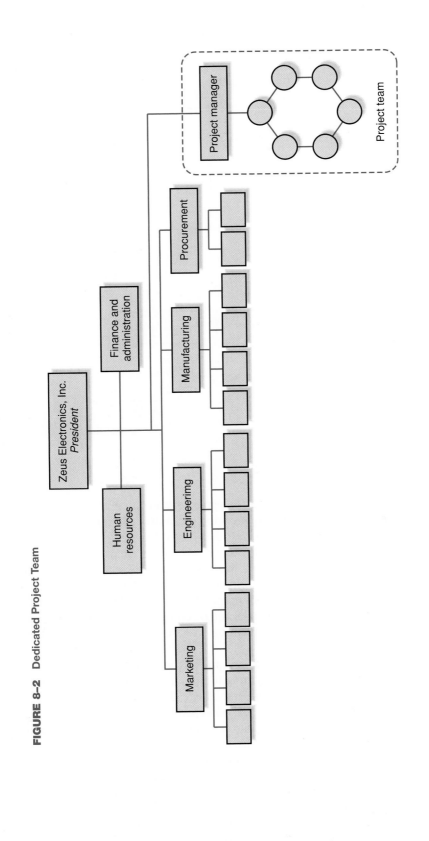

FIGURE 8–2 Dedicated Project Team

FIGURE 8–3 Project Organization Structure

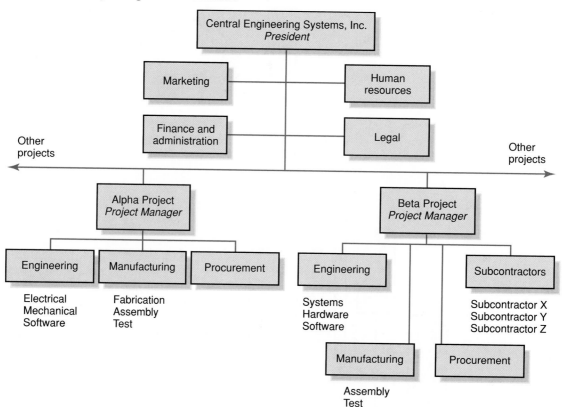

The interface between the parent organization and the project teams will vary. In some cases the parent organization prescribes administrative and financial control procedures over the project. In other cases, firms allow the project manager maximum freedom to get the project done given the resources originally assigned to the project. Both Apple and IBM used this approach to develop their new line of personal computers in the 1980s. At Apple, the Macintosh development team was isolated in a separate building, away from corporate noise and interference, and given the prime directive to develop a breakthrough computer as quickly as possible. Finally, some organizations are experimenting with self-managing project teams without a formal project manager.

In the case of firms where projects are the dominant form of business, such as a construction firm, a consulting firm, or a movie company, the entire organization is designed to support project teams. Instead of one or two special projects, the organization consists of sets of quasi-independent teams working on specific projects. The main responsibility of traditional functional departments is to assist and support these project teams. For example, the marketing department is directed at generating new business that will lead to more projects, while the human resource department is responsible for managing a variety of personnel issues as well as recruiting and training new employees. This type of organization is referred to in the literature as a *projectized* form of organization and is graphically portrayed in Figure 8–3.

As in the case of functional organization, the dedicated project team approach has strengths and weaknesses.[4] The following are recognized as strengths:

1. It is a relatively simple means for completing a project that does not directly disrupt ongoing operations. Other than taking away resources in the form of specialists assigned to the project, the functional organization remains intact with the project team operating independently.

2. There is a concentrated project focus often missing in the functional approach. The project manager has full authority over the project. Although the project manager must report to senior executives in the parent organization, there is a dedicated workforce whose sole function is to complete the project.

3. Projects tend to get done more quickly when dedicated teams are created. Perhaps the main reason for this is that participants devote their full attention to the project and are not distracted by other obligations and duties. Furthermore, response time tends to be quicker under this arrangement because most decisions are made within the team and are not deferred up the hierarchy.

4. A high level of motivation and cohesiveness often emerges within the project team. Participants share a common goal and personal responsibility toward the project and the team.

5. Assuming that the appropriate resources are assigned to the project team, a high level of cross-functional integration occurs. Specialists from different areas work closely together and, with proper guidance, become committed to optimizing the project not their respective areas of expertise.

In many cases, the project team approach is the optimum approach for completing a project when you view it solely from the standpoint of what is best for completing the project. Its weaknesses become more evident when the needs of the parent organization are taken into account:

1. Creating self-contained project teams to complete projects is expensive. Not only have you created a new management position (project manager), but resources are also assigned on a full-time basis. This can result in duplication of efforts across projects and a loss of economies of scale.

2. Sometimes dedicated project teams take on an entity of their own and a disease known as *projectitis* develops (see the accompanying Snapshot from Practice). A strong we–they divisiveness emerges between the project team and the parent organization. This divisiveness can undermine not only the integration of the eventual outcomes of the project into mainstream operations but also the assimilation of project team members back into their functional units once the project is completed.

3. Creating self-contained teams inhibits maximum technological expertise being brought to bear on problems. Technical expertise is limited somewhat to the talents and experience of the specialists assigned to the project. While nothing prevents specialists from consulting with others in the functional division, the we–they syndrome and the fact that such help is not formally sanctioned by the organization discourage this from happening.

4. Assigning full-time personnel to a project creates the dilemma of what to do with personnel after the project is completed. If other project work is not available, then the transition back to their original functional departments may be difficult because of their prolonged absence and the need to catch up with recent developments in their functional area.

Organizing Projects within a Matrix Arrangement

Matrix management is a hybrid organizational form in which a horizontal project management structure is "overlaid" on the normal functional hierarchy. In a matrix

Snapshot from Practice
PROJECTITIS: THE DARK SIDE TO PROJECT TEAMS

One of the advantages of creating dedicated project teams is that project participants from different functional areas can develop into a highly cohesive work team that is strongly committed to completing the project. While such teams often produce Herculean efforts in pursuit of project completion, there is a negative dimension to this commitment that is often referred to in the literature as *projectitis*. A we–they attitude can emerge between project team members and the rest of the organization. The project team succumbs to *hubris* and develops a holier-than-thou attitude that antagonizes the parent organization. People not assigned to the project become jealous of the attention and prestige being showered on the project team, especially when they believe that it is their hard work that is financing the endeavor. The tendency to assign project teams exotic titles such as "Silver Bullets" and "Tiger Teams," as well as give them special perks, tends to intensify the gap between the project team and the parent organization.

Such appears to have been the case with Apple's highly successful Macintosh development team. Steve Jobs, who at the time was both the chairman of Apple and the project manager for the Mac team, pampered his team with perks including at-the-desk massages, coolers stocked with freshly squeezed orange juice, a Bosendorfer grand piano, and first-class plane tickets. No other employees at Apple got to travel first class. Jobs considered his team to be the elite of Apple and had a tendency to refer to everyone else as "Bozos" who "didn't get it." Engineers from the Apple II division, which was the bread and butter of Apple's sales, became incensed with the special treatment their colleagues were getting.

One evening at Ely McFly's, a local watering hole, the tensions between Apple II engineers seated at one table and those of a Mac team at another boiled over. Aaron Goldberg, a long-time industry consultant, watched from his barstool as the squabbling escalated. "The Mac guys were screaming, 'We're the future!' The Apple II guys were screaming, 'We're the money!' Then there was a geek brawl. Pocket protectors and pens were flying. I was waiting for a notebook to drop, so they would stop and pick up the papers."[5]

Although comical from a distance, the discord between the Apple II and Mac groups severely hampered Apple's performance during the 1980s. John Sculley, who replaced Steve Jobs as chairman of Apple, observed that Apple had evolved into two "warring companies" and referred to the street between the Apple II and Macintosh buildings as "the DMZ" (demilitarized zone).[6]

system, there are usually two chains of command, one along functional lines and the other along project lines. Instead of delegating segments of a project to different units or creating an autonomous team, project participants report simultaneously to both functional and project managers.

Companies apply this matrix arrangement in a variety of different ways. Some organizations set up temporary matrix systems to deal with specific projects, while "matrix" may be a permanent fixture in other organizations. Let us first look at its general application and then proceed to a more detailed discussion of finer points. Consider Figure 8–4. There are three projects currently under way: A, B, and C. All three project managers (PM a-c) report to a director of project management, who supervises all projects. Each project has an administrative assistant, although the one for project C is only part time.

Project A involves the design and expansion of an existing production line to accommodate new metal alloys. To accomplish this objective, project A has assigned to it 3.5 people from manufacturing and 6 people from engineering. These individuals are assigned to the project on a part-time or full-time basis, depending on the project's needs during various phases of the project. Project B involves the development of a new product that requires the heavy representation of engineering, manufacturing, and

FIGURE 8–4 Matrix Organization Structure

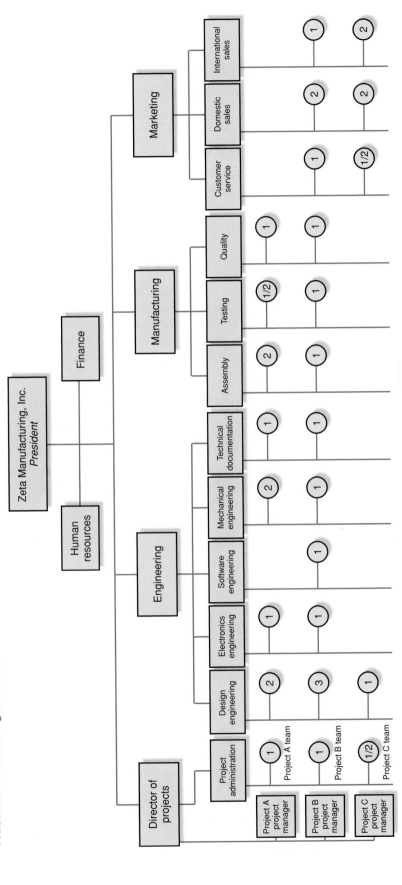

TABLE 8-1

DIVISION OF PROJECT MANAGER AND FUNCTIONAL MANAGER RESPONSIBILITIES IN A MATRIX STRUCTURE

Project manager	Negotiated issues	Functional manager
What has to be done?	Who will do the task?	How will it be done?
When should the task be done?	Where will the task be done?	
How much money is available to do the task?	Why will the task be done?	How will the project involvement impact normal functional activities?
How well has the total project been done?	Is the task satisfactorily completed?	How well has the functional input been integrated?

marketing. Project C involves forecasting changing needs of an existing customer base. While these three projects, as well as others are being completed, the functional divisions continue performing their basic, core activities.

The matrix structure is designed to optimally utilize resources by having individuals work on multiple projects as well as being capable of performing normal functional duties. At the same time, the matrix approach attempts to achieve greater integration by creating and legitimizing the authority of a project manager. In theory, the matrix approach provides a dual focus between functional/technical expertise and project requirements that is missing in either the project team or functional approach to project management. This focus can most easily be seen in the relative input of functional managers and project managers over key project decisions (see Table 8–1).

In principle every major project decision and action must be negotiated. The project manager is responsible for integrating functional input and overseeing the completion of the project. Functional managers are responsible for overseeing the functional contribution to the project.

Different Matrix Forms

In practice there are really different kinds of matrix systems, depending on the relative authority of the project and functional managers.[7] Weak, lightweight, or *functional matrix* are titles given to matrices in which the balance of authority strongly favors the functional managers. *Balanced,* or middleweight, *matrix* is used to describe the traditional matrix arrangement. Strong, heavyweight, or *project matrix* is used to describe a matrix in which the balance of authority is strongly on the side of the project manager.

The relative difference in power between functional managers and project managers is reflected along a number of related dimensions. One such dimension is level of reporting relationship. A project manager who reports directly to the CEO has more clout than a marketing manager who reports to the VP of marketing. Location of project activities is another subtle but important factor. A project manager wields considerably more influence over project participants if they work in his office than if they perform their project-related activities in their functional offices. Likewise, the percentage of full-time staff assigned to the project contributes to relative influence. Full-time status implies transfer of obligations from functional activities to the project.

Ultimately, whether the matrix is weak or strong, a functional or project matrix is determined by the extent to which the project manager has direct authority over participants. Authority may be determined informally by the persuasive powers of man-

Snapshot from Practice
CONCURRENT ENGINEERING

The impetus for the matrix organization originated in firms operating in high-tech areas that had to integrate several functional specialties to work on a set of projects and, because of re-source scarcity, wished to time-share expertise among individual projects. At the same time, the technical requirements of the project required a more holistic systems approach than was pos-sible in a functional organization. In earlier times, when a high-technology project such as a new-product development was initiated by a firm, it would start its sequential journey in the R&D de-partment. Concepts and ideas would be worked out and the results passed to the engineering department, which sometimes reworked the whole product. This result would be passed to man-ufacturing, where it might be reworked once more to ensure the product could be manufactured using existing machinery and operations. This sequential approach to product development re-quired a great deal of time, and it was not uncommon for the final product to be totally unrec-ognizable when compared with original specifications.

Given the increased importance of time-to-market, companies have abandoned the sequen-tial approach to product development and have adopted a more holistic approach called *con-current engineering.* In a nutshell, concurrent engineering entails the active involvement of all the relevant specialty areas throughout the design and development process. For example, this ap-proach was used by Chrysler Corporation to design its new line of SC cars including the popu-lar Neon sedan. From the very beginning specialists from marketing, engineering, design, man-ufacturing, quality assurance, and other relevant departments were involved in every stage of the project. Not only did the project meet all of its objectives, it was completed six months ahead of schedule.[8]

It should be noted that concurrent engineering can occur in the form of a dedicated project team or in a matrix structure. The only difference is that in the latter project, personnel do not work on the project on a full-time basis but rather divide their time and attention across multiple projects and functional responsibilities.

agers involved and the perceived importance of the project or formally by the pre-scribed powers of the project manager. Here is a thumbnail sketch of the three kinds of matrices:

- **Functional matrix**—This form is very similar to a functional approach with the exception that there is a formally designated project manager responsible for coordinating project activities. Functional managers are responsible for managing their segment of the project. The project manager basically acts as a staff assistant who draws the schedules and checklists, collects information on status of work, and facilitates project completion. The project manager has indirect authority to expedite and monitor the project. Functional managers call most of the shots and decide who does what and when the work is completed.

- **Balanced matrix**—This is the classic matrix in which the project manager is responsible for defining what needs to be accomplished while the functional managers are concerned with how it will be accomplished. More specifically, the project manager establishes the overall plan for completing the project, integrates the contribution of the different disciplines, sets schedules, and monitors progress. The functional managers are responsible for assigning personnel and executing their segment of the project according to the standards and schedules set by the project manager. The merger of "what and how" requires both parties to work closely together and jointly approve technical and operational decisions.

- **Project matrix**—This form attempts to create the "feel" of a project team within a matrix environment. The project manager controls most aspects of the project, including scope trade-offs and assignment of functional personnel. The project manager controls when and what specialists do and has final say on major project decisions. The functional manager has title over her people and is consulted on a need basis. In some situations a functional manager's department may serve as a "subcontractor" for the project, in which case they have more control over specialized work. For example, the development of a new series of laptop computers may require a team of experts from different disciplines working on the basic design and performance requirements within a project matrix arrangement. Once the specifications have been determined, final design and production of certain components (i.e., power source) may be assigned to respective functional groups to complete.

One final factor that determines the relative influence of project and functional managers is who is responsible for conducting performance appraisals and compensation decisions. In a functional matrix, the project manager is not likely to have any direct input in the evaluation of participants who worked on the project. This would be the sole responsibility of the functional manager. Conversely, in a project matrix, the project manager's evaluation would carry more weight than the functional manager's. In a balanced matrix, either input from both managers is sought, or the project manager makes recommendations to the functional manager, who is responsible for the formal evaluation of individual employees. Often companies will brag that they use a strong, project-oriented matrix only to find upon closer examination that the project managers have very little say over the evaluation and compensation of personnel.

Both matrix management in general and in its specific forms have unique strengths and weaknesses.[9] The advantages and disadvantages of matrix organizations in general are noted below, while only briefly highlighting specifics concerning different forms:[10]

1. Resources can be shared across multiple projects as well as within functional divisions. Individuals can divide their energy across multiple projects on an as-needed basis. This reduces duplication required in a pure project team structure.
2. A stronger project focus is provided by having a formally designated project manager who is responsible for coordinating and integrating contributions of different units. This helps sustain a holistic approach to problem solving that is often missing in the functional organization.

3. Because the project organization is overlaid on the functional divisions, the project has reasonable access to the entire reservoir of technology and expertise of functional divisions. Furthermore, unlike dedicated project teams, specialists maintain ties with their functional group, so they have a homeport to return to once the project is completed.

4. Matrix arrangements provide for flexible utilization of resources and expertise within the firm. In some cases functional units may provide individuals who are managed by the project manager. In other cases the contributions are monitored by the functional manager.

The strengths of the matrix structure are considerable. Unfortunately, so are the potential weaknesses. This is due in large part to the fact that a matrix structure is more complicated and the creation of multiple bosses represents a radical departure from the traditional hierarchical authority system:

1. The matrix approach is predicated on tension between functional managers and project managers who bring critical expertise and perspectives to the project. Such tension is viewed as a necessary mechanism for achieving an appropriate balance between complex technical issues and unique project requirements. While the intent is noble, the effect is sometimes analogous to opening Pandora's box. Legitimate conflict can spill over to a more personal level, resulting from conflicting agendas and accountabilities. Worthy discussions can degenerate into heated arguments that engender animosity among the managers involved.

2. Any situation in which equipment, resources, and people are being shared across projects and functional activities lends itself to conflict and competition for scarce resources. Infighting can occur among project managers, who are primarily interested in what is best for their project.

3. Matrix management violates the management principle of unity of command. Project participants have at least two bosses—their functional head and one or more project managers. Working in a matrix environment can be extremely stressful. Imagine what it would be like to work in an environment in which you are being told to do three conflicting things by three different managers.

4. In theory, the presence of a project manager to coordinate the project should accelerate the completion of the project. In practice, decision making can get bogged down as agreements have to be forged across multiple functional groups. This is especially true for the balanced matrix.

When the three variant forms of the matrix approach are considered, we can see that advantages and disadvantages are not necessarily true for all three forms of matrix. The project matrix is likely to enhance project integration, diminish internal power struggles, and ultimately improve control of project activities and costs. On the downside, technical quality may suffer because functional areas have less control over their contributions. Finally, projectitis may emerge as the members develop a strong team identity.

The functional matrix is likely to improve technical quality as well as provide a better system for managing conflict across projects because the functional manager assigns personnel to different projects. The problem is that functional control is often maintained at the expense of poor project integration. The balanced matrix can achieve better balance between technical and project requirements, but it is a very delicate system to create and manage and is more likely to succumb to many of the problems associated with the matrix approach.[11]

CHOOSING THE APPROPRIATE PROJECT MANAGEMENT STRUCTURE

There is growing empirical evidence that project success is directly linked to the amount of autonomy and authority project managers have over their projects (see the accompanying Research Highlight). However, most of this research is based on what is best for managing specific projects. It is important to remember what was stated in the beginning of the chapter—that the best system balances the needs of the project with those of the parent organization. Allen has cautioned that while certain structures may contribute to the success of a certain project, they may do so at the detriment of other organizational activities.[12] For example, most experts would agree the simplest

RESEARCH HIGHLIGHT
Relative Effectiveness of Different Project Management Structures

Larson and Gobeli studied the relative efficacy of different project management structures.[13] Their work is based on a sample of more than 1,600 project professionals and managers actively involved in project management within their organizations. Among the findings they report are the rated effectiveness of different structures for product development and construction projects. These results are summarized in Figure 8–5 and indicate a strong preference for either the project team or project matrix. Both the functional approach and the functional matrix were rated ineffective, and the balanced matrix was considered only marginally effective.

FIGURE 8–5 Rated Effectiveness of Different Project Structures by Type of Project

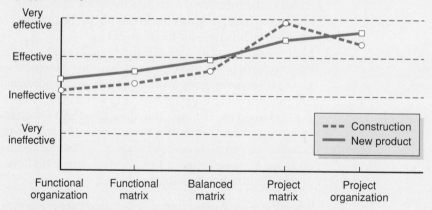

Because these ratings may have been tempered by self-interest, with project managers advocating forms that give them more formal authority, the ratings of project managers were compared with those of top management and functional managers. No significant differences were found; the functional matrix and functional organization were considered the least effective even by functional managers.

This research was published at a time when matrix management was receiving a lot of negative press and when popular management media were advocating the dedicated project team approach. A key finding was that matrix management can be as effective as a project team—if the project manager is given significant control over project activities. The support is not without reservations; as one project manager reported, "Matrix management works, but it sure is difficult at times. All matrix managers must keep up their health and take Stress Tabs."

and most effective way to organize a project is to create a full-time, dedicated project team. However, relying on this method to complete projects may adversely affect the parent organization if it robs the organization of essential personnel, engenders jealously between the parent organization and the project teams, and inhibits the assimilation of project personnel back into the parent company.

So what project structure should an organization use? First, there is little empirical or theoretical support for using the functional organization to manage projects. Common sense would tell us that even the most mundane project needs someone to assume a leadership role. The one exception would be for projects in which the major work is concentrated in a specific functional department and cross-functional coordination is minimal. Under these circumstances adequate project leadership can be provided by the normal chain of command. Furthermore, in these situations there can still be the sharing element of a matrix environment in that the boss determines how much time and energy each person devotes to the project and other duties.

Accepting that the functional organization is inadequate for managing most projects, then the question is one of whether organizations should use the dedicated team approach or a matrix arrangement. Even then they must decide whether to dedicate an entire organization to create a projectized organization or individual project teams. Likewise they have to decide what kind of matrix to use and whether it is a formal or informal arrangement.

A number of different factors need to be considered in choosing between a dedicated project team or a matrix approach to organizing projects. Still, we believe the decision ultimately rests on the trade-off between the simplicity, speed, and concentrated focus of a full-time project team and the flexibility and efficient use of resources of a matrix structure. As stated earlier, project management experts agree there is no quicker way to complete complex projects than to form a dedicated project team of appropriate experts who devote undivided attention to completing the project. Also recall that matrix structures evolved out of the necessity to share resources across multiple projects and functional domains while at the same time creating legitimate project leadership. For organizations that cannot afford to tie up critical personnel on individual projects, a matrix system would appear to be appropriate. At the same time the matrix is a more complicated system to manage, and it creates a dual management structure that can wreak havoc on the parent organization. While dedicated project teams are more expensive, they operate independently and therefore do not directly disrupt the parent organization. Management should only invest in creating a matrix system if successful project management is critical to company success and if they are personally committed to making it work.

When talking about project management structures, it is not always an "either-or" question. Many firms that are heavily involved in project management use dedicated project teams for special projects, while a matrix arrangement exists for the majority of the other projects. For example, Chaparral Steel, a mini-mill that produces steel bars and beams from scrap metal, classifies projects into three categories: advanced development, platform, and incremental. Advanced development projects are high-risk endeavors involving the creation of a breakthrough product or process. Platform projects are medium-risk projects involving system upgrades that yield new products and processes. Incremental projects are low-risk, short-term projects that involve minor adjustments in existing products and processes. At any point in time, Chaparral might have 40 to 50 projects under way, of which only 1 or 2 are advanced, 3 to 5 are platform projects, and the remainder are small, incremental projects. The incremental projects are almost all done within a functional matrix, with the project manager coordinating the work of functional subgroups. A project matrix is used to complete the platform projects, while dedicated project teams are typically created to complete the advanced development projects.[14] More and more companies are using this "mix and match" approach to managing projects.

ORGANIZATIONAL CULTURE

The decision for combining a discussion of project management structures and organizational cultures in this chapter can be traced to a conversation we, the authors, had with two project managers who work for a medium-sized information technology firm.

The managers were currently developing a new operating platform that would be critical to the future success of their company. When they tried to describe how this project was organized, one manager began to sketch out on a napkin a complicated structure involving 52 different teams, each with a project leader and a technical leader! With further probing to understand how this system worked, the manager stopped short and proclaimed, "The key to making this structure work is the culture in our company. This approach would never work at company Y, where I worked before. But because of our culture here we are able to pull it off."

This comment, our observations of other firms, and research suggest there is a strong connection between project management structure, organizational culture, and project success.[15] We have observed organizations successfully manage projects within the traditional functional organization because the culture encouraged cross-functional integration. Conversely we have seen matrix structures break down because the culture of the organization did not support the division of authority between project managers and functional managers. We have also observed companies relying on independent project teams because the dominant culture would not support the innovation and speed necessary for success.

What Is Organizational Culture?

Anyone who has traveled abroad has experienced the phenomenon of culture. The architecture is different from that at home. The food is not what the traveler commonly eats, nor do the natives necessarily adhere to a particular routine of breakfast, lunch, and dinner. People dress differently. They often speak a different language. Beneath these obvious differences, the traveler probably discerns sometimes subtle but significant differences in how people interact and spend their time. For example, one of the authors encountered such differences while working in Poland with several Polish colleagues to complete a significant segment of a project that was due by the end of the day. They were on the verge of completing the work when, at 4:00 P.M., everyone stopped what they were doing and went home. Unlike a work culture in the United States, where it was expected that everyone would stay to finish the work, there is a clear division between work time and personal time in Poland, and it was taboo to expect or require people to work beyond business hours.

Although perhaps less pronounced, organizational cultures are similar to cultures of different countries. Think about the differences in physical layout, dress, pace, and tone of communication encountered in your local bank, department store, or medical clinic. Likewise, anyone who has worked in several organizations encounters significant differences in the norms, values, and customs of individual organizations.

Organizational culture refers to a system of shared norms, beliefs, values, and assumptions which bind people together, thereby creating shared meanings.[16] This system is manifested by customs, norms, and habits that exemplify the values and beliefs of the organization. Culture reflects the personality of the organization and, similar to an individual's personality, can enable us to predict attitudes and behaviors of organizational members. Culture is also one of the defining aspects of an organization that sets it apart from other organizations even in the same industry.

Research suggests that there are 10 primary characteristics which, in aggregate, capture the essence of an organization's culture:[17]

1. **Member identity**—the degree to which employees identify with the organization as a whole rather than with their type of job or field of professional expertise.
2. **Team emphasis**—the degree to which work activities are organized around groups rather than individuals.
3. **Management focus**—the degree to which management decisions take into account the effect of outcomes on people within the organization.
4. **Unit integration**—the degree to which units within the organization are encouraged to operate in a coordinated or interdependent manner.
5. **Control**—the degree to which rules, policies, and direct supervision are used to oversee and control employee behavior.
6. **Risk tolerance**—the degree to which employees are encouraged to be aggressive, innovative, and risk-seeking.
7. **Reward criteria**—the degree to which rewards such as promotion and salary increases are allocated according to employee performance rather than seniority, favoritism, or other nonperformance factors.
8. **Conflict tolerance**—the degree to which employees are encouraged to air conflicts and criticisms openly.
9. **Means versus end orientation**—the degree to which management focuses on outcomes rather than on techniques and processes used to achieve those results.
10. **Open-systems focus**—the degree to which the organization monitors and responds to changes in the external environment.

As shown in Figure 8–6, each of these dimensions exists on a continuum. Assessing an organization according to these 10 dimensions provides a composite picture of the organization's culture. This picture becomes the basis for feelings of shared un-

FIGURE 8–6   Key Dimensions Defining an Organization's Culture

	1. Member identity	
Job	———————————	Organization
	2. Team emphasis	
Individual	———————————	Group
	3. Management focus	
Task	———————————	People
	4. Unit integration	
Independent	———————————	Interdependent
	5. Control	
Loose	———————————	Tight
	6. Risk tolerance	
Low	———————————	High
	7. Reward criteria	
Performance	———————————	Other
	8. Conflict tolerance	
Low	———————————	High
	9. Means-ends orientation	
Means	———————————	Ends
	10. Open-system focus	
Internal	———————————	External

derstanding that the members have about the organization, how things are done, and the way members are supposed to behave.

Culture performs several important functions in organizations. An organization's culture *provides a sense of identity* for its members. The more clearly an organization's shared perceptions and values are stated, the more strongly people can identify with their organization and feel a vital part of it. Identity generates commitment to the organization and reasons for members to devote energy and loyalty to the organization.

A second important function is that culture *helps legitimize the management system* of the organization. Culture helps clarify authority relationships and provides reasons why people are in a position of authority and why their authority should be respected. Furthermore, culture through myths, stories, and symbols helps people reconcile incongruities between ideal and actual behavior.

Most importantly, organizational culture *clarifies and reinforces standards of behavior.* Culture helps define what is permissible and inappropriate behavior. These standards span a wide range of behavior from dress code and working hours to challenging the judgment of superiors and collaborating with other departments. Ultimately, culture *helps create social order* within an organization. Imagine what it would be like if members didn't share similar beliefs, values, and assumptions—chaos! The customs, norms, and ideals conveyed by the culture of an organization provide the stability and predictability in behavior that is essential for an effective organization.

Although our discussion of organizational culture may appear to suggest one culture dominates the entire organization, in reality this is rarely the case. "Strong" or "thick" are adjectives used to denote a culture in which the organization's core values and customs are widely held and widely shared within the entire organization. Conversely, a "thin" or "weak" culture is one that is not widely shared or practiced within a firm.

Even within a strong organizational culture, there are likely to be subcultures often aligned within specific departments or specialty areas. As noted earlier in our discussion of project management structures, it is not uncommon for norms, values, and customs to develop within a specific field or profession such as marketing, finance, or operations. Similarly, countercultures can emerge within organizations that reflect a different set of values, beliefs, and customs—often in direct contradiction with the culture espoused by top management. How pervasive these subcultures and countercultures are affects the strength of the culture of the organization and the extent to which culture influences members' actions and responses.

Identifying Cultural Characteristics

Deciphering an organization's culture is a highly interpretative, subjective process that requires assessment of both current activities and past history. The student of culture cannot simply rely on what people report about their culture. The physical environment in which people work, as well as how people act and respond to different events that occur, must be examined. Figure 8–7 contains a worksheet for diagnosing the culture of an organization.[18] Although by no means exhaustive, the checklist often yields clues about the norms, customs, and values of an organization:

1. **Study the physical characteristics of an organization.** What does the external architecture look like? What image does it convey? Is it unique? Are the buildings and offices the same quality for all employees? Or are modern buildings and fancier offices reserved for senior executives or managers from a specific depart-

FIGURE 8–7 Organizational Culture
Diagnosis Worksheet

I. Physical Characteristics
Architecture, office layout, decor, attire

_____
_____
_____

II. Public Documents
Annual reports, internal newsletters, vision statements

_____
_____
_____

III. Behavior
Pace, language, meetings, issues discussed,
decision-making style, communication patterns, rituals

_____
_____
_____

IV. Folklore
Stories, anecdotes, heroines, heroes, villains

_____
_____
_____

ment? What are the customs concerning dress? What symbols does the organization use to signal authority and status within the organization? These physical characteristics can shed light on who has real power within the organization, the extent to which the organization is internally differentiated, and how formal the organization is in its business dealings.

2. **Read about the organization.** Examine annual reports, mission statements, press releases, and internal newsletters. What do they describe? What principles are espoused in these documents? Do the reports emphasize the people who work for the organization and what they do or the financial performance of the firm? Each emphasis reflects a different culture. The first demonstrates concern for the people who make up the company. The second may suggest a concern for results and the bottom line.

3. **Observe how people interact within the organization.** What is their pace—is it slow and methodical or urgent and spontaneous? What rituals exist within the organization? What values do they express? Meetings can often yield insightful information. Who are the people at the meetings? Who does the talking? To whom do they talk? How candid is the conversation? Do people speak for the organization or for the individual department? What is the focus of the meetings? How much time is spent on various issues? Issues that are discussed repeatedly and at length are clues about the values of the organization's culture.

4. **Interpret stories and folklore surrounding the organization.** Finally, either through talking directly to people from other organizations or in daily conversations with co-workers, an observer can begin to gain a deeper sense of an organization's culture. Pay particular attention to the stories and anecdotes that are passed on within the organization; they often yield useful evidence about the important qualities of the culture. Look for similarities among stories told by different people. The subjects highlighted in recurring stories often reflect what is important to an organization's culture. For example, many of the stories that are repeated at

Versatec, a Xerox subsidiary that makes graphic plotters for computers, involve their flamboyant cofounder, Renn Zaphiropoulos. According to company folklore, one of the very first things Renn did when the company was formed was to assemble the top management team at his home. They then devoted the weekend to handmaking a beautiful teak conference table around which all future decisions would be made. This table came to symbolize the importance of teamwork and maintaining high standards of performance, two essential qualities of the culture at Versatec.

Try to identify who the heroes and villains are in the folklore company. What do they suggest about the culture's ideals? Returning to the Versatec story, when the company was eventually purchased by Xerox many employees expressed concern that Versatec's informal, play hard/work hard culture would be overwhelmed by the bureaucracy at Xerox. Renn rallied the employees to superior levels of performance by arguing that if they exceeded Xerox's expectations they would be left alone. Autonomy has remained a fixture of Versatec's culture long after Renn's retirement.

It is also important to pay close attention to the basis for promotions and rewards. Are promotions based on accomplishments and performance or tenure and loyalty to the organization? What do people see as the keys to getting ahead within the organization? What contributes to downfalls? These last two questions can yield important insights into the qualities and behaviors which the organization honors as well as the cultural taboos and behavioral land mines that can derail a career. For example, one project manager confided that a former colleague was sent to project management purgatory soon after publicly questioning the validity of a marketing report. From that point on, the project manager was extra careful to privately consult the marketing department whenever she had questions about their data.

With practice an observer can assess how strong the dominant culture of an organization is and the significance of subcultures and countercultures. Furthermore, learners can discern and identify where the culture of an organization stands on the 10 cultural dimensions presented earlier and, in essence, begin to build a cultural profile for a firm. Based on this profile conclusions can be drawn about specific customs and norms that need to be adhered to as well as those behaviors and actions that violate the norms of a firm.

IMPLICATIONS OF ORGANIZATIONAL CULTURE FOR ORGANIZING PROJECTS

Project managers have to be able to operate in several, potentially diverse, organizational cultures. First, they have to interact with the culture of their parent organization as well as the subcultures of various departments (e.g., marketing, accounting). Second, they have to interact with the project's client or customer organizations. Finally, they have to interact in varying degrees with a host of other organizations connected to the project. These organizations include suppliers and vendors, subcontractors, consulting firms, government and regulatory agencies, and, in many cases, community groups. Many of these organizations are likely to have very different cultures. Project managers have to be able to read and speak the culture they are working in to develop strategies, plans, and responses that are likely to be understood and accepted.[19] Still, the emphasis of this chapter is on the relationship between organizational culture and project management structure, and it is necessary to defer further discussion of these implications until Chapters 9–11 which focus on leadership, team building, and partnering.

Earlier we stated that we believe there are strong relationships among project management structure, organizational culture, and successful project management. To explore these relationships further, let us return to the dimensions that can be used to characterize the culture of an organization. When examining these dimensions we could hypothesize that certain aspects of the culture of an organization would support successful project management while other aspects would deter or interfere with effective management. Figure 8–8 attempts to identify which cultural characteristics create an environment conducive to completing most complex projects involving people from different disciplines.

Note that, in many cases, the ideal culture is not at either extreme. For example, a fertile project culture would likely be one in which management balances its focus on the needs of both the task and the people. An optimal culture would balance concern with output (ends) and processes to achieve those outcomes (means). In other cases, the ideal culture would be on one end of a dimension or the other. For example, because most projects require collaboration across disciplines, it would be desirable that the culture of the organization emphasize working in teams and identifying with the organization, not just the professional domain. Likewise it would be desirable that the culture support a certain degree of risk taking and a reasonably high conflict tolerance.

One organization that appears to approach this ideal profile is 3M. 3M has received acclaim for creating an entrepreneurial culture within a large corporate framework. The essence of its culture is captured in phrases that have been chanted often by 3Mers throughout its history: "Encourage experimental doodling." "Hire good people and leave them alone." "If you put fences around people, you get sheep. Give people the room they need." Freedom and autonomy to experiment are reflected in the "15 percent rule," which encourages technical people to spend up to 15 percent of their time on projects of their own choosing and initiative. This fertile culture has contributed to 3M's branching out into more than 60,000 products and 40 separate product divisions.[20]

FIGURE 8–8 Cultural Dimensions of an Organization Supportive of Project Management

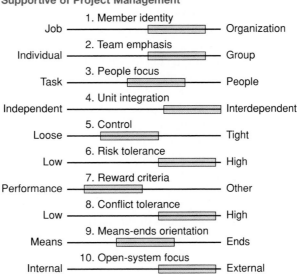

Snapshot from Practice
MATRIX PROBLEMS AT DEC

After a decade of declining sales and profits, Digital Equipment Corporation (DEC) was acquired in 1998 by Compaq Computer. Many analysts attributed the decline at DEC to management of the company's structure prior to the ousting of its founder and CEO, Kenneth H. Olsen, in 1992.

Olsen created a matrix structure to manage DEC's new-product development. In the early days of the computer industry, companies had the time and opportunity to perfect a product's technical capabilities because the product cycles were slow. In the matrix, rival product teams worked side by side on different designs. When one superior design emerged, it was chosen for further development. The winning teams became organizational heroes and rose quickly in the corporation, earning the right to lead future product teams and claim a larger share of the company resources. The other teams were disbanded so that their members could work on other products.

At first this system worked well and led to early successes. But soon DEC began to lose ground as a result of increased competition in the computer industry, which placed a premium on speed to market. As DEC faltered, resources tightened, and the product teams began to compete with each other for scarce company resources such as marketing and engineering support. Intense rivalries broke out among product teams. Many key members left because they felt that their careers were in jeopardy because DEC rewarded only winners.

As a result of the increased competition among teams, the product teams did not pool knowledge and expertise, and integration between functions declined. Instead of providing flexibility and efficient use of resources, the matrix structure at DEC resulted in inertia, infighting, and slow development time.[21]

The metaphor we choose to describe the relationship between organizational culture and project management is that of a riverboat trip. Culture is the river and the project is the boat. Organizing and completing projects within an organization in which the culture is conducive to project management is like paddling downstream: Much less effort is required, and the natural force of the river generates progress toward the destination. In many cases, the current can be so strong that steering is all that is required. Such is the case for projects that operate in a project-friendly environment where teamwork and cross-functional cooperation are the norms, where there is a deep commitment to excellence, and where healthy conflict is voiced and dealt with quickly and effectively.

Conversely, trying to complete a project in an organization in which several important features of the dominant culture inhibit effective project management is like paddling upstream: much more time, effort, and attention are needed to reach the destination. This would be the situation in cultures that discourage teamwork and cooperation, that have a low tolerance for conflict, where risks are to be avoided, and where getting ahead is based less on performance and more on cultivating favorable relationships with superiors. In such cases, the project manager and her people not only have to overcome the natural obstacles of the project but also have to overcome the prevailing negative forces inherent in the culture of the organization. (See the accompanying Snapshot from Practice box on matrix problems at DEC.)

The implications of this analogy are obvious but important. Greater project authority and resources are necessary to complete projects that encounter a strong, negative cultural current. Conversely, less formal authority and fewer dedicated resources are needed to complete projects in which the cultural currents generate behavior and cooperation essential to project success. The key issue is the degree of interdependency between the parent organization and the project team and the corresponding need to create a unique project culture conducive to successful project completion.

In cases where the prevalent organizational culture supports the behaviors essential to project completion, a weaker project management structure can be effective. For example, one of the major reasons Chaparral Steel is able to use a functional matrix to successfully complete incremental projects is that its culture contains strong norms for cooperation. Conversely, one of the reasons behind the failure of Kodak's "Factory of the Future" project in the mid-1980s was that the culture at that time did not support project management.[22]

When the parent organization possesses a dominant culture that inhibits collaboration and innovation among disciplines and groups of people, it is advisable to insulate the project team from the dominant culture by creating a self-sufficient, dedicated project team. If a dedicated project team is impossible because of resource constraints, then at least a project matrix should be used where the project manager has centralized control over the project. In both cases, the managerial strategy is to create a distinct subculture within the project team in which a new set of norms, customs, and values evolve that will be conducive to project completion.

Under extreme circumstances this project culture could even represent a counter-culture in that many of the norms and values are the antithesis of the dominant, parent culture. Such was the case of the original "Skunk Works" established by Kelly Johnson at Lockheed. Kelly and a small, isolated band of Lockheed mavericks developed the revolutionary U-2 spy plane during the early 1950s. Likewise when IBM decided to develop their personal computer quickly in 1980, they knew that the project could get bogged down by the overabundance of computer knowledge and bureaucracy in the company. They also realized that they would have to work closely with suppliers and make use of many non-IBM parts if they were to get to the market quickly. This was not the IBM way at the time, so IBM established the PC project team in a warehouse in Boca Raton, Florida, far from corporate headquarters and other corporate development facilities that existed within the organization.[23]

SUMMARY

This chapter examined two major characteristics of the parent organization that affect the implementation and completion of projects. The first is the formal structure of the organization and how it chooses to organize and manage projects. Although the individual project manager may have very little say as to how the firm chooses to manage projects, he must be able to recognize the options available as well as the inherent strengths and weaknesses of different approaches.

Three basic project management structures were described and assessed as to their weaknesses and strengths. Only under unique circumstances can a case be made for managing a project within the normal functional hierarchy. When thinking only in terms of what is best for the project, the creation of an independent project team is clearly favored. However, the most effective project management system appropriately balances the needs of the project with those of the parent organization. Matrix structures emerged out of the parent organization's need to share personnel and resources across multiple projects and operations while creating legitimate project focus. The matrix approach is a hybrid organizational form that combines elements of both the functional and project team forms in an attempt to realize the advantages of both.

Matrix management, while good in theory, has often proven difficult to implement. Many firms have abandoned a matrix after several years of experimentation, citing it as a totally unworkable structure prone to anarchy. Others have found it to be quite effective. These mixed results may, in part, be attributable to the fact that there are different kinds of matrices depending on the relative influence of the functional managers and the project managers.

The second major characteristic of the parent organization that was discussed in this chapter is the concept of organizational culture. Organizational culture is the pattern of beliefs and expectations shared by an organization's members. Culture includes the behavioral norms, customs, shared values, and the "rules of the game" for getting along and getting ahead within the organization. It is important for project managers to be "cultural sensitive" so that they can develop strategies and responses that are likely to be understood and accepted as well as avoid violating key norms that would jeopardize their effectiveness within the organization.

The interaction between project management structure and organizational culture is a complicated one. We have suggested that in certain organizations, culture encourages the implementation of projects. In this environment the project management structure used plays a less decisive role in the success of the project. Conversely, for other organizations in which the culture stresses internal competition and differentiation, just the opposite may be true. The prevailing norms, customs, and attitudes inhibit effective project management, and the project management structure plays a more decisive role in the successful implementation of projects. At a minimum, under adverse cultural conditions, the project manager needs to have significant authority over the project team; under more extreme conditions firms should use dedicated project teams to complete critical projects. In both cases, the managerial strategy should be to insulate project work from the dominant culture so that a more positive "subculture" can emerge among project participants.

The project management structure of the organization and the culture of the organization are major elements of the environment in which a project is initiated. Subsequent chapters will examine how project managers and professionals work within this environment to successfully complete projects.

REVIEW QUESTIONS

1. What are the relative advantages and disadvantages of the functional, matrix, and dedicated team approaches to managing projects?
2. What distinguishes a functional matrix from a project matrix?
3. Under what conditions would it be advisable to use a project matrix instead of a dedicated project team?
4. Why is it important to assess the culture of an organization before deciding what project management structure should be used to complete a project?
5. What do you believe is more important for successfully completing a project—the formal project management structure or the culture of the parent organization?

EXERCISES

1. This exercise takes a look at the culture of a successful high-tech company, Hewlett-Packard (HP). Explore its Web site (*http://www.hp.com/*). In particular click on the sections contained in "About Hewlett-Packard" (*http//www.hp.com/abouthp/AboutHP.html*), and especially review the section about the "Hewlett-Packard Way."
   a. What are the main elements of the HP way?

    b. How does the HP way help create an organizational culture that supports effective project management?

If you have difficulty accessing any of the Web addresses listed in the text, you can find up-to-date addresses on the home page of Dr. Erik Larson, co-author of this book, at *www.bus.orst.edu/faculty/larson.*

2. You work for LL Company, which manufacturers high-end optical scopes for hunting rifles. LL Company has been the market leader for the past 20 years and has decided to diversify by applying its technology to develop a top-quality binocular. What kind of project management structure would you recommend they use for this project? What information would you like to have to make this recommendation, and why?

3. Going to college is analogous to working in a matrix environment in that most students take more than one class and must distribute their time across multiple classes. What problems does this create for you? How does it affect your performance? How could the system be better managed to make your life less difficult and more productive?

ENDNOTES

1. Erik W. Larson and David H. Gobeli, "Matrix Management: Contradictions and Insights," *California Management Review,* vol. 29, no. 4 (Summer 1987), p. 137.

2. For a discussion of how internal differentiation inhibits organizational integration see Paul R. Lawrence and Jay W. Lorsch, *Organization and Environment* (Homewood, IL: Irwin, 1969); and M. Trice Harrison and Janice M. Beyer, *The Culture of Organizations* (Englewood Cliffs, NJ: Prentice Hall, 1993).

3. See Linn C. Stuckenbruck, *Implementation of Project Management* (Upper Darby, PA: Project Management Institute, 1981); Robert Youker, "Organizational Alternatives for Project Management," *Project Management Quarterly,* vol. 8 (March 1977), pp. 24–33; Vijay K. Verma, *Organizing Projects for Success: The Human Aspects of Project Management* (Newtown Square, PA: Project Management Institute, 1995); and Jack R. Meredith and Samuel J. Mantel, *Project Management: A Managerial Approach,* 3rd ed. (New York: Wiley, 1995).

4. *Ibid.*

5. Jim Carlton, *Apple: The Inside Story of Intrigue, Egomania, and Business Blunders* (New York: Random House, 1997), pp. 13–14.

6. John Sculley, *Odyssey: Pepsi to Apple . . . A Journey of Adventure, Ideas, and the Future* (New York: Harper & Row, 1987), pp. 270–79.

7. Erik W. Larson and David H. Gobeli, "Project Management Structures: Is There a Common Language?" *Project Management Journal,* vol. 16, no. 2 (June 1985), pp. 40–44; Preston G. Smith and Donald G. Reinertsen, *Developing Products in Half the Time* (New York: Van Nostrand Reinhold, 1995); and H. Kent Bowen, Kim B. Clark, Charles A. Holloway, and Steven C. Wheelwright, *The Perpetual Enterprise Machine* (New York: Oxford University Press, 1994).

8. O. Suris, "Competitors Blinded by Chrysler's Neon," *The Wall Street Journal* (January 10, 1994).

9. Erik W. Larson and David H. Gobeli, "Matrix Management: Contradictions and Insights," reference cited, pp. 126–37.

10. Linn C. Stuckenbruck, reference cited; Robert Youker, reference cited; Vijay K. Verma, reference cited; and Jack R. Meredith and Samuel J. Mantel, reference cited.

11. Erik W. Larson and David H. Gobeli, "Matrix Management: Contradictions and Insights," reference cited.

12. Thomas J. Allen, "Organization Structure, Information Technology, and R&D Productivity," *IEEE Transactions in Engineering Management,* vol. EM-31 (1984), pp. 212–17.

13. C. Gray, S. Dworatschek, D. H. Gobeli, H. Knoepfel, and E. W. Larson, "International Comparison of Project Organization Structures: Use and Effectiveness," *International Journal of Project Management,* vol. 8, no. 1 (February 1990), pp. 26–32; Erik W. Larson

and David H. Gobeli. "Organizing for Product Development Projects," *Journal of Product Innovation Management,* vol. 5 (1988), pp. 180–90; David H. Gobeli and Erik W. Larson, "Relative Effectiveness of Different Project Management Structures," *Project Management Journal,* vol. 18, no. 2 (June 1987), pp. 81–85.

14. H. Kent Bowen, Kim B. Clark, Charles A. Holloway, and Steven C. Wheelwright, reference cited.
15. See Stanley M. Davies and Paul R. Lawrence, *Matrix* (Reading, MA: Addison-Wesley, 1977); and Harold Kerzner, *In Search of Excellence in Project Management* (New York: Von Nostrand Reinhold, 1997).
16. T. E. Deal and A. A. Kennedy, *Corporate Cultures: The Rites and Rituals of Corporate Life* (Reading, MA: Addison-Wesley, 1982); and Harrison M. Trice and Janice M. Beyer, reference cited.
17. A. M. Pettegrew, "On Studying Organizational Culture," *Administrative Science Quarterly,* vol. 24, no. 4 (1979), pp. 570–81; G. Hofstede, B. Neuijen, D. D. Ohayv, and D. Sanders, "Measuring Organizational Culture: A Qualitative and Quantitative Study Across Twenty Cases," *Administrative Science Quarterly* (June 1990), pp. 286–316; C. A. O'Reilly, J. Chatman, and D. F. Caldwell, "People and Organizational Culture: A Profile Comparison Approach to Assessing Person-Organization Fit," *Academy of Management Journal,* vol. 34, no. 3 (September 1991), pp. 487–516; Edgar Schein, *Organizational Culture and Leadership: A Dynamic View* (San Francisco, CA: Jossey-Bass, 1985).
18. Edgar Schein, reference cited.
19. Michael Elmes and David Wilemon, "Organizational Culture and Project Leader Effectiveness," *Project Management Journal,* vol. 19, no. 4 (September 1989), pp. 54–63.
20. James C. Collins and Jerry I. Porras, *Built to Last: The Successful Habits of Visionary Companies* (New York: HarperCollins, 1994), pp. 150–58.
21. "Through the Mill," *The Economist,* vol. 33, no. 7880 (September 10, 1994), p. 76; and G. McWilliams, "Crunch Time at DEC," *Business Week* (May 4, 1992), pp. 30–33.
22. H. Kent Bowen, Kim B. Clark, Charles A. Holloway, and Steven C. Wheelwright, reference cited.
23. Preston G. Smith and Donald G. Reinertsen, reference cited.

CASE

Moss and McAdams Accounting Firm

Bruce Palmer had worked for Moss and McAdams (M&M) for six years and was just promoted to account manager. His first assignment was to lead an audit of Johnsonville Trucks. He was quite pleased with the five accountants who had been assigned to his team, especially Zeke Olds. Olds was an Army vet who returned to school to get a double major in accounting and computer sciences. He was on top of the latest developments in financial information systems and had a reputation for coming up with innovative solutions to problems.

M&M was a well-established regional accounting firm with 160 employees located across six offices in Minnesota and Wisconsin. The main office, where Palmer worked, was in Green Bay, Wisconsin. In fact, one of the founding members, Seth Moss, played briefly for the hometown NFL Packers during the late 1950s. M&M's primary services were corporate audits and tax preparation. Over the last two years the partners decided to move more aggressively into the consulting business. M&M projected that consulting would represent 40 percent of their growth over the next five years.

M&M operated within a matrix structure. As new clients were recruited, a manager was assigned to the account. A manager might be assigned to several accounts, depending on the size and scope of the work. This was especially true in the case of tax preparation projects, where it was not uncommon for a manager to be assigned to 8 to 12 clients. Likewise, senior and staff accountants were assigned to multiple account teams. Ruby Sands was the office manager responsible for assigning personnel to different accounts at the Green Bay office. She did her best to assign staff to multiple projects under the same manager. This wasn't always possible, and sometimes accountants had to work on projects led by different managers.

M&M, like most accounting firms, had a tiered promotion system. New CPAs entered as junior or staff accountants. Within two years, their performance was reviewed and they were either asked to leave or promoted to senior accountant. Sometime during their fifth or sixth year, a decision was made to promote them to account manager. Finally, after 10 to 12 years with the firm, the manager was considered for promotion to partner. This was a very competitive position. During the last five years, only 20 percent of account managers at M&M had been promoted to partner. However, once a partner, they were virtually guaranteed the position for life and enjoyed significant increases in salary, benefits, and prestige. M&M had a reputation for being a results-driven organization; partner promotions were based on meeting deadlines, retaining clients, and generating revenue. The promotion team based its decision on the relative performance of the account manager in comparison to his or her cohorts.

One week into the Johnsonville audit, Palmer received a call from Sands to visit her office. There he was introduced to Ken Crosby, who recently joined M&M after working nine years for a Big 5 accounting firm. Crosby was recruited to manage special consulting projects. Sands reported that Crosby had just secured a major consulting project with Springfield Metals. This was a major coup for the firm: M&M had competed against two Big 5 accounting firms for the project. Sands went on to explain that she was working with Crosby to put together his team. Crosby insisted that Zeke Olds be assigned to his team. Sands told him that this would be impossible because Olds was already assigned to work on the Johnsonville audit. Crosby persisted, arguing that Olds's expertise was essential to the Springfield project. Sands decided to work out a compromise and have Olds split time across both projects.

At this time Crosby turned to Palmer and said, "I believe in keeping things simple. Why don't we agree that Olds works for me in the mornings and you in the afternoons. I'm sure we can work out any problems that come up. After all, we both work for the same firm."

Six Weeks Later

Palmer could scream whenever he remembered Crosby's words, "After all, we both work for the same firm." The first sign of trouble came during the first week of the new arrangement when Crosby called, begging to have Olds work all of Thursday on his project. They were conducting an extensive client visit, and Olds was critical to the assessment. After Palmer reluctantly agreed, Crosby said he owed him one. The next week when Palmer called Crosby to request that he return the favor, Crosby flatly refused and said any other time but not this week. Palmer tried again a week later and got the same response.

At first Olds showed up promptly at 1:00 P.M. at Palmer's office to work on the audit. Soon it became a habit to show up 30 to 60 minutes late. There was always a good reason. He was in a meeting at Springfield and couldn't just leave, or an urgent task took longer than planned. One time it was because Crosby took his entire team out to lunch at the new Thai restaurant—Olds was over an hour late because of slow service.

In the beginning Olds would usually make up the time by working after hours, but Palmer could tell from conversations he overheard that this was creating tension at home.

What probably bothered Palmer the most were the e-mails and telephone calls Olds received from Crosby and his team members during the afternoons when he was supposed to be working for Palmer. A couple of times Palmer could have sworn that Olds was working on Crosby's project in his (Palmer's) office.

Palmer met with Crosby to talk about the problem and voice his complaints. Crosby acted surprised and even a little bit hurt. He promised things would change, but the pattern continued.

Palmer was becoming paranoid about Crosby. He knew that Crosby played golf with Olds on the weekends and could just imagine him badmouthing the Johnsonville project and pointing out how boring auditing work was. The sad fact was that there probably was some truth to what he was saying. The Johnsonville project was getting bogged down, and the team was slipping behind schedule. One of the contributing factors was Olds's performance. His work was not up to its usual standards. Palmer approached Olds about this, and Olds became defensive. Olds later apologized and confided that he found it difficult switching his thinking from consulting to auditing and then back to consulting. He promised to do better, and there was a slight improvement in his performance.

The last straw came when Olds asked to leave work early on Friday so that he could take his wife and kids to a Milwaukee Brewers baseball game. It turned out Springfield Metals had given Crosby their corporate tickets, and he decided to treat his team with box seats right behind the Brewers dugout. Palmer hated to do it, but he had to refuse the request. He felt guilty when he overheard Olds explaining to his son on the telephone why they couldn't go to the game.

Palmer finally decided to pick up the phone and request an urgent meeting with Sands to resolve the problem. He got up enough nerve and put in the call only to be told that Sands wouldn't be back in the office until next week. As he put the receiver down, he thought maybe things would get better.

Two Weeks Later

Sands showed up unexpectedly at Palmer's office and said they needed to talk about Olds. Palmer was delighted, thinking that now he could tell her what had been going on. But before he had a chance to speak, Sands told him that Olds had come to see her yesterday. She told him that Olds confessed that he was having a hard time working on both Crosby's and Palmer's projects. He was having difficulty concentrating on the auditing work in the afternoon because he was thinking about some of the consulting issues that had emerged during the morning. He was putting in extra hours to try to meet both of the projects' deadlines, and this was creating problems at home. The bottom line was that he was stressed out and couldn't deal with the situation. He asked that he be assigned full-time to Crosby's project. Sands went on to say that Olds didn't blame Palmer, in fact he had a lot of nice things to say about him. He just enjoyed the consulting work more and found it more challenging. Sands concluded by saying, "We talked some more and ultimately I agreed with him. I hate to do this to you, Bruce, but Olds is a valuable employee, and I think this is the best decision for the firm."

1. If you were Palmer at the end of the case, how would you respond?
2. What, if anything, could Palmer have done to avoid losing Olds?

3. What advantages and disadvantages of a matrix type organization are apparent from this case?
4. What could the management at M&M do to more effectively manage situations like this?

ORION Systems (A)*

The office erupted into cheers when it was announced over the PA system that ORION had just been awarded the government contract to build the next generation of high-speed, light-rail trains. Everyone came over to shake Mike Rosas's hand and congratulate him. It was well known that Rosas would be the project manager for this important project, which would be code named Jaguar. Once the celebration subsided, Rosas gazed out the window and thought about what he had just gotten himself into.

The Jaguar project would be a high-profile project that would affect procurement of future contracts with the government. Increased competition had raised performance expectations regarding completion time, quality, reliability, and cost. He knew that major changes in how ORION organized and managed projects would be necessary to meet the expectations of the Jaguar project.

Project Management at ORION

ORION was a division of a large aerospace company with 7,000 employees. ORION evolved from a project organization into a matrix structure to conserve costs and better utilize limited resources. At any point in time, ORION could be working on three to five large projects such as the Jaguar project and 30 to 50 smaller projects. Project managers negotiated personnel assignments with the VP of operations, who ultimately decided project assignments. It was not uncommon for an engineer to be working on two to three projects during a week.

Figure C8–1 portrays how new-product development projects were organized at ORION. Project management was limited only to the design and development of the new product. Once the final design and prototype were completed, they were turned over to manufacturing for production and delivery to the customer. A four-person management team oversaw the completion of the project and their responsibilities are briefly described here:

- *Project manager*—responsible for all aspects of design and development of the product.
- *Planning and control manager*—responsible for building an overall project network, scheduling, managing the budget, controlling and evaluating the design and development program, and preparing status reports.
- *Electronics system engineer*—responsible for providing technical expertise on electronic systems issues.

---

* Prepared by Shlomo Cohen.

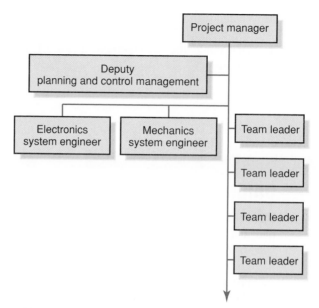

FIGURE C8–1 Organization of Product Development Projects at ORION

- *Mechanics system engineer*—responsible for providing technical expertise on mechanical system issues.

The core work was completed by 12 to 20 design teams. Each team had a leader, who was responsible for designing, developing, building, and testing a specific subsystem of the product. The size of individual teams varied from 5 to 15 engineers, depending on the scope of their work. These engineers split time across multiple projects.

Design engineers ran the show at ORION, and manufacturing, marketing, and other groups were expected to follow their lead. The special status of the design engineers was reinforced by the fact that they were actually paid on higher pay curves than the manufacturing engineers.

The overall product development and manufacturing process is captured in the master plan chart (Figure C8–2). New-product design and development evolves around five major reviews: system design review (SDR), preliminary design review (PDR), critical design review (CDR), test readiness review (TRR), and production readiness review (PRR).

Design and development work begins within the laboratory and progresses to field tests of specific subsystems and ultimately final product prototypes. Once completed, the design and prototype are turned over to manufacturing, which begins building the production line for the new product. Manufacturing also develops the necessary test equipment to confirm that manufactured components perform correctly. During this time, integrated logistical support (ILS) teams prepare product documentation, users' manuals, maintenance programs, and training programs for the customers who will be using the product. It typically takes ORION six to seven years to develop and manufacture a product such as the Jaguar.

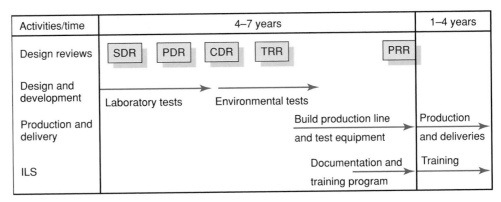

FIGURE C8–2   Traditional Master Plan at ORION

ORION just completed a major assessment of how projects are managed. Below is a brief description of some of the major problems that were identified:

- *Higher than expected production costs.* Once products were developed, there was a tendency for them to be "thrown over the wall" to manufacturing to produce. Very little design for manufacturability was done, and the transfer to production and the production ramp was complicated, inefficient, and stressful to the people in the plant.
- *Quality concerns.* Increased competition had raised customer expectations with regard to quality. Customers expected fewer defects and longer replacement schedules. ORION had a tendency to deal with quality issues after the fact, initiating quality improvements after the production process was set up. Not enough attention was devoted to incorporating quality considerations into the original design of products.
- *Problems with customer support.* User manuals and technical documentation sometimes failed to address all of a customer's concerns, and the follow-up training was not always adequately prepared. These problems contributed to increased costs in customer service and a decline in customer satisfaction.
- *Lack of strong project ownership.* While everyone accepted that a matrix arrangement was the only way to accommodate all the projects at ORION, the shifting back and forth of personnel across multiple projects took its toil on the progress of individual projects. Members often failed to identify with individual projects and develop the sense of excitement that contributed to superior performance. The shuffling of personnel slowed down progress because additional time had to be devoted to bringing returning members up to speed on current developments.
- *Scope creep.* ORION was renowned for its engineering prowess. However, there was a tendency for design engineers to get so absorbed with the science of the project that they lost focus on the practical considerations. This led to costly delays and sometimes design modifications that were inconsistent with customer requirements.

Rosas was aware of these and other concerns as he sat down with his staff to figure out the best way to organize the new Jaguar project.

1. What recommendations would you make to Rosas about organizing the Jaguar project, and why?
2. How would you change the organizational chart and master plan to reflect these changes?

ORION Systems (B)

Rosas's Plan

Rosas and his staff worked hard over the past week to develop a plan to establish a new standard for completing projects at ORION. The Jaguar project management team will be expanded to seven managers, who will be responsible for overseeing the completion of the project from design to delivery to the customer. A brief description of the responsibilities for the three new positions follows (see Figure C8–3):

- *Production manager*—responsible for raising production issues during the design phase; responsible for building and managing the production line.
- *ILS (integrated logistical support) manager*—responsible for all activities that require project/customer support after delivery including customer training, documentation, and equipment testing.
- *QA (quality assurance) manager*—responsible for implementing a quality program that will enhance the reliability, availability and maintainability of the product.

These seven managers (the three just described plus the four discussed in Part A) will coordinate the completion of the project and see that their respective disciplines are factored into all major decisions. Rosas, as project manager, will work toward achieving consensus, but he will have the authority to intervene and make decisions if necessary.

The core work will be completed by 35 teams. Each team will have a "leader," who will be responsible for designing, developing, building, and testing a specific subsys-

FIGURE C8–3   Proposed Project Organization for the Jaguar Project

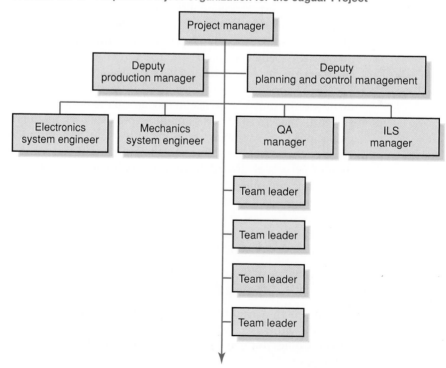

FIGURE C8–4 Jaguar Master Plan

Activities/time	3–4 years				1–4 years
Design reviews	SDR PDR	CDR		TRR	PRR
Design and development	Laboratory tests		Environmental tests		
Production and delivery		Build production line and test equipment			Production and delivery
ILS		Documentation/training program			Training

tem of the project. They will also be responsible for the quality and productivity of the subsystems and for doing the work on time and within budget.

Individual teams will consist of 5 to 12 members, and Rosas insists that at least half of each team be assigned to work full-time on the project. This will help ensure continuity and enhance commitment to the project.

The second key feature to the plan is the development of the overall master plan for the project. This involves abandoning the traditional sequential approach to product development and adopting a concurrent engineering approach to the project (see Figure C8–4).

Once the system design is reviewed and approved, different teams will begin working within the laboratory to design, develop, and test specific subsystems and components. Soon after this has begun the ILS team will start gathering information and preparing product documentation. Once the PDR is completed, the production teams will begin designing the necessary production lines. The CDR will include not only resolution of major technical questions but also a plan for manufacturing. Once the CDR is completed, project teams will begin field tests under a variety of different environmental conditions according to government specifications. Subsequent design refinements will be closely coordinated with manufacturing and ILS teams so that, ideally, ORION will be ready to begin producing the Jaguar upon completion of the PRR.

Rosas believes that the phasing of the production and documentation work along side the core development work will accelerate project completion, reduce production costs, and contribute to customer satisfaction.

1. What are the major changes between this plan and the way ORION has managed projects in the past?
2. How well do you believe these changes deal with the problems identified in Part A?
3. Who is likely to support this plan? Who is not likely to support this plan?

APPENDIX 8–1

How Culture Is Created and Communicated in Organizations

To understand, interpret, and even change the culture of an organization, it is useful to understand how that culture evolved and how it is communicated to its members. Most

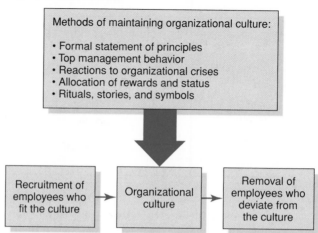

FIGURE A8–1   Mechanisms for Sustaining Organizational Culture

experts trace the origins of an organization's culture to the personality, values, and habits of the individual(s) responsible for founding the organization. For example, Bill Gates has been described as personally aggressive, competitive, highly disciplined, and willing to put in long hours on the job. These same characteristics have been used to describe the Microsoft organization, the software giant he founded and currently heads. While the roots of culture may be traced to the personality of the founding members, as organizations grow in size and encounter new challenges, their culture evolves and is sustained by a complex set of mechanisms summarized in Figure A8–1.[1]

Selection of New Members

The explicit goal of the recruitment process is to identify and hire individuals with the requisite skills, knowledge, and experience to perform jobs within an organization. Part of performing work within an organization is the ability to work with others and fit into the culture of the organization. Companies are paying increased attention to assessing the personal values and habits of applicants to determine whether they are compatible with the culture of the organization. For example, Compaq computers is known to hire candidates who are easy to get along with and who feel comfortable with the consensus decision-making style they use. They actively screen out loners or stellar performers with big egos. Conversely, Microsoft has a reputation for hiring aggressive, competitive employees.

The importance of selection as a means of sustaining or changing the culture of an organization cannot be underestimated. Experience has taught companies that it is much more difficult and costly to get rid of people who do not fit in than to invest extra time and effort to ensure that new hires are compatible with the culture of the organization. This is why it is not uncommon today for the selection and hiring process to be extended over a battery of interviews in which one of the primary objectives is to determine how well the applicant will "fit in."

Methods for Sustaining Culture

No matter how careful an organization is in recruiting and hiring personnel, new employees need to be indoctrinated in the culture of the organization. Just like all Marines go through boot camp to prove their worthiness and learn the "Marine Way," new employees experience a less intense socialization process, where they are tested and learn the norms, customs, and ideals of the organization.

Formal Statement of Principles

It has become fashionable for companies to explicitly publish their values and operating principles in company documents. For example, the Kaufman and Broad Home Corporation, located in Los Angeles, states its mission as follows:[2]

> We build homes to meet people's dreams.

Objectives
- We are fiercely determined to continue to succeed. We intend to provide the best quality housing for our customers, a superior return to our shareholders, and a chance for every employee to make a difference and share in our success.

Vision
- We strive to be the leading home builder in each market in which operate. We intend to lead the way in home building well into the twenty-first century.

Core Values
- It is our intention to deliver a quality product . . . 100 percent of the time.
- We believe that the true test of quality is customer satisfaction.
- There are no good excuses.
- We strive to be the cutting edge of product development and innovative design.
- We reward innovation and encourage reasonable and prudent risk taking.
- We don't just build homes, we build neighborhoods.
- This business is built around people. We want self-directed winners who have high personal integrity.
- This is a team business where we depend upon one another. We expect people to make a contribution.
- All people at Kaufman and Broad have clout. We all work for the same ultimate boss, our customers.
- Our subcontractors and suppliers are our partners. We demand a lot from them, especially high-quality work. We expect to work and prosper together.
- We respect the dignity of those with whom we deal. We always try to be fair.
- We are committed to steady growth and improved earnings; we will not overemphasize short-term results.

These corporate principles and philosophies are generally reviewed during new employee orientation sessions and are augmented by stories to underscore their significance. It should be noted that simply stating what the values and principles of a firm are will be meaningless unless they are visibly supported by the other methods.

Top Management Behavior

Just as the founder's personality is critical to the initial formation of a company's culture, many experts argue that top management plays a critical role in sustaining and shaping the culture of a firm. First, they serve as exemplars of the culture of the organization. As such, members look to them as role models to be emulated and to be analyzed to determine those qualities and habits the organization cherishes. Second, members interpret from top managers' actions what is truly important to the firm. For example, imagine the president of a firm announcing that improving customer satisfaction is the firm's number one priority. Now imagine the different impact this statement would have on the organization if, after this declaration, the president disappears behind a wall of business as usual as opposed to personally leading a series of focus groups to determine specific customer needs and complaints.

Reaction to Crisis

Organizations are sometimes confronted with defining moments in their history in which their values and priorities are tested and most clearly manifested. For example, during the mid-1980s the local Hewlett-Packard (HP) plant was operating at less than 40 percent capacity. Rumors abounded that there would be corresponding layoffs and massive transfers. However, one of the dominating principles of the culture at HP has always been a commitment to human resources. Instead of draconian layoffs, management of the plant responded by scheduling a nine-day work schedule over two weeks, representing a 10 percent cut in salary for everyone. They also encouraged employees to go on sabbaticals and pursue advanced degrees while maintaining benefits and job assurance. In doing so the firm sent a clear message to its employees about the importance of human resources. This response has become deeply ingrained in the corporation's folklore and, in turn, now serves to reinforce this aspect of its culture.

Allocation of Rewards and Status

Employees also learn about their organization's culture through its reward systems. The rewards and punishments attached to various behaviors convey to employees the priorities and values of both the individual manager and the organization.[3] Imagine the different signals that are being sent if a worthy subordinate who was justifiably critical of a top management proposal is promoted versus transferred to a less prestigious area within the firm. Likewise, what values are being communicated when an employee is discovered engaging in unethical behavior and is verbally reprimanded as opposed to being fired?

It is important to note that organizations may be quite ineffective in rewarding behavior consistent with their espoused values and principles. Employees are adroit at pointing out inconsistencies between what management says and does. These inconsistencies undermine management credibility as well as help create a weak culture that contributes to ineffective organizational performance.[4]

Rituals, Stories, and Symbols

A significant portion of an organization's culture is transmitted and reinforced symbolically. Symbolic communication is a sign or an act that means something more than itself—it is something invested with a particular, subjective meaning. Although symbolic communication is indirect, it can act as an "evocative" mechanism for rousing, channeling, and domesticating powerful emotions.[5] To appreciate how much feeling symbols evoke, consider the response to the raising of a national flag at the Olympics or the meaning of Yassir Arafat standing or not standing when the Israeli national anthem is being played.

Organizational Rituals Organizational rituals are defined as formal and customarily repeated acts that convey basic norms and values throughout the organization. The function of rituals is to give concrete expression to deeply held cultural values.[6] The variety of ritualistic behaviors includes the annual company picnic and Christmas party, employee morale surveys, TGIF gatherings, weekly staff meetings, and going-away parties. Companies that are committed to building a strong culture that supports their basic values and principles invest considerable attention in organizational rituals. Take, for example, the Sequent Corporation, an information technology firm located in Portland, Oregon. As it turns out, 85 percent of their business is typically shipped out during the last week of the quarter. It has become the custom for everyone at Sequent from the president to the janitor to volunteer to work one shift in the loading area during this time. According to the president, this custom reinforces a variety of important corporate values, including "We're in the business of building products," and "None of us is too big to get our hands dirty."

Stories, Myths, and Legends Many of the underlying beliefs and values of an organization's culture are expressed as legends and stories that become part of the organization's folklore. These stories and legends are a way of transmitting the existing culture from senior employees to new ones; they serve to emphasize important aspects of that culture.[7] For example, IBM employees pass on the story of a plant security supervisor who challenged Thomas Watson, Jr., who at the time was chairman of IBM's board. The supervisor, a 22-year-old woman, was responsible for making sure that no one entered the security areas without the proper *green* identification badge. One day, Watson approached the security door surrounded by his usual entourage. Although the supervisor knew who he was, she told him that she had been instructed not to let anyone enter without the security badge. The group accompanying Watson was taken aback. Would the young security guard be fired on the spot? "Don't you know who he is?" someone asked. Watson raised his hand for silence while one of the party strode off and returned with the appropriate badge. The message to IBM employees: No matter who you are, you obey the rules.[8]

Material Symbols Nike Corporate Headquarters in Portland, Oregon, doesn't look like normal head office operations. The first thing a visitor sees when driving into the grounds is a professionally groomed soccer field. Within the hall of the main building is a large mural of Michael Jordan. Intermixed within the network of modern offices are state-of-the-art athletic facilities for almost every sport imaginable. The employees are uniformly young and athletic. Fiercely contested basketball games are played during the workday. The entire operation communicates a play hard/work hard, competitive environment.

Size and layout of offices are other material symbols that reflect corporate values. For example, for many companies the size of an office and its floor number reflects how much status and real power the manager has. Conversely, many companies have tried to promote egalitarianism by opting for cubicle arrangements in which all departments are on the same floor and office space is standardized.

Removal of Deviants

Just as members assess those people who are being rewarded to determine what the organization values, they assess people who are asked to leave to identify what kind of people and behavior management disapproves of. It is perfectly natural for individuals to gossip about reasons a former member left. These explanations help clarify what is acceptable and unacceptable behavior. Whenever possible, management needs to spell out the reasons individuals were discharged or left voluntarily so that the correct causes are understood.

Appendix Summary

An organization's culture can have a profound impact on members' attitudes and behavior. Top management is devoting more time and attention to developing a unique culture that will provide them with a competitive advantage in today's business world.

Appendix Review Questions

1. What are the mechanisms that are used to sustain the culture of an organization?
2. Which mechanism do you believe has the biggest effect on the culture of an organization and why?

Appendix Exercise

Select an organization you have been or currently are a member of (e.g., work organization, athletic team, fraternity). Assess the organization's culture in terms of the roles that rituals and stories play in communicating the norms, expectations, and values of the organization. How are the cultural values communicated symbolically?

Appendix Endnotes

1. Edgar Schein, *Organizational Culture and Leadership: A Dynamic View* (San Francisco: Jossey-Bass, 1985).
2. Jeffrey Abrahams, *The Mission Statement Book* (New York: Ten-Speed Press, 1995), pp. 350–51.
3. Jeffrey Kerr and John W. Slocum, "Managing Corporate Culture through Reward Systems," *Academy of Management Executive,* vol. 1, no. 2 (May 1987), pp. 99–108.
4. Erik W. Larson and Jonathan King, "The Systemic Distortion of Information: An Ongoing Challenge to Management," *Organizational Dynamics,* vol. 24, no. 3 (Winter 1996), pp. 49–62.
5. T. C. Dandridge, "Symbols' Function and Use," in L. R. Pondy et al., eds., *Organizational Symbolism 1, Monographs in Organizational Behavior and Industrial Relations* (Greenwich, CT: JAI Press, 1983), p. 166.
6. T. E. Deal and A. A. Kennedy, *Corporate Cultures: The Rites and Rituals of Corporate Life* (Reading, MA: Addison-Wesley, 1982); and Harrison M. Trice and Janice M. Beyer, *The Culture of Organizations* (Englewood Cliffs, NJ: Prentice Hall, 1993).
7. Harrison M. Trice and Janice M. Beyer, reference cited.
8. W. Rogers, *Think* (New York: Sein & Day, 1969), pp. 153–54.

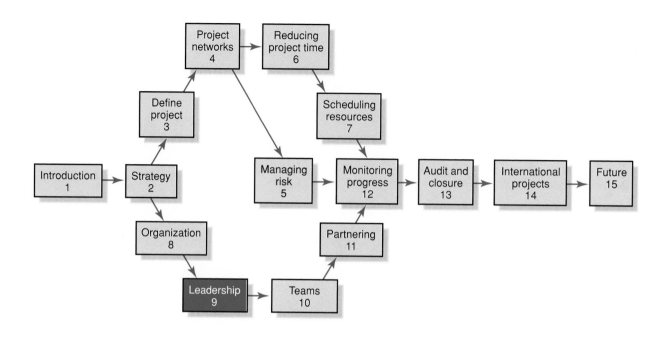

CHAPTER NINE

Leadership: Being an Effective Project Manager

*I couldn't wait to be the manager of my own project and run the project the way I
thought it should be done. Boy, did I have a lot to learn!*
—first-time project manager

This chapter is based on the premise that one of the keys to being an effective project manager is building cooperative relationships among different groups of people to complete projects. Project success does not just depend on the performance of the project team. Success or failure often depends on the contributions of top management, functional managers, customers, suppliers, contractors, and others.

The chapter begins with a brief discussion of the differences between leading and managing a project. The importance of managing project interfaces is then introduced. Managers require a broad influence base to be effective in this area. Different sources of influence are discussed and are used to describe how project managers build social networks. This management style necessitates constant interacting with different groups of people whom project managers depend on. Special attention is devoted to managing the critical relationship with top management and the importance of leading by example. The importance of gaining cooperation in ways that build and sustain the trust of others is emphasized. The chapter concludes by identifying personal attributes associated with being an effective project manager. Subsequent chapters will expand on these ideas in a discussion of managing the project team and working with people outside the organization.

MANAGING VERSUS LEADING A PROJECT

In a perfect world, the project manager would simply implement the project plan and the project would be completed. The project manager would work with others to formulate a schedule, organize a project team, keep track of progress, and announce what needs to be done next, and then everyone would charge along. Of course no one lives in a perfect world, and rarely does everything go according to plan. Project participants get testy; they fail to complement each other; other departments are unable to fulfill their commitments; technical glitches arise; work takes longer than expected. The project manager's job is to get the project back on track. A manager expedites certain activities; figures out ways to solve technical problems; serves as peacemaker when tensions rise; and makes appropriate trade-offs among time, cost, and scope of the project.

However, project managers do more than put out fires and keep the project on track. They also innovate and adapt to ever-changing circumstances. They often have to deviate from what was planned and introduce significant changes in the project scope and schedule to respond to unforeseen threats or opportunities. For example, customers' needs may change, requiring significant design changes midway through the project. Competitors may release new products that dictate switching the time, cost, and scope priorities of the project. Working relationships among project participants may break down, requiring a reformulation of the project team. Ultimately, what was planned or expected in the beginning may be very different from what was accomplished by the end of the project.

Project managers are responsible for integrating assigned resources to complete the project according to plan. At the same time they need to initiate changes in plans and schedules as persistent internal problems make plans unworkable or as unexpected external events require accommodation. In other words, managers want to keep the project going while making necessary adjustments along the way. According to Kotter these two different activities represent the distinction between management and leadership. Management is about coping with complexity, while leadership is about coping with change.[1] Good management brings about order and stability by formulating plans and objectives, designing structures and procedures, monitoring results against plans, and taking corrective action when necessary. Leadership involves recognizing and articulating the need to significantly alter the direction and operation of the project, aligning people to the new direction, and motivating them to work together to overcome hurdles produced by the change and to realize new objectives.

Strong leadership, while usually desirable, is not always necessary to successfully complete a project. Well-defined projects that encounter no significant surprises require little leadership, as might be the case in constructing a conventional apartment building in which the project manager simply administrates the project plan. Conversely, the higher the degree of uncertainty encountered on a project—whether in terms of changes in project scope, technological stalemates, breakdowns in coordination between people, and so forth—the more leadership is required. For example, strong leadership would be needed for a software development project in which the parameters are always changing to meet developments in the industry.

It takes a special person to perform both roles well. Some individuals are great visionaries who are good at exciting people about change. Too often though, these same people lack the discipline or patience to deal with the day-to-day drudgeries of managing. Likewise, there are other individuals who are very well organized and methodical but lack the ability to inspire others. Strong leaders can compensate for their managerial weaknesses by having trusted assistants who oversee and manage the details of the project. Conversely, a weak leader can complement his or her strengths by having assistants who are good at sensing the need to change and rallying project participants. Still, one of the things that makes good project managers so valuable to an organization is that they have the ability to both manage and lead a project. In doing so they recognize the need to manage project interfaces and build a social network that allows them to find out what needs to be done and obtain the cooperation necessary to achieve it.

MANAGING PROJECT INTERFACES

First-time project managers are eager to implement their own ideas and manage their people to successfully complete their project. What they soon find out is that project success depends on the cooperation of a wide range of individuals, many of whom do

Snapshot from Practice
THE PROJECT MANAGER AS CONDUCTOR

Metaphors convey meaning beyond words. For example, a meeting can be described as being difficult or "like wading through molasses." A popular metaphor for the role of a project manager is that of *conductor.* The conductor of an orchestra integrates the divergent sounds of different instruments to perform a given composition and make beautiful music. Similarly, the project manager integrates the talents and contributions of different specialists to complete the project. Both have to be good at understanding how the different players contribute to the performance of the whole. Both are almost entirely dependent upon the expertise and know-how of the players. The conductor does not have command of all the musical instruments. Likewise, the project manager usually possesses only a small proportion of the technical knowledge to make decisions. As such, the conductor and project manager both facilitate the performance of others rather than actually perform.

Conductors use their arms and baton and other nonverbal gestures to influence the pace, intensity, and involvement of different musicians. Likewise, project managers orchestrate the completion of the project by managing the involvement and attention of project members. Project managers balance time and process and induce participants to make the right decisions at the right time just as the conductor induces the wind instruments to perform at the right moment in a movement. Each controls the rhythm and intensity of work by managing the tempo and involvement of the players. Finally, each has a vision that transcends the music score or project plan. To be successful they must both earn the confidence, respect, and trust of their players.

not directly report to them. For example, during the course of a system integration project, a project manager was surprised by how much time she was spending negotiating and working with vendors, consultants, technical specialists, and other functional managers:

> Instead of working with my people to complete the project, I found myself being constantly pulled and tugged by demands of different groups of people who were not directly involved in the project but had a vested interest in the outcome.

Too often when new project managers do find time to work directly on the project, they adopt a hands-on approach to managing the project. They choose this style not because they are power-hungry egomaniacs but because they are eager to achieve results. They become quickly frustrated by how slowly things operate, the number of people that have to be brought on board, and the difficulty of gaining cooperation. Unfortunately, as this frustration builds, the natural temptation is to exert more pressure and get more heavily involved in the project.[2] These project managers quickly earn the reputation of "micro-managing" and begin to lose sight of the real role they play on guiding a project.

Some new managers never break out of this vicious cycle. Others soon realize that authority does not equal influence and that being an effective project manager involves managing a much more complex and expansive set of interfaces than they had previously anticipated. They encounter a web of relationships that requires a much broader spectrum of influence than they felt was necessary or even possible.

For example, a significant project, whether it involves renovating a bridge, creating a new product, or installing a new information system, will likely involve in one way or another working with a number of different groups of people.[3] First, there is the core group of specialists assigned to complete the project. This group is likely to be supplemented at different times by professionals who work on specific segments of the project. Second, there are the groups of people within the performing organization who are either directly or indirectly involved with the project. The most notable is top management, to whom the project manager is accountable. There are also other project managers, functional managers who provide resources and/or may be responsible for specific segments of the project, and administrative support services such as human resources, finance, etc. Depending on the nature of the project, there are a number of different groups outside the organization that influence the success of the project; the most important is the customer for which the project is designed (see Figure 9–1).

Each of these groups of individuals brings different expertise, standards, priorities, and agendas to the project. One of the things that distinguishes project management from regular management is the sheer breadth and complexity of the relationships that need to be managed. To be effective, a project manager must understand how these groups can affect the project and develop methods for managing the dependency. The nature of these dependencies is identified here:

- The **project team** is responsible for managing and completing project work. Most participants want to do a good job, but they are also concerned with their other obligations and how their involvement on the project will contribute to their personal goals and aspirations.
- **Project managers** naturally compete with each other for resources and the support of top management. At the same time they often have to share resources and exchange information.
- **Administrative support** groups, such a human resources, information systems, purchasing agents, and maintenance, provide valuable support services. At the same time they impose constraints and requirements on the project such as the documentation of expenditures and the timely and accurate delivery of information.
- **Functional managers,** depending on how the project is organized, can play a minor or major role toward project success. In matrix arrangements, they may be responsible for assigning project personnel, resolving technical dilemmas, and overseeing the completion of significant segments of the project work. Even in dedicated project teams, the technical input from functional managers may be useful, and accep-

FIGURE 9–1   Network of Relationships

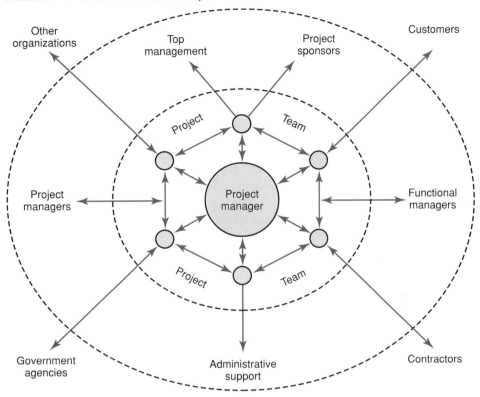

tance of completed project work may be critical to in-house projects. Functional managers want to cooperate up to a point, but only up to a certain point. They are also concerned with preserving their status within the organization and minimizing the disruptions the project may have on their own operations.

- **Top management** approves funding of the project and establishes priorities within the organization. They define success and adjudicate rewards for accomplishments. Significant adjustments in budget, scope, and schedule typically need their approval. They have a natural vested interest in the success of the project, but at the same time have to be responsive to what is best for the entire organization.

- **Project sponsors** champion the project and used their influence to gain approval of the project. Their reputation is tied to the success of the project, and they need to be kept informed of any major developments. They defend the project when it comes under attack and are a key project ally.

- **Subcontractors** may do all the actual work, in some cases, with the project team merely coordinating their contributions. In other cases, they are responsible for ancillary segments of the project scope. Poor work and schedule slips can affect work of the core project team. While contractors' reputations rest with doing good work, they must balance their contributions with their own profit margins and their commitments to other clients.

- **Government agencies** place constraints on project work. Permits need to be secured. Construction work has to be built to code. New drugs have to pass a rigorous battery of U.S. Food and Drug Administration tests. Other products have to meet safety standards, for example, Occupational Safety and Health Administration standards.

- **Other organizations,** depending on the nature of the project, may directly or indirectly affect the project. For example, suppliers provide necessary resources for completion of the project work. Delays, shortages, and poor quality can bring a project to a standstill. Public interest groups may apply pressure on government agencies. Customers often hire consultants and auditors to protect their interests on a project.

- **Customers** define the scope of the project, and ultimate project success rests in their satisfaction. Project managers need to be responsive to changing customer needs and requirements and to meeting their expectations. Customers are primarily concerned with getting a *good deal* and, as will be elaborated in Chapter 11, this naturally breeds tension with the project team.

These relationships are interdependent in that a project manager's ability to work effectively with one group will affect her ability to manage other groups. For example, functional managers are likely to be less cooperative if they perceive that top management's commitment to the project is waning. Conversely, the ability of the project manager to buffer the team from excessive interference from a client is likely to increase her standing with the project team.

The project management structure being used will influence the number and degree of external dependencies that will need to be managed. One advantage of creating a dedicated project team is that it reduces dependencies, especially within the organization, because most of the resources are assigned to the project. Conversely, a functional matrix structure increases dependencies, with the result that the project manager is much more reliant upon functional colleagues for work and staff.

The old-fashioned view of managing projects emphasized directing and controlling subordinates; the new perspective emphasizes managing project interfaces and anticipating change as the most important jobs.[4] Project managers need to be able to assuage concerns of customers, sustain support for the project at higher levels of the organization, quickly identify problems that threaten project work, while at the same time defend the integrity of the project and the interests of the project participants.

Within this web of relationships, the project manager must find out what needs to be done to achieve the goals of the project and build a cooperative network to accomplish it. Project managers must do so without the requisite authority to expect or demand cooperation. Doing so requires sound communication skills, political savvy, and a broad influence base.

INFLUENCE AS EXCHANGE

To successfully manage a project, a manager must adroitly build a cooperative network among divergent allies. Networks are mutually beneficial alliances that are generally governed by the law of reciprocity.[5] The basic principle is that "one good deed deserves another, and likewise, one bad deed deserves another." The primary way to gain cooperation is to provide resources and services for others in exchange for future resources and services. This is the age-old maxim: "Quid pro quo (something for something)." Or in today's vernacular: "You scratch my back, I'll scratch yours."

Cohen and Bradford[6] described the exchange view of influence as "currencies." If you want to do business in a given country, you have to be prepared to use the appropriate currency, and the exchange rates can change over time as conditions change. In

TABLE 9–1

COMMONLY TRADED ORGANIZATIONAL CURRENCIES

Task-related currencies

Resources	Lending or giving money, budget increases, personnel, etc.
Assistance	Helping with existing projects or undertaking unwanted tasks.
Cooperation	Giving task support, providing quicker response time, or aiding implementation.
Information	Providing organizational as well as technical knowledge.

Position-related currencies

Advancement	Giving a task or assignment that can result in promotion.
Recognition	Acknowledging effort, accomplishments, or abilities.
Visibility	Providing a chance to be known by higher-ups or significant others in the organization.
Network/contracts	Providing opportunities for linking with others.

Inspiration-related currencies

Vision	Being involved in a task that has larger significance for the unit, organization, customer, or society.
Excellence	Having a chance to do important things really well.
Ethical correctness	Doing what is "right" by a higher standard than efficiency.

Relationship-related currencies

Acceptance	Providing closeness and friendship.
Personal support	Giving personal and emotional backing.
Understanding	Listening to others' concerns and issues.

Personal-related currencies

Challenge/learning	Sharing tasks that increase skills and abilities.
Ownership/involvement	Letting others have ownership and influence.
Gratitude	Expressing appreciation.

Source: Adapted from A. R. Cohen and David L. Bradford, *Influence without Authority* (New York: John Wiley & Sons, 1990). Reprinted by permission of John Wiley & Sons, Inc.

the same way, what is valued by a marketing manager may be different from what is valued by a veteran project engineer, and you are likely to need to use different influence currency to obtain the cooperation of each individual. Although this analogy is a bit of an oversimplification, the key premise holds true that in the long run, "debit" and "credit" accounts must be balanced for cooperative relationships to work. Table 9–1 presents the commonly traded organizational currencies identified by Cohen and Bradford; they are then discussed in more detail in the following sections.

Task-Related Currencies

This form of influence comes directly from the project manager's ability to contribute to others accomplishing their work. Probably the most significant form of this currency is the ability to respond to subordinates' requests for additional manpower, money, or time to complete a segment of a project. This kind of currency is also evident in sharing resources with another project manager who is in need. At a more personal level, it may simply mean providing direct assistance to a colleague in solving a technical problem.

Providing a good word for a colleague's proposal or recommendation is another form of this currency. Because most work of significance is likely to generate some form of opposition, the person who is trying to gain approval for a plan or proposal can be greatly aided by having a "friend in court."

Another form of this currency includes extraordinary effort. For example, fulfilling an emergency request to complete a design document in two days instead of the normal four days is likely to engender gratitude. Finally, sharing valuable information that would be useful to other managers is another form of this currency.

Position-Related Currencies

This form of influence stems from the manager's ability to enhance others' positions within their organization. A project manager can do this by giving someone a challenging assignment that can aid their advancement by developing their skills and abilities. Being given a chance to prove yourself naturally generates a strong sense of gratitude. Sharing the glory and bringing to the attention of higher-ups the efforts and accomplishments of others generates goodwill.

Project managers confide that a key strategy useful for gaining the cooperation of professionals in other departments and organizations is figuring out how to make these people look good to their bosses. For example, a project manager was working with a subcontractor whose organization was heavily committed to total quality management (TQM). The project manager made it a point in top-level briefing meetings to point out how quality improvement processes initiated by the contractor contributed to cost control and problem prevention.

Another variation of recognition is enhancing the reputation of others within the firm. "Good press" can pave the way for lots opportunities, while "bad press" can quickly shut a person off and make it difficult to perform. This currency is also evident in helping to preserve someone's reputation by coming to the defense of someone unjustly blamed and making sure the right attributions are made.

Finally, one of the strongest forms of this currency is sharing contacts with other people. Helping individuals expand their own networks by introducing them to key people naturally engenders gratitude. For example, suggesting to a functional manager that he should contact Sally X if he wants to find out what is really going on in that department or to get a request expedited is likely to engender a sense of indebtedness.

Inspiration-Related Currencies

Perhaps the most powerful form of influence is based on inspiration. Most sources of inspiration derive from people's burning desire to make a difference and add meaning to their lives. Creating an exciting, bold vision for a project can elicit extraordinary commitment. For example, many of the technological breakthroughs associated with the introduction of the original Macintosh computer were attributed to the feeling that the project members had a chance to change the way people approached computers. A variant form of vision is providing an opportunity to do something really well. Being able to take pride in your work is a significant driving force for many people.

Often the very nature of the project provides a source of inspiration. Discovering a cure for a devastating disease, introducing a new social program that will help those in need, or simply building a bridge that will reduce a major traffic bottleneck can provide opportunities for people to feel good about what they are doing and that they are making a difference. The power of inspiration is that it operates as a magnet—pulling people as opposed to pushing people toward doing something.

Relationship-Related Currencies

These currencies have more to do with strengthening the relationship with someone than directly accomplishing the project tasks. The essence of this form of influence is forming a relationship that transcends normal professional boundaries and extends into the realm of friendship. Such relationships develop by giving personal and emotional backing. Picking people up when they are feeling down, boosting their confidence, and providing encouragement naturally breed goodwill. Sharing a sense of humor and making difficult times fun is another form of this currency. Similarly, engaging in non-work-related activities such as sports and family outings are another way relationships are naturally enhanced.

Perhaps the most basic form of this currency is simply listening to other people. Psychologists suggest that most people have a strong desire to be understood and that relationships break down because the parties stop listening to each other. Sharing personal secrets/ambitions and being a wise confidant also creates a special bond between individuals.

Personal-Related Currencies

This last form of currency deals with individual needs and an overriding sense of self-esteem. Some argue that self-esteem is a primary psychological need; the extent to which we can help others feel a sense of importance and personal worth will naturally generate goodwill. A project manager can enhance a colleague's sense of worth by sharing tasks that increase skills and abilities, delegating authority over work so that others experience ownership, and allowing individuals to feel comfortable stretching their abilities. This form of currency can also be seen in sincere expressions of gratitude for the contributions of others. Care, though, must be exercised in expressing gratitude since it is easily devalued when overused. That is, the first *thank you* is likely to be more valued than the twentieth.

The bottom line is that a project manager will be influential only insofar as she can offer something that others value. Furthermore, given the diverse cast of people a project manager depends on, it is important that she be able to acquire and exercise different influence currencies. The ability to do so will be constrained in part by the nature of the project and how it is organized. For example, a project manager who is in charge of a dedicated team has considerably more to offer team members than a manager who is given the responsibility of coordinating the activities of different professionals across different departments and organizations. In such cases, that manager will probably have to rely more heavily on personal and relational bases of influence to gain the cooperation of others.

SOCIAL NETWORK BUILDING

Mapping Dependencies

The first step to building a social network is identifying those on whom the project depends for success.[7] The project manager and his or her key assistants need to ask the following questions:

- Whose cooperation will we need?
- Whose agreement or approval will we need?
- Whose opposition would keep us from accomplishing the project?

Many project managers find it helpful to draw a map of these dependencies. For example, Figure 9–2 contains the dependencies identified by a project manager who was responsible for installing a new financial software system in her company.

It is always better to overestimate rather than underestimate dependencies. All too often, otherwise talented and successful project managers have been derailed because they were blindsided by someone whose position or power they had not anticipated. After identifying whom you will depend on, you are ready to "step into their shoes" and see the project from their perspective:[8]

- What differences exist between myself and the people on whom I depend (goals, values, pressures, working styles, risks)?
- How do these different people view the project (supporters, indifferent, antagonists)?
- What is the current status of the relationship I have with the people I depend on?
- What sources of influence do I have relative to those on whom I depend?

Once you start this analysis you can begin to appreciate what others value and what currencies you might have to offer as a basis on which to build a working relationship. You begin to realize where potential problems lie—relationships in which you have a current debit or no convertible currency. Furthermore, diagnosing another's point of view as well as the basis for their positions will help you anticipate their reactions and feelings about your decisions and actions. This information is vital for selecting the appropriate influence strategy and tactics and conducting win/win negotiations.

FIGURE 9–2 Dependencies for Financial Software Installation Project

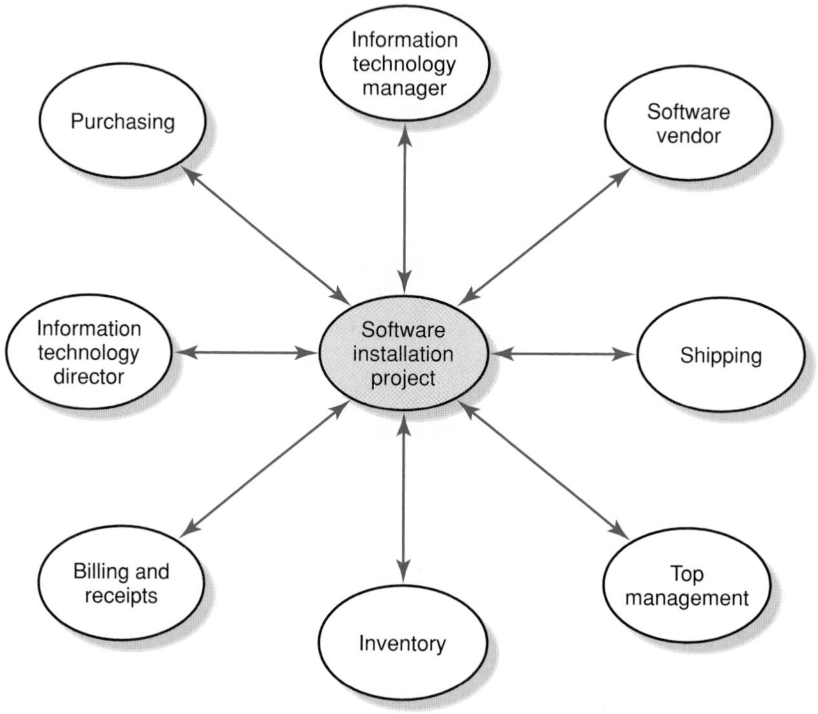

For example, after mapping her dependency network, the project manager who was in charge of installing the software system realized that she was likely to have serious problems with the manager of the receipts department, who would be one of the primary users of the software. She had no previous history of working with this individual but had heard through the grapevine that the manager was upset with the choice of software and that he considered this project to be another unnecessary disruption of his department's operation. Prior to project initiation the project manager arranged to have lunch with the manager, where she sat patiently and listened to his concerns. She invested additional time and attention to educate him and his staff about the benefits of the new software. She tried to minimize the disruptions the transition would cause in his department. She altered the implementation schedule to accommodate his preferences as to when the actual software would be installed and the subsequent training would occur. In turn, the receipts manager and his people were much more accepting of the change, and the transition to the new software went more smoothly than anticipated.

Management by Wandering Around (MBWA)

The preceding example illustrates the next step in building a supportive social network. Once you have established who the key players are that will determine success, then you initiate contact and begin to build a relationship with those players. Building this relationship requires a management style employees at Hewlett-Packard refer to as "management by wandering around" (MBWA) to reflect that managers spend the majority of their time outside their offices.[9] MBWA is somewhat of a misnomer in that there is a purpose/pattern behind the "wandering." Through face-to-face interactions, project managers are able to stay in touch with what is really going on in the project and build cooperative relationships essential to project success.

Effective project managers initiate contact with key players to keep abreast of developments, anticipate potential problems, provide encouragement, and reinforce the objectives and vision of the project. They are able to intervene to resolve conflicts and prevent stalemates from occurring. In essence, they "manage" the project. By staying in touch with various aspects of the project they become the focal point for information on the project. Participants turn to them to obtain the most current and comprehensive information about the project which reinforces their central role as project manager.

We have also observed less-effective project managers who eschew MBWA and attempt to manage projects from their offices and computer terminals. Such managers proudly announce an open-door policy and encourage others to see them when a problem or an issue comes up. To them no news is good news. What this does is allow their contacts to be determined by the relative aggressiveness of others. Those who take the initiative and seek out the project manager get too high a proportion of the project manager's attention. Those people less readily available (physically removed) or more passive get ignored. This behavior contributes to the adage, "Only the squeaky wheel gets greased," which produces resentment in those who believe they are more deserving.

While a significant amount of their time is devoted to the project team, effective project managers find the time to regularly interact with more distal stakeholders. They keep in touch with suppliers, vendors, top management, and other functional managers. In doing so they maintain familiarity with different parties, sustain friendships, discover opportunities to do favors, and understand the motives and needs of others. They remind people of commitments and champion the cause of their project. They also shape people's expectations. Through frequent communication they alleviate people's concerns about the project, dispel rumors, warn people of potential problems, and lay the groundwork for dealing with setbacks in a more effective manner.

Unless project managers take the initiative to build a network of supportive relationships, they are likely to see a manager (or other stakeholder) only when there is bad news or when they need a favor (e.g., they don't have the data they promised or the project has slipped behind schedule). Without prior, frequent, easy give-and-take interactions around nondecisive issues, the encounter prompted by the problem is likely to provoke excess tension. The parties are more likely to act defensively, interrupt each other, and lose sight of the common problem.

Experienced project managers recognize the need to build relationships before they need them. They initiate contact with the key stakeholders at times when there are no outstanding issues or problems and therefore no anxieties and suspicions. On these social occasions, they engage in small talk and responsive banter. Astute project managers also seek to make deposits in their relationships with potentially important stakeholders. They are responsive to others' requests for aid, provide supportive counsel, and exchange information. In doing so they are establishing credit in that relationship, which will allow them to deal with more serious problems down the road. When one person views another as pleasant, credible, and helpful based on past contact, he or she is more likely to be responsive to requests for help and less confrontational when problems arise.[10]

Veteran project managers also recognize that personal contact can be motivating. They confer status on the other person by sharing their scarcest resource—their time—with that person. For this to occur there must be a healthy give-and-take interchange. Project managers adapt their interaction pattern to that of the other. They do so by using the language and jargon of the other party. They don't always dominate the conversation with their own agenda, but frequently listen and respond to the other. Simple questions such as "How are things going?" or "Do you have any questions about the project?" can yield valuable information and establish goodwill at the same time. Inept project managers turn off others by failing to exchange pleasantries and dominating the conversation. The ineffectiveness of these interactions can easily be seen in the stiffness of the body language and the minimal exchange of information. In contrast, when a project manager is able to interact effectively, the interchange is naturally relaxing, and information flows freely. This behavior not only provides satisfaction but also yields better information and insights to the project manager.

Managing Upward Relations

Research consistently points out that project success is strongly affected by the degree to which a project has the support of top management.[11] Such support is reflected in an appropriate budget, responsiveness to unexpected needs, and a clear signal to others in the organization of the importance of cooperation. In most organizations priorities are communicated through normal channels. However, companies have found it necessary to take less orthodox approaches to signaling priorities. For example, at Sequent Computer Systems, president Casey Powell at one critical point handed out buttons. Most of the company were given green "How can I help" buttons, but people working on vital projects were given red "Priority" buttons. People with the green buttons were told to do anything to remove obstacles for those with the red buttons. Powell wore a green button. This simple, inexpensive technique clearly communicated project priorities throughout the entire organization.[12]

Visible top management support is not only critical for securing the support of other managers within an organization, but it also is a key factor in the project manager's ability to motivate the project team. Nothing establishes a manager's right to lead more

RESEARCH HIGHLIGHT
Improving the Performance of New-Product Teams

Ancona and Caldwell studied the performance of 45 new-product teams in five high-technology companies and produced some startling results.[13] The most significant was that internal team dynamics were not related to performance. That is, high-performance teams were not distinguished by clearer goals, smoother workflow among members, or greater ability to satisfy the individual goals of team members. What was related to team performance were level and intensity of external interactions between the project team and the rest of the organization. Ancona and Caldwell identified four key patterns of activity which contribute to creating a high performance team:

1. *Ambassador* activities are aimed at representing the team to others and protecting the team from interference. The project manager typically takes on this responsibility, which involves buffering the team from political pressures and building support for the project within the hierarchy of the company.
2. *Task coordinator* activities are aimed at coordinating the team's efforts with other units and organizations. Unlike the ambassador role, which is focused upward, these are more lateral activities and involve negotiating and interacting with interested parties within the organization.
3. *Scouts* act as a scout on an expedition; that is, they go out from the team to bring back information about what is going on elsewhere in the organization. This is a much less focused task than task coordinator.
4. *Guard* activities differ from the other activities in that they are intended to keep information and resources inside the team, preventing drainage out of the group. A key guard activity is keeping necessary information secret until it is appropriate to share it.

Ancona and Caldwell found that the importance of these activities varies during the product development life cycle if the project team is to be successful. For example, scouting activities are more critical during the creation phase, when the product idea is being formulated and the team is being developed. Ambassador activities are especially critical during the development phase, when product specifications have been agreed upon and the major task is developing a prototype.

Ancona and Caldwell caution that their findings do not mean that teamwork and the internal operations of a project team are not important to project success. Effective team dynamics are necessary to successfully integrate information from outside sources and coordinate activities across groups. Their research supports the adage that problems and opportunities often lie at the borders of projects, and that one of the primary jobs of a project manager is to manage the interface between his or her team and the rest of the organization.

than her ability to defend. To win the loyalty of team members, project managers have to be effective advocates for their projects. They have to be able to get top management to rescind unreasonable demands, provide additional resources, and recognize the accomplishments of team members.

Perhaps because of the importance of this connection, working relationships with upper management is a common source of consternation. Comments we have heard from project managers about upper management include the following:

They don't know how much it sets us back losing Neil to another project.

I would like to see them get this project done with the budget they gave us.

I just wish they would make up their minds as to what is really important.

While it may seem counterintuitive for a subordinate to "manage" a superior, smart project managers devote considerable time and attention to influencing and garnering the support of top management. Project managers have to accept profound differences in perspective and become skilled at the art of persuading superiors.

Many of the tensions that arise between upper management and project managers are a result of differences in perspective. Project managers become naturally absorbed with what is best for their project, while upper management is concerned with what is best for the entire organization. It is only natural for these two interests to conflict at times. For example, a project manager may lobby intensively for additional personnel only to be turned down because top management believes that the other departments cannot afford a reduction in staff. Although frequent communication can minimize differences, the project manager has to accept the fact that top management is inevitably going to see the world differently.

Once project managers accept that disagreements with superiors are more a question of perspective than substance, they can focus more of their energy on the art of persuading upper management. But before they can persuade superiors, they must first prove loyalty.[14] Loyalty in this context simply means that most of the time project managers have to show that they consistently follow through on requests and adhere to the parameters established by top management without a great deal of grumbling or fuss. Closely linked to loyalty is having credibility, which comes from an established track record of success. Once managers have proven loyalty to upper management, senior management is much more receptive to their challenges and requests.

Project managers have to cultivate strong ties with upper managers who are sponsoring the project. As noted earlier, these are high-ranking officials who championed approval and funding of the project; as such, their reputations are aligned with the project. Sponsors are also the ones who defend the project when it is under attack in upper circles of management. They shelter the project from excessive interference (see Figure 9–3). Project managers should *always* keep such people informed of any problems that may cause embarrassment or disappointment. For example, if costs are beginning to outrun the budget or a technical glitch is threatening to delay the completion of the project, managers make sure that the sponsors are the first to know.

When negotiating from a subordinate position for additional funds, resources, or extensions, project managers recognize that the timing of a request is critical. Asking for additional budget the day after disappointing third-quarter earnings are reported is going to be much more difficult than making a similar request four weeks later. Good project managers pick the optimum time to appeal to top management. They enlist their project sponsors to lobby their cause. They also realize there are limits to top management's accommodations. Here, the Lone Ranger analogy is appropriate—you have only so many silver bullets, so use them wisely.

When giving a status report to superiors, project managers must present the most positive image possible without stretching the truth. They should adapt their communication pattern to that of the senior group, making it a point to use buzzwords and jargon valued by superiors in their presentations. For example, one project manager recognized that top management had a tendency to use sports metaphors to describe business situations, so she framed a recent slip in schedule by admitting that "we lost five yards, but we still have two plays to make a first down." Smart project managers learn the language of top management and use it to their advantage.

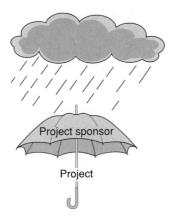

FIGURE 9–3 The Significance of a Project Sponsor

Finally, a few project managers admit ignoring chains of command. If they are confident that top management will reject an important request and that what they want to do will benefit the project, they do it without asking permission. While acknowledging that this is very risky, they claim that bosses typically won't argue with success.

Leading by Example

A highly visible, interactive management style is not only essential to building and sustaining cooperative relationships, it also allows project managers to utilize their most powerful leadership tool—their own behavior.[15] Often, when faced with uncertainty, people look to others for cues as to how to respond and demonstrate a propensity to mimic the behavior of superiors. A project manager's behavior symbolizes how other people should work on the project. Through her behavior a project manager can influence how others act and respond to a variety of issues related to the project. To be effective, project managers must "walk the talk" (see Figure 9–4). Six aspects of leading by example are discussed next.

FIGURE 9–4 Leading by Example

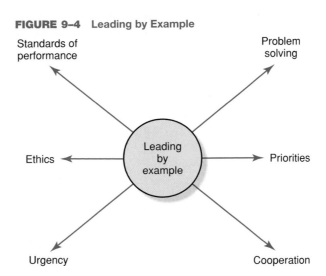

Priorities   Actions speak louder than words. Subordinates and others discern project managers' priorities by how they spend their time. If a project manager claims that this project is critical and then is perceived as devoting more time to other projects, then all his verbal reassurances are likely to fall on deaf ears. Conversely, a project manager who takes the time to observe a critical test instead of simply waiting for a report affirms the importance of the testers and their work. Likewise, the types of questions project managers pose communicate priorities. By repeatedly asking how specific issues relate to satisfying the customer, a project manager can reinforce the importance of customer satisfaction.

Urgency   Through their actions project managers can convey a sense of urgency, which can permeate project activities. This urgency in part can be conveyed through stringent deadlines, frequent status report meetings, and aggressive solutions for expediting the project. The project manager uses these tools like a metronome to pick up the beat of the project. At the same time, such devices will be ineffective if there is not also a corresponding change in the project manager's behavior.[16] If they want others to work faster and solve problems quicker, then they need to work faster. They need to hasten the pace of their own behavior. They should accelerate the frequency of their interactions, talk and walk more quickly, get to work sooner, and leave work later. By simply increasing the pace of their daily interaction patterns, project managers can reinforce a sense of urgency in others.

Problem Solving   How project managers respond to problems sets the tone for how others tackle problems. If bad news is greeted by verbal attacks, then others will be reluctant to be forthcoming. If the project manager is more concerned with finding out who is to blame instead of how to prevent problems from happening again, then others will tend to cover their tracks and cast the blame elsewhere.[17] If, on the other hand, project managers focus more on how they can turn a problem into an opportunity or what can be learned from a mistake, then others are more likely to adopt a more proactive approach to problem solving.

Cooperation   How project managers act toward outsiders influences how team members interact with outsiders. If a project manager makes disparaging remarks about the "idiots" in the marketing department, then this oftentimes becomes the shared view of the entire team. If project managers set the norm of treating outsiders with respect and being responsive to their needs, then others will more likely follow suit.

Standards of Performance   Veteran project managers recognize that if they want participants to exceed project expectations then they have to exceed others' expectations of a good project manager. They establish a high standard for project performance through the quality of their daily interactions. They respond quickly to the needs of others, carefully prepare and run crisp meetings, stay on top of all the critical issues, facilitate effective problem solving, and stand firm on important matters.

Ethics   How others respond to ethical dilemmas that arise in the course of a project will be influenced by how the project manager has responded to similar dilemmas. In many cases, team members base their actions on how they think the project manager would respond. If project managers deliberately distort or withhold vital information from customers or top management, then they are signaling to others that this kind of behavior is acceptable. Project management invariably creates a variety of ethical dilemmas; this would be an appropriate time to delve into this topic in more detail.

ETHICS AND PROJECT MANAGEMENT

Questions of ethics have already arisen in previous chapters that discussed padding of cost and time estimations, exaggerating pay-offs of project proposals, and so forth. Ethical dilemmas involve situations where it is difficult to determine whether conduct is right or wrong. Is it acceptable to falsely assure customers that everything is on track when, in reality, you are only doing so to prevent them from panicking and making matters worse?

In a survey of project managers, 81 percent reported that they encounter ethical issues in their work.[18] These dilemmas range from being pressured to alter status reports, backdate signatures, or shade documentation to mask the reality of project progress to falsifying cost accounts, compromising safety standards to accelerate progress, and approving shoddy work.

Project management is complicated work, and, as such, ethics invariably involve gray areas of judgment and interpretation. For example, it is difficult to distinguish deliberate falsification of estimates from genuine mistakes or the willful exaggeration of project payoffs from genuine optimism. It becomes problematic to determine whether unfulfilled promises were deliberate deception or an appropriate response to changing circumstances.

To provide greater clarity to business ethics, many companies and professional groups publish a code of conduct. The PMI code of ethics is presented in Appendix 9–1 to this chapter. Cynics see these documents as simply window dressing, while advocates argue that they are important, albeit limited, first steps. In practice, personal ethics do not lie in formal statutes but at the intersection of one's work, family, education, profession, religious beliefs, and daily interactions.[19] Most project managers report that they rely on their own private sense of right and wrong—what one project manager called his "internal compass."[20] One common rule of thumb for testing whether a response is ethical is to ask, "Imagine that whatever you did was going to be reported on the front page of your local newspaper. How would you like that? Would you be comfortable?"

Unfortunately, Nazi war crimes have demonstrated the willingness of highly trained professionals to abdicate personal responsibility for horrific actions and to obey the directives of organizational hierarchies. Top management and the culture of an organization play a decisive role in shaping members' beliefs of what is right and wrong. Many organizations encourage ethical transgressions by creating a "win at all cost" mentality. The pressures to succeed obscure consideration of whether the ends justify the means. Other organizations place a premium on "fair play" and command a market position by virtue of being trustworthy and reliable.

Discussing business ethics is like opening Pandora's box. What can be pointed out is that many project managers claim that ethical behavior is its own reward. By following your own internal compass your behavior expresses your personal values. Others suggest that ethical behavior is doubly rewarding.[21] You not only are able to fall asleep at night but you also develop a sound and admirable reputation. As will be explored in the next section, such a reputation is essential to establishing the trust necessary to exercise influence effectively.

BUILDING TRUST: THE KEY TO EXERCISING INFLUENCE

We all know people who have influence but whom we do not trust; these individuals are often referred to as "political animals" or "jungle fighters." While these individuals are often very successful in the short run, the prevalent sense of mistrust prohibits long-term efficacy. Successful project managers not only need to be influential, they also need to exercise influence in a manner that builds and sustains the trust of others.

The significance of trust can be discerned by its absence. Imagine how different a working relationship is when you distrust the other party as opposed to trusting them. When people distrust each other, they often spend inordinate amounts of time and energy attempting to discern hidden agendas and the true meaning of communications and then securing guarantees to promises. They are much more cautious with each other and hesitant to cooperate.

Conversely, trust is the "lubricant" that maintains smooth and efficient interactions. When you are trusted, people are more likely to take your actions and intentions at face value when circumstances are ambiguous. Cohen and Bradford[22] note that with trust, people will be less stringent about whether you are paying back in kind; they will extend you a larger line of credit and be more liberal in your repayment terms. Such flexibility is critical to project managers, especially during times of organizational change and uncertainty, when it is by definition more difficult to establish "fair exchange rates."

Trust is an elusive concept. It is hard to nail down in precise terms why some project managers are trusted and others are not. One popular way to understand trust is to see it as a function of character and competence.[23] Character focuses on personal motives (i.e., does he or she want to do the right thing?), while competence focuses on skills necessary to realize motives (i.e., does he or she know the right things to do?).

Stephen Covey resurrected the significance of character in leadership literature in his best selling *Seven Habits of Highly Effective People.*[24] Covey criticized popular management literature as focusing too much on shallow human relations skills and manipulative techniques, which he labeled the personality ethic. He argues that at the core of highly effective people is a character ethic that is deeply rooted in personal values and principles such as dignity, service, fairness, the pursuit of truth, and respect.

One of the distinguishing traits of character is consistency. When people are guided by a core set of principles, they are naturally more predictable because their actions are consistent with these principles. Another feature of character is openness. When people have a clear sense of who they are and what they value, they are more receptive to others. This trait provides them with the capacity to empathize and the talent to build consensus among divergent people. Finally, another quality of character is a sense of purpose. Managers with character are driven not only by personal ambitions but also for the common good. Their primary concern is what is best for their organization and the project, not what is best for themselves. This willingness to subordinate personal interests to a higher purpose garners the respect, loyalty, and trust of others.

The significance of character is summarized by the comments made by two team members about two very different project managers.

> At first everyone liked Joe and was excited about the project. But after a while, people became suspicious of his motives. He had a tendency to say different things to different people. People began to feel manipulated. He spent too much time with top management. People began to believe that he was only looking out for himself. It was HIS project. When the project began to slip he jumped ship and left someone else holding the bag. I'll never work for that guy again.

My first impression of Jack was nothing special. He had a quiet, unassuming management style. Over time I learned to respect his judgment and his ability to get people to work together. When you went to him with a problem or a request, he always listened carefully. If he couldn't do what you wanted him to do, he would take the time to explain why. When disagreements arose he always thought of what was best for the project. He treated everyone by the same rules; no one got special treatment. I'd jump at the opportunity to work on a project with him again.

Character alone will not engender trust. We must also have confidence in the competency of the individual before we really trust them.[25] We all know well-intended managers whom we like but do not trust. Although we may befriend these managers, we don't like to work with or for them. Competence is reflected at a number of different levels. First, there is task-related knowledge and skills reflected in the ability to answer questions, solve technical problems, and excel in certain kinds of work. Second, there is competence at an interpersonal level demonstrated in being able to listen effectively, communicate clearly, resolve arguments, provide encouragement, and so forth. Finally, there is organizational competence. This includes being able to run effective meetings, set meaningful objectives, reduce inefficiencies, and build a social network. Too often there is a tendency for young engineers and other professionals to place too much value on task or technical competence. They underestimate the significance of organizational skills. Veteran professionals, on the other hand, recognize the importance of management and place a greater value on organizational and interpersonal skills.

One problem new project managers experience is that it takes time to establish a sense of character and competency. Character and competency are often demonstrated when they are tested, such as when a tough call has to be made or when difficult problems have to be solved. Veteran project managers have the advantage of reputation and an established track record of success. Although endorsements from credible sponsors can help a young project manager create a favorable first impression, ultimately he or she will have to demonstrate character and competence during the course of their dealings with others in order to gain their trust.

So far this chapter has addressed the importance of building a network of relationships to complete the project based on trust and reciprocity. The next section examines the nature of project management work and the personal qualities needed to excel at it.

QUALITIES OF AN EFFECTIVE PROJECT MANAGER

Project management is, at first glance, a misleading discipline in that there is an inherent logic in the progression from formulating a project scope statement, creating a WBS, developing a network, adding resources, finalizing a plan, and reaching milestones. However, when it comes to actually implementing and completing projects, this logic quickly disappears, and project managers encounter a much messier world, filled with inconsistencies and paradoxes. Effective project managers have to be able to deal with the contradictory nature of their work. Some of those contradictions are listed here:

- **Innovate and maintain stability.** Project managers have to put out fires, restore order, and get the project back on track. At the same time they need to be innovative and develop new, better ways of doing things. Innovations unravel stable routines and spark new disturbances that have to be dealt with.

Snapshot from Practice
PROFILE OF A PROSPECTIVE PROJECT COORDINATOR

Martin F. Malkin, the executive director of the planning and management department of MSDRL (Merck, Sharp, and Dohme Research Laboratories), oversaw 14 project coordinators. In addition to formal job descriptions, Malkin created a list of special talents project managers must bring to the job.[26] Be:

1. Able to juggle many balls in the air at the same time but know which balls can be dropped when priorities demand it.

2. The consummate separator of the wheat from the chaff but still be able to use the chaff.

3. Able to remain intelligent, objective, neutral at all times even when you know the limitations of people presenting strategies.

4. A person who can talk with kings—and cabbages—and be called a good listener by both.

5. Pesky, persistent but effective, and above all, correct.

6. Able to have both ears to the ground at the same time and never be surprised.

7. Able, at times, to possess the discretion of a clam.

8. Able to show favoritism but never be accused of playing favorites.

9. Able to live without recognition but survive with scorn.

10. Dependable but independent.

11. Able to suffer fools gladly, but take notes.

12. Trusted but not necessarily trusting.

- **See the big picture while getting your hands dirty.** Project managers have to see the big picture and how their project fits within the larger strategy of their firm. There are also times when they must get deeply involved in project work and technology. If they don't worry about the details, who will?

- **Encourage individuals but stress the team.** Project managers have to motivate, cajole, and entice individual performers while at the same time maintaining teamwork. They have to be careful that they are considered fair and consistent in their treatment of team members while at the same time treating each member as a special individual.

- **Hands-off/Hands-on.** Project managers have to intervene, resolve stalemates, solve technical problems, and insist on different approaches. At same time they have to recognize when it is appropriate to sit on the sidelines and let other people figure out what to do.

- **Flexible but firm.** Project managers have to be adaptable and responsive to events and outcomes that occur on the project. At the same time they have to hold the line at times and tough it out when everyone else wants to give up.

- **Team versus organizational loyalties.** Project managers need to forge a unified project team whose members stimulate one another to extraordinary performance. But at the same time they have to counter the excesses of cohesion and the team's resistance to outside ideas. They have to cultivate loyalties to both the team and the parent organization.

Managing these and other contradictions requires finesse and balance. Finesse involves the skillful movement back and forth between opposing behavioral patterns.[27] For example, most of the time project managers actively involve others, move by increment, and seek consensus. There are other times when project managers must act as autocrats and take decisive, unilateral action. Balance involves recognizing the danger of extremes and that too much of a good thing invariably becomes harmful. For example, many managers have a tendency to always delegate the most stressful, difficult assignments to their best team members. This habit often breeds resentment among those chosen ("why am I always the one who gets the tough work?") and never allows the weaker members to develop their talents further.

There is no one management style or formula for being an effective project manager. The world of project management is too complicated for formulas. Successful project managers have a knack for adapting styles to specific circumstances of the situation.

So, what should one look for in an effective project manager? Many authors have addressed this question and have generated list after list of skills and attributes associated with being an effective manager.[28] When reviewing these lists, one sometimes gets the impression that to be a successful project manager requires someone with superhuman powers. While we agree that not everyone has the right stuff to be an effective project manager, there are some core traits and skills that can be developed to successfully perform the job. Nine of these traits are noted below.

1. **Systems thinker.** Project managers must be able to take a holistic rather than a reductionist approach to projects. Instead of breaking up a project into individual pieces (planning, budget) and managing it by understanding each part, a systems perspective focuses on trying to understand how relevant project factors collectively interact to produce project outcomes. The key to success then becomes managing the interaction between different parts and not the parts themselves.[29]

2. **Personal integrity.** Before you can lead and manage others, you have to be able to lead and manage yourself.[30] Begin by establishing a firm sense of who you are, what you stand for, and how you should behave. This inner strength provides the buoyancy to endure the ups and downs of the project life cycle and the credibility essential to sustaining the trust of others.

3. **Proactive.** Good project managers take action before it is needed to prevent small problems from escalating into major concerns. They spend the majority of their time working within their sphere of influence to solve problems and not dwelling on things they have little control over.[31] Project managers can't be whiners.

4. **High tolerance of stress.** Project management is not for the meek. Deadline pressures, technical uncertainties, and dealing with a variety of difficult, even stubborn professionals can generate a great deal of stress. People vary in their tolerance of stress. Physical exercise, a healthy diet, and a supportive homefront are necessary to endure the rigors of project management.

5. **General business perspective.** Because the primary role of a project manager is to integrate the contributions of different business and technical disciplines, it is important that a manager have a general grasp of business fundamentals and how the different functional disciplines interact to contribute to a successful business.

6. **Good communicator.** This one appears on every list and with good reason. Project managers have to be able to communicate with a wide variety of individuals. They not only have to be able to convey their ideas in an easily understandable manner, but they must also be empathic listeners, capable of drawing out the true meaning in what others are trying to say to them.

7. **Effective time management.** Time is a manager's scarcest resource. Project managers have to be able to budget their time wisely and quickly adjust their priorities. They need to balance their interactions so no one feels ignored.

8. **Skillful politician.** Project managers have to be able to deal effectively with a wide range of people and win their support and endorsement of their project. They need to be able to sell the virtues of their project without compromising the truth.

9. **Optimist.** Project managers have to display a can-do attitude. They have to be able to find rays of sunlight in a dismal day and keep people's attention positive. A good sense of humor and a playful attitude are often a project manager's greatest strength.

These nine traits are not all inclusive, but they describe traits possessed by "superstar" project managers. It is possible for anyone to develop an awareness and sensitivity for each trait with a positive effort toward self-improvement. Successful project managers appear to have a personal "continuous improvement program" for each of the traits discussed.

SUMMARY

To be successful, project managers must build a cooperative network among a diverse set of allies. They begin by identifying who the key stakeholders on a project are, followed by a diagnosis of the nature of the relationships, and the basis for exercising influence. Effective project managers are skilled at acquiring and exercising a wide range of influence. They use this influence and a highly interactive management style to monitor project performance and initiate appropriate changes in project plans and direction. They do so in a manner that generates trust, which is ultimately based on others' perceptions of their character and competence.

Project managers are encouraged to keep in mind the following suggestions:

• *Build relationships before you need them.* Identify key players and what you can do to help them before you need their assistance. It is always easier to receive a favor after you have granted one. This requires the project manager to see the project in systems terms and to appreciate how it affects other activities and agendas inside and outside the organization. From this perspective they can identify opportunities to do good deeds and garner the support of others.

• *Be leery of the Golden Rule.* Many managers boil down managing to this basic premise: "Do unto others as you would wish them to do unto you." While there is a lot of wisdom embedded in this saying, there is one potential dangerous flaw. Others may not want what you want or need what you need. What is fair to you may not be perceived as fair by others. Empathy is needed to put yourself in their shoes to understand their specific desires and needs.

• *Trust is sustained through frequent face-to-face contact.* Trust withers through neglect. This is particularly true under conditions of rapid change and uncertainty that naturally engender doubt, suspicion, and even momentary bouts of paranoia. Project managers must maintain frequent contact with key stakeholders to keep abreast of developments, assuage concerns, engage in reality testing, and focus attention on the project. Frequent face-to-face interactions affirm mutual respect and trust in each other.

Ultimately, exercising influence in an effective and ethical manner begins and ends with how you view the other parties. Do you view them as potential partners or obstacles to your goals? If obstacles, then you wield your influence to manipulate and gain compliance and cooperation. If partners, you exercise influence to gain their commitment and support. People who view social network building as building partnerships see every interaction with two goals: resolving the immediate problem/concern and improving the working relationship so that next time it will be even more effective. Experienced project managers realize that "what goes around comes around" and try at all cost to avoid antagonizing players for quick success.

REVIEW QUESTIONS

1. Why is a conductor of an orchestra an appropriate metaphor for being a project manager? What aspects of project managing are not reflected by this metaphor? Can you think of other metaphors that would be appropriate?
2. What does the exchange model of influence suggest you do to build cooperative relationships to complete a project?
3. What differences would you expect to see between the kinds of influence currencies that a project manager in a functional matrix would use and the influence a project manager of a dedicated project team would use?
4. Why is it important to build a relationship before you need it?
5. Why is it critical to keep the project sponsor informed?
6. Why is trust a function of both character and competence?
7. Which of the nine traits/skills associated with being an effective project manager is the most important? The least important? Why?

EXERCISES

1. Access the Keirsey Temperament Sorter Questionnaire at *http://sunsite.unc.edu/personality/ keirsey.html*. Respond to the interactive questionnaire to identify your temperament type. Read supportive documents associated with your type. What does this material suggest are the kinds of projects that would best suit you? What does it suggest your strengths and weaknesses are as a project manager? How can you compensate for your weaknesses?

   If you have difficulty accessing any of the Web addresses listed here or elsewhere in the book, you can find up-to-date addresses on the home page of Dr. Erik Larson, coauthor of this book, at *www.bus.orst.edu/faculty/larson*.
2. You are organizing an AIDS benefit concert in your hometown that will feature local heavy metal rock groups and guest speakers. Draw a dependency map identifying the major groups of people that are likely to affect the success of this project. Who do you think will be most cooperative? Who do you think will be the least cooperative? Why?
3. You are the project manager responsible for the overall construction of a new international airport. Draw a dependency map identifying the major groups of people that are likely to affect the success of this project. Who do you think will be most cooperative? Who do you think will be the least cooperative? Why?
4. Identify an important relationship (co-worker, boss, friend) in which you are having trouble gaining cooperation. Assess this relationship in terms of the influence currency model. What kinds of influence currency have you been exchanging in this relationship? Is the "bank account" for this relationship in the "red" or the "black"? What kinds of influence would be appropriate for building a stronger relationship with that person?
5. Each of the following three mini-case scenarios involve ethical dilemmas associated with project management. How would you respond to each situation, and why?

Jack Nietzche

You returned from a project staffing meeting in which future project assignments were finalized. Despite your best efforts, you were unable to persuade the director of project management to promote one of your best assistants, Jack Nietzche, to a project manager position. You feel a bit guilty because you dangled the prospect of this promotion to motivate Jack. Jack responded by putting in extra hours to ensure that his segments of the project were completed on time. You wonder how Jack will react to this disappointment. More importantly, you wonder how his reaction might affect your project. You have five days remaining to meet a critical deadline for a very important customer. While it won't be easy, you believed you would be able to complete the project on time. Now you're not so sure. Jack is halfway through completing the documentation phase, which is the last critical activity. Jack can be pretty emotional at times, and you are worried that he will blow up once he finds he didn't get the promotion. As you return to your office, you wonder what you should do. Should you tell Jack that he isn't going to be promoted? What should you say if he asks about whether the new assignments were made?

Seaburst Construction Project

You are the project manager for the Seaburst construction project. So far the project is progressing ahead of schedule and below budget. You attribute this in part to the good working relationship you have with the carpenters, plumbers, electricians, and machine operators who work for your organization. More than once you have asked them to give 110 percent, and they have responded.

One Sunday afternoon you decide to drive by the site and show it to your son. As you point out various parts of the project to your son, you discover that several pieces of valuable equipment are missing from the storage shed. When you start work again on Monday you are about to discuss this matter with a supervisor when you realize that all the missing equipment is back in the shed. What should you do? Why?

The Project Status Report Meeting

You are driving to a project status report meeting with your client. You encountered a significant technical problem on the project that has put your project behind schedule. This is not good news because completion time is the number one priority for the project. You are confident that your team can solve the problem if they are free to give their undivided attention to it and that with hard work you can get back on schedule. You also believe if you tell the client about the problem, she will demand a meeting with your team to discuss the implications of the problem. You can also expect her to send some of her personnel to oversee the solution to the problem. These interruptions will likely further delay the project. What should you tell your client about the current status of the project?

ENDNOTES

1. John P. Kotter, "What Leaders Really Do," *Harvard Business Review,* vol. 68, no. 3 (May–June 1990), pp. 103–11.
2. Linda A. Hill, *Becoming a Manager: Mastery of a New Identity* (Boston: Harvard Business School Press, 1992).
3. Vijay K. Verma, *Organizing Projects for Success: The Human Aspects of Project Management,* vol. 1 (Newtown Square, PA: Project Management Institute, 1995), pp. 45–73.
4. Leonard R. Sayles, *The Working Leader* (New York: Free Press, 1993); and Richard E. Walton, "From Control to Commitment in the Work Place," *Harvard Business Review,* vol. 63, no. 3 (March–April 1985), pp. 77–84.
5. See R. E. Kaplan, "Trade Routes: The Manager's Network of Relationships," *Organizational Dynamics,* vol. 12, no. 4 (Spring 1984), pp. 37–52; and W. E. Baker, *Networking*

Smart: How to Build Relationships for Personal and Organizational Success (New York: McGraw-Hill, 1994).

6. A. R. Cohen and David L. Bradford, *Influence without Authority* (New York: John Wiley & Sons, 1990).

7. John P. Kotter, "Power, Dependence, and Effective Management," *Harvard Business Review,* vol. 55, no. 4 (July–August 1977), pp. 125–36.

8. _____. *Power and Influence: Beyond Formal Authority* (New York: The Free Press, 1985).

9. Tom Peters, *Thriving on Chaos: Handbook for a Management Revolution* (New York: Alfred A. Knopf, 1988).

10. This discussion is based on Leonard R. Sayles, *Leadership: Managing in Real Organizations* (New York: McGraw-Hill, 1989), pp. 70–78.

11. See, for example, Jeffrey L. Pinto and D. P. Sleven, "Critical Success Factors in Successful Project Implementation," *IEEE Transactions in Engineering Management,* vol. 34, no. 1 (1987), pp. 22–27; and Jeffrey L. Pinto and Samuel K. Mantel, "The Causes of Project Failure," *IEEE Transactions in Engineering Management,* vol. 37, no. 4 (1990), pp. 269–76.

12. James M. Kouzes and Barry Z. Posner, *The Leadership Challenge* (San Francisco: Jossey-Bass, 1987).

13. Deborah G. Ancona and David Caldwell, "Improving the Performance of New Product Teams," *Research Technology Management,* vol. 33, no. 2 (March–April 1990), pp. 25–29.

14. Leonard R. Sayles, reference cited, pp. 136–45.

15. Tom Peters, reference cited, pp. 411–34; and James M. Kouzes and Barry Z. Pozner, *The Leadership Challenge,* reference cited, pp. 189–216.

16. Tom Peters, reference cited, pp. 471–78.

17. Erik Larson and Jonathan B. King, "The Systemic Distortion of Information: An Ongoing Management Challenge," *Organizational Dynamics,* vol. 24, no. 3 (Winter 1996), pp. 49–62.

18. Jeannette Cabanis, "A Question of Ethics: The Issues Project Managers Face and How They Resolve Them," *PMNetwork* (December 1996), pp. 19–24.

19. J. L. Badaracco, Jr. and A. P. Webb, "Business Ethics: A View from the Trenches," *California Management Review,* vol. 37, no. 2 (Winter 1995), pp. 8–28.

20. David J. Robb, "Ethics in Project Management: Issues, Practice, and Motive," *PMNetwork* (December 1996), pp. 13–18.

21. Jeannette Cabanis, reference cited, p. 20.

22. A. R. Cohen and David L. Bradford, reference cited.

23. See J. J. Gabarro, *The Dynamics of Taking Charge* (Boston: Harvard Business School Press, 1987); and James M. Kouzes and Barry Z. Posner, *Credibility: How Leaders Gain and Lose It. Why People Demand It* (San Francisco: Jossey-Bass, 1993).

24. Stephen R. Covey, *The Seven Habits of Highly Effective People* (New York: Simon & Schuster, 1989).

25. See Rosabeth M. Kanter, "Power Failure in Management Circuits," *Harvard Business Review* (July–August 1979), pp. 65–75; and Barry Z. Posner and John R. Kouzes, reference cited.

26. John E. Englehart, Martin F. Malkin, and Richard Rhodes, "From the Laboratory to the Pharmacy: Therapeutic Drug Development at Merck Sharp & Dohme Research Laboratories," *PMNetwork,* vol. 3, no. 6 (August 1989), p. 21.

27. Leonard R. Sayles, reference cited, p. 296.

28. For other lists of characteristics of effective project managers, see Barry Z. Posner, "What It Takes to Be an Effective Project Manager," *Project Management Journal* (March 1987), pp. 51–55; Aaron J. Shenhar and Brian Nofziner, "A New Model for Training Project Managers," *Proceedings of the 28th Annual Project Management Institute Symposium* (1997), pp. 301–6; Avraham Shtub, Jonathan F. Bard, and Shlomo Globerson, *Project Management: Engineering, Technology, and Implementation* (Englewood Cliffs, NJ:

Prentice Hall, 1994); and Robert K. Wysocki, Robert Beck, and David B. Crane, *Effective Project Management* (New York: John Wiley & Sons, 1995).

29. For a practical elaboration of what it means to be a systems thinker, see Peter M. Senge, *The Fifth Discipline* (New York: Doubleday, 1990).

30. See Warren Bennis, *On Becoming a Leader* (Reading, MA: Addison-Wesley, 1989).

31. For a more extensive discussion of the habit of being proactive, see Stephen R. Covey, reference cited, pp. 65–94.

CASE

Western Oceanography Institute

It was already 72 degrees when Astrid Young pulled into the parking lot at the Western Oceanography Institute (WOI). The radio announcer was reminding listeners to leave out extra water for their pets because the temperature was going to be in the high 90s for the third straight day. Young made a mental note to call her husband, Jon, when she got to her office and make sure that he left plenty of water outside for their cat, Figaro. Young was three-quarters of the way through the Microsoft NT conversion project. Yesterday had been a disaster, and she was determined to get back on top of things.

Astrid Young

Astrid Young was a 27-year-old graduate of Western State University (WSU) with a BS degree in management information systems. After graduation she worked for five years at Evergreen Systems in Seattle, Washington. While at WSU she worked part-time for an oceanography professor, Ahmet Green, creating a customized database for a research project he was conducting. Green was recently appointed director of WOI, and Young was confident that this prior experience was instrumental in her getting the job as information services (IS) director at the Institute. Although she took a significant pay cut, she jumped at the opportunity to return to her alma mater. Her job at Evergreen Systems had been very demanding. The long hours and extensive traveling had created tension in her marriage. She was looking forward to a normal job with reasonable hours. Besides, Jon would be busy pursuing his MBA at Western State. While at Evergreen, Young worked on Y2000 projects and installed NT servers. She was confident that she had the requisite technical expertise to excel at her new job.

Western Oceanography Institute was an independently funded research facility aligned with Western State University. Approximately 60 full- and part-time staff worked at the Institute. They worked on research grants funded by the National Science Foundation (NSF) and the United Nations (UN), as well as research financed by private industry. There were typically 7 to 8 major research projects under way at any one time as well as 20 to 25 smaller projects. One-third of the Institute's scientists had part-time teaching assignments at WSU and used the Institute to conduct their own basic research.

First Four Months at WOI

Young worked at the Institute for four months prior to initiating the NT conversion project. She made a point of introducing herself to the various groups of people upon her arrival at the Institute. Still, her contact with the staff had been limited. She spent most of her time becoming familiar with WOI's information system, training her staff, responding to unexpected problems, and planning the conversion project. Young suffered from food allergies and refrained from informal staff lunches at nearby restaurants. She stopped regularly attending the biweekly staff meetings in order to devote more time to her work. She now only attended the meetings when there was a specific agenda item regarding her operation.

Last month the system was corrupted by a virus introduced over the Internet. She devoted an entire weekend to restoring the system to operation. A recurring headache was one of the servers code named "Poncho" that would occasionally shut down for no apparent reason. Instead of replacing it, she decided to nurse Poncho along until it was replaced by the new NT system. Her work was frequently interrupted by frantic calls from staff researchers who needed immediate help on a variety of computer-related problems. She was shocked at how computer illiterate some of the researchers were and how she had to guide them through some of the basics of e-mail management and database configuration. She did find time to help Assistant Professor Amanda Johnson on a project. Johnson was the only researcher to respond to Young's e-mail announcing that the IS staff was available to help on projects. Young created a virtual project office on the Internet so that Johnson could collaborate with colleagues from institutes in Italy and Thailand on a UN research grant. She looked forward to the day when she could spend more time on fun projects like that.

Young had a part-time team of five student assistants from the computer science department. At first she was not sure how freely she could delegate work to the students, and she closely supervised their work. She quickly realized that they were all very bright, competent workers who were anxious to leverage this work experience into a lucrative career upon graduation. She admitted that she sometimes had a hard time relating to students who were preoccupied with fraternity bashes and X-games. She lost her temper only once, and that was at Samantha Eggerts for failing to set up an adequate virus screening system that would have prevented the Internet corruption that occurred. She kept a close eye on Eggerts's work after that, but in time, Eggert proved her worth. Young saw a lot of herself in Eggerts's work habits.

The Microsoft NT Conversion Project

Young laid the groundwork for the NT conversion project in her recruitment interview with the director by arguing that conversion was a critical skill she would bring to the position. Once hired she was able to sell the director and his immediate staff on the project, but not without some resistance. Some associate directors questioned whether it was necessary to go through another conversion so soon after the Windows 95 conversion 16 months ago. Some of the researchers lobbied that the money would be better spent on installing a centralized air-conditioning system at WOI. Ultimately, the director signed off on the project after Young assured him that the conversion would be relatively painless and the Institute would then have a state-of-the-art information system.

The conversion was scheduled to take eight weeks to complete and consisted of four major phases: server setup, network installation, data migration, and workstation conversion. The project would be completed during the summer so that the student assistants could work full time on the project. Young and her student team would first need to purchase and set up seven new NT servers. They would then create a new local area network (LAN). Next they would migrate data to the new Oracle NT database. Finally, they would convert the existing 65 client computers into NT workstations capable of functioning on the new system. Young had been actively involved in four similar conversions when working at Evergreen Systems and was confident that she and her team could complete the project with a minimum of technical problems. She also believed that this conversion would not be traumatic to the staff at the Institute because the NT interface was very similar to the Windows 95 interface.

Young knew that in order for the project to be considered successful, there needed to be minimum disruption of daily staff functions. She held a staff briefing meeting to outline the scope of the project and the impact it would have on the Institute's operations. She was disappointed by the light attendance at the meeting. One problem was the irregular hours staff worked at WOI. Several of the researchers were night owls who preferred to work late into the night. Other staff traveled frequently. She ended up holding two other briefing meetings, including one in the evening. Still the attendance was less than desired.

The staff's major concerns were the amount of downtime that would occur and whether the software and databases they were currently using would work on the new system. Young assured them that most of the downtime would occur on the weekends and would be posted well in advance. The only disruption would be two hours necessary to convert their existing computer into a workstation. Young invested extra energy in researching the compatibility issue and sent an e-mail to everyone listing the software that was known to not work in the NT system. The only software problems involved specially written DOS v2.1 or older programs that would not function in the new NT operating environment. In one case, she assigned a student to rewrite and enhance the present program for a researcher. In the other case, she was able to persuade the staff member to use a newer, better program.

Young sent a second e-mail asking staff members to clean up their hard drives and get rid of old, obsolete files because the new NT software would take up considerably more space than the Windows 95 operating system. In some cases, she replaced existing hard drives with bigger drives so that this would not be a problem. She circulated a workstation conversion schedule by e-mail so that staff could pick a preferred time for when their computer would be down and when her assistants could upgrade the computer into a workstation. Seventy percent of the staff responded to the e-mail request, and she and her staff contacted the remaining staff by telephone to schedule the conversion.

The first six weeks of the project went relatively smoothly. The NT servers arrived on time and were installed and configured on schedule. The completion of the network was delayed three days when the fire marshal showed up earlier than planned to inspect the electrical wiring. Young had never met the marshal before and was surprised at how nit-picking he was. They failed the inspection, and it took three days to reschedule and pass inspection. Word about failing the fire inspection circulated the hallways at the Institute. One joker put a Smokey the Bear sign on the IS office door. Young later found out that as a result of a recent fire in town, the fire marshals had been instructed to be extra vigilant in their inspections.

Data migration to the new Oracle database took a little longer than planned because the new version was not as compatible with the old version as advertised. Still, this only added three days to the project. The project was entering the fourth and final phase—conversion of client computers into NT workstations. This phase involved her staff deleting the old operating system and installing new operating software in each computer at the Institute. Young had scheduled two hours per machine and had organized a daily workload of 10 computers so that adequate backup could be made just in case something went wrong.

Young chose to convert the director's office first and told Green that everything was going according to plan. Soon the project began to experience nagging problems. First, some of the staff forgot when they were scheduled to be converted. The team had to wait for them to abandon what they were doing so they could convert the computer. Second, the drivers on some of the computers were not compatible, and the team had to devote extra time downloading new drivers off the Internet. Third, a few of the staff failed to create adequate hard drive space to accommodate the new NT software. In most cases, the team worked with the staff member to delete or compress unnecessary files. One time the staff member could not be found, and Young had to decide which files to delete. This wasn't a problem since the hard drive contained computer games and ancient Word Perfect files. To compound matters, midway through the third day, one of the student assistants, Steve Stills, was diagnosed with a moderate case of carpal tunnel and was told to take two weeks off from computer work.

After three days only 22 computers had been converted to NT stations. Young ended the day by sending an e-mail to the remaining users apologizing for the delays and posting a revised schedule for their system configuration.

The Call

Young and her staff were working diligently on converting computers into NT workstations when she received an urgent call from the director's secretary requesting that she drop everything and come downstairs to the staff meeting. The secretary's voice appeared tense, and Young wondered what was up. As she gathered her things, the student assistant, Eggerts, cleared her throat and confided that there may be problems with some of the Institute's Web sites. She discovered yesterday that some of the links in the Web pages created using Netscape weren't working in the Microsoft environment. Young demanded to know why she wasn't told about this sooner. Eggerts confessed that she thought she had fixed the problem last night. Young told her that they would talk about this when she got back and left.

Young entered the meeting room and immediately recognized that there were more than the usual faces in attendance. The director welcomed her by saying, "We're glad you could find the time to visit with us. My staff meeting has just erupted into a series of complaints about your NT conversion project. As it turns out Dr. Phillips over here can't access his documents because his Word Perfect file mysteriously disappeared. Dr. Simon's geothermal assessment program, which he has used for the past seven years, doesn't seem to work anymore. Now it appears that the Web site we use to coordinate our research with the Oslo Institute is a mess. Everyone is complaining about how the revised installation schedule is going to disrupt work. I want to know why I wasn't informed about these problems. These guys want to lynch me for approving your project!"

1. How would you respond to the director?
2. What mistakes did Young make that contributed to the problems at the end of the case?
3. How could she have managed the conversion project better?

Code of Ethics for the Project Management Profession

PREAMBLE: Project Management Professionals, in the pursuit of their profession, affect the quality of life for all people in our society. Therefore, it is vital that Project

Management Professionals conduct their work in an ethical manner to earn and maintain the confidence of team members, colleagues, employees, clients, and the public.

ARTICLE I: Project Management Professionals shall maintain high standards of personal and professional conduct and:

a. Accept responsibility for their actions.

b. Undertake projects and accept responsibility only if qualified by training or experience, or after full disclosure to their employers or clients of pertinent qualifications.

c. Maintain their professional skills at the state-of-the-art and recognize the importance of continued personal development and education.

d. Advance the integrity and prestige of the profession by practicing in a dignified manner.

e. Support this code and encourage colleagues and co-workers to act in accordance with this code.

f. Support the professional society by actively participating and encouraging colleagues and co-workers to participate.

g. Obey the laws of the country in which work is being performed.

ARTICLE II: Project Management Professionals shall, in their work:

a. Provide the necessary project leadership to promote maximum productivity while striving to minimize costs.

b. Apply state-of-the-art project management tools and techniques to ensure quality, cost, and time objectives as set forth in the plan are met.

c. Treat fairly all project team members, colleagues, and co-workers, regardless of race, religion, sex, age, or national origin.

d. Protect project team members from physical and mental harm.

e. Provide suitable working conditions and opportunities for project team members.

f. Seek, accept, and offer honest criticism of work, and properly credit the contribution of others.

g. Assist project team members, colleagues, and co-workers in their professional development.

ARTICLE III: Project Management Professionals shall, in their relations with employers and clients:

a. Act as faithful agents or trustees for their employers or clients in professional or business matters.

b. Keep information on the business affairs or technical processes of an employer or client in confidence while employed, and later, until such information is properly released.

c. Inform their employers, clients, professional societies, or public agencies of which they are members or to which they may make any presentations, of any circumstance that could lead to a conflict of interest.

d. Neither give nor accept, directly or indirectly, any gift, payment, or service of more than nominal value to or from those having business relationships with their employers or clients.

e. Be honest and realistic in reporting project quality, cost, and time.

ARTICLE IV: Project Management Professionals shall, in fulfilling their responsibilities to the community:

a. Protect the safety, health, and welfare of the public, and speak out against abuses in these areas affecting the public interest.
b. Seek to extend public knowledge and appreciation of the project management profession and its achievements.

Source: Reprinted from "A Guide to the Project Management Institute Body of Knowledge (PMBOK)," *Exposure Draft* (August 1994), p. 66, with permission of the Project Management Institute Headquarters, Four Campus Boulevard, Newton Square, PA 19073-3299 USA, a worldwide organization for advancing the state-of-the-art in project management.

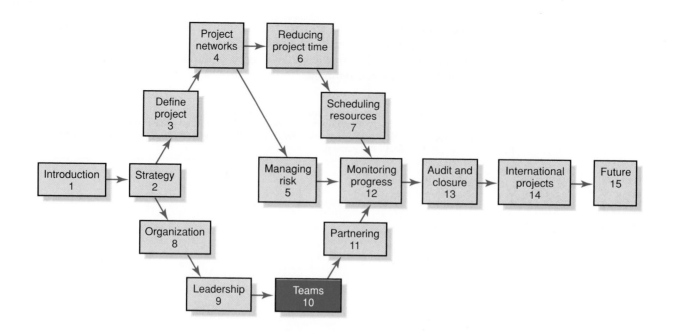

Managing Project Teams

The Five-Stage Team Development Model
Situational Factors Affecting Team Development
Building High-Performance Project Teams
Managing Virtual Project Teams
Project Team Pitfalls
Summary

CHAPTER TEN

Managing Project Teams

The difference in productivity between an average team and a turned-on, high-performing team is not 10 percent, 20 percent, or 30 percent, but 100 percent, 200 percent, even 500 percent!
—Tom Peters, management consultant and writer[1]

The magic and power of teams is captured in the term "synergy," which is derived from the Greek word *sunergos:* "working together." There is positive and negative synergy. The essence of positive synergy can be found in the phrase, "The whole is greater than the sum of the parts." Conversely, negative synergy occurs when the whole is less than the sum of the parts. Mathematically, these two states can be symbolized by the following equations:

$$\text{Positive Synergy } 1 + 1 + 1 + 1 + 1 = 10$$

$$\text{Negative Synergy } 1 + 1 + 1 + 1 + 1 = 2 \text{ (or even } -2)$$

Synergy perhaps can best be seen on a football field, a soccer pitch, or a basketball court. For example, the Chicago Bulls have dominated professional basketball during the 1990s. Admittedly in Michael Jordan they had, if not the greatest, then one of the best players to ever play the game. Still, it wasn't until management found players to complement Jordan's abilities and Jordan himself accepted the fact that he had to play a team game that their reign of championships began. Positive synergy could be seen in how routinely the Bulls executed a fast break, where the combined actions of all five players produced an unchallenged slam dunk, or in their aggressive, denial defense, which stifled the performance of a much taller and more talented opponent. Negative synergy can be plainly seen in cellar-dwelling NBA teams where players ignore wide-open teammates to launch wild 3-point shots or when two or three members fail to hustle back on defense leaving a lone teammate to defend a 3-on-1 fast break. Teams that exhibit negative team synergy are often characterized as being underachievers, while champions become synonymous with teams that exhibit positive synergy.

Although less visible than in team sports, positive and negative synergy can also be observed and felt in the daily operations of project teams. Here is a description from one project manager we interviewed:

Instead of operating as one big team we fractionalized into a series of subgroups. The marketing people stuck together as well as the systems guys. A lot of time was wasted gossiping and complaining about each other. When the project started slipping behind schedule, everyone started covering their tracks and trying to pass the blame on to others. After a while

293

we avoided direct conversation and resorted to e-mail. Management finally pulled the plug and brought in another team to salvage the project. It was one of the worst project management experiences in my life.

This same manager fortunately was also able to recount a more positive experience:

There was a contagious excitement within the team. Sure we had our share of problems and setbacks, but we dealt with them straight on and, at times, were able to do the impossible. We all cared about the project and looked out for each other. At the same time we challenged each other to do better. It was one of the most exciting times in my life.

The following is a set of characteristics commonly associated with high-performing teams that exhibit positive synergy:[2]

1. The team shares a sense of common purpose, and each member is willing to work toward achieving project objectives.
2. The team identifies individual talents and expertise and uses them, depending on the project's needs at any given time. At these times, the team willingly accepts the influence and leadership of the members whose skills are relevant to the immediate task.
3. Roles are balanced and shared to facilitate both the accomplishment of tasks and feelings of group cohesion and morale.
4. The team exerts energy toward problem solving rather than allowing itself to be drained by interpersonal issues or competitive struggles.
5. Differences of opinion are encouraged and freely expressed.
6. To encourage risk taking and creativity, mistakes are treated as opportunities for learning rather than reasons for punishment.
7. Members set high personal standards of performance and encourage each other to realize the objectives of the project.
8. Members identify with the team and consider it an important source of both professional and personal growth.

High-performing teams become champions, create break-through products, exceed customer expectations, and get projects done ahead of schedule and under budget. They are bonded together by mutual interdependency and a common goal or vision. They trust each other and exhibit a high level of collaboration.

THE FIVE-STAGE TEAM DEVELOPMENT MODEL

Just as infants develop in certain ways during their first months of life, many experts argue that groups develop in a predictable manner. One of the most popular models identifies five stages through which groups develop into effective teams:[3]

1. **Forming.** During this initial stage the members get acquainted with each other and understand the scope of the project. They begin to establish ground rules by trying to find out what behaviors are acceptable with respect to both the project (what role they will play, what performance expectations are) and interpersonal relations (who's really in charge). This stage is completed once members begin to think of themselves as part of a group.
2. **Storming.** As the name suggests, this stage is marked by a high degree of internal conflict. Members accept that they are part of a project group but resist the constraints that the project and group put on their individuality. There is conflict over who will control the group and how decisions will be made. As these conflicts are

resolved, the project manager's leadership becomes accepted, and the group moves to the next stage.

3. **Norming.** The third stage is one in which close relationships develop and the group demonstrates cohesiveness. Feelings of camaraderie and shared responsibility for the project are heightened. The norming phase is complete when the group structure solidifies and the group establishes a common set of expectations about how members should work together.

4. **Performing.** The team operating structure at this point is fully functional and accepted. Group energy has moved from getting to know each other and how the group will work together to accomplishing the project goals.

5. **Adjourning.** For conventional work groups, performing is the last stage of their development. However, for project teams, there is a completion phase. During this stage, the team prepares for its own disbandment. High performance is no longer a top priority. Instead attention is devoted to wrapping up the project. Responses of members vary in this stage. Some members are upbeat, basking in the project team's accomplishments. Others may be depressed over loss of camaraderie and friendships gained during the project's life.

This model has several implications for those managing project teams. The first is that the project manager needs to devote initial attention to helping the group evolve quickly to the productive fourth (performing) phase. The second implication for project managers is that the model provides a framework for the group to understand its own development. Project managers have found it useful to share the model with their teams. It helps members accept the tensions of the storming phase, and it directs their focus to moving toward the more productive phases. The final implication is that it stresses the importance of the norming phase, which contributes significantly to the level of productivity experienced during the performing phase. Project managers, as we shall see, have to take an active role in shaping group norms that will contribute to ultimate project success.

SITUATIONAL FACTORS AFFECTING TEAM DEVELOPMENT

Experience and research indicate that high-performance project teams are much more likely to develop under the following conditions:[4]

- There are 10 or fewer members per team.
- Members volunteer to serve on the project team.
- Members serve on the project from beginning to end.
- Members are assigned to the project full time.
- Members are part of an organization culture that fosters cooperation and trust.
- Members report solely to the project manager.
- All relevant functional areas are represented on the team.
- The project involves a compelling objective.
- Members are located within conversational distance of each other.

In reality, it is rare that a project manager is assigned a project that meets all of these conditions. For example, many projects' requirements dictate the active involvement of more than 10 members and may consist of a complex set of interlocking teams comprising more than 100 professionals. In many organizations, functional managers or central manpower offices assign project members with little input from the project manager. To optimize resource utilization, team member involvement may be part

RESEARCH HIGHLIGHT
The Punctuated Equilibrium Model of Group Development

Gersick's research suggests that groups don't develop in a universal sequence of stages as suggested by the five-phase model.[5] Her research, which is based on the systems concept of *punctuated equilibrium,* found that the *timing* of when groups form and actually change the way they work is highly consistent. What makes this research appealing is that it is based on studies of more than a dozen field and laboratory task forces assigned to complete a specific project. This research reveals that each group begins with a unique approach to accomplishing its project that is set in its first meeting and includes the behavior and roles that dominate phase I. Phase I continues until one-half of the allotted time for project completion has expired (regardless of actual amount of time). At this midpoint, a major transition occurs that includes the dropping of the group's old norms and behavior patterns and the emergence of new behavior and working relationships that contribute to increased progress toward completing the project. The last meeting is marked by accelerated activity to complete the project. These findings are summarized in Figure 10–1.

FIGURE 10–1 The Punctuated Equilibrium Model of Group Development

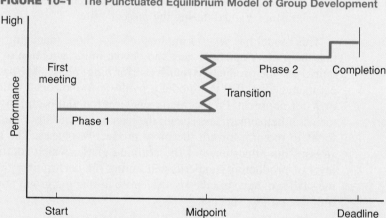

The remarkable discovery in these studies was that each group experienced its transition at the same point in its calendar—precisely halfway between the first meeting and the completion deadline—despite the fact that some groups spent as little as an hour on their project while others spent six months. It was as if the groups universally experienced a midlife crisis at this point. The midpoint appeared to work like an alarm clock, heightening members' awareness that time was limited and they needed to get moving. Within the context of the five-stage model, it suggests that groups begin by combining the forming and norming stages, then go through a period of low performing, followed by storming, then a period of high performing, and finally adjourning.

Gersick's findings suggest that there are natural transition points during the life of teams in which the group is receptive to change and that such a moment naturally occurs at the scheduled midpoint of a project. However, a manager does not want to have to wait 6 months on a complicated 12-month project for a team to get its act together! Here it is important to note that Gersick's groups were working on relatively small-scale projects, i.e., a 4-person bank task force in charge of designing a new bank account in one month and a 12-person medical task force in charge of reorganizing two units of a treatment facility. In most cases no formal project plan was established. If anything, the results point to the importance of good project management and the need to establish deadlines and milestones. By imposing a series of deadlines associated with important milestones, it is possible to create multiple transition points for natural group development. For example, a 12-month construction project can be broken down into six to eight significant milestones with the challenge of meeting each deadline producing the prerequisite tension for elevating team performance.

time, and/or participants may move in and out of the project team on an as-needed basis. In the case of ad hoc task forces, no member of the team works full time on the project. In many corporations an NIH (not invented here) culture exists that discourages collaboration across functional boundaries. Team members often report to different managers, and, in some cases, the project manager will have no direct input over performance appraisals and advancement opportunities of team members. Key functional areas may not be represented during the entire duration of the project but may only be involved in a sequential manner. Not all projects have a compelling objective. It can be hard to get members excited about mundane projects such as a simple product extension or a conventional apartment complex. Finally, team members are often scattered across different corporate offices and buildings or, in the case of a virtual project, across the entire globe.

It is important for project managers and team members to recognize the situational constraints they are operating under and do the best they can. It would be naive to believe that every project team has the same potential to evolve into a high-performance team. Under less-than-ideal conditions, it may be a struggle just to meet project objectives. Ingenuity, discipline, and sensitivity to team dynamics are essential to maximizing the performance of a project team.

BUILDING HIGH-PERFORMANCE PROJECT TEAMS

Project managers play a key role in developing high-performance project teams. They recruit members, conduct meetings, establish a team identity, create a common sense of purpose or a shared vision, create and manage a reward system that encourages teamwork, orchestrate decision making, resolve conflicts that emerge within the team, and lead team-building sessions (see Figure 10–2). Project managers take advantage of situational factors that naturally contribute to team development while improvising around those factors that inhibit team development. In doing so they exhibit a highly interactive management style that exemplifies teamwork and, as discussed in the previous chapter, manage the interface between the team and the rest of the organization.

Recruiting Project Members

The process of selecting and recruiting project members will vary across organizations. Two important factors affecting recruitment are the importance of the project and the management structure being used to complete the project. Often for high-priority projects that are critical to the future of the organization, the project manager will be given virtual carte blanche to select whomever he or she deems necessary. For less significant projects, the project manager will have to persuade personnel from other areas within the organization to join the team. In many matrix structures, the functional manager controls who is assigned to the project; the project manager will

FIGURE 10–2   Creating a High-Performance Project Team

have to work with the functional manager to obtain necessary personnel. Even in a project team where members are selected and assigned full time to the project, the project manager has to be sensitive to the needs of others. There is no better way to create enemies within an organization than to be perceived as unnecessarily robbing other departments of essential personnel.

Experienced project managers stress the importance of asking for volunteers. However, this desirable step oftentimes is outside the manager's control. Still, the value of having team members volunteer for the project as opposed to being assigned cannot be overlooked. Agreeing to work on the project is the first step toward building personal commitment to the project.[6] Such commitment will be essential to maintain motivation when the project hits hard times and extra effort is required.

When selecting and recruiting team members, project managers naturally look for individuals with the necessary experience and knowledge/technical skills critical for project completion. At the same time, there are less obvious considerations that need to be factored into the recruitment process:[7]

- *Problem-solving ability.* If the project is complex and fuzzy, then a manager wants people who are good at working under uncertainty and have strong problem identification and solving skills. These same people are likely to be bored and less productive working on straightforward projects that go by the book.
- *Availability.* Sometimes the people who are most available are not the ones wanted for the team. Conversely, if members recruited are already overcommitted, they may not be able to offer much.
- *Technological expertise.* Managers should be wary of people who know too much about a specific technology. They may be technology buffs who like to study but have a hard time settling down and doing the work.
- *Credibility.* The credibility of the project is enhanced by the reputation of the people involved in the project. Recruiting a sufficient number of "winners" lends confidence to project.
- *Political connections.* To begin to establish a cooperative relationship with a significant, but potentially uncooperative stakeholder group, managers would be wise to recruit individuals who already have a good working relationship with that group. This is particularly true for projects operating in a matrix environment in which a significant portion of the work will be under the domain of a specific functional department and not the core project team.
- *Ambition, initiative, and energy.* These qualities can make up for a lot of shortcomings in other areas and should not be underestimated.

After reviewing needed skills, the manager should try and find out through the corporate grapevine who is good, who is available, and who might want to work on the project. Some organizations may allow direct interviews. Once key people are recruited, it is wise to have them involved in the interviewing and recruiting process of other team members. Often a manager will have to expend political capital to get highly prized people assigned to the project.

In matrix environments, the project manager will have to request appointments with functional managers to discuss project requirements for staffing. The following documents should be available at these discussions: an overall project scope statement, endorsements of top management, and a description of the tasks and general schedule that pertain to the people from their departments. Managers need to be precise as to what attributes they are seeking and why they are important. Good negotiation skills are necessary at this meeting. Functional managers should be encouraged to suggest names of people within their departments as candidates. If the project manager is asked to suggest names, it might be wise to say, "Well, I would really like Pegi Young, but I know how critical her work is. How about Billy Talbot?" If the conversation goes this way, the project manager may be able to cut a deal then and there and will want to be sure to put the agreement in writing immediately after the meeting as a memorandum of understanding.

If, on the other hand, the functional manager balks at the suggestions and the meeting is not progressing, the project manager should adroitly terminate the conversation with an understanding that the matter will be discussed again in a few days. This technique demonstrates persistence and a desire to do what it takes to resolve the issue. Ultimately, of course, the project manager will have to settle on the best offer. Managers should exercise care not to reveal how different members of the team were selected. The project might be crippled at the start if reluctantly assigned members are identified and the team perceives differences in attitude and commitment.

Conducting Project Meetings

The First Project Team Meeting   Research on team development confirms what we have heard from project managers: The first project kick-off meeting is critical to the early functioning of the project team. According to one veteran project manager:

> The first team meeting sets the tone for how the team will work together. If it is disorganized, or becomes bogged down with little sense of closure, then this can often become a self-fulfilling prophecy for subsequent group work. On the other hand, if it is crisply run, focusing on real issues and concerns in an honest and straightforward manner, members come away excited about being part of the project team.

There are typically three objectives project managers try to achieve during the first meeting of the project team. The first is to provide an overview of the project, including the scope and objectives, the general schedule, method, and procedures. The second is to begin to address some of the interpersonal concerns captured in the team development model: Why are we here? Who are the other team members? How does each person fit in? What are we doing? Why? The third and most important objective is to begin to model how the team is going to work together to complete the project. The project manager must recognize that first impressions are important; her behavior will be carefully monitored and interpreted by team members. This meeting should serve as an exemplary role model for subsequent meetings and reflect the leader's style.

The meeting itself comes in a variety of shapes and forms. It is not uncommon in major projects for the kickoff meeting to involve one or two days, often at a remote site away from interruptions. This retreat provides sufficient time for preliminary introduction, to begin to establish ground rules, and to define the structure of the project. One advantage of offsite kickoff meetings is that they provide ample opportunity for informal interaction among members during breaks, meals, and evening activities; such informal interactions are critical to forming relationships.

However, many organizations do not have the luxury of holding elaborate retreats. In other cases the scope of project and level of involvement of different participants does not warrant such an investment of time. In these cases, the key operating principle should be KISS (keep it simple stupid!) Too often when constrained by time, project managers try to accomplish too much during the first meeting; in doing so, issues do not get fully resolved, and members come away with an information headache. Managers must remember that there are limits to how much information any one individual can absorb and that there will be opportunities in future meetings to establish ground rules and procedural matters. The primary goal is to run a productive meeting,

Snapshot from Practice
MANAGING MARTIANS

Courtesy of NASA.

Donna Shirley's 35-year career as aerospace engineer reached a pinnacle in July 1997 when Sojourner—the solar-powered, self-guided, microwave-oven-sized rover—was seen exploring the Martian landscape in Pathfinder's spectacular images from the surface of the red planet. The event marked a milestone in space exploration: No vehicle had ever before roamed the surface of another planet. Shirley, a manager at the Jet Propulsion Laboratory's Mars Exploration Program, headed the mostly male team that designed and built Sojourner. In her insightful memoir, *Managing Martians,* written with Danelle Morton, she makes the following observation about managing creative teams:

> When you are managing really brilliant, creative people, at some point you find it's impossible to command or control them because you can't understand what they are doing. Once they have gone beyond your ability to understand them, you have a choice to make as a manager. You can limit them and the project by your intelligence, which I think is the wrong way to do it. Or you can trust them and use your management skills to keep them focused on the goal.
>
> A lot of bad managers get threatened when their "subordinates" know more than they do. They either hire people who are inferior to them so they can always feel in control or they bottleneck people who know something they don't so they can maintain control. The whole project suffers from the manager's insecurities.

Source: Donna Shirley and Danelle Morton, *Managing Martians* (New York: Broadway Books, 1998), pp. 88–89.

and objectives should be realistic given the time available. If the meeting is only one hour, then the project manager should simply review the scope of the project, discuss how the team was formed, and provide an opportunity for members to introduce themselves to the team.

Establishing Ground Rules   Whether as part of an elaborate first meeting or during followup meetings, the project manager must quickly begin to establish operational ground rules for how the team will work together. These ground rules involve not only organizational and procedural issues but also normative issues on how the team will interact with each other. Although specific procedures will vary across organizations and projects, some of the major issues that need to be addressed include the following:

Planning Decisions

- How will the project plan be developed?
- What tools will be used to support the project?
- Will a specific project management software package be used? If so, which one?
- Who will enter the planning information?
- Who in addition to the team will be working on the plan?
- What are the specific roles and responsibilities of all the participants?
- Who needs to be informed of decisions? How will they be kept informed?
- What are the relative importance of cost, time, and performance?
- What are the deliverables of the project planning process?
- What format is appropriate for each deliverable?
- Who will approve and sign off at the completion of each deliverable?
- Who receives each deliverable?

Tracking Decisions

- How will progress be assessed?
- At what level of detail will the project be tracked?
- How will team members get data from each other?
- How often will they get this data?
- Who will generate and distribute reports?
- Who needs to be kept informed about project progress, and how will they be informed?
- What content/format is appropriate for each audience?
- Meetings
  - Where will meetings be located?
  - What kind of meetings will be held?
  - Who will "run" these meetings?
  - How will agendas be produced?
  - How will information be recorded?

Managing Change Decisions

- How will changes be instituted?
- Who will have change approval authority?
- How will plan changes be documented and evaluated?

Relationship Decisions

- What department or organizations will the team need to interact with during the project?
- What are the roles and responsibilities of each organization (reviewer, approver, creator, user)?
- How will all involved parties be kept informed of deliverables, schedule dates, expectations, etc.?
- How will the team members communicate among themselves?
- What information will and won't be exchanged?

Checklists like this are only a guide; items should be added or deleted as needed. Many of these procedures will have already been established by precedent and will only have to be briefly reviewed. For example, *Microsoft Project* or *Primavera* may be the standard software tool for planning and tracking. Likewise, a specific firm is likely to have an established format for reporting status information. How to deal with other issues will have to be determined by the project team. When appropriate, the project manager should actively solicit input from the project team members and draw upon their experience and preferred work habits. This process also contributes to their buying into the operational decisions. Decisions should be recorded and circulated to all members.

During the course of establishing these operational procedures, the project manager, through word and deed, should begin working with members to establish the norms for team interaction. Below are examples of some of the norms researchers have found associated with high performance teams.[8]

- There are no sacred cows: members should feel free to raise any relevant issues.
- Confidentiality is maintained; no information is shared outside the team unless all agree to it.
- It is acceptable to be in trouble, but it is not acceptable to surprise others. Tell others immediately when deadlines or milestones will not be reached.
- There is zero tolerance for bulling a way through a problem or an issue.
- Agree to disagree, but when a decision has been made, regardless of personal feelings, move forward.
- Respect outsiders, and do not flaunt one's position on the project team.
- Hard work does not get in the way of having fun.

One way of making these norms more tangible is by creating a project team charter that goes beyond the scope statement of the project and states in explicit terms the norms and values of the team. This charter should be a collaborative effort on the part of the core team. Project managers can lead by proposing certain tenets, but they need to be open to suggestions from the team. Once there is general agreement as to the rules of conduct, each member signs the final document to symbolize commitment to the principles it contains. Unfortunately, in some cases this becomes a meaningless ritual because the charter is signed and filed away, never to be discussed again. To have a lasting effect, the charter has to be a legitimate part of the project monitoring system. Just as the team reviews progress toward project objectives, the team assesses the extent to which members are adhering to the principles in the charter.

Project managers play a major role in establishing team norms through personal example. If they freely admit mistakes and share what they have learned from them, other team members will begin to do the same. At the same time, project managers need to intervene when they believe such norms are being violated. They should talk to offenders privately and clearly state their expectations. The amazing thing about groups is that once a group is cohesive, with well-established norms, the members will police themselves so that the manager doesn't have to be the heavy. For example, one project manager confided that his team had a practice of having a small bean bag present at every meeting. If any one member felt that a colleague was shooting hot air or shading the truth, he or she was obligated to toss the bean bag at the speaker.

Managing Subsequent Project Meetings   The project kickoff meeting is one of several kinds of meetings required to complete a project. Other meetings include status report meetings, problem-solving meetings, and audit meetings. Issues unique to these meetings will be discussed in subsequent chapters. For now, here are some general guidelines for running effective meetings.[9] They speak directly to the person chairing the meeting:

- Start meetings on time regardless of whether everyone is present.
- Prepare and distribute an agenda prior to the meeting.
- Identify an adjournment time.
- Periodically take time to review how effective previous meetings have been.
- Solicit recommendations and implement changes.
- Assign good recordkeeping.
- Review the agenda before beginning, and tentatively allocate time for each item.
- Prioritize issues so that adjustments can be made given time constraints.
- Encourage active participation of all members by asking questions instead of making statements.
- Summarize decisions, and review assignments for the next meeting.
- Prepare and distribute a summary of the meeting to appropriate people.
- Recognize accomplishments and positive behavior.

Meetings are often considered an anathema to productivity, but this does not have to be the case. The most common complaint is that meetings last too long. Establishing an agenda and adjournment time helps participants budget discussion time and provides a basis for expediting the proceedings. Recordkeeping can be an unwelcome, tedious task. Utilizing laptop computers to record decisions and information can facilitate the communication process. Careful preparation and consistent application of these guidelines can make meetings a vital part of projects.

Establishing a Team Identity

One of the challenges project managers often face in building a team is the lack of full-time involvement of team members. Specialists work on different phases of the project and spend the majority of their time and energy elsewhere. They are often members of multiple teams, each competing for their time and allegiance. Project expert David Frame points out that for many of these specialists a specific project is an abstraction; as a consequence their level of motivation suffers. Project managers need to try to make the project team as tangible as possible to the participants by developing a unique team identity to which participants can become emotionally attached.[10] Team meetings, co-location of team members, team names, and team rituals are common vehicles for doing so.

- *Effective use of meetings.* Periodic project team meetings provide an important forum for communicating project information. A less obvious function of project meetings is to help establish a concrete team identity. During project meetings, members see that they are not working alone. They are part of a larger project team, and project success depends on the collective efforts of all the team members. Timely gatherings of all the project participants help define team membership and reinforce a collective identity.
- *Co-location of team members.* The most obvious way to make the project team tangible is to have members work together in a common space. This is not always possible in matrix environments where involvement is part time and members are working on other projects and activities. A worthwhile substitute for co-location is the creation of a project office, sometimes referred to as the project war room or clubhouse. Such rooms are the common meeting place and contain the most significant project documentation. Frequently, their walls are covered with Gantt charts, cost

Snapshot from Practice[11]

"RAT FAX" GALVANIZES ELITE TEAM AT NEWSPAPER

Knight-Ridder's *Tallahassee Democrat,* like many American newspapers in the late 1980s, was struggling to survive in the face of declining revenues. Fred Mott, the general manager of the *Democrat,* was convinced that the key to the newspaper's future was becoming more customer-focused. Despite his best efforts, little progress was being made toward becoming a customer-driven newspaper. One area that was particularly problematic was advertising, where lost revenues due to errors could be as high $10,000 a month.

Fred Mott decided to create a team of 12 of his best workers from all parts of the newspaper. They became known as the ELITE team because their mission was to "ELIminate The Errors." At first the team spent a lot of time pointing fingers at each other rather than coming to grips with the error problems at the newspaper. A key turning point came when one member produced what became known as "the rat tracks fax" and told the story behind it. It turns out a sloppily prepared ad arrived through a fax machine looking like "a rat had run across the page." Yet the ad passed through the hands of seven employees and probably would have been printed if it had not been totally unreadable. The introduction of this fax broke the ice, and the team started to admit that everyone—not everyone else—was at fault. Then, recalls one member, "We had some pretty hard discussions. And there were tears at those meetings."

The emotional responses galvanized the group to the task at hand and bonded them to one another. The ELITE team looked carefully at the entire process by which an ad was sold, created, printed, and billed. When the process was examined, the team discovered patterns of errors, most of which could be attributed to bad communication, time pressures, and poor attitude. They made a series of recommendations that completely transformed the ad process at the *Democrat.* Under ELITE's leadership, advertising accuracy rose sharply and stayed above 99 percent. Lost revenues from errors dropped to near zero. Surveys showed a huge positive swing in advertiser satisfaction.

The impact of ELITE, however, went beyond numbers. The ELITE team's own brand of responsiveness to customer satisfaction spread to other parts of the newspaper. In effect this team of mostly frontline workers spearheaded a cultural transformation at the newspaper that emphasized a premium on customer service.

---

graphs, and other output associated with project planning and control. These rooms serve as a tangible sign of project effort.

- *Creation of project team name.* The development of a team name such as the "A-Team" or "Casey's Crusaders" is a common device for making a team more tangible. Frequently an associated team logo is also created. Again the project manager should rely on the collective ingenuity of the team to come up with the appropriate name and logo. Such symbols then can be affixed to stationery, T-shirts, coffee mugs, etc., to help signify team membership.

- *Team rituals.* Just as corporate rituals help establish the unique identity of a firm, similar symbolic actions at the project level can contribute to a unique team subculture. For example, on one project members were given ties with stripes that corresponded to the number of milestones on the project.[12] After reaching each milestone, members would gather and cut the next stripe off their ties to signify progress. On another project, Katz reports it was common practice for Digital Equipment's alpha chip design team to recognize people who found a bug in the design by giving them a phosphorescent toy roach. The bigger the bug that was discovered, the bigger the toy roach received.[13] Such rituals help set project work apart from mainstream operations and reinforce a special status.

Creating a Shared Vision

Unlike project scope statements, which include specific cost, completion dates, and performance requirements, a *vision* involves the less tangible aspects of project performance. It refers to an image a project team holds in common about how the project will look upon completion, how they will work together, and/or how customers will accept the project. At its simplest level, a shared vision is the answer to the question, "What do we want to create?"[14] Not everyone will have the same vision, but the images should be similar. Visions come in a variety of shapes and forms; they can be captured in a slogan or a symbol or can be written as a formal vision statement.

What a vision is, is not as important as what it does. A vision inspires members to give their best effort. Moreover, a shared vision unites professionals with different backgrounds and agendas to a common aspiration. It helps motivate members to subordinate their individual agendas and do what is best for the project. As psychologist Robert Fritz puts it, "In the presence of greatness, pettiness disappears."[15] Visions also provide focus and help communicate less tangible priorities, helping members make appropriate judgment calls. Finally, a shared vision for a project fosters commitment to the long term and discourages expedient responses that collectively dilute the quality of the project.

Visions can be surprisingly simple. For example, the vision for a new car could be expressed as a "pocket rocket." Compare this vision with the more traditional product description—"a sports car in the mid-price range." The "pocket rocket" vision provides a much clearer picture of what the final product should be. Design engineers would immediately understand that the car will be both small and fast and that the car should be quick at the getaway, nimble in the turns, and very fast in the straight-aways. Obviously, many details would have to be worked out, but the vision would help establish a common framework for making decisions.[16]

There appear to be four essential qualities of an effective vision (see Figure 10–3): First, its essential qualities must be able to be communicated. A vision is worthless if it only resides in someone's head. Second, it has to make strategic sense, given the objectives, constraints, resources, and opportunities inherent within the project. Visions have to be challenging but also realistic. For example, a task force directed at overhauling the curriculum at the college of business at a state university is likely to roll its eyes if the dean announces that their vision is to design a curriculum to compete

FIGURE 10–3 Requirements for an Effective Project Vision

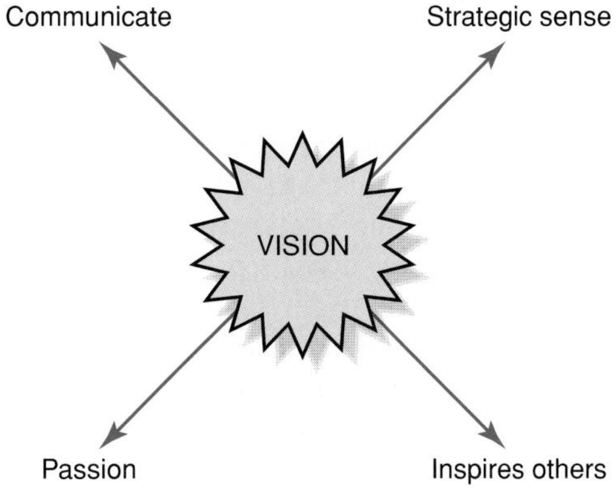

Communicate

Strategic sense

VISION

Passion

Inspires others

with the business schools at Harvard and Stanford. Conversely, developing the best undergraduate business program in that state may be a realistic vision for that task force. Third, the project manager has to believe in the vision. Passion for the vision is an essential element of an effective vision. Finally, it should be a source of inspiration to others.

Once a project manager accepts the importance of building a shared vision, the next question is how to get a vision for a particular project. First, project managers don't get visions. They act as catalysts and midwives for the formation of a shared vision of a project team.[17] In many cases visions are inherent in the scope and objectives of the project. People get naturally excited about being the first ones to bring a new technology to the market or solving a problem that is threatening their organization. Even with mundane projects, there are often ample opportunities for establishing a compelling vision. One way is to talk to various people involved in the project and find out early on what gets them excited about the project. For some it may be doing a better job than on the last project or the satisfaction in the eyes of the customers when the project is over. Many visions evolve reactively in response to competition. For example, the Kodak team responsible for developing the single-use FunSaver camera was driven by the vision of beating a similar effort by Fuji to the market.[18]

Some experts advocate engaging in formal vision building meetings.[19] These meetings generally involve several steps, beginning with members identifying different aspects of the project and generating ideal scenarios for each aspect. For example, on a construction project the scenarios may include "no accidents," "no lawsuits," "winning a prize," or "how we are going to spend our bonus for completing the project ahead of schedule." The group reviews and chooses the scenarios that are most appealing and translates them into vision statements for the project. The next step is to identify strategies for achieving the vision statements. For example, if one of the vision statements is that there will be no lawsuits, members will identify how they will have to work with the owner and subcontractors to avoid litigation. Next, members volunteer to be the keeper of the flame for each statement. The vision, strategies, and the name of the responsible team member are published and distributed to relevant stakeholders.

In more cases than not, shared visions emerge informally. Project managers collect information about what excites participants about the project. They test bits of their working vision in their conversations with team members to gauge the level of excitement the early ideas elicit in others. To some extent they engage in basic market research. They seize opportunities to galvanize the team, such as a disparaging remark by an executive that the project will never get done on time or the threat of a competing firm launching a similar project. Consensus in the beginning is not essential. What is essential is a core group of at least one-third of the project team that is genuinely committed to the vision. They will provide the critical mass to draw others aboard. Once the language has been formulated to communicate the vision, then the statement needs to be a staple part of every working agenda, and the project manager should be prepared to deliver a "stump" speech at a moment's notice.[20] When problems or disagreements emerge, all responses should be consistent with the vision.

Much has been written about visions and leadership. Critics argue that vision is a glorified substitute for shared goals. Others argue that it is one of the things that separates leaders from managers. The key is discovering what excites people about a project, being able to articulate this source of excitement in an appealing manner, and finally protecting and nurturing this source of excitement throughout the duration of the project.

Managing Project Reward Systems

Project managers are responsible for managing the reward system that encourages team performance and extra effort. One advantage they have is that often project work is inherently satisfying, whether it is manifested in an inspiring vision or simple sense of accomplishment. Projects provide participants with a change in scenery, a chance to learn new skills, and an opportunity to break out of their departmental cocoon. Another inherent reward is what was referred to in *The Soul of the New Machine*[21] as "pinball"—project success typically gives team members an option to play another exciting game.

Still, many projects are underappreciated, boring, interfere with other more significant priorities, and are considered an extra burden. In some of these cases, the biggest reward is finishing the project so that team members can go back to what they really enjoy doing and what will yield the biggest personal payoffs. Unfortunately, when this attitude is the primary incentive, project quality is likely to suffer. In these circumstances, external rewards play a more important role in motivating team performance.

Most project managers we talk to advocate the use of group rewards. Because most project work is a collaborative effort, it only makes sense that the reward system would encourage teamwork. Recognizing individual members regardless of their accomplishments can distract from team unity. Project work is highly interdependent, so it can become problematic to distinguish who truly deserves additional credit. Cash bonuses and incentives need to be linked to project priorities. It makes no sense to reward a team for completing their work early if controlling cost was the number one priority.

One of the limitations of lump-sum cash bonuses is that all too often they are consumed by the household budget to pay the dentist or mechanic. To have more value, rewards need to have lasting significance.[22] Many companies convert cash into vacation rewards, sometimes with corresponding time off. For example, there is one firm that rewarded a project team for getting the job done ahead of schedule with a four-day, all-expenses-paid trip to Walt Disney World for the members' entire families. That vacation not only will be remembered for years, but it also recognizes spouses and children who, in a sense, also contributed to the project's success. Similarly, other firms have been known to give members home computers and entertainment centers. Wise project managers negotiate a discretionary budget so that they can reward teams surpassing milestones with gift certificates to popular restaurants or tickets to sporting events. Impromptu pizza parties and barbecues are also used to celebrate key accomplishments.

Sometimes project managers have to use negative reinforcement to motivate project performance. For example, Ritti recounts the story of one project manager who was in charge of the construction of a new, state-of-the-art manufacturing plant.[23] His project team was working with a number of different contracting firms. The project was slipping behind schedule, mostly because of a lack of cooperation among the different players. The project manager did not have direct authority over many key people, especially the contractors from the other companies. He did, however, have the freedom to convene meetings at his convenience. So the project manager instituted daily "coordination meetings," which were required of all the principals involved, at 6:00 A.M. The meetings continued for about two weeks until the project got back on schedule. At that time the project manager announced that the next meeting was canceled, and no further sunrise meetings were ever rescheduled.

While project managers tend to focus on group rewards, there are times when they need to reward individual performance. This is done not only to compensate extraordinary effort but also to signal to the others what exemplary behavior is. Experienced project managers recognize the need to develop an informal reward system that is independent of the formal one prescribed by the company. Managers are adroit at utilizing different influence currencies (see Chapter 9) to create a favorable bank account in the minds of project participants. More specifically, among the rewards they use to motivate and recognize individual contributions are the following:[24]

- **Letters of commendation.** While project managers may not have responsibility for their team members' performance appraisals, they can write letters commending their project performance. These letters can be sent to the workers' supervisors to be placed in their personnel files.
- **Public recognition for outstanding work.** Superlative workers should be publicly recognized for their efforts. Some project managers begin each status review meeting with a brief mention of project workers who have exceeded their project goals.
- **Job assignments.** Good project managers recognize that, while they may not have much budgetary authority, they do have substantial control over who does what, with whom, when, and where. Good work should be rewarded with desirable job assignments. Managers should be aware of member preferences and, when appropriate, accommodate them.
- **Flexibility.** Being willing to make exceptions to rules, if done judiciously, can be a powerful reward. Allowing members to work at home when a child is sick or excusing a minor discretion can engender long lasting loyalty.

We reiterate that individual rewards should be used judiciously, and the primary emphasis should be on group incentives. Nothing can undermine the cohesiveness of a team more than members beginning to feel that others are getting special treatment or that they are being treated unfairly. Camaraderie and collaboration can quickly vanish only to be replaced by bickering and obsessive preoccupation with group politics. Such distractions can absorb a tremendous amount of energy that otherwise would be directed toward completing the project. Individual rewards typically should be used only when everyone in the team recognizes that a member is deserving of special recognition.

Orchestrating the Decision-Making Process

Project managers must orchestrate decision making within the project team to complete projects. Some decisions are easy, such as deciding what information should be contained in the user's manual. Others are much more difficult, such as deciding to discontinue a course of action that is just not working the way it should. Frequently, the project team will encounter novel problems that require creative solutions. Project managers need to manage the decision making on a project by getting the right people together to make the right decisions at the right time. At the same time, not all decisions require active team involvement. Some decisions can and should be made by individuals. Project managers need to oversee the decision-making process so that good decisions are made in a timely manner.

Choosing the Decision-Making Approach   Vroom, Yetton, and Jago developed a framework for helping managers choose the decision-making process most appropriate for various problem situations.[25] We adapted this framework to a project environment so that it does not simply apply to the project manager but also to any team member confronted with a decision. The framework is based on five alternative decision-making options. Note that the level of participation increases with each option:

Snapshot from Practice
MANAGING LOW-PRIORITY PROJECTS

So far the discussion of team building has been directed primarily to significant projects that command the attention and involvement of assigned members. But what about projects that have low priority for team members: The perfunctory task forces that members begrudgingly join? The committee work people get assigned to do? The part-time projects that pull members away from the critical work they would rather be doing? Projects that cause members to privately question why they are doing this?

There is no magic wand available that can be used to transform mildly interested, part-time project teams into high-performance teams. We interviewed several project managers about such project scenarios. They all agreed that these can be very difficult and frustrating assignments and that there are limits to what is possible. Still, they offered tips and advice for making the best of the situation. Most of these tips focus on building commitment to the project when it does not naturally exist.

One project manager advocated orchestrating a large "time" investment upfront on such projects—either in the form of a lengthy meeting or a significant early assignment. He viewed this as a form of down payment that members would forfeit if they didn't carry the project to completion.

Others emphasize interjecting as much fun into activities as possible. Here rituals discussed under building team identity come into play. People become committed because they enjoy working together on the project. One project manager even confided that the perfect attendance at her project meetings was due primarily to the quality of the doughnuts she provided.

Another strategy is to make the benefits of the project as real to the team members as possible. One project manager escalated commitment to a mandated accidents prevention task force by bringing accident victims to a project meeting. Another project manager brought the high-ranking project sponsor to recharge the team by reinforcing the importance of the project to the company.

Most project managers emphasized the importance of building a strong personal relationship with each of the team members. When this connection occurs, members work hard not so much because they really care about the project but because they don't want to let the project manager down. Although not couched in influence currency terms, these managers talked about getting to know each member, sharing contacts, offering encouragement, and extending a helping hand when needed.

Finally, all project managers cautioned that nothing should be taken for granted on low-priority projects. They recommend reminding people about meetings and bringing extra copies of materials to meetings for those who have forgotten them or can't find them. Project managers should remain in frequent contact with team members and remind them of their assignments. One manager summed it up best when he said, "Sometimes it all boils down to just being a good nag."

A1. The individual solves the problem or makes the decision alone, using information available at that time.

A2. The individual obtains necessary information from team members. The individual may or may not tell other team members what the problem is before obtaining the information from them. The team members provide the necessary information but do not generate or evaluate alternatives.

C1. The individual shares the problem with relevant team members individually, getting their ideas and suggestions without bringing them together as a group. The individual makes a decision based on his or her interpretation of the information.

C2. The individual shares the problem with the team, collectively obtaining their ideas and suggestions. The individual makes a decision based on his or her interpretation of the information.

G. The individual shares the problem with the team and engages the group in consensus, seeking to arrive at a final decision everyone can agree on.

Vroom and Jago use a flowchart similar to the one in Figure 10–4 to help individuals analyze problem situations and choose the most appropriate decision-making methods.[26] Key issues involve the quality requirements of the decision, the availability and location of relevant information, and the commitments needed to fully implement the decision. The model does not apply to urgent problems that require immediate attention, such as responding to an emergency. Still the model does assume that time is important and that it takes longer for a group of individuals to reach a decision than for one individual. Therefore, group decision making is recommended only when the nature of the problem situation dictates it.

FIGURE 10–4   Modified Vroom and Jago Decision Process Flowchart
(*Source:* Reprinted from Victor H. Vroom and Arthur G. Jago, *The New Leadership* (Englewood Cliffs, NJ: Prentice Hall, 1988), p. 184. Used by permission of the authors.)

Problem Attributes		Key Questions
QR	Quality requirement	How important is the technical quality of this decision?
CR	Commitment requirement	How important is project team commitment to the decision?
II	Individual's information	Do you have sufficient information to make a high-quality decision?
ST	Problem structure	Is the problem well structured?
CP	Commitment probability	If you were to make the decision by yourself, is it reasonably certain that others would be committed to the decision?
GC	Goal congruence	Do members share the project goals to be attained in solving this problem?
CO	Team conflict	Is conflict among project team members over preferred solutions likely?
TI	Team information	Do project team members have sufficient information to make a high-quality decision?

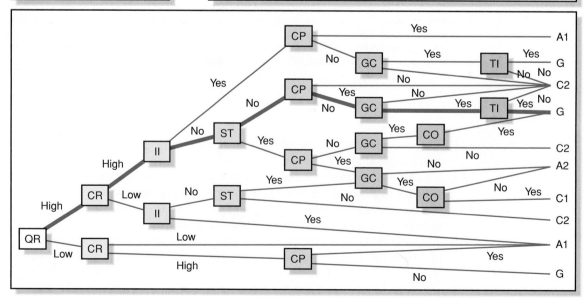

To understand how the flowchart works, let's apply it to a specific decision scenario. Assume you are the project manager responsible for leading a small team of dedicated IS professionals charged with developing a working prototype of a Web-based electronic ordering system. The project is at the scheduled halfway point and is five days behind schedule. You are worried that you will not be able to complete the project on time. You are considering your options. One option is to accept that the project will be late and revise the schedule accordingly. This would mean that the team would not receive a bonus for meeting the deadline. Another option would be to secure an additional programmer to work on the coding. Your team has different opinions about the status of the project. Some fear that there may be a basic flaw in the original configuration that is contributing to the delays. Others argue that "bugs" are inevitable and the worst is over. A few even volunteered to work on weekends to get back on schedule.

Now use the flow chart in Figure 10–4 to identify the appropriate decision-making process for dealing with this problem. The first box on the left is QR (quality requirement). You must decide whether the importance of quality requirements is high or low. After you make that decision, go to the next box, or CR (commitment required). Once again you must make a decision about the importance of having members committed to the final decision. After you have made that decision, you face another decision and then another. As you make each decision, follow the proper line to the next box. Eventually, at the far right side of Figure 10–4, you will arrive at the recommended decision-making process to use, given your previous eight decisions. Check and see whether your decisions correspond with what the authors chose (see Table 10–1).

Project managers can use this framework to choose how to approach decision making on specific problems. They can assess the decision-making processes on the project. Are different team members choosing the most appropriate approach when confronted with a problem? Are we wasting valuable time in meetings discussing

---

TABLE 10–1

DECISION ANALYSIS

Attribute	Key question	Answers
QR	How important is the technical quality of the decision?	Highly important
CR	How important is project team commitment to the decision?	Highly important
II	Do you have sufficient information to make a high-quality decision?	Probably not
ST	Is the problem well-structured?	No
CP	If you were to make the decision by yourself, is it reasonably certain that others would be committed to the decision?	Probably not
GC	Do members share the project goals to be attained by solving this problem?	Yes
TI	Do project team members have sufficient information to make a high-quality decision?	Probably yes

Answer

G (group consensus decision making)

problems that do not require everyone's involvement? Managers can share this framework with the team to develop norms and standards for problem solving.

Most decisions on a project do not require a formal team meeting to discuss alternatives and determine solutions. Instead decisions are made in real time as part of the daily interaction between project managers and team members. Through active MBWA, project managers consult team members, solicit ideas, determine optimum solutions, and create a sense of involvement that builds trust and commitment to decisions. Still, projects often encounter problems, such as the one depicted in the examples, that require the active involvement of the entire project team as well as other relevant stakeholders. Suggestions for managing group decision making are provided next.

Facilitating Group Decision Making　According to Vroom and Jago, group decision making should be used when it will improve the quality of important decisions. This is often the case with complex problems that require the collective input of a variety of different specialists. Group decision making should also be used when strong commitment to the decision is needed and there is a low probability of acceptance if only one person makes the decision. Participation is used to reduce resistance and secure support for the decision. Group decision making would be called for with controversial problems that could have a major effect on project activities or when trust is low within the project team.

Project managers play a pivotal role in guiding the group decision-making process. They must remind themselves that their job is not to make a decision but to facilitate the discussion within the group so that the team reaches a consensus on the best possible solution. Consensus within this context does not mean that everyone supports the decision 100 percent, but that they all agree what the best solution is under the circumstances. Facilitating group decision making essentially involves four major steps. Each step is briefly described here with suggestions for how to manage the process:[27]

1. **Problem identification.** The project manager needs to be careful not to state the problem in terms of choices (e.g., should we do X or Y?). Rather the project manager should identify the underlying problem to which these alternatives and probably others are potential solutions. This allows group members to generate alternatives, not just choose among them. One useful way of defining problems is to consider the gap between where a project is (i.e., the present state) and where it should be (desired state). For example, the project may be four days behind schedule or the prototype weighs two pounds more than the specifications. Whether the gap is small or large, the purpose is to eliminate it. The task of the group is to find one or more courses of action that will the change the existing state into the desired one.

   If one detects defensive posturing during the problem identification discussion, then it may be wise to postpone the problem-solving step if possible. This allows for emotions to subside and members to gain a fresh perspective on the issues involved.

2. **Generating alternatives.** Once there is general agreement as to the nature of the problem(s), then the next step is to generate alternative solutions. If the problem requires creativity, then brainstorming is commonly recommended. Here the team generates a list of possible solutions on a flipchart or blackboard. During that time the project manager establishes a moratorium on criticizing or evaluating ideas. Members are encouraged to "piggyback" on other's ideas by extending them or combining ideas into a new idea. The object is to create as many alternatives as

possible no matter how outlandish they may appear to be. Some project managers report that for really tough problems they have found it beneficial to conduct such sessions away from the normal work environment; the change in scenery stimulates creativity.

3. **Reaching a decision.** The next step is to evaluate and assess the merits of alternative solutions. During this phase it is useful to have a set of criteria for evaluating the merits of different solutions. In many cases the project manager can draw upon the priorities for the project and have the group assess each alternative in terms of its impact on cost, schedule, and performance as well as reducing the problem gap. For example, if time is critical, then the solution that solves the problem as quickly as possible would be chosen.

 During the course of the discussion the project manager attempts to build consensus among the group. This can be a complicated process. Project managers need to provide periodic summaries to help the group keep track of its progress. They must protect those members who represent the minority view and ensure that such views get a fair hearing. They need to guarantee that everyone has an opportunity to share opinions and no one individual or group dominates the conversation. It may be useful to bring a two-minute timer to regulate the use of air time. When conflicts occur, managers need to apply some of the ideas and techniques discussed in the next section.

 Project managers need to engage in consensus testing to determine what points the group agrees on and what are still sources of contention. They are careful not to interpret silence as agreement; they confirm agreement by asking questions. Ultimately, through thoughtful interaction, the team reaches a "meeting of the minds" as to what solution is best for the project.

4. **Followup.** Once the decision has been made and implemented, it is important for the team to find the time to evaluate the effectiveness of the decision. If the decision failed to provide the anticipated solution, then the reasons should be explored and the lessons learned added to the collective memory bank of the project team.

Managing Conflict within the Project Team

Disagreements and conflicts naturally emerge within a project team during the life of the project.[28] Participants will disagree over priorities, allocation of resources, the quality of specific work, solutions to discovered problems, and so forth. Some conflicts support the goals of the group and improve project performance. For example, two members may be locked in a debate over a design trade-off decision involving different features of a product. They argue that their preferred feature is what the primary customer truly wants. This disagreement may force them to talk to or get more information from the customer, with the result that they realize neither feature is highly valued, but instead the customer wants something else. On the other hand, conflicts can also hinder group performance. Initial disagreements can escalate into heated arguments with both parties storming out of the room and refusing to work together.

 The demarcation between functional and dysfunctional conflict is neither clear nor precise. In one team, members may exchange a diatribe of four-letter expletives and eventually resolve their differences. Yet in another project team, such behavior would create irreconcilable divisions and would prohibit the parties from ever working together productively again. The distinguishing criterion is how the conflict affects project performance, not how individuals feel. Members can be upset and dissatisfied with the interchange, but as long as the disagreement furthers the objectives of the project, then the conflict is functional. Project managers should recognize that conflict is an inevitable and even a desirable part of project work; the key is to encourage functional conflict and manage dysfunctional conflict.[29]

Encouraging Functional Conflict   A shared vision can transcend the incongruities of a project and establish a common purpose to channel debate in a constructive manner. Without shared goals there is no common ground for working out differences. In the previous example involving the design trade-off decision, when both parties agreed that the primary goal was to satisfy the customer, there was a basis for more objectively resolving the dispute. Therefore, agreeing in advance which priority is most important—cost, schedule, or scope—can help a project team decide what response is most appropriate.

Sometimes it's not the presence of conflict, but the absence of conflict that is the problem. Oftentimes as a result of compressed time pressures, self-doubt, and the desire to preserve team harmony, members are reluctant to voice objections. This hesitation robs the team of useful information that might lead to better solutions and the avoidance of critical mistakes. Project managers need to encourage healthy dissent in order to improve problem solving and innovation. They can demonstrate this process by asking tough questions and challenging the rationale behind recommendations. They can also orchestrate healthy conflict by bringing in people with different points of view to critical meetings.

Project managers can legitimize dissent within the team by designating someone to play the role of devil's advocate or by asking the group to take 15 minutes to come up with all the reasons the team should not pursue a course of action. Functional conflict plays a critical role in obtaining a deeper understanding of the issues and coming up with the best decisions possible.

One of the most important things project managers can do is model an appropriate response when someone disagrees or challenges their ideas. They need to avoid acting defensively and instead encourage critical debate. They should exhibit effective listening skills and summarize the key issues before responding. They should check to see if others agree with the opposing point of view. Finally, project managers should value and protect dissenters. Organizations have a tendency to create too many yes-men, and the emperor needs to be told when he doesn't have any clothes on.

Managing Dysfunctional Conflict   Managing dysfunctional conflict is a much more challenging task than encouraging functional conflict. First, dysfunctional conflict is hard to identify. A manager might have two highly talented professionals who hate each other's guts, but in the heat of competition they produce meritorious results. Is this a pleasant situation? No. Is it functional? Yes, as long as it contributes to project performance. Conversely, sometimes functional conflict degenerates into dysfunctional conflict. This change occurs when technical disagreements evolve into irrational, personality clashes or when failure to resolve an issue causes unnecessary delays in critical project work.

The second major difficulty managers face is that there is often no easy solution to dysfunctional conflict. Project managers have to decide among a number of different strategies to manage it; here are five possibilities:[30]

1. **Mediate the conflict.** The manager intervenes and tries to negotiate a resolution by using reasoning and persuasion, suggesting alternatives and the like. One of the keys is trying to find common ground. In some cases the project manager can make the argument that the win/lose interchange has escalated to the point that it has become lose/lose for everyone and now is the time to make concessions.

2. **Arbitrate the conflict.** The manager imposes a solution to the conflict after listening to each party. The goal is not to decide who wins but to have the project win. In doing so, it is important to seek a solution that allows each party to save face; otherwise the decision may provide only momentary relief. One project manager admits that she has had great success using a King Solomon approach to resolving conflict. She confided she announces a solution that neither party will like and gives the opponents two hours to come up with a better solution they can both agree on.

3. **Control the conflict.** Reducing the intensity of the conflict by smoothing over differences or interjecting humor is an effective strategy. If feelings are escalating, the manager can adjourn the interaction and hope cooler heads prevail the next day. If the conflict continues to escalate, project assignments may need to be rearranged if possible so that two parties don't have to work together.

4. **Accept it.** In some cases the conflict will outlive the life of the project and, though a distraction, it is one the manager has to live with.

5. **Eliminate the conflict.** Sometimes the conflict has escalated to the point that it is no longer tolerable. In this case the manager removes the members involved from the project. If there is a clear villain then only he or she should be removed. If, as is often the case, both parties are at fault, then it would be wise if possible to eliminate both individuals. Their removal would give a clear signal to the others on the team that this kind of behavior is unacceptable.

In summary, project managers establish the foundation for functional conflict by establishing clear roles and responsibilities, developing common goals or a shared vision, and using group incentives that reward collaboration. Project managers have to be adroit at reading body language to identify unspoken disagreement. They also have to keep in touch with what is going on in a project to identify small problems that might escalate into big conflicts. Well-timed humor and redirecting the focus to what is best for the project can alleviate the interpersonal tensions that are likely to flare up on a project team.

Leading Team-Building Sessions

Sometimes during the course of a long project the project manager recognizes the need for a formal team-building session devoted to improving the work processes of the team.[31] This meeting is particularly appropriate if she senses that the team is approaching a transition point in its development. The goal of such a session is to improve the project team's effectiveness through better management of project demands and group processes. It is an inward look by the team at its own performance, behavior, and culture for the purpose of eliminating dysfunctional behaviors and strengthening functional ones. The project team critiques its performance, analyzes its way of doing things, and attempts to develop strategies to improve its operation.

Oftentimes an external consultant is hired, or an internal staff specialist is assigned to facilitate the session. This process brings a more objective, outside perspective to the table, frees the project manager to be part of the process, and provides a specialist trained in group dynamics. Furthermore, if preliminary information is to be collected, team members may be more candid and open to an outsider. One caveat about using outside consultants is that too often managers resort to this as a method for dealing with a problem that they have been unable or unwilling to deal with. The marching order to the consultant is "fix my team for me." What the managers fail to recognize is that one of the keys to fixing the team is improving the working relationship between themselves and the remainder of the team. For such sessions to be effective, project managers have to be willing to have their own role scrutinized and be receptive to changing their own behavior and work habits based on the comments and suggestions of the project team.

Consultants use a wide variety of team-building techniques to elevate team performance. Here is a brief description of one of the more common approaches. The first step is to gather information and make a preliminary diagnosis of team performance. Whether through individual interviews or in a group forum, the consultant asks general questions about the project team performance, that is, what obstacles are getting in the way of the team being able to perform better? This information is summarized in terms of themes. When everyone has understood the themes, the group ranks them in terms of both their importance and the extent the team has ownership over them. This last dimension is critical. *Ownership* refers to whether the team has direct influence over the issue. For example, a team probably has little influence over delivery of contracted supplies, but they do control how quickly they inform each other of sudden changes in plans. If the group becomes preoccupied with issues outside their control, the meeting can quickly evolve into a demoralizing gripe session. Therefore, the most important issues they have direct control over become the subjects of the agenda. During the course of the meeting, much interpersonal and group process information will be generated, and that is examined too. Thus, the group works on two sets of items: the agenda items and the items that emerge from the interaction of the participants. This is where the expertise of the external facilitator becomes critical for identifying interaction patterns and their implications for team performance.

As important problems are discussed, alternatives for action are developed. The team-building session concludes by deciding on specific action steps for remedying problems and setting target dates for who will do what, when. These assignments can be reviewed at project status meetings or at a special followup session.

It has become fashionable to link team-building activities with outdoor experiences.[32] The outdoor experience—whether it is whitewater rafting down the Rogue River in Oregon or rock climbing in Colorado—places group members in a variety of physically challenging situations that must be mastered through teamwork, not individual effort. By having to work together to overcome difficult obstacles, team members are supposed to experience increased self-confidence, more respect for another's capabilities, and a greater commitment to teamwork. No empirical data are available to support such exotic endeavors other than the enthusiastic support of the participants. Such activities are likely to provide an intense common experience that may accelerate the social development of the team. Such an investment of time and money communicates the importance of teamwork and is considered by some a perk for being on the project. At the same time, unless the lessons from these experiences can be immediately transferred to actual project work, their significance is likely to vanish.

MANAGING VIRTUAL PROJECT TEAMS

Building a high-performance project team among a mixture of part-time and full-time members is a challenging task. Consider how much more challenging it is to build a team when members cannot engage in face-to-face interactions. Such would be the case for a virtual project team in which the team members are geographically situated so that they may seldom, if ever, meet face-to-face as a team. For example, Hewlett-Packard's integrated circuit business headquarters and a portion of the R&D facilities are located in Palo Alto, California; the two wafer fabrication operations are located in Corvallis, Oregon, and Fort Collins, Colorado; and the packaging assembly process is primarily in Singapore and Korea. It is not uncommon for professionals at each of these locations to be involved in the same project. When team members are spread across different time zones and continents, the opportunity for direct communication is severely limited. Electronic communication such as the Internet, e-mail, and tele-conferencing takes on much more importance in virtual projects because this is the primary means of communication.

Two of the biggest challenges involved in managing a virtual project team are developing trust and effective patterns of communication.[33] Trust is crucial to virtual project management. Unlike working as a traditional team, where members can see whether someone has done what they say they have done, virtual team members depend on the word of distant members. At the same time, it can be difficult to trust someone whom you may have met only one or two times or not at all. Geographical separation also prohibits the informal social interactions that are often essential to building camaraderie among team members. As one virtual team member put it, "You can't have a beer together over the Internet."

So how can a project manager facilitate the development of trust within a virtual team? First, if it is impossible to hold a face-to-face meeting in the beginning, managers need to orchestrate the exchange of social information—who everyone is and some personal background information during the initial electronic interchange. Second, they need to set clear roles for each team member. Ideally, specific tasks should be assigned to each member so that they can make an immediate contribution to the project. Project reports and technical information need to be freely shared electronically as well as jokes, logos, and mottos. Most project software can be linked directly to the Internet, and project Web sites can evolve into electronic clubhouses for the project members. Finally, the project manager must consistently display enthusiasm and an action orientation in all messages; this spirit will hopefully spread to other team members.

The second major challenge for managing a virtual project team is to establish effective patterns of communication. E-mail and faxes are great for communicating facts—but not the feelings behind the facts; nor do they allow for real-time communication. Conference calls and project chat rooms can help, but they also have their limitations. Videoconferencing is a significant improvement over nonvisual electronic forms of communication. Still, it is a very expensive medium, and real-time interaction is available on only the most advanced and expensive systems. Even with the best system, managers have to overcome the problem of time zone differences, cultural nuances, and finding a convenient time for people to conference. Here are some tips for alleviating communication problems and enhancing the performance of virtual teams:[34]

1. **Include face-to-face time if at all possible.** Hold an initial meeting for all team members so they can meet each other and socialize. Hold subsequent meetings at key junctures in the project. These meetings will help establish ties among team members and facilitate effective problem solving.
2. **Keep team members informed on how the overall project is going.** Use shareware or develop a central access point such as either a Web site or LAN account to provide members with updated project schedules. Team members need to know where they fit in the big picture.
3. **Don't let team members vanish.** Virtual teams often experience problems getting in touch with each other. Use an Internet scheduling software to store member's calendars.

4. **Establish a code of conduct to avoid delays.** Team members need to agree not only on what, when, and how information will be shared but also on how and when they will respond to it. Develop a priority system to distinguish messages that require immediate response from those with longer time frames.

5. **Establish clear norms and protocols for surfacing assumptions and conflicts.** Because most communication is nonvisual, project managers cannot watch body language and facial expressions to develop a sense of what is going on. They need to probe deeper when communicating to force members to explain their viewpoints, actions, and concerns more clearly; they must double check comprehension.

To a large extent managing a virtual project team is no different from managing a regular project team. The key is working within the constraints of the situation to develop effective ways for team members to interact and combine their talents to complete the project.

PROJECT TEAM PITFALLS

High-performance project teams can produce dramatic results. However, like any good thing, there is a dark side to project teams that managers need to be aware of. We referred to this phenomenon as *projectitis* in Chapter 8. In this section we examine in more detail some of the pathologies that high-performance project teams can succumb to and highlight what project managers can do to reduce the likelihood of these problems occurring.

Groupthink

Janis first identified *groupthink* as a factor that influenced the misguided 1961 Bay of Pigs invasion of Cuba.[35] His term refers to the tendency of members in highly cohesive groups to lose their critical evaluative capabilities. This malady appears when pressures for conformity are combined with an illusion of invincibility to suspend critical discussion of decisions. As a result decisions are made quickly with little consideration of alternatives; often the practice leads to fiascoes that, after the fact, appear totally improbable. Some of the symptoms of groupthink include the following:

- *Illusion of invulnerability.* The team feels invincible. It is marked by a high degree of esprit de corps, an implicit faith in its own wisdom, and an inordinate optimism that allows group members to feel complacent about the quality of their decisions.
- *Whitewash of critical thinking.* The group members discuss only a few solutions, ignoring alternatives; they fail to examine the adverse consequences that could follow their preferred course of action; and they too quickly dismiss any alternatives that, on the surface, appear to be unsatisfactory.
- *Negative stereotypes of outsiders.* "Good guy/bad guy" stereotypes emerge in which the group considers any outsiders who oppose their decisions as the bad guys, who are perceived as incompetent and malicious and whose points are unworthy of serious consideration.
- *Direct pressure.* When a team member does speak out or question the direction in which the team is headed, direct pressure is applied to the dissenter. He or she is reminded that speed is important and that the aim is agreement, not argument.

Bureaucratic Bypass Syndrome

Project teams are often licensed to get things done without having to go through normal protocols of the parent organization. Bypassing bureaucratic channels is appealing and invigorating. However, if bypassing becomes a way of life, it results in the rejection of bureaucratic policies and procedures, which provide the glue for the overall organization. A team that operates outside the organization may alienate other workers who are constrained by the norms and procedures of the organization; eventually, these outside bureaucrats will find ways to put up roadblocks and thwart the project team.[36]

Entrepreneur's Disease

Project teams can be intoxicating in the same way that startup ventures are. Such intoxication is exciting and contributes greatly to the success of the team. But abuse can occur as the team makes decisions based on what is best for the project and not for the parent organization. The team becomes myopic in its focus and often views the constraints imposed by the parent organization as something to be overcome. When this attitude occurs on developmental projects, the team members, enthralled with their accomplishments, sometimes quit the parent organization and start their own business. While starting a new venture may be good for the project team, it does little for the parent organization that sponsored and financed the development work.

Team Spirit Becomes Team Infatuation

High-performance project teams can be a tremendous source of personal satisfaction. The excitement, chaos, and joy generated by working on a challenging project can be an invigorating experience. Leavitt and Lipman-Blumen even go so far as to say that team members behave like people in love.[37] They become infatuated with the challenge of the project and the talent around them. This total preoccupation with the project and the project team, while contributing greatly to the remarkable success of the project, can leave in its wake a string of broken professional and personal relationships that contribute to burnout and disorientation upon completion of the project.

Going Native

Going native is a phrase first used by the British Foreign Service during colonial times to describe agents who assumed the customs, values, and prerogatives of their foreign country assignment. They did so to the point that they were no longer representing the best interests of the British government but rather those of the natives. This same phenomenon can occur within project teams working abroad or in those who become closely identified with their customers. In essence, the customer's interests take precedence over the parent organization's interests. This change in viewpoint can lead to excessive scope creep and open defiance of corporate policy and interests.

Dealing with these maladies is problematic because, in most cases, they are a distortion of a good thing, rather than a simple evil. Awareness is the first step for prevention. The next step is to take preemptive action to reduce the likelihood of these pitfalls occurring. For example, managers can reduce the isolation of the project team by creating work-related connections outside the project team. These interactions naturally occur in a matrix environment where members work on multiple projects and maintain ties to their home department. Likewise, the isolation of dedicated project teams can be reduced by the timely involvement of external specialists. In either case, the active involvement of relevant members of the parent organization at project status meetings can help maintain the link between the project and the rest of the organization. If the team appears to be suffering from groupthink, then the project manager can encourage functional conflict by playing a devil's advocate role to encourage dissent. Finally, formal team-building sessions may reveal dysfunctional norms and refocus the attention of the team on project objectives.

SUMMARY

Project managers must often work under less-than-ideal conditions to develop a cohesive team committed to working together and completing the project to the best of their abilities. They have to recruit personnel from other departments and manage the temporary involvement of team members. They have to bring strangers together and quickly establish a set of operational procedures that unite their efforts and contributions. They have to be skilled at managing meetings so that they do not become a burden but rather a vehicle for progress. Project managers need to forge a team identity and a shared vision, which command the attention and allegiance of participants. They need to use group incentives to encourage teamwork while recognizing when it is appropriate to single out individuals for special recognition. Project managers have to encourage functional conflict that contributes to superior solutions while being on guard against dysfunctional conflict that can break a team apart. In doing these things, they have to be careful not to do too good a job and avoid the pitfalls of excessive group cohesion.

While agendas, charters, visions, rewards, and so forth are important tools and techniques, it has been emphasized both in this chapter and in Chapter 9 that the most important tool a project manager has to build an effective project team is his or her own behavior. Just as the founding members of an organization shape the culture of the organization, the project manager shapes and influences the internal culture of the project team. A positive example can define how team members respond to changes, how they handle new tasks, and how they relate to one another and the rest of the organization. There is no easy way to lead by example. It requires personal conviction, discipline, sensitivity to team dynamics, and a constant awareness of how personal actions are perceived by others.

REVIEW QUESTIONS

1. Which of the two models of team development does the best job of describing how groups evolve? Why?
2. What are the elements of an effective project vision? Why are they important?
3. Why should a project manager emphasize group rewards over individual rewards?
4. What is the difference between functional and dysfunctional conflict on a project?
5. When would it be appropriate to hold a formal team-building session on a project?
6. What are the unique challenges to managing a virtual project team?
7. What can a project manager do to avoid some of the pitfalls of a highly cohesive project team?

EXERCISES

1. The following activities are based on a recently completed group project that you have been involved in. This project may have been a student project, a work project, or an extracurricular project.
   a. Analyze the development of the team in terms of the five-phase model and the punctuated equilibrium model. Which model does the best job of describing how the team evolved?
   b. Analyze the group in terms of the nine situational factors that influence team development. What factors positively contributed to group performance? What factors negatively contributed to group performance? How did the group try to overcome the negative factors? What could you have done differently to overcome these negative factors?
   c. Analyze how effectively the group managed meetings. What did the group do well?

What didn't the group do well? If the group were formed again, what specific recommendations would you make about how the group should manage meetings?

2. Apply the Vroom and Jago decision-making model to identify which decision-making approach you should use for each of the following problem scenarios. Do you agree with the choice?

   a. You are the project leader for Casino Night on campus, a charitable event organized by your group to raise money for the homeless. The event was a big success, garnering a net profit of $3,500. Before the event your team researched nearby organizations that support the homeless and to whom the money could be given. You narrowed the choices to the "Chunk of Coal House" and "St. Mary's Soup Kitchen." Eventually your group decided that the funds be given to Chunk of Coal. You are about to write a check to its director when you read in the local newspaper that the Chunk of Coal House has terminated operations. Which decision-making approach should you use decide what to do with the money?

   b. You are a golf course designer hired by Trysting Tree Golf Club to renovate their golf course. You have worked closely with the board of directors of the club to develop a new layout that is both challenging and aesthetically pleasing. Everyone is excited about the changes. The project is nearly 75 percent complete when you encounter problems on the 13th hole. The 13th hole at Trysting Tree is a 125-yard par three in which golfers have to hit their tee shots over a lake to a modulated green. During the construction of the new tee box, workers discovered that an underground spring runs beneath the box to the lake. You inspected the site and agreed with the construction foreman that this could create serious problems, especially during the rainy winter months. After surveying the area, you believe the only viable option would be to extend the hole to 170 yards and create elevated tees on the adjacent hillside. Which decision-making approach should you use to decide what to do about the 13th hole?

ENDNOTES

1. Tom Peters, *A Passion for Excellence,* video (Palo Alto, CA: The Tom Peters Group, 1985).

2. See Edgar H. Schein, *Process Consultation* (Reading, MA: Addison-Wesley, 1969), pp. 42–43; and Rensis Likert, *New Patterns of Management* (New York: McGraw-Hill, 1961), pp. 162–77.

3. B. W. Tuchman, "Developmental Sequence of Small Groups," *Psychological Bulletin,* vol. 63 (1965), pp. 384–99; and B. W. Tuchman and M. C. Jensen, "Stages of Small Group Development Revisited," *Group and Organizational Studies,* vol. 2 (1977), pp. 419–27.

4. George C. Homans, *Social Behavior: Its Elementary Forms* (New York: Harcourt Brace Jovanovich, 1961); M. Sherif, *Group Conflict and Cooperation: Their Social Psychology* (Chicago: Aldine Publishing Co., 1967); J. J. Seta, P. B. Paulus, and J. Schkade, "Effects of Group Size and Proximity under Cooperative and Competitive Conditions," *Journal of Personality and Social Psychology,* vol. 98, no. 2 (1976), pp. 47–53; A. Zander, *Making Groups Effective* (San Francisco: Jossey-Bass, 1982); and G. Preston Smith and Donald G. Reinertsen, *Developing Products in Half the Time* (New York: Van Nostrand Reinhold, 1995).

5. Connie J. Gersick, "Time and Transition in Work Teams: Toward a New Model of Group Development," *Academy of Management Journal,* vol. 31, no. 1 (March 1988), pp. 9–41; and Connie J. Gersick, "Making Time Predictable Transitions in Task Groups," *Academy of Management Journal,* vol. 32, no. 2 (June 1989), pp. 274–309.

6. Gerald R. Salancik, "Commitment and the Control of Organizational Behavior and Belief," *Psychological Foundations of Organizational Behavior,* ed. B. M. Staw (New York: Wiley, 1977), pp. 202–7.

7. These considerations are based in part on Bennet P. Lientz and Kathryn P. Rea, *Project Management for the 21st Century* (San Diego: Academic Press, 1995), pp. 118–19.

8. Jon R. Katzenbach and Douglas K. Smith, "The Discipline of Teams," *Harvard Business Review,* vol. 71, no. 2 (March/April 1993), pp. 111–21; Lee G. Bolman and Terrence E. Deal, "What Makes a Team Work?" *Organizational Dynamics,* vol. 21, no. 2 (Autumn 1992), pp. 34–45; and Ralph Katz, "How a Team at Digital Equipment Designed the 'Alpha' Chip," *The Human Side of Managing Technological Innovation,* ed. Ralph Katz (New York: Oxford Press, 1997), pp. 137–48.

9. David I. Cleland, "Team Building: The New Strategic Weapon," *PMNetwork,* vol. 11, no. 1 (January 1997), pp. 29–31; Peter M. Scholtes, *The Team Handbook: How to Use Teams to Improve Quality* (Madison, WI: Joiner Associates, 1991).

10. J. D. Frame, *Managing Projects in Organizations* (San Francisco: Jossey-Bass, 1995), pp. 101–3.

11. Jon R. Katzenbach and Douglas K. Smith, *The Wisdom of Teams* (Boston: Harvard Business School Press, 1993), pp. 67–72. Copyright McKinsey & Co., Inc.

12. This anecdote was provided by Dr. Frances Hartman, University of Calgary, Alberta.

13. Ralph Katz, reference cited.

14. Peter M. Senge, *The Fifth Discipline* (New York: Doubleday, 1990), pp. 205–33.

15. Quoted in *ibid.,* p. 209.

16. Kent H. Bowen, Kim B. Clark, Charles A. Holloway, and Steven C. Wheelwright, *The Perpetual Enterprise Machine* (New York: Oxford Press, 1994), p. 72.

17. Bryan Smith, "Building Shared Visions: How to Begin," *The Fifth Discipline Fieldbook: Strategies and Tools for Building a Learning Organization,* eds. Peter M. Senge, Charlotte Roberts, Richard B. Ross, Bryan J. Smith, and Art Kleiner (New York: Doubleday, 1994), pp. 312–27.

18. Kent H. Bowen et al., reference cited, p. 87.

19. Peg Thoms, "Creating a Shared Vision with a Project Team," *PMNetwork* (January 1997), pp. 33–35.

20. Tom Peters, *Thriving on Chaos: Handbook for a Management Revolution* (New York: Knopf, 1988), pp. 399–410.

21. Tracy Kidder, *The Soul of a New Machine* (New York: Avon Books, 1981), pp. 221–32.

22. G. Preston Smith and Donald G. Reinertsen, reference cited, p. 129.

23. Richard R. Ritti, *The Ropes to Skip and the Ropes to Know: Studies in Organizational Behavior,* 5th ed. (New York: Wiley), pp. 89–90.

24. J. D. Frame, reference cited, pp. 103–4.

25. Victor H. Vroom and Phillip W. Yetton, *Leadership and Decision Making* (Pittsburgh: Pittsburgh University Press, 1973); and Victor H. Vroom and Arthur G. Jago, *The New Leadership* (Englewood Cliffs, NJ: Prentice Hall, 1988).

26. Vroom and Jago, reference cited, p. 184.

27. This discussion is based on N. R. F. Maier's classic research: N. R. F. Maier, *Problem Solving Discussion and Conferences* (New York: McGraw-Hill, 1963); and N. R. F. Maier, *Problem Solving and Creativity in Individuals and Groups* (Belmont, CA: Brooks-Cole, 1970).

28. For a discussion of how conflicts relate to project life cycle, see H. J. Thamhain and D. L. Wilemon, "Conflict Management in Project Life Cycle," *Sloan Management Review,* vol. 16, no. 3 (Summer 1975), pp. 31–41.

29. Stephen P. Robbins, *Managing Organizational Conflict: A Nontraditional Approach* (Englewood Cliffs, NJ: Prentice Hall, 1974).

30. James Ware, "Some Aspects of Problem-Solving and Conflict Resolution in Management Groups," *Managing Behavior in Organizations: Text, Cases, Readings,* eds. Leonard A. Schelsinger, Robert G. Eccles, and John L. Gabarro (New York: McGraw-Hill, 1983), pp. 101–15.

31. This section is based on William G. Dyer, *Team Building: Issues and Alternatives* (Reading, MA: Addison-Wesley, 1987).

32. For example, see Chuah B. Hwa, "Leadership Training via Outdoor Activities," *The New Strait Times* (April 1993), p. 1.

33. John R. Adams and Laura L. Adams "The Virtual Projects: Managing Tomorrow's Team Today," *PMNetwork* (January 1997), pp. 37–41; Jaclyn Kostner, *Knights of the Tele-Round Table* (New York: Warner Books, 1994); and Anthony M. Townsend, Samuel DeMarie, and Anthony R. Hendrickson, "Virtual Teams: Technology and the Workplace of the Future," *Academy of Management EXECUTIVE,* vol. 12, no. 3 (August 1998), pp. 17–29.

34. Diane L. Coutu, "Organization: Trust in Virtual Teams," *Harvard Business Review,* vol. 76, no. 3 (May–June 1998), pp. 20–21; and David Gould, "Leading Virtual Teams," *Boeing Manager Magazine* (May 1997), pp. 7–14.

35. Irving L. Janis, *Groupthink* (Boston: Houghton Mifflin, 1982), p. 36.

36. This section is based in part on Robert Johansen, David Sibbet, Suzyn Benson, Alexia Martin, Robert Mittman, and Paul Saffo, *Leading Business Teams: How Teams Can Use Technology and Group Process Tools to Enhance Performance* (Reading, MA: Addison-Wesley, 1991), pp. 93–98.

37. Harold J. Leavitt and Jean Lipman-Blumen, "Hot Groups," *Harvard Business Review,* vol. 73 (1995), pp. 109–16.

CASE

Kerzner Office Equipment

Amber Briggs looked nervously at her watch as she sat at the front of a large table in the cafeteria at Kerzner Office Equipment. It was now 10 minutes after 3:00 and only 10 of the 14 members had arrived for the first meeting of the Kerzner anniversary task force. Just then two more members hurriedly sat down and mumbled apologies for being late. Briggs cleared her throat and started the meeting.

Kerzner Office Equipment

Kerzner Office Equipment is located in Charleston, South Carolina. It specializes in the manufacture and sales of high-end office furniture and equipment. Kerzner enjoyed steady growth during its first five years of existence with a high-water employment mark of more than 1,400 workers. Then a national recession struck, forcing Kerzner to lay off 25 percent of its employees. This was a traumatic period for the company. Justin Tubbs was brought in as the new CEO, and things began to slowly turn around. Tubbs was committed to employee participation and redesigned operations around the concept of self-managing teams. The company soon introduced an innovative line of ergonomic furniture designed to reduce back strain and carpal tunnel. This line of equipment proved to be a resounding success, and Kerzner became known as a leader in the industry. The company currently employs 1,100 workers and has just been selected for the second straight time by the *Charleston Post and Courier* as one of the 10 best local firms to work for in South Carolina.

Amber Briggs

Amber Briggs is a 42-year-old human resource specialist who has worked for Kerzner for the past five years. During this time she has performed a variety of activities involving recruitment, training, compensation, and team building. David Brown, vice president of human resources, assigned Briggs the responsibility for organizing Kerzner's 10th anniversary celebration. She was excited about the project because she would report directly to top management.

She was briefed by CEO Tubbs as to the purpose and objectives of the celebration. Tubbs stressed that this should be a memorable event and that it was important to

FIGURE C10–1   Celebration Task Force

Agenda

3:00	Introductions
3:15	Project overview
3:30	Ground rules
3:45	Meeting times
4:00	Adjourn

celebrate Kerzner's success since the dark days of the layoffs. Moreover, he confided that he had just read a book on corporate cultures and believed that such events were important for conveying the values at Kerzner. He went on to say that he wanted this to be an employee celebration—not a celebration conjured up by top management. As such, she would be assigned a task force of 14 employees from each of the major departments to organize and plan the event. Her team was to present a preliminary plan and budget for the event to top management within three months. When discussing budgets, Tubbs revealed that he felt the total cost should be somewhere in the $150,000 range. He concluded the meeting by offering to help Briggs in any way he could to make the event a success.

Soon thereafter Briggs received the list of the names of the task force members, and she contacted them either by phone or e-mail to arrange today's meeting. She had to scramble to find a meeting place. Her cubicle in human resources was too small to accommodate such a group, and all the meeting rooms at Kerzner were booked or being refurbished. She settled on the cafeteria because it was usually deserted in the late afternoon. Prior to the meeting she posted the agenda on a flipchart (see Figure C10–1) adjacent to the table. Given everyone's busy schedules, the meeting was limited to just one hour.

The First Meeting

Briggs began the meeting by saying, "Greetings. For those who don't know me, I'm Amber Briggs from human resources and I've been assigned to manage the 10th anniversary celebration at Kerzner. Top management wants this to be special event—at the same time they want it to be our event. This is why you are here. Each of you represents one of the major departments, and together our job is to plan and organize the celebration." She then reviewed the agenda and asked each member to introduce themselves. The tall, red-haired woman to the right of Briggs broke the momentary silence by saying, "Hi, I'm Cara Miller from Plastics. I guess my boss picked me for this task force because I have a reputation for throwing great parties."

In turn each member followed suit. Below is a sampling of their introductions:

"Hi, I'm Mike Wales from maintenance. I'm not sure why I'm here. Things have been a little slow in our department, so my boss told me to come to this meeting."

"I'm Megan Plinski from domestic sales. I actually volunteered for this assignment. I think it will be a lot of fun to plan a big party."

"Yo, my name is Nick Psias from accounting. My boss said one of us had to join this task force, and I guess it was my turn."

"Hi, I'm Rick Fennah. I'm the only one from purchasing who has been here since the beginning. We've been through some rough times, and I think it is important to take time and celebrate what we've accomplished."

"Hi, I'm Ingrid Hedstrom from international sales. I think this is a great idea, but I should warn you that I will be out of the country for most of the next month."

"I'm Abby Bell from engineering. Sorry for being late, but things are a bit crazy in my department."

Briggs circled the names of the two people who were absent and circulated a roster so that everyone could check to see if their phone numbers and e-mail addresses were correct. She then summarized her meeting with Tubbs and told the group that he expected them to make a formal presentation to top management within 10 weeks. She acknowledged that they were all busy people and that it was her job to manage the project as efficiently as possible. At the same time, she reiterated the importance of the project and that this would be a very public event: "If we screw up everyone will know about it."

Briggs went over the ground rules and emphasized that from now on meetings would start on time and that she expected to be notified in advance if someone was going to be absent. She summarized the first part of the project as centering on five key questions: when, where, what, who, and how much? She created a stir in the group when she responded to a question about cost by informing them that top management was willing to pay up to $150,000 for the event. Megan quipped, "This is going to be one hell of a party."

Briggs then turned the group's attention to identifying a common meeting time. After jousting for 15 minutes, she terminated the discussion by requesting that each member submit a schedule of free time over the next month by Friday. She would use this information and a new planning software to identify optimal times. She ended the meeting by thanking the members for coming and asking them to begin soliciting ideas from co-workers about how this event should be celebrated. She announced that she would meet individually with each of them to discuss their role on the project. The meeting was adjourned at 4:00 P.M.

1. Critique Briggs's management of the first meeting. What, if anything, should she have done differently?
2. What barriers is she likely to encounter in completing this project?
3. What can she do to overcome these barriers?
4. What should she do between now and the next meeting?

Franklin Equipment, Ltd.*

Franklin Equipment, Ltd. (FEL), with headquarters and main fabrication facilities in Saint John, New Brunswick, was founded 75 years ago to fabricate custom-designed large machines for construction businesses in the Maritime Provinces. Over the years its product lines became strategically focused on creating rock-crushing equipment for

---

* Prepared by John A. Drexler, Jr.

dam and highway construction and for a few other markets that require the processing of aggregate. FEL now designs, fabricates, and assembles stationary and portable rock-crushing plants and services its own products and those of its competitors.

In the 1970s, FEL began to expand its market from the Maritime Provinces to the rest of Canada. FEL currently has several offices and fabrication facilities throughout the country. More recently, FEL has made a concerted effort to market its products internationally.

Last month, FEL signed a contract to design and fabricate a rock-crushing plant for a Middle East construction project, called Project Abu Dhabi. Charles Gatenby secured this contract and has been assigned as project manager. This project is viewed as a coup because FEL has wanted to open up markets in this area for a long time and has had difficulty getting prospective customers to realize that FEL is a Canadian firm and not from the United States. Somehow these customers view all North American vendors as the same and are reluctant to employ any of them because of international political considerations.

A project of this scope typically starts with the selection of a team of managers responsible for various aspects of the design, fabrication, delivery, and installation of the product. Manager selection is important because the product design and fabrication vary with the unique needs of each customer. For example, the terrain, rock characteristics, weather conditions, and logistical concerns create special problems for all phases of plant design and operations. In addition, environmental concerns and labor conditions vary from customer to customer and from region to region.

In addition to the project manager, all projects include a design engineer; an operations manager, who oversees fabrication and onsite assembly; and a cost accountant, who oversees all project financial and cost reporting matters. Each of these people must work closely together if a well-running plant is to be delivered on time and within cost constraints. Because international contracts often require FEL to employ host nationals for plant assembly and to train them for operations, a human resource manager is also assigned to the project team. In such cases, the human resource manager needs to understand the particulars of the plant specifications and then use this knowledge to design selection procedures and assess particular training needs. The human resource manager also needs to learn the relevant labor laws of the customer's country.

FEL assigns managers to project teams based on their expertise and their availability to work on a particular project given their other commitments. This typically means that managers without heavy current project commitments will be assigned to new projects. For instance, a manager finishing one project will likely be assigned a management position on a new project team. The project manager typically has little to say about who is assigned to his or her team.

Because he secured Project Abu Dhabi and has established positive working relationships with the Abu Dhabi customer, Gatenby was assigned to be project manager. Gatenby has successfully managed similar projects. The other managers assigned to Project Abu Dhabi are Bill Rankins, a brilliant design engineer, Rob Perry, operations manager with responsibility for fabrication and installation, Elaine Bruder, finance and cost accounting manager, and Sam Stonebreaker, human resource manager. Each of these managers has worked together on numerous past projects.

A few years ago, FEL began contracting for team facilitator services from several consulting firms to help new project teams operate effectively. Last month, FEL recruited Carl Jobe from one of these consulting firms to be a full-time internal consultant. A number of managers, including Gatenby, were so impressed with Jobe's skills that they convinced FEL top management of the need to hire a permanent internal facilitator; Jobe was the obvious choice.

Because Gatenby was instrumental in hiring Jobe at FEL, he was excited at the prospect of using Jobe to facilitate team building among Project Abu Dhabi team members. Gatenby was very proud of having secured this project and had expected to be appointed project manager. He knew that this project's success would be instrumental in advancing his own career.

Gatenby told Jobe, "This project is really important to FEL and to me personally. I really need for you to help us develop into a team that works well together to achieve the project's goals within budget. I've observed your success in developing teams on other projects, and I expect you'll do the same for Project Abu Dhabi. I'll take care of you if you help me make this work."

Jobe outlined for Gatenby how he would proceed. Jobe would begin by interviewing team members individually to learn their perceptions of each other and of the promises and pitfalls of being involved in this project. Meetings of the entire team would follow these interviews using the information he collected to help establish a team identity and a shared vision.

Jobe interviewed Bruder first. She expressed skepticism about whether the project could succeed. During the interview, Bruder appeared to be distant, and Jobe could not figure out why he had not established good rapport with her. Bruder intimated that she expected a lot of cost overruns and a lot of missed production deadlines. But not knowing Jobe well, Bruder was reluctant to identify any specific barriers to the project's success. While she would not directly say so, it was clear to Jobe that Bruder did not want to be a part of Project Abu Dhabi. Jobe left this interview confused and wondering what was going on.

Jobe's next interview was with Perry, the operations manager. Perry has worked at FEL for 15 years, and he immediately came to the point: "This project is not going to work. I cannot understand why upper management keeps assigning me to work on projects with Rankins. We simply cannot work together, and we don't get along. I've disliked him from day one. He keeps dropping the fact that he has earned all these advanced degrees from Purdue. And he keeps telling us how things are done there. I know he's better educated than I am, and he's really smart. But I'm smart too and am good at what I do. There's no need for Rankins to make me feel like an idiot because I don't have a degree. Jobe, I'll be honest with you. Rankins has only been here for five years, but I hold him personally responsible for my problem with alcohol, and for its resulting effect on my marriage. I got divorced last year, and it's Rankins's fault."

Jobe next talked with Rankins, who said, "I don't care what you do. Perry and I simply can't work closely together for the nine months it will take to get it done. One of us will kill the other. Ever since I arrived at FEL, Perry has hated my guts and does everything he can to sabotage my designs. We usually worry about customers creating change orders; here it's the fabrication and operations manager who is responsible for them. Perry second-guesses everything I do and makes design changes on his own, and these are always bad decisions. He is out of control. I swear he stays awake at nights thinking up ways to ruin my designs. I don't have this problem with any other manager."

Jobe left these interviews thoroughly discouraged and could not imagine what would come up in his interview with Stonebreaker. But Stonebreaker was quite positive: "I enjoy these international projects where I get to travel abroad and learn about different cultures. I can't wait to get started on this."

Jobe asked Stonebreaker about the ability of various team members to work together. Stonebreaker replied, "No problem! We've all worked together before and have had no problems. Sure, there have been ruffled feathers and hurt feelings between Rankins and Perry. Rankins can be arrogant and Perry stubborn, but it's never been anything that we can't work around. Besides, both of them are good at what they do—both professionals. They'll keep their heads on straight."

Jobe was even more bewildered. Gatenby says this project's success rides on Jobe's facilitation skills. The finance manager appears to want off this project team. The design engineer and operations manager admit they detest each other and cannot work together. And the human resources manager, having worked on projects with Perry and Rankins before, expects a rosy working relationship and anticipates no problems.

Jobe had a second meeting with Gatenby. Before discussing the design of the team building sessions, he asked questions to learn what Gatenby thought about the ability of team members to work together. Gatenby admitted that there has been very bad blood between Perry and Rankins, but added, "That's why we hired you. It's your job to make sure that the history between those two doesn't interfere with Project Abu Dhabi's success. It's your job to get them to work well together. Get it done."

Their dialogue toward the end of this meeting progressed as follows:

> *Jobe*: "Why do you expect Rankins and Perry to work well together, given their history? What incentives do they have to do so?"
>
> *Gatenby*: "As you should know, FEL requires formal goal setting between project managers and functional managers at the beginning of each project. I've already done this with Bruder, Stonebreaker, Perry, and Rankins. Perry and Rankins have explicit goals stating they must work well together and cooperate with each other."
>
> *Jobe*: "What happens if they do not meet these goals?"
>
> *Gatenby*: "I've already discussed this with top management. If it appears to me after two months that things are not working out between Perry and Rankins, FEL will fire Rankins."
>
> *Jobe*: "Does Perry know this?"
>
> *Gatenby*: "Yes."

1. Evaluate the criteria FEL uses to assign managers to project teams. What efficiencies do these criteria create? What are the resulting problems?
2. Why is it even more important that project team members work well together on international projects such as Project Abu Dhabi?
3. Discuss the dilemma that Jobe now faces.
4. What should Jobe recommend to Gatenby?

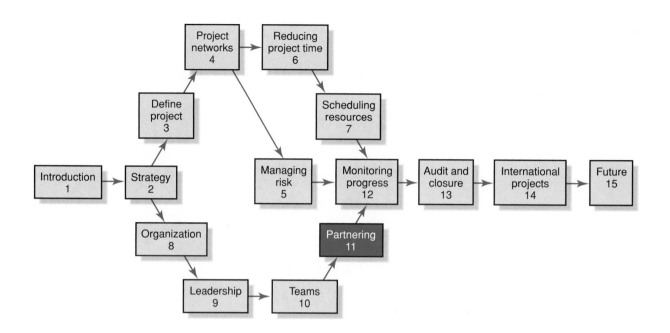

Partnering: Managing Interorganizational Relations

Introduction to Project Partnering
Preproject Activities—Setting the Stage for Successful Partnering
Project Implementation—Sustaining Collaborative Relationships
Project Completion—Celebrating Success
Why Project Partnering Efforts Succeed or Fail
The Art of Negotiating
A Note on Managing Customer Relations
Summary
Appendix 11–1: Contract Management

CHAPTER ELEVEN

Partnering: Managing Interorganizational Relations

. . . being a good partner has become a key corporate asset. I call it a company's collaborative advantage. In the global economy, a well-developed ability to create and sustain fruitful collaborations gives companies a significant competitive leg up.
—Rosabeth Moss Kanter[1]

It is rare in today's downsized world to find significant projects that are being completed totally in-house. Outsourcing or contracting significant segments of project work to other companies is commonplace. For example, nine states attempting to unify the accounting of all their state agencies did not have the internal resources to implement such a large project. Hence, project teams were formed consisting of personnel from software, hardware, and accounting firms to implement the projects. Small high-tech firms outsource research to determine what features customers value in new products they are developing. Even industry giants such as Microsoft and Intel commonly hire independent firms to test new products they are developing.

Contracting project work has long been the norm in the construction industry, where firms hire general contractors who, in turn, hire and manage cadres of subcontractors to create new buildings and structures. For example, the Chunnel project, which created a transportation tunnel between France and England, involved more than 250 organizations. Contracting is not limited to large projects. For example, an insurance company worked with an outside contractor to develop an answering service that directs customers to specific departments and employees. The trend for the future suggests that more and more projects will involve working with people from different organizations.

This chapter extends the previous two chapters' discussion of building and managing relations by focusing specifically on issues surrounding working with people from other organizations to complete a project. The term *partnering* is used to describe this process. Partnering is a process for transforming contractual arrangements into a cohesive, collaborative team that deals with issues and problems encountered in implementing projects to meet a customer's need. First, the genesis of project partnering and its major assumptions are reviewed. This introduction is followed by a general description of the partnering process and the barriers to collaboration. The focus then shifts to the art of negotiating, which is at the heart of effective partnering. Negotiating skills and techniques for resolving disagreements and reaching optimal solutions are then presented. The chapter closes with a brief note on managing customer relations.

In addition, an appendix on contract management is included to suggest some differences in the nature of partnering arrangements—given a particular type of contract.

INTRODUCTION TO PROJECT PARTNERING

The term *partnering,* as it relates to projects, emerged during the 1980s in the construction industry. During this period a report conducted by the Construction Industry Institute concluded that "the U.S. Construction Industry is ill."[2] The report went on to document the general decline in productivity over the past two decades. Delays in construction were common and expensive, and litigation related to design and construction was rising at an exponential rate. As one building contractor put it, "The only people making money in construction are the lawyers." In addition, the U.S. construction industry experienced difficulty in securing overseas contracts. Representatives from several countries have stated, "U.S. construction companies were not even considered because of the fear of litigation during and after completion of the project."

The industry response was to test the concept of "partnering" by a few adventurous owners and construction firms. The intent was to keep the formal contract intact but change the way the owner and construction firms interact during project implementation. A variety of definitions of partnering are found in the literature. Two of the more popular ones are noted here:

> Partnering is a long-term commitment between two or more organizations for the purpose of achieving specific business objectives by maximizing the effectiveness of each participant's resources. This requires changing traditional relationships to a shared culture without regard to organizational boundaries. The relationship is based upon trust, dedication to common goals, and an understanding of each other's individual expectations and values. Expected benefits include improved efficiency and cost-effectiveness, increased opportunity for innovation, and the continuous improvement of quality products and services.[3]

> Project partnering is a method of transforming contractual relationships into a cohesive, cooperative project team with a single set of goals and established procedures for resolving disputes in a timely manner.[4]

Partnering is more than a set of goals and procedures; it is a state of mind, a philosophy on how to conduct business with other organizations. Partnering represents a commitment from all the participants working on a project to respect, trust, and collaborate. Today, partnering is used across all industries because it makes good business sense.

Partnering is based on the assumption that the traditional adversarial relationship between owner and contractor(s) is ineffective and self-defeating. The basis for this adversarial posturing centers on the inherent conflict between the cost to the owner and the profit to the contractor. This is essentially a zero-sum game in which one party's gain is the other party's loss. The apparent conflict of interest predisposes owners and contractors to be suspicious of the motives and actions of each other. For the owners, this suspicion manifests itself by oppressively monitoring the contractor's performance, challenging each and every request to make an adjustment in plans or budget, and forcing compliance by withholding funds. Contractors respond by exploiting loopholes in the contract, withholding or manipulating information, or taking advantage of the owner's ignorance to inflate cost estimates and charging for unnecessary work.

Suspicion and mistrust prevent effective problem solving. Mistakes and problems are often hidden. When they surface, a game of "hot potato" is played as to who is responsible for correcting them. When conflicts emerge they are often deferred up the hierarchy. This creates costly delays as well as, at times, questionable responses because upper management is often too removed from the situation to make an effective decision. Many disputes end up in court as each side realizes that the only way to protect its interests is through litigation. To some extent litigation becomes a self-fulfilling prophecy. Managers spend almost as much time preparing a case as doing the work. The tragedy is that often small problems mushroom into major obstacles because problems were not resolved at inception.

Partnering naturally emerged as people began to realize that the traditional win/lose adversarial relationship between owner and contractor degenerates into a costly lose/lose situation for all the parties. Furthermore, partnering assumes that the parties share sufficient common goals to warrant a more collaborative relationship. For example, both contractors and owners want projects completed on time and safely. Neither party wants rework. Both parties would prefer to avoid costly litigation. Each party would like to reduce costs while at the same time improve quality.

Major benefits can be enjoyed when partnering arrangements extend across multiple projects and are long term. For example Bechtl, Inc., began a partnering arrangement with Union Carbide in 1988 to provide engineering, procurement, and construction services for all major projects involving Union Carbide's chemical and plastics group. Among the many advantages for establishing a long-term partnership are the following:[5]

- **Reduced administrative costs**—The costs associated with bidding and selecting a contractor are eliminated. Contract administration costs are reduced as partners become knowledgeable of their counterpart's legal concerns.
- **More efficient utilization of resources**—Contractors have a known forecast of work while owners are able to concentrate their workforce on core businesses and avoid the demanding swings of project support.
- **Improved communication**—As partners gain experience with each other, they develop a common language and perspective, which reduces misunderstanding and enhances collaboration.
- **Improved innovation**—The partners are able to discuss innovation and associated risks in a more open manner and share risks and rewards fairly.
- **Improved performance**—Over time partners become more familiar with each other's standards and expectations and are able to apply lessons learned from previous projects to current projects.

The existence of common goals, the prohibitive costs of the adversarial approach, and the benefits that can be shared provide an opportunity for transforming a competitive situation into a more collaborative relationship. The differences between the traditional approach and the partnering approach to managing contracted relationships are summarized in Table 11–1.[6]

Partnering requires more than a simple handshake. Partnering typically entails a considerable up-front investment in time and resources to forge a common team identity among participants from different organizations. It also involves the creation of mechanisms designed to sustain and expand collaboration over the course of the project. The actual partnering process can take many different shapes and forms, depending on the nature of the project and contract, the number of organizations involved, and their prior experience working together. Still, our experience suggests that there are several core elements associated with most first-time partnering endeavors.[7] These elements are summarized in Figure 11–1.

TABLE 11–1

KEY PRACTICES IN PARTNERING RELATIONSHIPS VERSUS TRADITIONAL PRACTICES

Key practices in partnering relationships	Traditional practices
Mutual trust forms the basis for strong working relationships.	Suspicion and distrust; each party is wary of the motives for actions by the other.
Shared goals and objectives ensure common direction.	Each party's goals and objectives, while similar, are geared to what is best for them.
Joint project team exists with high level of interaction.	Independent project teams; teams are spatially separated with managed interactions.
Open communications avoid misdirection and bolster effective working relationships.	Communications are structured and guarded.
Long-term commitment provides the opportunity to attain continuous improvement.	Single project contracting is normal.
Objective critique is geared to candid assessment of performance.	Objectivity is limited due to fear of reprisal and lack of continuous improvement opportunity.
Access to each other's organization resources is available.	Access is limited with structured procedures and self-preservation taking priority over total optimization.
Total company involvement requires commitment from CEO to team members.	Involvement is normally limited to project-level personnel.
Integration of administrative systems equipment takes place.	Duplication and/or translation takes place with attendant costs and delays.
Risk is shared jointly among the partners, which encourages innovation and continuous improvement.	Risk is transferred to the other party.

FIGURE 11–1 Project Partnering Framework

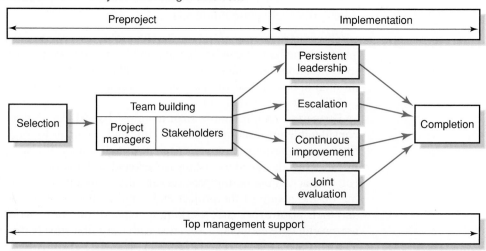

Snapshot from Practice
THE KODAK ORION PROJECT[8]

An excellent example of multinational companies employing partnering on a project is the Orion Project: Kodak, Fuji, Canon, Minolta, and Nikon joined forces to create a new camera technology. This project developed a new film cassette that drops into a camera without threading or adjusting. The cassette can also be used for storing negatives, rather than having loose negatives as is currently the case. No one firm had the total competency or resources to develop the new technology and, moreover, be sure others in the industry would adopt the technology. Research strongly suggested customers would readily accept and use the new technology. Hence the benefits provided a compelling reason for major players in the industry to develop a strong bond because of the shared vision of a new photo system that would be truly exciting and have a major impact on company performance and the photo industry.

The partnering arrangement did not just happen. Partners were selected by their belief in a shared vision, ability to pursue separate goals and still support and contribute to the partnership, and skills that complement each other. The companies worked cooperatively and voluntarily shared progress reports. The number of partners was restricted to five. Top management support was persistent and visible. All partners were able to develop their own products using the new-technology platform, and they launched them on the agreed date of April 22, 1996.

PREPROJECT ACTIVITIES—SETTING THE STAGE FOR SUCCESSFUL PARTNERING

Selecting a Partner(s)

Ideally contractors and even owners are selected based on an established track record of partnering on previous projects. Owners select only contractors with an interest and expertise in partnering. Contractors also screen potential work according to the owner's commitment to partnering principles. In some cases partnering provisions are explicitly stated in an advertised "invitation for bid" (IFB) and are a formal part of the contract. In other cases, the decision to pursue a partnering approach is made after the contract is awarded.

In either case, the first step is to get the commitment of the top management of all the firms involved to use the partnering process. For example, in the case of one public works contract, the owner arranged a meeting with the general contractor. At this meeting the owner congratulated the contractor for winning the contract and expressed a desire to manage the project according to partnering principles. The owner described in detail how this partnership would work and the benefits each would enjoy. The owner was careful to frame the proposal as an invitation and indicated that the contractor was free to choose whether to try partnering. Partnering will not work unless all sides freely commit themselves to implementation. Intimidation, shallow inducements, or halfhearted commitments on the part of either party will likely lead to failure.

Team Building: The Project Managers

Once top management from the major parties agree to try partnering, the next step is to begin to build a collaborative relationship among the key people from each organization who will actually be responsible for managing the project. This typically involves the lead representatives or project managers from the different organizations. For experienced managers this may simply involve meeting to review mutual objectives and outline the implementation of the partnering process. For less experienced managers this may involve more elaborate activities. For example, on one $34 million project, top management decided to send the managers to a weeklong leadership conference where they were exposed to principles of teamwork and effective communication. The training not only reinforced collaborative concepts but more importantly accelerated the evolution of their relationship from strangers to partners. The managers became bonded by a common, exhilarating experience and the development of a common set of project goals.

Team Building: The Stakeholders

Once the principal managers establish a personal commitment to partnering, the next step is to expand this commitment to the other key managers and specialists who will be working together on the project. Team-building workshops are held prior to project implementation that involve all the key players from the different firms, for example, engineers, architects, lawyers, specialists, and other staff. In many cases, firms find it useful to hire an outside consultant to design and facilitate the sessions. Such a consultant is typically well-versed in interorganizational team building and can provide an impartial perspective to the workshop. In other cases, the project managers jointly design and lead the sessions.

The length and design of the team-building sessions will depend on the experience, commitment, and skill level of the participants. For example, one project, in which the owner and the contractors were relatively inexperienced but committed to partnering, utilized a three-day workshop. The first day was devoted to ice-breaking activities and establishing the rationale behind partnering. The conceptual foundation was supported by exercises and minilectures on teamwork, synergy, win/win, and constructive feedback. The second day began by examining the problems and barriers that have prevented collaboration in the past. Representatives from the different organizations were separated and each asked the following:

- What actions do the other groups engage in that create problems for us?
- What actions do we engage in that we think create problems for them?
- What recommendations would we make to improve the situation?

The groups shared their responses and asked questions on points needing clarification.[9] Agreements and disparities in the lists were noted and specific problems were identified. Once problem areas were noted, each group was assigned the task of identifying its specific interests and goals for the project. Goals were shared across groups, and special attention was devoted to establishing what goals they had in common. Recognition of shared goals is critical for transforming the different groups into a cohesive team.[10]

Members from the different organizations were put into smaller mixed groups composed of their counterparts from the other organizations. For example, all of the lawyers were put in one group. These groups were assigned specific problems germane to their area of responsibility and asked to work out a recommended solution for each problem. The second day concluded with each group reporting their solutions to the entire group for review and agreement.

The final day of the workshop was devoted to consolidating the efforts of the previous day into a series of agreements and procedures to guide the partnering process. The session culminated with the creation of a project charter signed by all of the participants. This charter states their common goals for the project as well as the procedures that will be used to achieve these goals (see Figure 11–2 for an example of the first page of a project charter).

Carefully setting the stage for successful project implementation is imperative. Too often managers become preoccupied with the plans and technical challenges of the project and assume that people issues will work themselves out over time. Partnering recognizes that people issues are as important if not more important than technical issues. After all, who solves technical problems? Partnering accepts that one of the major barriers to effective collaboration is that participants come from different organizational cultures with different standards, habits, and priorities. The team-building sessions provide an opportunity for people to discuss differences and similarities and to begin to build a relationship with their counterparts before the project starts. At best, a common team culture begins to emerge that is based on successfully completing the project. At worst, participants develop a shared understanding so that cultural differences can coexist while jointly achieving the common objectives of the project.

PROJECT IMPLEMENTATION—SUSTAINING COLLABORATIVE RELATIONSHIPS

One of the objectives of the team-building sessions is to establish a "we" as opposed to "us and them" attitude among the different participants toward the project. Some companies reinforce this point by having the management teams from the different organizations work at the same location. A second objective of the sessions is to establish in advance mechanisms designed to ensure that this collaborative spirit is able to withstand the problems and setbacks that will invariably occur on the project. These mechanisms require the unwavering, consistent, and fanatical support of senior management. Among the most significant mechanisms are problem resolution, continuous improvement, joint evaluation, and persistent leadership.

Problem Resolution

Escalation is the primary control mechanism for dealing with and resolving problems. The basic principle is that problems should be resolved at the lowest level within a set

FIGURE 11–2 Project Partnering Charter

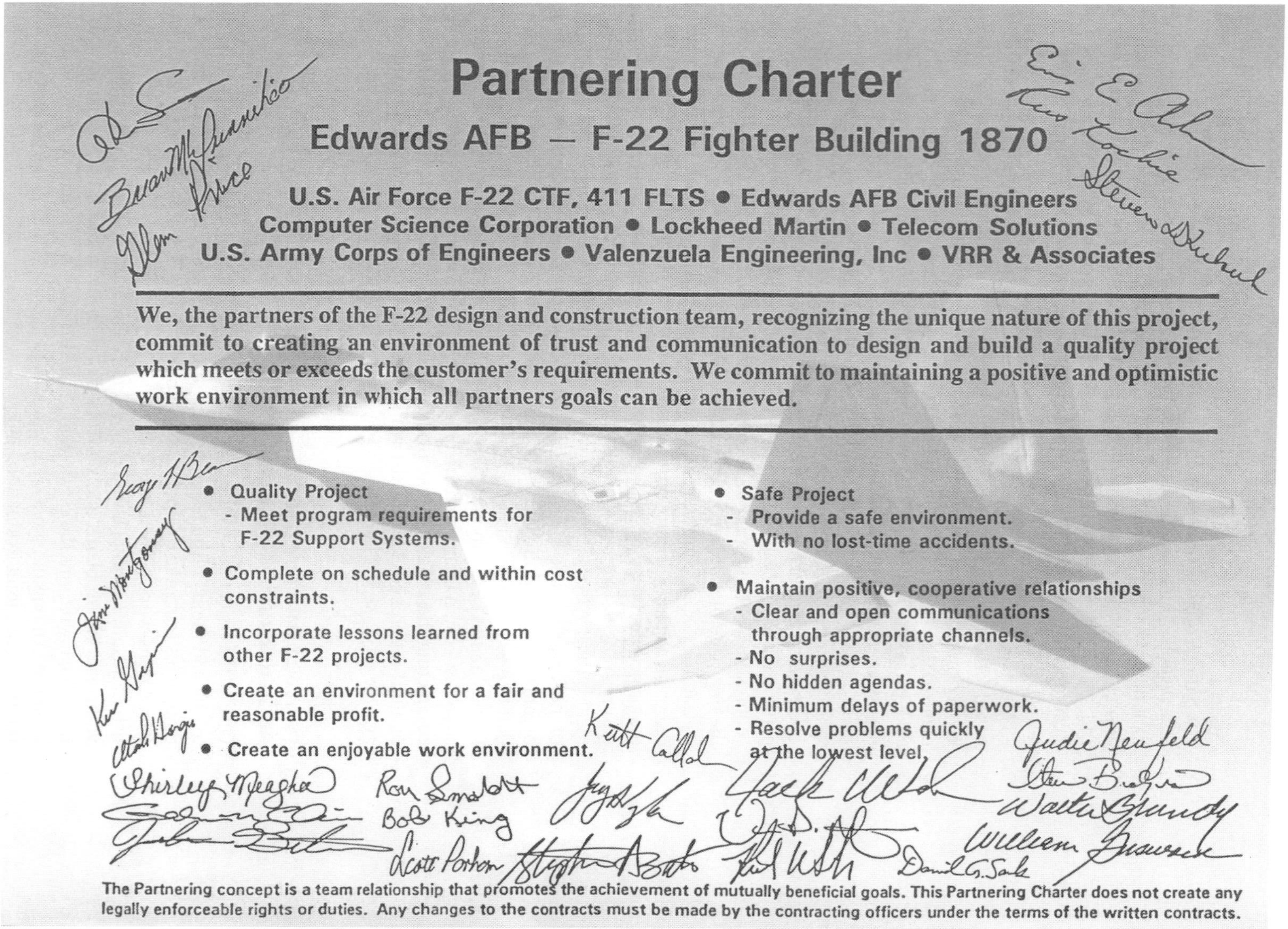

Partnering Charter

Edwards AFB — F-22 Fighter Building 1870

U.S. Air Force F-22 CTF, 411 FLTS • Edwards AFB Civil Engineers
Computer Science Corporation • Lockheed Martin • Telecom Solutions
U.S. Army Corps of Engineers • Valenzuela Engineering, Inc • VRR & Associates

We, the partners of the F-22 design and construction team, recognizing the unique nature of this project, commit to creating an environment of trust and communication to design and build a quality project which meets or exceeds the customer's requirements. We commit to maintaining a positive and optimistic work environment in which all partners goals can be achieved.

- Quality Project
  - Meet program requirements for F-22 Support Systems.
- Complete on schedule and within cost constraints.
- Incorporate lessons learned from other F-22 projects.
- Create an environment for a fair and reasonable profit.
- Create an enjoyable work environment.
- Safe Project
  - Provide a safe environment.
  - With no lost-time accidents.
- Maintain positive, cooperative relationships
  - Clear and open communications through appropriate channels.
  - No surprises.
  - No hidden agendas.
  - Minimum delays of paperwork.
  - Resolve problems quickly at the lowest level.

The Partnering concept is a team relationship that promotes the achievement of mutually beneficial goals. This Partnering Charter does not create any legally enforceable rights or duties. Any changes to the contracts must be made by the contracting officers under the terms of the written contracts.

time limit (i.e., 24 hours), or they are "escalated" to the next level of management. If so, the principals have the same time limit to resolve the problem, or it gets passed on to the next higher level. No action is not an option. Nor can one participant force concessions from the other by simply delaying the decision. There is no shame in pushing significant problems up the hierarchy; at the same time, managers should be quick to point out to subordinates those problems or questions that they should have been able to resolve on their own.

Continuous Improvement

Partnering assumes that continuous improvement is a joint effort to eliminate waste and pursue opportunities for cost savings. Risks as well as benefits are typically shared 50/50 between the principals, with the owner adhering to a fast-track review to withstand the problems and setbacks that will invariably occur in the project/approval process. The Snapshot from Practice box on page 341 shows an alternative arrangement from a project involving two partners and an owner.

Joint Evaluation

All involved parties meet on a regular basis to review and evaluate the partnering process. Specific criteria relating to the effectiveness of the partnering process such as teamwork and timely problem resolution are evaluated. This provides a forum for identifying problems not only with the project but also with working relationships so that they can be resolved quickly and appropriately. Evaluation of the partnering process usually includes a periodic survey. Comparison of survey responses period by period identifies areas of improvement and potential problems. See Figure 11–3 for a partial example of a survey.

Persistent Leadership

Project managers and their subordinates must "walk the talk" and consistently display a collaborative as opposed to confrontational response to problem solving. This is especially true early in the project, where mutual trust will be tested by how the partners respond to the first disagreements or setbacks that emerge. Project managers have to reward those within their own organization who adhere to the principles of partnering as well as admonish those who resort to more adversarial practices.

PROJECT COMPLETION—CELEBRATING SUCCESS

Once the project is completed, management needs to jointly review accomplishments as well as disappointments and derive lessons to be applied to future projects. This formal review of project execution is typically accompanied by a more festive celebration (picnic or banquet) involving all the participants. Top management takes advantage of this social function to recognize special contributions. Such a festivity provides a sense of closure and reaffirms the collaborative nature of the project.

WHY PROJECT PARTNERING EFFORTS SUCCEED OR FAIL

Organizational downsizing and concentration on utilizing core competencies has already increased the use of outside sources to assist or implement projects. The trend for the future suggests partnering will be more common. The challenge is to get the project completed on time, within budget, and to customer specifications. Although

FIGURE 11–3 Sample Partnering Evaluation

Evaluation of partnering process: attitudes, teamwork, process.
(Collected separately from owner and contractor participants, compared, and
aggregated.)

1. Communications between the owner/contractor personnel are

1	2	3	4	5
Difficult, guarded				Easy, open, up front

2. Top management support of partnering process is

1	2	3	4	5
Not evident or inconsistent				Obvious and consistent

3. Problems, issue, or concerns are

1	2	3	4	5
Ignored				Attacked promptly

4. Cooperation between owner and contractor personnel is

1	2	3	4	5
Cool, detached, unresponsive, removed				Genuine, unreserved, complete

5. Responses to problems, issues, or concerns frequently become

1	2	3	4	5
Personal issues				Treated as project problems

the results achieved from successful partnering can be phenomenal, we have noticed three areas that lead to the breakdown of the partnering arrangement and one area that is frequently overlooked.

The first and most significant problem is with senior management—the owner and contractor. The owner and contractor must have compelling reasons to make the partnering relationship work. Although most partnering arrangements start out with good intentions, when senior management fails to keep on top of the project and partnership, the seeds for failure are planted. The breakdown typically begins with a problem that needs resolution. A minor problem is escalated instead of solving the problem at the first level. Team members are hesitant to accept risk. The owner and contractor fail to return the problem to the first level where it should have been solved. Soon all problems are escalated and the relationship deteriorates as both sides hurl accusations and begin defensive posturing. Senior management must give clear signals that team members are empowered and encouraged to make decisions at the lowest possible level. The same problem occurs when senior management fails to resolve an escalated problem within the time limits set. Senior management is not leading the way. Senior management support of the partnering process cannot be ad hoc; leadership and commitment must be 100 percent and constant. Partnering will only be successful if senior management works at it!

Snapshot from Practice
INCENTIVE SYSTEM FOR A PARTNERING PROJECT

The snapshot describes conversations with the project manager of the project.

The project was to design and build a high technology oil drilling ship for the North Sea. The ship would be capable of finding the selected location within less than one meter and hold the location for drilling. The project included the owner and two major partners. Early, precontract meetings indicated all three were interested in the benefits partnering could offer. All three wanted to complete the project on time, within budget, and to meet specifications.

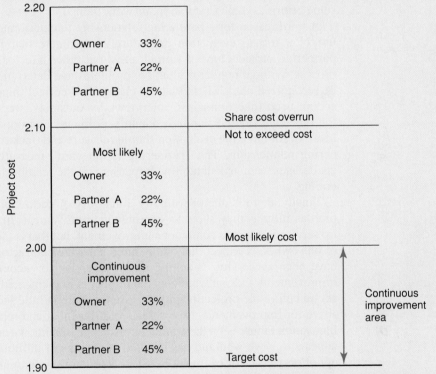

After several meetings, the owner and partners agreed to a simple incentive system to encourage continuous improvement during project implementation. The crux of the system centered on sharing *proportionally* any savings in total project cost or in cost overruns. The proportions for the project were determined by the money value each controlled—the owner, 33 percent, and 22 percent and 45 percent respectively, for the partners.

The project manager used the above exhibit to explain the numbers and process to all stakeholders. The partners agreed to three cost levels—*not-to-exceed cost, most likely cost,* and *target cost.* The manager said, "Getting to these agreed costs was sticky, but we did it." The project manager related that everyone came out a winner! The project was on time, under target cost, and met specifications and expectations. He believed success can be attributed to primarily three factors:

1. The incentive system forced the owner to join the effort.
2. Sharing was proportional to cost responsibility.
3. The three project teams were joined, housed in one location. Responsibility for project implementation, control, and improvements was charged to the merged project team.

He suggested that the last factor of merging the three independent teams in one location seems to be the key that significantly increases the chances of partnering success.

A second major reason partnering arrangements break down is the failure to adequately deal with cultural differences among the contributing organizations. Differences in management styles, terminology, operating procedures, and perspectives of time can result in culture shock that frustrates the development and maintenance of good rapport between the participants. The key is to try to merge these cultural differences into a common team culture that is based on successfully completing the project. This process begins with the team-building sessions but must be a priority agenda item throughout the duration of the project. Much of the material on developing a high-performance team discussed in the previous chapter must be applied. Each organization must also be careful to select and place savvy professionals in key positions who are adept at forging relationships with people who do not necessarily share the same priorities, time orientation, or work habits.

A third reason for a partnering relationship to deteriorate is the absence or lack of use of a formal evaluation procedure. We estimate that fewer than 20 percent of partnering projects have a formal, effective procedure for evaluating the partnering process. Without regular evaluation, problems and deterioration of the process cannot be recognized until it is too late to change and correct things. Regardless of the procedure used (questionnaires, interviews by outsiders, weekly evaluation meetings), the procedure should regularly identify problems and opportunities at the operating level. In addition, the evaluation should measure and track the overall state of the partnering relationship. The "partnering report card" measures team performance and encourages team accountability. It measures if the relationship is improving or degenerating.

Finally, there is one opportunity a majority of partnering arrangements fail to exploit as fully as they should—continuous improvement. In many partnering projects lip service is given to continuous improvement, but that is the extent of it. In the words of one owner, "I expect that of any hired software contractor." The key, for those who have been successful, is setting up an incentive to encourage a contractor to seek improvements and innovation as the project is implemented. A procedure needs to be set up before the project begins. In essence there is little incentive for a contractor to strive for improvements, except for repeat business and reputation. All of the risk of innovation failure is on the contractor. An approach known as the "50/50 percent split" appears to work well and has resulted in savings of millions of dollars across a variety of projects—for example, R&D, construction, time to market. This procedure has the owner and contractor share the costs (risks) for any innovation and rewards on a 50/50 basis.

Partnering is a conscious effort on the part of management to form collaborative relationships with personnel from different organizations to complete a project. For partnering to work, the individuals involved need to be effective negotiators capable of merging interests and discovering solutions to problems that contribute to the ultimate success of the project and the partnership. The next section addresses some of the key skills and techniques associated with effective negotiation.

THE ART OF NEGOTIATING

Effective negotiating is critical to successful partnering. All it takes is one key discussion to break down and unravel a partnering arrangement. At the same time, negotiating is pervasive through all aspects of project management work. Project managers must negotiate support and funding from top management. They must negotiate staff and technical input from functional managers. They must coordinate with other project managers and negotiate project priorities and commitments. They must negotiate within their project team to determine assignments, deadlines, standards, and priorities. Project managers must negotiate prices and standards with vendors and suppliers. A firm understanding of the negotiating process, skills, and tactics is essential to project success.

Many people approach negotiating as if it is a competitive contest. Each negotiator is out to win as much as he or she can for his or her side. Success is measured by how much is gained compared with the other party. While this may be applicable when negotiating the sale of a house, it is not true for project management. *Project management is not a contest.* First, the people working on the project, whether they represent different companies or departments within the same organization, are not enemies or competitors but rather allies or partners. They have formed a temporary alliance to complete a project. For this alliance to work requires a certain degree of trust, cooperation, and honesty. Second, although the parties within this alliance may have different priorities and standards, they are bound by the success of the project. If conflicts escalate to the point where negotiations break down and the project comes to a halt, then everyone loses. Third, unlike bartering with a street vendor, the people involved on project work have to continue to work together. Therefore, it behooves them to resolve disagreements in a way that contributes to the long-term effectiveness of their working relationship. Finally, as pointed out in the previous chapter, conflict on a project can be good. When dealt with effectively it can lead to innovation, better decisions, and more creative problem solving.

Project managers accept this noncompetitive view of negotiation and realize that negotiation is essentially a two-part process: The first part deals with reaching an agreement; the second part is the implementation of that agreement.[11] It is the implementation phase, not the agreement itself, that determines the success of negotiations. All too often, managers reach an agreement with someone only to find out later that they failed to do what they agreed to do or that their actual response fell far short of expectations. Experienced project managers recognize that implementation is based on satisfaction not only with the outcome but also with the process by which the agreement was reached. If someone feels they have been bullied or tricked into doing something, this feeling will invariably be reflected by halfhearted compliance and passive resistance.

Veteran project managers do the best they can to merge individual interests with what is best for the project and come up with effective solutions to problems. Fisher and Ury from the Harvard Negotiation Project champion an approach to negotiating that embodies these goals.[12] It emphasizes developing win/win solutions while protecting yourself against those who would take advantage of your forthrightness. Their approach is called *principle negotiation* and is based on four key points listed in Table 11–2 and discussed in the following sections.

TABLE 11–2
PRINCIPLE NEGOTIATION
1. Separate the people from the problem
2. Focus on interests, not positions
3. Invent options for mutual gain
4. When possible, use objective criteria

Separate the People from the Problem

Too often personal relations become entangled with the substantive issues under consideration. Instead of attacking the problem(s), people attack each other. Once people feel attacked or threatened their energy naturally goes to defending themselves, and not to solving the problem. The key, then, to is to focus on the problem—not the other person—during the negotiation. Avoid personalizing the negotiation and framing the negotiation as a contest. Instead, try to keep the focus on the problem to be resolved. In Fisher and Ury's words: *Be hard on the problem, soft on the people.*

By keeping the focus on the issues and not the personalities, negotiators are better able to let the other person blow off steam. On important problems it is not uncommon for people to become upset, frustrated, and angry. However, one angry attack produces an angry counterattack, and the discussion quickly escalates into a heated argument, an emotional chain reaction. In some cases people use anger as a means of intimidating and forcing concessions because the other person wishes to preserve the relationship. When people become emotional, negotiators should keep a cool head and remember the old German proverb, "Let anger fly out the window." In other words, in the face of an emotional outburst, imagine opening a window and letting the heat of the anger out the window.[13] Avoid taking things personally, and redirect personal attacks back to the question at hand. Don't react to the emotional outburst, but try to find the issues that triggered it. Skilled negotiators keep their cool under stressful times and, at the same time, build a bond with others by empathizing and acknowledging common sources of frustration and anger.

While it is important to separate the people from the problem during actual negotiations, it is beneficial to have a friendly rapport with the other person prior to negotiating. Friendly rapport is consistent with the social network tenet introduced in Chapter 9 of building a relationship before you need it. Reduce the likelihood of misunderstandings and getting off on the wrong foot by having a history of interacting in a friendly, responsive manner with the other person. If, in the past, the relationship has been marked by healthy give-and-take, in which both parties have demonstrated a willingness to accommodate the interests of the other, then neither individual is likely to adopt an immediate win/lose perspective. Furthermore, a positive relationship adds a common interest beyond the specific points of contention. Not only do both parties want to reach an agreement that suits their individual interests, but they also want to do so in a manner that preserves their relationship. Each is therefore more likely to seek solutions that are mutually beneficial. Conversely, if the relationship has been dominated by one individual who takes more than she gives, then the resentment and mistrust that have been slowly building over time will naturally spill into the immediate interaction.

Focus on Interests, not Positions

Negotiations often stall when people focus on positions:

> I'm willing to pay $10,000. No, it will cost $15,000.
>
> I need it done by Monday. That's impossible, we can't have it ready until Wednesday.

While such interchanges are common during preliminary discussions, managers must prevent this initial posturing from becoming polarized. When such positions are stated, attacked, and then defended, each party figuratively begins to draw a line they will not cross. This line creates a win/lose scenario in which someone has to lose by crossing the line in order to reach an agreement. As such, the negotiations can become a war of wills, with concessions being seen as a loss of face.

The key is to focus on the interests behind your positions (what you are trying to achieve) and separate these goals from your ego as best you can. Not only should you be driven by your interests, but you should try to identify the interests of the other party. Ask why it will cost so much or why it can't be done by Monday. At the same time, make your own interests come alive. Don't just say that it is critical that it done by Monday; explain what will happen if it isn't done by Monday.

Sometimes when the true interests of both parties are revealed, there is no basis for conflict. Take, for example, the Monday versus Wednesday argument. This argument could apply to a scenario involving a project manager and the production manager of a small, local firm that was contracted to produce prototypes of a new generation of computer mouse. The project manager needs the prototypes on Monday to demonstrate to a users' focus group. The production manager said it would be impossible. The project manager said this would be embarrassing because marketing had spent a lot of time and effort setting up this demonstration. The production manager again denied the request and added that he already had to schedule overtime to meet the Wednesday delivery date. However, when the project manager revealed that the purpose of the focus group was to gauge consumers' reactions to the color and shape of the new devices, not the finished product, the conflict disappeared. The production manager told the project manager that she could pick up the samples today if she wanted because production had an excess supply of shells.

When focusing on interests, it is important to keep in mind that one of the habits of effective interpersonal communication is, *Seek first to understand, then to be understood*. This involves what Covey calls empathetic listening, which allows a person to fully understand another person's frame of reference—not only what they are saying but also how they feel.[14] Covey asserts that people have an inherent need to be understood. He goes on to observe that satisfied needs do not motivate human behavior, only unsatisfied needs do. People try to go to sleep when they are tired, not when they are rested. The key point is that until the other party believes they are being understood, they will expend time and energy trying to bring about that understanding. They will repeat their points and reformulate their arguments. If, on the other hand, you satisfy this need by seeking first to understand, then the other party is free to understand your interests and focus directly on the issues at hand. Seeking to understand requires discipline and compassion. Instead of responding to the other person by asserting your agenda, respond by summarizing both the facts and feelings behind what the other person has said and checking the accuracy of comprehension.

Invent Options for Mutual Gain

Once the individuals involved have identified their interests, then they can explore options for mutual gain. This is not easy. Stressful negotiations inhibit creativity and free exchange. What is required is collaborative brainstorming in which people work together to solve the problem in a way that will lead to a win/win scenario. The key to brainstorming is separating the inventing from the deciding. Begin by taking 15 minutes to generate as many options as possible. No matter how outlandish any option is, it should not be subject to criticism or immediate rejection. People should feed off the ideas of others to generate new ideas. When all the possible options are exhausted, then sort through the ideas that were generated to focus on those with the greatest possibilities.

Clarifying interests and exploring mutual options creates the opportunity for dovetailing interests. Dovetailing means one person identifies options that are of low cost to them but of high interest to the other party. This is only possible if each party knows what the other's needs are. For example, in negotiating price with a parts supplier, a project manager learned from the discussion that the supplier was in a cash flow squeeze after purchasing a very expensive fabrication machine. Needed cash was the primary reason the supplier had taken such a rigid position on price. During the brainstorming session, one of the options presented was to prepay for the order instead of the usual payment on delivery arrangement. Both parties seized on this option and reached an amicable agreement in which the project manager would pay the supplier for the entire job in advance in exchange for a faster turnaround time and a significant price reduction. Such opportunities for win/win agreements are often overlooked because the negotiators become fixated on solving their problems and not on opportunities to solve the other person's problems.

When Possible, Use Objective Criteria

Most established industries and professions have developed standards and rules to help deal with common areas of dispute. Both buyers and sellers rely on the blue book to establish price parameters for a used car. The construction industry has building codes and fair practice policies to resolve proof of quality and safe work procedures. The legal profession uses precedents to adjudicate claims of wrongdoing.

Whenever possible, you should insist on using external, objective criteria to settle disagreements. For example, a disagreement arose between a regional airlines firm and the independent accounting team entrusted with preparing the annual financial statement. The airline firm had made a significant investment by leasing several used airplanes from a larger airline. The dispute involved whether this lease should be classified as an operating or capital lease. This was important to the airline because if the purchase was classified as an operating lease, then the associated debt would not have to be recorded in the financial statement. However, if the purchase was classified as a capital lease, then the debt would be factored into the financial statement and the debt/equity ratio would be much less attractive to stockholders and would-be investors. The two parties resolved this dispute by deferring to formulas established by the Financial Accounting Standards Board. As it turns out the accounting team was correct, but, by deferring to objective standards, they were able to deflect the disappointment of the airline managers away from the accounting team and preserve a professional relationship with that firm.

Dealing with Unreasonable People

Most people working on projects realize that in the long run it is beneficial to work toward mutually satisfying solutions. Still, occasionally you encounter someone who has a dominant win/lose attitude about life and will be difficult to deal with. Fisher and Ury recommend that you use negotiation jujitsu when dealing with such a person.[15] That is, when the other person begins to push, don't push back. As in the martial arts, avoid pitting your strengths against theirs directly; instead use your skill to step aside and turn their strength to your ends. When someone adamantly sets forth a position, neither reject it nor accept it. Treat it as a possible option and then look for the interests behind it. Instead of defending your ideas, invite criticism and advice. Ask why it's a bad idea and discover the other's underlying interest.

Those who use negotiation jujitsu rely on two primary weapons. They ask questions instead of making statements. Questions allow for interests to surface and do not provide the opponent with something to attack. The second weapon is silence. If the other person makes an unreasonable proposal or attacks you personally, just sit there and don't say a word. Wait for the other party to break the stalemate by answering your question or coming up with a new suggestion.

The best defense against unreasonable, win/lose negotiators is having what Fisher and Ury call a strong BATNA (best alternative to a negotiated agreement). They point out that people try to reach an agreement to produce something better than the result of not negotiating with that person. What those results would be (BATNA) is the true benchmark for determining whether you should accept an agreement. A strong BATNA gives you the power to walk away and say, "No deal unless we work toward a win/win scenario."

Your BATNA reflects how dependent you are on the other party. If you are negotiating price and delivery dates and can choose from a number of reputable suppliers, then you have a strong BATNA. If on the other hand there is only one vendor who can supply you with specific, critical material on time, then you have a weak BATNA. Under these circumstances you may be forced to concede to the vendor's demands. At the same time, you should begin to explore ways of increasing your BATNA for future negotiations. This can be done by reducing your dependency on that supplier. Begin to find substitutable material or negotiate better lead times with other vendors.

Negotiating is an art. There are many intangibles involved. This section has reviewed some time-tested principles of effective negotiating based on the groundbreaking work of Fisher and Ury. Given the significance of negotiating, you are encouraged to read their book as well as others on negotiating.[16] In addition, attending training workshops can provide an opportunity to practice these skills. You should also take advantage of day-to-day interactions to sharpen negotiating acumen.

A NOTE ON MANAGING CUSTOMER RELATIONS

In Chapter 2 it was emphasized that ultimate success is not determined by whether the project was completed on time, within budget, or according to specifications, but whether the customer is satisfied with what has been accomplished. Customer satisfaction is the bottom line. In today's competitive world where information flows freely, reputation is essential to long-term success. As advocates of the total quality revolution are quick to point out, there is about an 8:1 ratio between the communication of customer dissatisfaction and satisfaction. This means that for every satisfied customer who shares his satisfaction regarding a particular product or service with another person, a dissatisfied customer is likely to share her dissatisfaction with eight other people.[17] Bad news travels faster and farther than good news. Project managers need to cultivate positive working relations with clients to ensure success and preserve their reputations.

Customer satisfaction is a complex phenomenon. One simple but useful way of viewing customer satisfaction is in terms of met expectations.[18] According to this model, customer satisfaction is a function of the extent to which perceived performance (or outcome) exceeds expectations. Mathematically, this relationship can be represented as the ratio between perceived performance and expected performance (see Figure 11–4). When performance falls short of expectations (ratio < 1), the customer is dissatisfied. If the performance matches expectations (ratio = 1), the customer is satisfied. If the performance exceeds expectations (ratio > 1), the customer is very satisfied or even delighted.

FIGURE 11–4 The Met-Expectations Model of Customer Satisfaction

$$\underset{\text{Dissatisfied}}{0.90} = \frac{\text{Perceived performance}}{\text{Expected performance}} = \underset{\text{Very satisfied}}{1.10}$$

High customer satisfaction is the goal of most projects. However, profitability is another major concern. Exceeding expectations typically entails additional costs. For example, completing a construction project two weeks ahead of schedule may involve significant overtime expenses. Similarly, exceeding reliability requirements for a new electronic component may involve considerably more design and debugging effort. Under most circumstances, the most profitable arrangement occurs when the customer's expectations are only slightly exceeded. Returning to the mathematical model, with all other things being equal, one should strive for a satisfaction ratio of 1.05, not 1.5!

The met-expectations model of customer satisfaction highlights the point that whether a client is dissatisfied or delighted with a project is not based on hard facts and objective data but on perceptions and expectations. For example, a customer may be dissatisfied with a project that was completed ahead of schedule and under budget if he thought the work was poor quality and that his fears and concerns were not adequately addressed by the project team. Conversely, a customer may be very satisfied with a project that was over budget and behind schedule if she felt the project team protected her interests and did the best job possible under adverse circumstances.

Project managers must be skilled at managing customer expectations and perceptions. Too often they deal with these expectations after the fact when they try to alleviate a client's dissatisfaction by carefully explaining why the project cost more or took longer than planned. A more proactive approach is to begin to shape the proper expectations up front and accept that this is an ongoing process throughout the life of a project. Project managers need to direct their attention to both the customer's base expectations, the standard by which perceived performance will be evaluated, and to the customer's perceptions of actual performance. The ultimate goal is to educate clients so that they can make a valid judgment as to project performance as well as reduce chances for misunderstandings that can lead to disappointment and dissatisfaction.

Managing customer expectations begins during the preliminary project approval phase of negotiations. It is important to avoid the temptation to oversell the virtues of a project to win approval because this may create unrealistic expectations that may be too difficult, if not impossible, to achieve. At the same time, project proponents have been known to lower customer expectations by underselling projects. If the estimated completion time is 10 to 12 weeks, they will promise to have the project completed within 12 to 14 weeks, therefore increasing the chances of exceeding customer expectations by getting the project completed early.

Once the project is authorized, the project manager and team need to work closely with the client organization to develop a well-defined project scope statement that clearly states the objectives, parameters, and limits of the project work. The project scope statement is essential to establishing customer expectations regarding the project. It is critical that all parties are in agreement as to what is to be accomplished and that everyone is reading as best they can from the same page. It is also important to share significant risks that might disrupt project execution. Customers do not like surprises, and if they are aware in advance of potential problems they are much more likely to be accepting of the consequences.

Once the project is initiated it is important to keep customers abreast of project progress. The days when you would simply take orders from customers and tell them to return when the project is done are over. More and more organizations and their project managers are treating their customers as de facto members of the project team and are actively involving them in key aspects of project work. They consult with customers on important technical decisions to ensure that solutions are consistent with customer needs. Project managers need to keep customers informed of project developments so that customers can make adjustments in their own plans. When circumstances dictate changing the scope or priorities of the project, project managers need to be quick to spell out as best they can the implications of these changes to the customers so that they can make an informed choice. Active customer involvement allows customers to naturally adjust their expectations in accordance with the decisions and events that transpire on a project, while at same time, the customer's presence keeps the project team focused on the customer's objectives for the project.

Active customer involvement also provides a firmer basis for assessing project performance. The customer not only sees the results of the project but also acquires glimpses of the effort and actions that produced those results. Naturally project managers want to make sure these glimpses reflect favorably on their project teams, so they exercise extra care that customer interactions are handled in a competent and professional manner. In some respects, customer perceptions of performance are shaped more by how well the project team deals with adversity than by actual performance. Project managers can impress customers with how diligently they deal with unexpected problems and setbacks. Likewise, industry analysts have noted that customer dissatisfaction can be transformed into customer satisfaction by quickly correcting mistakes and being extremely responsive to customer concerns.

Managing customer relations on a project is a broad topic; we have only highlighted some of the central issues involved. This brief segment concludes with two words of advice passed on by veteran project managers:

Speak with one voice. Nothing erodes confidence in a project more than for a customer to receive conflicting messages from different project members. The project manager should remind team members of this fact and work with them to ensure that appropriate information is shared with customers.

Speak the language of the customer. Too often project members respond to customer inquiries with technical jargon that exceeds the customer's vocabulary. Project managers and members need to describe problems, trade-offs, and solutions in ways that the customer can understand.

SUMMARY

More and more companies are seeking cooperative arrangements with each other to compete in today's business world. Project partnering represents a proactive response to many of the challenges associated with working with people from different organizations. Before the project is started, significant time and effort are invested up front to build relationships among stakeholders and develop agreed-upon procedures and provisions for dealing with problems and opportunities before they happen. These procedures typically include joint assessments of how well the partnering arrangement is working, escalation guidelines for resolving disputes in a timely and effective manner, and provisions for process improvement and risk sharing. Persistent leadership is required to make partnering work. Project managers must "walk the talk" and consistently display a collaborative response to problems. Similarly, top management must consistently and visibly champion the principles of openness, trust, and teamwork.

Partnering is not limited to contracted relationships. More and more companies are applying the partnering approach to managing internal projects involving different subsidiaries and departments. For example, in a large high-tech firm a team made up of 49 individuals from multiple disciplines used partnering to establish a more cohesive, cooperative relationship to implement their section of a project.

Effective negotiating skills are essential to making partnering work. People need to resolve differences at the lowest level possible in order to keep the project on track. Veteran project managers realize that negotiating is not a competitive game and work toward collaborative solutions to problems. They accomplish this by separating people from the problem, focusing on interests and not positions, inventing options for mutual gain, and relying on objective criteria whenever possible to resolve disagreements. They also recognize the importance of developing a strong BATNA, which provides them with the leverage necessary to seek collaborative solutions.

Customer satisfaction is the litmus test for project success. Project managers need to take a proactive approach to managing customer expectations and perceptions. They need to actively involve customers in key decisions and keep them abreast of important developments. Active customer involvement keeps the project team focused on the objectives of the project and reduces misunderstandings and dissatisfaction.

REVIEW QUESTIONS

1. Why should contractors and owners want to enter a partnering arrangement with each other?
2. Why do proponents of partnering claim that it is a proactive approach to managing projects?
3. What does the term "escalate" refer to, and why is it essential to project partnering success?
4. Why is the principle negotiation approach recommended for negotiating agreements on projects?
5. What does the acronym BATNA refer to, and why is it important to being a successful negotiator?
6. How can a project manager influence customer expectations and perceptions?

CASE

Partnering—The Accounting Software Installation Project

Sitting in her office, Karin Chung is reviewing the past four months of the large corporate accounting software installation project she has been managing. Everything seemed so well planned before the project started. Each company division had a task force that provided input into the proposed installation along with potential problems. All the different divisions had been trained and briefed on exactly how their division would interface and use the forthcoming accounting software. All six contractors, which included one of the Big Five consulting companies, assisted in developing the work breakdown structure—costs, specifications, time.

Karin hired a consultant to conduct a one-day partnering workshop attended by the major accounting heads, a member of each task force group, and key representatives from each of the contractors. During the workshop, several different team-building exercises were used to illustrate the importance of collaboration and effective communication. Everyone laughed when Karin fell into an imaginary acid pit during a human bridge-building exercise. The workshop ended on an upbeat note with everyone signing a partnering charter that expressed their commitment to working together as partners to complete the project.

Two Months Later

One task force member came to Karin to complain that the contractor dealing with billing would not listen to his concerns about problems that could occur in the Virginia division when billings are consolidated. The contractor had told him, the task force member, he had bigger problems than consolidation of billing in the Virginia division. Karin replied, "You can settle the problem with the contractor. Go to her and explain how serious your problem is and that it will have to be settled before the project is completed."

Later in the week in the lunchroom she overheard one consulting contractor bad-mouthing the work of another—"never on time, interface coding not tested." In the hallway the same day an accounting department supervisor told her that tests showed the new software will never be compatible with the Georgia division's accounting practices.

While concerned, Karin considered these problems typical of the kind she had encountered on other smaller software projects.

Four Months Later

The project seemed to be falling apart. What happened to the positive attitude fostered at the prepartnering workshop? One contractor wrote a formal letter complaining that another contractor was sitting on a coding decision that was delaying their work. The letter went on: "We cannot be held responsible or liable for delays caused by others." The project was already two months behind, so problems were becoming very real and serious. Karin finally decided to call a meeting of all parties to the project and partnering agreement.

She began by asking for problems people were encountering while working on the project. Although participants were reluctant to be first for fear of being perceived as a complainer, it was not long before accusations and tempers flared out of control. It was always some group complaining about another group. Several participants complained that others were sitting on decisions that resulted in their work being held up. One consultant said, "It is impossible to tell who's in charge of what." Another participant complained that although the group met separately on small problems, it never met as a total group to assess new risk situations that developed.

Karin felt the meeting had degenerated into an unrecoverable situation. Commitment to the project and partnering appeared to be waning. She quickly decided to stop the meeting and cool things down. She spoke to the project stakeholders: "It is clear that we have some serious problems, and the project is in jeopardy. The project must get back on track, and the backbiting must stop. I want each of us to come to a meeting Friday morning with concrete suggestions of what it will take to get the project back on track and specific actions of how we can make it happen. We need to recognize our mutual interdependence and bring our relationships with each other back to a win/win environment. When we do get things back on track, we need to figure out how to stay on track."

1. Why does this attempt at project partnering appear to be failing?
2. If you were Karin, what would you do to get this project back on track?
3. What action would you take to keep the project on track?

EXERCISES

1. Break into groups of 4–5 students. Assign half of the groups the role of Owner and the other half the role of Contractor.

   Owners: After saving for many years you are about to hire a contractor to build your "dream home." What are your objectives for this project? What concerns or issues do you have about working with a general contractor to build your home?

Contractors: You specialize in building customized homes. You are about to meet with prospective owners to begin to negotiate a contract for building their "dream home." What are your objectives for this project? What concerns or issues do you have about working with the owners to build their home?

Each Owner group meets with another Contractor group and shares their objectives, concerns, and issues.

Identify what objectives, issues, and concerns you have in common and which ones are unique. Discuss how you could work together to realize your objectives. What would be the keys to working as partners on this project?

2. Enter "partnering" in an Internet search engine and browse different web sites containing information on partnering (you may have to narrow your search to "project partnering" or "construction partnering"). Who appears to be interested in partnering? What kinds of projects is partnering being applied to? Does partnering mean the same thing to different people?

ENDNOTES

1. Rosabeth M. Kanter, "Collaborative Advantage: The Art of Alliances," *Harvard Business Review* (July–August 1994), p. 96.

2. Referenced in S. Leonard DiDonato, "Contract Disputes: Alternatives for Dispute Resolution (Part 1)," *PM Network* (May 1993), pp. 19–23.

3. Construction Industry Institute, "In Search of Partnering Excellence," Special Report 17-1 (July 1991), p. 2.

4. Charles Cowan, Clifford Gray, and Erik Larson, "Project Partnering," *Project Management Journal,* vol. 12, no. 4 (December 1992), p. 5. Note: A significant portion of the material on partnering implementation is drawn from this article.

5. Construction Industry Institute, reference cited, pp. 8–10.

6. Charles Cowan, Clifford Gray, and Erik Larson, reference cited, p. 6; Construction Industry Institute, reference cited, p. 5.

7. Research on project partnering includes Charles Cowan, Clifford Gray, and Erik Larson, reference cited; "Project Partnering: Results of a Study of 280 Construction Projects," *Journal of Management Engineering,* vol. 11, no. 2 (March/April 1995), pp. 30–35; Erik Larson and Clifford Gray, "Project Partnering in the Construction Industry: The Wave of the Future," *National Productivity Review* (Winter 1994/95), pp. 15–24; Erik Larson, "Partnering on Construction Projects: A Study of the Relationship between Partnering Activities and Project Success," *IEEE Transactions in Engineering Management,* vol. 44, no. 2 (May 1997), pp. 188–95; and Erik Larson and John A. Drexler, "Barriers to Project Partnering: Report from the Firing Line," *Project Management Journal,* vol. 28, no. 1 (March 1997), pp. 46–52.

8. For a more detailed description see Chris E. Adams, "Industrial Cooperation in a Competitive Environment—The Story of the Advanced Photo System," *Proceedings of 28th Annual Project Management Institute 1997 Seminars and Symposium* (Newtown Square, PA: Project Management Institute, 1997), pp. 907–12; and Chris Adams, "A Kodak Moment," *PM Network,* vol. 12, no. 1 (1998), pp. 21–28. The Orion project was named Project of the Year by the Project Management Institute.

9. This is a classic example of intergroup team building; see William Dyer, *Teambuilding: Concepts and Issues* (Reading, MA: Addison-Wesley, 1987).

10. *Ibid.*

11. Deborah S. Kezsbom, Donald L. Schilling, and Katherine A. Edward, *Dynamic Project Management* (New York: Wiley, 1989), p. 255.

12. The majority of this segment on negotiating is based on Roger Fisher and William Ury, *Getting to Yes: Negotiating Agreement without Giving In,* 2nd ed. (New York: Penguin Books, 1991).

13. This parable was referenced in Robert E. Quinn, Sue R. Faerman, Michael P. Thompson,

and Michael R. McGrath, *Becoming a Master Manager: A Competency Framework* (New York: Wiley, 1990), p. 290.

14. For a more in-depth discussion of this habit see Stephen R. Covey, *The Seven Habits of Highly Effective People* (New York: Simon and Schuster, 1990), pp. 235–60.

15. Roger Fisher and William Ury, reference cited.

16. Other books on negotiating we would recommend include Peter Economy, *Business Negotiating Basics* (Burr Ridge, IL: Irwin Professional Publishing, 1994); Roy J. Lewicki, Joseph A. Litterer, David M. Saunders, and John W. Minton, *Negotiation: Readings, Cases, and Exercises,* 2nd ed. (Burr Ridge, IL: Irwin, 1993); Roger Fisher and Scott Brown, *Getting Together: Building a Relationship that Gets to Yes* (Boston: Houghton Mifflin, 1988); James A. Wall, *Negotiation: Theory and Practice* (Glenview, IL: Scott Foresman, 1985); and Herb Cohen, *You Can Negotiate Anything* (Secaucus, NJ: Lyle Stuart, Inc., 1980).

17. Karl Albrecht and Ron Zemke, *Service America!* (Homewood, IL: Dow-Jones Irwin, 1985), pp. 6–7.

18. A. Parasuraman, Valarie A. Zeithaml, and Leonard L. Berry, *A Conceptual Model of Service Quality and Its Implications for Future Research* (Cambridge, MA: Marketing Science Institute, 1984).

APPENDIX 11–1

Contract Management

Because most interorganizational work on projects is contractual in nature, this appendix discusses the different kinds of contracts that are used, their strengths and weaknesses, and how contracts shape the motives and expectations of different participants.

A contract is a formal agreement between two parties wherein one party (the contractor) obligates itself to perform a service and the other party (the client) obligates itself to do something in return, usually in the form of a payment to the contractor. For example, an insurance firm contracted with a consulting firm to reprogram segments of their information system to conform to the year 2000.

A contract is more than just an agreement between parties. A contract is a codification of the private law, which governs the relationship between the parties to it. It defines the responsibilities, spells out the conditions of its operations, defines the rights of the parties in relationship to each other, and grants remedies to a party if the other party breaches its obligations. A contract attempts to spell out in specific terms the transactional obligations of the parties involved as well as contingencies associated with the execution of the contract. An ambiguous or inconsistent contract is difficult to understand and enforce.

There are essentially two different kinds of contracts. The first is the "fixed-price" contract in which a price is agreed upon in advance and remains fixed as long as there are no changes to scope or provisions of the agreement. The second is a "cost-plus" contract in which the contractor is reimbursed for all or some of the expenses incurred during the performance of the contract. Unlike the fixed-price contract, the final price is not known until the project is completed. Within these two types of contracts, several variations exist.[1]

Fixed-Price Contracts

Under a fixed-price (FP) or lump-sum agreement, the contractor agrees to perform all work specified in the contract at a fixed price. Clients are able to get a minimum price by putting out the contract to competitive bid. Advertising an invitation for bid (IFB) that lists customer requirements usually results in low bids.[2] Prospective contractors can obtain IFB notices through various channels. In the case of large business organizations and government agencies, potential contractors can request to be included on the bidder's list in the area of interest. In other cases, IFBs can be found by scanning appropriate industry media such as newspapers, trade journals, and the *Commerce Business Daily.* In many cases, the owner can put restrictions on potential bidders, such as requiring that they be ISO 9000 certified.

With fixed-contract bids, the contractor has to be very careful in estimating target cost and completion schedule because once agreed upon, the price cannot be adjusted. If the contractor overestimates the target cost in the bidding stage, they may lose the contract to a lower-priced competitor; if the estimate it too low, they may win the job but make little or no profit.

Fixed-price contracts are preferred by both owners and contractors when the scope of the project is well defined with predictable costs and low implementation risks. Such might be the case for producing parts or components to specifications, executing training programs, or orchestrating a banquet. With fixed-price contracts, clients do not have to be concerned with project costs and can focus on monitoring work progress and performance specifications. Likewise, contractors prefer fixed-price contracts because the client is less likely to request changes or additions to the contract. Fewer potential changes reduce project uncertainty and allow the contractors to more efficiently manage their resources across multiple projects.

The disadvantage of a fixed-price contract for owners is that it is more difficult and more costly to prepare. To be effective, design specifications need to be spelled out in sufficient detail to leave little doubt as to what is to be achieved. Because the contractor's profit is determined by the difference between the bid and the actual costs, there is some incentive for contractors to use cheaper quality materials, perform marginal workmanship, or extend the completion date to reduce costs. The client can counteract these by stipulating rigid end-item specifications and completion date and by supervising work. In many cases, the client will hire a consultant who is an expert in the field to oversee the contractor's work and protect the client's interest.

The primary disadvantage of a fixed-price contract for contractors is that they run the risk of underestimating. If the project gets into serious trouble, cost overruns may make the project unprofitable, and, in some cases, may lead to bankruptcy. To avoid this, contractors have to invest significant time and money to ensure that their estimates are accurate.

Contracts with long lead times such as construction and production projects may include escalation provisions that protect the contractor against external cost increases in materials, labor rates, or overhead expenses. For example, the price may be tied to an inflation index, so it can be adjusted to sudden increases in labor and material prices, or it may be redetermined as costs become known. A variety of redetermination contracts are used: Some establish a ceiling price for a contract and permit only downward adjustments, others permit upward and downward adjustments; some establish one readjustment period at the end of the project, others use more than one period. Redetermination contracts are appropriate where engineering and design efforts are difficult to estimate or when final price cannot be estimated for lack of accurate cost data.

While, in principle, redetermination contracts are used to make appropriate adjustments in cost uncertainties, they are prone to abuse. A contractor may win an initial low bid contract, initiate the contracted work, and then "discover" that the costs are much higher than expected. The contractor can take advantage of redetermination provisions and a client's ignorance to justify increasing the actual cost of the contract. The contract evolves into a cost-plus contract.

To alleviate some of the disadvantages of a fixed-price contract while maintaining some certainty as to final cost, many fixed-price contracts contain incentive clauses designed to motivate contractors to reduce costs and improve efficiency. For example, a contractor negotiates to perform the work for a target price based on target cost and a target profit. A maximum price and maximum profit are also established. If the total cost ends up being less than the target cost, the contractor makes a higher profit up to the profit maximum. If there is a cost overrun, the contractor absorbs some of the overrun until a profit floor is reached.

Profit is determined according to a formula based on a cost-sharing ratio (CSR). A CSR of 75/25, for example, indicates that for every dollar spent above target costs, the client pays 75 cents and the contractor pays 25 cents. This provision motivates contractors to keep costs low since they pay 25 cents on every dollar spent above the expected cost and earn 25 cents more on every dollar saved below the expected cost. Fixed-price incentive contracts tend to be used for long-duration projects with fairly predictable cost estimates. The key is being able to negotiate a reasonable target cost estimate. Unscrupulous contractors have been known to take advantage of the ignorance of the client to negotiate an unrealistically high target cost and use performance incentives to achieve excessive profits.

Cost-Plus Contracts

Under a cost-plus contract the contractor is reimbursed for all direct allowable costs (materials, labor, travel) plus an additional fee to cover overhead and profit. This fee is negotiated in advance and usually involves a percentage of the total costs. On small projects this kind of contract comes under the rubric "time and materials contract" in which the client agrees to reimburse the contractor for labor cost and materials. Labor costs are based on an hourly or daily rate, which includes direct and indirect costs as well as profit. The contractor is responsible for documenting labor and materials costs.

Unlike fixed contracts, cost-plus contracts put the burden of risk on the client. The contract does not indicate what the project is going to cost until the end of the project. Contractors are supposed to make the best effort to fulfill the specific technical requirements of the contract but cannot be held liable, in spite of their best efforts, if the work is not produced within the estimated cost and time frame. These contracts are often criticized because there is little formal incentive for the contractors to control costs or finish on time because they get paid regardless of the final cost. The major factor motivating contractors to control costs and schedule is the effect overruns have on their reputation and their ability to secure future business. The government has curtailed use of cost-plus contracts in favor of incentive contracts in response to abuse by contractors.

The inherent weakness of cost-plus contracts has been compensated for by a variety of incentive clauses directed at providing incentives to contractors to control costs, maintain performance, and avoid schedule overruns. Contractors are reimbursed for costs, but instead of the fee being fixed, it is based on an incentive formula and subject to additional provisions. This is very similar to fixed-price incentive contracts, but instead of being based on a target cost, the fee is based on actual cost, using a cost-sharing formula.

Most contracts are concerned with the negotiated cost of the project. However, given the importance of speed and timing in today's business world, more and more contracts involve clauses concerning completion dates. To some extent schedule incentives provide some cost-control measures because schedule slippage typically but not always involves cost overruns. Schedule incentives/penalties are stipulated depending on the significance of time to completion for the owner. For example, the contract involving the construction of a new baseball stadium is likely to contain stiff penalties if the stadium is not ready for opening day of the season. Conversely, time-constrained projects in which the number one priority is getting the project completed as soon as possible are likely to include attractive incentives for completing the project early. For example, a software firm that is anxious to get a new product to market may offer a testing firm a sizable bonus for each day the tests are completed ahead of schedule.

Contract Change Control System

A contract change control system defines the process by which the contract may be modified. It includes the paperwork, tracking systems, dispute resolution procedures, and approval levels necessary for authorizing changes. There are a number of reasons a contract may need to be changed. Clients may wish to alter the original design or scope of the project once the project is initiated. This is quite common as the project moves from concept to reality. For example, an owner may wish to add windows after inspecting the partially completed homesite. Market changes may dictate adding new features or increasing the performance requirements of equipment. Declining financial resources may dictate that the owner cut back on the scope of the project. The contractor may initiate changes in the contract in response to unforeseen legitimate problems. A building contractor may need to renegotiate the contract in the face of excessive groundwater or the lack of availability of specified materials. In some cases, external forces may dictate contract changes, such as a need to comply with new safety standards mandated by the federal government.

There need to be formal, agreed-upon procedures for initiating changes in the original contract. Contract change orders are subject to abuse. Contractors sometimes take advantage of owners' ignorance to inflate the costs of changes to recoup profit lost from a low bid. Conversely, owners have been known to "get back" at contractors by delaying approval of contract changes, thus delaying project work and increasing the costs to the contractor. All parties need to agree upon the rules and procedures for initiating and making changes in the original terms of the contract in advance.

Contract Management in Perspective

Contract management is not an exact science. For decades, the federal government has been trying to develop a more effective contract administration system. Despite their best efforts, abuses are repeatedly exposed in the news media. The situation is similar to trying to take a wrinkle out of an Oriental rug. Efforts to eliminate a wrinkle in one part of the rug invariably create a wrinkle in another part. Likewise, each new revision in government procurement procedures appears to generate a new loophole that can be exploited. There is no perfect contract management system. Given the inherent uncertainty involved in most project work, no contract can handle all the issues that emerge. Formal contracts cannot replace or eliminate the need to develop effective working relationships between the parties involved that are based on mutual goals, trust, and cooperation. For this reason, the earlier discussion of project partnering and effective negotiating is very important.

Appendix Review Questions

1. What are the fundamental differences between fixed-price and cost-plus contracts?
2. For what kinds of projects would you recommend that a fixed-price contract be used? For what kinds of projects would you recommend that a cost-plus contract be used?

Appendix Endnotes

1. For a broad overview of the contracting process, see Harold Kerzner and Hans J. Thamhain, *Project Management for Small and Medium Businesses* (New York: Van Nostrand Reinhold Co., 1984), pp. 193–230. For more detailed information on contract management, see M. Martin, C. Teagarden, and C. Lambreth, *Contract Administration for the Project Manager* (Upper Darby, PA: Project Management Institute, 1983); P. Cavendish and M. Martin, *Negotiating and Contracting for Project Management* (Upper Darby, PA: Project Management Institute, 1982); and J. Downey, R. Gilbert, and P. Gilbert, *Successful Interior Projects: Through Effective Contract Documents* (R. S. Means, 1995).
2. It is beyond the scope of this book to discuss submitting proposals and bids. For information on these subjects, see J. Fraser, *Professional Project Proposals* (Aldershot, U.K.: Gower/Ashgate, 1995); R. Barakat, "Writing to Win New Business," *PM Network* (November 1991); and Jim M. Beveridge and J. I. Velton, *Creating Superior Proposals* (Talent, OR: J. M. Beveridge Associates, 1978).
3. D. C. Weston and G. E. Gibson, "Partnering-Project Performance in U.S. Army Corps of Engineers," *Journal of Management Engineering,* vol. 9, no. 4 (1993), pp. 410–25.

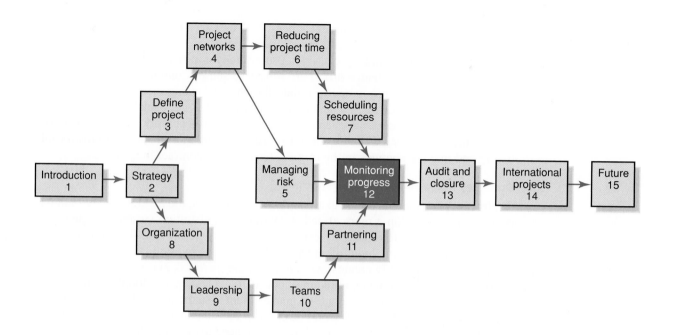

CHAPTER TWELVE

Progress and Performance Measurement and Evaluation

How does a project get one year late?
. . . One day at a time.
—Frederick P. Brooks[1]

Evaluation and control are part of every project manager's job. Control by "walking around" and/or "involvement" can overcome most problems in small projects. However, in larger projects informal control is difficult, and formal control is a crucial necessity. Project evaluation and control require a single information system that measures project progress and performance against a project plan that supports delivery of a product or service on time, on budget, and in the form requested by the customer. The system should alert management to potential problems before it is too late to correct them. A short description of the steps required to develop an evaluation and control system is presented next. The description of the steps is followed by the details of an integrated project information system used by practicing project managers.

CONTROL PROCESS

Except for accounting controls, project control is not performed well in most organizations. Control is one of the most neglected areas of project management. Control holds people accountable, allows for traceability, keeps focus. Control has negative connotations for many and is frequently resisted. Commonly heard phrases, such as "the system stifles flexibility," "it takes too much effort for the return," and "the data are too old to be of use," are manifestations of resistance to control. Favorite excuses of project managers in manufacturing firms are "accounting is not interested in managing projects per se" and "the project software is not compatible with the accounting system," so control may be almost ignored. Construction is frequently an exception; their accounting systems are set up for job-costing of tasks, labor, and materials. Their format is similar to that of project management software and may only require a simple coding system to integrate project management software with the accounting software for many construction firms.

Most people who work in an environment in which the control system is effective cannot imagine how to manage without the control system. They are able to perceive the benefits individually as well as for the organization as a whole. In essence, those who minimize the importance of control are passing up a great opportunity to be effective managers and, perhaps, allow the organization to gain a competitive edge.

Basically, measurement and evaluation of project performance require a control process consisting of the following four steps:

1. Setting a baseline plan.
2. Measuring progress and performance.
3. Comparing plan against actual.
4. Taking action.

Each of the control steps is described in the following paragraphs.

Step 1: Setting a Baseline Plan   The baseline plan provides us with the elements for measuring performance. The baseline is derived primarily from the work breakdown structure (WBS) database. The WBS defines the work in discrete work packages that are tied to deliverables and organization units. In addition, each work package defines the work, duration, and budget. From the WBS the project network schedule is used to time-phase all work, resources, and budgets into a baseline plan.

Step 2: Measuring Progress and Performance   Time and budgets are quantitative measures of performance that readily fit into the integrated information system. Qualitative measures such as meeting customer technical specifications and product function are most frequently determined by onsite inspection or actual use. This chapter is limited to quantitative measures of time and budget. Measurement of time performance is relatively easy and obvious. That is, is the critical path early, on schedule, or late; is the slack of near-critical paths decreasing to cause new critical activities? Measuring performance against budget (e.g., money, units in place, labor hours) is more difficult and is *not* simply a case of comparing actual versus budget. A concept called "earned value" is necessary to get a realistic estimate of performance against a time-phased budget. Earned value will be defined as the budgeted cost of the work performed (BCWP).

Step 3: Comparing Plan against Actual   Because plans seldom materialize as expected, it becomes imperative to measure deviations from plan to determine if action is necessary. Periodic monitoring and measuring the status of the project allow for comparisons of actual versus expected plans. It is crucial that the timing of status reports be frequent enough to allow for early detection of variations from plan and early corrections of causes. Usually status reports should take place every one to four weeks to be useful and allow for proactive correction.

Step 4: Taking Action   If deviations from plans are significant, corrective action will be needed to bring the project back in line with the original or revised plan. In some cases, conditions or scope can change, which, in turn, will require a change in the baseline plan to recognize new information.

The remainder of this chapter will discuss performance and monitoring systems for controlling time and cost performance. Time performance and monitoring are discussed first, then an integrated project cost/schedule system.

MONITORING TIME PERFORMANCE

A major goal of progress reporting is to catch any negative variances from plan as early as possible to determine if corrective action is necessary. Fortunately, monitoring schedule performance is relatively easy. The project network schedule, derived from the WBS/OBS, serves as the baseline to compare against actual performance. Gantt charts (bar charts) and control charts are the typical tools used for communicating project schedule status. As suggested in Chapter 4, the Gantt chart is the most favored, used, and understandable. Adding actual and revised time estimates to the Gantt chart gives a quick overview of project status on the report date.

Figure 12–1 presents an updated Gantt chart for a project in period 7. The solid black bar below the original schedule bar represents the actual start and finish times for completed activities or any portion of an activity completed (see activities A, B, C, D, and E). For example, the actual start time for activity C is period 2; the actual finish time is period 6; the actual duration is 4 time units, rather than 5 scheduled time periods. Activities in process show the actual start time until the present; the extended bar represents the remaining scheduled duration (see activities D and E). The remaining expected duration for activities D and E are shown with the square hatched bar.

FIGURE 12–1   Gantt Chart Showing Schedule Status

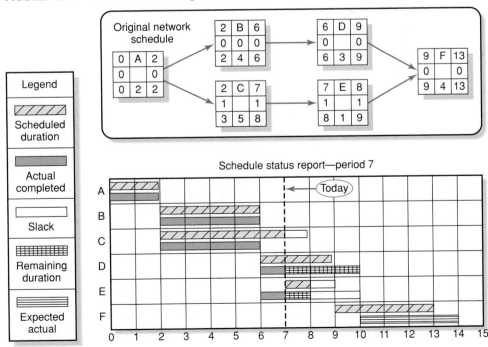

Activity F, which has not started, shows a revised estimated actual start (10) and finish time (14) using a parallel line bar.

Note how activities can have durations that differ from the original schedule, as in activities D and E. Either the activity is complete and the actual is known, or new information suggests the estimate of time be revised and reflected in the status report. In activity D the revised duration is expected to be 4 time units, which is 1 time period longer than the original schedule. Although sometimes the Gantt chart does not show dependencies, when it is used with a network, the dependencies are easily identified if tracing is needed.

The control chart is another tool used to monitor past project schedule performance and current performance and to estimate future schedule trends. Figure 12–2 depicts a project control chart. The chart is used to plot the difference between the scheduled time on the critical path at the report date with the actual point on the critical path. Although Figure 12–2 shows the project was behind early in the project, the plot suggests corrective action brought the project back on track. If the trend is sustained, the project will come in ahead of schedule. Because the activity scheduled times represent average durations, four observations trending in one direction indicate there is a very high probability that there is an identifiable cause. The cause should be located and action taken if necessary. Control charts are also frequently used to monitor progress toward milestones. Control chart trends are very useful for giving warning of potential problems so appropriate action can be taken if necessary.

Milestones are significant project events that mark major accomplishments. To be effective, milestones need to be concrete, specific, measurable events. Milestones must be easily identifiable by all project stakeholders—for example, product testing complete. Control charts very similar to the example shown in Figure 12–2 are often used to record and communicate project progress toward a milestone.

Schedule slippage of one day seldom receives a great deal of attention. However, one day here and another there soon add up to large delay problems. It is well known that once work gets behind, it has a tendency to stay behind because it is difficult to

FIGURE 12-2 Project Schedule Control Chart

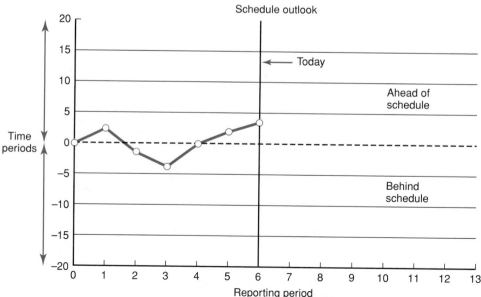

Snapshot from Practice
STATUS REPORTS AT MICROSOFT*

At Microsoft each software product has a corresponding project status report. Project teams send these reports each month to Bill Gates and other top executives as well as to the managers of all related projects. The status reports are brief and have a standard format. Gates can read most of them quickly and still spot potential project delays or changes he does not want. He especially looks for schedule slips, cutting too many product features, or the need to change a specification. Gates usually responds to the relevant managers or developers directly by electronic mail. Status reports are an important mechanism for communicating between top management and projects. As Gates explains:

"I get all the status reports. Right now there might be a hundred active projects. . . . [The status reports] contain the schedule, including milestones dates, and any change in spec, and any comments about 'Hey we can't hire enough people,' or 'Jeez, if this OLE (Object Linking and Embedding) 2 Mac release isn't done, we're just going to have to totally slip' . . . They know [their report] goes up to all the people who manage all the other groups that they have dependencies with. So if they don't raise it in the status report and then two months later they say something, that's a breakdown in communication. . . . The internal group is totally copied on those things, so it's sort of the consensus of the group."

*Michael A. Cusumano, *Microsoft Secrets* (New York: The Free Press, 1995), pp. 28–29.

make up. Examples of causes of schedule slippage are unreliable time estimates, minor redesign, scope creep, and unavailable resources. Using slack early in a path may create a problem for someone responsible for a later activity; flexibility and potential opportunities are reduced. For these reasons, having frequent and clearly defined monitoring points for work packages can significantly improve the chances of catching schedule slippage early. Early detection reduces the chance of small delays growing to large ones and thereby reducing opportunities for correction action to get back on schedule.

Gantt and control charts serve well as means for tracking and trending schedule performance. Their easy-to-understand visual format make them favorite tools for communicating project schedule status—especially to top management who prefer less detail. Another system that integrates cost and schedule and ties directly to the WBS/OBS is presented next.

AN INTEGRATED COST/SCHEDULE SYSTEM

The format for this cost/schedule system was pioneered by the U.S. Department of Defense (DOD) in the 1960s. Cost overruns and the lack of consistency among contractors served as a major motivation for the DOD to search for a system to track schedule and cost in large project contracts.[2] Basically, the system brings discipline to the process of measuring project progress. The private sector was quick to recognize the worth of the system as a totally integrated project management system. It is probably safe to say project managers in every major country are using some form of the system. It is not limited to construction or contracts. The system is being used on internal projects in the manufacturing, pharmaceutical, and high-tech industries. For example, organizations such as EDS, NCR, Levi Strauss, Tektronics, and Disney have used earned-value systems to track projects. The basic framework of the system is withstanding the test of time. Most project management software includes the original framework; many systems have added industry-specific variations to more precisely track progress and costs. This chapter presents the "generic" core of an integrated cost/schedule information system. Carefully note that the system depends on a well-developed plan and schedule similar to those presented in Chapters 3, 4, and 7.

The Need for an Earned-Value (EV) System

The system depends on an accounting concept called "earned value." Systems that only compare actuals against budget fail to measure what work was actually accomplished for the money spent. Such systems fail to include the *time* variable as part of the equation. An example of a hypothetical project will demonstrate the need for using earned value. A high-tech firm is implementing an R&D project. The original plan calls for completion of the project in 10 months at a cost of exactly $200,000 per month for a total cost of $2.0 million. After five months, top management wishes to assess the status of the project. The following information is available:

- Actual costs for the first five months are $1.3 million.
- Planned budget costs for the first five months are $1.0 million.

Management might draw the conclusion the project has a $300,000 cost overrun. This could be a correct conclusion, but it may not be. It is possible the project is way ahead of schedule and the $300,000 represents payments to labor working ahead of schedule. It is possible we may have both a cost overrun and be behind schedule. These data do not tell the full story.

   Using the same high-tech example with another set of outcome data, we again see the data are inadequate to draw accurate conclusions five months into the project:

- Actual costs for the first five months are $800,000.
- Planned costs for the first five months are $1.0 million.

These data can lead to the conclusion the project is costing less than expected by $200,000. Is this true? If the project is behind schedule, the $200,000 may represent planned work that has not started. It is possible the project is behind schedule and also over in cost. From the data in these two examples, it is easy to understand why real-world systems using only actual and planned costs can mislead management and customers in evaluating project progress and performance. This cost variance (budget-to-actual) alone is inadequate. It does not measure how much work was accomplished for the money spent. Earned value overcomes the problems described by keeping track of schedules and budgets against time.

Outline for an Integrated Cost/Schedule System

Following five careful steps ensures that the cost/schedule system is integrated. These steps are outlined here. Steps 1, 2, and 3 are accomplished in the planning stage. Steps 4 and 5 are sequentially accomplished during the execution stage of the project.

1. Define the work using a WBS. This step involves developing documents that include the following information:
   a. Scope.
   b. Work packages.
   c. Deliverables.
   d. Organization units.

    e. Resources.

    f. Budgets for each work package.

2. Develop work and resource schedules.

    a. Time-phase work packages into a network.

    b. Schedule resources to activities.

3. Develop a time-phased budget using work packages included in an activity. The cumulative values of these budgets will become the baseline and will be called the budgeted cost of the work scheduled (BCWS). The sum should equal the budgeted amounts for all the work packages in the cost accounts.

4. At the work package level, collect the actual costs for the work performed. These costs will be called the actual cost of the work performed (ACWP). Collect the budgeted values for the work actually accomplished. These will be called earned value or budgeted cost of the work performed (BCWP).

5. Compute the schedule variance (SV = BCWP – BCWS) and cost variance (CV = BCWP – ACWP). Prepare hierarchical status reports for each level of management—from work package manager to customer or project manager. The reports should also include project rollups by organization unit and deliverables. In addition, actual time performance should be checked against the project network schedule.

Figure 12–3 presents a schematic overview of the integrated information system, which includes the techniques and systems presented in earlier chapters. Those who have tenaciously labored through the early chapters can smile! Steps 1 and 2 are already carefully developed.

Development of Project Baselines

The baseline serves as an anchor point for measuring performance. The baseline is a concrete document and commitment; it is the planned cost and expected schedule per-

FIGURE 12–3   Project Management Information System Overview

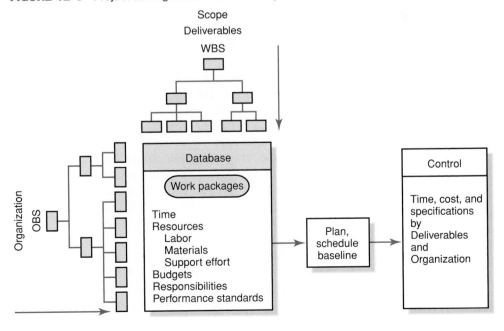

FIGURE 12–4 Baseline Data Relationships

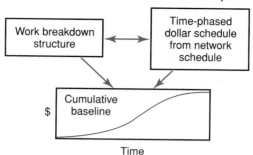

formance against which actual cost and schedule performance are measured. It can also serve as a basis for developing cash flows and awarding progress payments. Development of the project baseline is properly part of the planning process. The baseline is included in this chapter because it is the major input to the cost/schedule system to be described. The building blocks or data for development of the baseline have already been set in place. The placement of work packages in the activities of the network essentially assigns start times for those work packages; it also *time-phases the budgets* that are tied to the work packages. Budgets are ultimately expressed in monetary units—for example, dollars, yen, marks, pounds. These time-phased budgets are added along a project timeline to create the project baseline. The cumulative sum of all these time-phased budgets should equal the sum of all the work packages found in the cost accounts. Figure 12–4 depicts the relationship of the data used to create the baseline.

What Costs Are Included in Baselines?

The baseline BCWS is the sum of the cost accounts, and each cost account is the sum of the work packages in the cost account. Three costs are typically included in baselines—labor and equipment, materials, and level of effort (LOE). LOE costs are typically found in project direct overhead costs (see Chapter 3).

Level of effort costs represent time-related activities. These activities, such as administrative support, computer support, legal, public relations, etc., exist for a work package, segment of the project, or the duration of the project and represent direct project overhead. Because these LOE costs are very different, it is common to separate LOE costs from costs for labor, materials, and equipment and to compute separate variances for them.[3] The ability to control LOE costs is minimal, which is the reason they are included in direct project overhead costs. LOE costs can also be tied to a hammock activity that covers a segment of a project. When LOE costs are tied to work packages that have no measurable outputs, their costs are budgeted as a rate per unit of time (e.g., $200 per day). LOE work packages should represent a very small portion of project costs (1 to 10 percent). There are a few rare circumstances that warrant high LOE costs. For example, the cost of having a crew on site on the Alaskan pipeline exceeds the direct cost of their actual work. This cost of providing housing, food, and 10 days, leave for every 23 days of work was counted as LOE cost and exceeded the 10 percent level. The nuclear industry faces a similar situation with crews working in "hot spots." After workers are exposed to a fixed number of REMs (Roentgen equivalent man), they are required to stop working until the number decreases to a safe level. During this waiting period, the individuals are paid; this waiting cost is considered an

LOE cost. These examples are extreme and under normal circumstances LOE costs should be minimized as much as possible.

Most work packages should be discrete, of short time span, and have measurable outputs. Usually the major costs are labor, machines, and/or materials. If materials are a significant portion of the cost of work packages, they can be budgeted in separate work packages and cost accounts (see Appendix 12–2).

Rules for Placing Costs in Baselines

The major reasons for creating a baseline are to monitor and report progress and to estimate cash flow. Therefore, it is crucial to integrate the baseline with the performance measurement system. Costs are to be placed (time-phased) in the baseline exactly as managers expect them to be "earned." This approach facilitates tracking costs to their point of origin. In practice, the integration is accomplished by using the same rules in assigning costs to the baseline as those used to measure progress using earned value. Three of the most common rules are described here. The first two rules are used to reduce the overhead costs of collecting detailed data.

- **0/100 percent rule.** This rule assumes credit is earned for having performed the work once it is completed. Hence, 100 percent of the budget is earned when the work package is completed. This rule is used for work packages having very short durations.
- **50/50 rule.** This approach allows 50 percent of the value of the work package budget to be earned when it is started and 50 percent to be earned when the package is completed. This rule is popular for work packages of short duration and small total costs.
- **Percent complete rule.** This method is the rule used most frequently by practicing project managers. The best method for assigning costs to the baseline under this rule is to establish frequent checkpoints over the duration of the work package and assign completion percentages in dollar terms. For example, units completed could be used to assign baseline costs and later to measure progress. Units might be lines of code, drawings completed, cubic yards of concrete in place, prototypes complete, etc. This approach to percent complete adds "objectivity" to the subjective observation approaches often used. When measuring percent complete in the monitoring phase of the project, it is common to limit the amount earned to 80 percent until the work package is 100 percent complete.

Another rule used in practice is the milestone rule. This rule can be used for work packages with long durations marked by distinct, measurable, sequential events. When each event is reached, the preassigned earned value is credited. Because the milestone rule uses the same principles as the percent complete rule (separate, measurable events versus small discrete work elements), it will not be explored in detail here or in the exercises.

These rules are assigned by project planners/managers familiar with the work. The rules are used to integrate the baseline budget plan with monitoring performance over the life of the project.

Methods of Variance Analysis

Generally the method for measuring accomplishments centers on two key computations:

1. Comparing earned value with the expected schedule value.
2. Comparing earned value with the actual costs.

TABLE 12-1

GLOSSARY OF TERMS

BCWS	Budgeted cost of the work scheduled. A cost estimate of the resources scheduled in a time-phased cumulative baseline.
BCWP	Budgeted cost of the work performed. The earned value or original budgeted cost for work actually completed.
ACWP	Actual cost of the work completed. The sum of the costs incurred in accomplishing work.
SV	Schedule variance (BCWP – BCWS).
CV	Cost variance (BCWP – ACWP).
BAC	Budgeted cost at completion. The total budgeted cost of the baseline or project cost accounts.
EAC	Estimated costs at completion. Includes costs to-date plus *revised* estimated costs for the work remaining.
FAC	Computed forecasted costs at completion.
VAC	Variance at completion (BAC – EAC or BAC – FAC). Indicates expected actual over- or underrun at completion.

These comparisons can be made at the project level or down to the cost account level. Project status can be determined for the latest period, all periods to date, and estimated to the end of the project.

To the uninitiated, the terms used in practice appear horrendous and intimidating. However, once a few basic terms are understood, the intimidation index evaporates rapidly. Table 12–1 presents a glossary of terms used in analysis.

Assessing the current status of a project using the earned-value cost/schedule system requires three data elements—BCWS, BCWP, and ACWP. From these data the SV and CV are computed each reporting period, as shown in the glossary. *A positive variance indicates a desirable condition, while a negative variance suggests problems.*

Cost variance tells us if the work accomplished costs more or less than was planned at any point over the life of the project. If labor and materials have not been separated, cost variance should be reviewed carefully to isolate the cause to either labor or materials—or to both.

Schedule variance presents an overall assessment of *all* work packages in the project scheduled to date. It is important to note schedule variance contains *no* critical path information. Schedule variance measures progress in dollars rather than time units. Therefore, it is unlikely that any translation of dollars to time will yield accurate information telling if any milestone or critical path is early, on time, or late (even if the project occurs exactly as planned). *The only accurate method for determining the true time progress of the project is to compare the project network schedule against the actual network schedule to measure if the project is on time* (refer to Figure 12–2). However, SV is very useful in assessing the direction all the work in the project is taking—after 20 or more percent of the project has been completed.

Figure 12–5 presents a sample cost/schedule graph with variances identified for a project at the current status report date. Note the graph also focuses on what remains to be accomplished and any favorable or unfavorable trends. The "today" label marks the report date (time period 25) of where the project has been and where it is going. Because our system is hierarchical, graphs of the same form can be developed for different levels of management. The top line represents the actual costs (ACWP) incurred

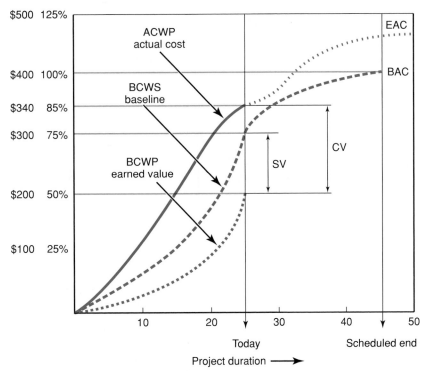

FIGURE 12–5   Cost/Schedule Graph

for the project work to date. The middle line is the baseline (BCWS) and ends at the scheduled project duration (45). The bottom line is the budgeted value of the work actually completed to date (BCWP) or the earned value. The dotted line extending the actual costs from the report date to the new estimated completion date represents revised estimates of *expected* actual costs; that is, additional information suggests the costs at completion of the project will be different from what was planned. Note that the project duration has been extended and the variance at completion (VAC) is negative (BAC – EAC).

Another interpretation of the graph uses percentages. At the end of period 25, 75 percent of the work was scheduled to be accomplished. At the end of period 25, the value of the work accomplished is 50 percent. The actual cost of the work completed to date is $340, or 85 percent of the total project budget. The graph suggests the project will have about a 12 percent cost overrun and be 5 time units late. The current status of the project shows the cost variance (CV) to be over budget by $140 (BCWP – ACWP = 200 – 340 = –140). The schedule variance (SV) is negative $100 (BCWP – BCWS = 200 – 300 = –100), which suggests the project is behind schedule. Before moving into an example, consult Figure 12–6 to practice interpreting the outcomes of cost/schedule graphs. Remember, BCWP is your anchor point.

DEVELOPING A STATUS REPORT: A HYPOTHETICAL EXAMPLE

Assumptions

Working through an example demonstrates how the baseline serves as the anchor from which the project can be monitored using earned-value techniques. Because the

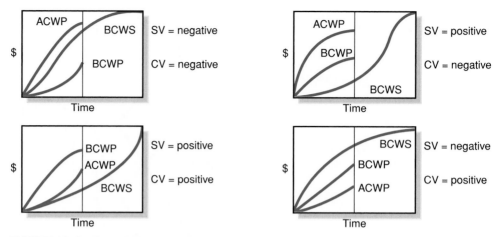

FIGURE 12–6   Earned-Value Review Exercise

process becomes geometrically complex with the adding of project detail, some simplifying assumptions are made in the example to more easily demonstrate the process:

1. Assume each cost account has only one work package, and each cost account will be represented as an activity on the network.
2. The project network early start times will serve as the basis for assigning the baseline values.
3. Except when the 0/100 rule or 50/50 rule is used, baseline values will be assigned linearly, unless stated differently. (Note: In practice costs can be assigned any way which is consistent with actual expected conditions.)

FIGURE 12–7   Hypothetical Work Breakdown Structure

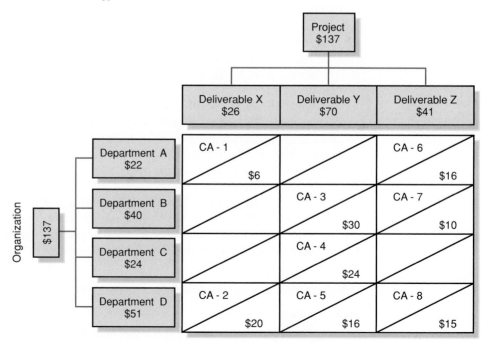

4. From the moment work on an activity begins, some actual costs will be incurred each period until the activity is completed.

Baseline Development

Figure 12–7 presents a simple work breakdown structure (WBS/OBS) for the example. There are three deliverables (X, Y, Z), and four departments (A, B, C, D) are responsible. The total for all the cost accounts (CA) is $137. Figure 12–8 depicts the project network with the ES, LS, EF, LF, and slack times. This network information is used to time-phase the project baseline. Figure 12–9 presents a worksheet with the baseline developed using the earned-value rules decided by the project planners. Remember, the rules used should be "exactly" as managers plan to monitor and measure schedule and cost performance. The rules used are the three basic ones:

1. 100 percent of budget when completed.
2. 50/50 percent when started and finished.
3. Observed percent complete.

For example, activity 3 uses the earned-value 50/50 rule and assigns $15 when started in period 3–4 and $15 when finished in period 5–6 for a total budget value of $30. Activity 4 uses the percent complete rule and disperses the costs linearly over the expected duration of the activity. The cumulative baseline for the project is $137. These values are plotted on Figure 12–11 as BCWS or baseline. The time-phased budget ends in period 12, the scheduled completion date.

Development of the Status Report

A status report is analogous to a camera snapshot of a project at a specific point in time. The status report uses earned value to measure schedule and cost performance. Measuring earned value begins at the work package level. Work packages are in one of three conditions on a report date:

FIGURE 12–8 Project Network Plan

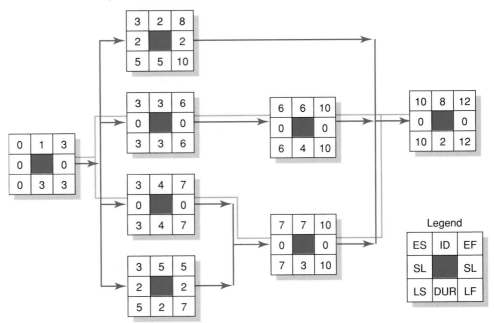

FIGURE 12-9 Project Baseline Budget

	Schedule information						Baseline budget needs — Time period															
Earned-value rule	Activity/ work package	Duration	ES	LF	Slack	Total BCWS	0	1	2	3	4	5	6	7	8	9	10	11	12	13	14
1	1	3	0	3	0	6				6											
2	2	5	3	10	2	20					10				10						
2	3	3	3	6	0	30					15		15								
3	4	4	3	7	0	24					6	6	6	6							
1	5	2	3	7	2	16						16									
3	6	4	6	10	0	16								4	4	4	4				
1	7	3	7	10	0	10											10				
1	8	2	10	12	0	15													15		
	Total BCWS by period						0	0	0	6	31	22	21	10	14	4	14		15		
	Cumulative BCWS by period						0	0	0	6	37	59	80	90	104	108	122	122	137		

1. Not yet started.
2. Finished.
3. In-process or partially complete.

Earned values for the first two conditions present no difficulties. Work packages that are not yet started earn 0 percent of the BCWS (budget). Packages that are completed earn 100 percent of their BCWS (budget). In-process packages apply one of the three earned-value rules used to develop the baseline to measure earned value (BCWP).

Figure 12–10 presents a worksheet for developing a status report at the end of period 4. The following information has been gathered for the status report:

1. Activity 1 is complete.
2. Activities 2, 3, 4, and 5 are in process.
   a. Activity 3 now has a duration of 5 time units.
   b. Activity 4 now has a duration of 5 time units.
3. Activities 2, 3, 4, 5, and 6 have revised cost estimates.
4. Activity 4 is 66 percent complete in budget dollars.
5. Activities 6, 7, and 8 are not yet started and will be late.

The earned-value rule for each activity in Figure 12–10 is found in the shaded circle on the left. For example, activity 4 uses rule 3—percent complete—to measure earned value. Activity 5 uses rule 1. The shaded rows indicate the ACWP; under each actual row is the earned-value row. For example, activity 1 has actual values of $1, $3, and $4 in periods 0 through 3. Because activity 1 is complete, the earned value is 100 percent of the BCWS (budget). Activities 2 and 3 are in process and use the 50/50 rule. Hence, the earned value to date for activity 2 is $10 (50 percent of $20), and the earned value for activity 3 is $15 (50 percent of $30). Activity 4 is 66 percent complete; the earned value is $16 (66 percent of $24). Because activities 6, 7, and 8 are not yet started, they earn 0 percent of their respective budgets.

In Figure 12–10, revised estimates have been gathered from the field and built into the status report to estimate cost at completion (EAC). Often these revised estimates of expected costs differ from the original planned budget in terms of timing and money amounts. For example, activity 3 now has an expected duration of 5 time units and expected costs of 35. Activity 4 is 66 percent complete in one time period, but it still has 4 time periods remaining with additional costs expected in periods 5–6 (6) and 7–8 (12).

The ACWP and BCWP totals for each period are shown. These values are cumulative. The cumulative ACWP to date is $32; the cumulative BCWP to date is $47. Given these cumulative values, the cost variance (CV = BCWP – ACWP) is positive $15 (47 – 32 = 15). The schedule variance (SV = BCWP – BCWS) is positive $10 (47 – 37 = 10). The BCWS is found in the baseline. (See Figure 12–7; the BCWS at the status report date is $37.) Because both variances are positive, the project to date *appears* to be in a favorable situation. A careful look at activity 3 and the network tells us the activity will require 5 time units to complete, rather than 3 planned time units. Also, activity 4 is now expected to require 5 actual time units rather than 4. *Remember, SV is in dollars and is not an accurate measure of time;* however, it is a fairly good indicator of the status of the whole project in terms of being ahead or behind schedule. Only the project network and actual work schedule can give an accurate assessment of schedule performance down to the work package level.

Given the revised cost estimates and schedules, the finished project will not come in on time or on budget unless corrective action can alter future trends. The project du-

FIGURE 12-10 Updated Status Report

Status end of period 4	Earned-value rule	Activity/work package	Duration	Total BCWS	Actual and earned value by period			ACWP / BCWP		Revised cost estimate to complete										EAC
					1	2	3	ACWP (4)	BCWP (4)	5	6	7	8	9	10	11	12	13	14	
Complete	①	1	3	6	1	3	4	8	6											8
In process	②	2	5	20			4	4	10			11	3							18
In process	②	3	⌿3 5	30			6	6	15		10	10	10							35
66% complete	③	4	⌿4 5	24			12	12	16		6	12								30
In process	①	5	2	16			2	2	0	16										18
Not started	③	6	4	16									5	5	5	5				20
Not started	①	7	3	10											10					10
Not started	①	8	2	15														15		15

					1	2	3			5	6	7	8	9	10	11	12	13	14	
ACWP totals					1	4	24			20	11	21	25	5	5	5	0	15		
Cumulative ACWP total					1	8	32			52	63	84	109	114	119	134	139	139	154	
BCWP totals					0	6	41													
Cumulative BCWP total					0	6	47													

Cost variance 47 − 32 = +15

Schedule variance 47 − 37 = +10

ration is estimated to finish in time period 14 rather than 12. The variance at completion (VAC = BAC – EAC = 137 – 154) is a cost overrun of – $17.

Figure 12–11 presents a cost/schedule graph derived from the worksheet. This graph represents the data found in Figures 12–9 and 12–10. A glance at the graph suggests that at the end of period 4, project schedule and cost performance look favorable. However, after period 4 the expected performance should give the customer and project manager some concern. The graph shows the project will be 2 periods late and have a cost overrun of –$17. Graphs of the same form can be developed for separate sections of the project. Note: The example again shows how the traditional method that uses only actual (ACWP = $32) and budget (BCWS = $37) can be misleading. Using the traditional method, the conclusion could be that the project is behind schedule and on cost or under cost and/or schedule. Actually, the project is *currently* ahead of schedule and under cost.

Figure 12–12 presents a project cost summary report. This report is similar in form to the output of some computer software programs. Note the data through period 4 represent the cost variance: +$15 (47 – 32 = +15). The variance at completion (VAC) is –$17 (137 – 154 = –17).

Figure 12–13 shows an oversimplified project rollup at the end of period 4. The rollup is by deliverables and organization units. All deliverables look favorable on schedule and cost variance. Department A has a cost overrun of –$2. In more complex projects the crosstabs of cost accounts by deliverables and organization units can be very revealing and more profound.

This example contains the basics for developing a status report—baseline development and measuring schedule and cost variance. In our example, performance analysis had only one level above the cost account level. Because all data are derived from

FIGURE 12–11 Cost/Schedule Graph

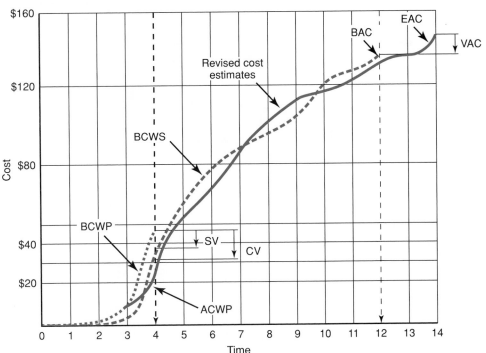

Activity	Work performed to date			Total cost at completion		
	Earned budget value (BCWP)	Actual cost (ACWP)	Cost over/under run	Original cost budget (BCWS)	Latest revised cost	Cost over/under run
1	6	8	(−2)	6	8	(−2)
2	10	4	6	20	18	2
3	15	6	9	30	35	(−5)
4	16	12	4	24	30	(−6)
5	0	2	(−2)	16	18	(−2)
6				16	20	(−4)
7				10	10	0
8				15	15	0
Total	47	32	+15	137	154	(−17)

FIGURE 12–12 Project Cost Summary Report

FIGURE 12–13 Period 4 Project Rollup by Deliverables, Organization, and Cost Account

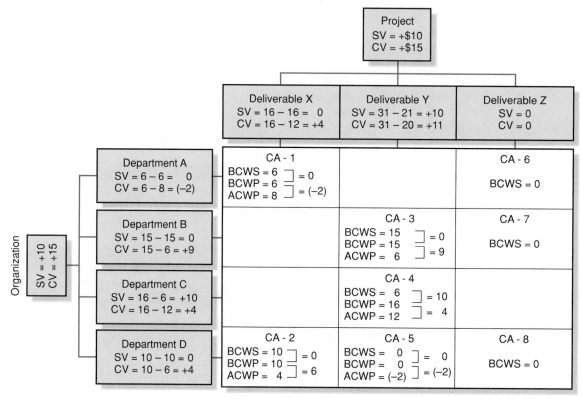

the detailed database, it is relatively easy to determine progress status at all levels of the work and organization breakdown structures. Fortunately, this same current database can provide additional views of the current status of the project and forecast costs at the completion of the project. Approaches for deriving additional information from the database are presented next.

INDEXES

Indexes are typically used at the cost account level and above. In practice, the database is also used to develop indexes that allow the project manager and customer to view progress from several angles. An index of 1.00 (100 percent) indicates progress is as planned. An index greater than 1.00 shows progress is better than expected. An index less than 1.00 suggests progress is poorer than planned and deserves attention.

Performance Indexes

There are two indexes of performance efficiency. The first index measures *cost* efficiency of the work accomplished to date:

$$\text{Cost performance index (CPI)} = \text{BCWP/ACWP} = 47/32 = 1.47$$

The CPI of $1.47 show that $1.47 worth of work planned to date has been completed for each $1.00 actually spent—a favorable situation indeed. The CPI is the most accepted and used index. It has been tested over time and found to be the most accurate, reliable, and stable.[4]

The second index is a measure of *scheduling* efficiency to date:

$$\text{Scheduling performance index (SPI)} = \text{BCWP/BCWS} = 47/37 = 1.27$$

The schedule index indicates $1.27 worth of work has been accomplished for each $1.00 worth of scheduled work to date. Table 12–2 presents the interpretation of the indexes.

Percent Complete Index

These next indexes compare the to-date progress to the end of the project. The implications underlying use of these indexes are that conditions will not change, no improvement or action will be taken, and the information in the database is accurate. The first index looks at percent complete in terms of budget amounts:

$$\text{Percent complete index (PCI-B)} = \text{BCWP/BAC} = 47/137 = 0.34 \ (34\%)$$

This PCI indicates the work accomplished represents 34 percent of the total budgeted (BAC) dollars to date. Observe that this calculation does not include actual costs

---

TABLE 12–2

INTERPRETATION OF INDEXES

Index	Cost (CPI)	Schedule (SPI)
>1.00	Under cost	Ahead of schedule
= 1.00	On cost	On schedule
<1.00	Over cost	Behind schedule

incurred. Because actual dollars spent do not guarantee project progress, this index is favored by many project managers when there is a high level of confidence in the original budget estimates.

The second index views percent complete in terms of actual dollars spent to accomplish the work to date and the actual expected dollars for the completed project (EAC). The application of this view is written as

$$\text{Percent complete index (PCI-C)} = \text{ACWP/EAC} = 32/154 = 0.21 \ (21\%)$$

This percent complete indicates 21 percent of the project is completed, when viewed from the actual dollars spent to complete the work to date and the revised actual expected costs to complete the project. Some managers favor this index because it contains actual and revised estimates that include newer, more complete information.

These two views of percent complete present different views of the "real" percent complete. Management must be careful to use all input sources to have a full grasp of the progress of the project.

Technical Performance Measurement

Measuring technical performance is as important as measuring schedule and cost performance. Although technical performance is often assumed, the opposite can be true. The ramifications of poor technical performance frequently are more profound—something works or it doesn't if technical specifications are not adhered to. Assessing technical performance of a system, facility, or product is often accomplished by examining the documents found in the scope statement and/or work package documentation. These documents should specify criteria and tolerance limits against which performance can be measured. For example, the technical performance of a software project suffered because the feature of "drag and drop" was deleted in the final product. Conversely, the prototype of an experimental car exceeded the miles per gallon technical specification and, thus, its technical performance. It is very difficult to specify how to measure technical performance because it depends on the nature of the project. Suffice it to say, measuring technical performance must be done. Project managers must be creative in finding ways to control this very important area.

Software for Project Cost/Schedule Systems

Software developers have created sophisticated schedule/cost systems for projects that track and report budget, actual, earned, committed, and index values. These values can be labor hours, materials, and/or dollars. This information supports cost and schedule progress, performance measurements, and cash flow management. Recall from Chapter 3 that budget, actual, and committed dollars usually run in different time frames (see Figure 3–9). A typical computer-generated status report includes the following information outputs:

1. Revised costs at completion (EAC).
2. New forecast costs at completion (FAC).
3. Actual paid this period (ACWP).
4. Cumulative total paid to date (ACWP).
5. Schedule variance (BCWP/BCWS) by cost account and WBS and OBS.
6. Cost variance (BCWP/ACWP) by cost account and WBS and OBS.
7. Indexes—cost, schedule, total percent complete.
8. Paid and unpaid commitments.

The variety of software packages, with their features and constant updating, is too extensive for inclusion in this text. Software developers and vendors have done a superb job of providing software to meet the information needs of most project managers. Differences among software in the last decade have centered on improving "friendliness" and output that is clear and easy to understand. Anyone who understands the concepts and tools presented in Chapters 3 through 7 and Chapter 12 should have little trouble understanding the output of any of the popular project management software packages.

FORECASTING FINAL PROJECT COST

Early questions raised by management are: Are we on budget? What will the final project cost be? If the project is small or moderate in size, and a good look-ahead system for revising cost estimates exists, the EAC procedure suggested earlier in the chapter is probably adequate to estimate final costs. However, if the project is a large one, revised cost estimates far into the future are less reliable or nonexistent. One method that has gained acceptance and proven to be accurate and reliable in forecasting final project costs uses the CPI performance index (CPI = BCWP/ACWP). The equation for this forecasting model (FAC) is as follows:

$$ETC = \frac{\text{Work remaining}}{CPI} = \frac{BAC - BCWP}{BCWP/ACWP}$$

$$FAC = ETC + ACWP$$

where

ETC = estimated cost to complete.
CPI = cumulative cost performance index to date.
BCWP = cumulative budgeted cost of work completed to date.
ACWP = cumulative actual cost of work completed to date.
BAC = total budget of the baseline.
FAC = forecasted total cost at completion.

For example, if we assume the following information is available, the forecast cost at completion (FAC) is computed as follows:

Total baseline budget (BAC) for the project	$5,000
Cumulative earned value (BCWP) to date	1,600
Cumulative actual cost (ACWP) to date	2,000

$$FAC = \frac{\$5,000 - \$1,600}{\$1,600/\$2,000} + \$2,000 = \frac{\$3,400}{0.8} + \$2,000 = \$4,250 + \$2,000$$

$$= \$6,250$$

The final project cost forecast is $6,250. Research data[5] indicate that on large projects that are more than 20 percent complete, the model performs well with an error of less than 10 percent. This model can also be used for WBS and OBS cost accounts that have been used to forecast remaining and total costs. It is important to note that this model assumes conditions will not change, the cost database is reliable, BCWP and ACWP are cumulative, and past project progress is representative of future progress. This objective forecast represents a good starting point or benchmark that management can use to compare other forecasts that include other conditions and subjective judgments.

OTHER CONTROL ISSUES

The Costs and Problems of Data Acquisition

The accompanying Snapshot from Practice captures some of the frequent issues surrounding resistance to data collection of percent complete for earned value systems. Similar pseudo-percent complete systems have been used by others.[6] Such pseudo-percent complete approaches appear to work well in multiproject environments that include several small and medium-sized projects. Assuming a one-week reporting period, care needs to be taken to develop work packages with a duration of about one week long so problems are identified quickly. For large projects, there is no substitute for using a percent complete system that depends on data collected through observation at clearly defined monitoring points.

Baseline Changes

Changes during the life cycle of projects are inevitable and will occur. Some changes can be very beneficial to project outcomes; changes having a negative impact are the ones we wish to avoid. Careful project definition can minimize the need for changes. The price for poor project definition can be changes that result in cost overruns, late schedules, low morale, and loss of control. Change comes from external sources or from within. Externally, for example, the customer may request changes that were not included in the original scope statement and that will require significant changes to the project and thus to the baseline. Or the government may render requirements that were not a part of the original plan and that require a revision of the project scope. Internally, stakeholders may identify unforeseen problems or improvements that change the scope of the project. In rare cases scope changes can come from several sources. For example, the Denver International Airport automatic baggage handling system was an afterthought supported by several project stakeholders that included the Denver city government, consultants, and at least one airline customer. The additional $2 billion in costs were staggering, and the airport opening was delayed 16 months. If this automatic baggage scope change had been in the original plan, costs would have been only a fraction of the overrun costs, and delays would have been reduced significantly.

Generally, project managers should resist baseline changes. Baseline changes should be allowed only if it can be proven the project will fail without the change or the project will be improved significantly with the change. This statement is an exaggeration, but it sets the tone for approaching baseline changes. In the field, if the change results in a significant effect on the project and requires a scope change, the baseline can be changed. The effect of the change on the scope and baseline should be accepted and signed off by the project customer. Figure 12–14 depicts the cost impact of a scope change on the baseline at a point in time—"today." Line A represents a scope change that results in an increase in cost. Line B represents a scope change that decreases cost. Quickly recording scope changes to the baseline keeps the computed earned values valid. Failure to do so results in misleading cost and schedule variances.

Care should be taken to not use baseline changes to disguise poor performance on past or current work. A common signal of this type of baseline change is a constantly revised baseline that seems to match results. Practitioners call this a "rubber baseline" because it stretches to match results. Most changes will not result in serious scope changes and should be absorbed as positive or negative variances. Retroactive changes for work already accomplished should not be allowed. Transfer of money among cost accounts should not be allowed after the work is complete. Unforeseen changes can be handled through the contingency reserve. The project manager typically makes this decision. In some large projects, a partnering "change review team," made up of members of the project and customer teams, makes all decisions on project changes.

Snapshot from Practice
A PSEUDO–EARNED VALUE PERCENT COMPLETE APPROACH

A consultant for the U.S. Forest Service suggested the use of earned value to monitor the 50-plus timber sale projects taking place concurrently in the district. As projects were completed, new ones were started. Earned value was tried for approximately nine months. After a nine-month trial, the process was to be reviewed by a task force. The task force concluded the earned value system provided good information for monitoring and forecasting project progress; however, the costs and problems of collecting timely percent complete data were unacceptable because there were no funds available to collect such data.

The level of detail dilemma was discussed, but no suggestions satisfied the problem. The discussion recognized that too little data fail to offer good control, while excessive reporting requires paperwork and people, which are costly. The task force concluded progress and performance could be measured using a pseudo-version of percent complete while not giving up much accuracy for the total project. This modified approach to percent complete required that very large work packages (about 3 to 5 percent of all work packages in a project) be divided into smaller work packages for closer control and identification of problems sooner. It was decided work packages of about a week's duration would be ideal. The pseudo-version required only a telephone call and "yes/no" answers to one of the following questions to assign percent complete:

Has work on the work package started?	No = 0%
Working on the package?	Yes = 50%
Is the work package completed?	Yes = 100%

Data for the pseudo-earned value, percent complete system was collected for all 50-plus projects by an intern working fewer than eight hours each week.

Contingency Reserve

Plans seldom materialize in every detail as estimated. Because perfect planning doesn't exist, some contingency funds should be agreed upon before the project commences to cover the unexpected. The size of the contingency reserve should be related to the uncertainty and risk of schedule and cost estimate inaccuracies. For example, if the project represents little that is new to the project team, the contingency reserve

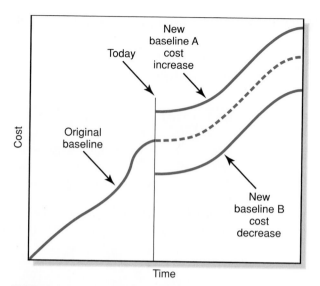

FIGURE 12–14   Scope Changes to a Baseline

might be 1 to 2 percent of the total cost of the project. Conversely, if the project represents something that is new to all team members, the reserve might be 5 to 20 percent of the total cost. A rule of thumb used by a construction management firm centers around the percent of design complete when the project begins. For example, if 30 percent of design is completed when the project begins, a contingency reserve of 25 percent is included as a hedge against uncertainty; if 60 percent of design is complete, the reserve is 15 percent; if design is 95 percent complete, a 10 percent reserve is included. Contingency reserve funds represent flexibility for the project manager so he or she can move the project forward.

Contingency reserve is not a free lunch for all who come. Reserve funds should only be released by the project manager on a very formal and documented basis. Recall that *budget reserve* contingency funds are not for scope changes. Scope changes are covered by *management reserve* funds. Chapter 5 provides a detailed description of budget and management contingency reserves. The trend today is to allow all stakeholders to know the size of the contingency reserve (even subcontractors). This approach is built on trust, openness, and the self-discipline of the project stakeholders who are all focused on one set of goals.

Scope Creep

Large changes in scope are easily identified. It is the "minor refinements" that eventually build to be major scope changes that can cause problems. These small refinements are know in the field as *scope creep*. For example, the customer of a software developer requested small changes in the development of a custom accounting software package. After several minor refinements, it became apparent the changes represented a significant enlargement of the original project scope. The result was an unhappy customer and a development firm that lost money and reputation.

Although scope changes are usually viewed negatively, there are situations when scope changes result in positive rewards. Scope changes can represent significant opportunities. In product development environments, adding a small feature to a product can result in a huge competitive advantage. A small change in the production process may get the product to market one month early or reduce product cost.

Scope creep is common early in projects—especially in new-product development projects.[7] Customer requirements for additional features, new technology, poor design assumptions, etc., all manifest pressures for scope changes. Frequently these changes are small and go unnoticed until time delays or cost overruns are observed. Scope creep affects the organization, project team, and project suppliers. Scope changes alter the organization's cash flow requirements in the form of fewer or additional resources, which may also affect other projects. Frequent changes eventually wear down team motivation and cohesiveness. Clear team goals are altered, become less focused, and cease being the focal point for team action. Starting over again is annoying and demoralizing to the project team because it disrupts project rhythm and lowers productivity. Project suppliers resent frequent changes because they represent higher costs and have the same effect on their team as on the project team.

The key to managing scope creep is change control. (Chapter 5 discusses the process. See Figure 5–5 to review key variables to document in project changes.) First, the original baseline must be well defined and agreed upon with the project customer. Before the project begins, it is imperative that clear procedures be in place for authorizing and documenting scope changes by the customer or project team. If a scope change is necessary, the impact on the baseline should be clearly documented—for example, cost, time, dependencies, specifications, responsibilities, etc. Finally, the scope change must be quickly added to the original baseline to reflect the change in budget and schedule; these changes and their impacts need to be communicated to all project stakeholders.

SUMMARY

The best information system does not result in good control. Control requires the project manager to *use* information to steer the project through rough waters. Control and Gantt charts are useful vehicles for monitoring time performance. The cost/schedule system allows the manager to have a positive influence on cost and schedule in a timely manner. The ability to influence cost decreases with time; therefore, timely reports identifying adverse cost trends can greatly assist the project manager in getting back on budget and schedule. The integrated cost/schedule model provides the project manager and other stakeholders with a snapshot of the current and future status of the project. The benefits of the cost/schedule model are as follows:

1. Measures accomplishments against plan and deliverables.
2. Provides a method for tracking directly to a problem work package and organization unit responsible.
3. Alerts all stakeholders to early identification of problems, and allows for quick, proactive corrective action.
4. Improves communication because all stakeholders are using the same database.
5. Keeps customer informed of progress, and encourages customer confidence that the money spent is resulting in the expected progress.
6. Provides for accountability over individual portions of the overall budget for each organizational unit.

REVIEW QUESTIONS

1. How does earned value give a clearer picture of project schedule and cost status than a simple plan versus actual system?
2. How does a baseline facilitate integrating the planning and controlling of projects?
3. Why is it important for project managers to resist changes to the project baseline? Under what conditions would a project manager make changes to a baseline? When would a project manager not allow changes to a baseline?

4. How does a project rollup help identify project cost and schedule problems?
5. Costs can be aggregated or disaggregated horizontally and vertically. What are the advantages of this system?
6. What are the differences among BAC, EAC, and FAC?

EXERCISES

1. Given the following information for the latest period (5), answer the questions below:
   - Actual costs to date are $550.
   - The original budget through period 5 was $350.
   - The revised costs for the project at completion (EAC) are $9,000.
   - The sum of the earned values to date is $400.
   - The total original budget (BAC) for the project was $7,000.
   - The reserve/contingency fund has not been used.
   a. What is the schedule variance at the end of period 5?
   b. What is the cost variance at the end of period 5?
   c. Given the current information, will the project finish on schedule and on budget? Justify your answer.

2. Fiberoptik Ltd. is installing fiber-optic lines into two identical ENTEL production facilities in different counties in the United Kingdom. Both projects have cost estimates of £50,000 per week and are scheduled to be completed in 30 weeks. The following actual and earned value data (in thousands of pounds) have been collected for each project for eight weeks:

Week	Project 1 actual	Project 1 earned value	Project 2 actual	Project 2 earned value
1	45	45	45	45
2	50	50	40	35
3	50	50	50	55
4	60	55	60	65
5	60	65	55	60
6	50	45	45	50
7	40	35	55	40
8	50	40	60	60

Compare the schedule and cost variance for each project at the end of week 8. Compute the cost and percent complete index. What can you say about the performance for each project?

Note: For the following earned-value exercises 3 through 6, make the following assumptions:
1. Assign costs linearly when percent complete rule 3 is used in baselines and status reports.
2. Assume if work is in process, actual direct costs are being incurred each period.
3. Use the earned-value rules below for all exercises:
   a. 100% of budget when complete.
   b. 50% when started and 50% when finished.
   c. Observed percent complete in dollars.
4. All EAC figures are *revised* estimates, not forecasted. FAC is only used in computer outputs.

---

3. Given the following information, develop a project baseline and prepare a status report for period 7. From your status report, determine if the project is ahead or behind schedule. How

many time periods? How much is the project under or over budget? What is the forecasted completion date? Cost? Explain in detail to the project manager what the information means.

Additional information at the end of period 7:
- Activity 3 has been observed to be 50 percent complete in dollars.
- Activities 1 and 2 are complete.
- Activities 3 and 4 are in process with revised cost and duration information.
- Activities 5, 6, 7, 8, and 9 have not started.
- Activities 5 and 8 have revised cost information.

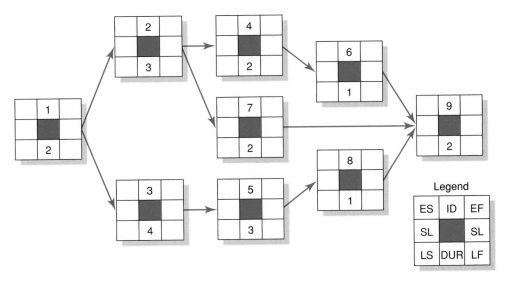

Schedule information / Baseline budget needs

Earned-value rule	Activity/work package	Duration	ES	LF	Slack	Total BCWS	1	2	3	4	5	6	7	8	9	10	11	12	13	14
3	1	2	0	2	0	10	5	5												
2	2	3	2	7	2	8			4	4										
3	3	4	2	6	0	16			4	4	4	4								
2	4	2	5	9	2	12						6	6							
3	5	3	6	9	0	12							4	4	4					
1	6	1	7	10	2	7								7						
2	7	2	5	10	3	4						2	2							
1	8	1	9	10	0	9										9				
3	9	2	10	12	0	16											8	8		
	Total BCWS by period																			
	Cumulative BCWS by period																			

Earned value analysis worksheet

Status end of period 7	Earned-value rule	Activity/ work package	Duration	Total BCWS	Actual and earned value by period								ACWP / BCWP		Revised cost estimate to complete								EAC
					1	2	3	4	5	6	7	ACWP	7BCWP	8	9	10	11	12	13	14	
Finished	③	1	2	10	5	5							10								10
					5	5							10								
Finished	②	2	3	8	5	5	4	4					8								8
50% complete	③	3	4→5	16				3	3	6	9		21	3							24
In process	②	4	2→3	12					5	5	5			5	5	5	5				
Not started	③	5	3	12											5	7					
Not started	①	6	1	7											7						
Not started	②	7	2	4										2	2						
Not started	①	8	1	9														10			
Not started	③	9	2	15															7	8	

ACWP totals

Cumulative ACWP total

BCWP totals

Cumulative BCWP total

Cost variance _____

Schedule variance _____

4. Given the information provided, complete a baseline and status report for the end of period 5. Your status report should include the SV, CV, CPI, SPI, PCI(B), PCI(C), a cost summary report, and a project cost graph. What is the forecasted completion date? Cost? Using your well-labeled project graph, explain to the project owner what the current and future expected status of the project are at the end of period 5.

Additional information at the end of period 5:
- Activities 1, 2, 3, 4, and 5 are complete.
- Activities 1, 2, 3 and 9 have revised time durations.
- Activities 6 and 7 are in process with revised cost information.
- Activities 8 and 9 have not started.
- Activities 8 and 9 have revised cost information.

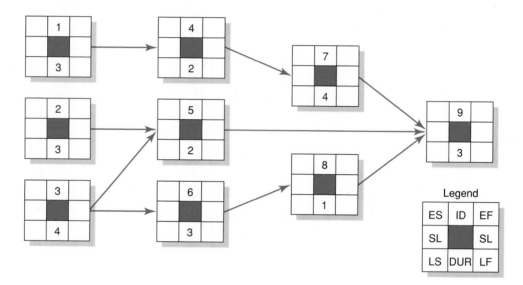

Baseline budget needs

	Schedule information							Time period													
Earned-value rule	Activity/ work package	Duration	ES	LF	Slack	Total BCWS	1	2	3	4	5	6	7	8	9	10	11	12	13	14
③	1	3	0	3	0	12	4	4	4											
①	2	3	0	7	4	10			10											
②	3	4	0	5	1	20														
②	4	2	3	5	0	8														
③	5	2	4	9	3	10														
①	6	3	4	8	1	15														
③	7	4	5	9	0	16														
①	8	1	7	9	1	9							9							
③	9	3	9	12	0	18														
						Total BCWS by period														
						Cumulative BCWS by period														

Status end of period 5   **Actual and earned value by period**   **Revised cost estimate to complete**

Status end of period 5	Earned-value rule	Activity/work package	Duration	Total BCWS	0	1	2	3	4	5 BCWP	ACWP	BCWP	6	7	8	9	10	11	12	EAC
Finished	③	1	~~3~~ 2	12	4	4					8	8								8
Finished	①	2	~~3~~ 2	10	6	6					12									16
Finished	②	3	~~4~~ 3	20	8	8	12													
Finished	②	4	2	8	6	6	5	5												
Finished	③	5	2	10			5	5												
In process	①	6	3	15			10	7	7				5							
25% complete	③	7	4	16				10	5				6	6	1					
Not started	①	8	1	9									10							
Not started	③	9	~~3~~ 2	18										9	10					
ACWP totals																				
Cumulative ACWP total																				
BCWP totals																				
Cumulative BCWP total																				

Cost variance _____

Schedule variance _____

Project Cost Summary Report

Activity/ work package	Work performed to date			Total cost at completion		
	Earned budget value (BCWP)	Actual cost (ACWP)	Cost over/under run	Original cost budget (BCWS)	Latest expected actual (EAC)	Cost over/under run
1						
2						
3						
4						
5						
6						
7						
8						
9						
Total						

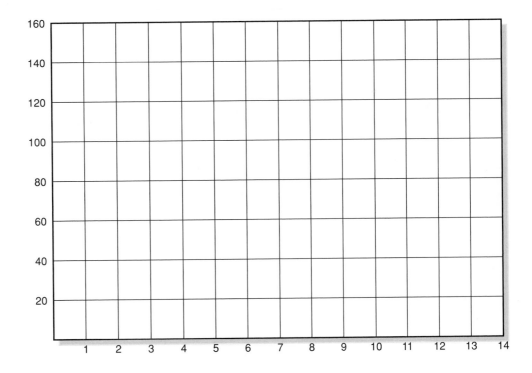

5. Given the following information, develop a project baseline and prepare a status report for period 5. Is the project ahead or behind schedule? How many time periods? How much is the project under or over budget? What is the forecasted completion date? Cost? Compute the project ratios. Explain in detail to the project manager what the managerial implications of your reports are.

Additional information at the end of period 5:
- Activities 1 and 2 are complete.
- Activities 2, 3, and 4 have revised durations.
- Activities 3 and 4 are in process.
- Activities 5, 6, and 7 have not started.
- Activities 3, 4, 5, and 6 have revised cost information.

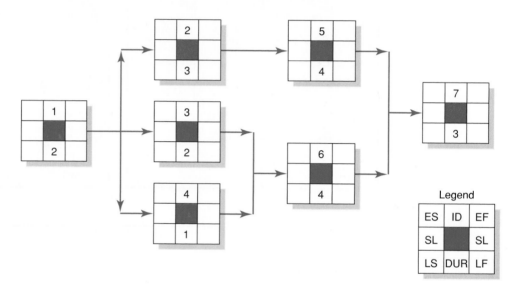

Schedule information | **Baseline budget needs**

Earned-value rule	Activity/work package	Duration	ES	LF	Slack	Total BCWS	0	1	2	3	4	5	6	7	8	9	10	11	12
③	1	2	0	2	0	20		10	10										
①	2	3	2	5	0	10					10								
②	3	2	2	5	1	10			5	5									
①	4	1	2	5	2	5			5										
③	5	4	5	9	0	16													
③	6	4	4	9	1	24													
②	7	3	9	12	0	10													
	Total BCWS by period																		
	Cumulative BCWS by period																		

Time period

Status end of period 5	Earned-value rule	Activity/work package	Duration	Total BCWS	Actual and earned value by period						ACWP	BCWP	Revised cost estimate to complete										EAC
					0	1	2	3	4	5		5	6	7	8	9	10	11	12	13	14	15	
Finished	③	1	2	20		10 / 10	20 / 10					30											30
Finished	①	2	1̶ 1	10		10 / 10			12			20											12
In process	②	3	2̶ 3	10				6	6			2	3										15
In process	①	4	1̶ 4	5										2	2								
Not started	③	5	4	16									2	2	2								
Not started	③	6	4	24											4	4	4	4					
Not started	②	7	3	10															5		5		
ACWP totals																							
Cumulative ACWP total																							
BCWP totals																							
Cumulative BCWP total																							

Cost variance _____

Schedule variance _____

6. Given the information provided, complete a baseline and status report for the end of period 7. Your status report should include the SV, CV, CPI, SPI, PCI(B), PCI(C), a cost summary report, and a project cost graph. What is the forecasted completion date? Cost? Use your project graph to explain to the project owner what the current and future expected status of the project are at the end of period 7.

Additional information at the end of period 7:
- Activities 1 and 2 are finished and "actuals" missed budget.
- Activities 3, 4, and 6 are in process.
- Activity 3 has been observed to be 60 percent complete in dollars.
- Activity 6 has been observed to be 75 percent complete in dollars, and cost to complete has been revised.
- Activities 5 and 7 have not started.
- Activities 4, 5, and 6 have revised cost information.

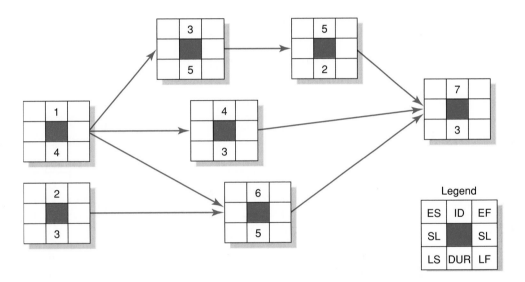

Schedule information | Baseline budget needs

Earned-value rule	Activity/work package	Duration	ES	LF	Slack	Total BCWS	0	1	2	3	4	5	6	7	8	9	10	11	12	13	14
(2)	1	4	0	4	0	28		14			14											
(1)	2	3	0	6	3	9			9													
(3)	3	5	4	9	0	50																
(1)	4	3	4	11	4	18																
(1)	5	2	9	11	0	10												10				
(3)	6	5	4	11	2	20																
(2)	7	3	11	14	0	24																
	Total BCWS by period																					
	Cumulative BCWS by period																					

Time period

Status end of period 7	Earned-value rule	Activity/work package	Duration	Total BCWS	0	1	2	3	4	5	6	7 BCWP	ACWP	8	9	10	11	12	13	14	15	EAC
Finished	②	1	4	28		14			13				27									27
Finished	①	2	3̶4	9		14	14	20	9				28									20
60% complete	③	3	5	50					10	10	10	10		10	10							50
In process	①	4	3̶4	18					10	10	5	5		5								30
Not started	①	5														10	5					
75% complete	③	6							6	6	12	3		3	3							
Not started	②	7																12		12			

Actual and earned value by period (period columns 1–7, BCWP / ACWP)

Revised cost estimate to complete (period columns 8–15)

ACWP totals

Cumulative ACWP total

BCWP totals

Cumulative BCWP total

Cost variance _____

Schedule variance _____

Project Cost Summary Report

Activity/ work package	Work performed to date			Total cost at completion		
	Earned budget value (BCWP)	Actual cost (ACWP)	Cost over/under run	Original cost budget (BCWS)	Latest expected actual (EAC)	Cost over/under run
1	28	27	+1	28	27	+1
2						
3						
4						
5						
6						
7						
Total						

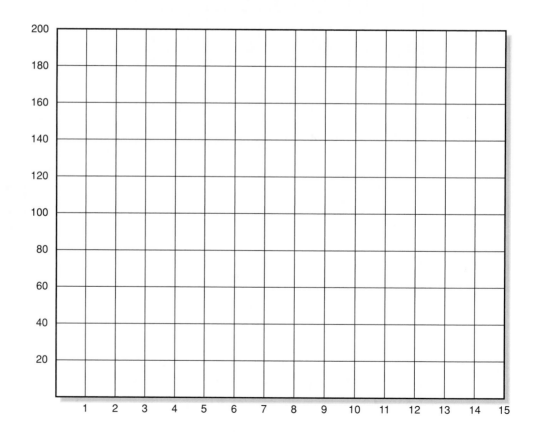

ENDNOTES

1. Frederick P. Brooks, *The Mythical Man-Month* (Reading, MA: Addison-Wesley, anniversary ed., 1997), p. 153.
2. There are many publications on the system. A good discussion is found in *Cost/Schedule Control Systems Criteria: Joint Implementation Guide* (Departments of the Air Force, the Army, the Navy, and the Defense Logistics Agency), published by the U.S Department of Defense, Washington, DC, 1987. Also see *Performance Measurement for Selected Acquisition,* Department of Defense instruction no. 500.2, part 11, section B, attachment 2 (Washington, DC: U.S. Department of Defense, 1991).
3. For a good description of types and timing of costs, see David H. Hamburger, "Three Perceptions of Cost—Cost Is More Than a Four Letter Word," *Project Management Journal* (June 1986), pp. 51–58.
4. Fleming W. Quentin and Joel M. Koppelman, "The Earned Value Concept: Back to Basics," *PM Network,* vol. 8, no. 1 (January 1994), pp. 27–29. See also Fleming W. Quentin and Joel M. Koppelman, "Forecasting the Final Cost and Schedule Results," *PM Network,* vol. 10, no. 1 (January 1996), pp. 13–19; Fleming W. Quentin and Joel M. Koppelman, "The Earned Value Body of Knowledge," *pmNetwork,* vol. 11, no. 5 (May 1996), pp. 11–15; and David S. Christensen, "Using Performance Indexes to Evaluate the Estimate at Completion," *Journal of Cost Analysis* (Spring 1994), p. 19.
5. *Ibid.*
6. Daniel M. Brandon, Jr., "Implementing Earned Value Easily and Effectively," *Project Management Journal,* vol. 29, no. 2 (June 1998), pp. 11–18.
7. S. Craig Keifer, "Scope Creep . . . Not Necessarily a Bad Thing," *pmNetwork,* vol. 10, no. 5 (May 1996), pp. 33–35.

CASE

Scanner Project

You have been serving as Electroscan's project manager and are now well along in the project. Develop a narrative status report for the board of directors of the chain store that discusses the status of the project to date and at completion. Be as specific as you can using numbers given and those you might develop. Remember, your audience is not familiar with the jargon used by project managers and computer software personnel; therefore, some explanation may be necessary. Your report will be evaluated on your detailed use of the data, your total perspective of the current status and future status of the project, and your recommended changes (if any).

Electroscan, Inc.
555 Acorn Street, Suite 5
Boston, Massachusetts

29 In-store Scanner Project
(thousands of dollars)
Actual Progress as of January 1

Name	BCWS	BCWP	ACWP	SV	CV	BAC	FAC
Scanner project	420	395	476	−25	−81	915	1103
H 1.0 Hardware	92	88	72	−4	16	260	213
H 1.1 Hardware specifications (DS)	20	20	15	0	5	20	15
H 1.2 Hardware design (DS)	30	30	25	0	5	30	25
H 1.3 Hardware documentation (DOC)	10	6	5	−4	1	10	8
H 1.4 Prototypes (PD)	2	2	2	0	0	40	40
H 1.5 Test Prototypes (T)	0	0	0	0	0	30	30
H 1.6 Order circuit boards (PD)	30	30	25	0	5	30	25
H 1.7 Preproduction models (PD)	0	0	0	0	0	100	100
OP 1.0 Operating system	195	150	196	−45	−46	330	431
OP 1.1 Kernel specifications (DS)	20	20	15	0	5	20	15
OP 1.2 Drivers	45	55	76	10	−21	70	97
OP 1.2.1 Disk drivers (DEV)	25	30	45	5	−15	40	60
OP 1.2.2 I/O drivers (DEV)	20	25	31	5	−6	30	37
OP 1.3 Code software	130	75	105	−55	−30	240	336
OP 1.3.1 Code software (C)	30	20	40	−10	−20	100	200
OP 1.3.2 Document software (DOC)	45	30	25	−15	5	50	42
OP 1.3.3 Code interfaces (C)	55	25	40	−30	−15	60	96
OP 1.3.4 Beta test software (T)	0	0	0	0	0	30	30
U 1.0 utilities	87	108	148	21	−40	200	274
U 1.1 Utilities specifications (DS)	20	20	15	0	5	20	15
U 1.2 Routine utilities (DEV)	20	20	35	0	−15	20	35
U 1.3 Complex utilities (DEV)	30	60	90	30	−30	100	150
U 1.4 Utilities documentation (DOC)	17	8	8	−9	0	20	20
U 1.5 Beta test utilities (T)	0	0	0	0	0	40	40
S 1.0 System integration	46	49	60	3	−11	125	153
S 1.1 Architecture decisions (DS)	9	9	7	0	2	10	8
S 1.2 Integration hard/soft (DEV)	25	30	45	5	−15	50	75
S 1.3 System hard/software test (T)	0	0	0	0	0	100	150
S 1.4 Project documentation (DOC)	12	10	8	−2	2	20	12
S 1.5 Integration acceptance testing (T)	0	0	0	0	0	30	30

SOFTECH, Ltd.—Part A

Softech, Ltd., has contracted with a transportation company (Kypros Transport, ASA) to develop two custom computer programs for monitoring, tracking, and scheduling their ship (project 1) and truck (project 2) fleets. Fundamentally, both projects are nearly identical in structure and can be implemented concurrently; each should take about three years to complete. Kypros Transport will buy the necessary equipment when the programs are tested and accepted. There is a potential followup contract to develop a similar software program for the cargo planes (project 3). The follow-up project (project 3) cannot start until projects 1 and 2 are up and running and accepted by Kypros Transport. The basic idea is simple. At any point in time, Kypros Transport wishes to know the exact location; cargo by type, weight, size, and customer details; schedule; etc. Satellites, global positioning system (GPS) locators, and electronic transfer of information will be used and are available to Softech already. These projects are major and will consume about 50 percent of Softech's people resources. It is expected that successful management of time and budget will result in banner profits and award of the cargo plane program (project 3).

Softech is now six months into projects 1 and 2 (July 1). Problems seem to be appearing on the horizon. Project managers from projects 1 and 2 are reporting to senior management. Each project manager reports problems with swapping resources between the two projects. Each project manager reports they are pretty sure they are on schedule and budget because actual costs appear to be running ahead of budget for each project. Kypros is complaining to senior management that there has been little contact with the project managers.

Softech's senior management is apprehensive and somewhat alarmed. Coordination between projects seems nearly nonexistent. Are they ahead of schedule or over cost and behind schedule? When will the projects be finished? Will the projects be under or over budget? The future of Softech, Ltd., depends on the success of these two major projects for survival, and they should ensure the award of the followup contract, which will be pure gravy because of its similarity to the truck and ship projects. Their worries are further intensified by a request from the El-Hahzar Bank financing Softech's projects for a status and progress report next month.

Senior management has asked the managers of projects 1 and 2 to get together and come up with a verifiable, total integrated system that coordinates both projects and measures progress of each project.

The two project managers have hired you as a consultant to help with their problem. They need a quick overview action proposal from you now so they can spend the weekend coming up with changes they may need to make to get the projects under control. (You will be asked later to develop a complete proposal after input from their weekend meetings.) Be as specific and detailed as you can in the time and space allotted. Good luck on your new assignment!

SOFTECH, Ltd.—Part B

One change since July is the development of an earned-value format for the Softech projects. The first computer reports for the two projects are attached. You are free to develop any other numerical information you feel appropriate and rearrange the information given in any form you wish for your appendix.

Develop a narrative status report for the board of directors of Kypros Transport and the El-Hahzar Bank that discusses the status of the two projects to date and at completion. Be as specific as you can using numbers given and those you might develop. Remember, your audience is not familiar with the jargon used by project managers and computer software personnel; therefore, some explanation may be necessary. Your report will be evaluated on your detailed use of the data, your total perspective of the current status and future status of the project, and your recommended changes.

Softech, LTD
Nottingham Building, Suite 4
5555 Oxford, UK

Truck Tracking Software Project
(thousands of pounds)
Actual Progress as of December 31

Name	BCWS	BCWP	ACWP	SV	CV	BAC	FAC
Truck tracking project	1015	915	985	−100	−70	4700	5060
D 1.0 Design	180	130	180	−50	−50	210	291
D 1.1 Set specifications	150	100	140	−50	−40	170	238
D 1.1.1 Hardware (D)	75	55	75	−20	−20	80	109
D 1.1.2 Software (D)	75	45	65	−30	−20	90	130
D 1.2 Review specifications (D)	25	25	30	0	−5	30	36
D 1.3 Document new features (DOC)	5	5	10	0	−5	10	20
C 1.0 Code	570	550	550	−20	0	2980	2980
C 1.1 Write software	550	500	510	−50	−10	2900	2958
C 1.1.1 Develop outline (C)	300	310	290	10	20	400	374
C 1.1.2 Code subroutines (C)	200	170	190	−30	−20	1500	1676
C 1.1.3 Code interfaces (C)	50	20	30	−30	−10	1000	1500
C 1.2 Edit and publish notes (DOC)	10	40	30	30	10	50	38
C 1.3 First draft manual (DOC)	10	10	10	0	0	20	20
C 1.4 Final draft manual (DOC)	0	0	0	0	0	10	10
T 1.0 Test	0	0	0	0	0	900	900
T 1.1 Test beta site (T)	0	0	0	0	0	300	300
T 1.2 Test interfaces (T)	0	0	0	0	0	100	100
T 1.3 Test alpha sites (T)	0	0	0	0	0	500	500
MF 1.0 Manufacture (outsource) (P)	15	15	15	0	0	150	150
ST 1.0 Service & Training	250	220	240	−30	−20	460	502
ST 1.1 Prepare class modules (ST)	100	100	100	0	0	100	100
ST 1.2 Select customer personnel (ST)	0	0	0	0	0	60	60
ST 1.3 Provide training (ST)	0	0	0	0	0	100	100
ST 1.4 Setup & staff free number (ST)	150	120	140	−30	−20	200	233

Softech, LTD
Nottingham Building, Suite 4
5555 Oxford, UK

Ship Tracking Software Project
(thousands of pounds)
Actual Progress as of December 31

Name	BCWS	BCWP	ACWP	SV	CV	BAC	FAC
Ship tracking project	735	690	815	−45	−125	3620	4276
D 1.0 Design	150	110	180	−40	−70	170	278
D 1.1 Set specifications	120	80	140	−40	−60	130	228
D 1.1.1 Hardware (D)	80	60	75	−20	−15	90	113
D 1.1.2 Software (D)	40	20	65	−20	−45	40	130
D 1.2 Review specifications (D)	25	25	30	0	−5	30	36
D 1.3 Document new features (DOC)	5	5	10	0	−5	10	20
C 1.0 Code	420	465	490	45	−25	2080	2192
C 1.1 Write software	400	410	450	10	−40	2000	2195
C 1.1.1 Develop outline (C)	200	200	210	0	−10	1000	1050
C 1.1.2 Code subroutines (C)	150	170	190	20	−20	750	838
C 1.1.3 Code interfaces (C)	50	40	50	−10	−10	250	313
C 1.2 Edit and publish notes (DOC)	10	50	35	40	15	50	35
C 1.3 First draft manual (DOC)	10	5	5	−5	0	20	20
C 1.4 Final draft manual (DOC)	0	0	0	0	0	10	10
T 1.0 Test	0	0	0	0	0	900	900
T 1.1 Test beta site (T)	0	0	0	0	0	300	300
T 1.2 Test interfaces (T)	0	0	0	0	0	100	100
T 1.3 Test alpha sites (T)	0	0	0	0	0	500	500
MF 1.0 Manufacture (outsource) (P)	15	15	15	0	0	150	150
ST 1.0 Service & Training	150	100	130	−50	−30	320	416
ST 1.1 Prepare class modules (ST)	50	50	50	0	0	100	100
ST 1.2 Select customer personnel (ST)	0	0	0	0	0	20	20
ST 1.3 Provide training (ST)	0	0	0	0	0	100	100
ST 1.4 Setup & staff free number (ST)	100	50	80	−50	−30	100	160

Computer-Controlled Conveyor Belt Project

PART 4

1. Develop a financial requirements schedule over the life of the project—the BCWS.
2. Print out the total costs for each activity/work package (and each deliverable, if possible).
3. Print out the total financial schedule for each month.

Remember, your financial schedule should follow your resource schedule (Chapter 7), not the original network. Because the project has not started yet all of your variances, schedule, cost, earned value (BCWP), and actual cost (ACWP) should be zero.

Once you are confident that you have the final schedule, save the file as a baseline. (Hint: Save a backup file just in case without baseline!)

PART 5

Prepare status reports for each of the first four quarters of the project given the information provided here. This requires saving your resource schedule as a baseline and inserting the appropriate status report date in the program. Assume that no work has been completed on the day of the status report.

First Quarter, April 1

Table A12–1 summarizes the information regarding activities accomplished to date.

TABLE A12-1				
APRIL 1, YEAR 1				
Activity	Start date	Finish date	Actual duration	Remaining duration
Architectural decisions	1/1/y1	1/26/y1	26	0
Hardware specifications	1/27/y1	3/12/y1	45	0
Hardware design	3/13/y1		18	53
Kernel specifications	1/27/y1	2/20/y1	25	0
Disk drivers	2/22/y1		37	63
Memory management	2/22/y1		37	53
Operating system Documentation	3/10/y1	3/31/y1	22	0
Utilities specifications	2/22/y1	3/9/y1	16	0
Complex utilities	3/10/y1		22	65

Note: The manager of the external development team that was hired to perform routine utilities reported that due to commitments to other projects they would be able to start on that activity 4/16/y1.

1. Print out a status report for the first quarter in table form that shows the BCWS, BCWP, ACWP, BAC, EAC, SV, and CV for each work package, deliverable, and the whole project (the WBS).

Questions

How is the project progressing in terms of cost and schedule? What activities have gone well? What activities have not gone well?

What is the forecasted cost at completion (FAC)? What is the budgeted cost for the work remaining?

2. Compute the performance indexes (PCI-S and PCI-C).

Be sure to save your file after each quarterly report and use it to build the next report!

Second Quarter, July 1

Table A12–2 summarizes the information regarding activities accomplished since the last report.

TABLE A12-2

JULY 1, YEAR 1

Activity	Start date	Finish date	Actual duration	Remaining duration
Hardware design	3/13/y1	5/17/y1	65	0
Hardware Documentation	5/18/y1	6/16/y1	30	0
Disk drivers	2/22/y1	6/1/y1	100	0
Memory management	2/22/y1	5/27/y1	95	0
Routine utilities	4/16/y1	6/29/y1	75	0
Complex utilities	3/10/y1	6/27/y1	110	0
Utilities documentation	6/17/y1		14	18

Note: On April 1 top management reassigned one of the design teams to another higher priority project which caused the utilities documentation activity to be delayed until 6/17/y1.

3. Print out a status report for the second quarter in table form that shows the BCWS, BCWP, ACWP, BAC, EAC, SV, and CV for each work package, deliverable, and the whole project (the WBS).

Questions

How is the project progressing in terms of cost and schedule? What activities have gone well? What activities have not gone well? What is the present and future impact of having only one design team?

What is the forecasted cost at completion (FAC)? What is the budgeted cost for the work remaining?

4. Compute the performance indexes (PCI-S and PCI-C).

Third Quarter, October 1

Table A12–3 summarizes the information regarding activities accomplished since the last report.

TABLE A12–3

OCTOBER 1, YEAR 1

Activity	Start date	Finish date	Actual duration	Remaining duration
Utilities documentation	6/17/y1	7/18/y1		
Integration first phase	7/19/y1	9/21/y1	65	
Prototypes	9/22/y1		9	71
Serial I/O drivers	9/22/y1		9	122

5. Print out a status report for the third quarter in table form that shows the BCWS, BCWP, ACWP, BAC, EAC, SV, and CV for each work package, deliverable, and the whole project (the WBS).

Questions

How is the project progressing in terms of cost and schedule? What activities have gone well? What activities have not gone well?

What is the forecasted cost at completion (FAC)? What is the budgeted cost for the work remaining?

6. Compute the performance indexes (PCI-S and PCI-C).

Fourth Quarter, January 1, Year 2

Table A12–4 summarizes the information regarding activities accomplished since the last report.

TABLE A12–4

JANUARY 1, YEAR 2

Activity	Start date	Finish date	Actual duration	Remaining duration
Prototypes	9/22/y1	12/5/y1	75	0
Serial I/O drivers	9/22/y1		101	9

7. Print out a status report for the fourth quarter in table form that shows the BCWS, BCWP, ACWP, BAC, EAC, SV, and CV for each work package, deliverable, and the whole project (the WBS).

Questions

How is the project progressing in terms of cost and schedule? What activities have gone well? What activities have not gone well?

What is the forecasted cost at completion (FAC)? What is the budgeted cost for the work remaining?

8. Compute the performance indexes (PCI-S and PCI-C).

PART 6

You have received revised estimates for the remaining activities at the end of the fourth quarter:

- Serial I/O drivers will be completed on 1/9/y2.
- System hardware/software tests will start on 1/10/y2 and take 25 days.
- Order circuit boards will start on 2/4/y2 and take 3 days.
- Assemble preproduction model will begin on 3/2/y2 and take 35 days.
- Project documentation is expected to start on 2/4/y2 and will take 65 days.
- Network interface is expected to start on 2/4/y2 and will take 85 days.
- Shell is expected to start on 2/4/y2 and will take 75 days.
- Integrated acceptance test is expected to start on 4/29/y2 and will take 65 days.

1. What is the new EAC for the project? How long should the project take given these revised estimates?
2. Management is insisting that the project be done no later than June 13 or else. They are willing to add additional manpower to development teams to speed up completion of the project. The cost will be an additional $50 per hour for each development team. You have forecasted that the impact of adding development manpower on the remaining activities:
   - System hardware/software tests will start on 1/7/y2 and take 15 days.
   - Assemble preproduction model will begin on 3/2/y2 and take 25 days.
   - Project documentation will take 55 days.
   - Network interface will take 80 days.
   - Shell will take 65 days.
   - Integrated acceptance test will take 50 days.
3. Decide which activities you would add the additional development manpower to (at a cost of +$50 an hour) in order to meet the June 13 deadline. (Note: A development team would be added to the assembly team in order to expedite the system hardware/software tests.) What would the EAC be for the revised schedule? Can the project be completed by June 13? How soon can it be completed?
4. You are asked to explain the actual and estimated future performance of your project to top management. Past experience has taught you that they are not impressed with reams of computer output of tables and graphs. They prefer a two- to four-page written summary of present and forecasted status of the project and the managerial implications of problems identified. You may wish to use presentation software for your meeting.

Project Material Price and Usage Variance

Project material variances arise when the price and/or usage of a material item differ from what was budgeted. When materials are a major cost, the cost variance (CV) can be separated into price and usage variance to trace to causes. Project materials cost variance is a combination of both price and usage variance.

Price variance (PV) occurs when the budgeted price of material items differs from the actual price. The formula is expressed as follows:

$$PV = (\text{Budgeted price} - \text{Actual price}) \times \text{Actual quantity used}$$

Price variances arise for reasons such as poor price estimates, changes in prices, expediting arrival of materials, etc.

Usage variance (UV) occurs when the quantity of a material item consumed differs from the quantity budgeted. Usage variance is computed as follows:

$$UV = (\text{Budgeted quantity} - \text{Actual quantity used}) \times \text{Budgeted price}$$

Usage variance occurs when more or fewer materials are needed than budgeted and/or when schedules are ahead or behind.

To illustrate project price and usage materials variance and how they are related, suppose a consultant has found the data provided here:

Cost variance (CV)	(–$21,000)
Budgeted price per unit of material	$520
Actual price paid per unit used	$500
Actual units used	250 units
Budgeted quantity to date	200 units

From the data, it is clear that less was paid for each unit than was planned. What is the impact of this price change?

$$
\begin{aligned}
PV &= (\text{Budgeted price} - \text{Actual price}) \times \text{Actual quantity used} \\
&= (\$520 - \$500) \times 250 \\
&= \$20 \times 250 \\
&= \$5,000
\end{aligned}
$$

The data also indicate more units were used than planned to date:

$$
\begin{aligned}
UV &= (\text{Budgeted quantity} - \text{Actual quantity used}) \times \text{Budgeted price} \\
&= (200 - 250) \times \$520 \\
&= (-50) \times \$520 \\
&= (-\$26,000)
\end{aligned}
$$

Thus, price accounted for a $5,000 favorable influence on the cost variance, while usage accounted for an unfavorable variance of –$26,000. Together, the resultant cost variance at report date for this material is an unfavorable variance of –$21,000 [(–26,000) + (+5,000)].

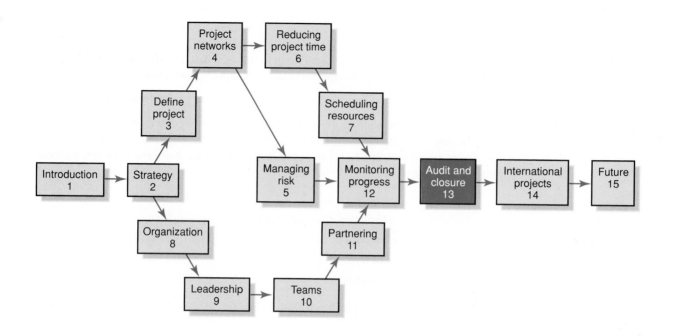

Project Audit and Closure

The Project Audit Process
The Audit Report
Project Closure
Team, Team Member, and Project Manager Evaluations
Summary

CHAPTER THIRTEEN

Project Audit and Closure

Those who cannot remember the past are condemned to fulfill it.
—George Santayana, 1863–1952

Mistakes are made; the unexpected happens; conditions change. In organizations that have several projects going on concurrently, it is prudent to have periodic reality checks on current and recently completed projects and their role in the organization's future. The post-project audit includes three major tasks:

1. Evaluate if the project delivered the expected benefits to all stakeholders. Was the project managed well? Was the customer satisfied?
2. Assess what was done wrong and what contributed to successes.
3. Identify changes to improve the delivery of future projects.

The project audit and report are instruments for supporting continuous improvement and organization learning.

Unfortunately, it is estimated that about 90 percent of all projects are not seriously reviewed or audited. In addition, lessons learned are not recorded for improving management of future projects. Failure to consistently audit projects and report findings is an opportunity lost. We have observed that the 10 percent of projects that are seriously audited appear to be done by extremely well-managed organizations which are vigorously committed to continuous improvement and organization learning.

Project audits are more than the status reports suggested in Chapter 12, which check on project performance. Status reports are analogous to viewing the project through a telescope. Audits are analogous to viewing the project through field glasses—a wide-angle view of the project in its bigger organizational environment. Project audits do use performance measures and forecast data. But project audits are more inclusive. Project audits review why the project was selected. Project audits include a reassessment of the project's role in the organization's priorities. Project audits include a check on the organizational culture to ensure it facilitates the type of project being implemented. Project audits assess if the project team is functioning well and is appropriately staffed. Audits of projects in process should include a check on external factors that might change where the project is heading or its importance—for example, technology, government laws, competitive products. Project audits include a review of all factors relevant to the project and to managing future projects.

411

Project audits can be performed while a project is in process and after a project is completed. There are only a few minor differences between these audits.

- **In-process project audits.** Project audits early in projects allow for corrective changes if they are needed on the audited project or others in progress. In-process project audits concentrate on project progress and performance and check if conditions have changed. For example, have priorities changed? Is the project mission still relevant? In rare cases, the audit report may recommend closure of a project that is in process.
- **Post-project audits.** These audits tend to include more detail and depth than in-process project audits. Project audits of completed projects emphasize improving the management of future projects. These audits are more long-term oriented than in-process audits. Post-project audits do check on project performance, but the audit represents a broader view of the project's role in the organization; for example, were the strategic benefits claimed actually delivered?

The depth and detail of the project audit depend on many factors. Some are listed in Table 13–1. Because audits cost time and money, they should include no more time or resources than are necessary and sufficient. Early in-process project audits tend to be perfunctory unless serious problems or concerns are identified. Then, of course, the audit would be carried out in more detail. Because in-process project audits can be worrisome and destructive to the project team, care needs to be taken to protect project team morale. The audit should be carried out quickly, and the report should be as positive and constructive as possible. Post-project audits are more detailed and inclusive and contain more project team input.

In summary, plan the audit, and limit the time for the audit. For example, in post-project audits, for all but very large projects, a one-week limit is a good benchmark. Beyond this time, the marginal return of additional information diminishes quickly. Small projects may require only one or two days and one or two people to conduct an audit.

The priority team functions well in selecting projects and monitoring performance—cost and time. However, reviewing and evaluating projects and the process of managing projects is usually delegated to independent audit groups.[1] Each audit group is charged with evaluating and reviewing *all* factors relevant to the project and to managing future projects. The outcome of the project audit is a report.

The process for conducting the project audit and preparing the written report are discussed in the first two sections of this chapter. Conditions and approaches for

TABLE 13–1

FACTORS INFLUENCING AUDIT DEPTH AND DETAIL

Organization size

Project importance

Project type

Project risk

Project size

Project problems

project closure of in-process and completed projects are discussed in the third section of the chapter. The final section discusses evaluations of the team, its members, and the project manager.

THE PROJECT AUDIT PROCESS

Initiation and Staffing

Initiation of the audit process depends primarily on organization size and project size along with other factors. However, every effort should be made to make the project audit a normal process rather than a surprise notice. In small organizations and projects where face-to-face contact at all levels is prevalent, an audit may be informal and only represent another staff meeting. But even in these environments the content of a formal project audit should be examined and covered with notes made of the lessons learned. In medium-sized organizations that have several projects occurring simultaneously, initiation can come from a formal project review group, from the project priority team, or be automatic. For example, in the latter case, all projects are audited at specific stages in the project life cycle—perhaps when a project is 10 to 20 percent complete in time or money, 50 percent complete, and after completion. The automatic process works well because it removes the perceptions that a project has been singled out for evaluation and that someone might be on a witch hunt. In large projects, the audit may be planned for major milestones.

There are rare circumstances that require an unplanned project audit, but they should be few and far between. For example, in a project that involved the development of a very large computer accounting system for multiple locations, one major consulting firm (of many) gave notice of withdrawal from the project, with no apparent reason. The project customer became alarmed that perhaps there was a serious fundamental problem in the project that caused the large consulting firm to drop out. A project audit identified the problem. The problem was one of sexual harassment by members of a small consulting firm toward members of the larger consulting firm. The small consulting firm engagement was terminated and replaced with a firm of similar expertise. The larger firm agreed to remain with the project. There are many other avenues to identify and solve such problems, but this example occurred as reported. Other circumstances, internal and external to the project, can cause an unplanned audit—for example, large cost or time overruns, change in project managers, or coverups. Regardless, unplanned audits should be avoided except in unusual circumstances.

A major tenant of the project audit is that the outcome must represent an independent, outside view of the project. Maintaining independence and an objective view is difficult, given that audits are frequently viewed as negative by project stakeholders. Careers and reputations can be tarnished even in organizations that tolerate mistakes. In less forgiving organizations, mistakes can lead to termination or exile to less significant regions of an organization. Of course, if the result of an audit is favorable, careers and reputations can be enhanced. Given that project audits are susceptible to internal politics, some organizations rely on outside consulting firms to conduct the audits. Regardless, it is imperative the audit leader possess the following characteristics:

1. No direct involvement or direct interest in the project.
2. Respect (perceived as impartial and fair) of senior management and other project stakeholders.

3. Willingness to listen.
4. Independence and authority to report audit results without fear of recriminations from special interests.
5. Perceived as having the best interests of the organization in making decisions.
6. Broad-based experience in the organization or industry.

Other audit members should have similar characteristics even if they are selected for their special expertise. Some project team members will need to be included in the audit evaluation. Post-project audits have a stronger representation of project team members than in-process project audits because of the slightly different orientation. The concern that team members will come to the audit with strong biases is usually overstated. In general, project team members are genuinely interested in improving the future project management process; they make every attempt to be objective.

Thus, when project audits are planned there is time to carefully select the audit staff. The size of the audit group depends on the organization size, project size, and project importance. An audit report recording the lessons learned can have dramatic results in improving future projects. After an organization has determined when to conduct audits and who will conduct them, it can charge the audit team with gathering information and analyzing it.

Information and Data Collection and Analysis

The traditional content model for a project audit presents two perspectives. One evaluates the project from the view of the organization. The second perspective represents the project team's evaluative view. The organization perspective is developed by a small group primarily made up of persons not having a direct interest in the project. The project team perspective is developed by a group composed primarily of team members along with persons independent of the project to ensure the evaluation is objective.

Each organization and project is unique. Therefore, many factors need to be considered. For example, the industry, project size, newness of technology, and project experience can influence the nature of the audit. However, information and data are gathered to answer questions similar to those suggested next.

Organization View

1. Was the organizational culture supportive and correct for this type of project? Why? Why not?
2. Was senior management's support adequate?
3. Did the project accomplish its intended purpose?
   a. Is there a clear link to organizational strategy and objectives?
   b. Does the priority system reflect importance to the future of the organization?
   c. Has the environment (internal or external) changed the need for the project's completion (if project is still in process)?
4. Were the risks for the project appropriately identified and assessed? Were contingency plans used? Were they realistic? Have risk events occurred that have an impact greater than anticipated?
5. Were the right people and talents assigned to this project?
6. If the project was completed, have staff been fairly assigned to new projects?
7. What does evaluation from outside contractors suggest?
8. Did the technology required overextend current technological competencies?
9. Were the project startup and hand-off successful? Why? Is the customer satisfied?

Project Team View

1. Were the project planning and control systems appropriate for this type of project? Should all similar size and type of projects use these systems? Why/why not?
2. Did the project conform to plan? Is the project over or under budget and schedule? Why?
3. Were interfaces with project stakeholders adequate and effective?
4. If the project is completed, have staff been fairly assigned to new projects?
5. Did the team have adequate access to organizational resources—people, budget, support groups, equipment? Were there resource conflicts with other ongoing projects? Was the team managed well?
6. What does evaluation from outside contractors suggest?

The audit group should not be limited to these questions.[2] The audit group should include other questions related to their organization and project type—e.g., research and development, marketing, information systems, construction, facilities. The generic questions above, although overlapping, represent a good starting point and will go a long way toward identifying project problem and success patterns.

Guidelines for Conducting a Project Audit

The following guidelines should improve chances for a successful audit:

1. First and foremost, the philosophy must be that the project audit is not a witch-hunt.
2. Comments about individuals or groups participating in the project are no-no's. Keep to project issues, not what happened or by whom.
3. Audit activities should be intensely sensitive to human emotions and reactions. The inherent threat to those being evaluated should be reduced as much as possible.
4. The project manager should be notified of the impending audit.
5. Accuracy of data should be verifiable or noted as subjective, judgmental, or hearsay.
6. Senior management should announce support for the project audit and see that the audit group has access to all information, project participants, and (in most cases) project customer.
7. The attitude toward a project audit and its aftermath depend on the modus operandi of the audit leadership and group. The objective is not to prosecute. The objective is to learn and conserve valuable organization resources where mistakes have been made. Friendliness, empathy, and objectivity encourage cooperation and reduce anxiety.
8. The audit should be completed as quickly as is reasonable.
9. The audit leader should be given access to senior management above the project manager.

THE AUDIT REPORT

General Requirements

The major goal of the audit report is to improve the way future projects are managed. Succinctly, the report attempts to capture needed changes and lessons learned from a current or finished project. The report serves as a training instrument for project managers of future projects.

Audit reports need to be tailored to the specific project and organizational environ-

Snapshot from Practice
OPERATION EAGLE CLAW

© 1999 Michael McGrath.

On November 4, 1979, a mob in Iran stormed the U.S. Embassy and took 52 Americans hostage. After six months of failed negotiation, the decision was made to execute Operation Eagle Claw, a joint military effort to free the U.S. hostages.

The plan called for eight Navy RH-53D helicopters to fly 600 miles to a remote site in Iran, code named Desert One. Under the cover of darkness, the helicopters would be refueled by KC-130 tankers. The helicopters would then fly the assault force to a spot near the outskirts of Tehran where they would meet up with special agents already in the country. The agents would lead them to a safe house to await the assault on the embassy the next night. Upon rescuing the hostages, the assault team would escort the hostages to a nearby airfield that had been secured by a second attack team where they would be flown to safety.

What actually happened was far different from what was planned.

The helicopter pilots were ordered to fly at or below 200 feet to avoid radar. This caused them to run into "haboobs" or dust storms. Two helicopters malfunctioned and turned back. The remainder battled the dust storms and arrived at Desert One an hour late. The rescue attempt was dealt its final blow when it was discovered that a third helicopter had a hydraulic leak and was inoperable. Only five aircraft were serviceable and six were needed, so the mission was aborted. Things got worse, though, when one of the helicopters moved into position to refuel and collided with a KC-130 plane. Both aircraft burst into flames. All told, eight soldiers died and dozens were injured. The Iranians scattered the hostages around the country afterward, making any further rescue attempts impossible.

The Armed Services routinely conduct audits of every exercise and operation. Given the gravity of the situation, a special six-member commission was appointed by the Joint Chiefs of Staff to investigate the failed operation. They discovered a number of issues that contributed to the failure. One issue was the selection of air crew. Navy and Marine pilots with little experience in long-range overland navigation or refueling were selected though more than a hundred qualified Air Force pilots were available. Another issue was the lack of a comprehensive mission rehearsal program. From the beginning, training was not conducted in a truly joint manner; it was compartmentalized by service and held in scattered locations across the United States. The limited rehearsals that were conducted assessed only portions of the total mission. Also at issue was the number of helicopters used. The commission concluded that 10 and perhaps 12 helicopters should have been launched to guarantee the minimum six required for completion of the mission. Finally, the hopscotch method of ground refueling was criticized. If the planners had chosen to use enroute air fueling, the entire Desert One scenario could have been avoided. The final report of the commission contained several important recommendations designed to prevent such a tragedy from occurring again.[3]

ment. Nevertheless, a generic format for all audits facilitates development of an audit database and a common outline for those who prepare audit reports and the managers who read and act on their content. A very general outline common to those found in practice is as follows:

1. Classification of project.
2. Analysis of information gathered.
3. Recommendations.
4. Lessons learned.
5. Appendix.

Classification   Each project audit is categorized because there are differences in the way projects with different characteristics are managed and handled in an organization. A prospective project manager of a software coding project will have little interest in the construction of a clean room or recycling of inkjet reservoirs for printers. A prospective project manager of a small project will not be as interested in a computer project planning and control system as a project manager who is going to manage a very large project. The classification of projects by characteristics allows prospective readers and project managers to be selective in the use of the report content. Typical classification categories include the following:

- Project type—e.g., development, marketing, systems, construction.
- Size—monetary.
- Number of staff.
- Technology level—low, medium, high, new.
- Strategic or support.

Other classifications relevant to the organization should be included.

Analysis   The analysis section includes succinct, factual review statements of the project. For example,

- Project mission and objectives.
- Procedures and systems used.
- Organization resources used.

Recommendations   Usually audit recommendations represent major corrective actions that should take place. However, it is equally important to recommend positive successes that should be continued and used in future projects. Post-project audits may be the place to give credit to the project team for an outstanding contribution.

Lessons Learned   These do not have to be in the form of recommendations. Lessons learned serve as reminders of mistakes easily avoided and actions easily taken to ensure success. In practice, new project teams reviewing audits of past projects similar to the one they are about to start have found audit reports very useful. Team members will frequently remark later, "The recommendations were good, but the 'lessons learned' section really helped us avoid many pitfalls and made our project implementation smoother." In the accompanying Snapshot from Practice, this Bell Canada project involved a business transformation process of bringing more than 500 independent projects under one generic project management process umbrella. This project was especially challenging because most managers had little project management experience. The lessons learned demonstrate some of the difficulties and insights gained by the implementation team trying to integrate project management into the culture of the organization.

Snapshot from Practice
LESSONS LEARNED: BELL CANADA BUSINESS TRANSFORMATION PROJECT

Managing the team's expectations of the planning process was crucial. Team members needed to understand that frustrations, "surprises," and recycling were a normal part of planning. Planning is hard work, and more effort spent in planning would improve the success factor.

The teams were often scattered along functional lines. This made reporting and identifying roles and responsibilities very difficult for the project manager. Project team structure was also challenged by the geography, cross-functional membership, and two organizations (Bell Canada and Bell Sygma) playing equal roles. The understanding and use of organization structure played a key role in the planning and implementation of the project.

The level of coaching required by the project manager once the project plan was implemented was more than anticipated. Understanding and using the processes for day-by-day project management were challenging when team members returned to their work environments.

Not all consultants hired were successful. Some consultants would offer recommendations too quickly after their arrival. As a result, most of these early recommendations were not applicable to our project. Subsequently, the senior consultant or a member of the team accompanied all new consultants for the first few days to familiarize them with the project and our specific areas of concern.

The primary hiring skills for consultants were (1) project management skills, (2) proven and recent experience in managing IT projects, and (3) facilitation skills. It turned out that if facilitation skills were lacking, it did not matter how strong the first two skill sets were, the consultant could not succeed.

There is a fine line between what *must* be done and what *should* be done in these situations. It was a struggle to maintain a pragmatic, minimalist approach in applying project management with novice teams, especially without supporting infrastructure in place. Even with the short-term process that was established, we had to pull back on some of the initial requirements (structure of the WBS, post-planning review, and uninterrupted planning). In many cases the consultants' desire to "do it right" often had to give way to "getting it done."

Some of the BT projects would have not been approved had there been proper planning in the first phase of the project. Knowing the true cost of development and implementation could have resulted in a nonviable business case from a financial perspective.[4]

Appendix   The appendix may include backup data or details of analysis that would allow others to follow up if they wished. It should not be a dumping ground used for filler; only critical pertinent information should be attached.

Summary Booklet   Finally, it is good to keep a small summary booklet of major lessons learned. Give references to archived audit reports if additional information is desired. This process may appear a bit formal, but people use these summaries and archives when they are available—more frequently than most would believe.

Audit Summary

Again, the major objective of the audit report is to improve the way future projects are managed in the organization. The immediate recommendations and lessons learned are extremely valuable to near-term future projects. For example, having project audits and lessons learned available shortens the lengthy learning curve project teams go through when they begin a new project. But perhaps more importantly, in the longer run after several audit reports are harvested, dramatic changes begin to happen in the organization because of the common threads among the reports. For example, the result of three post-project audits in one organization revealed teams were "throwing their part of the project over the fence" to the next team in the sequence with little or no coordination. The resultant change was to include a member of the receiving team on the team passing the project on so that problems could be identified and corrected before passing to the next team.

If the project audit reports are not hidden in someone's office drawer but actually used, the results over a two- or three-year period can be startling and dramatic. Project audit reports can have a powerful, positive influence on the effectiveness of the organization and on the professional development of all members of the organization.

PROJECT CLOSURE

Every project comes to an end, eventually. On some projects the end may not be as clear as would be hoped. Although the scope statement may define a clear ending for a project, the actual ending may or may not correspond. Fortunately, a majority of projects are blessed with a well-defined ending. Regular project audits and a priority team will identify those projects that should have endings different from those planned.

Conditions for Project Closure

Normal   The most common circumstance for project closure is simply a completed project. Although some modifications in scope, cost, and time may have emerged during implementation, most projects are completed near plan. Traditionally, there is a colossal ending and all stakeholders celebrate with awards, accolades, and recognition for special efforts. The project is transferred to the customer, and the project is closed down.

Premature   For a few projects, the project may be completed early with some parts of the project eliminated. For example, in a new-product development project, a marketing manager may insist on production models before testing:

> Give the new product to me now, the way it is. Early entry into the market will mean big profits! I know we can sell a bizzillion of these. If we don't do it now, the opportunity is lost!

The pressure is on to finish the project and send it to production. Before succumbing to this form of pressure, the implications and risks associated with this decision should be carefully reviewed and assessed by senior management and all stakeholders. Too frequently, the benefits are illusory, dangerous, and carry large risks. Why have the original project scope and objectives changed? If early project closure occurs, it should have the support of all project stakeholders. This decision should be left to the audit group, project priority team, or senior management.

Perpetual   Some projects never seem to end. That is, the project appears to develop a life of its own.[5] Although these projects are plagued with delays, they are viewed as desirable when they finally are completed. The major characteristic of this kind of project is constant "add-ons." The owner or others continuously require more small changes that will improve the project outcome—product or service. These changes typically represent "extras" perceived as being part of the original project intent. Examples are adding features to software, to product design, to systems, or to construction projects. Constant add-on changes suggest a poorly conceived project scope.

More care in upfront definition of the project scope and limitations will reduce the add-on phenomenon.

At some point the project manager or audit group needs to call the project design locked to bring closure. Although these projects are exhibiting scope, cost, and schedule creep, facing the fact that the project should be brought to an end is not an easy chore. Project managers or audit/priority groups have several alternatives available. They can redefine the project end or scope so that closure is forced. They can limit budget or resources. They can set a time limit. All alternatives should be designed to bring the project to an end as quickly as possible to limit additional costs and still gain the positive benefits of a completed project. The audit group should recommend methods for bringing final closure to this type of project. Failed projects are usually easy to identify and easy for an audit group to close down. However, every effort should be made to communicate the technical reasons for termination of the project; project participants should not be left with an embarrassing stigma of working on a project that failed.

Failed Project   In rare circumstances projects simply fail—for a variety of reasons. For example, developing a prototype of a new technology product may show the original concept to be unworkable. Or in the development of a new pharmaceutical drug, the project may need to be abandoned because side effects of the drug are deemed unacceptable.

Changed Priority   The priority team continuously revises project selection priorities to reflect changes in organizational direction. Normally these changes are small over a period of time, but periodically major shifts in organization require dramatic shifts in priorities. In this transition period, projects in process may need to be altered or canceled. Thus, a project may start with a high priority but see its rank erode or crash during its project life cycle as conditions change. For example, a computer game company found their major competitor placed a 64-bit, 3-D game on the market while their product development projects still centered on 32-bit games. From that moment on, 32-bit game projects were considered obsolete and met sudden deaths. (Meredith and Mantel termed this type of closure "termination by murder."[6]) The priority team of this company revised organization priorities. Audit groups found it easy to recommend closure for many projects, but those on the margin or in "gray areas" still presented formidable analysis and difficult decisions.

In some cases the original importance of the project was misjudged; in some the needs have changed. In other situations implementation of the project is impractical or impossible. Because the audit group and priority team are periodically reviewing a project, the changed perception of the project's role (priority) in the total scheme of things becomes apparent quickly. If the project no longer contributes significantly to organization strategy, the audit group or priority team needs to recommend the project be terminated. In many termination situations, these projects are integrated into related projects or routine daily operations.

Clearly changes in technology and needs can occur while projects are being implemented. Does this change the project priority? The situation becomes a new resource allocation problem. Will the additional costs of incorporating the new technology into the current project still keep the project at the same priority level with current alternative projects? When the answer is yes, these changes should be reflected in scope changes and their impact on schedule and budget noted. If the answer is no, the audit group will probably recommend termination. (Note that costs to this point are sunk costs, so the decision rests on future costs and project benefits.)

Termination of "changed priority" projects is no easy task. The project team's perception may be that the project priority is still high in relation to other projects. Egos and, in some cases perhaps, jobs are on the line. Individuals or teams feel success is just over the horizon. Giving up is tantamount to failure. Normally, rewards are given for staying with a project when the chips are down, not giving up. Such emotional issues make project termination difficult.

There is little advantage to placing blame on individuals. Other modes should be used to "justify" early project closure or to identify a project problem—for example, customer needs or tastes have changed, technology is ahead of this project, or competition has a better, more advanced product or service. These examples are external to the organization and perceived as beyond anyone's control. Another approach that weakens close team loyalty is changing team members or the project manager. This approach tends to minimize team commitment and makes closing the project easier, but it should only be used as a last resort. Minimizing embarrassment should be a primary goal for a project review group closing down an unfinished project.

Signals for Continuing or Early Project Closure

Persons who are preparing to join a project audit group for the first time would find it rewarding to read a few studies that identify barriers to project success and the antithesis, factors that contribute to success. Knowledge of these factors will suggest areas to review in an audit. These factors signal where problems or success patterns might exist. In rare cases their existence may signal problems and the need for an in-process project to be terminated early.

A number of studies have examined this area.[7] There is surprising conformity among these studies. For example, all of these studies (and others) rank poor project definition (scope) as a major barrier to project success. There is no evidence these factors have changed over the years, although some differences in relative importance have been noted in different industries. Table 13–2 presents the barriers identified by 1,654 participating project managers in a survey by Gobeli and Larson.[8] The signals noted in Table 13–2 can be useful to audit groups in their preliminary review of in-process projects or even in post-project audits.

The Closure Decision

For an incomplete project, the decision to continue or close down the project is fundamentally an organizational resource allocation decision. Should the organization commit additional resources to complete the project and realize the project objectives? This is a complex decision. The rationale for closing or proceeding is often based on many cost factors that are primarily subjective and judgmental. Thus, care needs to be taken to avoid inferences concerning groups or individuals. The audit report needs to focus on organizational goals, changing conditions, and changing priorities requiring reallocation of scarce organizational resources.

When the audit group or priority team suggests closure, the announcement may need to come from a CEO position if the effect is large or if key egos are involved. But, in most cases, the closure decision is left to the audit group or priority team. Prior to announcement of closure, a plan for future assignment of the project team members should be in place.

Project Closure Process

As the project nears the end of its life cycle, people and equipment are directed to other activities or projects. Carefully managing the closure phase is as important as

TABLE 13-2

BARRIERS TO PROJECT SUCCESS

Activity*	Barrier	Incidence (%)
Planning 32%	Unclear definition	16%
	Poor decision making	9
	Bad information	3
	Changes	4
Scheduling 12%	Tight schedule	4
	Not meeting schedule	5
	Not managing schedule	3
Organizing 11%	Lack of responsibility or accountability	5
	Weak project manager	5
	Top management interference	1
Staffing 12%	Inadequate personnel	5
	Incompetent project manager	4
	Project member turnover	2
	Poor staffing process	1
Directing 26%	Poor coordination	9
	Poor communication	6
	Poor leadership	5
	Low commitment	6
Controlling 7%	Poor followup	3
	Poor monitoring	2
	No control system	1
	No recognition of problems	1

* To interpret the table, note that 32 percent of the 1,654 participants reported the barriers under "Planning," 12 percent reported the barriers under "Scheduling," and so on.

any other phase of the project. The major challenges for the project manager and team members are over. Getting the project manager and team members to wrap up the odds and ends of closing down the project is sometimes difficult. For example, accounting for equipment and completing final reports are perceived as boring by project professionals who are action-oriented individuals. They are looking forward to new opportunities and challenges. The major activities found in project terminations are developing a plan, staffing, communicating the plan, and implementing the plan.

The typical close-out plan includes answers to questions similar to these:

- What tasks are required to close the project?
- Who will be responsible for these tasks?
- When will closure begin and end?
- How will the project be delivered?

Staffing is usually not a significant issue if the termination is not a sudden hatchet job. If the project is suddenly canceled early, before completion, it may be judicious to seek someone other than the project manager to close out the project. In successful, completed projects, the project manager is the likely choice for closing down the project. In this case it is best to have the project manager's next assignment known; this will serve as an inducement to terminate the project as quickly as possible and move on to new challenges.

Communicating the termination plan and schedule early allows the project team to (1) accept the psychological fact the project will end and (2) prepare to move on. The ideal scenario is to have the team member's next assignment ready when the termination is announced. Conversely, a major dilemma in the termination phase is that project participants are looking forward to future projects or other opportunities. The project manager's challenge is to keep the project team focused on the project activities and delivery to the customer until the project is complete. Project managers need to be careful to maintain their enthusiasm for completing the project and hold people accountable to deadlines, which are prone to slip during the waning stages of the project.

Implementing the close-down plan includes several wrap-up activities. Many organizations develop lengthy lists for closing projects as they gain experience. These are very helpful and ensure nothing is overlooked.[9] Implementing close down includes the following six major activities:

1. Getting delivery acceptance from the customer.
2. Shutting down resources and releasing to new uses.
3. Reassigning project team members.
5. Closing accounts and seeing all bills are paid.
6. Evaluating the project team, project team members, and the project manager.

Figure 13–1 depicts a partial closedown checklist for the Euro conversion project for a space company.

Orchestrating the closure of a project is truly a difficult task and a challenge to the manager's leadership ability. Implementing closure usually takes place in an emotionally charged web of happiness from successful completion of the project and sadness that newly forged friendships are now being severed as individuals go their separate ways. It is customary in organizations to arrange a celebration of the completion of the project; this could range from an informal pizza party after work to a more formal banquet including speeches and awards or certificates of recognition for participants. Such a festivity provides a sense of closure and emotional release for the participants as they bid farewell to each other. For less successful projects, this ending can take the form of a ceremonial wake; even though the atmosphere may be less than festive, such an event can also provide a sense of closure and help people move on with their lives.

TEAM, TEAM MEMBER, AND PROJECT MANAGER EVALUATIONS

Auditing includes performance evaluations of the project team, individual team members, and the project manager. Evaluation of performance is essential to encourage changes in behavior, to support individual career development, and to support continuous improvement through organization learning. Evaluation implies measurement against specific criteria. Experience corroborates that before commencement of the project the stage must be set so all expectations, standards, supportive organization culture, and constraints are in place; if not, the effectiveness of the evaluation process will suffer.

Project _____ *Euro Conversion* _____   Customer _____ *Finance Department* _____

Project manager _____ *Hans Kramer* _____   Completion date _____ *12 December XX* _____

	Due date	Person responsible	Notes
1. Document finance department acceptance	16/12	Hans	
2. Customer training in Euro software	28/12	Joan	Train all departments before conversion
3. Archive all			
Schedules/actuals	31/12	Maeyke	
Budgets/actual costs	31/12	Maeyke	
Changes	31/12	Maeyke	
4. Close out all accounts with vendors	31/12	Guido	
5. Close out all work orders	31/12	Mayo	
6. Close out partner accounts	31/12	Guido	
7. Reassign project staff	16/12	Sophie	
8. Evaluation of			
Vendors	31/12	Mayo	Use standard questionnaire for vendors
Staff members	31/12	Sophie	Have HR department develop and administer
9. Final report and lessons learned meeting	4/1	Hans	Send notice to all stakeholders
10. Lessons learned archive to database	10/1	Maeyke	Contact IS department
tribute awards		Sophie	Notify all stakeholders

FIGURE 13–1   European Space Launch, AG—Project Closure Checklist

In a macro sense the evidence today suggests that performance evaluation in each of these realms is not done well. The major reasons cited by practitioners are twofold:

1. Evaluations of individuals are still left to supervisors of the team member's home department.
2. Typical measures of team performance center on time, cost, and specifications.

Most organizations do not go beyond these measures, although they are important and critical. Organizations should consider evaluating the team-building process, effectiveness of group decision and problem-solving processes, group cohesion, trust among team members, and quality of information exchanged. Addressing evaluation of teams, team members, and project managers is extremely complex and project dependent. The discussion that follows touches on some of the major issues and approaches found in practice.

Team Evaluation

Before an auditing of the project team can be effective and useful, a minimum core of conditions needs to be in place before the project begins (see Chapter 10). Some conditions are listed here in the form of questions:

1. Do standards for measuring performance exist? (You can't manage what you can't measure.) Are the goals clear for the team and individuals? Challenging? Attainable? Lead to positive consequences?
2. Are individual and team responsibilities and performance standards known by all team members?
3. Are team rewards adequate? Do they send a clear signal that senior management believes the synergy of teams is important?
4. Is a clear career path for successful project managers in place?
5. Does the team have discretionary authority to manage short-term difficulties?
6. Is there a relatively high level of trust emanating from the organization culture?
7. Team evaluation should go beyond time, cost, and specifications. Are there criteria beyond these triple threat criteria?[11] The "characteristics of highly effective teams" from Chapter 10 can easily be adapted as measurements of team effectiveness.

These "in-place conditions" will support any evaluation approach for teams and their members.

In practice the actual team evaluation process takes many forms—especially when evaluation goes beyond time, budget, and specifications. The typical mechanism for evaluation of teams is a survey administered by a consultant, a staff member from the human resources department, or through computer e-mail. The survey is normally restricted to team members, but, in some cases, other project stakeholders interacting with the team may be included in the survey. When the results are tabulated, the team meets with senior management, and the results are reviewed. An example of a partial survey is found in Table 13–3.

This session is comparable to the team-building sessions described in Chapter 10 except that the focus is on using the survey results to assess the development of the team, its strengths and weaknesses, and the lessons that can be applied to future project work. The results of team evaluation surveys are helpful in changing behavior, stressing the importance of supporting the team approach, and continuous improvement.

TABLE 13–3

SAMPLE TEAM EVALUATION AND FEEDBACK SURVEY

Using the scale below, assess each statement.

	Disagree				**Agree**
1. The team shared a sense of common purpose, and each member was willing to work toward achieving project objectives.	1	2	3	4	5
2. Respect was shown for other points of view. Differences of opinion were encouraged and freely expressed.	1	2	3	4	5
3. All interaction among team members occurred in a comfortable, supportive atmosphere.	1	2	3	4	5

Individual Team Member and Project Manager Evaluation

Team evaluation is crucial, but at some point a project manager is likely to be asked to evaluate the performance of individual members. Such an evaluation will typically be required as part of the closure process and will then be incorporated in the annual performance appraisal system of the organization. These evaluations constitute a major element of an individual's personnel file and often form the basis for making decisions about promotions, future job assignments, merit pay increases, and other rewards.[12]

Organizations vary in the extent to which project managers are actively involved in performing the appraisal process. In organizations where projects are managed within a functional organization or functional matrix, the individual's area manager, not the project manager, is responsible for assessing performance. The area manager may solicit the project manager's opinion of the individual's performance on a specific project; this will be factored into the individual's overall performance. In a balanced matrix, the project manager and the area manager jointly evaluate an individual's performance. In project matrix and project organizations in which the lion's share of the individual's work is project related, the project manager is responsible for appraising individual performance. One new process, which appears to be gaining wider acceptance, is the multirater appraisal or the "360-degree feedback," which involves soliciting feedback concerning team members' performance from all the people their work affects. This would include not only project and area managers, but also peers, subordinates, and even customers.[13]

Performance appraisals generally fulfill two important functions. The first is developmental in nature; the focus is on identifying individual strengths and weaknesses and developing action plans for improving performance. The second is evaluative and involves assessing how well the person has performed in order to determine salary or merit adjustments. These two functions are not compatible. Employees, in their eagerness to find out how much pay they will receive, tend to tune out constructive feedback on how they can improve their performance. Likewise, managers tend to be more concerned with justifying their decision than engaging in a meaningful discussion on how the employee can improve his or her performance. It is difficult to be both a coach and a judge. As a result, several experts on performance appraisal systems recommend that organizations separate performance reviews, which focus on individual improvement, and pay reviews, which allocate the distribution of rewards.[14] In some matrix organizations, project managers conduct the performance reviews, while area managers are responsible for pay reviews. In other cases, performance reviews are part of the project closure process, and pay reviews are the primary objective of the annual performance appraisal. Other organizations avoid this dilemma by allocating only group rewards for project work. The remaining discussion is directed at reviews designed to improve performance because pay reviews are often outside the jurisdiction of the project manager.

Performance Reviews

Organizations employ a wide range of methods to review individual performance on a project. In general, all review methods of individual performance center on the technical and social skills brought to the project and team. Some organizations rely simply on an informal discussion between the project manager and the project member. Other organizations require project managers to submit written essays that describe and assess an individual's performance on a project. Many organizations use rating scales similar to the team evaluation survey in which the project manager rates the individual according to a certain scale (i.e., from 1 to 5) on a number of relevant performance dimensions (i.e., teamwork, customer relations). Some organizations augment these rating schemes with behaviorally anchored descriptions of what constitutes a 1 rating, a 2 rating, and so forth. Each method has its strengths and weaknesses, and, unfortunately, in many organizations the appraisal systems were designed to support mainstream operations and not unique project work.[15] The bottom line is that project managers have to use the performance review system mandated by their organization as best they can.

Regardless of the method, the project manager needs to sit down with each team member and discuss his or her performance. Here are some general tips for conducting performance reviews:

- Always begin the process by asking the individual to evaluate his or her own performance. First, this approach may yield valuable information that you were not aware of. Second, the approach may provide an early warning for situations in which there is disparity in assessments. Finally, this method reduces the judgmental nature of the discussion.
- Avoid, when possible, drawing comparisons with other team members; rather, assess the individual in terms of established standards and expectations. Comparisons tend to undermine cohesion and divert attention away from what the individual needs to do to improve performance.
- When you have to be critical, focus the criticism on specific examples of behavior rather than on the individual personally. Describe in specific terms how the behavior affected the project.
- Be consistent and fair in your treatment of all team members. Nothing breeds resentment more than if, through the grapevine, individuals feel that they are being held to a different standard than are other project members.
- Treat the review as only one point in an ongoing process. Use it to reach an agreement as to how the individual can improve his or her performance.

Managers and subordinates both may dread a formal performance review. Neither side feels comfortable with the evaluative nature of the discussion and the potential for misunderstanding and hurt feelings. Much of this anxiety can be alleviated if the project manager is doing her job well. Project managers should be constantly giving team members feedback throughout the project so that individual team members should have a pretty good idea how well they have performed and how the manager feels before the formal meeting.

Snapshot from Practice
THE 360-DEGREE FEEDBACK

More and more companies are discarding the traditional superior-subordinate performance feedback process and replacing it with 360-degree feedback systems. The 360-degree feedback approach gathers behavioral observations from many sources within the organization and includes employee self-assessment. The individual completes the same structured evaluation process that superiors, project team members, peers and, in many cases, external customers use to evaluate his performance. Survey questionnaires, augmented by a few open-ended questions, are typically used to gather information.

Summary results are compared against organizational strategies, values, and business objectives. The feedback is communicated to the individual with the assistance of the company's human resource department or an outside consultant. The technique is used by a growing number of firms including General Electric, AT&T, Mobil Oil, Nabisco, Hewlett-Packard, and Warner-Lambert.

The objective of the 360-degree process is to identify areas for individual improvement. When anonymous feedback solicited from others is compared with the individual's self-evaluations, the individual may form a more realistic picture of her strengths and weaknesses. This may prompt behavioral change if the weaknesses identified were previously unknown to the individual. Such appears to be the case for Jerry Wallace, an up-and-coming manager at General Motors. "The strongest message I got was that I need to delegate more," he says, "I thought I'd been doing it. But I need to do it more and sooner. My people are saying, 'Turn me loose.'"

Many firms obtain feedback from internal and external project customers. For example, a client may evaluate a project manager or member of the project team according to, "How effectively does the individual get things done without creating unnecessary adversarial relationships?" Incorporating customer feedback in the evaluation process underscores collaboration and the importance of client expectations in determining project success.

William J. Miller, a program director at Du Pont, helped install a 360-degree feedback system for 80 scientists and support people. "A high or low score didn't predict a scientist's ability to invent Teflon," says Miller. "But what feedback did was really improve the ability of people to work in teams. Their regard for others and behaviors that were damaging and self-centered are what changed."[16]

While in many cases the same process that is applied to reviewing the performance of team members is applied to evaluating the project manager, many organizations augment this process, given the importance of the position to their organization. This is where conducting the 360-degree review is becoming more popular (see the accompanying Snapshot from Practice). In project-driven organizations, directors or vice presidents of project management will be responsible for collecting information on a specific project manager from customers, vendors, team members, peers, and other managers. This approach has tremendous promise for developing more effective project managers.

SUMMARY

Project audits enhance individual and organizational change and improvement. In this chapter processes for conducting project audits and developing the report were examined. Project closures and the importance of conducting team and individual evaluations were also reviewed. Key points of the chapter include the following:

• It is better to have automatic times or points when audits will take place. Surprises should be avoided.

- Audits of projects (especially those in process) need to be conducted carefully and with sensitivity to human reactions. The audit should focus on issues, problems, and successes and avoid references to groups or individuals.
- The audit is best staffed with individuals independent of the project.
- Audit reports need to be used and accessible.
- Audits support an organizational culture that vigorously promotes continuous improvement and organizational learning.
- Project closures should be planned and orderly regardless of the type of closure.
- Certain "core conditions" should be in place to support team and individual evaluation.
- Both individual and team evaluations should be conducted, and performance reviews should be separated from pay or merit reviews.

Competitive conditions appear to be forcing more organizations to adopt continuous improvement and organization learning. Regular use of project audits has yielded dramatic improvements in the way projects are managed. As more members of these organizations are learning from project mistakes and what is contributing to project successes, the process of managing projects is continuously improving in their respective organizations. The major instrument for implementing this philosophy will be the project audit and report. It is highly probable that the use of project audits will increase significantly in the future. This observation is in line with Chapter 15, which suggests that in the future, more organizations will adopt the philosophy of continuous improvement and organizational learning.

REVIEW QUESTIONS

1. How does the project audit differ from the performance measurement control system discussed in Chapter 12?
2. What major information would you expect to find in a project audit?
3. Why is it difficult to perform a truly independent, objective audit?
4. What personal characteristics and skills would you look for in selecting a project audit leader?
5. Comment on the following statement: "We cannot afford to terminate the project now. We have already spent more than 50 percent of the project budget."
6. Why should you separate performance reviews from pay reviews? How?

EXERCISE

Imagine you are conducting an audit of the International Space Station project. Research press coverage and the Internet to collect information on the current status of the project. What are the successes and failures to date? What forecasts would you make about the completion of the project, and why? What recommendations would you make to top management of the program, and why?

ENDNOTES

1. For a discussion of separating the audit group from the project priority team, see R. Balachandra and A. J. Raelin, "How to Decide When to Abandon a Project," *Research Management,* vol. 23, no. 4 (July 1980), pp. 24–29.
2. For an extensive list and another view, see C. K. Buell, "When to Terminate a Research and Development Project," *Research Management,* vol. 10, no. 4 (July 1987), pp. 275–84.
3. D. M. Giangreco and Terry A. Griswold, *Delta: America's Elite Counterterrorist Force* (New York: Motorbooks International, 1992).

4. Catherine Daw and Suzanne Sills, "Kick-Starting Project Management for a $1.7B Transformation Program in Bell Canada," *Proceedings of 28th Annual Project Management Institute 1997 Seminars and Symposium* (Newtown, PA: Project Management Institute, 1997), p. 728.

5. Berry M. Staw and Jerry Ross, "Knowing When to Pull the Plug," *Harvard Business Review* (March–April 1987), pp. 68–74.

6. Jack Meredith and Samuel J. Mantel Jr., *Project Management: A Managerial Approach,* 3rd ed. (New York: Wiley and Sons, 1995), p. 632.

7. David B. Gobeli and Erik Larson, "Barriers Affecting Project Success," in *1986 Proceedings Project Management Institute: Measuring Success* (Upper Darby, PA: Project Management Institute, 1986), pp. 22–29; David B. Ashley, Clive S. Lurie, and Edward J. Jaselskis, "Determinants of Construction Project Success," *Project Management Journal,* vol. 18, no. 2 (June 1987), p. 72; and Jefferey K. Pinto and Dennis P. Slevin, "Critical Success Factors Across the Project Life Cycle," *Project Management Journal,* vol. 19, no. 3 (June 1988), p. 72.

8. David B. Gobeli and Erik Larson, "Barriers Affecting Project Success," reference cited.

9. For a detailed checklist, see Russell D. Archibald, *Managing High-Technology Programs and Projects* (New York: John Wiley & Sons, 1992), pp. 364–70.

10. Joseph Fusco, "Better Policies Provide the Key to Implementing Project Management," *Project Management Journal,* vol. 28, no. 3 (September 1997), p. 38.

11. Donald D. Pippett and James F. Peters, "Team Building and Project Management: How Are We Doing?" *Project Management Journal,* vol. 26, no. 4 (December 1995), pp. 29–37.

12. Paul C. Dinsmore, "You Get What You Pay For," *PM Network,* vol. 12, no. 2 (1998), pp. 21–22.

13. For a description of this method, see H. H. House and L. P. Price, "The Return Map: Tracking Product Teams," *Harvard Business Review* (January–February 1991), pp. 37–46.

14. See, for example, K. E. Romanoff, "The Ten Commandments of Performance Management," *Personnel,* vol. 66, no. 1 (1989), pp. 24–26; Gary P. Latham and K. N. Wexley, *Increasing Productivity through Performance Appraisal,* 2nd ed. (Reading, MA: Addison-Wesley, 1994); and H. H. Myere, E. A. Kay, and J. R. P. French, Jr., "Split Role in Performance Appraisal," *Harvard Business Review* 43 (1965), pp. 123–29.

15. For a review of different performance appraisal methods, see Stephen J. Carroll and Craig E. Schneier, *Performance Appraisal and Review Systems* (New York: Scott Foresman & Co., 1982); J. Smither, *Performance Appraisal: State of the Art Methods for Performance Management* (San Francisco: Jossey-Bass, 1998); and Gary P. Latham and K. N. Wexley, reference cited.

16. Adapted from Brian O'Reilly, "360 Feedback Can Change Your Life," *Fortune* (October 17, 1994), pp. 93–100; and Robert Hoffman, "Ten Reasons You Should Be Using 360 Degree Feedback," *HRMagazine* (April 1995), pp. 82–85.

CASE

Maximum Megahertz Project

Olaf Gundersen, the CEO of Wireless Telecom Company, is in a quandary. Last year he accepted the Maximum Megahertz Project suggested by six up-and-coming young R&D corporate stars. Although Olaf did not truly understand the technical importance of the project, the creators of the project needed only $600,000, so it seemed like a good risk. Now the group is asking for $800,000 more and a six-month extension on a project that is already four months behind. However, the team feels confident they can turn things around. The project manager and project team feel that if they hang in there a little longer they will be able to overcome the roadblocks they are encountering—especially those that reduce power, increase speed, and use a new technology battery. Other managers familiar with the project hint that the power pack problem might be solved, but "the battery problem will never be solved." Olaf believes he is locked into this project; his gut feeling tells him the project will never materialize, and he should get out. John, his human resource manager, suggested bringing in a consultant to axe the project. Olaf is thinking maybe he should do that on this project if it needs to be terminated.

Olaf decided to call his friend, Dawn O'Connor, the CEO of an accounting software company. He asked her, "What do you do when project costs and deadlines escalate drastically? How do you handle doubtful projects?" Her response was, "Let another project manager look at the project. Ask: 'If you took over this project tomorrow, could you bring the project in on time and within budget with the extended time and additional money?' If the answer is no, I call my top management team together and have them review the doubtful project in relation to other projects in our project portfolio." Olaf feels this is good advice.

Unfortunately the Maximum Megahertz Project is not an isolated example. Over the last five years there have been three projects that were never completed. "We just seemed to pour more money into them, even though we had a pretty good idea the projects were dying. The cost of those projects was high; those resources could have been better used on other projects." Olaf wonders, "Do we ever learn from our mistakes? How can we develop a process that catches errant projects early? More importantly, how do we ease a project manager and team off an errant project without embarrassment?" Olaf certainly does not want to lose the six bright stars on the Maximum Megahertz Project.

Olaf is contemplating how his growing telecommunications company should deal with the problem of identifying projects that should be terminated early, how to allow good managers to make mistakes without public embarrassment, and how they all can learn from their mistakes.

Give Olaf a plan of action for the future that attacks the problem. Be specific and provide examples that relate to Wireless Telecom Company.

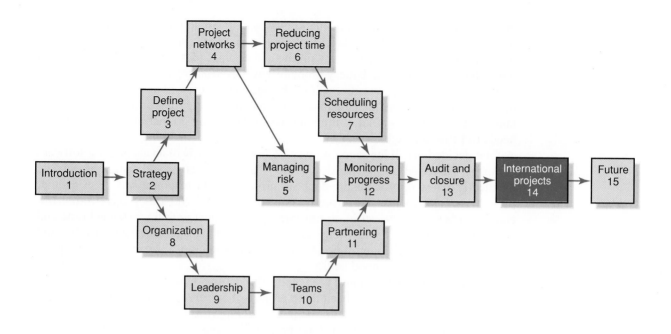

International Projects

Assessing the Motivation for International Projects
Environmental Factors
Project Site Selection
Cross-Cultural Considerations: A Closer Look
Selection and Training for International Projects
Summary

CHAPTER FOURTEEN

International Projects

The principal benefit of living abroad is that it enables us to get glimpses of ourselves as others see us and to realize that others' views are more accurate than ours. Progress begins with grasping the truth about ourselves, however unpleasant it may be.[1]
—Russel Ackoff

Projects are frequently classified as domestic, overseas, foreign, or global. A domestic project is one performed in its native country for a resident firm (a construction firm building a bridge in its state). An overseas project is one executed in a foreign country for a native firm (a Swedish company building a truck factory in the United States for their native company). A foreign project is executed in a foreign country for a foreign firm (a U.S. firm developing an information system in Malaysia for Malaysian banks). A global project consists of teams formed from professionals spanning multiple countries, continents, and cultures with their work integrated for the entire enterprise (e.g., multinational enterprise developing a global distribution system). Global teams are a crisscross of functions, work locale, markets, culture, and products. Today, these distinctions become blurred as the world economy and organizations become more integrated.

This chapter targets the international project manager who must resettle in a foreign environment to manage the project. These project managers typically face a difficult set of problems—for example, absence from home, friends, and sometimes family; personal risks; missed career opportunities; foreign language, culture, and laws; adverse conditions. Of course there are positives—for example, increased income, increased responsibilities, career opportunities, foreign travel, new lifetime friends. How the international project manager approaches and handles the project problems encountered in the host country often determines the success or failure of a project.

There is no generally accepted framework or road map for project managers given international assignments. Few guidelines exist for project managers working in environments far removed from past experiences and comfort zones. Nonetheless, as companies continue to become more globally focused, project managers who seek a challenge, who are willing to work under unusual conditions, who are flexible, and who view the trend as an opportunity will find the opportunities and rewards are exciting and growing exponentially. Project managers in the new millennium may spend most of their career in foreign countries working with foreign organizations.

This chapter focuses on five major issues surrounding the management of international projects. The first is the importance of understanding the forces that motivate

433

organizations to send people abroad to work on projects. Second, major environmental factors that impact project selection and implementation are briefly highlighted. Third, an example of how organizations decide where to expand globally is provided. Fourth, the challenge of working in a strange and foreign culture is addressed. Finally, how companies select and train professionals for international projects is discussed. Although by no means comprehensive, this chapter attempts to provide a solid understanding of the major issues and challenges confronting the international project manager.

ASSESSING THE MOTIVATION FOR INTERNATIONAL PROJECTS

Project managers need to have a keen understanding of their firm's competitive position in its global industry. Assessing the firm's strengths, weaknesses, available resources, and management's attitude toward growth can be used to motivate project stakeholders. Typical questions a project manager might explore include the following:

- Why is the firm looking globally?
- Does the firm have inadequate core competencies requiring an alliance or merger project?
- Is demand growing in other developing nations so that a global presence is necessary to succeed?
- How do past success factors match with global ventures?
- Are financial resources adequate? Is financing available at home or abroad?
- Are the board of directors and senior management committed to this global venture?
- What is the firm's level of experience with multicultural projects?
- Do the risk levels for this project match the firm's profile for risk?

There are many other situational questions that will be directly linked to a specific project and that need answers. Answers to macro questions such as those just suggested provide a view of the forces pushing the firm to select and implement a specific project. A project manager who understands the overall picture and the role and importance of her project will be better prepared to tackle the global project. An additional factor that will help the project manager gain perspective for her project is the major criteria used by the firm to select their specific project. This total perspective should clarify the project objectives, provide a basis for informing host-country nationals of the background and intent of the project, and serve as a foundation for motivating project stakeholders.

ENVIRONMENTAL FACTORS

The major challenge international project managers face is the reality that what works at home may not work in a foreign environment. Too often project managers impose practices, assumed to be superior, from their home country on host-country nationals without questioning applicability to the new environment. Although there are similarities between domestic and international projects, it is a fact that good management practices vary across nations and cultures. It is these differences that can turn an international project into a nightmare. If potential international project managers have a keen awareness of differences in the host country's environment from their own domestic environment, dangers and obstacles of the global project can be reduced or avoided. There are several basic factors in the host country's environment that may al-

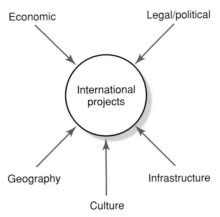

FIGURE 14–1 Environmental Factors
Affecting International Projects

ter how projects will be implemented: legal/political, geographical, economic, infrastructure, and culture (see Figure 14–1).

Legal/Political

Expatriate project managers should operate within the laws and regulations of the host country. Political stability and local laws strongly influence how projects will be implemented. Typically, these laws favor protection of local workers, suppliers, and environment. For example, how much control will be imposed from government agencies? What is the attitude of federal and state bureaucracies toward regulations and approval policies that can cause project delays? How much government interference or support can one expect? For example, an expatriate project manager based in Ho Chi Minh City observed:

> There is a common saying among the barflies about doing business in Vietnam: "The government interprets the law for its friends, and applies the law to strangers." Vietnam is no place for strangers to do business. The foreign investment law is tailored to approve investments based on the government's view of how a company and its project will further certain economic and social objectives.[2]

The constraints imposed by national and local laws need to be identified and adhered to. Are local ecological laws restrictive? Will manufacturing a new product in a computer chip plant require exporting toxic waste materials? What are the pollution standards? How will labor laws affect the use of indigenous workers to complete the project? Given that laws that affect business vary widely across countries, qualified legal assistance is essential.

Political stability is another key factor in deciding to implement a project in a foreign country. What are the chances that there will be a change in the party in power during the project? Are the tax provisions and government regulations stable or subject to change with the winds of political change? How are laws made, and what is the past record of fairness? How are labor unions treated in the political realm? Does labor unrest exist? Is there a chance for a coup d'état?

Crime is another factor. The growing presence of the Russian Mafia has discouraged many foreign firms from setting up operations in the former Soviet Union. International terrorism is a fact of life in today's world. American and other foreign businesses operate under the threat of attack by extremist groups. Security precautions are a major cost consideration not only in dollars and cents but also in the psychological well-being of personnel sent abroad.

Geography

One factor that is often underestimated until project personnel actually arrive at a foreign destination is the geography of the country. Imagine what it is like to deplane from a modern aircraft and encounter the 105-degree heat and 90 percent humidity of Jakarta, Indonesia, or three feet of fresh snow and –25-degree temperatures in Kokkla, Finland. Whether it is the wind, the rain, the heat, the jungle, or the desert, more than one project manager has asserted that their greatest challenge was overcoming the "elements." Mother Nature cannot be ignored.

The planning and implementation of a project must take into account the impact the country's geography will have on the project. For example, a salvage operation off the coast of Greenland can only be scheduled one month out of the year because the waterway is frozen over during the remainder of the year. Construction projects in Southeast Asia have to accommodate the monsoon season when rainfall can be as high as 50 inches per month. Geography does not just affect outdoor projects. It can have an indirect effect on "indoor" projects. For example, one information systems specialist reported that his performance on a project in Northern Sweden declined due to sleep deprivation. He attributed his problems to the 20 hours of daylight this part of the world experiences during summer months. Finally, extreme weather conditions can make extraordinary demands on equipment. Projects can grind to a halt because of equipment breakdown under the brunt of the elements. Working under extreme conditions typically requires special equipment, which increases the costs and complexity of the project.

Before beginning a project in a foreign land, project planners and managers need to study carefully the unique characteristics of the geography of that country. They need to factor into project plans and schedules such items as climate, seasons, altitude, and natural geographical obstacles.

Economic

How business is conducted in the host country can influence project success. Basic economic factors in foreign countries and regions influence choices of site selection and how business will be conducted for potential projects. The gross domestic product (GDP) of a country suggests the level of development of a country. A faltering economy may indicate fewer sources of capital funding. For example, changes in protectionist strategies of a host country, such as import quotas and tariffs, can quickly alter the viability of projects. Other factors such as balance of payments, currency fluctuations, hyperinflation, population growth, education level of workforce, and market size can influence project choices and operations. For example, the economic downturn in Southeast Asia during the late 1990s saw local economies in Thailand, Malaysia, and Indonesia being devastated by inflation rates in excess of 60 percent. A company can protect against currency fluctuations by hedging or tying costs to a strong currency such as the U.S. dollar, British pound, or Euro. Still, the social upheaval caused by such dramatic economic events cannot be underestimated.

Bartering is a form of compensation that is still used by some countries and organizations. For example, one project in Africa was paid in goat skins. The goat skins were eventually sold to an Italian manufacturer of gloves. Another project along the Caspian Sea was paid for in oil. There is a small group of firms that specialize in bartering for project contractors. These intermediaries charge a commission to sell the

Snapshot from Practice
THE FILMING OF *APOCALYPSE NOW*

In February 1976, Francis Ford Coppola took his Hollywood film crew to the Philippines to shoot *Apocalypse Now,* a film adaptation of Joseph Conrad's *Heart of Darkness* within the context of the Vietnam conflict. The Philippines was chosen because the terrain was similar to Vietnam's, and the government was willing to rent its helicopter force for the movie. At the time, the U.S. military was unwilling to cooperate on a film about Vietnam. An additional advantage was cheap labor. Coppola was able to hire more than 300 laborers at $1 to $3 per day to construct elaborate production sets, including an impressive Cambodian temple. *Apocalypse Now* was scheduled for 16 weeks of shooting at a budget of $12 to $14 million.

Months earlier, George Lucas, of *Star Wars* fame, warned Coppola against filming the movie in the Philippines. He said, "It's one thing to go over there for three weeks with five people and scrounge some footage with the Filipino Army, but if you go over there with a big Hollywood production, the longer you stay the more in danger you are of getting sucked into the swamp." His words turned out to be prophetic.

A civil war was going on between government forces and communist rebels. Shooting was repeatedly interrupted because the Philippine military ordered their helicopter pilots to leave the set and fly to the mountains to fight the rebels.

In May 1976, a typhoon struck the Philippine Islands, destroying most of the movie sets. The film team was forced to shut down production and returned to the United States for two months.

The lead character was played by Martin Sheen, who suffered a serious heart attack under the stress and heat of the filming and had to return to the United States. Coppola scrambled to film the scenes that did not required Sheen, but eventually production came to a standstill until Sheen's return nine weeks later.

The entire project proved to be a traumatic experience for Coppola, who had enjoyed Academy Award success with his previous *Godfather* movies, "There were times when I thought I was going to die, literally, from the inability to move the problems I had. I would go to bed at four in the morning in a cold sweat."

Film production ended in May 1977 after more than 200 days of shooting. The final cost was about $30 million. To date, *Apocalypse Now* has earned more than $150 million throughout the world.[3]

bartered goods (e.g., oil) for the contractor. However, dealing with commodities can be a risky enterprise.

Skills, educational level, and labor supply prevalent in a host country can determine the choice of a project site. Is project selection driven by low wage levels or availability of technically skilled talent? For example, you can hire three computer programmers in India for the price of one programmer in the United States. Conversely, many high-tech companies are willing to endure the additional expense of setting up joint projects in Switzerland and Germany to take advantage of their engineering prowess.

Infrastructure

Infrastructure refers to a country's or community's ability to provide the services required for a project. Infrastructure needs for a project could be communication, transportation, power, technology, and education systems. For example, developing an electric steel plant to be near a major market requires a reliable supply of electric power. If reliable power is not sufficient, other alternatives need to be considered. Software projects across borders are common today; however, they depend on reliable telecommunication networks. These networks simplify and facilitate project coordination and management among project stakeholders in different locations. If the project depends on a high ratio of vendor suppliers, good roads, and other transportation modes such as air and seaports, a good infrastructure will be imperative.

An example of a project that failed to take into account the needs and infrastructure of the host nation involved a U.S. company that was awarded the contract for building a hospital in an African nation. The local African officials wanted a "low-tech" health care facility that would take local traditions into consideration. Because their relatives generally accompanied patients, space had to be provided for them, too. Electricity was not reliably supplied, and it was doubtful whether well-educated doctors would want to spend careers out in the countryside away from the city. Therefore, the locals wanted a hospital for basic care with minimum technology. The construction company doing the building, on the other hand, had a preconceived notion of what a hospital should be and was not going to be accused of building a second-rate facility. It built a modern hospital that could have stood in any U.S. city. The building was completed; however, even after several years it was not used because the electricity was not sufficient, the air-conditioning could not be used, and doctors refused to live in the rural area.

Organizations need to consider the needs of the families of personnel they send overseas. Will the facilities and living conditions for the expatriate families place an undue hardship on families? Will schooling for children be available? The welfare and comfort of expatriate families play an important role in retaining good project managers and promoting their peak performance.

Culture

Visiting project managers must accept and respect the customs, values, philosophies, and social standards of their host country. Global managers recognize that if the customs and social cultural dimensions of the host country are not accommodated, projects will not succeed. Too many project audits and final reports of international projects reflect challenges and problems linked to cultural differences.

For most project managers, the biggest difference in managing an international project is operating in a national culture where things are done differently. For example, most developed nations use the same project management techniques (CPM, risk analysis, trade-off analysis). However, how activity work is performed can be very different in the host country.

Will English be the operating language, or will the project manager need to be fluent in the foreign language? Will translation services be available and sufficient? Communication problems—because of language differences—often become a major problem in carrying out even simple tasks. Although the use of translators can help tremendously, their use does not solve the communication problem completely because something is lost in translation.

Will religious factors influence the project? For example, religious factors touched the spouse of a Scandinavian project manager responsible for building a water desalination plant from sea water in a Middle East country. She was restricted to the living compound for families of foreign guest workers. Going outside the compound to a nearby city meant covering her head, arms, and legs and being accompanied by another woman or, preferably, a man. A physical altercation in the city concerning her clothing was traumatic for her. She left the country and returned home. Her husband requested a transfer back home three months later. The loss of the original project manager from the project required the assigned project manager to establish relationships with the project team and host country's nationals to get the project moving smoothly again. Of all the factors, working within the host culture is most often the greatest challenge for project managers. It will be dealt with in detail later in this chapter.

PROJECT SITE SELECTION

As the project manager studies the factors contributing to site selection, he will see that inherent in all of these factors is the risk level senior management and directors are willing to accept for the potential rewards of a successful international project. One approach for the project manager to digest, clarify, and understand the factors leading to the selection of a specific project is to use a risk matrix similar to those found in Chapter 5. The major difference lies in the selection of the risk factors for different project sites.

Figure 14–2 presents a truncated matrix for project site selection of the construction of a laser printer factory in Singapore, India, or Ireland. In this example, political stability, worker skill and supply, culture compatibility, infrastructure, government support, and product-to-market advantage were the major assessment factors. Each project site is compared against each factor. Figure 14–3 depicts a further breakdown

FIGURE 14–2 Assessment Matrix Project Site Selection

Score legend

5 = excellent
3 = acceptable
1 = poor

	Political stability	Worker skill, supply	Culture compatibility	Infrastructure	Government support	Product-to-market advantage
Singapore	5	4	4	4	4	3
India	3	4	3	3	3	3
Ireland	5	4	5	5	5	5

FIGURE 14–3 Evaluation Matrix Breakdown for Infrastructure

Score legend

5 = excellent
3 = acceptable
1 = poor

	Transportation	Educated workforce	Utilities	Telecommunications	Vendor suppliers
Singapore	5	4	5	5	4
India	3	4	4	4	2
Ireland	5	4	5	5	5

of the infrastructure evaluation factor. In this example, transportation, educated workforce, utilities, telecommunications, and vendor suppliers are considered important to evaluating the infrastructure for each site. The scores given in Figure 14–3 are used to assign values to the infrastructure factor of the assessment matrix, Figure 14–2. In this project, Ireland was the choice. Clearly, Singapore and Ireland were very close in terms of infrastructure and several other factors. However, the major assessment factor of using Ireland to access the EEC (product-to-market advantage) turned the decision.

Given the macro-economic factors, the firm's strategic posture toward global projects, and the major considerations for selecting this project, it is imperative the project manager quickly become sensitized to the foreign cultural factors that can spell project success or failure.

CROSS-CULTURAL CONSIDERATIONS: A CLOSER LOOK

The concept of culture was introduced in Chapter 8 as referring to the unique personality of a particular firm. More specifically, culture was defined as a system of shared norms, beliefs, values, and customs that bind people together, creating shared meaning and a unique identity. *Culture* is a concept created for descriptive purposes and depends on the group that is the focus of attention. For example, within a global context culture can refer to certain regions (i.e., Europeans, Arabs), to specific nations (i.e., French, Thai), or to certain ethnic or religious groups (i.e., Kurds, African-Americans). This chapter looks at national cultures; we freely recognize that many cultural characteristics are borderless and that there is considerable variation within any one country. Still, national cultures provide a useful anchor for understanding different habits, customs, and values around the world.

Right or wrong, Americans have a reputation for not being able to work effectively in foreign cultures. (When we use the term "American," we are referring to people from the United States; we apologize to our friends in Canada and Central and South America.) In the 1960s, the term "Ugly American" encapsulated the apparent indifference of Americans to native cultures when working or traveling abroad. Americans are often criticized for being parochial; that is, they view the world solely through their own eyes and perspectives. People with a parochial perspective do not recognize that other people have different ways of living and working effectively. American parochial attitudes probably reflect the huge domestic market of the United States, the geographic isolation of the United States, and the reality that English is becoming the international business language in many parts of the world.

It is important that Americans working on international projects anticipate cultural differences. Take, for example, a project manager from a large North American construction company who was given responsibility to select a site for the design and construction of a large fish processing plant in a West African country. The manager assessed potential sites according to the availability of reliable power, closeness to transportation, nearness to the river for access of fishing boats from the Atlantic Ocean, proximity to main markets, and availability of housing and people for employment. After evaluating alternative sites, the project manager chose the optimum location. Just prior to requesting bids from local contractors for some of the site preparation, the manager discovered, in talking to the contractors, that the site was located on ground considered sacred by the local people, who believed this site was the place where their gods resided. None of the local people upon whom the project manager was depending for staff would ever consider working there! The project manager quickly revised his choice and relocated the site. In this case, he was lucky that the cultural gaffe was discovered prior to construction. Too often these errors are realized only after a project is completed.[4]

Some argue that Americans have become less parochial. International travel, immigration, movies, and the popularity of such international events as the Olympics have made more Americans sensitive to cultural differences. While Americans may be more worldly, there is still a tendency for them to believe that American cultural values and ways of doing things are superior to all others. This ethnocentric perspective is reflected in wanting to conduct business only on their terms and stereotyping other countries as lazy, corrupt, or inefficient. Americans need to make a serious effort to appreciate other ways of approaching work and problems in other countries.

Finally, American project managers have earned a reputation abroad for being very good at understanding technology but not good at understanding people.[5] As one Indonesian engineer put it, "Americans are great at solving technical problems, but they tend to ignore the people factor." For example, Americans tend to underestimate the importance that relationship building plays in conducting business in other countries. Americans have a tendency to want to get down to work and let friendships evolve in the course of their work. In most other cultures just the opposite is true. Before a foreigner works with you, they want to get to know you as a person. Trust is not established by credentials but rather evolves from personal interaction. Business deals often require a lengthy and elaborate courtship. For example, it may take five to eight meetings before Arab managers are even willing to discuss business details.

Two of the biggest adjustments Americans typically have to make in working abroad is adapting to the general pace of life and the punctuality of people. In America "time is money," and a premium is placed on working quickly. Other cultures do not share Americans' sense of urgency and are accustomed to a much slower pace of life. They can't understand why Americans are always in such a hurry. Punctuality varies across cultures. For example, Americans will generally tolerate someone being 5 to 10 minutes late. Conversely, among Peruvians, the period before an apology or explanation for being late is expected might be 45 minutes to an hour!

While working on multicultural projects, managers sometimes encounter ethical dilemmas that are culturally bound. For example, the 1999 Olympic site selection scandal featured the sordid details of committee members peddling their votes for a wide range of gifts (i.e., university scholarships for their children, extravagant trips). In many societies such "bribes"or "tributes" are expected and the only way to conduct meaningful business. Moreover, many cultures will not grant a female project manager the same respect they will a male project manager. Should U.S. management increase project risk or violate its own sex-discrimination policy?

These cultural differences are just the tip of the iceberg. There are numerous "How to Do Business in . . . " books written by people who have traveled and worked abroad. Although these books may lack rigor, they typically do a good job of identifying local customs and common mistakes made by outsiders. On the other hand, anthropologists have made significant contributions to our understanding of why and how the cultures of societies are different (see the accompanying Research Highlight). Students of international project management are encouraged to study these works to gain a deeper understanding of the root causes of cultural diversity.[6]

So what can be said to prepare people to work on international projects? The world is too diverse to do justice in one chapter to all the cultural variations managers are likely to encounter when working on international projects. Instead, a sample of some of these differences will be highlighted by discussing working on projects in four

Anthropologists Kluckhohn and Strodtbeck assert that cultural variations reflect how different societies have responded to common issues or problems throughout time[7] (see Figure 14–4). Five of the issues featured in their comparative framework are discussed here.

- *Relation to nature*—This issue reflects how people relate to the natural world around them and to the supernatural. Should people dominate their environment, live in harmony with it, or be subjugated to it? North Americans generally strive to harness nature's forces and change them as they need. Other societies, as in India, strive to live in harmony with nature. Still other societies see themselves at the mercy of physical forces and/or subject to the will of a supreme being. Life in this context is viewed as predetermined, preordained, or an exercise in chance.
- *Time orientation*—Does the culture focus on the past, present, or future? For example, many European countries focus on the past and emphasize maintaining tradition. North Americans, on the other hand, are less concerned with tradition and tend to focus on the present and near future. Paradoxically, Japanese society, while rich with tradition, has a much longer time horizon.
- *Activity orientation*—This issue refers to a desirable focus of behavior. Some cultures emphasize "being" or living in the moment. This orientation stresses experiencing life and seeking immediate gratification. Other cultures emphasize "doing" and emphasize postponing immediate gratification for greater accomplishment. A third alternative is the "control" orientation, where people restrain their desires by detaching themselves from objects. The activity dimension affects how people approach work and leisure and the extent to which work-related concerns pervade their lives. It is reflected in the age-old question, "Do we live to work or work to live?"
- *Basic nature of people*—Does a culture view people as good, evil, or some mix of these two? In many Third World countries, people see themselves as basically honest and trustworthy. Conversely, some Mediterranean cultures have been characterized as taking a rather evil view of human nature. North Americans are somewhere in between. They see people as basically good but stay on guard so as not to be taken advantage of.
- *Relationships among people*—This issue concerns the responsibility one has for others. Americans, for instance, tend to be highly individualistic and believe everyone should take care of him- or herself. In contrast, many Asian societies emphasize concern for the group or community he or she is a member of. A third variation is hierarchical, which is similar to the group except that in these societies groups are hierarchically ranked, and membership is essentially stable over time. This is a characteristic of aristocratic society and caste systems.

The Kluckhohn and Strodtbeck framework provides a basis for a deeper understanding of cultural differences. At the same time, they warn that not all members of a culture practice the same behavior all the time, and, as in the United States, there is likely to be considerable variation within a given culture.

FIGURE 14–4 Kluckhohn-Strodtbeck's Cross-Cultural Framework

Cultural issue	Variations		
Relationship to nature	Domination	Harmony	Subjugation
Time orientation	Past	Present	Future
Activity orientation	Being	Doing	Controlling
Nature of people	Good	Evil	Mixed
Relationships among people	Individualist	Group	Hierarchical

Note: The line indicates where the United States tends to fall along these issues.

Snapshot from Practice
PROJECT MANAGEMENT X-FILES

Americans tend to discount the significance of luck and believe that good fortune is generally a result of hard work. In other cultures, luck takes on greater significance and has supernatural ramifications. For example, in many Asian cultures certain numbers are considered lucky, while others are unlucky. In Hong Kong the numbers 7, 3, and especially 8 (which sounds like the word for prosperity) are considered lucky, while the number 4 is considered unlucky (because it is pronounced like the word "death"). Hong Kong businesspeople go to great lengths to avoid the number 4. For example, there is no fourth floor in office and hotel buildings. Business executives have been known to reject ideal sites in heavily congested Hong Kong because the address would contain the number 4. They pay premium prices for suitable sites containing addresses with the lucky numbers. Likewise, Hong Kong business managers avoid scheduling important events on the fourth day of each month and prefer to arrange critical meetings on the eighth day.

Hong Kong is also a place where the ancient art of *Feng shui* (literally "wind water") is practiced. This involves making sure a site and buildings are aligned in harmony with the earth's energy forces so that the location will be propitious. Feng shui practitioners are often called in on construction projects to make sure that the building is aligned correctly on the site. In some cases, the technical design of the building is changed to conform to the recommendations of such experts. Similarly, Feng shui experts have been known to be called in when projects are experiencing problems. Their recommendations may include repositioning the project manager's desk or hanging up mirrors to deflect the flow of unharmonious influences away from the building or site of the project.

In cultures where luck is believed to play a role in business, people who discount luck may not only insult the luck seekers, they may risk being thought negligent in not paying enough attention to what is viewed as a legitimate business concern.

different countries: Mexico, France, Saudi Arabia, and China. We apologize to our readers outside the United States because briefings are presented from the viewpoint of a U.S. project manager working in these countries. Still, in an effort not to be too ethnocentric, we present a fifth scenario for foreign project managers assigned to working in the United States. Although by no means exhaustive, these briefings provide a taste of what it is like to work in and with people from these countries.

Working in Mexico

America developed historically in an environment where it was important for strangers to be able to get along, interact, and do business. On the American frontier almost everyone was a stranger, and people had to both cooperate and keep their distance. The New England Yankee sentiment that "Good fences make good neighbors" expresses this American cultural value well. Conversely, Mexico developed historically in an environment where the only people to trust were family and close friends—and by extension, people who were known to those whom you knew well. As a consequence, personal relationships dominate all aspects of Mexican business. While Americans are generally taught not to do business with friends, Mexicans and other Latin Americans are taught to do business with no one but friends.

The significance of personal relationships has created a *compadre* system in which Mexicans are obligated to give preference to relatives and friends when hiring, contracting, procuring, and sharing business opportunities. North Americans often complain that such practices contribute to inefficiency in Mexican firms. While this may or may not be the case, efficiency is prized by Americans, while Mexicans place a higher value on friendship.

Mexicans tend to perceive Americans as being "cold." They also believe that most Americans look down on them. Among the most effective things an American can do to prevent being seen as a typical *Gringo* is to take the time and effort in the beginning of a working relationship to really get to know Mexican counterparts. Because family is all important to Mexicans, a good way for developing a personal relationship is exchanging information about each other's family. Mexicans will often gauge people's trustworthiness by the loyalty and attention they devote to their family.

The *mañana* syndrome reflects another cultural difference between Americans and Mexicans. Mexicans have a different concept of time than Americans do. Mexicans feel confined and pressured when given deadlines; they prefer open-ended schedules. They generally consider individuals to be more important than sticking to a schedule. If a friend drops in at work, most Mexicans will stop and talk, regardless of how long it takes, and even if chatting makes their work late.

Finally, as in many other cultures, Mexicans do not share Americans' confidence that they control their own destiny. While Americans are taught, "When the going gets tough, the tough get going," Mexicans are taught, "Taking action without knowing what is expected or wanted can have dangerous consequences." Mexicans tend to be more cautious and want to spend more time discussing risks and potential problems that Americans might dismiss as improbable or irrelevant.

Other useful guidelines for working with Mexicans on projects include the following:

1. Americans tend to be impersonal and practical when making arguments; Mexicans can be very passionate and emotional when arguing. They enjoy a lively debate.
2. Where Americans tend to use meetings as the place to work things out publicly, Mexicans tend to see meetings as the place where persons with authority ratify what has been decided during informal private discussions.
3. While Mexicans can be emotional, they tend to shy away from any sort of direct confrontation or criticism. A long silence often indicates displeasure or disagreement.
4. Although Mexicans tend to prefer a more distant relationship between workers and managers than Americans do, they still value managers who treat them in a friendly but dignified manner.

5. Titles are extremely important in Mexico and are always used when a person is introducing him- or herself or being introduced. Pay as much attention to remembering a person's title as to remembering their name.[8]

Working in France

Some Americans consider the French the most difficult to work with among Europeans. This feeling probably stems from a reflection of the French culture, which is quite different from that in the United States.

In France one's social class is very important. Social interactions are constrained by class standing, and during their lifetime most French people do not encounter much change in social status. Unlike an American, who through hard work and success can move from the lowest economic stratum to the highest, a successful French person might, at best, climb one or two rungs up the social ladder. Additionally, the French are very status conscious and like to provide signs of this status, such as knowledge of literature and arts; a well-designed, tastefully decorated house; and a high level of education.

The French tend to admire or be fascinated with people who disagree with them; in contrast, Americans are more attracted to those who agree with them. As a result, the French are accustomed to conflict and, during negotiations, accept the fact that some positions are irreconcilable and must be accepted as such. Americans, on the other hand, tend to believe that conflicts can be resolved if both parties make an extra effort and are willing to compromise. Also, the French often determine a person's trustworthiness based on their firsthand, personal evaluation of the individual's character. Americans, in contrast, tend to evaluate a person's trustworthiness on the basis of past achievements and other people's evaluations.

The French are often accused of lacking an intense work ethic. For example, many French workers frown on overtime and on average they have one of the longest vacations in the world (four to five weeks annually). On the other hand, the French enjoy a reputation for productive work, a result of the French tradition of craftsmanship. This tradition places a greater premium on quality rather than on getting things accomplished quickly.

Most French organizations tend to be highly centralized with rigid structures. As a result, it usually takes longer to carry out decisions. Because this arrangement is quite different from the more decentralized organizations in the United States, many U.S. project managers find the bureaucratic red tape a source of considerable frustration.

In countries like the United States, a great deal of motivation is derived from professional accomplishments. The French do not tend to share this same view of work. While they admire American industriousness, they believe that quality of life is what really matters. As a result they attach much greater importance to leisure time, and many are unwilling to sacrifice the enjoyment of life for a dedication to project work.

Cautions to remember with the French include these:

1. The French value punctuality. It is very important to be on time for meetings and social occasions.
2. Great importance is placed on neatness and taste. When interacting with French businesspeople, pay close attention to your own professional appearance and appear cultured and sophisticated.
3. The French can be very difficult to negotiate with. Often, they ignore facts, no

matter how convincing they may be. They can be quite secretive about their position. It is difficult to obtain information from them, even in support for their position. Patience is essential for negotiating with them.

4. French managers tend to see their work as an intellectual exercise. They do not share the American view of management as an interpersonally demanding exercise, where plans have to be constantly "sold" upward and downward using personal skills.

5. The French generally consider managers to be experts. They expect managers to give precise answers to work-related questions. To preserve their reputation, some French managers act as if they know the answers to questions even when they don't.[9]

Working in Saudi Arabia

Project management has a long tradition in Saudi Arabia and other Arab countries. Financed by oil money, European and American firms have contributed greatly to the modernization of Arab countries. Despite this tradition, foreigners often find it very hard to work on projects in Saudi Arabia. A number of cultural differences can be cited for this difficulty.

One is the Arabian view of time. In North America, it is common to use the cliché, "The early bird gets the worm." In Saudi Arabia, a favorite expression is, "Bukra insha Allah," which means, "Tomorrow if God wills," an expression that reflects the Saudis' approach to time. Unlike Westerners, who believe they control their own time, Arabs believe that Allah controls time. As a result, when Saudis commit themselves to a date in the future and fail to show up, there is no guilt or concern on their part because they have no control over time in the first place. In planning future events with Arabs, it pays to hold lead time to a week or less, because other factors may intervene or take precedence.

An associated cultural belief is that destiny depends more on the will of a supreme being than on the behavior of individuals. A higher power dictates the outcome of important events, so individual action is of little consequence. As a result, progress or the lack of progress on a project is considered more a question of fate than effort. This leads Saudis to rely less on detailed plans and schedules to complete projects than Americans do.

Another important cultural contrast between Saudi Arabians and Americans is emotion and logic. Saudis often act on the basis of emotion; in contrast, those in an Anglo culture are taught to act on logic. During negotiations, it is important not only to share the facts but also to make emotional appeals that demonstrate your suggestion is the right thing to do.

Saudis also make use of elaborate and ritualized forms of greetings and leave-takings. A businessperson may wait far past the assigned meeting time before being admitted to an Saudi office. Once there, the individual may find a host of others present; one-on-one meetings are rare. Moreover, during the meeting there may be continuous interruptions. Visitors arrive and begin talking to the host, and messengers may come in and go out on a regular basis. The businessperson is expected to take all this activity as perfectly normal and to remain composed and ready to continue discussions as soon as the host is prepared to do so.

Initial meetings are typically used to get to know the other party. Business-related discussions may not occur until the third or fourth meeting. Business meetings typically conclude with an offer of coffee or tea. This is a sign that the meeting is over and that future meetings, if there are to be any, should now be arranged.

Saudis attach a great deal of importance to status and rank. When meeting with them, defer to the senior person. It is also important never to criticize or berate anyone publicly. This causes the individual to lose face; the same is true for the person who makes these comments. Mutual respect is expected at all times.

Other useful guidelines for working in an Arab culture such as Saudi Arabia include the following:

1. It is important never to display feelings of superiority because this makes the other party feel inferior. No matter how well someone does something, the individual should let the action speak for itself and not brag or draw attention to himself.

2. A lot of what gets done is a result of going through administrative channels in the country. It is often difficult to sidestep a lot of this red tape, and efforts to do so can be regarded as disrespect for legal and governmental institutions.

3. Connections are extremely important in conducting business. More important people get fast service from less important people. Close relatives take absolute priority; nonrelatives are kept waiting.

4. Patience is critical to the success of business negotiations. Time for deliberations should be built into all negotiations to prevent a person from giving away too much in an effort to reach a quick settlement.

5. Important decisions are usually made in person and not by correspondence or telephone. While Saudis seek counsel from many people, the ultimate power to make a decision rests with the person at the top, and this individual relies heavily on personal impressions, trust, and rapport.[10]

Working in China

In recent years the People's Republic of China (PRC, or China, for short) has slowly moved away from isolation to encourage more business with the rest of the world. While China holds tremendous promise, many Western firms have found working on projects in China to be a long, grueling process that often results in failure. One of the primary reasons for problems is the failure to appreciate Chinese culture.

Chinese society, like those of Japan and Korea, is influenced by the teachings of Confucius (551–478 B.C.). Unlike America, which relies on legal institutions to regulate behavior, in Confucian societies the primary deterrent against improper or illegal behavior is shame or loss of face. Face is more than simply reputation. There is a Chinese saying that, "Face is like the bark of a tree; without its bark, the tree dies." Loss of face not only brings shame to individuals but also to family members. A member's actions can cause shame for the entire family, hampering that family from working effectively in Chinese society.

In China "whom you know is more important than what you know." The term *guanxi* refers to personal connections with appropriate authorities or individuals. China observers argue that *guanxi* is critical for working with the Chinese. Many outsiders criticize *guanxi,* considering it to be like nepotism where decisions are made regarding contracts or problems based on family ties or connections instead of an objective assessment of ability.

Many believe that the quickest way to build *guanxi* relationships is through tendering favors. Gift-giving, entertainment at lavish banquets, questionable payments, and overseas trips are common. While Westerners see this as nothing short of bribery, the Chinese consider it essential for good business. Another common method for outsiders to acquire *guanxi* is by hiring local intermediaries, who use their connections to create contacts with Chinese officials and businesspeople.

In dealing with the Chinese, you must realize they are a collective society in which people pride themselves on being a member of a group. For this reason, you should never single out a Chinese for specific praise because this is likely to embarrass the individual in front of his peers. At the same time, you should avoid the use of "I" because it conveys that the speaker is drawing attention to himself or herself.

Chinese do not appreciate loud, boisterous behavior, and when speaking to each other they maintain a greater physical distance than is typical in America. Other cautions include the following:

1. Once the Chinese decide who and what is best, they tend to stick to their decisions. So while they may be slow in formulating a plan, once they get started they make good progress.
2. Reciprocity is important in negotiations. If Chinese give concessions, they expect some in return.
3. The Chinese tend to be less animated than Americans. They avoid open displays of affection and physical contact; they are more reticent and reserved than Americans.
4. The Chinese place less value on the significance of time and often get Americans to concede concessions by stalling.
5. In Confucian societies those in position of power and authority are obligated to assist the disadvantaged. In return they gain face and a good reputation.[11]

Working in the United States

In the world of international projects, professionals from other countries will come to the United States to manage projects. To them, the United States is a foreign assignment. They will have to adapt their management style to the new environment they find in the States.

Immigration has made the United States a melting pot of diverse cultures. While many are quick to point out the differences between North and South, Silicon Valley and Wall Street, social anthropologists have identified certain cultural characteristics that shape how many Americans conduct business and manage projects.

Mainstream Americans are motivated by achievement and accomplishment. Their identity and, to a certain extent, their self-worth are measured by what they have achieved. Foreigners are often astounded by the material wealth accumulated by Americans and the modern conveniences most Americans enjoy. They are also quick to point out that Americans appear too busy to truly enjoy what they have achieved.

Americans tend to idolize the self-made person who rises from poverty and adversity to become rich and successful. Most Americans have a strong belief that they can influence and create their future, that with hard work and initiative, they can achieve whatever they set out to do. Self-determination and pragmatism dominate their approach to business.

Although Americans like to set precise objectives, they view planning as a means and not an end. They value flexibility and are willing to deviate from plans and improvise if they believe change will lead to accomplishment. Obstacles on a project are to be overcome, not worked around. Americans think they can accomplish just about anything, given time, money, and technology.

Americans fought a revolution and subsequent wars to preserve their concept of democracy, so they resent too much control or interference, especially by governments. While more an ideal than practice, there is deep-rooted belief in American management philosophy that those people who will be affected by decisions should be involved in making decisions. Many foreign businesspeople are surprised at the amount of autonomy and decision-making authority granted to subordinates. Foreign personnel have to learn to interact with American professionals below their rank in their own organizations.

Businesspeople from different African, Asian, and Latin American countries are amazed and often somewhat distressed at the rapid pace of America. "Getting things done" is an American characteristic. Americans are very time-conscious and efficient. They expect meetings to start on time. They tinker with gadgets and technological systems, always searching for easier, better, more efficient ways of accomplishing things. American professionals are often relentless in pursuing project objectives and expect that behavior of others also.

Americans in play or business generally are quite competitive, reflecting their desire to achieve and succeed. Although the American culture contains contradictory messages about the importance of success (i.e., "It's not whether you win or lose but how you play the game" versus "nice guys finish last"), winning and being number one are clearly valued in American society. Foreigners are often surprised at how aggressively Americans approach business with adversarial attitudes toward competitors and a desire to not just meet but to exceed project goals and objectives.

Other guidelines and cautions for working with Americans on projects include:

1. More than half of U.S. women work outside the home; females have considerable opportunity for personal and professional growth, guaranteed by law. It is not uncommon to find women in key project positions. Female professionals expect to be treated as equals. Behavior tolerated in other countries would be subject to harassment laws in the States.
2. In the United States, gifts are rarely brought by visitors in a business situation.
3. Americans tend to be quite friendly and open when first meeting someone. Foreigners often mistake this strong "come-on" for the beginning of a strong reciprocal friendship. This is in contrast to many other cultures where there is more initial reserve in interpersonal relations, especially with strangers. For many foreigners, the American comes on too strong, too soon, and then fails to follow up with the implicitly promised friendship.
4. Although in comparison to the rest of the world Americans tend to be informal in greeting and dress, they are a non-contact culture (e.g., they avoid embracing in public usually) and Americans maintain certain physical/psychological distance with others (e.g., about two feet) in conversations.
5. American decision making is results oriented. Decisions tend to be based on facts and expected outcomes, not social impact.[12]

Summary Comments about Working in Different Cultures

These briefings underscore the complexity of working on international projects. It is common practice to rely on intermediaries—often natives who are foreign educated—to bridge the gap between cultures. These intermediaries perform a variety of functions. They act as translators. They use their social connections to expedite transactions and protect the project against undue interference. They are used to sidestep the touchy bribery/gift dilemma (see the accompanying Snapshot from Practice). They serve as cultural guides, helping outsiders understand and interpret the foreign culture. In today's world, there are a growing number of consulting firms that perform these functions by helping foreign clients work on projects in their country.

The international briefings also highlight the importance of project managers doing their homework and becoming familiar with the customs and habits of the host coun-

Snapshot from Practice
DEALING WITH CUSTOMS

Will corruption influence the project? Bribes are illegal in the United States, but in some countries they are they usual way to do business. For example, one American project manager in a foreign country requested that a shipment of critical project equipment be sent "overnight rush." Two days later, inquiries to the sender confirmed the materials had been delivered to the nearby airport. Further inquiries to the port found the shipment "waiting to pass customs." Locals quickly informed the American that money paid to the chief customs inspector would expedite clearance. The American project manager's response was, "I will not be held hostage. Bribes are illegal!" Two more days of calling government officials did not move the shipment from customs. The manager related his problem to a friendly businessman of the host nation at a social affair. The local businessman said he would see if he could help. The shipment arrived the next morning at 10:00 A.M. The American called his local business friend and thanked him profusely. "I owe you one." "No," replied the local. "You owe me a $50 dinner when I visit you in the States." The use of an intermediary in such situations may be the only avenue available to a manager to reduce the stress and personal conflict with the U.S. value system.

try they are going to be working in. As far as possible, the project should be managed in such a way that local-country norms and customs are honored. However, there are limits to the extent to which you should accommodate foreign cultures. *Going native* is generally not an alternative. After all, it took a Russian his entire life to learn how to be a Russian. It would be foolish to think an outsider could learn to be one in six months, two years, or perhaps ever.

The remainder of this chapter focuses on the selection and training of project personnel for international projects. But before these issues are discussed, this section concludes with a discussion of the phenomenon of culture shock, which can have a profound effect on a foreigner's performance on a project in a strange culture.

Culture Shock

> My first few weeks in Chiang Mai [Thailand] were filled with excitement. I was excited about the challenge of building a waste treatment plant in a foreign country. I was fascinated with Thai customs and traditions, the smells and sights of the night market. Soon I noticed a distinct change in my attitude and behavior. I started having problems sleeping and lacked energy. I became irritable at work, frustrated by how long things took to accomplish, and how I couldn't seem to get anything accomplished. I started staying up late at night watching CNN in my hotel room.

This engineer is experiencing what many would call "culture shock." *Culture shock* is a natural psychological disorientation that most people suffer when they move into a culture different from their own.[13] The culture shock cycle has four stages (see Figure 14–5):

1. *Honeymoon*—You start your overseas assignment with a sense of excitement. The new and the unusual are welcomed. At first it is amusing not to understand or be understood. Soon a sense of frustration begins to set in.
2. *Irritability and hostility*—Your initial enthusiasm is exhausted, and you begin to notice that differences are greater than you first imagined. You become frustrated

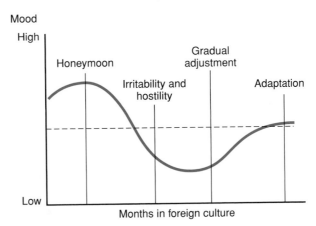

FIGURE 14–5 Culture Shock Cycle

by your inability to get things done as you are accustomed to. You begin to lose confidence in your abilities to communicate and work effectively in the different culture.

3. *Gradual adjustment*—You begin to overcome your sense of isolation and figure out how to get things done in the new culture. You acquire a new perspective of what is possible and regain confidence in your ability to work in the culture.

4. *Adaptation*—You recover from your sense of psychological disorientation and begin to function and communicate in the new culture.

Culture shock is not a disease but a natural response to immersing yourself in a new environment. Culture shock results from a breakdown in your selective perception and effective interpretation system. At a subliminal level, your senses are being bombarded by a wide variety of strange sounds, sights, and smells. At the same time, the normal assumptions you are accustomed to using in your home culture to interpret perceptions and to communicate intentions no longer apply. When this happens, whether in a business context or in normal attempts to socialize, confusion and frustration set in. The natives' behavior does not seem to make sense, and, even more importantly, your behavior does not produce expected results. Frustration occurs because you are used to being competent in such situations and now find you are unable to operate effectively.

Culture shock is generally considered a positive sign that the professional is becoming involved in the new culture instead of remaining isolated in an expatriate ghetto. The significant question is how best to manage culture shock, not how to avoid it. The key appears to be managing the stress associated with culture shock.

Stress-related culture shock takes many forms: disappointment, frustration, withdrawal, anxiety, and physiological responses such as fatigue, sleeplessness, and headaches. Stress is induced by the senses being overwhelmed by foreign stimuli and the inability to function effectively in a strange land. Stress is exacerbated when one encounters disturbing situations that, as a foreigner, are neither understood nor condoned. For example, some North Americans are appalled by the poverty in many developing countries.

There are a wide range of stress management techniques for coping with culture shock. One method does not necessarily work any better than another; success depends on the particular individual and situation involved. Some people engage in regular physical exercise programs, some practice meditation and relaxation exercises, and others find it healthy to keep a journal.

Many effective international managers create "stability zones."[14] They spend most of their time immersed in the foreign culture but then briefly retreat into an environment—a stability zone—that closely recreates home. For example, when one of the authors was living in Kraków, Poland, with his family, we would routinely go to the Polish movie houses to see American movies with Polish subtitles. The two hours spent hearing English and seeing a familiar environment on the screen had a soothing effect on everyone.

On the project, managers can reduce the stress caused by culture shock by recognizing it and modifying their expectations and behavior accordingly. They can redefine priorities and develop more realistic expectations as to what is possible. They can focus their limited energy on only the most important tasks and relish small accomplishments.

After three to six months, depending on the individual and assignment, most people come up from their culture shock "low" and begin living a more normal life in the foreign country. They talk to acquaintances from the host country and experienced outsiders from their own culture to find out how to behave and what to expect. Little by little they learn how to make sense of the new environment. They figure out when "yes" means "yes" and when it means "maybe" and when it means "no." They begin to master the language so that they can make themselves understood in day-to-day conversations.[15]

The vast majority of people eventually make the adjustment, although for some people it can take much longer than three to six months. A smaller number never recover, and their international experience turns into a nightmare. Some exhibit severe stress symptoms (e.g., alcoholism, drug abuse, nervous breakdown) and must return home before finishing their assignment.

Professionals can use project work as a bridge until they adjust to their new environment. Unfortunately, spouses who do not work do not have this advantage. When spouses are left to cope with the strange environment on their own, they often have a much more difficult time overcoming culture shock. The effect on spouses cannot be underestimated. The number one reason expatriate managers return home is that their spouses failed to adjust to the new environment.[16]

Project professionals working overseas accept that they are in a difficult situation and that they will not act as effectively as they did at home, especially in the initial stages. They recognize the need for good stress management techniques, including stability zones. They also recognize that it is not an individual problem and invest extra time and energy to help their spouse and family manage the transition. At the same time, they appreciate that their colleagues are experiencing similar problems and are sensitive to their needs. They work together to manage the stress and pull out of a culture shock low as quickly as possible.

It is somewhat ironic, but people who work on projects overseas experience culture shock twice. Many professionals experience the same kind of disorientation and stress when they return home, although it is usually less severe. For some, their current job has less responsibility and is boring compared with the challenge of their overseas assignment. For others, they have problems adjusting to changes made in the home organization while they were gone. This can be compounded by financial shock when the salary and fringe benefits they became accustomed to in the foreign assignment are now lost, and adjusting to a lower standard of living is difficult. It typically takes six months to a year before managers operate again at full effectiveness after a lengthy foreign assignment.[17]

SELECTION AND TRAINING FOR INTERNATIONAL PROJECTS

When professionals are selected for overseas projects and they do not work out, the overall costs can be staggering. Not only does the project experience a serious setback, but the reputation of the firm is damaged in the region. This is why many firms have developed formal screening procedures to help ensure the careful selection of personnel for international projects. Organizations examine a number of characteristics to determine whether an individual is suitable for overseas work. They may look for work experience with cultures other than one's own, previous overseas travel, good physical and emotional health, a knowledge of a host nation's language, and even recent immigration background or heritage. Prospective candidates and their family members are often interviewed by trained psychologists, who assess their ability to adapt and function in the new culture.

While there is growing appreciation for screening people for foreign assignments, the number one reason for selection is that the personnel assigned are the best people available for the technical challenges of the project.[18] Technical know-how takes precedence over cross-cultural sensitivity or experience. As a consequence, training is critical to fill in the cultural gaps and prepare individuals to work in a foreign land.

Training varies widely, depending on the individual, company, nature of the project, and cultures to work with. Project professionals assigned to foreign countries should have a minimal understanding of the following areas:

- Religion.
- Dress codes.
- Education system.
- Holidays—national and religious.
- Daily eating patterns.
- Family life.
- Business protocols.
- Social etiquette.
- Equal opportunity.

An example of a short-term training program is the one developed by Underwriter Laboratories, Inc., to train staff who travel to Japan to work with clients on projects. The program is designed around a series of mini-lectures that cover topics ranging from how to handle introductions to the proper way to exchange gifts to the correct way of interpreting Japanese social and business behavior. The two-day program consists of lectures, case studies, role plays, language practice, and a short test on cultural terminology; it concludes with a 90-minute question-and-answer period. At the end of the program, participants have a fundamental understanding of how to communicate with the Japanese. More importantly, they know the types of information they lack and how to go about learning more to become effective intercultural communicators.

Other training programs are more extensive. For example, Peace Corps volunteers undergo an intense two- to four-month training program in their country of service. The training includes classes on the history and traditions of the country, intensive language instruction, and cross-cultural training as well as home-stays with local families. Many companies outsource training to one of the many firms specializing in overseas and intercultural training.

Figure 14–6 attempts to link the length and type of training with the cultural fluency required to successfully complete the project.[19] Three different learning approaches are highlighted:

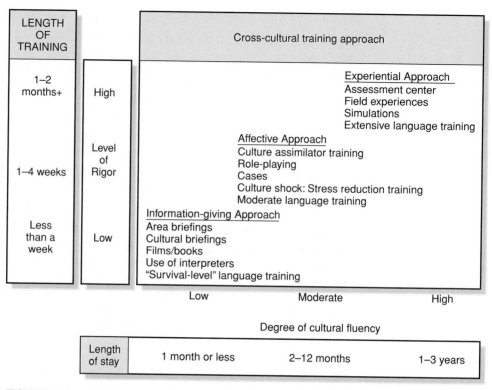

FIGURE 14–6 Relationship between Length and Rigor of Training and Cultural Fluency Required

1. The "information-giving" approach—the learning of information or skills from a lecture-type orientation.
2. The "affective approach"—the learning of information/skills that raise the affective responses on the part of the trainee and result in cultural insights.
3. The "behavioral/experiential" approach—variant of the affective approach technique that provides the trainee with realistic simulations or scenarios.

According to this framework, the length and level of training would depend on the degree of cultural fluency required to be successful. In general, the longer the person is expected to work in the foreign country, the more intensive the training should be. Length of stay should not be the only consideration; high levels of cultural fluency, and therefore more extensive training, may be required to perform short-term, intense projects. In addition, location is important. Working in Australia will likely require less cultural fluency than working on a project in Pakistan.

While English is rapidly becoming the international language for business in many parts of the world, you should not underestimate the value of being able to speak the language of the host country. At a minimum you should be able to exchange basic pleasantries in the native tongue. Most foreigners consider this a sign of respect, and even if you stumble they appreciate the effort.

In many situations translators are used to facilitate communication. While time-consuming, this is the only way to communicate with non–English-speaking personnel. Be careful in the selection of translators, and do not just assume they are competent. For example, one of the authors enlisted the help of a Polish translator to conduct a meeting with some Polish managers. After the meeting the translator, who taught English at a local university, asked if the author "had good time." I responded that I felt things went well. The translator repeated her question. Puzzled, I reaffirmed that I felt things went well. After the interchange was repeated several times, the translator finally grabbed my wrist, pointed at my watch, and asked again if I "had good time?" Doubts arose concerning the accuracy of the meeting translation!

SUMMARY

The number of international projects continues to increase, and nothing on the horizon suggests things will change in the new millennium. More and more project managers will be needed to implement international projects. There are few guidelines for the fledgling international project manager. Preparing for international projects can be enhanced through training. As a general background, potential international project managers can benefit from a basic international business course that sensitizes them to the forces of change in the global economy and to cultural differences. Learning a foreign language is also strongly recommended.

Further training specific to the host country is a very useful pre-project endeavor. The length and type of training usually depend on the duration of the project manager's assignment. Review Figure 14–3. Still, self-learning, on-the-job training, and experience are the best teachers for international project managers.

Preparing for a specific international project requires serious pre-project homework. Understanding the motivation of the firm in selecting the project and its site provides important insights. What basic political, geographic, economic, and infrastructure factors were key considerations? How will they impact the implementation of the project?

Finally, preparation and understanding the cultural differences of the host country go a long way toward making positive first impressions with the nationals and managing the project. International projects have distinct personalities. All people are not the same. Differences within and among countries and cultures are numerous and complex. Project managers need to accept these differences and treat them as real— or live with the consequences. The way we do it at home may not work in the foreign assignment. The challenge is to get the project completed on time and on budget within the cultural environment of the host country. Americans are regarded as friendly by our neighbors in the global village, but Americans are also noted to be insensitive to differences in local cultures and customs and awkward in our use of languages other than English. Although most attention in foreign projects is focused on technical efforts and their cost, the project must be carried out within the environment of the country's social customs, work practices, government controls, and religious beliefs. In most cultures, sincerity and flexibility will pay off.

REVIEW QUESTIONS

1. How do environmental factors affect project implementation?
2. What role do local intermediaries play in helping an outsider complete a project?
3. Why is it important to honor the customs and traditions of a country when working on an international project?
4. What is culture shock? What can you do to reduce the negative effects of culture shock?
5. How should you go about preparing yourself for an international project?

EXERCISES

1. Interview someone who has worked or lived in a foreign country for more than two months.
   a. What was their experience with culture shock?
   b. What did they learn about the culture of the country they lived in?
   c. What advice would they give to someone who would be working on a project in that country?

2. Try as best you can to apply the Kluckhohn-Strodtbeck cross-cultural framework to the four countries discussed in this chapter: Mexico, France, Saudi Arabia, and China. Where do you think these countries lie on each of the cultural issues?

ENDNOTES

1. Russel L. Ackoff, *Ackoff's Fables: Irreverent Reflections on Business and Bureaucracy* (New York: Wiley, 1991), p. 221.

2. Micahel J. Scown, "Managers Journal: Barstool Advice for the Vietnam Investor," *Asian Wall Street Journal* (July 15, 1993).

3. Adapted from the documentary, *Hearts of darkness, a Filmmaker's Apocalypse* (1997).

4. This incident was cited in Henry W. Lane and Joseph J. DiStefano, *International Project Management,* 2nd ed. (Boston: PWS-Kent Publishing, 1992), p. 27.

5. Phillip B. Arms and Elmer Lucas, "How Do Foreign Clients Really See American Project Managers?" *Proceedings of the 1978 Annual Seminar/Symposium on Project Management* (Newtown Square, PA: Project Management Institute, 1978), pp. IIK-1–7.

6. See for example, Gerte Hofstede, *Cultures Consequences: International Difference in Work-Related Values* (Beverly Hills, CA: Sage Publishing, 1980); Edward T. Hall, *The Silent Language* (New York: Doubleday, 1959); F. Kluckhohn and F. L. Strodtbeck, *Variations in Value Orientations* (Evanston, IL: Row, Peterson, 1961).

7. F. Kluckhohn, and F. L. Strodtbeck, reference cited.

8. Adapted from S. A. Hellwig, L. A. Samovar, and L. Skow, "Cultural Variations in Negotiation Styles," in L. A. Samovar and R. E. Proter, eds., *Intercultural Communications: A Reader,* 2nd ed. (Belmont, CA: Wadsworth, 1994), pp. 286–92; E. Kras, *Management in Two Cultures: Bridging the Gap between U.S. and Mexican Managers,* rev. ed. (Yarmouth, ME: Intercultural Press, 1995); and *International Straight Talk on Mexico,* video (Waxahachie, TX: William Drake, 1996).

9. Adapted from K. D. Schmidt, *Doing Business in France* (Menlo Park, CA: SRI International, 1987); Phillip R. Harris and Robert T. Moran, *Managing Cultural Differences,* 3rd ed. (Houston, TX: Gulf Publishing, 1991); and T. J. Griffen and W. R. Daggatt, *The Global Negotiator: Building Strong Business Relations Anywhere in the World* (New York: Harper Business, 1990).

10. Adapted from Phillip R. Harris and Robert T. Moran, reference cited; and S. A. Hellwig, L. A. Samovar and L. Skow, reference cited.

11. Adapted from Phillip R. Harris and Robert T. Moran, reference cited; and Irene Y. M. Yeung and Rosalie L. Tung, "Achieving Business Success in Confucian Societies: The Importance of Guanxi (Connections)," *Organizational Dynamics,* vol. 25, no. 2 (Autumn 1996), pp. 54–65.

12. Adapted from Phillip R. Harris and Robert T. Moran, reference cited; J. P. Fiegg and L. E. Yaffe, *Adjusting to the U.S.A.: Orientation for International Students* (Washington, DC: Meridian House International, 1997); and Dragan Z. Milosevic, "Echoes of the Silent Language of Project Management," *Project Management Journal,* vol. 30, no. 1 (March 1999), pp. 27–39.

13. Ingemar Torbiorn, *Living Abroad* (New York: Wiley, 1982).

14. I. Ratiu, "Thinking Internationally: A Comparison of How International Executives Learn," *International Studies of Management and Organization,* vol. 13, no. 1–2 (Spring–Summer 1983), pp. 139–50.

15. Nancy J. Adler, *International Dimensions of Organizational Behavior,* 2nd ed. (Boston: PWS-Kent Publishing, 1991), p. 230.
16. R. L. Tung, "Expatriate Assignments: Enhancing Success and Minimizing Failure," *The Academy of Management Executive,* vol. 1, no. 2 (1987), pp. 117–26.
17. Nancy J. Adler, reference cited, p. 234.
18. Mark E. Mendenhall, Edward Dunbar, and Gary R. Oddou, "Expatriate Selection, Training, and Career-Pathing: A Review and Critique," *Human Resource Management,* vol. 26, no. 3 (Fall 1987), pp. 331–45.
19. Adapted from *ibid.*

CASE

AMEX, Hungary

Michael Thomas shouted, "Sasha, Tor-Tor, we've got to go! Our driver is waiting for us." Thomas's two daughters were fighting over who would get the last orange for lunch that day. Victoria ("Tor-Tor") prevailed as she grabbed the orange and ran out the door to the Mercedes Benz waiting for them. The fighting continued in the back seat as they drove toward the city of Budapest, Hungary. Thomas finally turned around and grabbed the orange and proclaimed that he would have it for lunch. The back seat became deadly silent as they made their way to the American International School of Budapest.

After dropping the girls off at the school, Thomas was driven to his office in the Belváros area of Budapest. Thomas worked for AMEX Petroleum and had been sent to Budapest four months earlier to set up business operations in central Hungary. His job was to establish 10 to 14 gas stations in the region by purchasing existing stations, building new ones, or negotiating franchise arrangements with existing owners of stations. Thomas jumped at this project. He realized that his career at AMEX was going nowhere in the United States, and if he were going to realize his ambitions, it would be in the "wild, wild east" of the former Soviet empire. Besides, Thomas's mother was Hungarian, and he could speak the language. At least he thought he could until he arrived in Budapest and realized that he had greatly exaggerated his competence.

As he entered the partially refurbished offices of AMEX, he noticed that only three of his staff were present. No one knew where Miklos was, while Margit reported that she would not be at work today because she had to stay at home to take care of her sick mother. Thomas asked Béla why the workmen weren't present to work on finishing the office. Béla informed him that the work had to be halted until they received approval from the city historian. Budapest, anxious to preserve its historical heritage, required that all building renovations be approved by the city historian. When Thomas asked Béla how long it would take, Béla responded, "Who knows—days, weeks, maybe even months." Thomas muttered "great" to himself and turned his attention to the morning business. He was scheduled to interview prospective employees who would act as station managers and staff personnel.

The interview with Ferenc Erkel was typical of the many interviews he held that morning. Erkel was a neatly dressed, 42-year-old, unemployed professional who could speak limited English. He had a masters degree in international economics and had worked for 12 years in the state-owned Institute for Foreign Trade. Since being laid off two years ago, he has been working as a taxicab driver. When asked about his work at the Institute, Erkel smiled sheepishly and said that he pushed paper and spent most of the time playing cards with his colleagues.

To date Thomas had hired 16 employees. Four quit within three days on the job, and six were let go after a trial period for being absent from work, failing to perform duties, or showing a lack of initiative. Thomas thought that at this rate it would take him over a year just to hire his staff.

Thomas took a break from the interview schedule to scan the *Budapest Business Journal,* an English newspaper that covered business news in Hungary. Two items caught his eye. One article was on the growing threat of the Ukrainian Mafia in Hungary, which detailed extortion attempts in Budapest. The second story was that inflation had risen to 32 percent. This last item disturbed Thomas because at the time only one out of every five Hungarian families owned a car. AMEX's strategy in Hungary depended on a boom in first-time car owners.

Thomas collected his things and popped a few aspirin for the headache he was developing. He walked several blocks to the Kispipa restaurant where he had a supper meeting with Hungarian businessman Zoltán Kodaly. He had met Kodaly briefly at a reception sponsored by the U.S. consulate for American and Hungarian businesspeople. Kodaly reportedly owned three gas stations that Thomas was interested in.

Thomas waited, sipping bottled water for 25 minutes. Kodaly appeared with a young lady who could not have been older than 19. As it turned out Kodaly had brought his daughter Annia, who was a university student, to act as translator. While Thomas made an attempt to speak in Hungarian at first, Kodaly insisted that they use Annia to translate.

After ordering the house specialty, *szekelygulas,* Thomas immediately got down to business. He told Kodaly that AMEX was willing to make two offers to him. They would like to either purchase two of his stations at a price of $150,000 each, or they could work out a franchise agreement. Thomas said AMEX was not interested in the third station located near Klinikak because it would be too expensive to modernize the equipment. Annia translated, and as far as Thomas could tell she was doing a pretty good job. At first Kodaly did not respond and simply engaged in side conversations with Annia and exchanged pleasantries with people who came by. Thomas became frustrated and reiterated his offer. Eventually Kodaly asked what he meant by franchising, and Thomas tried to use the local McDonald's as an example of how it worked. He mentioned that Kodaly would still own the stations, but he would have to pay a franchisee fee, share profits with AMEX, and adhere to AMEX procedures and practices. In exchange AMEX would provide petroleum and funds to renovate the stations to meet AMEX standards.

Toward the end of the meal Kodaly asked what would happen to the people who worked at the stations. Thomas asserted that according to his calculation the stations were overstaffed by 70 percent and that to make a profit, at least 15 workers would have to be let go. This statement was greeted with silence. Kodaly then turned the conversion to soccer and asked Thomas if it was true that in America girls play "football." Thomas said that both of his daughters played AYSO soccer in America and hoped to play in Hungary. Kodaly said girls don't play football in Hungary and that Annia was an accomplished volleyball player. Thomas pressed Kodaly for a response to his offer, but Kodaly rose and thanked Thomas for the meal. He said he would think about his offer and get back in touch with him.

Thomas left the Kispipa wondering if he would ever see Kodaly again. He returned to his office where an urgent message was waiting from Tibor. Tibor was responsible for retrofitting the first station Thomas had purchased for AMEX. The new tanks had not arrived from Vienna, and the construction crew had spent the day doing nothing. After several phone calls he found out that the tanks were being held at the border by customs. This irritated him because he had been assured by local officials that everything had been taken care of. He asked his secretary to schedule an appointment with the Hungarian trade office as soon as possible.

At the end of the day he checked his e-mail from the States. There was a message from headquarters asking about the status of the project. By this time he had hoped to have his office staffed and up and running and at least three stations secured. So far he had only one-third of his staff, his office was in shambles, and only one station was being retrofitted. Thomas decided to wait until tomorrow to respond to the e-mail.

Before returning home Thomas stopped off at the English Pub, a favorite hangout for expats in Budapest. There he met Jan Krovert, who worked for a Dutch company that was building a large discount retail store on the outskirts of Badapest. Thomas and Krovert often talked about being "strangers in a strange land" at the pub. Thomas talked about the interviews and how he could just see in their eyes that they didn't have the drive or initiative to be successful. Krovert responded that Hungary has high unemployment but a shortage of motivated workers. Krovert confided that he no longer interviewed anyone over the age of 30, claiming that what fire they had in their bellies was burned out after years of working in state-run companies.

1. What are the issues confronting Thomas in this case?
2. How well is Thomas dealing with these issues?
3. What suggestions would you have for Thomas in managing this project?

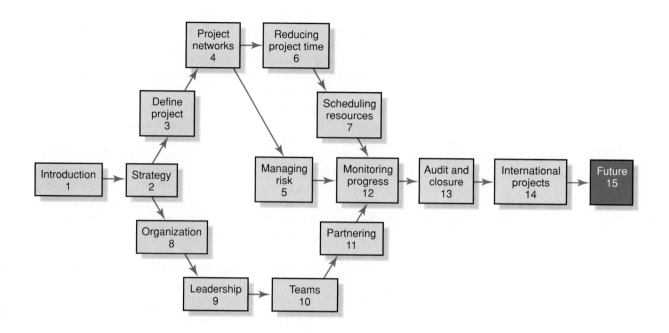

The Process of Project Management and the Future

Emergence of Project-Driven Organizations
Future, Positive Trends
Unresolved Issues
Career Paths in Project Management
Conclusions
Summary

CHAPTER FIFTEEN

The Process of Project Management and the Future

A great wind is blowing and that gives you either imagination or a headache.
—Catherine the Great, Empress of Russia, 1726–1796

Before we look toward the future we need to look at the past. During the 1960s and 1970s, project management emerged as a critical-path-based network planning technique for building complex vehicles and products such as submarines and space crafts. The introduction of microcomputer software in the 1980s made computerized planning and control tools available to all kinds of projects and organizations. Project management received wide acclaim as a platform for developing new products and services. The 1990s saw an expansion of project management into mainstream business. Project planning and control methods still dominate the discipline, but the human side to managing projects has taken on greater importance. The scope of project management has expanded to touch every fiber of the organization to include such hot topics as continuous improvement, concurrent engineering, strategic change, and multiproject management.

In the new millennium, project management appears to be ideally positioned to meet many of the challenges confronting global business enterprises. This chapter begins by briefly reviewing the major forces that are contributing to the growth and importance of project management. The chapter identifies some emerging trends and speculates on what the process of managing projects will be like in the twenty-first century. Unresolved issues confronting the field are also identified and discussed. Because the premise is that project management has a bright future, it is appropriate to conclude with some suggestions on how to pursue a career in project management.

EMERGENCE OF PROJECT-DRIVEN ORGANIZATIONS

Assessment of the future process of managing projects begins with identification of the forces of change. (Some of these forces were mentioned in Chapter 1.) These megaforces are typically beyond the control of individual managers or organizations; they represent changes in the basic fabric of society—sweeping across all nations.

The compression of the *product life cycle* is perhaps the most prodigious force driving changes in the process of managing projects. Only 50 years ago the average life cycle of all products was in the neighborhood of 15 to 20 years. Today, business executives estimate the life cycle to be close to three years for all products. Managers in high-technology firms estimate the life cycle to be closer to six months. Clearly, the velocity of new-product development has increased geometrically. Short life cycles increase the number of projects an organization will need to handle simultaneously. It is not unusual for organizations to have more than 100 projects occurring simultaneously. Resource shortages and conflicts can become rampant in this environment. How will time-to-market be reconciled with resources? These outcomes have created problems that will alter the way projects are selected and managed. Each new product is a new project!

Another megaforce closely linked with the product life cycle is the *knowledge/technology explosion.* It is a popular belief that more knowledge has been created in the last two or three decades than in the history of the human race. Although these numbers are difficult to verify, the magnitude is obvious to all. Today 33 percent of the GNP comes from new-knowledge products. Improved knowledge and technology support innovation. Innovation results in new projects!

Global competition touches every part of our world. No country or product is immune from this turbulent force. Surviving and being successful in the savage competition witnessed today intensifies the need for sustained innovation and process improvements. Organizations that are best at innovations and process improvements win. These activities represent projects!

These forces as well as others are not only increasing the sheer number of projects but also making project management the dominant vehicle for business growth and survival in the future. Perhaps noted project management expert, Paul Dinsmore, sums it up best when he predicts that in the future ". . . companies will perceive themselves not as hierarchical, functional organizations, but as fast-tracking entrepreneurial enterprises, made up of a 'portfolio of projects'—ever-changing and ever-renewable—all of which need to be done 'faster, cheaper, better.' "[1]

Dinsmore is describing what was referred to in the first chapter as the emergence of project-driven organizations. Such organizations will integrate strategy, project selection, culture, and processes consistently on all projects. Project-driven organizations will use projects as the major instrument to accomplish the organizational vision, goals, and strategies. The linkages between organizational direction, strategy, and projects will be well defined. Project-driven organizations will very carefully select a prioritized portfolio of projects, which will clearly guide the organization toward its ever-changing needs. These organizations enhance cooperation, enhance group performance, and enhance continuous improvement and renewal. Stakeholder skill requirements will shift from technical skills to a razor-sharp understanding and use of business skills and processes. Project-driven organizations provide the environment for quickly adapting to change and uncertainties of the volatile environment in which they exist.

FUTURE, POSITIVE TRENDS

As projects become the focal point of business, organizations will naturally adapt and change to support more effective project management. The remainder of this section lists and then describes some of the positive changes we believe will occur as organizations evolve toward being project-driven enterprises. Many of these changes are already evident in leading-edge corporations.

• **Organizational culture will support organizational learning.**

The organizational culture of most successful firms of the future will be one that supports flexibility, places a high importance on projects, and maintains a sustained effort by members to learn and improve processes. The challenge for senior management is to get members to adopt and commit to a culture that supports continuous improvement, renewal, and organizational learning. This belief should be the primary focus and commitment permeating the entire organization.

Top management will need to create a clear vision for the organization to keep the efforts of all its members moving in the same direction. A compelling vision serves as a motivating mechanism, acts as a self-discipline force in allocating scarce organization resources, and points to activities that will be rewarded. Organizations without a transparent vision statement supported by all its members seldom perform well financially.[2]

Because future organizations will need to react quickly to forces of change—usually in the form of innovation and continuous improvement—the organizational culture will exhibit rules and standards that guarantee quick response. A few organizations are picking up the classic format used by 3M Corporation for several decades. For example, 3M has an expectation that 25 percent of revenues will come from products developed in the last five years. This standard gives a clear message of expectations to all members of the organization. Other organizations are now creating similar approaches to signal the need for new products and services and process improvements. A format similar to that of 3M rests on a philosophy of trust and confidence in an organization's members. This principle means senior management gives up power. Access to information is available to all members. Communication among members is encouraged. Hierarchical structures give way to horizontal structures in which teams manage product, process, and system improvements. The collaborative spirit and mutual respect for project team members is evident to any observer.

• **Matrix organizational design will be institutionalized.**

The use of project teams within a matrix organizational structure will be accepted as simply "the way we do things around here." Dedicated project teams will coexist alongside part-time project teams, with project work being the core activity of most businesses. Professionals will move in and out of projects on an as-needed basis. Traditional turf battles between functional areas and between functional managers and project managers will subside as project success becomes the focal point of the organization. Many organizations will rely on project management offices (PMO) to coordinate projects, perform project audits, and manage the project managers. As the project management culture becomes more ingrained in organizations, PMOs will evolve into "centers of excellence" for project management. These centers will focus on institutionalizing best project management practices and developing the project management capacity of the firm.[3]

• **Cross-border, cross-cultural projects will increase.**

The mega mergers of the 1990s and the new millennium will compel project managers to develop a global perspective. The resultant restructuring of companies will force project managers to work with their counterparts in different countries. Managing global teams working together on one project from several distant sites will require the project manager to change management style to accommodate this unique project

Snapshot from Practice
THE PROJECT MANAGEMENT PROGRAM OFFICE[4]

As more and more companies embrace project management as a critical vehicle for realizing corporate objectives, they are creating centralized project management offices (PMOs) to oversee and improve the management of projects. PMO functions vary widely by organization and need. In some cases, they serve as a simple clearinghouse for project management information. In other cases, they recruit, train, and assign managers to specific projects. As PMOs mature and evolve over time, they become full-service providers of project management expertise within a firm. The different services PMOs may provide include the following:

- Creating and maintaining the internal project management information system.
- Recruiting and selecting project managers both within and outside the organization.
- Establishing standardized project planning and reporting methodologies.
- Training personnel in project management techniques and tools.
- Auditing ongoing and recently completed projects.
- Developing comprehensive risk management programs.
- Providing in-house project management consulting and mentoring services.
- Maintaining an internal project management library containing critical documents, including project plans, funding papers, test plans, audit reports, and so forth.
- Establishing and benchmarking *best practices* in project management.
- Maintaining and tracking the portfolio of projects within an organization.

A good example of how project management offices evolve is the global project office (GPO) at Citibank's Global Corporate Bank. GPO originated at the grass-roots level within the small world of Operations and Technology for Global Cash Management. Committed to bringing order to the chaos of managing projects, GPO instituted training programs and professional project management practices on a very small scale. Soon the success of GPO-supported projects caught the eye of upper management. Within three years the department was expanded to offer a full range of PMO services across Citibank's entire banking operation. GPO's mission is to establish project management as a core competency throughout the entire Citibank organization.

---

environment. For example, how will you bring in a project on time in a country in which bureaucratic government officials are slow to respond; or how do you manage communication and build trust in a global team made up of several diverse ethnic backgrounds? It seems inevitable that project managers must prepare for the challenge of operating in countries that have unfamiliar business practices and prepare for the challenge of dealing with unfamiliar behavior patterns of differing ethnic groups. The discussion of international project management in Chapter 14 serves as a good starting point to prepare for the inescapable increase in cross-border, cross-cultural projects.

- **Systematic project selection and priority systems will be established.**

In the future projects will be strongly linked to strategic need. The connection between strategic goals and a project will be transparent to all members of the organization. Competition among projects for organizational resources will require a centralized project priority system to allocate resources. Project proposals will come from a variety of sources—teams, individuals, customers. The priority system will be managed by a multilevel management steering committee. The committee will use the priority system to allocate resources to projects that contribute the most value added, that balance risk, and that allow priorities to change when conditions change. The portfolio of projects will be future-oriented toward organizational goals and business plans. The portfolio will carefully match organizational resources to skill capacities. Overcommitment of individuals to three to five projects will be discouraged, thereby avoiding project delays and burnout. Today, forward-oriented organizations try as much as possible to place individuals on a single project rather than spreading their effort over several projects simultaneously. The creation and implementation of a project priority system will be considered a major responsibility of top management.

- **Integrative project management information systems will be established.**

Software developers will satisfy the demand for friendlier project management software to manage both single and multiple projects. The software will provide easy access to core project management planning tools such as Gantt charts, network diagrams, and responsibility matrices as well as customized features for dealing with risk management, critical chain issues, and organizational cost systems. These software packages will be fully linked to Internet technology to provide wide access to key information. Project Web sites will be used to centralize project information. The use of groupware (e.g., Lotus Notes™) to allow geographically dispersed teams to work together and share information will increase.

Individual project management software will feed into a more complex project management information system that monitors multiple projects and coordinates resource allocation. Many of these systems will have a customized interface with the central information system of an organization. In other cases, the firm's centralized information system will be totally designed to manage and support projects.

- **Evaluation and reward systems will support effective project management.**

Reward and evaluation systems will be aligned to support successful project management. These systems will combine team incentives with individual assessments. For example, one evaluation and reward system cuts the reward pie into three weighted pieces: 25 percent, 50 percent, and 25 percent. Twenty-five percent of the reward is allocated to the contribution of the team's project to the organization's goals. Fifty percent depends on an individual's contribution to the team as determined by fellow team members. Twenty-five percent results from the member's performance in his or her area of expertise (e.g., accounting, engineering, marketing). Peer performance reviews and 360-degree reviews will become the norm (if legal restrictions are not imposed). The effectiveness of team members evaluating other project members is illustrated in a recent interview with a Hewlett-Packard executive about the Internet. The reporter asked the executive if he was concerned about members of his organization spending too much time surfing the Net rather than working. The reply was immediate and succinct: "Oh no, team members would quickly take care of that problem; they wouldn't allow it."

- **Project audits will become an integral part of the management system.**

Organizations will have a well-established system for auditing project performance. Significant, long-term projects will undergo scheduled, in-process audits to ensure satisfactory progress and corrective changes as needed. Veteran project managers approaching the ends of their careers will lead post-project audits. Top management will rely heavily on information and recommendations drawn from these audits to initiate changes to improve the process of managing projects. Lessons learned from individual projects will be a vital part of the organization's efforts toward continuous improvement.

Snapshot from Practice
THE INTERNATIONAL SPACE STATION PROJECT (ISS)

Courtesy of NASA.

Hopefully, by 2006 the space station assembly will be complete and functional 220 miles above the earth at a cost of more than $40 billion. The station will cover an area of approximately two football fields and have a housing unit the size of a jumbo jet. This space station will conduct research concerning human life and production of products in space. The complexity of the space station and the coordination required among 16 partner nations is daunting.

Russia launched the first piece of the space station on November 20, 1998. This module provides power for future assembly operations. On December 3 of the same year, the United States launched the first space component hub, which serves as the connector for other pieces of the station. This hub also serves as housing for up to seven astronauts. In total it is planned that 34 space deliveries will transport more than 900,000 pounds of materials needed to assemble the completed station. It is estimated that 144 to 160 two-person space walks and 1,800 hours of construction will be needed to assemble the station.

The project has had a bumpy ride to date, and more problems are expected before the project is complete. The project is billions of dollars over budget; the total cost could reach $96 billion. The collapse of the Russian economy has caused delays on their development of a major module of the station. Financial support has been needed to get the Russian effort back on track. Redesign has been continual because of the multiple needs of the partners of the 16 nations; these changes have resulted in costly delays. Some of the risks have been underestimated, and reassessment has suggested failures along the way are inevitable—delivery vehicles blowing up, docking problems, even someone killed during construction. There have been calls to "pull the plug" on the project. Nevertheless, the project moves forward.

Snapshot from Practice (concluded)

The ESA (European Space Agency) is coordinating several ISS projects linked to the development of an ATV (automatic transfer vehicle—not related to all-terrain vehicles), which will supply nine tons of cargo and fuel to the space station. These projects, which include countries and companies from France, Germany, Russia, Italy, will take place in their respective countries under the guidance of ESA. DaimlerChrysler will produce the estimated 15 ATVs scheduled for delivery between 2003 and 2013. Standard penalty clauses for late delivery are in place. Incentive provisions for continuous improvement of mission success and payload mass are included in this multination endeavor.[5]

Problems are deemed surmountable, and plans to complete the assembly by 2006 are in place. It is expected that the world-class laboratory will lead to discoveries that will touch the lives of everyone in the world. Perhaps the lessons learned will be as valuable as the discoveries.

- **Managing project interfaces will take on greater significance.**

Project managers will spend less time managing the project and will pay more attention to managing the interface between the project and the rest of the organization. Stakeholder management will take on increased importance as project managers try to simultaneously meet the demands of different interest groups and preserve the integrity of the project. It will become widely accepted that one of the primary jobs of a project manager is to control and adjust the scope of the project to meet customer expectations. Project managers will spend less time overseeing and directing the implementation of the project. Instead the professional workforce and collaborative culture will encourage a "make it so" leadership style in which the manager defines what needs to be done and team members are empowered to figure how best to do it.[6]

- **Partnering will be the norm for managing interorganizational projects.**

Organizations will develop long-term relationships with other organizations to jointly complete projects. Like matrix management, partnering will simply become the way people work together on projects. As such, there will be less of a need to invest in intensive upfront team building because collaboration will already be the mind-set of participants. Contracts and associated incentive clauses will focus more on sharing risk, mutual gain, and profit sharing. Likewise, partnering mechanisms such as joint evaluation, escalation, and continuous improvement will become established industrywide and will simply have to be adapted to the particulars of the project.

- **Ad hoc project teams will become more widespread.**

More projects will be completed by temporary project teams whose members act as independent contractors. Organizations will hire individual project managers or leaders, who will then recruit appropriate team members from outside the organization to complete the project. Once their part of the project is completed, the specialists become free agents seeking other project employment opportunities. Free agency will place a premium on professional networking because contacts will be critical to secure future work.

These changes will not occur overnight. As noted in Chapter 1, it usually takes several years for an organization to evolve into a project-driven organization. Why does it take so long? One reason is simply organizational inertia. It is difficult for complex social organizations to institute significant changes while at the same time maintaining business efficacy. "How do we find time to change when we are so busy just keeping our heads above water?" A second reason is resistance to change. For many managers the shift from a hierarchical, functional organization to a flatter, project-driven organization represents a loss of power, authority, and prestige. People with power do not like to lose it, and they often use their power to preserve their status and position. A third reason is the lack of strong top management support. Most of today's CEOs have very little formal project management experience. They achieved their success by working their way up a functional hierarchy. Embracing project management as a core activity will require a paradigm shift in how executives view their organization. This pattern will change as project managers ascend to the ranks of top management.

Many organizations will struggle to adapt their project management systems; the driving forces for change will not dissipate. Those organizations that successfully ride the winds of change and accelerate the institutionalization of a project-driven organization will have a competitive advantage in the twenty-first century.

UNRESOLVED ISSUES

While we are fairly confident in our observations and resulting inferences, there are still some unresolved issues confronting project management. Two of these involve virtual project management and the management of projects under high levels of uncertainty:

• **How far can virtual project management evolve?**

In Chapter 10 we introduced the subject of virtual project teams in which members primarily interact electronically. Today, most project communication is limited to e-mail, teleconferencing, faxes, and, in some cases, videoconferencing. As telecommunication systems become more reliable worldwide and videoconferencing with high-definition resolution becomes readily available, project teams will be able to hold meetings in which geographically separated members visually interact with each other; e-mail will be augmented by video messages. Similarly, telephone conversations will be replaced by direct video interaction using PCs.

Some companies, with access to the latest technology, are experimenting with 24-hour product design teams. These teams have members scattered across the time zones so that work on a project is nonstop. For example, team members work on the project during normal hours in New York and then electronically pass their work to members in Hawaii, who are beginning their workday when the New York team is about to go home. The Hawaiian team passes their work to a team in Bangkok, Thailand, who, in turn, pass their work to a team situated in Copenhagen, Denmark. The Danish team passes its work to the New York team, and the cycle is repeated. Although it is too early to say how successful this tag-team approach to project management will be, it exemplifies the potential that exists given the information technology that is available today.

Clearly in the world of the future, project professionals will have access to technology to reduce the barriers of distance and time and improve their ability to interact in a virtual domain. The question is, What are the limits to virtual project management? What kinds of projects and under what circumstances will virtual project management best work? Or not work? Will different skill sets and personal characteristics be required to work in a virtual environment? What protocols, habits, and procedures need to be developed to successfully manage a virtual project team? Will visual, video interaction enhance the development of trust among physically separated team members? Conversely, new technology often produces unintended side effects (smog in the case of the gasoline engine; carpal tunnel in the case of PCs). What are the potential negative physical and psychological side effects of working in a virtual environment? How will workers respond if their sleep is periodically interrupted by urgent calls from Krakow, Poland, or if they have to make sure they are home from the movies at 11:00 P.M. so they can participate in a video project meeting?

Answers to these questions and others will emerge as organizations experiment with virtual project management.

• How do we manage projects under high levels of uncertainty?

Research on project success and failure consistently points to poor planning as a major reason behind project failures. The general recommendation is that more time and attention should be devoted to clearly defining the scope of the project and developing the project plan. However, poor planning may not simply be a result of a lack of effort but rather due to the inherent difficulty of planning a project under conditions of high uncertainty. For example, software development projects are notorious for being completed way over budget and behind schedule. Is this a result of poor planning? Or an innate characteristic of project work that involves tightly coupled activities, trial-and-error problem solving, and shifting design parameters?

Modern project management planning tools and techniques are well suited to accomplishing projects in which the scope is well defined. They are less well suited to managing projects with vaguely defined or unstable scopes. Purists would argue that this is a moot point because, by definition, project management involves only endeavors with well-defined objectives. While this is a neat "academic" solution to the problem, it does not mirror the reality of project management today. More and more people are engaged in projects in which, by intent, the initial scope is broadly defined or subject to significant change. Customers' needs change. Top management strategies and priorities change. Innovations create the impossible. Competitors change the playing field. In today's business world, certainty is a luxury, and a premium is placed on flexibility.

The key question is how to effectively manage projects with loosely defined or *unstable scopes* accompanied by high levels of *uncertainty*. How do managers plan a project for which they are not sure what the final outcome will be? How do they develop a project control system that is both flexible and responsive yet, at the same time, ensures accountability and yields reliable projections? How do they avoid paralysis through overanalysis yet, at the same time, engage in prudent risk management? How do they know when it is appropriate to freeze the scope or design of the project and begin formal implementation? Conversely, using uncertainty as an excuse for not planning and flying into the wind by the seat of the pants is an invitation for disaster.

The next decade should see a whirlwind of attention to the problem of managing projects with ill-defined project scopes and project uncertainties. Answers to the problem are not obvious. Some of the ideas and techniques will be short-term fads. Others will withstand the test of time and make significant contributions to the project management body of knowledge.

Snapshot from Practice
HARVESTING PROJECT LEADERS[7]

Executives "don't have a clue about how to grow project managers," says Gopal Kapur, president of the Center for Project Management, a consulting agency in San Ramon, California. "Project managers do not grow on trees. You have to understand the process of gardening before you can grow something." Kapur advocates that corporations develop internal programs to develop project managers.

The Federal Reserve Bank of St. Louis has had such a program for more than a year, and it's helped the bank grow 45 new project managers. It combines hands-on work in medium- to low-risk projects with classroom training. A new project manager is guided by a veteran leader, who acts as a coach or mentor. Gary Arnold, manager of learning and development services, calls that a very critical piece of the program. The coach/mentor can offer advice based on experience.

Typically, Arnold says, project manager wannabes are sent to the classroom for a few days before they apply some skills. But the Federal Reserve Bank found that the opposite works better and starts them off in the trenches. This way they experience firsthand the need to master key project management tools and concepts.

CAREER PATHS IN PROJECT MANAGEMENT

There is no set career path for becoming a project manager. Career avenues vary from industry to industry, organization to organization, and from profession to profession. What can be said is that advancement occurs incrementally. You don't simply graduate and become a project manager. As in other careers you have to work your way up to the position. For example, in project-based organizations such as construction firms, you may begin by working on several projects as an assistant engineer, then take an assignment as a project analyst. From there you are promoted to principal engineer, advance to assistant project manager, assume the role of project manager over a small project, and then continue to bigger, riskier projects. In other organizations, project management careers run parallel with functional advancement with many crossovers. For example, at Intel a management information systems (MIS) specialist might start his career as a designer, then take an assignment as a project specialist, later work as a project manager, and then return to a functional position as head of a department or a product manager.

Other people find that their project management responsibilities expand as they move up the organization's hierarchy. For example, a former marketing student began her career as an assistant buyer for a large retail company. She then became area sales manager at a specific store and became involved on a part-time basis in a series of projects acting as a facilitator of focus groups. She was promoted to buyer and eventually became a store manager. In her current position she coordinates a variety of projects ranging from improving the sales acumen of her salesforce to altering the physical layout of the store. Although the title of project manager does not appear in her job description, more than 50 percent of her work involves managing projects.

One aspect of project managing that is unique is the temporary nature of assignments. With line appointments, promotions are for the most part permanent and there is a natural, hierarchical progression to positions with greater authority and responsibility. In the example of the former marketing student, she progressed from assistant buyer to sales manager to buyer to store manager. Only under very unusual circumstances would she regress to being a buyer. Conversely, tenure is rarely granted to project managers. Once the project is completed, the manager may return to his previous department, even to a lesser position. Or, depending on the projects available, he may be assigned to manage a more or less significant project. Future work depends on what projects are available at the time the individual is available and how well the last project went. A promising career can be derailed by one unsuccessful project.

If you are considering pursuing a career in project management, you should first find out what specific project job opportunities exist in your company. You should talk to people in project management positions and find out how they got to where they are and what advice they can give you. Because career paths, as noted earlier, vary from organization to organization, you need to be attuned to the unique pathways within your company. For example, retail companies naturally assign marketing managers to projects.

Once you have concluded that you wish to pursue a career in project management, or see project management as an avenue for advancement, you need to share your aspirations with your immediate superior. Your superior can champion your ambitions, sanction additional training in project management, and assign immediate work that will contribute to your project skill base.

Most project managers have never received formal training in project management. They mastered the job through on-the-job training, buttressed by occasional workshops on specific project topics such as project scheduling or negotiating contracts. It wasn't until recently that universities started offering courses on project management outside of schools of engineering; to date there are only a handful of degree programs in project management. Regardless of your level of training you will likely need to supplement your education. Many large companies have in-house training programs on project management. For example, Hewlett-Packard has more than 32 training modules in its project management curriculum, which is organized around five levels of experience: project team, new project manager, project manager, experienced project manager, and manager of project managers. Take advantage of professional workshops, which can cover a range of specific project management tools and topics. Continued education should not be restricted to project management. Many technical professionals return to universities to complete an MBA or take night classes in management to expand their general business background.

Many professionals find it beneficial to join the Project Management Institute (PMI).[8] Membership entitles you to subscriptions to PMI publications including the academic *Project Management Journal* and the *PM Network,* a trade magazine. PMI sponsors workshops and national forums on project management. When you join PMI you also become a member of one of the more than 200 local chapters across North America. These chapters meet on a monthly basis and provide project managers with opportunities to network and learn from each other. In addition, PMI, as part of its effort to advance the profession, certifies mastery of project manager competency through a formal examination that covers the entire body of knowledge of project management. Passing the exam and being certified as a "Project Management Professional" is a clearly visible way to signal your competence and interest.

As you accumulate knowledge and techniques, you need to apply them to your immediate job situation. Most people's jobs entail some form of project, whether realizing a mandated objective or simply figuring out ways to improve the quality of performance. Gantt charts, responsibility matrices, CPM networks, and other project management tools can be used to plan and implement these endeavors. It may also be wise to look outside the workplace for opportunities to develop project management skills. Active involvement in your local community can provide numerous opportunities to manage projects. Organizing a local soccer tournament, managing a charitable fund-raising event, or coordinating the renovation of the neighborhood park can allow you to practice project management. Furthermore, given the volunteer nature of most of these projects, they can provide you with an excellent training ground to sharpen your ability to exercise influence without formal authority.

Regardless of how competent and worthy you are, your project management skills must be visible to others for them to be recognized. Many project managers' careers began by volunteering for task forces and small projects. Ideally you should select task forces and projects that allow you access to higher-ups and other departments within your organization, providing you with opportunities to develop contacts. Even in a subordinate position you can take advantage of project review meetings to demonstrate to your bosses and peers that you have the necessary skills for project planning and control.

In pursuing your ambition you should continually be on the lookout for a mentor. Most fast-track managers acknowledge that mentors played a significant role in their advancement.[9] Mentors are typically superiors who take a special interest in you and your career. They use their clout to champion your ambitions and act as a personal coach, teaching you "the ropes to skip and the ropes to know." This special treatment does not come without a price. Mentors typically require fervent loyalty and superior performance; after all, the mentor's reputation rests on your performance. How do you find a mentor? Most people say it just happens. But it doesn't happen to everyone. Mentors typically seek A+ workers, not C workers, and you must make your abilities known to others.

Many organizations have instituted formal mentoring programs in which experienced project managers are assigned to promising young managers. Although the relationship may not evolve to the personal level experienced with an informal mentor, designated mentors play a very similar role in coaching and championing one's professional progress. You should take advantage of this opportunity to learn as much as you can from these seasoned veterans.

Ultimately your goal is to accumulate a portfolio of project management experiences that broaden your skill base and reputation. Early on you should choose, when possible, projects with the greatest learning opportunities. Pick projects more for the quality of the people working on them than for the scope of the projects. There is no better way to learn how to be an effective project manager than by watching one at work. Keep a diary of your observations and review and refine lessons learned. Later, as your confidence and competency grow, you should try to get involved in projects that will enhance your reputation within the firm. Remember the comments about customer satisfaction. You want to exceed your superiors' expectations. Avoid run-of-the-mill projects or assignments. Seek high-profile projects that have some risks and tangible payoffs.[10] At the same time, be careful to be involved in projects commensurate with your abilities.

Finally, despite your efforts you may find that you are not making satisfactory progress toward your career goals. If this is your appraisal, you may wish to seriously consider moving to a different company or even a different industry that might provide more project management opportunities. Hopefully you have managed to accumulate sufficient project management experience to aid in your job search. One advantage of project work over general management is that it is typically easier to highlight and "sell" your accomplishments.[11]

CONCLUSIONS

By studying this text you have been exposed to the major elements of the process of managing projects. When you apply these ideas and techniques to real project situations, we offer three suggestions.

1. Maintain a sense of the big picture. Engage regularly in what some have called "helicopter management," which means expand your perspective beyond immediate concerns and assess how the project fits in the larger scheme of things. Project managers need to constantly assess how the project fulfills the mission and strategy of the firm, how the project is affecting the rest of the organization, whether the expectations of stakeholders are changing, and what key project interfaces have to be managed.
2. Remember that successful project management is essentially a balancing act. Project managers need to balance the soft (people) side of project management with the hard (technical) side, the demands of top management with the needs of team members, short-term gain with long-term need, and so forth.
3. Project management is the wave of the future. Change produces career opportunities that are often not available during normal times. We encourage you to take advantage of these opportunities by developing your project management skills and knowledge. It is not too late to catch the first wave.

SUMMARY

The twenty-first century should be the Golden Age for project management. Not only will there be an increased demand for project management skills and know-how, but organizations will evolve and change to support more effective project management. Instead of trying to get projects done despite everything else, the organization's culture, structure, reward system, and administrative systems will be reengineered to support successful project management. Mastery of the process of managing projects will be critical to business growth and survival.

The project manager of the new millennium will be a businessperson with responsibilities that encompass the total organization. The past 30 years have seen the transition from a technically oriented project manager to one skilled in all aspects of business. Worldwide competition will direct projects toward technology transfer, infrastructure, consumer goods, environment/ecological, defense, and fundamental needs. The future project manager will be comfortable in foreign or domestic settings and will understand the needs of people in all social settings. The project-driven organization will recognize the project manager as an agent of change and, from their ranks, select the senior managers of tomorrow.

Twenty years from now career paths in project management should be more clearly defined. Until then people wishing to pursue a career in project management should take advantage of the transition and improvise within the constraints of their situation to develop their project management skills. They should volunteer to work on task forces, take advantage of training opportunities, and apply project management tools and techniques to their work. They should signal to their superiors their interest in project management and garner project assignments. Over time they should accumulate a portfolio of project management experiences that establishes their skill base and reputation as someone who gets things done quickly and done right.

ENDNOTES

1. Paul C. Dinsmore, "Toward a Corporate Project Management Culture: Fast Tracking into the Future," *Proceedings of the Project Management Institute 28th Annual Seminars and Symposium* (Newton Square, PA: Project Management Institute, 1997), p. 450.

2. See Lawrence C. Rhyne, "The Relationship of Strategic Planning to Financial Performance," *Strategic Management Journal,* vol. 7 (September/October 1986), pp. 423–36; Richard B. Robinson, Jr., "The Importance of 'Outsiders' in Small Firm Strategic Planning," *Academy of Management Journal,* vol. 25, no. 1 (March 1982), pp. 80–93; Jonathan B. Welch, "Strategic Planning Could Improve Your Price Share," *Long Range Planning* (April 1984), pp. 144–47; J. S. Bracker and J. N. Pearson, "Planning and Financial Performance of Small Manufacturing Firms," *Strategic Management Journal* (November/December, 1986), pp. 503–22; and Donald W. Beard and Gregory G. Dess, "Corporate Business Strategy, Business Level Strategy, and Firm Performance," *Academy of Management Journal,* vol. 24, no. 4 (December 1981), pp. 663–88.

3. These predictions are contained in Paul C. Dinsmore, reference cited, pp. 447–51.

4. William Gradante and Donald Gardner, "Managing Projects from the Future, Not from the Past," *Proceedings of the 29th Annual Project Management Institute 1998 Seminars and Symposium* (Newtown Square, PA: Project Management Institute, 1998), pp. 289–94; and Thomas R. Block and J. Davidson Frame, *The Project Office—A Key to Managing Projects Effectively* (Menlo Park, CA: Crisp Publications, 1998).

5. Michael A. Taverna, "Europe Advances ATV Development for ISS," *Aviation Week and Space Technology* (November 30, 1998), p. 29.

6. This leadership style has been popularized by the television show, "Star Trek: The Next Generation," which is the subject of Robert Wess and Bill Ross, *Make It So: Leadership Lessons From Star Trek—Next Generation* (New York: Pocket Books, 1995).

7. Rick Saia, "Harvesting Project Leaders," *Computerworld,* vol. 31, no. 29 (July 21, 1997), p. 1.

8. You can contact PMI at Project Management Institute, Four Campus Blvd., Newtown Square, PA 19073 or at their Web site: *www.pmi.org.*

9. For some useful advice on how to find a mentor, see Harvey Mackay, *Dig Your Well Before You're Thirsty* (New York: Doubleday, 1997). For information on the mentoring process, see Kathy E. Kram, *Mentoring at Work: Developmental Relationships in Organizational Life* (Glenview, IL: Scott, Foresman & Co., 1985).

10. Bennet P. Lientz and Kathryn P. Rea, *Project Management for the 21st Century* (San Diego Academic Press, 1995), p. 296.

11. MacKay, reference cited.

Glossary

activity Task(s) of the project that consumes time while people/equipment either work or wait.

activity duration Estimate of time (hours, days, weeks, months, etc.) necessary to complete a project task.

actual cost of the work performed (ACWP) Actual cost of the work performed in a given time period. The sum of the costs incurred in accomplishing work.

AOA Activity-on-arrow method for drawing project networks. The activity is shown as an arrow.

AON Activity-on-node method for drawing project networks. The activity is on the node (rectangle).

backward pass The method used to compute the late start and finish times for each activity in the project network.

balanced scorecard method Model that measures the long-run results of major program activities in four areas—customer, internal, innovation and learning, and financial.

balanced matrix A matrix structure in which the project manager and functional managers share roughly equal authority over the project. The project manager decides what needs to be done; functional managers are concerned with how it will be accomplished.

bar chart A graphic presentation of project activities depicted as a time-scaled bar line (also called a Gantt chart).

baseline A concrete document and commitment; it represents the first real plan with cost, schedule, and resource allocation. The planned cost and schedule performance are used to measure actual cost and schedule performance. Serves as an anchor point for measuring performance.

brainstorming Generating as many ideas/solutions as possible without critical judgment.

budget at completion (BAC) Budgeted cost at completion. The total budgeted cost of the baseline or project cost accounts.

budgeted cost of the work performed (BCWP) The value for completed work measured in terms of the planned budget for the work. The earned value or original budgeted cost for work actually completed.

budget reserve Reserves set up to cover identified risks that may occur and influence baseline tasks or costs. These reserves are typically controlled by the project manager and the project team. See management reserves.

burst activity An activity that has more than one activity immediately following it.

chart of accounts   A hierarchical numbering system used to identify tasks, deliverables, and organizational responsibility in the work breakdown structure.

concurrent engineering or simultaneous engineering   Cross-functional teamwork in new-product development projects that provides product design, quality engineering, and manufacturing process engineering all at the same time.

consensus decision making   Reaching a decision that all involved parties basically agree with and support.

contingency plan   A plan that covers possible identified project risks that may materialize over the life of the project.

contingency reserves   Usually an amount of money or time set aside to cover identified and unforeseen project risks.

contract   A formal agreement between two parties wherein one party (the contractor) obligates itself to perform a service and the other party (the client) obligates itself to do something in return, usually in the form of a payment to the contractor.

cost account   A control point of one or more work packages used to plan, schedule, and control the project. The sum of all the project cost accounts represents the total cost of the project.

cost performance index (CPI)   The ratio of budgeted costs to actual costs (BCWP/ACWP).

cost-plus contract   A contract in which the contractor is reimbursed for all direct allowable costs (materials, labor, travel) plus an additional fee to cover overhead and profit.

cost variance (CV)   The difference between BCWP and ACWP (CV = BCWP − ACWP). Tells if the work accomplished cost more or less than was planned at any point over the life of the project.

crash time   The shortest time an activity can be completed (assuming a reasonable level of resources).

critical path   The longest activity path(s) through the network. The critical path can be distinguished by identifying the collection of activities that all have the same minimum slack.

critical path method (CPM)   A scheduling method based on the estimates of time required to complete activities on the critical path. The method computes early, late, and slack times for each activity in the network. It establishes a planned project duration, if one is not imposed on the project.

culture shock   A natural psychological disorientation that most people suffer when they move to a culture different from their own.

dedicated project team   An organizational structure in which all of the resources needed to accomplish a project are assigned full-time to the project.

duration (DUR)   The time needed to complete an activity, a path, or a project.

dummy activity   An activity that does not consume time; it is represented on the AOA network as a dashed line. A dummy activity is used to ensure a unique identification number for parallel activities and used to maintain dependencies among activities on the project network.

dysfunctional conflict   Disagreement that does not improve project performance.

early start   The earliest an activity can start. It is the largest early finish of all its immediate predecessors (ES = EF − DUR).

early finish   The earliest an activity can finish if all its preceding activities are finished by their early finish times (EF = ES + DUR).

escalation   A control mechanism for resolving problems in which people at the lowest appropriate level attempt to resolve a problem within a set time limit or the problem is "escalated" to the next level of management.

estimated cost at completion (EAC)   The sum of actual costs to-date plus revised estimated costs for the work remaining in the WBS.

event   A point in time when an activity(s) is started or completed. It does not consume time.

fixed-price or "lump-sum" contract   A contract in which the contractor agrees to perform all the work specified in the contract at a predetermined, fixed price.

forecast at completion (FAC) The forecasted cost at completion—using forecast equation.

float See slack.

forward pass The method for determining the early start and finish times for each activity in the project network.

free slack The maximum amount of time an activity can be delayed from its early start (ES) without affecting the early start (ES) of any activity immediately following it.

functional conflict Disagreement that contributes to the objectives of the project.

functional matrix A matrix structure in which functional managers have primary control over project activities and the project manager coordinates project work.

functional organization A hierarchical organizational structure in which departments represent individual disciplines such as engineering, marketing, purchasing.

Gantt chart See bar chart.

going native Adopting the customs, values, and prerogatives of a foreign culture.

Golden Rule Do unto others as you would wish them to do unto you.

groupthink A tendency of members in highly cohesive groups to lose their critical evaluative capabilities.

hammock activity A special-purpose, aggregate activity that identifies the use of fixed resources or costs over a segment of the project—e.g., a consultant. Derives its duration from the time span between other activities.

implementation gap The lack of consensus between the goals set by top management and those independently set by lower levels of management. This lack of consensus leads to confusion and poor allocation of organization resources.

infrastructure Basic services (i.e., communication, transportation, power) needed to support project completion.

insensitive network A network in which the critical path is likely to remain stable during the life of the project.

lag The amount of time between the end of one activity and the start of another. A duration assigned to the activity dependency. The minimum amount of time a dependent activity must be delayed to begin or end.

lag relationship The relationship between the start and/or finish of a project activity and the start and/or finish of another activity. The most common lag relationships are (1) finish-to-start, (2) finish-to-finish, (3) start-to-start, and (4) start-to-finish.

late finish The latest an activity can finish and not delay a following activity (LF = LS + DUR).

late start The latest an activity can start and not delay a following activity. It is the largest late finish (LF) of all activities immediately preceding it (LS = LF – DUR).

law of reciprocity People are obligated to grant a favor comparable to the one they received.

level of effort (LOE) Work packages that represent time-related activities. These activities, such as administrative support, computer support, legal, public relations, etc. exist for a segment or the duration of the project. LOE work packages have no measurable outputs.

management by walking around (MBWA) A management style in which managers spend majority of their time outside their offices interacting with key people.

management reserve A percentage of the total project budget reserved for contingencies. The fund exists to cover unforeseen, new problems—not unnecessary overruns. The reserve is designed to reduce the risk of project delays. Management reserves are typically controlled by the project owner or project manager. See budget reserves.

matrix Any organizational structure in which the project manager shares responsibility with the functional managers for assigning priorities and for directing the work of individuals assigned to the project.

mentor Typically a more experienced manager who acts as a personal coach and champions a person's ambitions.

merge activity An activity that has more than one activity immediately preceding it.

met expectations model Customer satisfaction is a function of the extent to which perceived performance exceeds expectations.

milestone   An event that represents significant, identifiable accomplishment toward the project's completion.

Monte Carlo simulation   A method of simulating project activity durations using probabilities. The method identifies the percentage of times activities and paths are critical over thousands of simulations.

net present value (NPV)   A minimum desired rate of return discount (e.g., 15 percent) is used to compute present value of all future cash inflows and outflows.

negative reinforcement   A motivational technique in which negative stimuli are removed once desired behavior is exhibited.

network   A logic diagram arranged in a prescribed format (e.g., AOA or AON) consisting of activities, sequences, interrelationships, and dependencies.

objective   An end you seek to create or acquire. Should be specific, measurable, realistic, assignable, and include a time frame for accomplishment.

organization breakdown structure (OBS)   A structure used to assign responsibility for work packages.

organizational culture   A system of shared norms, beliefs, values, and assumptions held by an organization's members.

organizational politics   Actions by individuals or groups of individuals to acquire, develop, and use power and other resources to obtain preferred outcomes when there is uncertainty or disagreement over choices.

parallel activity   One or more activities that can be carried on concurrently or simultaneously.

partnering   See project partnering.

path   A sequence of connected activities.

payback method   The time it takes to pay back the project investment (Investment/net annual savings). The method does not consider the time value of money or the life of the investment.

precedence diagram method   A method used to construct a project network that uses nodes (e.g., a rectangle) to represent activities and connecting arrows to indicate dependencies.

priority system   The process used to select projects. The system uses selected criteria for evaluating and selecting projects that are strongly linked to higher-level strategies and objectives.

principle of negotiation   A process of negotiation that aims to achieve win/win results.

project   A complex, nonroutine, one-time effort to create a product or service limited by time, budget, and specifications.

project interfaces   The intersections between a project and other groups of people both within and outside the organization.

project kick-off meeting   Typically the first meeting of the project team.

project life cycle   The stages found in all projects—definition, planning, execution, and delivery.

project management office (PMO)   A centralized unit within an organization or department that oversees and improves the management of projects.

project partnering   A non-binding method of transforming contractual relationships into a cohesive, cooperative project team with a single set of goals and established procedures for resolving disputes in a timely manner.

project matrix   A matrix structure in which the project manager has primary control over project activities and functional managers support project work.

project sponsor   Typically a high-ranking manager who champions and supports a project.

project vision   An image of what the project will accomplish.

projectitis   A social phenomenon in which project members exhibit inappropriately intense loyalty to the project.

projectized organization   An organizational structure in which core work is accomplished by project teams.

positive synergy   A characteristic of high-performance teams in which group performance is greater than the sum of individual contributions.

risk   The chance that an undesirable project event will occur and the consequences of all its possible outcomes.

resource   Any person, groups, skill, equipment or material used to accomplish a task, work package, or activity.

resource-constrained project   A project that assumes resources are limited (fixed) and therefore time is variable.

responsibility matrix   A matrix whose intersection point shows the relationship between an activity (work package) and the person/group responsible for its completion.

"sacred cow"   A project that is a favorite of a powerful management figure who is usually the champion for the project.

slack   Time an activity can be delayed before it becomes critical.

schedule variance (SV)   The difference between the planned dollar value of the work actually completed and the value of the work scheduled to be completed at a given point in time (SV = BCWP – BCWS). Schedule variance contains no critical path information.

schedule performance index (SPI)   The ratio of the work performed to work scheduled (BCWP/BCWS).

scope statement   A definition of the end result or mission of a project. Scope statements typically includes project objectives, deliverables, milestones, specifications, and limits and exclusions.

splitting   A scheduling technique in which work is interrupted on one activity and the resource is assigned to another activity for a period of time, then reassigned to work on the original activity.

systems thinking   A holistic approach to viewing problems that emphasizes understanding the interactions among different problem factors.

task   See activity.

team-building   A process designed to improve the performance of a team.

time-constrained project   A project that assumes time is fixed and, if resources are needed, they will be added.

Total slack   The amount of time an activity can be delayed and not affect the project duration (TS = LS – ES or LF – EF).

360-degree feedback   A multirater appraisal system based on performance information that is gathered from multiple sources (superiors, peers, subordinates, customers).

virtual project team   Spatially separated project team whose members are unable to communicate face to face. Communication is usually by electronic means.

variance at completion (VAC)   Indicates expected actual cost over- or underrun at completion (VAC = BAC – EAC).

work breakdown structure (WBS)   A hierarchical method that successively subdivides the work of the project into smaller detail.

work package   A segment of work within a cost account. It includes cost, time, technical specifications, and a list of tasks that need to be accomplished.

Acronyms

ACWP	Actual cost of work performed	IFB	Invitation to bid
AOA	Activity on arrow	LF	Late finish
AON	Activity on node	LS	Late start
BAC	Budget at completion	MBWA	Management by wandering around
BCWP	Budgeted cost of work performed	NIH	Not invented here
BCWS	Budgeted cost of work scheduled	NPV	Net present value
C-C	Critical chain approach to project planning and management	OBS	Organization breakdown structure
		PCI	Percent complete index
CPI	Cost performance index	PCI-B	Percent complete index—budget costs
CPM	Critical path method	PCI-C	Percent complete index—actual costs
CV	Cost variance	PDM	Precedence diagram method
DUR	Duration	PERT	Project evaluation review technique
EAC	Estimate at completion (with revised cost estimates)	PMO	Project management office
		PV	Price variance
EF	Early finish	RM	Responsibility matrix
ES	Early start	SL	Slack
ETC	Estimate to complete	SPI	Schedule performance index
EV	Earned value	SV	Schedule variance
FAC	Forecast at completion	TF	Total float
FF	Free float	UV	Usage variance
FAC	Forecast at completion (formula)	VAC	Variance at completion
KISS	Keep it simple, stupid	WBS	Work breakdown structure

Project Management Tool Equations

$$t_e = \frac{a + 4m + b}{6}$$

$$\sigma_{t_e} = \left(\frac{b - a}{6}\right)$$

$$(PCI - B) = \frac{BCWP}{BAC}$$

$$CV = BCWP - ACWP$$

$$CPI = \frac{BCWP}{ACWP}$$

$$FAC = \frac{(BAC - BCWP)}{\left(\frac{BCWP}{ACWP}\right)} + ACWP$$

$$\sigma_{T_E} = \sqrt{\Sigma \sigma_{t_e}^{\,2}}$$

$$z = \frac{T_S - T_E}{\sqrt{\Sigma \sigma_{t_e}^{\,2}}}$$

$$(PCI - C) = \frac{ACWP}{EAC} \text{ or } \frac{ACWP}{FAC}$$

$$SV = BCWP - BCWS$$

$$SPI = \frac{BCWP}{BCWS}$$

$$VAC = BAC - FAC \text{ or } BAC - EAC$$

Index